CITIES OF EMPIRE

CITIES OF EMPIRE

The British Colonies and the Creation of the
Urban World

TRISTRAM HUNT

Metropolitan Books
Henry Holt and Company
New York

Metropolitan Books
Henry Holt and Company, LLC
Publishers since 1866
175 Fifth Avenue
New York, New York 10010

Metropolitan Books® and m® are registered trademarks of
Henry Holt and Company, LLC.

Originally published in the U.K. in 2014 under the title
Ten Cities that Made an Empire
by Allen Lane, London.

Library of Congress Cataloging-in-Publication Data

Hunt, Tristram, 1974– author.
[Ten cities that made an empire]
Cities of empire : the British colonies and the creation of the urban world / Tristram
Hunt.
        pages cm
"Originally published in England in 2014 under the title Ten Cities that Made an
Empire by Allen Lane, London."
Includes bibliographical references and index.
ISBN 978-0-8050-9308-7 (hardback) — ISBN 978-0-8050-9600-2 (electronic book)
  1. Great Britain—Colonies—History—Case studies. 2. Cities and towns—
Case studies. 3. Metropolitan areas—Case studies. 4. Imperialism—History—Case
studies. I. Title.
DA16.H86 2014b
941—dc23
2014030024

Henry Holt books are available for special promotions and premiums.
For details contact: Director, Special Markets.

First U.S. Edition 2014

Printed in the United States of America

1 3 5 7 9 10 8 6 4 2

To M.D.E.H.

Contents

List of Illustrations

INSERTS

1. Paul Revere and Christian Remick, *A View of Part of the Town of Boston in New England and British ships of war landing troops*, 1768. (Photograph: Historic New England, Boston/The Bridgeman Art Library)
2. Paul Revere, *The Bloody Massacre perpetrated in King Street Boston on March 5th, 1770*. (Photograph: Library of Congress Prints and Photographs Division, Washington, DC)
3. Sidney Smith, *A View of John Hancock's House across Boston Common in 1768*. (Photograph: New York Public Library/The Bridgeman Art Library)
4. John Singleton Copley, *Samuel Adams*, 1770. Museum of Fine Arts, Boston. (Photograph: De Agostini Picture Library/The Bridgeman Art Library)
5. Teapot, probably made in Derby, Staffordshire, c. 1765–1770s. The Colonial Williamsburg Foundation. Museum Purchase (accession # 1953–417, image #DS90–557).
6. The Boston Tea Party, illustration from Rev. W. D. Cooper, *The History of North America*, 1789. (Photograph: Library of Congress Prints and Photographs Division, Washington, DC)
7. St Nicholas Abbey, Barbados. (Photograph: Spectrum/Heritage Images/Scala, Florence)
8. Anon, *View of Bridgetown and Carlisle Bay ('Governor Robinson Going to Church')*, c. 1742. By courtesy of the Barbados Museum & Historical Society

TEXT ILLUSTRATIONS

List of Maps

Acknowledgements

For their generous assistance with the research, writing and production of this book, the author would like to thank James Baker, Chris Bayly, Sara Bershtel, Paul Bew, Vivian Bickford, Chloe Campbell, Georgina Capel, Michael V. Carlisle, James Cronin, Thi Dinh, Richard Duguid, Donald Futers, Carrie Gibson, Julia Hobsbawm, Riva Hocherman, Julian and Marylla Hunt, Jennifer Huntington, Shruti Kapila, Peter Kilfoyle, Alan Lockey, Cecilia Mackay, Carrie Martin, Rana Mitter, Ruaridh Nicoll, Michael Parkinson, Stuart Proffitt, Gaye Blake Roberts, Hannah O'Rourke, Miri Rubin and the Department of History, Queen Mary, University of London, Claire Sandars, Ben Shephard, Owen Stanwood, Rory Stewart, Phil Tinline, Juliet Thornback, Imogen Walford, Ian Wason, David Watson, Alison Wedgwood, Benjamin Wegg-Prosser, Jon Wilson.

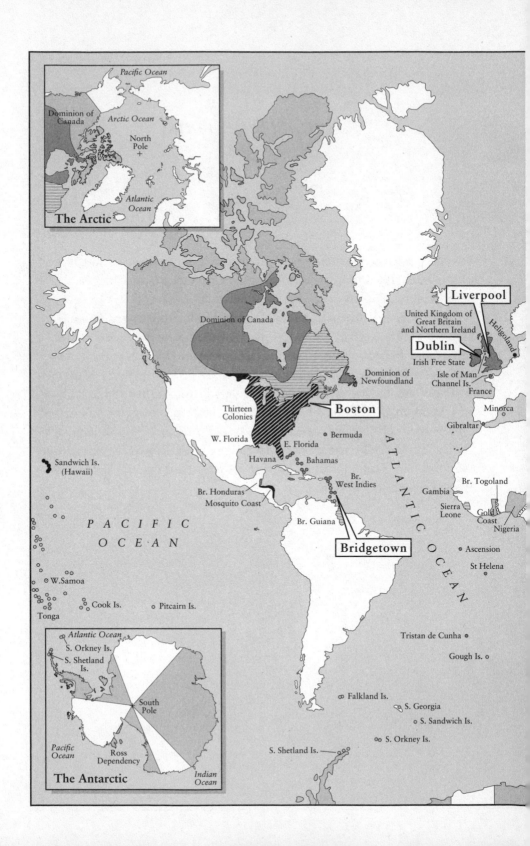

The Arctic

Pacific Ocean

Dominion of Canada

Arctic Ocean

North Pole +

Atlantic Ocean

Dominion of Canada

Sandwich Is. (Hawaii)

PACIFIC OCEAN

W. Samoa

Tonga

Cook Is.

Pitcairn Is.

The Antarctic

Atlantic Ocean

S. Orkney Is.

S. Shetland Is.

South Pole

Pacific Ocean

Ross Dependency

Indian Ocean

Thirteen Colonies

W. Florida

Boston

E. Florida

Havana

Bahamas

Bermuda

Dominion of Newfoundland

United Kingdom of Great Britain and Northern Ireland

Liverpool

Heligoland

Dublin

Irish Free State

Isle of Man

Channel Is.

France

Minorca

Gibraltar

Br. West Indies

Bridgetown

Br. Honduras
Mosquito Coast

Br. Guiana

ATLANTIC OCEAN

Gambia

Sierra Leone

Br. Togoland

Gold Coast

Nigeria

Ascension

St Helena

Tristan de Cunha

Gough Is.

Falkland Is.

S. Georgia

S. Sandwich Is.

S. Orkney Is.

S. Shetland Is.

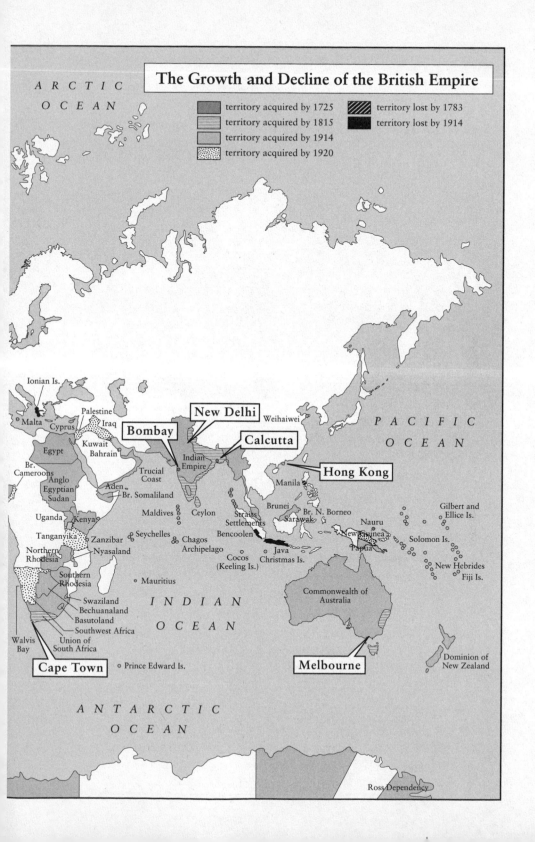

The Growth and Decline of the British Empire

- territory acquired by 1725
- territory acquired by 1815
- territory acquired by 1914
- territory acquired by 1920
- territory lost by 1783
- territory lost by 1914

ARCTIC OCEAN

PACIFIC OCEAN

Ionian Is.
Malta
Cyprus
Palestine
Iraq
Egypt
Kuwait
Bahrain
Bombay
New Delhi
Weihaiwei
Calcutta
Br. Cameroons
Anglo Egyptian Sudan
Trucial Coast
Aden
Br. Somaliland
Indian Empire
Hong Kong
Manila
Uganda
Kenya
Maldives
Ceylon
Brunei
Br. N. Borneo
Gilbert and Ellice Is.
Tanganyika
Zanzibar
Seychelles
Straits Settlements
Sarawak
Nauru
Northern Rhodesia
Nyasaland
Chagos Archipelago
Bencoolen
New Guinea
Solomon Is.
Southern Rhodesia
Cocos (Keeling Is.)
Java
Christmas Is.
Papua
New Hebrides
Fiji Is.
Mauritius
Swaziland
Bechuanaland
Basutoland
Southwest Africa
Walvis Bay
Union of South Africa
INDIAN OCEAN
Commonwealth of Australia
Cape Town
Prince Edward Is.
Melbourne
Dominion of New Zealand

ANTARCTIC OCEAN

Ross Dependency

CITIES OF EMPIRE

Introduction

On a sharp winter's day in December 2010, the Hong Kong Association and Society held its annual luncheon in London's Hyde Park. The venue, of course, was the Mandarin Oriental Hotel, part of the Jardine Matheson group, perched lucratively amidst the billionaires' playground of Knightsbridge, and all the great tai-pans of British corporate life were in attendance. However, the Association's guest of honour was not some old China hand, flown in from the Hong Kong Club, to wax lyrical about Britain's 'easternmost possession'. Instead, it was the tall, suave and studiously loyal ambassador of the People's Republic of China, His Excellency Mr Liu Xiaoming.

In syrupy diplomatese, Beijing's man in London spoke rhapsodically of the 'Pearl of the Orient' and the achievements of British business in building up the colony, and then reaffirmed his government's commitment to the vision of Hong Kong proclaimed by Deng Xiaoping: one country, two systems. Communist China would not impose 'Mao Zedong thought' on Hong Kong. Instead, it was determined to preserve freedom of speech, the rule of law, private property rights and, above all, the low-tax, free-trade model that underpinned the once-imperial city's prosperity. The future of this 'international city' was as a global finance centre and, for British companies, as a bridge to mainland China. A pleasing statement of business as usual, the message was smartly tailored to the merchant princes of the Mandarin Oriental.

Thirteen years earlier, when Britain's ninety-nine-year lease on Hong Kong came to an end, there was little evidence of such Sino-British harmony. Then, it was all tears and angst, pride and regret. At the stroke of midnight the Union Jack was lowered to the strains of 'God Save the Queen', the Hong Kong police ripped the royal insignia from their

3

uniforms, and Red Army troops poured over the border. Britain's last governor, Chris Patten, recorded the final, colonial swansong in all its lachrymose glory: its 'kilted pipers and massed bands, drenching rain, cheering crowds, a banquet for the mighty and the not so mighty, a goose-stepping Chinese honour guard, a president and a prince'. Steaming out of Victoria Harbour, as the Royal Marines played 'Rule, Britannia!' and 'Land of Hope and Glory', on the last, symbolic voyage of the Royal Yacht *Britannia*, 'we were leaving one of the greatest cities in the world, a Chinese city that was now part of China, a colony now returned to its mighty motherland in rather different shape to that in which it had become Britain's responsibility a century and a half before'.[1]

In London, responses to the handover ran the gamut, from anguished to humbled, emblematic, in a way, of the conflicted reexamination of Britain's colonial legacy that has been underway for some years. At the shrill end of the spectrum: 'The handover of Hong Kong to China strikes many westerners as a disgrace and a tragedy,' thundered *The*

The end of the line. Her Majesty's Ship the Royal Yacht *Britannia* sails at Hong Kong harbour, 23 June 1997. The ship, which became the floating base for Prince Charles, arrived a week before the territory was to be handed back to China after more than 150 years of British rule (1997).

Economist. 'Never before has Britain passed a colony directly to a Communist regime that does not even pretend to respect conventional democratic values.'[2] Historian Paul Johnson, writing in the *Daily Mail*, concurred: 'The surrender of the free colony of Hong Kong to the totalitarian Communist government is one of the most shameful and humiliating episodes in British history.' The scuttle from Victoria Harbour gave Fleet Street just the cue it needed for an enjoyable bout of colonial self-indulgence. 'All the rest of our empire has been given away on honourable terms,' continued Johnson. 'All the rest of our colonies were meticulously prepared for independence, by setting up model parliaments ... and by providing a judiciary professionally educated on British lines to maintain the rule of law.' Shamefully, the same could not be said of Hong Kong.[3]

Other brave commentators suggested there might be a more complex pre-history to this handover. Author Martin Jacques thought the ceremony showed, 'no sense of contrition, of humility, of history. This was British hypocrisy at its most rampant and sentimental.'[4] Instead of a moment of self-regard and imperial nostalgia, the journalist Andrew Marr thought this final, colonial retreat should have been an opportunity for a new British identity to emerge. 'So enough Last Posts and folded Union Flags. Enough "Britannia" and enough weary self-deprecation from the Prince of Wales. We should not leave Hong Kong with too much regret.'[5]

In his memoirs, Prime Minister Tony Blair admits to a startling failure to appreciate the historic significance of the return of Hong Kong to China, as a rising, newly prosperous country sought to take its place in the world and shed the memory of its 'century of humiliation' at the hands of British, French and American forces.* After President

---

* A visit to the landmark 'Road to Regeneration' exhibition at Beijing's National Museum of China clarifies any doubt about the central place of the Opium Wars and the loss of Hong Kong in the Communist Party narrative of contemporary China's progress. 'After Britain started the Opium War in 1840, the imperial powers descended on China like a swarm of bees, looting our treasures and killing our people,' reads the official account. 'They forced the Qing government to sign a series of unequal treaties that granted them economic, political and cultural privileges and sank China gradually into a semi-colonial, semi-feudal society.' The anti-imperialist struggle was the beginnings of China's 'search for a path to salvation [in Maoist socialism]'.

Jiang Zemin teased the jet-lagged and jejune British premier about his poor knowledge of William Shakespeare

> he then explained to me that this was a new start in UK/China relations and from now on, the past could be put behind us. I had, at that time, only a fairly dim and sketchy understanding of what the past was. I thought it was all just politeness in any case. But actually, he meant it. They meant it.[6]

However, one member of the British delegation remained determined to cling on to the past. In a confidential diary entry entitled 'The Great Chinese Takeaway', His Royal Highness the Prince of Wales laid bare his despair at seeing the Crown colony returned to the mainland. Watching another piece fall from his family inheritance, the prince lamented the 'ridiculous rigmarole' of meeting the 'old waxwork' Jiang Zemin, and the horror of watching an 'awful Soviet-style' ceremony in which 'Chinese soldiers goose-step on to the stage and haul down the Union Jack'. Charles Philip Arthur George Mountbatten-Windsor knew all too well that, when his time came to assume the throne, the loss of Hong Kong meant Britain's imperial role would be long past. 'Such is the end of Empire, I sighed to myself.'[7]

As Great Britain's formal empire finally receded into the distance, the public debate about the legacies and meaning of that colonial past has grown only more agonized.[8] Famously, in his 2003 book *Empire: How Britain Made the Modern World*, the historian Niall Ferguson made a stirring and influential case for the British Empire as the handmaiden of globalization and force for progress. 'No organization has done more to promote the free movement of goods, capital and labour than the British Empire in the nineteenth and early twentieth centuries. And no organization has done more to impose Western norms of law, order and governance around the world,' he wrote. Since globalization and the modern world were, for Ferguson, a 'good thing', this also meant the British Empire – for all its messy crimes and misdemeanours – was equally praiseworthy. 'Without the spread of British rule around the world, it is hard to believe that the structures of liberal capitalism would have been so successfully established in so many different economies.' Much of the chaos of the twentieth century was, he suggested, a product of the decline of transnational empires. And he went on to urge the White House of President George W. Bush to take up what Kipling called 'the white man's burden' and show some imperial leadership. For Ferguson, the British Empire offered the most salient guide for Washington's diplomats and generals as they sought to craft their own Pax Americana across the Middle East.[9]

As critics pointed out, there were numerous problems with Ferguson's version of empire: its Whiggish focus on the heroic age of Victorian achievement to the exclusion of the more amoral adventurism of the eighteenth century or bloody counter-insurgencies of the twentieth century; its unwillingness to chart the broader impact of colonialism on indigenous peoples; its concentration on the free-trade period of British imperialism as the Empire's defining ethos; and its dichotomous, good *versus* bad balance-sheet approach to the past.

Yet just as unhelpful a side-effect of Ferguson's case was that it provoked an equal and opposite reaction from scholars and commentators who sought, by way of contrast, to cast British imperialism as a very bad thing. In the context of political opposition to perceived American imperialism at the turn of the twenty-first century, discussion about the British Empire (particularly on the political left) was reduced to slavery, starvation and extermination; loot, land and labour. In the words of the left-wing author Richard Gott, 'the rulers of the British empire will one day be perceived to rank with the dictators of the twentieth century as the authors of crimes against humanity on an infamous scale'.[10]

Much of Gott's case has received official endorsement in recent years with a series of public acknowledgements by European governments of colonial crimes. In 2004 Germany apologized for the massacre of 65,000 Herero people in what is now Namibia; in 2008 Italy announced that it was to pay reparations to Libya for injustices committed during its thirty-year rule of the north African state (judged by *Time* magazine to be 'an unprecedented act of contrition by a former European colonial power'); in 2011 the Dutch government apologized for the killing of civilians in the 1947 Rawagede massacre in Indonesia; and in 2012 the President of France, François Hollande, officially acknowledged the role of the Parisian police in massacring some 200 Algerians during a 1961 rally.[11] Then, in 2013, the United Kingdom government (having apologized for the Great Famine of 1845–52 and expressed official regret over Britain's role in the Atlantic slave trade) was forced by a High Court judgement to announce a £20 million compensation package for 5,228 Kenyan victims of British abuse during the 1950s Kenya Emergency or Mau Mau Rebellion. 'The British government recognizes that Kenyans were subject to torture and other forms of ill-treatment at the hands of the colonial administration,' Foreign Secretary William Hague told the House of Commons. 'The British Government sincerely regrets that these abuses took place and that they marred Kenya's progress towards independence.'[12]

The danger now is that, as the legacy of Empire moves into the realm of official apologies, law suits and compensation settlements, the space for detached historical judgement has perceptibly narrowed. For the history of Empire is always more complicated than the simple binary of ruler and ruled – as episodes such as the loss of America in 1776, the tortured psychology of the settlers of the White Dominions, or the endlessly unclear place of Ireland within the British imperial imagination demonstrated. What is more, as Linda Colley has suggested, 'one of the reasons why we all need to stop approaching empire in simple "good" or "bad" thing terms, and instead think intelligently and enquiringly about its many and intrinsic paradoxes, is that versions of the phenomenon are still with us'.[13]

The most compelling of those phenomena still with us is the chain of former colonial cities dotted across the globe. From the Palladian glories of Leinster House in Dublin to the Ruskinian fantasia of the Victoria Terminus in Mumbai to the stucco campanile of Melbourne's Government House to the harbour of Hong Kong, the footprint of the old British Empire remains wilfully in evidence. After sporting pastimes and the English language (to which might be added Anglicanism, the parliamentary system and Common Law), Jan Morris has described urbanism as 'the most lasting of the British imperial legacies'.[14] And this imperial heritage is now being preserved and restored at a remarkable rate as postcolonial nations engage in a frequently more sophisticated conversation about the virtues and vices, the legacies and burdens of the British past and how they should relate to it today.

This book seeks to explore that imperial story through the urban form and its material culture: ten cities telling the story of the British Empire. It charts the changing character of British imperialism through the architecture and civic institutions, the street names and fortifications, the news pages, plays and ritual. And it is the very complexity of this urban past which allows us to go beyond the 'good' and 'bad' cul-de-sac of so much imperial debate. The history of colonialism covered in this study suggests a more diffuse process of exchange, interaction and adaptation. The historian John Darwin has described Empire as 'not just a story of domination and subjection but something more complicated: the creation of novel or hybrid societies in which notions of governance, economic assumptions, religious values and morals, ideas about property, and conceptions of justice, conflicted and mingled, to be reinvented, refashioned, tried out or abandoned'.[15] This nuanced account of negotiation and exchange is nowhere more obvious than in the advanced intellectual and cultural environment of the British imperial city – in the Indo-Saracenic architecture of Bombay, the east African mosques of Cape Town, or the Bengali Renaissance which British scholarship helped to foster in Calcutta.

The history of these cities also exposes how the justifications and understandings of imperialism changed across time and space. As English and then British imperial ambitions developed from the late sixteenth century, so the intellectual rationale of the leading advocates of Empire evolved. The motivation of the planters in early seventeenth-century Ulster would have seemed entirely foreign to the free-traders of nineteenth-century Hong Kong or to the White Dominion troops fighting for Empire in the First World War. Yet the presence of these often cumulative and sometimes competing sets of motives does not mean that the British Empire lacked ideology. There has been a long and often disingenuous history of imperial commentators expressing their amazement at the full extent of Britain's colonial ambitions. In 1762 Horace Walpole marvelled at how 'a peaceable, quiet set of tradesfolks' had become the 'heirs-apparent to the Romans and overrunning East and West Indies'. In the nineteenth century, the Cambridge historian J. R. Seeley famously described the British Empire as the product of 'a fit of absence of mind'. And a more recent history of Empire suggests it all emerged through a process of 'anarchic individualism'.[16] In fact, during every stage in the development of Britain's imperial ambitions there were political philosophies, moral certainties, theologies and ideologies at hand to promote and explain the extension of Britain's global reach. At times Britain was a mercantilist empire, at other times a free-trading empire; in certain periods, Great Britain was involved in a process of promoting Western civilization, at others in protecting multicultural relativism; for a good period prior to the 1807 abolition of the slave trade, Britain regarded itself as an empire of righteous exploitation, and afterwards part of a selfless crusade for liberty. As Joseph Conrad's Marlow acerbically notes in Conrad's peerless novella of colonial realism *Heart of Darkness*, it was an *idea* that had to redeem the practice of empire at any particular point: 'An idea at the back of it; not a sentimental pretence, but an idea; and an unselfish belief in the idea – something you can set up, and bow down before, and offer a sacrifice to.'[17] Down the centuries, it is possible to trace contentious debates in public, press and parliament about the purpose and nature of imperialism: its costs and benefits, its relationship to British identity and its strategic and economic requirements. There were complaints that Empire benefited a narrow mercantile elite at the expense of the public purse; that it involved arbitrary and abusive systems of political rule that threatened historic British liberties; or that it was Britain's divine mission to spread commerce and Christianity abroad.

The ambition of this book is also to explain how those ideologies of Empire were made flesh through the urban form and habits of city life. As the historian Partha Chatterjee has written, 'empire is not an abstract universal category . . . It is embodied and experienced in actual locations'.[18] The shifting justifications and contested understandings of Empire shaped the design and planning, the sport and pastimes, the rhetoric and politics of Britain's colonial cities. The manner in which settlers and indigenous residents interacted and the way in which those dynamics shaped the fabric and culture of the city allows for a more accurate account of the day-to-day realities of imperialism. Urban history helps to move us beyond casting the indigenous victims of colonialism as just that – passive recipients of metropolitan, European designs in which they had neither voice nor influence.

Working chronologically and then (broadly) geographically from west to east, the following chapters trace the history of these cities, their ruling ideas and their place within the story of British imperialism. We begin with Boston as the entry-point into the First British Empire, which stretched along the Atlantic seaboard of America, and the remarkable cultural affiliation which existed between the mother country and Massachusetts right up to the American Revolution of 1776. Bridgetown, Barbados highlights the importance of the slave trade in the financing of both British imperialism and then industrialization during the seventeenth and eighteenth centuries. Dublin is the third city of this Atlantic triangle, highlighting the complex place of Ireland within British imperial history as well as London's late eighteenth-century ambition to unite the British Isles before embarking upon its grander global ambitions.

Any such aspirations depended upon the ability of the Royal Navy to see off competing imperial powers, and the fight against the Dutch to take the city of Cape Town is a microcosm of the broader, geo-political struggle that the forces of Western Europe played out across the high seas. With the capture of Cape Town, Britain's 'Swing to the East' was secure, and Calcutta, the capital of British India, next introduces the East India Company and the beginnings of the Raj. If Calcutta signified mercantilism, then Hong Kong was a testament to free trade, standing as a monument to the new ideologies of laissez-faire and the instrument of Britain's 'informal empire' in China. For all the lofty rhetoric, however, the colony's finances were dependent upon the distribution of opium across the Middle Kingdom. To begin with, the poppies came from Bengal, until the advent of Malwa opium brought the city of Bombay into the drug economy. Opium and then cotton production turned Bombay into one of the first industrial cities of the British Empire and, accompanying it, all the attendant problems of urban sanitation and mass immigration. The history of Victorian Bombay chronicles the mid-nineteenth-century relationship between colonial modernity and industrial capitalism.

Melbourne was another port in that global, commercial nexus: the development of the 'Queen-city of the south' signals the emergence of finance capital in British imperialism and highlights the very different place the White Dominions (Canada, Australia, New Zealand, South Africa) had within the colonial firmament; the colony of Victoria was one strand of a 'crimson thread of kinship' uniting the Anglo-Saxon family. By contrast, the Edwardian Raj was about the assertion of power and authority, and no city in the world symbolized this imperial sensibility with more grandeur and world-historic self-regard than New Delhi. It was built as a monument to eternal imperial governance and yet barely finished it became the capital of an independent India. The final chapter analyses the end of Empire and the harrowing effect which decolonization had on a colonial city within the British Isles. Few places prospered more aggressively from Britain's imperial markets and global reach than Liverpool, and no city suffered more wretchedly from the end of Empire. The Janus face of Empire, its dual ability both to enrich and undo, is only now being overcome along the docks and wharfs of an otherwise often silent River Mersey.

In one sense, an account of imperialism pursued through urban history is obvious. While colonization might have begun as a rural pursuit, primarily involved in the extraction of mineral or agricultural wealth from foreign lands, it could not prosper without the development of an urban infrastructure to ship the riches back home. Initially, this meant the establishment of ports – such as Bridgetown for sugar, Boston for fisheries or Melbourne for gold – and then the emergence of more complicated economies around them, from ship-building to financial services to foodstuffs, leisure and retail. With these early settlements came the first springs of civic ambition. In the pioneering Ulster plantations of the late sixteenth century, there were grand plans to erect a new capital, Elizabetha. Similarly, the promoters of the Berkeley Plantation in Virginia in 1619 commissioned their representative Captain John Woodleefe 'to erect and build a town called Barkley and to settle and plant our men and diverse other inhabitants there, to the honour of Almighty God, the enlarging of Christian religion, and to the augmentation and revenue of the general plantation in that country, and the particular good and profit of ourselves, men and servants as we hope'.[19] Neither of those planned cities came to fruition. But in colonies which did contain significant commercial and strategic assets, the resources allocated to cities by central authorities rapidly escalated to cover the erection of garrisons, and places of worship, the establishment of industry and all the accoutrements of settler life. Nine out of ten of the cities in this book began their imperial lives as port economies.[20]

Most of them also attest to the defining attributes of colonial cities, as first set out by the urban historian Anthony D. King: power primarily in the hands of a non-indigenous minority; the relative superiority of this minority in terms of technological, military and organizational power; and the racial, cultural and religious differences between predominantly European, Christian settlers and the indigenous majority.[21] In these terms, a history of British imperial cities could be matched by an account of their German, Spanish or, most usefully, French counterparts – with the development of, say, Pondicherry, Casablanca or Saigon offering equivalent insights into French imperial development. Of course, the impulses were different for each colonial power, and the totalizing nature of France's 'civilizing mission' was recorded much more deliberately in those cities' urban design and architecture.

Yet, whether it is Hong Kong or Mumbai, or indeed Shanghai or Dubai (two cities not included in this study), it is notable how Britain's imperial cities currently play a far more significant role in world affairs than those of any other former European power. At the peak of British imperial dominion, in the late nineteenth and early twentieth centuries, the economic and cultural driver of Empire was a chain of major colonial cities – Bombay, Singapore, Melbourne. The advent of the steamship and telegram network, the cutting of the Suez Canal and increase in shipping, the acceleration of global trade in the lead-up to the First World War and the role of these cities as entrepôt and export hubs gave them a powerful, semi-autonomous place within the imperial hierarchy as engines of global growth. Funds from London, Paris and Berlin finance houses were sunk into major infrastructure schemes – docks, railways, trams – as well as used to open up the colonial hinterland.

Today, one hundred years on, the world is witnessing a revival of the global city-state. Not only does the majority of the world's population now live in urban areas (with tens of millions – across Africa, China and India – accelerating the rate of urbanization each passing year), the top twenty-three 'megacities' contribute by themselves some 14 per cent of global GDP.[22] Urban theorist Saskia Sassen has identified 'global cities' – those cities that function as 'command points in the organization of the world economy', provide 'key locations for specialized service firms' and operate as 'sites of production, including the production of innovations . . . and markets for the products and innovations produced' – as the economic powerhouses of the modern era.[23] And, rather like the port cities of the European empires, they operate increasingly outside the traditional framework of the nation state. In an era of instant communications and capital asset flows, global cities such as London, New York and Shanghai are international entities in their own right; the advice from branding agencies and management consultants is for companies to think of future markets in terms of cities rather than countries. If today the twentieth-century nation state is under pressure from globalization, the transnational power of world cities – operating through their own cultural and economic networks – is enjoying its own resurgence.

Alongside a twenty-first-century girdle of global cities, the language of colonial cities has also come back to life. In recent years, the Stanford University economist Paul Romer has made the case for 'Charter Cities'. 'My idea is to build dozens, perhaps hundreds, of cities, each run by a new partnership between a rich country and a poor country,' he has explained. 'The poor country would give up some land for the city, while a developed country like Britain or Canada could contribute a credible judicial system that anchors the rule of law.' Sound familiar? Romer is willing to admit that 'to some this sounds like colonialism'. But there is no need to worry. 'The developed partner country need not rule directly: residents of the city can administer the rules, so long as the well-established judiciary retains the final say, just as the Privy Council does for some members of the Commonwealth.'[24]

If constructing a new generation of colonial cities might seem far-fetched, then what is happening in the former cities of the British Empire also strikes many critics as an unwelcome updating of discredited systems of colonial inequality.* The difference is that this

* Partha Chatterjee has suggested the revival of colonial themes in postcolonial countries is itself the broader product of a new era of technocratic elitism. 'We are being told that it is a sign of our growing self-confidence as a nation that we can at last acknowledge, without shame or guilt, the good the British did for us,' he wrote in

time it is class rather than race shaping the urban fabric, as the segregation of the colonial period provides the antecedent for modern forms of apartheid now moulding the downtown districts, neighbourhoods and suburbs of postcolonial cities. Anthropologist and historian Mike Davis has condemned the restitution of 'older logics of imperial control' in developing cities. 'Throughout the Third World, postcolonial elites have inherited and greedily reproduced the physical footprints of segregated colonial cities,' he writes. 'Despite rhetorics of national liberation and social justice, they have aggressively adapted the racial zoning of the colonial period to defend their own class privileges and spatial exclusivity.'[25]

Similarly, in the cities of the metropole, the end of formal Empire has not meant the disappearance of colonial influence. The late Edward Said once asked, 'Who in India or Algeria today can confidently separate out the British or French component of the past from present actualities; and who in Britain or France can draw a clear circle around British London or French Paris that would exclude the impact of India or Algeria upon these two imperial cities?'[26] So too with the port of Liverpool, the docks of Glasgow, the 'merchant quarter' of Bristol and the workshops of Birmingham. From the iconography of St George's Hall, Liverpool, to Jamaica Street in Glasgow, to the funds supporting Matthew Boulton's Soho House in Birmingham, the lineages of Empire continue to find a resonance in the contemporary civic fabric.

Increasingly, the British are beginning to appreciate that imperialism was not just something 'we' did to other people overseas, but a long, complex process that transformed the culture, economy and identity of the British Isles. As Nicholas B. Dirks has argued, 'fundamental notions of European modernity – ideas of virtue, corruption, nationalism, sovereignty, economic freedom, governmentality, tradition, and history itself – derive in large part from the imperial

---

2005. 'I suspect it is something else. The more popular democracy deepens in India, the more its elites yearn for a system in which enlightened gentlemen could decide, with paternal authority, what was good for the masses. The idea of an Oxford graduate of 22 going out to rule over the destiny of 100,000 peasants in an Indian district can stir up many noble thoughts in middle-class Indian hearts today.' See Partha Chatterjee, 'Those Fond Memories of the Raj', in *Empire and Nation* (New York, 2010).

encounter'.[27] Once again, these transformations can be charted most obviously in our cities. In contrast to a barren conversation about Empire being a 'good' or 'bad' thing, we might reflect instead on how the processes of imperial exchange took place on these shores.

Not least because, as Prince Charles so painfully reflected, the final embers of Empire are almost extinguished. As a Member of Parliament, I see at first hand the uncomfortable realism of this position during the monthly ritual of parliamentary questions to the secretary of state for the Foreign and Commonwealth Office. While the architecture and iconography of the Palace of Westminster remain replete with the glories of Empire, question time is often little more than a rhetorical exercise in thwarted ambition: backbench Members of Parliament rise up demanding to know what Her Majesty's Government will 'do' about tensions in the South China Seas or the occupied West Bank or the situation in Kashmir, as if the despatch of a Palmerstonian gunboat was still a credible option. The bombast tends to deflate when ministers dutifully respond with some warm words about the role of the European Union or the United Nations, or spell out the stark limitations of Britain's military capacity. And when the British political class cannot have its way, its natural reflex point is a paroxysm of soul-searching about 'our place in the world'. In the summer of 2013, a dispute with Spain over border entry into the British territory of Gibraltar (on the 300th anniversary of the Treaty of Utrecht, which ceded the Rock to Great Britain) and the decision by the House of Commons not to support military intervention in Syria was immediately framed within the context of colonial loss and imperial retreat.

Out beyond Westminster, the end of Empire is equally redolent – not least in my own parliamentary constituency of Stoke-on-Trent Central. In the latter half of the eighteenth century, Josiah Wedgwood had been instrumental in commissioning the Trent and Mersey Canal to transport ceramic tableware from the Potteries to the port of Liverpool, then to be shipped out across the Empire. And his competitors followed suit, with the sturdy designs of Spode, Royal Doulton and the Empire Porcelain Company soon providing dinner services for colonial compounds from Canada to Australia. The booming pot banks of Stoke-on-Trent supplied the ceramics of Empire right up to the 1960s, while Herbert Minton's eponymous tiles could be found beautifying the most far-flung of colonial projects – perhaps most wonderfully, Sir George Gilbert Scott's convocation hall (Cowasji Jehangir) at the University of Bombay. This is not Stoke-on-Trent's only connection with Bombay, as it was in Burslem that the sculptor John Lockwood Kipling learned his craft and decided to name his son 'Rudyard' after a local beauty spot just north of the Six Towns. Rudyard Kipling, the finest poet of Empire, would describe his birth-place of Bombay as the 'Mother of cities to me', but his name is a reminder of his link to an altogether different colonial place.

In the postwar decades, the impact of Empire returned to Stoke-on-Trent in the form of extensive migration from Pakistan and India (most notably, the Mirpur district of disputed Kashmir), but the lucrative business of imperial production collapsed. The protected markets of the Commonwealth were thrown open to global competition. As with the cotton mills of Manchester and the port of Liverpool, the relative decline of the pottery industry in Stoke-on-Trent is connected to the end of Empire. Only a generation ago, the social and economic foundations of Stoke-on-Trent – as of so many parts of the UK – were bound up with a colonial identity which has now simply disappeared.

Indeed, barely a generation ago, that connection to Empire was central to the history and identity of my own family. My father was born in 1941 at a quintessential site of Kipling's Raj – the cool climes of Ootacamund, an Indian hill station in the Nilgiris Hills of Tamil Nadu. So-called 'Snooty Ooty' (now, Udhagamandalam), with its bungalows, club, Gothic Revival Anglican church, and beagles' pack, was where the officers and wives of the Indian Civil Service retreated from the blistering heat of the plains. One such officer was Roland Hunt CMG, my grandfather, despatched to Madras with his wife Pauline as a sub-collector after a year of Empire Studies – which involved a spot of Tamil and then learning to ride round the Oxford Parks – to administer British colonialism for what he and his colleagues regarded as the foreseeable future. In fact, his string of diplomatic postings perfectly mirrored the death-throes of the British Empire. When Indian independence arrived, he progressed to the High Commissions of Pakistan, South Africa and Malaya – where he assisted in the transition to Malaysia and (family legend has it) rewrote Benjamin Britten's score for the new national anthem, side by side on the piano stool, with the founding prime minister, Tunku Abdul Rahman. His final appointments followed the expansion of the Commonwealth, with the former colonies of Uganda and Trinidad and Tobago concluding his career as high commissioner. In retirement, the colonial legacy lingered. Visiting Roland and Pauline's bungalow in Pangbourne, Berkshire, was to enter a visual dreamscape of Empire: prints of Madras's Fort St George and Calcutta's Fort William; editions of Kipling and Conrad; the traditional colonial ephemera of drums, rugs, diplomatic photographs and oriental artefacts. But to me, as a young boy, it appeared a civilization as ancient and distant, in its way, as the Aztecs, the Egyptians or the classical Greeks.

None of this means that Empire as a global force has ended. If the formal dominion of the old European empires has indeed faded, competing nations have emerged to fill the vacuum. In the twenty-first century, it is China and India who are on the rise, dictating a broader pivot in world affairs from the Atlantic to the Pacific – both of them exerting geopolitical ambition and challenging the remnants of Anglo-American hegemony. One of the undercurrents in this book is the playing out of this uneasy transition, from a decaying colonial legacy to the assertive impact of emerging nations in former cities of Empire. For the myriad ways in which cities restore or erase, condemn or commemorate their colonial pasts is itself another stage in the compelling and continuing history of Empire.

I

Boston

'A City upon a Hill'

As evening fell on 16 December 1773, with thousands pressed into the square pew boxes and overflowing balconies of the whitewashed Old South Meeting House, brewer and politician Samuel Adams stepped forward to announce that 'he could think of nothing further to be done – that they had now done all they could for the Salvation of the Country'. The wealthy Boston merchant John Hancock agreed, erupting in frustration: 'Let every man do what is right in his own eyes!' Fifteen minutes later, the war whoops began.

It was the signal the 'patriots' had been waiting for. Secreted across Boston – in living rooms and parlours, workshops and shipyards – men had covered their faces, donned disguises and readied their weapons. Men like James Brewer, a pump- and blockmaker, whose wife had blackened his face with burnt cork; the blacksmith's apprentice Joshua Wyeth; the carpenter Amos Lincoln; the boat builder Samuel Nowell; and the lemon importer Edward Proctor. Anxious about what the ensuing hours might bring, these 'Sons of Liberty' steeled themselves for a potentially deadly clash with British troops.

Dressed as Mohawk Indians, they gathered together a hundred strong outside the Meeting House, then surged south-east through the narrow Boston lanes, shouting like Indians and whistling like boatswains, along Milk Street and Hutchinsons Street, and down to the docks, where the *Dartmouth*, the *Eleanor* and the *Beaver* sat at anchor alongside Griffin's Wharf. The crowds followed in a torchlit procession, before coming to a stop at the waterfront, silent as they watched the 'Mohawks' board the ships, brush past the crews and uncover their cargo.

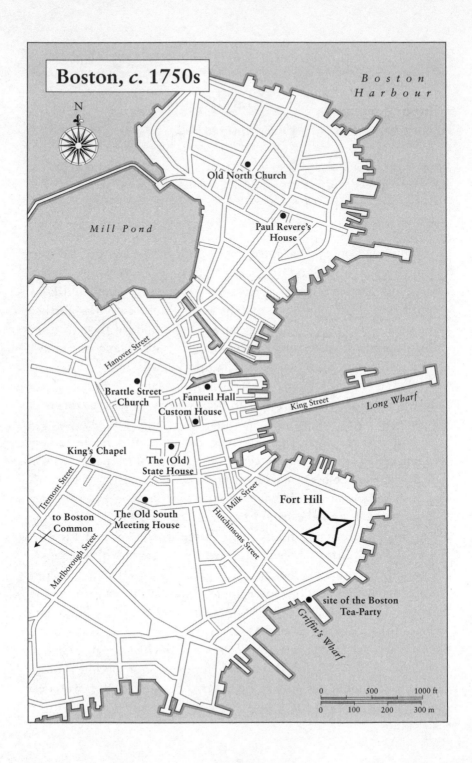

Boston, *c.* 1750s

N

*Boston
Harbour*

Old North Church

Paul Revere's
House

Mill Pond

Hanover Street

Brattle Street
Church

Fanueil Hall
Custom House

King Street

Long Wharf

King's Chapel

The (Old)
State House

Milk Street

Fort Hill

Tremont Street

to Boston
Common

The Old South
Meeting House

Hutchinsons Street

Marlborough Street

site of the Boston
Tea-Party

Griffin's Wharf

| 0 | 500 | 1000 ft |
| 0 | 100 | 200 | 300 m |

The night's quiet was shattered by the sound of axes heaving into wooden crates, the fixing of tackle and hauling of chests – and then the splash of tons of tea leaves cascading into the waters of Boston harbour. For hour after hour – within sight of the 64th Regiment stationed at Fort William, and in easy range of the guns of Admiral John Montagu's flagship, HMS *Captain* – the Mohawk stevedores unloaded the valuable cases of black and green Bohea, Singlo, Hyson and Congou tea. 'We were merry in an under tone,' Joshua Wyeth recalled, 'at the idea of making so large a cup of tea for the fishes.' Over 340 chests, containing over 46 tons of tea priced at almost £10,000, were dumped into Boston harbour.

As they fell, the splintered crates and sodden tea leaves formed an eighteenth-century oil-slick rising and falling with the Boston tides, lapping the Dorchester coastline all the way down to the British soldiers stationed at Fort William. The Atlantic currents never took the tea leaves back to Britain, but they had no need to. News of the 1773 'Boston Tea-Party' soon reached London – and Westminster's response to this audacious assault on British property would set in train the events of the American Revolution.[1]

Today, over 230 years later, Boston, Massachusetts is still defined by that revolutionary moment. It is the city of the 'Freedom Trail' where, beginning at Boston Common under the golden dome of the State House and snaking all the way up to the Bunker Hill Monument in Charlestown, you can walk the story of liberation, pursued by historical re-enactors. And be it Paul Revere House, Old North Church or USS *Constitution* – 'Old Ironsides' – the urban narrative is powerfully consistent: here was a city which stoically laboured under the heel of British colonialism until the greed and arrogance of the occupiers finally forced the citizens to turn freedom-fighters.

The reupholstered Faneuil Hall is branded 'Cradle to Liberty'; the Boston Historical Society exhibition at the Old State House is a Whiggish tale entitled 'From Colony to Commonwealth'. At the Museum of Fine Arts, that heritage of freedom is reaffirmed with its magnificent collection of John Singleton Copley portraits, depicting the likes of Paul Revere, Samuel Adams and John Hancock in suitably heroic poses. Adams, caught in the aftermath of the 1770 'Boston Massacre' (the fatal shooting of five Bostonians by British soldiers),* is especially striking, as he points melodramatically to the 1691 Massachusetts charter, every inch the wronged constitutionalist.

Implicit within the history is a residual anti-British sentiment which has become an important facet of modern Boston's identity. Mass Irish immigration to Massachusetts in the aftermath of the mid-nineteenth-century Great Famine helped to cement an implicit antagonism towards the redcoats and lobsterbacks across the pond. It certainly did no harm for city politicians to play to anti-British populism, and few managed it more successfully than the Kennedy clan. Even as US ambassador to Great Britain, stationed in London in the run-up to the Second World War, Joseph P. Kennedy, the grandson of Irish emigrants, could barely suppress his distaste for the UK. Much of that prejudice cascaded down the generations, and Massachusetts Senator Ted Kennedy's support for Sinn Fein always worked well with his Irish-Catholic Boston base. In less salubrious parts of South Boston there were often nickels and dimes to be found in pub collection tins for NORAID and 'the cause'.

But turn east from the Old South Meeting House, under the dreary skyscrapers of modern 'Washington Street' towards the Old State House and a different Boston peeks out of the past. There, either side of the eighteenth-century balcony from which the Declaration of Independence was read in July 1776, stands a glistening, golden lion and a rearing, silver unicorn. The coat of arms of the British royal family was ripped down in the aftermath of Independence but replaced in 1882, and it is that crest which highlights the hidden history of imperial Boston. For this city, right up to the moment of revolution, was renowned as one of the most ardently British and comfortably colonial of imperial satellites. Its birth and growth signalled the coming of the British urban footprint across the globe, whilst its unexpected rebellion in 1773 marked the first great rupture in the imperial story. There is no stop along the Freedom Trail for the less straightforward elements of this history of colonialism: before it became the revolutionary citadel of 1773, Boston was a fiercely royal city, a true Protestant redoubt. You would not know it from the John Hancock

* See below, pp. 58ff.

Tower, Franklin Street or Congress Street, but in the bones of Boston can be found some of the earliest traces of a British imperial identity.

THE LIGHT OF THE WORLD

Modern Boston's origins do not begin with its namesake in Lincolnshire, but rather in the Stour valley, that Arcadian stretch of 'Constable country' running through Cambridgeshire, Suffolk and Essex. In the early 1600s, this was a place of piety and godliness, of strict worship and careful magistracy, where drink and 'rough sports' were banned and preaching and prayer encouraged. Among the governing East Anglian merchant, legal and landowning classes, the call to Reformation had been answered most purposefully. They would come to be known as the Puritans – Protestants who focused on the pure word of Christian faith drawn from the pages of scripture, considered themselves in a much more personal relationship with God and eschewed what they regarded as the rituals, hierarchies and idolatry of the Church of England. Their mission was to lead England out of the lingering, crypto-Catholic darkness which had corrupted the Anglican church since the Reformation of 1534. Among the islands of godliness lining the Stour valley was, for example, Colchester in Essex – described by one admirer in the late 1590s as a 'town [which], for the earnest profession of the gospel, [was] like unto the city upon a hill; and as a candle upon a candlestick'.[2]

This was the stern spiritual environment in which the future governor of Massachusetts John Winthrop was brought up. His father, Adam Winthrop, had been a small-holder, lawyer and squire of Groton Manor, Suffolk – as well as a committed supporter of the Puritan cause. His son proved equally strict in his piety, as a barrister at Gray's Inn, and then a middling landowner and magistrate. Yet all around him, from the 1610s, Winthrop spied evidence of God's displeasure at work. The dual curse of erastianism (state interference in ecclesiastical matters) and Arminianism (which rejected strict Protestant doctrines of predestination) was undermining the true church, whilst the authorities appeared ever more indulgent to the unChristian pastimes of the 'rude sort'. On the European Continent, a great struggle between true religion and popery, the forces of light and dark, had opened in 1618 with the start of the Thirty Years' War, but Britain, under King James I and VI, was reluctant to intervene. The godly saw ahead of them a fearful Counter-Reformation, coordinated by the Catholic Spanish empire, threatening the very survival of Protestant England, and yet few in the Stuart court seemed to appreciate the eschatological immediacy.

By 1628, in his pamphlet *Reasons for the Plantation in New England,* Winthrop was dismissing England as 'this sinful land' which was growing 'weary of her inhabitants, so as man which is the most precious of all Creatures, is here more vile and base, than the earthe they tread upon'.[3] With his family's personal salvation at risk, Winthrop started to contemplate an Exodus. He need not have chosen America. Plantations had already emerged by the late 1500s as far afield as Ulster and Bermuda, with the dual ambition of profit and Protestantism. Land was carved out from the wilderness or expropriated from indigenous residents, handed over to enterprising colonial settlers, who then 'planted' labourers on to the fields and farmed it for profit. It was an early form of colonialism usefully combining systems of patronage with the informal extension of state power. Winthrop himself had numerous family ties to Ireland and, in the early 1620s, was considering emigrating to his brother-in-law's plantation at Montrath, in County Laois, in the middle of Ireland. At the time, the main possibility across the Atlantic was Jamestown, Virginia, settled in 1607 (christened in honour of Queen Elizabeth I, the 'Virgin Queen'), and, after its conversion to a royal colony in 1624, a model of loyal Anglicanism. Alternatively, there was the struggling colony of Plymouth, founded in 1620 by the 'Pilgrim Fathers', who had fled religious persecution in England first to the Netherlands and then to America, determined to separate themselves from the corrupt, decaying Old World. These struggling outposts formed part of a broader, incremental 'New England' society of European colonists encompassing Cape Ann, Rhode Island, parts of Connecticut and New Haven.

It was this wooded, storm-battered littoral of the eastern seaboard of America, with its promise of religious freedom and personal salvation, that offered the greatest hope for England's Puritans during the anxious Stuart years. In 1623 a 'Council for New England' had been established to promote the creation of further colonies, and, as one of the first histories of Boston recounts it,

On the 19th of March, 1627–8, Sir Henry Rosewell and Sir John Young [Puritan landowners and colonists], with their associates near Dorchester, in England, purchased of the Council for New England a patent for that part of the country situated between three miles to the northward of the Merrimac River and three miles to the southward of the Charles River, and in length from the Atlantic Ocean to the South Sea. Under this charter, 'the Governor and Company of the Massachusetts Bay in New England' commenced the settlement of the Massachusetts* colony.[4]

Like the Virginia Company, the Massachusetts Bay Company, formed in 1629, was a joint-stock corporation which received its rights to settle and trade in America from the Crown. But the vital difference was that the Massachusetts Bay leaders moved the location of their patent from London to New England, allowing them to build a self-governing commonwealth, over the sea, free from day-to-day royal interference. For the Council for New England was composed of a well-connected network of Puritan merchants and divines, who were keen to exploit Atlantic fishing opportunities but also to promote colonialism as a safe haven for true religion. In time, it was hoped the exercise of pure Protestantism in America would inspire and rescue the English church from its present woes. God's will had revealed itself: here was the perfect vehicle for Winthrop to escape Old England for New. He invested heavily in the Massachusetts Bay Company before, in October 1629, being elected its governor.

As his ship *Arbella* set sail out of Southampton for Cape Ann harbour in the spring of 1630, Winthrop took the opportunity to preach a lay sermon, 'The model of Christian charity', to his fellow passengers. He took as his text the Book of Matthew, 5:14–16:

* The name was taken from a local Indian tribe, part of the Algonquin people.

Ye are the light of the world. A city that is set on an hill cannot be hid. Neither do men light a candle, and put it under a bushel, but on a candlestick; and it giveth light unto all that are in the house. Let your light so shine before men, that they see your good works, and glorify your Father which is in heaven.

Aboard the ship's deck, the governor set out his ambitions for the colony and its elect membership, 'a company professing ourselves fellow members of Christ'. Central to Winthrop's vision of his prosperous, godly commonwealth was the seventeenth-century notion of a Covenant with God: 'We are entered into a covenant with Him for this work.' As a body of pilgrims dependent upon God's grace for their survival, they had to agree to work together, live together and worship the same God together. The colony, as an exemplary Christian community, was the corpus through which God could be most perfectly served. If the Lord 'shall please to hear us, and bring us in peace to the place we desire, then he hath ratified this Covenant . . . and will expect a strict performance of the articles'.⁵ If they achieved the purpose for which God had planned, 'We must consider that we shall be as a City upon a Hill; the eyes of all people are upon us.' Long before any notion of America's manifest destiny, the city of Boston had been marked out for special purposes. 'This Year [1630] it pleased God of his rich grace to Transport over into the Bay of the Massachusets divers honourable Personages, and many worthy Christians,' recalled Nathaniel Morton, the secretary of the Colony of Plymouth, 'whereby the Lord began in a manifest manner and way to make known the great thoughts which he had of Planting the Gospel in this remote and barbarous Wilderness.'⁶

Unfortunately, the Protestant Wind was not as benign as they had hoped, and it initially deposited the *Arbella* in Salem, which, according to the deputy governor Thomas Dudley, 'pleased us not'. They found the colony there in a 'sad and unexpected condition', with its dwindling residents barely able to make it through the winter.⁷ So they moved from Salem to another settlement at Charles Town and then, searching for a decent water supply, crossed the Charles River to join the reclusive Puritan William Blaxton (or Blackstone) in the Indian settlement of Shawmutt on the land known as Trimontaine, because of its three peaks. In September 1630, this settlement upon three hills was renamed Boston in honour of their brother and fellow pilgrim Isaac Johnson of Boston, in the county of Lincolnshire, who had died in Salem.

The advantages of the place were immediately apparent. 'His situation is very pleasant, being a Peninsula, hemmed in on the South-side with the Bay of Roxberry, on the north side with Charles-River, the Marshes on the back side being not half a quarter of a mile over; so that a little fencing will secure their cattle from the wolves,' was how William Wood described it in an early brochure, *New England's Prospect*.

> This neck of land is not above four miles in compass; in form almost square, having on the south-side, at one corner, a great broad hill, whereon is planted a fort, which can command any ship as she sails into any harbour within the still Bay. On the north side is another hill, equal in bigness, whereon stands a Windmill. To the north-west is a high mountain with three little rising hills on the top of it, wherefore it is called the Tramount.[8]

Winthrop set to work on his Garden of Eden, keen to find God's favour in the enterprise. 'Plantations in their beginnings have work enough . . .' he wrote in a letter, 'there being buildings, fencings, clearing and breaking up of ground, lands to be attended, orchards to be planted, highways and bridges and fortifications to be made, and all things to do, as in the beginning of the world.'[9] The Genesis analogy seemed apposite since, by the time Winthrop began tilling the soil, Massachusetts must have felt like a virgin landscape thanks to the decimation of the native Indian population. Indeed, he predicted as much in his 1629 Plantation pamphlet: 'God hath consumed the natives with a great plague in those parts, so as there be few inhabitants left.' The arrival of European settlers had indeed sparked an epidemic of smallpox, measles and influenza among the coastal Algonquian societies against which they lacked any immunity. By 1633 settlers already outnumbered Indians in the Massachusetts Bay area, and by 1700 the native population was reduced to about 10 per cent of what it had been before European contact.[10] 'So if we leave them sufficient for their own use, we may lawfully take the rest, there being more than enough for them and for us,' concluded Winthrop.[11]

With minimal Native American resistance to Winthrop's initial plans, the first identifiable outlines of Boston came into being. The lands and islands of the outer and inner harbours became populated with grazing cattle and sheep, with farmlands and orchards. It was hard, dangerous work. In December 1638 there was 'so great a tempest of wind and snow all the night and the next day, as had not been since our time'. As a result,

> Five men and youths perished between Mattapan and Dorchester . . . Anthony Dick, in a bark of thirty tons, cast away upon the head of Cape Cod. Three were starved to death with the cold; the other two got some fire and so lived there, by such food as they saved, seven weeks, till an Indian found them, etc.[12]

The Boston magistrate and keen diarist Samuel Sewall similarly noted the 'extream cold' of January 1686, 'so that the Harbour frozen up, and to the Castle. This day so cold that the Sacramental Bread is frozen pretty hard, and rattles sadly as broken into the Plates.'[13]

In the Boston promontory, the narrow 'neck' of which was regularly flooded by tidal surges, cutting the growing town off from the mainland, a windmill soon appeared atop the north hill (Copp's Hill or Mill Hill), 'grinding out the rich yellow corn of Indian origin, raised on nearly every garden lot on the peninsula'. A fire-pot suspended on a beacon was planted on Treamount or Tramount hill, to warn of impending dangers, and on the third hill, a wooden fort. These were the sites that greeted the growing number of Puritan migrants, fleeing the persecution of King Charles I's Archbishop Laud for the promised land of New England. In 1634, some seventeen emigrant ships arrived in Boston; thirty-two in 1635; and another twenty in 1638, landing a total of nearly 21,000 new settlers across the colony. They set to work constructing the first forms of a conurbation: market squares, a public park (the origin of today's Boston Common), roads, docks, meeting-houses and churches. Education and literacy were so elemental to the Puritan ethos that quite quickly the Boston Grammar School was established, and, in 1636, the Massachusetts Bay Company allocated £400 (more than half of the entire colony tax levy for 1635) to the establishment of Harvard College, named after the Puritan minister John Harvard, who on his deathbed donated £780 and his own library to the new institution. The college was located nearby at New-town (later renamed Cambridge) on a 'spacious plain' at the edge of salt marshes and designed to be as close a copy of a Cambridge University college as possible.[14] Harvard's purpose was to supply Massachusetts with a home-grown crop of Christian ministers and make it unnecessary to call upon unreliable Anglicans from England. In ensuing decades, Boston would add to its infrastructure with a bridge across the Charles River, a 670-metre defensive barricade in the harbour, town houses, pebbled streets, wharfs and more meeting-houses. For Winthrop's companions, such progress was all a sign of divine grace: nature was being tamed and a godly citadel erected. As Captain Edward Johnson put it in his celebrated tract of 1654, *Wonder-Working Providence of Zion's Saviour in New England,*

> The chiefe Edifice of this City-like Towne is crowded on the Sea-bankes, and wharfed out with great industry and cost, the buildings beautifull and large, some fairly set forth with Brick, Tile, Stone and Slate, and orderly placed with comly streets, whose continuall inlargement presages some sumptuous City. The wonder of this moderne Age, that a few yeares should bring forth such great matters by so meane a handfull . . . But now behold the admirable Acts of Christ; at this his peoples landing, the hideous Thickets in this place were such that Wolfes and Beares nurst up their young from the eyes of all beholders, in those very places where the streets are full of Girles and Boys sporting up and downe, with a continued concourse of people.[15]

Such earthly success was a reflection of true Christian sentiment, but it had to be worked at continuously. Around every corner, Winthrop saw the Devil's hand at work, as one of his journal entries from July 1632 describes:

> At waterton there was . . . a great combate betweene a mouse & a snake, & after a longe fight, the mouse prevayled & killed the snake; the Paster of Boston mr willson a verye sincere holy man hearinge of it, gave this Interpretation, that, the snake was the devill, the mouse was a poore contemptible people which God had brought hether, which should overcome Sathan heere & disposesse him of his kingdome.[16]

To assist salvation, Massachusetts's early government was almost theocratic. The franchise for the colony's assembly was not property holding, as in England, but church membership, and to join one of the many churches an individual had to evince positive signs of grace. It was compulsory for everyone to attend their parish church, and the power of ministers seamlessly extended from the ecclesiastical to the civil, the clapboard meeting-houses the setting for both religious devotion and legal transactions. The Stour valley's pious magistracy was now transposed to New England as a sharp culture of discipline cracked down on cards, dice, music, sports, saints' days and slander (especially against the church). In 1633 the Massachusetts Bay Company enacted a law stating 'that no person, householder or other, shall spend his time idly or unprofitably, under pain of such punishment as the Court shall think meet to inflict'.[17] In 1634 tobacco-taking in taverns was banned; in 1647 shovel-board in 'houses of common entertainment' was outlawed; and in 1664 'rude singing' was declared illegal. Unsurprisingly, most visitors found Boston's public culture grimly Puritanical. In 1699, the Englishman Edward Ward thought the Bostonians 'very busie in detecting one another's failings; and he is accounted, by their Church Governors, a Meritorious Christian, that betrays his Neighbour to a Whipping-post'.[18] This religio-civic theocracy was also highly antagonistic toward any sign of religious disharmony. For all their demands for toleration in England, when the heterodox views of religious radicals such as the Separatist Roger Williams and antinomian Anne Hutchinson threatened to disrupt Boston's stability, they were swiftly drummed out of the Bay Colony. It was never a wise decision to flout such punishments either: between 1659 and 1661 four Quakers were hanged for returning after banishment. There was a Covenant to be upheld, and political pluralism played no part in it.

In the light of these saints' attempt to erect a godly commonwealth, Boston's rapidity in backing the parliamentary cause during the English Civil War is unsurprising. The dynastic, business and religious connections between the American colonists and the English Roundheads ran deep and, in May 1643, reference to King Charles I was dropped altogether from the colony's oath of allegiance. According to Winthrop, the king 'had violated the privileges of parliament, and made war upon them, and thereby lost much of his kingdom and many of his subjects; whereupon it was thought fit to omit that part of it for the present'.[19]

Winthrop passed away in 1649, when the outcome of the English Revolution was unclear, but he bequeathed to the public culture of Boston a deep hostility towards Roman Catholicism, monarchical absolutism and all the other misdemeanours of the Stuart monarchy. Attempts by the Stuart Crown in the late 1670s to impose a new charter on the colony, abolish the Massachusetts Bay Company and establish a Dominion of New England under direct royal rule had led to violent clashes across Boston as Puritan ministers whipped up fears of another Popish plot led by untrustworthy London courtiers. It was small wonder that, in London, Massachusetts in general and Boston in particular were fast gaining a reputation as a haven for radical dissenters. A British customs agent, William Dyre, described New Englanders in the 1680s as 'raging furious fanatic Whigs . . . Rebellious and unnatural hators and warriors Against the true mother church'.[20] Indeed, the very crowning of the crypto-Catholic King James II had been greeted with signs of foreboding in Boston. 'The King is Proclaimed; 8 Companies, the Troop, and several Gentlemen on horseback assisted,' Samuel Sewall wrote on 20 April 1685. 'This day a child falls upon a Knife which runs through its cheek to the Throat, of which inward Wound it dies, and is buried on Wednesday.'[21]

So relief at the fall of King James and the triumph of the Dutch Protestant William of Orange in 1688 was overwhelming. As soon as news of the Glorious Revolution arrived in New England, Boston led the way with a band of rebels seizing the royal governor and dissolving the hated Dominion. Yet at the same time as the colony revived its old forms of self-government, Boston developed a novel sense of fealty towards the Crown after all those decades of hostility towards the Stuarts. With King William III on the throne, Boston's Puritans finally felt there was a godly monarch culturally attuned to New England's religious and political ethos. That sense of divergence from England, which had marked out the foundation of Massachusetts in the 1630s, began to ebb as the spiritual and political interests of Crown and colony aligned. Increasingly, the evangelical leaders of late seventeenth-century Boston could see themselves as part of a shared, global endeavour to resist popery, protect true religion and promote English liberty alongside their Protestant monarch. In reality, William III would continue with much of the Stuarts' policy of centralizing control over the American colonies: the rewritten Massachusetts charter of 1691 shifted the franchise qualification from church membership to property holding and kept the governorship a Crown appointment. Inevitably, this created the risk of a clash between the royal prerogative of the governor (usually, a former British army officer) and the autonomy of the Massachusetts House of Representatives (elected by male colonists since 1629), but at the turn of the eighteenth century such tensions were non-existent. The remarkable, natural sympathy which sprang up between elites in Massachusetts and the mother country – shared beliefs in the liberties of Magna Carta, the terrifying spectre of French and Spanish Catholicism, the wretchedness of the Stuarts and the virtues of the 1688 constitutional settlement – overshadowed any theoretical constitutional incompatibility. For now, Boston was delighted to be a part of Britain's emergent, Atlantic empire.[22]

THE GREAT MART AND STAPLE

What did that 'empire' look like in the late seventeenth century? The word itself was a translation from the Latin *imperium* and was taken to mean control over trade and sea as much as land. Indeed, a sea-based empire was looked on more favourably by colonial advocates: in contrast to the military dictatorship of the land empire of Rome or the corruption visited upon Spain by its possessions in the Americas, an empire of the seas brought more benign and flexible connotations. For merchants and courtiers in London thinking about England's *imperium* abroad, the contours of influence would have entailed the Caribbean plantations of Jamaica and Barbados (see Chapter 2), Ireland (see Chapter 3), the Chesapeake colonies of Maryland and Virginia, outposts in Newfoundland and in Hudson Bay, the coming towns of Philadelphia, New York and Charlestown, and then the New England settlements. It was a disparate, inchoate,

Atlantic empire. For whilst colonies shared an unified imperial authority in the form of the British monarch, judgements over who was in practical charge – who exercised 'dominium' or territorial control – were more opaque. In different corners of this empire, the running of the colonies varied from joint-stock corporations to royal governors to local assemblies to individual patentees. Taken together, the beginnings of the British Empire were an unruly mix of tobacco plantations, whaling stations, fishing ports, cane fields, forts and cities. Beyond their loyalty to the Crown, the only effective source of imperial unity was the quickening pace of transatlantic commerce.

Trade certainly changed Boston, as Winthrop's 'city on the hill' slowly emerged from its Puritan chrysalis. Of course, there still existed a strict culture of public piety, and the city remained a place of religious sanctuary during the final Stuart years. 'In about 1682,' Josiah Franklin, a cloth dyer of Banbury, Oxfordshire, sought asylum in Boston. 'The conventicles [having] been forbidden by law, and frequently disturbed, induced some considerable men of his acquaintance to remove to that country, and he was prevailed with to accompany them thither, where they expected to enjoy their mode of religion with freedom.'[23] But within the growing city it was proving harder and harder to retain that closeted, Puritan sense of purpose and prophetic function. 'The democratic leaven was at work,' as one nineteenth-century history put it. 'The ampler scope for individual energy, and the sudden accession of political rights and commercial importance, began to tell upon manners.'[24] This was one of the inadvertent consequences of Calvinist theology. With worldly success regarded as a sign of God's grace, a culture of industriousness and enterprise had gripped Boston from its earliest days. Material riches and rapid urban improvements felt like God fulfilling His side of the Covenant, and proved a source of intense spiritual satisfaction. Ever increasing numbers of the elect were drawn towards the fulfilling business of wealth creation. But for those pilgrims still inspired by Winthrop's more ascetic vision of the acting out of God's purpose the changing face of Boston resembled Mammon triumphant. 'The Lord he speaks in particular to Boston,' the influential cleric Increase Mather was informed by one angry correspondent in 1677, and calls you to a thorough reformation in your Town, you being set up as a Beacon upon the top of a mountain . . . your candlesticks should give light to all the neighbour Towns and Churches round about you: But when they see your famous Town abound with drunkennesse, swearing, excesse in apparel, etc. what encouragement is there for Towns round about you to follow your example?[25]

These were no idle accusations. By the 1670s, New England was coming to be known as 'the great Mart and Staple' of the Atlantic world, and the Boston economy was expanding steadily, even beginning to rival the well-established British ports of Hull, Liverpool, Bristol and Glasgow. Wealth came from the seas – in particular, the Atlantic cod caught in vast numbers off the Maine, New England and Newfoundland coasts. In 1716, some 6.5 million fish were caught and processed in New England; by 1765 that had risen to near 19 million.[26] Boston prospered by exporting both cured cod to Europe (the Spanish port of Bilbao became the major Mediterranean market, Mammon overcoming any religious scruples at trade with Catholics) and lower-quality dried, salted cod to the Caribbean, as well as re-exporting the catches from Newfoundland and Nova Scotia. Cod became the commodity upon which a new trading economy was built as the fishing fleets sailed back into Boston harbour from their Atlantic journeys laden with fruit, wine, molasses, spices and coffee from Europe and the West Indies. To 'the Islands of America and with Spain', the Massachusetts merchants carried 'flour, salt beef, salt pork, cod, staves, salt salmon, salt mackerel, onions, and oysters salted in barrels . . . and for their return, they bring Sugar, Cotton Wood, Molasses, Indigo, Sago'.[27] A typical fortune was that made by leading Boston merchant John Erving. His grandson, Robert C. Winthrop, described this everyday tale of Massachusetts wealth creation:

A few dollars earned on a commencement day, by ferrying passengers over Charles River, when there was no bridge – shipped to Lisbon in the shape of fish, and from thence to London in the shape of fruit, and from thence brought home to be reinvested in fish, and to be re-entered upon the same triangular circuit of trade – laid the foundations of the largest fortunes of the day.[28]

Some merchants also started to return to Boston with slave cargoes, beginning the British colony's traffic in human bondage and the start of the African diaspora in America. By the 1720s, Boston was host to a slave population of around 400, rising quickly to 1,400 by the 1740s – some 8.5 per cent of the city's population.[29]

Boston's merchants invested more and more of their profits from cod into the lucrative business of slaving – but also into whaling, whale oil, oysters and lobsters, potash, animal products and timber (including barrels, staves and boards). In effect, the city became the trading centre of New England and a North American hub for shipping and ship-building thanks to its rapid, eight-week sailing distance from the British Isles. As early as the 1640s Bostonians were boasting how 'besides many boats, shallops, hoys, lighters, pinnaces, we are in a way of building ships of a hundred, two hundred, three hundred, four hundred tons. Five of them already at sea; many more in hand at this present.'[30] By the second quarter of the eighteenth century, the city's waterfront had been transformed into a vast shipyard of rope-makers, shipjoiners, riggers and carpenters, teeming with tonnage ready for trade across the Atlantic. Abutting the shipyards was an expanding number of sugar refineries, for the imported molasses from the West Indies, and rum distilleries. Other industries such as flour milling, small-scale manufacturing, tanneries and taverns all helped to avoid an over-dependence on the shipping trade.

This prosperity was reflected in an improving urban fabric. 'Their streets are many and large, paved with Pebbles; the Materials of their Houses are Brick, Stone, Lime, handsomely contrived, and when any new Houses are built, they are made conformable to our New Buildings in London since the fire [of 1666],' noted the visiting bookseller John Dunton towards the end of the seventeenth century.[31] By then Boston was growing fast, from a town of 6,000 residents in the 1680s to 16,000 by the 1740s, densely hemmed into some sixty roads and forty lanes. 'The Town hath indeed Three Elder Sisters in this Colony, but it hath wonderfully outgrown them all; and her Mother, Old Boston, in *England* also,' the Reverend Cotton Mather (son of Increase Mather) boasted in 1702. 'Yea, within a few Years after the first Settlement it grew to be The Metropolis of the Whole English America.'[32] For some, the rapid urbanization was all a little stressful. 'Who can study in Boston streets?' asked John Adams, the future United States president and a prickly Boston lawyer, in 1759. 'My Eyes are so diverted with Chimney Sweeps, Carriers of Wood, Merchants, Ladies, Priests, Carts, Horses, Oxen, Coaches, Market men and Women, Soldiers, Sailors, and my Ears with the Rattle Gabble of them all that I can't think long enough in the Street upon any one Thing to start and pursue a Thought.'[33]

Above street level, the skyline was transformed into a set-piece battle between God and Mammon. On the side of divinity rose the spires of the city's sixteen churches, from the 'Brownist' Old Church (the faith of the earliest, *Mayflower* pilgrims) to the Brattle Square Presbyterian Church ministering to Scots-Irish Calvinists, to the more mainstream Old South (Congregationalist) Meeting House to those of the Anabaptists, Episcopalians and Quakers. Commerce, by contrast, planted a forest of masts in the harbour, where ships waited to unload at the 166 wharfs stretched out along the waterfront. The English historian Daniel Neal described 'the masts of ships here' (in 1719) as 'a kind of Wood of Trees like that we see upon the River of Thames about Wapping and Limehouse'. The most impressive of the wharfs was the half-mile Long Wharf, whose line of warehouses was topped off with a battery and had the effect of seamlessly stretching King Street (now State Street) into the bay waters. Today, the wharf's constrained, corporate atmosphere – with an ugly Marriott Hotel and Starbucks, an aquarium and luxury yacht offices – gives little sense of the commerce, hustle and dockside grandeur which allowed 'Ships of the greatest burthen' to unload 'without the help of Boats or Lighters'.[34] Here was where goods, peoples, ideas and British officialdom first landed in Boston.

The city which spread out before these arrivals had none of the orderly town-planning or civic grandeur of Philadelphia or New York. Instead, the chaotic demands of commerce and trade shaped the cityscape, making Boston a maze of narrow lanes, crooked streets, haphazard pathways and docklands. What was most obvious in the urban pattern was a clear distinction between a more nautical, plebeian North End and a spacious, leafy South End, where large lots provided homes for the finer members of the merchant class. In the south, according to a pseudonymous 'Mr Bennett' of the 1740s, 'both the ladies and gentlemen dress and appear as gay, in common, as courtiers in England on a coronation or birthday. And the ladies here visit, drink tea, and indulge every little piece of gentility to the height of the mode, and neglect the affairs of their families with as good a grace as the finest ladies in London.' The bookseller John Dunton greatly admired the 'gardens and orchards' of the south, and the evening promenade on Boston Common, 'where the Gallants a little before sunset walk with their Marmalet Madams, as we do in Moorfield, etc.'.[35]

Yet eighteenth-century colonial Boston was also strikingly intimate: a 3-kilometre stretch of land, encircled by water, in which rich and poor, godly and ungodly, smuggler and custom official all had to rub along. Today, after centuries of land reclamation and construction has decapitated the 'Three Hills' and pushed the city boundaries deep into the harbour on the east and the Charles River on the west, it is difficult to reimagine the much narrower, almost stifling contours of pre-industrial Boston. Then there was no East Boston or South Boston, no dry docks, dams and mass of bridges. It was a place of coves and bays, rivers and necks which at no point was more than a kilometre from the water.

And the density of the city nursed its elevated civil society. The wealth of the 'codfish aristocracy' combined with the Puritan ethos of the city's founders to produce a remarkably educated citizenry, who were kept up to date with contemporary controversies by an unrivalled range of bookshops, printing presses, journals and newspapers. 'There are five Printing-Presses in Boston, which are generally full of Work, by which it appears that Humanity and the Knowledge of Letters flourish more here than in all the other English Plantations put together,' said the visiting historian Daniel Neal.[36] The letters of John Dunton, on his visit to Boston in the 1680s, are further testimony to the extensive literary life in the colony. Recounting his social rounds, he lists visits to the bookseller John Usher ('He is very rich, and Merchandizes; very witty; and has got a great Estate by book-selling'); Joseph Bruning, a 'Dutch book-seller from Holland' ('he valu'd a good-book, who-ever printed it'); the 'Scotch book-seller, one Campbel' ('a Brisk young fellow, that dresses All-a-Mode'); Mr Andrew Thorncomb, 'a book-seller from London' whom Ladies adored for

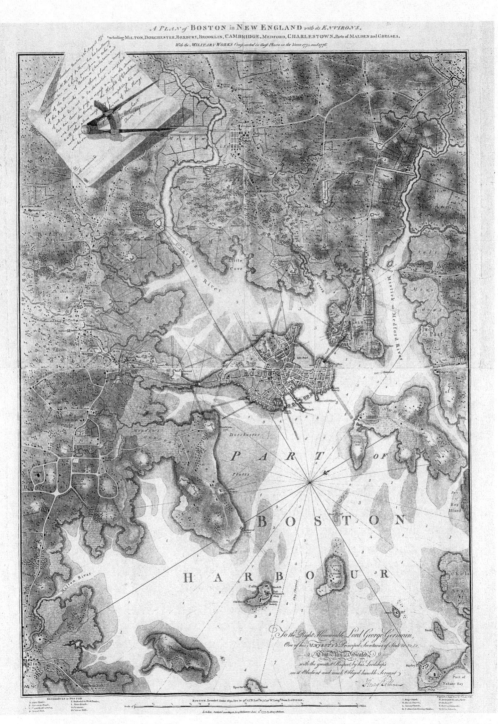

A plan of Boston in New England with its environs, by Henry Pelham (1777).

'his excellent singing and variety of Songs'; and, finally, Samuel Green the printer ('a man of good Sense, and understanding').[37] Dunton was always delighted to visit his friends' homes, but Boston also provided a sophisticated network of civic institutions, from Masonic lodges to shipping associations, from the townhouse (or town hall) to the Merchants' Exchange. Then there were the coffee-houses and estimated 150 taverns – such as the Bunch of Grapes, Green Dragon, Rose & Crown, the Royal Exchange, the Two Palaverers – providing a more rough and ready setting for the political and religious controversies of the day.[38] All in all, Daniel Neal felt able to conclude, 'a Gentleman from *London* would almost think himself at home at *Boston*, when he observes the Numbers of people, their Houses, their Furniture, their Tables, their Dress and Conversation, which perhaps is as splendid and showy as that of the most considerable Tradesmen in London'.[39]

THY CITIES SHALL WITH COMMERCE SHINE

Just as the wealth of London and numerous English county towns, such as Bristol and Cheltenham, in the eighteenth century was part and parcel of colonialism, so Boston's economy was dependent on that amorphous, Atlantic *imperium* which had begun to emerge during the 1600s. 'TRADE, without enlarging the *British* Territories, has given us a kind of additional Empire,' wrote the playwright and *Spectator* journalist Joseph Addison in 1711. Indeed, following the 1707 Act of Union between England and Scotland, the phrase 'British Empire' – as in John Oldmixon's book *The British Empire in America* (1708) – became much more regularly employed as trade fostered some sense of shared interest and political community across Britain's congeries of territories. It was still taken to mean a mercantilist consortium of mutual commercial advantage, with the prospering colonies of America part of a broader vision of common enrichment covering Old World and New. But there was now more of a sense of growing metropolitan control over the outlying colonies. The legal axis of Addison's 'additional Empire' was the Navigation Acts, a series of laws which had been first passed in the 1650s dictating that all colonial, merchant traffic be transported via British ports and British ships. So-called enumerated products – such as tobacco, sugar, cotton and rice – had first to be shipped to either England or Scotland before then passing on to their final destination, an imperial trading system designed to enrich the mother country by denying the Dutch and French any bilateral commerce with British possessions. The Navigation Acts produced a closed trading system which bound New and Old England together in a shared sense of mercantile endeavour, cultural affinity and equal citizenship. The mutual benefits of this 'empire of goods' was apparent to Philadelphia and Boston as well as Glasgow and Liverpool.[40] The bonds of imperial loyalty, as one scholar puts it, 'depended upon commerce, upon the free flow of goods, and not upon coercion'.[41]

Yet the British Empire in the eighteenth century was not unfamiliar with some external coercion. A rolling succession of conflicts, variously known as King William's War (or the Nine Years' War), Queen Anne's War (War of the Spanish Succession), King George's War (War of the Austrian Succession) and the French and Indian War (Seven Years' War), turned the Atlantic into a global theatre of conflict enveloping the British, French and Spanish Empires in a century-long battle for supremacy. 'The Empire of the Seas is ours; we have been many ages in possession of it; we have had many sea-fights, at a vast effusion of blood, and expences of treasure, to preserve it; and preserve it we still must, at all Risks and Events, if we have a Mind to preserve ourselves,' was the common-enough view of one patriotic publication in 1738.[42]

The demands of these world wars transformed the European state, leading to the expansion of the navy and army, vastly enlarged tax revenue and the exporting of conflict beyond the Continent and into the colonies. It also had a cultural impact: the war state, and the chauvinism it engineered, seeded a deeper conception of the British Empire as an enterprise involved in more than trade. With British armed forces and free-spirited merchants engaged in a global struggle against the absolutist, Catholic monarchies of France and Spain, the Empire came to be imagined as something Protestant, commercial, maritime and dedicated to liberty. This was the imperial vision of Britain which would be celebrated in James Thomson's masque hit of 1740, 'Rule,

Britannia!' And it was a widening conception of Empire enthusiastically embraced in eighteenth-century Boston:

> To thee belongs the rural reign;
> Thy cities shall with commerce shine:
> All thine shall be the subject main,
> And every shore it circles thine.
> 'Rule, Britannia! rule the waves:
> 'Britons never will be slaves.'

It was exactly this notion of combined, Protestant enterprise for which Massachusetts had embraced the new monarchy of King William III in 1688. John Adams recorded in his diary on 3 April 1778 a conversation with an 'inquisitive sensible' Dutch merchant who claimed that Holland 'regarded England as the Bulwark of the Protestant Religion and the most important Weight in the Ballance of Power in Europe against France', with which Adams heartily agreed.[43] And in 1763, he felt compelled to state how 'the liberty, the unalienable, indefeasible rights of men, the honor and dignity of human nature, the grandeur and glory of the public, and the universal happiness of individuals, were never so skilfully and successfully consulted as in that most excellent monument of human art, the common law of England'.[44]

Such ideological conviction was only natural in a Boston that found itself on the front line in the Franco-British power struggle. In March 1744, France had joined Spain in the War of the Austrian Succession against the nation they came to call perfidious Albion. The response of the British authorities in America was to push north into Canada and try to capture the French fortress at Louisburg, on Cape Breton Island, the so-called 'Gibraltar of the New World'. Controlling entry to the St Lawrence River – and hence access to Quebec – was regarded by the British as vital to preventing a French encirclement of its thirteen American colonies, from Canada in the north to Mississippi in the south. In June 1745 Admiral Peter Warren, heavily aided by colonial militia, captured Louisburg in a brilliant naval assault – to the delight of Boston's political and merchant elite.

The Louisburg démarche was just a skirmish in the British Empire's broader battle against Bourbon France, which by the mid-1700s was being played out from Canada in the north to the islands of St Lucia and St Vincent in the Caribbean south. Victory in Canada and the Americas was regarded by British military strategists as essential for supremacy over the French on the European continent. It was a zero-sum game, as one contemporary polemicist acknowledged: 'The French . . . know that the source of power lies in riches, and that the source of the English riches lies in America. They know that in proportion we are weakened there, in the same proportion they are strengthened.' And this was equally understood within the Thirteen Colonies which made up British America by the 1730s.* The Boston physician and polemicist William Clarke warned in 1755 that if Britain's colonies were lost, the French navy 'would increase to such a degree of superiority over that of Great Britain, as must entirely destroy her commerce, reduce her from her present state of independency to be at last nothing more than a province of France'.[45] Another Bostonian, Thomas Hancock, was equally adamant that ridding America of the French 'will be the salvation of England, for in forty years this very America will absolutely take all the manufactory of England . . . whoever keeps America will in the end (whether French or English) have the Kingdom of England'.[46]

The 1763 Franco-British Peace of Paris seemed to settle the matter: having lost Quebec to General Wolfe, the French were forced to cede control of Canada after a century of colonial dominance. As the spectre of Bourbon encirclement of Anglo-Saxon America eased, few were more delighted than one Benjamin Franklin, son of Josiah Franklin, the cloth dyer from Banbury who had sought asylum in Boston back in the 1680s. 'No one can rejoice more sincerely than I do, on the reduction of Canada,' the young Franklin wrote,

> this not merely as I am a colonist, but as I am a Briton. I have long been of opinion, that the foundations of the future grandeur and stability of the British Empire lie in America; and though like other foundations, they are low and little seen, they are nevertheless broad and strong enough to support the greatest political structure human wisdom ever erected.[47]

* Virginia (1607), New York (1626), Massachusetts Bay (1630), New Hampshire (1630), Maryland (1634), Connecticut (1636), Rhode Island and Providence Plantations (1636), Delaware (1638), North Carolina (1653), New Jersey (1660), South Carolina (1670), Pennsylvania (1682) and Georgia (1733).

There was good reason for the likes of Clarke, Hancock and Franklin to identify themselves as both Britons and supporters of this common, Atlantic project – for the city of Boston was doing spectacularly well out of it. The House of Hancock was, in many respects, typical. The Hancock family's connections to Boston stretch back to Nathaniel Hancock, who landed in America in 1634 and sired a line of celebrated Congregationalist ministers. As Boston began to shed its Puritan heritage, the family moved into commerce, and by the 1730s Thomas Hancock was running the city's most lucrative general store with annual sales in excess of £10,000. At the beginning, Hancock serviced Boston's literary culture by trading in publishing, stationary and book-binding, before expanding into domestic wares and consumables, then commodity trading and even investment banking. His real breakthrough, however, was to make some deft political connections in London and exploit the transatlantic trading routes: he exported rum, beef, cotton and other commodities to the cut-off whaling towns of New England, before picking up whale oil and bone for England, and then returning with consumer durables from Europe (not all of it declared) for the Boston middling classes. Hancock's enormous profits were evident for all to see in his Beacon Hill house, which stood on the edge of Boston Common on land now occupied by the Massachusetts State House. It was a three-storey Georgian mansion, renowned for its mahogany furniture, English 'flockwork' wallpaper, more than fifty glass windows and two-acre garden complete with peach, apricot and mulberry orchard.[48]

If one digs a little deeper, it quickly becomes apparent that much of Hancock's profit was entirely dependent upon British imperial aggrandizement. For all Thomas Hancock's peaceable commerce, from as early as the 1740s he was helping to provision the Royal Navy and British army in their various campaigns. Sudden surges in demand, limited supplies, lack of infrastructure and the need for the right type of contact – all these conditions of a war economy were ably exploited by the well-resourced Hancock. When Admiral Vernon launched his expedition against the Spanish cities of Porto Bello in Panama and Cartagena in Colombia as part of the War of the Austrian Succession, Hancock supplied them with beef and pork. When the British assault on Louisburg was being prepared, Hancock was the man to feed, transport and clothe the troops. (It made him £100,000 and the richest man in Boston.) And when Halifax and other Canadian bases needed to be supported in the early 1750s from a French counter-attack, Hancock delivered lumber and carpenters, transports and fishing vessels. At the outset of the French and Indian War in 1755, Governor Lawrence of Novia Scotia appointed Hancock sole supplier for the expedition against Fort Beausejour thanks to his ready terms of credit. He sold arms, imported wheat from Philadelphia and revealed himself to be the most fervently patriotic of colonists: 'For God's sake then let us Root the French blood out of America.' And so when General James Wolfe launched his expedition up the St Lawrence to capture Quebec in 1759, the House of Hancock took care of the draught-oxen, teamsters for the artillery, provision of the fleet and other cargo logistics. By 1760, Thomas Hancock and his Boston corporation were one of the world's leading suppliers for the British colonial project.[49]

It was not only Hancock who prospered in this manner. In 1754 the three wealthiest men in Boston were the three largest war contractors for the British army and navy – Thomas Hancock, the quartermaster Charles Apthorp and the Lisbon fish-exporter John Erving. And the war economy trickled down to the ship-builders, the fishermen (whose monopolies were secured), the tanners, the glove-makers, the bakers, the artisans and those businesses which simply benefited from the influx of credit brought about by the war. As the conflicts rolled on, the demand for food, clothing, transport, alcohol and armaments kept the Boston economy humming. While there were periods of retrenchment and depression following the peace treaties, and Boston's ship-building felt increasing competition from other ports, by the mid-eighteenth century the city had established itself as a major commercial metropolis within the British Empire.

What was more, Boston's residents were keen to show off their riches. 'Went over the House to view the Furniture, which alone cost a thousand Pounds sterling,' wrote John Adams after a dinner party at the house of the Boston merchant Nick Boylstone. 'A seat it is for a noble Man, a Prince. The Turkey Carpets, the painted Hangings, the Marble Tables, the rich Beds with crimson Damask Curtains and Counterpins, the beautiful Chimney Clock, the Spacious Garden, are the most magnificent of any Thing I have ever seen.'[50] Boston might have been an export economy, shipping natural resources across the Atlantic, but it was also an aggressive importer. Beginning in the 1740s the American market for imported goods – buttons, ribbons, jewels, books, toys, musical instruments, carpets and draperies – began to take off. Between 1750 and 1773 it rose 120 per cent, and in the five years 1768–72 alone American imports from England grew by 43 per cent.[52] 'A vast demand is growing for British manufactures,' Benjamin Franklin remarked in 1751, 'a glorious market wholly in the Power of Britain.'[53]

And he should know. When Josiah Franklin discovered that in Boston 'his dying trade would not maintain his family,' he became a tallow-chandler, producing soap and candles from a shop on Fort Street (Milk Street), round the corner from the Old South Meeting House where his fifteenth child, Benjamin, was christened. As perhaps the most famous son of a city built on the Book of Matthew, Benjamin Franklin's first job was 'cutting wick for candles, filling the dipping mold and the molds for cast candles, attending the shop, going on errands etc.'. Unfortunately, Franklin 'disliked the trade, and had a strong inclination for the sea, but my father declared against it'.[54] His brothers would also soon declare against him and, after falling out over a joint publishing enterprise, Benjamin Franklin fled his Boston apprenticeship for Philadelphia. But the Franklin family business was typical of Boston's expanding consumer economy. Rather than making their own soap and candles, Bostonians were now heading to the shops for their household goods, their fashion items and their perishable foodstuffs. Milliners, hairdressers, silversmiths (such as Paul Revere), glove-makers and silk merchants were the new emblems of the Boston economy. Into the great wharfs and warehouses of the waterfront came the latest consumer accessories from England. But of all the imports introduced into America via the Navigation Acts, by far the most popular and lucrative was tea.

Europeans had been drinking tea – along with hot chocolate and coffee – from the late sixteenth century. Imported from China, both green and black tea leaves, grown on the bohea hills, gained in popularity over the ensuing centuries. The caffeine, taste and ritual of tea proved an immediate hit in Europe's royal courts, especially when the bitter taste began to be sweetened by Caribbean sugar. Thanks to the corporate muscle of the East India Company, hurrying its precious crates from the port of Canton to the wharfs of London, the price of a cup of tea started to fall away during the 1700s, until it stopped being a beverage of the elite and became a major staple of British commercial and cultural life. In 1768 tea represented almost 50 per cent of the East India Company's total turnover.

America drank deep on this global commodity, with the ports of Boston, Philadelphia and New York among the thirstiest customers for the East India Company's cargo. Estimates put the licit and illicit imports of tea from England at over £200,000 a year by the 1770s, with each American annually drinking more than a pound of tea. It was a universal drink which was found in almost every colonial household, crossing the boundaries of social class: in the 1750s even the inmates of Philadelphia's poor house insisted on having bohea tea. And in middle-class drawing rooms, on lacquered furniture, the custom of tea drinking became a significant component of household ritual, with its brewing, serving and sipping a litmus test of middle-class etiquette. 'Tea became a ritual of family solidarity, sustenance and politeness.'[55]

Needless to say, the correct tea party demanded the right kind of consumer accessories, and in the cities of the eastern seaboard the British ceramics industry found an enticing new market. The pioneering Stoke-on-Trent potter Josiah Wedgwood was among the first to provide the American middling classes with the cups, saucers, milk-jugs, sugar pots and teapots (let alone the tea caddies, sugar tongs and spoons) they decided they needed to drink a cup of tea. In the archives of the Wedgwood Museum is a letter from Wedgwood's Liverpool merchants, Thomas Bentley and Samuel Boardman, dated 25 September 1764, requesting over 1,600 pieces for immediate export including Cauliflower and Pineapple moulded wares, black glazed wares, tortoiseshell dishes and fifty dozen white plates. 'Above you have a copy of a small order we have just received from Boston in New England from the very careful man who has sent in cash to pay from them,' Boardman added, 'and they probably send us more if they are served to his satisfaction.' It no doubt helped future sales that Wedgwood would himself become a leading proponent of American independence. Ever the entrepreneur, he even saw good sales in it. 'What do you think of sending Mr Pitt [Lord Chatham, defender of the colonists] on Crockery Ware to America; a quantity certainly might be sold there now, and some advantage made of the American prejudice in favour of that great man.'[56]

The Staffordshire pottery, the bohea tea, the sugar, silverware and delicate table-cloths all helped to bestow an Anglicized identity on the Boston middling classes. Gone was that oppositional, Puritan culture which had inspired the first founders of Boston, who developed an urban sensibility so consciously distinct from Stuart England. Instead, there now flourished on either side of the Atlantic a shared Georgian society, shaped by the literature of Addison and Pope, entertained by the witticisms of Swift and Defoe, informed by *The Spectator* and other fashionable journals 'from London'. The pages of Boston's five newspapers in the 1730s were dominated by news from the capital, Edinburgh or Dublin, with important society information on the noteworthy weddings, births and funerals of the day there. Boston's ninety-five booksellers, libraries, myriad societies, shops and taverns – the world of John Dunton – helped to nurture an authentically colonial culture which naturally regarded itself as a component part of the British Empire. A Parisian visitor to the city thought that 'in their whole manner of living, the Americans resemble the English. Punch, warm and cold, before dinner; excellent beef and Spanish and Bordeaux wines, cover their tables, always solidly and abundantly served'.[57] Here was the 'colonization of taste', in which furniture, ceramics and tea managed subtly to unite Massachusetts and the other twelve colonies with their mother country across the Atlantic. It was a powerfully uniform material culture which meant that 'on the eve of the American Revolution, Americans were more English than they had been in the past since the first years of the colonies'.[58]

Yet it would be a mistake to regard such English tastes as the passive product of a consumer society. Boston was also an imperial city in its ritual and public culture. It had been settled by John Winthrop in the 1630s as a consciously anti-royalist redoubt – a place of refuge for true Protestants fearful of the Catholic ambitions of the Stuart monarchy. It didn't think twice about supporting the Roundhead cause in the 1640s or the Glorious Revolution of 1688; its Puritan faith, democratic ethos and commercial ambitions marked it as an obviously parliamentary metropolis. As we have seen, that changed in

1688 with the accession of the faithful Protestant King William III and the willingness of his Hanoverian successors to wage a global war against the Catholic empires of Spain and France. The consequence was that in the 1700s Bostonians could start to understand themselves as Britons not thanks to any parliamentary connection but rather as royal subjects. It was the Crown which connected up the British Empire; if anything, the burghers of Boston were rather hostile to the growing interference, taxation and regulation which emanated from Westminster politicians. Instead, they displayed far more affection for the Hanoverian kings than most of their indigenous British subjects. In the judgement of one recent history, the eighteenth-century political culture of Massachusetts 'was decidedly monarchical and imperial, Protestant and virulently anti-Catholic, almost to the moment of American independence'.[59]

Just as the Hanoverian monarchy embedded itself through a calendar of public rites in Great Britain, so accession dates, coronations, birthdays and deaths provided a regular cycle for celebrating the Protestant succession in Boston. Along Orange Street, Marlborough Street and Hanover Street, Boston played host to some twenty-six annual events embedding the monarchy in the everyday life of Massachusetts. 'We ... do now with full Voice and Consent of Tongue and Heart, Publish and Proclaim That the High and Mighty Prince George, Prince of Wales; is now ... become our only Lawful and Rightful Liege Lord GEORGE the Third ... To Whom we acknowledge all Faith and constant Obedience, with all heart and humble Affection,' was the proclamation read from the courthouse on 30 December 1760 to 'a vast Concourse of People of all Ranks'.[60] There then followed days of loyal revelry, cannonades, bell-ringing, illuminations and fireworks marking the accession of King George III – a long way from Winthrop's more Cromwellian vision for Boston. In 1765, the city partied again, celebrating the birthday of the Prince of Wales 'with the greatest demonstrations of joy, and with marks of unfeigned loyalty'. 'Every apartment in town rung with pious and loyal ejaculations,' commented the *Pennsylvania Gazette*, '"God bless our true British King" – "Long Live their Majesties" – "Heaven preserve the Prince of Wales, and all the Royal Family."'[61]

By the 1760s, royalist sentiments were an everyday part of public culture. 'The merchants made a dinner for Captain Gideon at the Coffee house and a very Genteel Entertainment it was,' the Exeter-born Boston merchant John Rowe noted in his diary for 2 December 1766. 'After Dinner the following toasts were Drank. 1. The King 2. The Queen and Royal Family 3.The Parliament of Great Britain 4. His Majesty's Ministry 5. The Earl of Chatham [etc.].'[62]

Loyalism was not limited to the upper orders. Two years earlier, John Rowe had witnessed 'a sorrowful accident' take place:

> The wheel of the carriage that the Pope was fixed on run over a Boy's head and he died instantly. The Sheriff, Justices, Officers of the Militia were ordered to destroy both South and North End Popes. In the afternoon they got the North End Pope pulled to pieces. They went to the South End but could not conquer upon which the South End people brought out their pope and went in Triumph to the Northward and at the Mill Bridge a Battle begun between the people of Both Parts of the Town.[63]

What Rowe was describing was Pope's Day in Boston, the annual 5 November Guy Fawkes celebrations which combined a ritual display of anti-popery with violent neighbourhood factionalism. On the one hand, the Pope's Day public holiday gave licence to the most obvious and participative form of monarchical triumphalism, allowing a city-wide expression of anti-Catholic, anti-Stuart fervour and a celebration of Protestantism, liberty and the loyalties of Empire. It bound the Boston labouring classes – the apprentices, carpenters, sailors and tavern-keepers – to the heroic history and purpose of the British monarchy. On the other hand, it also served as a yearly vehicle for the sometimes deadly rivalry of Boston's North End and South End. By the 1760s, this communal antagonism constituted a vast civic ritual, with floats and effigies of Hanoverian hate-figures (popes, Guy Fawkes, the Stuart Pretender, even Admiral Byng)* paraded through the Boston streets, before then culminating in an all-out brawl on Boston Common at day's end. For the precious John Rowe, the ritual and carnival was all getting too much by 1766. 'This is a Day of Confusion in Boston,' he noted sourly, 'occasioned by a foolish custom of

---

* Admiral John Byng was widely held responsible for the loss of Minorca in 1756 at the start of the Seven Years' War. He was court-martialled and executed in 1757.

Carrying about the pope and the Devill etc. on a large carriage through the streets of this Town. Indeed three very large ones made their appearance this day.'[64] For all its vernacular chaos, Pope's Day was, in fact, another component of loyal, royal Boston: testament to a colonial city contentedly embedded within the British Empire, an urban expression of the Empire's Atlantic strengths, commercial focus and increasingly global reach.

The cultural affinity was evident in the streets and squares of Boston. After spending extensively on sewerage systems and decent streets in the 1720s and '30s, a construction spree gripped the city. 'The buildings in Boston are in general good,' reported the visiting Anglican clergyman Andrew Burnaby in 1759. 'The streets are open and spacious, and well-paved; and the whole has much the air of some of our best country towns in England.' In addition to a growing number of Georgian mansions and domestic developments across the city (as well as in the surrounding towns of Cambridge, Dorchester and Milton), there was a more confident 'public architecture' in the city modelled on the designs of James Gibbs and Christopher Wren in London. The Governor's Palace, the courthouse, the exchange and Faneuil Hall were all regarded as fine additions to the city, but the real gem was agreed to be the King's Chapel on Tremont Street – 'exceedingly elegant and fitted up in the Corinthian taste', as Burnaby described the church. 'There is also an elegant private concert-room, highly finished in the Ionic manner.'[65] Indeed, such was the expansive dignity of Boston's architecture, with its 'lofty and regular' edifices and 'spires and cupolas intermixt at proper distances', it now had as much the air of Old England as New. As the French military chaplain Abbé Robin admiringly described it in a letter to a friend in 1781, Boston 'did not seem to us a modern settlement so much as an ancient city'.[66]

AMERICA IS JOSEPH

Yet in Old England itself, Members of Parliament were beginning to fret about the exact place of America within *their* understanding of Empire. The autonomous confidence of the Thirteen Colonies seemed to grate with British *amour propre*. In 1764 the British bureaucrat and American imperialist Thomas Pownall suggested his colleagues understand 'that our kingdom may be no more considered as the mere kingdom of this isle, with many appendages of provinces, colonies, settlements, and other extraneous parts'. Instead, it was now 'a grand marine dominion' and, as such, needed a new political structure 'consisting of our possessions in the Atlantic and in America united into a one interest, in a one centre where the seat of government is'.[67] The 1766 Declaratory Act had granted the British parliament the power 'to bind the Colonies and People of *America*, Subjects of the Crown of *Great Britain*, in all cases whatsoever', and the role of the royal governor was now recast as enforcing the writ of parliament rather than co-existing with colonial legislatures. That was not how they saw it in Boston: a city with its own Parliamentary Charter of 1691, its own House of Representatives, its annual 'Town Meetings' (held in Faneuil Hall), vibrant meeting-houses and a democratic political culture which stretched back to its covenanting past. For all their loyal toasts to the king and queen, the citizens of Boston and settlers of Massachusetts were also adamant that their political freedoms rested in the chambers of their self-governing assemblies, not upon the whim of royal governors.[68]

When Britain and America were in harmony, such competing ideas mattered little, but in fractious times they were engines of misunderstanding. After the capture of Quebec, the 1763 Peace of Paris and the end of Franco-British hostilities, the misunderstandings multiplied. The expansion of British imperial power and a growing military infrastructure needed to service multiple wars produced a doubling of the national debt and demanded new sources of revenue. Many in London – not least the new prime minister, George Grenville – felt that the merchants and financiers of the American east coast had done well out of British imperial power and could now look forward to a stable trading future. So they should pay for it. To keep the French at bay, military numbers were to be expanded in America from 4,000 to 10,000 regular troops, and it was only right that the colonists should help foot the bill – just as George III's other subjects in England, Wales and Scotland did so. After years of gentle subsidy which had allowed Boston, New York and Philadelphia to grow fat on colonial commerce, America needed to contribute to its own defence. The logic of the case seemed entirely sensible to Benjamin Franklin, who, then acting as the Pennsylvanian Assembly's agent in London, accepted that the Crown might need 'to keep troops in America henceforward, to maintain its conquests, and defend the colonies; and that the Parliament may establish some revenue arising out of the American trade, to be applied supporting these troops'.[69] Advocates of this course suggested it was best to regard the colonies as analogous to English 'counties palatinate' – jurisdictions without parliamentary representation but integral members of the English body politic.[70]

But for the business interests of Bostonians, parliament's grounds for taxation could not have been more unfortunately chosen. They began with the 1764 Sugar Act, which actually dropped the duty on imported molasses but raised it on sugar and legislated for a more effective tax collection system in the hope of countering the smuggler economy. Boston's distillers were hit hard. 'There was not a man on the continent of America who does not consider the Sugar Act, as far as it regards molasses, as a sacrifice made of the northern colonies to the superior interest in Parliament of the West Indies,' grumbled John Adams.[71] Then came the 1765 Stamp Act, which slapped extra taxes on pretty much all printed material – every newspaper, journal, pamphlet, almanac (such as those published by Benjamin Franklin's brother), diploma and legal document – even on packs of playing cards. For such a fiercely literary city as Boston, this meant a substantial new expense imposed in the midst of a postwar slump. The response was, as John Rowe recalled, swift and violent. On 14 August 1765,

> a great number of people assembled at Deacon Elliot's Corner this morning to see the Stamp Officer hung in Effigy with a Libel on the Breast, on Deacon Elliot's tree and along side him a Boot stuffed with representation . . . this stamp officer hung up all Day – at night they cut him down, layd him out and carried in Triumph amidst the acclamations of many thousands who were gathered together on that occasion. They proceeded from the South End down the Main Street, through the Town House and Round by Oliver's Dock – they pull'd down a New Building which some people thought was building for a Stamp Office and did some Mischief to Mr Andrew Oliver's house.[72]

After hanging effigies at the 'Liberty Tree' (an elm tree in the South End) and ransacking the stamp master Andrew Oliver's house, the mob came for his brother-in-law and chief justice of the Massachusetts superior court, Thomas Hutchinson. His elegant North End mansion was gutted – every expensive window smashed; the crockery, drapes and furniture looted – and his life almost taken. In many ways, this sudden urban violence was no different to the kind of 'moral economy' bread riots which many British cities experienced during the course of the eighteenth century: a popular outburst to 'unfair' price rises or taxes.[73] Oliver, Hutchinson and the loyalist community within Boston – now identified as 'enemies of liberty' – saw a more sinister force at play.

'Spent this evening with Mr. Samuel Adams at his House,' recorded John Adams in his diary on 30 December 1772.

> He affects to despize Riches, and not to dread Poverty. But no Man is more ambitious of entertaining his Friends handsomely, or of making a decent, an elegant Appearance than he. He has lately new covered and glased his House and painted it, very neatly, and has new papered, painted and furnished his Rooms. So that you visit at a very genteel House and are very politely received and entertained.[74]

This urbane host, up to date with all the London fashions, was the man behind the 'Boston Caucus', the long-standing political wing of the city's labouring classes, which was now blamed for running the mobs attacking Oliver and Hutchinson. Samuel Adams had been baptized at the New South Congregational Church (in 1722) and was the son of an equally devout nonconformist father, 'Deacon' Samuel Adams Senior. But politics, as well as religion, featured prominently in the Adams household thanks to a failed investment in a land bank followed by punitive law suits, all of which the family blamed on arbitrary interventions by Crown authorities. In 1729 Samuel Adams Senior was elected a member of the Boston Town Meeting as part of the Boston Caucus, and in the 1750s, after Boston Latin School and Harvard College, his son took on a sinecure as a tax collector for the Town Meeting and then followed his father into the Caucus. His previous profession as lawyer, accountant, businessman and brewer had not worked out. Even as a tax collector he ended up owing the town of Boston £8,000 in back payments.

Over time, Samuel Adams Senior and Junior worked their personal animus towards British officialdom into a broader critique of colonial rule. Writing as 'A Puritan' in the Boston newspaper, *Independent Advertiser*, Samuel Adams Junior played on a growing sense of economic insecurity among the labouring classes and sought to connect that anxiety to London's oppressive taxation policies. In doing so, he drew upon the Bostonian self-identity as 'free-born Englishman' with the rights of Magna Carta and liberty under the law. From its origins in the 1630s theirs was a colony of settlement, not exploitation; a joint endeavour across the ocean. But the Westminster parliament, with its growing demands for colonial taxation, was both undermining a Boston economy already laden with war debts and striking at the heart of the legal and political privileges which flowed from the colonies' founding Charters. At root, Massachusetts was being taxed without being represented in the legislative assembly which was imposing the levies – and this was surely contrary to the British constitution, mystically unwritten though it was. 'If taxes are laid upon us in any shape without our having a legal Representation where they are laid,' Adams asked in 1764, 'are we not reduced from the Character of free Subjects to the miserable State of tributary Slaves?'[75] Adams was far more than a gifted polemicist – he was also a first-rate politician able to marshal public opinion, manage mob dynamics and secure election to the Massachusetts House of Representatives. In the midst of an economic downturn, in a city with a tradition of voluble street politics and a merchant elite ever more hostile to the demands of parliament (but not king), the Boston Caucus came to pose a powerful challenge to the imperial settlement.

At this point, uncharacteristically, British politicians opted for peaceable compromise. On 16 May 1766 the brigantine *Harrison* docked at Boston harbour with copies of the repeal of the Stamp Act. The relief across the city was tangible. After the effigy burning, house looting and politicking of recent months, Boston could resume its natural role as a loyal, royal city. 'This day is the Joyfull Day indeed for all America and all the people are to Rejoice,' recorded John Rowe in his diary on 19 May 1766. 'Dined at Colo Ingersoll's with 28 Gentlemen – we drank fifteen Toasts and very Loyal they were and suited to the Occasion. In the evening there were very grand Illuminations all over

the Town. In the Common there was an Obelisk very beautifully decorated and very grand fireworks were displayed.'[76] Indeed, the repeal
allowed for another outburst of monarchical fervour with huge 'Figures of their Majesties' erected on Boston Common for all to celebrate.
Two months later, there was even a thanksgiving service for the repeal
of the Stamp Act. John Adams was in the congregation.

> Mr Wibirt's [text] was Genesis 50th. 20th. – 'But as for you, ye thought
> evil against me; but god meant it unto good, to bring to pass, as it is this
> Day, to save much People alive.' – America is Joseph, the King Lords
> and Commons – Josephs Father and Brothers. Our Forefathers sold
> into Egypt, i.e. Persecuted into America, etc. Wibirt shone, they say.[77]

But the repeal of the Stamp Act and the loss of income to the
Exchequer only intensified the problem of funding the colonies, containing the French and supporting both a military infrastructure and
legal system (of customs officials, judges and governors) needed to
underpin parliamentary sovereignty. The young chancellor of the
exchequer, Charles Townshend, supported by Prime Minister Grenville, came up with an alternative solution in the form of the
1767 Revenue Act. The so-called 'Townshend duties' imposed an
import tax (rather than the Stamp Tax's direct tax on indigenous produce) on all glass, paper, lead, paint and tea shipped into the American
colonies. And these new taxes came with a Board of Customs Commissioners designed to end Boston's dockside grey economy and
finally put the imperial finances on a stable footing. Needless to say,
the duties were met with an indignant response. Because for all of
Samuel Adams's protestations of constitutional propriety and lawful-
ness, the Boston economy was in fact heavily dependent upon illegal
smuggling and the avoidance of duties. 'We have been so long habitu-
ated to illicit trade that people in general see no evil in it,' Thomas
Hutchinson censoriously commented.[78] He estimated that some
three-quarters of the consumer goods brought into America were
done so illegally. And the high-yielding crates of Chinese tea were
amongst the most regularly smuggled goods.

In Boston, the imposition of new taxes on established imports
instantly politicized the waterfront and, with it, Boston's relationship
with the mother country. Within a matter of weeks, the customs

officials, the Royal Navy and the tax collectors who patrolled the wharfs and jetties metamorphosed from an irksome but necessary bureaucracy to the aggressive arm of a foreign government. The British Empire imperceptibly shifted from an enterprise of which Boston was a part to something approaching an oppressive, occupying force. On a more psychological level, the taxing of those consumer goods which had connected Boston with Britain, which had made Massachusetts part of the Georgian world, also undermined an important component of their imperial identity as Britons. That consumer bond across the Atlantic – drinking from the same ceramics, wearing the same silks, reading the same novels – was under fiscal assault by the British government. And the response of Boston was to strike back at precisely that 'empire of goods' which had so Anglicized their city.

The Townshend duties sparked a wave of non-consumption and 'non-importation' activism which stressed frugality and asceticism as the only means to make London mend its ways. Lists were drawn up of superfluous consumer goods – ceramics, furniture, clocks, draperies and finery – which any righteous Boston citizen should have the moral purpose to resist. With smart political acumen, Samuel Adams called upon Boston's Puritan heritage to encourage his compatriots to deny themselves the 'baubles of Britain'. The language of commerce was shifting: what had once connected the Americans with the greatest trading nation of the world, in peaceable and prosperous union, was now regarded as a luxurious, corrupting self-indulgence. Even the House of Hancock, the leading trading family of North America, was forced into backing the boycott. After the death of Thomas Hancock in 1764 the business had passed into the hands of his nephew, the raffish but shrewd John Hancock, who wisely thought it best to ally himself with Samuel Adams and the Boston Caucus rather than suffer the fate of a Thomas Hutchinson. 'It is surprising to me that so many attempts are made on your side to Cramp our Trade, new Duties every day increasing,' he wrote in ostentatious protest to his London associate in 1767. 'In short we are in a fair way of being Ruin'd. We have nothing to do but unite and come under a Solemn agreement to stop importing any goods from England.'[79]

In 1767, public virtue not private consumption became the touchstone of patriotism. In December the Boston Town Meeting instructed its representatives in the general assembly to acknowledge its fears over 'the distressed Circumstances of this Town, by means of the amazing growth of Luxury, and the Embarrassments of our Trade; and having also the strongest apprehensions that our invaluable Rights and Liberties as Men and British Subjects, are greatly affected by a late Act of the British Parliament'; they urged their representatives 'to encourage a spirit of Industry and Frugality among the People'.[80] Above all, that meant an end to tea. The drink that had defined a shared British sensibility and became a template for manners was now demonized as a symbol of enslavement and luxury. The students of Harvard College vowed to abstain; the coffee-houses served up all sorts of new, revolting non-tea concoctions. But it was the women of Boston, having once brewed the pot, sieved the tea and poured the milk, who placed themselves at the forefront of this consumer boycott. They wrote to the newspapers, created trouble in shops selling tea, circulated lists of importing merchants, and urged the city's menfolk to show the same kind of reserve in the tavern that they themselves were exhibiting at the tea table.[81]

The response of the British authorities to such commercial disobedience was not subtle. 'On Friday, September 30th, 1768, the ships of WAR, armed Schooners, Transports, etc. Came up the Harbour and Anchored round the TOWN: their Cannon loaded, a Spring on their Cables, as for a regular Siege,' recounted the North End silversmith Paul Revere. 'At noon on Saturday, October the 1st the fourteenth and twenty-ninth Regiments, a detachment from the 59th Regiment and Train of Artillery, with two pieces of Cannon, landed on the Long Wharf; then Formed and Marched with insolent Parade, Drums beating, Fifes playing, and Colours flying, up King Street.'[82] Revere went on to craft a very precise little silver engraving depicting the troops processing up the Long Wharf, the warships bobbing in the harbour and 'the city on the hill' looking every inch the godly bastion under attack from a tyrannical empire.

With the fifty-gun warship HMS *Romney* sitting at anchor, 700 British grenadiers encamped on the Common and customs officials boarding ships and raiding wharfs at whim, Boston came to feel like a city under siege. It was only a matter of time before violence erupted. The capture of John Hancock's sloop *Liberty* on the charge of smuggling Madeira, followed by the arrest of Hancock and the requisition of *Liberty*, could have sparked off a wave of attacks on customs commissioners. But Hancock himself was wealthy and smart enough to swallow the losses. Instead, the spark came in March 1770 with a fight outside the customs house on King Street, when a wigmaker's apprentice taunted Captain-Lieutenant John Goldfinch over an unpaid bill. Months of escalating brawling and abuse between bored soldiers and the Boston mob culminated in a confused fire-fight which resulted in five fatal shootings. Among the dead were the sixteen-year-old shipwright's apprentice Christopher 'Kit' Monk, the mixed-race mariner Crispus Attucks and the Irish leatherworker Patrick Carr.

As the crack of gunshot ricocheted into the March air, the tight, tiny city of Boston erupted: bells rung and the streets swarmed as if a fire had engulfed it. Even the placid, trimming John Rowe was perturbed by such incendiary violence.

> This night the 29th Regiment on Duty. A Quarrel between the soldiers and Inhabitants. A Great Number Assembled in King Street. A Party of the 29th under the Command of Captain Preston fired on the People – they killed five – wounded several others, particularly Mr Edward Payne in his Right Arm. Captain Preston bears a good Character – he was taken in the night and Committed also seven more of the 29th – the inhabitants are greatly enraged and not without Reason.[83]

John Adams rushed from a dining club in the South End when he heard the news.

> In the Street we were informed that the British Soldiers had fired on the Inhabitants, killed some and wounded others near the Town house . . . I walked down Boylstons Alley into Brattle Square, where a Company or two of regular soldiers were drawn up in Front of Dr. Coopers old Church with their Musquets all shouldered and their Bayonetts all fixed.[84]

Today, all that marks the site of the 'Boston Massacre', as it was quickly inscribed, is a slightly grubby circle of stones underneath a traffic light on a busy junction at the top of State Street (no longer King Street). But in the immediate aftermath of 5 March 1770, it became a place of pilgrimage and commemoration. Paul Revere produced another engraving depicting the execution of the innocents, while the British soldiers themselves were quickly escorted off the Boston peninsula (to Fort William on Castle Island) for their own safety. Three days later, John Rowe 'attended the funeral of the unhappy people that were killed on Monday last. Such a Concourse of people I never saw before – I believe ten or twelve thousand.'[85]

AN EPOCH IN HISTORY

After the fury of the 'Massacre' came another period of retreat and reflection. The trigger-happy soldiers were placed on trial (with John Adams and Josiah Quincy conducting the defence), parliament overturned the Townshend duties in April 1770, and Boston, in response, ended its non-consumption boycott. On the surface, Anglo-American relations returned to an even keel. But there lurked one unresolved issue: the price of a cup of tea. Townshend had grudgingly removed duties on glass, paint, paper and the rest, but he refused to rescind the tax on tea. First, because the finances of the East India Company – the major tea exporter to America – were in difficulties, and a tea tax would help subsidize this government-backed business. And, second, because the British parliament was adamant that it had the right to tax the colonies: to abandon every levy was to jettison a principle of imperial finance which had increasingly global ramifications. This was the thinking behind the 1773 Tea Act, which provided a tax rebate to the East India Company on tea shipped to America, reducing the cost of tea but retaining both the principle of taxation and a solid income for the Exchequer. The new prime minister, Lord North, regarded it as an ideal compromise – the rebate cut the price of tea for the caffeine-loving colonists, but also kept the East India Company afloat, and the 'empire of goods' ticking over.

Samuel Adams saw it differently. The Tea Act not only threatened to undercut Boston's lucrative tea-smuggling industry (by allowing the East India Company to supply its cargo at much lower rates), it also cemented the principle of colonial taxation. And out of that taxation would be funded a growing army of customs commissioners, soldiers, lawyers and governors all intent on undermining Magna Carta rights in the Thirteen Colonies. Tea was just the first sip; if it was swallowed then the Townshend duties would be back and the principle of no taxation without representation lost for ever. Boston would become a subject of, rather than partner in, Empire. 'The Monopoly of Tea, is, I dare say, but a small Part of the Plan they have formed to strip us of our Property,' was how the Pennsylvanian lawyer John Dickinson saw it, exposing the tensions of his Atlantic identity. 'But thank GOD, we are not Sea Poys, nor Marattas, but *British Subjects*, who are born to Liberty, who know its Worth, and who prize it high.'[86] 'We won't be their Negroes,' agreed John Adams (with no hint of irony). 'I say we are as handsome as old England folks, and so should be as free.'[87] But Lord North was equally resolute that there must be no retreat on tea. After the repeal of the Stamp Act and the Townshend duties, Westminster had to show its imperial resolve and stop surrendering to the threats of Boston. On each side of the Atlantic, the positions on the Tea Act became entrenched – and sailing across the ocean came 'the accursed dutiable' cargo.

'This morning Captain Scot arrived from London,' John Rowe noted on 17 November 1773. 'He brings advice that Hall, Loring, Coffin and Bruce are to Bring the Tea from the East India Company – this a measure that is Generally disapproved and will Remain a Great Occasion of Disagreement between England and America.'[88] Eleven days later, the *Dartmouth*, the *Eleanor* and the *Beaver* docked at Griffin's Wharf with their 46 tons of East India Company tea. As a part owner of the *Eleanor*, Rowe had extra reason to be worried. Immediately, the fly-posters went up.

> Friends, Brethren, Countrymen! That worst of Plagues The Detestable Tea, ship'd for this Port by the East India Company is now arriv'd in this harbour, the Hour of Destruction or manly Opposition to the Machinations of Tyranny Stares you in the Face: every Friend to his Country to himself and to Posterity is now called upon to meet at Fanewill Hall at nine of Clock this Day (at which time the Bells will begin to Ring) to make a United and Successful Resistance to this last worst and most Destructive Measure of Administration.

Under Boston port authority rules, the owners of the vessels had twenty days (until 17 December) to pay their customs dues or have the entire cargo seized – spelling instant bankruptcy for the unfortunate merchants. By contrast, Samuel Adams and his Boston Caucus, now operating under the soubriquet 'Sons of Liberty', were equally adamant that the tea should not be unloaded and hence become subject to the tax. They wanted the tea returned to London on the very same vessels, devoid of all duties. 'To let it be landed, would be giving up the Principle of Taxation by Parliamentary Authority, against which the Continent have struggled for ten years,' agreed John Adams, 'and subjecting ourselves and our Posterity forever to Egyptian Taskmasters – to Burthens, Indignities, to Ignominy, Reproach and Contempt, to Desolation and Oppression, to Poverty and Servitude.'[89]

Once again, Boston's heritage of biblical liberation was revived. Samuel Adams summoned the Winthrop legacy by urging a 'Solemn League and Covenant' against the forces of British oppression. The spirit of liberty which had swept the *Arbella* into Massachusetts and bound Boston's founder into a sacred covenant was called forth to do God's bidding and fight tyranny. If Boston was to remain free, the tea could not be landed.

Poor Thomas Hutchinson, promoted from chief justice to royal governor in 1771, was ill-equipped to manage such a quickening political crisis. In the past, he had quietly criticized the Stamp Act and other clumsy interventions from Westminster; he believed in the traditional, cordial, informal agreement which had co-existed between the legislatures in Britain and Boston. But he also believed in the rule of law and he would not allow the *Dartmouth*, *Eleanor* and *Beaver* to slink back to England without having been cleared by the customs house. Located at a safe distance from disorderly Boston in a house on Unquity Hill in upstate Milton, Massachusetts, Hutchinson had little idea of just how incendiary his refusal would be on the streets of his agitated, angry, fearful city. When, on the freezing evening of 16 December 1773 – the night before the deadline for paying the customs duties – Hutchinson's decision that the cargo be unloaded was relayed to the thousands pressed into the pews of the Old South

Meeting House, the cry went up 'Boston Harbor a tea-pot this night!' It was then that the war whoops began, the 'Mohawks' appeared, and British suzerainty of Boston was effectively lost.

The morning after, John Adams thought the Tea-Party a stunning, signal affair. 'This is the most magnificent Movement of all', he wrote.

> There is a Dignity, a Majesty, a Sublimity, in this last Effort of the Patri-ots, that I greatly admire. The people should never rise, without doing something to be remembered – something notable. And striking. This Destruction of the Tea is so bold, so daring, so firm, intrepid and inflex-ible, and it must have so important Consequences, and so lasting, that I can't but consider it as an Epocha in History.[90]

He had rarely written a truer word. Within two years Britain and its colonies were at war. In one of his final diary entries, John Rowe caught the moment – on 19 April 1775 – with chronological clarity. 'Last night the Grenadiers and Light Companies belonging to the several Regiments in this Town were ferry'd over Charles River and landed on Phipps Farm in Cambridge from whence they Proceeded on their way to Concord, where they arrived early this day. On their march they had a Skirmish with some Country People at Lexington.'[91] The shot that was 'heard around the world' (as Ralph Waldo Emerson first described it) had been fired, and Boston was behind the trigger. The cack-handed British response to the Tea-Party – an escalating ser-ies of Coercive Acts designed to emasculate Boston's democracy and isolate its economy – had pushed the city into open rebellion. The city upon a hill, the great mart and staple, the finest English country town outside England had become in the words of Lord North 'the ring-leader of all violence and opposition to the execution of the laws of this country'.[92]

The imperial city transformed itself into a revolutionary citadel, with devastating consequences for the emergent British Empire. Those loyal Bostonians, who had once counted themselves the most fervent subjects of the British Crown, the keenest promoters of British *impe-rium*, now recast themselves as anti-colonial freedom-fighters. Boston, that candle upon a candle-stick, was now a light to the world for a very different vision of liberty. The First Empire, the Thirteen Colo-nies, was about to be lost. In London, the diplomat and politician the

Duke of Manchester instantly realized the significance of events in Boston, Concord and Lexington. He mournfully informed the House of Lords that, 'the page of future history will tell how Britain planted, nourished, and for two centuries preserved' a British empire across the Atlantic. And how,

> strengthened by her sons, she rose to such a pitch of power, that this little island proved too mighty for the greatest efforts of the greatest nations ... Historic truth must likewise relate, within the same little space of time, how Britain fell to half her greatness; how strangely lost, by misjudging ministers, by rash-advised councils, our gracious sovereign, George III, saw more than half his empire crumble beneath his sceptre.[93]

2

Bridgetown

'A sweet Spot of Earth'

In the year 1773, some months after my arrival in Barbados, I, one morning, saw the body of a negro man, who had been run through, the foregoing night, it was said, with a spit . . . The naked body of a murdered man lying neglected, or treated, in all respects, like a dead dog, must needs be a new and a shocking spectacle to any European youth, especially to a country youth from Britain, on his first arrival in a land of slavery.

This was just a taste of Barbadian brutality.

Among many other negroes, who bore more or less the marks of ill treatment, one of the first objects who presented himself to my view was a negro man whose whole body, his face not wholly excepted, was covered with scars . . . One of his legs was loaded with an iron ring or boot, at least half an inch thick, and upwards of two inches broad . . . I asked by what authority his owner thus treated him, and was answered, that he was his owner's property, who had a right to treat him as he pleased.[1]

As private secretary to the governor of Barbados, the young William Dickson was to bear witness to the full, sadistic reality of the British Empire's slave economy. As he recounted in horrified page after page of his abolitionist polemic of 1789, *Letters on Slavery*, the practice was fundamental to the running of the tiny colony known as 'the civilised island, Barbados'. And whilst the most heinous abuses took place amid the cane fields and boiling rooms of the sugar plantations hidden from polite gaze, the cities of the British Caribbean were not wholly immune to the human suffering underpinning their prosperity.

Indeed, at the pinnacle of upper Broad Street, in the commercial heart of the Barbadian capital Bridgetown, stood the Cage. Originally built in the 1650s as a temporary prison for indentured white servants or drunken sailors, it had by the late 1700s become a wood and wire holding pen for runaway slaves and black offenders awaiting punishment. Any slave caught outside their plantation or on the streets of Bridgetown without a good excuse between 9 p.m. and 5 a.m. would be imprisoned in the Cage and then brought before magistrates (the rule of law being such a defining feature of the Empire) and whipped if they 'deserved' it. The owner of the slave was required to pay fifteen shillings to have his slave released from the Cage, and another fifteen shillings for the expenses incurred by the whipping.

Conditions inside were not pleasant. 'Such are the situation, construction, and want of ventilation of the Cage, as to render it unfit for permanent confinement of one single human creature, and if it were properly constructed and ventilated, not more than twelve ought to be confined there,' declared a report from the Speaker of the Barbados House of Assembly. 'In this wretched and miserable hole, shocking to relate eighty five persons have been confined at one time. If they lay down at all, they must have been lain tier upon tier, at least four deep.' The solution, of course, was not to close the Cage, but to move it from 'their most populous street', where the stench and noise was off-putting, to 'some other and more convenient part of Bridgetown'. Removed to the Pier Head, the depredations of slavery could safely be placed out of sight and out of mind.[2]

Yet, the Cage's position at the centre of Bridgetown – the site is now a 'Chefette's' fast-food outlet, its history commemorated by a 'Slave Route' plaque – was entirely appropriate since it so graphically conveyed the economic basis of Barbados. The city of Boston and the Thirteen Colonies of America had left the British Empire on the question of tea, while Bridgetown and the British Caribbean had bound themselves ever tighter to Britain thanks to tea's sweet accompaniment, sugar. As America edged away from Empire in the second half of the eighteenth century, the West Indies nestled closer. In the words of the Marxist scholar and one-time prime minister of Trinidad, Eric

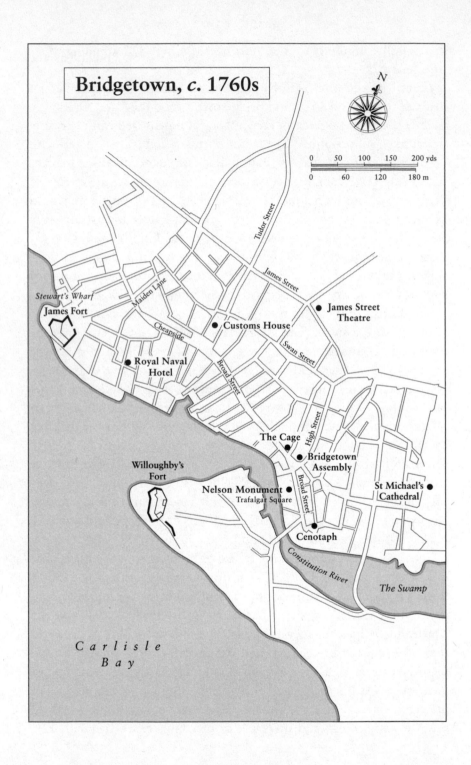

Bridgetown, *c.* 1760s

N

0   50   100   150   200 yds
0   60   120   180 m

Tudor Street

James Street

Stewart's Wharf

Maiden Lane

James Fort

Cheapside

Customs House

James Street
Theatre

Swan Street

Royal Naval
Hotel

Broad Street

The Cage

High Street

Bridgetown
Assembly

Willoughby's
Fort

Nelson Monument
Trafalgar Square

Broad Street

St Michael's
Cathedral

Cenotaph

Constitution River

The Swamp

C a r l i s l e
B a y

Williams, the Caribbean would take the place of New England as 'the hub of Empire'. The great economist Adam Smith was even clearer, declaring in *The Wealth of Nations* (1776) that 'the profits of a sugar plantation in any of our West Indian colonies are generally much greater than those of any other cultivation that is known either in Europe or America'.[3] There was a growing appreciation, on both sides of the Atlantic, that West Indian wealth creation offered a new model for imperial hegemony built around aggressive exploitation and the monopolization of trade. 'If then this small colony is so useful to Great Britain, as from hence it appears to be, of how much more consequence must all her colonies together be found?' asked Henry Frere, a member of the council of Barbados in 1768. 'From their resources the colonies claim a share of the merit of having raised Great Britain to be one of the first kingdoms in Europe for power and opulence, as she is undoubtedly the first country in the world for affording every convenience and blessing of life.'[4]

The doomed future prophesied by the Duke of Manchester after the loss of Boston, of the Empire crumbling beneath the sceptre of King George III, did not take place following American independence. Instead, the British Empire grew, diversified and prospered. And whereas the residents of the Thirteen Colonies had come to identify themselves as an increasingly separate 'American' people, the planters and settlers of Barbados were happy to continue to count themselves as citizens of the British Empire. 'It is to Great Britain alone that our West Indian planters consider themselves as belonging,' was how the planters' ally Bryan Edwards described their stance in the 1760s. He added, 'even such of them as have resided in the West Indies from their birth, look on the islands as their temporary abode only, and the fond notion of being able to go home (as they emphatically term a visit to England) year after year animates their industry and alleviates their misfortune'.[5]

Barbados was called by settlers and colonial officials alike 'little England'. The most easterly of the Caribbean islands, it was among the first to be colonized and long held its own as an imperial pace-setter. It was 'the mother colony, the centre to which newly-formed colonies looked for labour, experienced planters, capital, and leadership in matters of imperial politics and trade'.[6] The Englishness of the island – its cathedrals, parliament, parishes, cricket pitches, garrisons and gardens – would become a source of intense pride. 'On no one of our foreign possessions is the print of England's foot more strongly impressed than on Barbados,' wrote the nineteenth-century historian J. A. Froude. 'It has been ours for two centuries and three-quarters, and was organized from the first on English traditional lines, with its constitution, its parishes and parish churches and churchwardens, and schools and parsons, all on the old model; which the unprogressive inhabitants have been wise enough to leave undisturbed.'[7]

Well might the Victorians look back on the settlement of Barbados with admiration. For the wealth and riches which flowed from sugar and slavery played an essential role in Britain's rise to global pre-eminence. The port cities of the Caribbean – led by Bridgetown, Barbados, Kingston, Jamaica and, for the French, Port-au-Prince, Haiti – were the conduits for funnelling back profits from plantations and human trafficking. This was where the prices were set, the goods off-loaded, and the harvests from the rural hinterland expropriated to Europe. The 'seaport towns,' as one army engineer put it in 1698, '[were] the very doors of the islands'.[8] And the staggering returns from the West Indies colonies funded the acceleration of the British Empire, the beginnings of the Industrial Revolution and the expansion of the Royal Navy. Like Boston before her, eighteenth-century Bridgetown assumed an entrepôt role in Britain's Atlantic empire of trade and of the emergent global struggle against the rival imperial forces of France, Spain and the Netherlands. In many ways, it was just as intimate an extension of England as Georgian Boston – but, unlike Massachusetts, Barbados remained loyal to Empire to the very end.

Two hundred years later, on the eve of the island's independence in 1966, the travel writer Patrick Leigh Fermor thought such fealty still very much in evidence. He described postwar Bridgetown as 'a completely English town, a town on the edge of London, and the wide clean streets ... almost as full of the white as of the coloured Barbadians'.[9] In Leigh Fermor's day, Bridgetown's statue of Admiral Lord Nelson – built after the Battle of Trafalgar to stand opposite the Cage on Broad Street – looked out over a Trafalgar Square and a carefully codified imperial space of parliament buildings, an Anglican cathedral and a Whitehall-style Cenotaph. All of it was designed to celebrate the intimate connection with the mother country, and the intense colonial loyalties of the Barbadian or Bajan people.

Today, much of that has changed. Trafalgar Square has become National Heroes Square (commemorating those Barbadians who died in the twentieth-century world wars), while shoppers along Broad Street barely give Horatio a second glance, his tired-looking plinth overshadowed by a bland, three-storey office block. Twenty-first-century Bridgetown is a crowded, commercial, traffic-clogged port, an American-flavoured, international metropolis of tax-free shopping and offshore banking, as well as one of the political and legal hubs of the Caribbean. The economy of Barbados is now almost entirely oriented around the tourists arriving on cruise ships chugging into Carlisle Bay and the flights touching down at Grantley Adams International Airport.

Yet you only have to chart the number of British Airways and Virgin Atlantic arrivals to sense that something of the old Empire economics – the Caribbean dependency upon foreign capital – remains. Take a trip up the so-called Platinum Coast, lining the Caribbean Sea from Bridgetown to Speightstown, past the Four Seasons hotel complex, the Sandy Lane beach resort, the Cliff restaurant and up to the exclusive Port Ferdinand marina, and you see British investment in Barbados at work. Barbados itself is happy to exploit this empathy for the island and its 'little England' identity, with a well-managed series of historical attractions based around the Plantation House and a sepia version of the colonial past. Inevitably in this sun-drenched vista the gruesome history of Barbadian slavery is by-passed for a more palatable heritage of rum-tasting, plantation living and cricket. Today, Bridgetown might be a confident city of the Commonwealth, but in the fraying remnants of the garrison fort, St Michael's Cathedral and Carlisle Wharf the colonial memory and its British money are still reverberating.

THE ENGINE

Just as with Winthrop's vision of Massachusetts Bay as a 'Garden of Eden', Barbados was never the virgin isle which European chroniclers liked to imagine. In fact, it had been settled as early as 2000 BC by

Amerindians, travelling northwards from the Orinoco River Basin out of South America (modern-day Venezuela), with a community that could have reached 10,000-strong on the island they called Ichirouganian. The Amerindians were the first to introduce pottery to the island and were still around in the 1520s to spy Portuguese and then Spanish explorers pass en route to Brazil. But increased slave-raiding missions by those Spanish *conquistadores* forced the 'Caribs' (as the Europeans christened them) to flee Barbados in the second half of the sixteenth century for more defensible outposts in the Windward Islands. So when in 1625 Captain John Powell arrived to claim Barbados on behalf of King James I, he found a deserted isle which he thought ideal for agricultural settlement. Two years later, his younger brother Henry Powell began the colonial process in earnest when he stepped off the *William and John* into the crystal Caribbean Sea and established a settlement in what is today Holetown. Backing for the expedition came from a City of London syndicate led by the financiers Sir Peter and Sir William Courteen, who were more interested in profits than any New England attempts at furthering Puritanism. Their plan was to fund some eighty pioneer colonists – hired as company employees-cum-tenant farmers – to begin producing crops on the island.

Among those first settlers accompanying Henry Powell in 1627 was one Henry Winthrop, son of John Winthrop, hoping to make his own fortune overseas. 'I do intend God willing to stay here on this island called Barbados in the West Indies and here I and my servants to join in the planting of tobacoo which three years I hope will be very profitable to me,' he wrote optimistically to his uncle in August 1627. The Courteens were offering new colonists £100 as an annual wage, and young Winthrop planned to import a few servants on £5 or £6 a year to run his own plantation. 'The island is the pleasantest island in all the West Indies,' he continued. Apart from his fellow Englishmen, it was deserted 'save a matter of 50 slaves of Indian and black [heritage], we have a crop of tobacco in the ground and I hope with God's blessing the next time I send for England to send over 500 or a thousand weight of tobacco'. Sadly, when he did send back the tobacco, his father was far from impressed. John Winthrop thought the rolls were so 'very ill conditioned, fowle, full of stalkes and evil coloured' that he could not unload them at even five shillings a pound. Clearly, Massachusetts would be a more promising prospect.[10]

The Courteens had more immediate problems, however, than the wilting tobacco plants. As news spread of potential Caribbean riches, a London-funded land grab ensued – settling St Christopher's (St Kitt's) in 1624, Nevis in 1628, Montserrat and Antigua in 1632. (Jamaica was to follow under Oliver Cromwell's anti-Spanish naval strategy – or 'western design' – in the 1650s.) In July 1627, King Charles I removed the Courteens from the Caribbean and, in a sign of a quickening appreciation of the Caribbean's riches, granted letters patent for the settlement of Barbados and other 'Caribee islands' to his court favourite James Hay, the first Earl of Carlisle. Granted possession and title of 'Lord Proprietor' of Barbados, Carlisle ruled the island from afar through a series of governors, alongside an assembly established in 1639 to represent the growing number of planters on the island who had managed to buy their properties' freehold. Until it was redesignated a Crown colony in the 1660s, this curious constitutional settlement shaped Barbados's unique political ethos: a combination of high levels of self-government with adamantine colonial loyalty.[11]

Every colony needed a capital and in 1630 one of Carlisle's earliest deputies, Governor Hawley, chose the site of the 'Indian Bridgetown', down the coast from Holetown, as the legal and administrative centre for Carlisle's possession. Hawley built a law court, after which arrived the House of Assembly, and then accompanying governmental and commercial establishments. The location was not particularly popular. 'The Choice of the place to build this Town upon, seems to have been directed more by Convenience than Health,' was how one 1700s visitor accounted for it. 'For the Ground thereabouts being a little lower within Land than the Sea-Banks, the Spring-Tides flow over, and make a great part of the Flat a Bog, or Marsh: From which there us'd formerly to ascend noxious Vapours, that contributed very much to the Unhealthiness of the Place.'[12] But the capital had to be on the western, Caribbean side of the island rather than the stormy, Atlantic littoral, and the natural harbour of what is today Carlisle Bay was an obvious attraction. It also enjoyed a navigable river point, where a primitive bridge had been erected, and was the site for the convergence of three major Amerindian island paths. But the swamps around the area, known as 'the Bridge' or 'the Bridgetown', made it a gamble. 'A town ill situate, for if they had considered health, as they did convenience, they would never have set it there; or if they had any intention at first to have built a Town there, they could not have been so improvident as not to foresee the main inconveniences that must ensue by making choice of so unhealthy a place to live in,' was how the first Barbadian historian, Richard Ligon, put it in 1647. 'But one house being set up, another was erected, and so a third, and a fourth, till at last it came to take the name of a town; divers storehouses being there built to stow their goods in for their convenience, being near the harbour.'[13]

By 1657 there were already 400 houses, some 2,000 residents and over forty streets, some of which are still recognizable in the city today – such as James Street, Swan Street, Tudor Street and High Street. While the sewage unfortunately lingered, the city's swamps were slowly drained and the 'unwholesome fumes' began to ease. Indeed, the elegance of Bridgetown became noteworthy. 'Bridgetown is a fine large town and the streets are straight, wide and clean,' was how the French Roman Catholic missionary Père Labat described it in the 1690s. 'The houses are all well built in the English fashion with many glass windows, and are splendidly furnished. In a word, they have an appearance of dignity, refinement and order, that one does not see in the other islands and which indeed would be hard to find anywhere.'[14] But it certainly wasn't Henry Winthrop's tobacco plant – or the cotton, indigo and ginger which other settlers had tried to harvest in the 1630s and '40s – which was behind such wealth. Rather, it was the white gold of sugar.

Along an unsigned, unpaved, bumpy road, set amid acre after acre of swaying cane plants atop the hills of the southern Barbados parish of St George, barely 11 kilometres from Bridgetown, sits Drax Hall. Whereas other plantation houses such as nearby Sunbury have turned themselves into tourist traps for plantation nostalgia, Drax is a private house at the centre of what remains a commercial sugar operation. Littering the outside of this austere, gabled mansion are tractors, farm tools, chemical drums and trailers – as well as the crumbling remnants of an old windmill and boiling house. The funds behind this plantation can be traced back to the 1640s, when the Barbadian pioneer James Drax realized that tobacco or cotton was never going to yield the riches he dreamed of. Cutting his losses, he set off for Recife, in Brazil, to see for himself the cultivation of a crop which was said to promise truly remarkable returns. For the planting and manufacturing of sugar cane had been taking place in Pernambuco, Brazil and the North Guiana coasts for many decades under Dutch and Portuguese management. What Drax brought back to Barbados was the skill of refining and – by working with Sephardic Jewish merchants, who were the early lynchpins in the international sugar trade out of Brazil – the networks to sell it into Europe. He imported the cane plant from New Guinea (where it grew naturally), farmed it on his Barbados estates and then copied the technology developed by Dutch planters in Brazil to make sugar. However, turning the cane into sugar was a slow, painful process, taking 'divers yeeres paines, care, patience and industry, with the disbersing of vast sums of money'. And Drax's early crops were 'so moist, and full of molasses, and so ill cur'd, as they were hardly worth the bringing home for England'.[15] Indeed, the early history of Barbados is a chronicle of fires, epidemics, wrecked harvests and hurricanes, a colonial economy being built up through arduous struggle a world away from today's luxury island resort. But Drax stuck with it and, helped by the soil, climate and trade winds of Barbados (ensuring rapid export times to Europe), he began an agricultural revolution of profound significance for both Caribbean and British imperial history.

Even now the production of sugar is a complicated and fraught endeavour. The sugar-cane plant needs to be harvested from the fields during the dry months of January–May, cut by machete and placed on to carts (drawn by donkeys in the 1600s), and then its juice extracted as quickly as possible. Today, this is done through vast, mechanized horizontal rollers, but in the seventeenth century it was crushed by pushing it through vertical rollers powered first by oxen and then, from the mid-1700s, by the 500 windmills which dotted the hills and peaks of Barbados. The pure cane juice had then to be siphoned off and taken to the boiling house, usually next to the mill, for a complicated procedure of heating, skimming of impurities, and boiling down to a dark, textured sugar base. At the end of this production line, involving a relentless cycle of cane deliveries, roaring furnaces, heavy machinery and intense heat, the planter was left with muscovado – a raw brown sugar – and a liquid by-product, molasses. The sugar was then dried out before being packed into hogshead barrels and taken to Bridgetown for export. The molasses would be sold, at home and abroad, to rum distilleries and for animal feed.

All in all, it was a highly advanced industrial process for the early modern era, and the language of the sugar mill – *engenho* (Portuguese) or *ingenio* (Spanish), literally 'the engine' – hinted at its novel, mechanized nature. And it was by this process that a tiny, wild island on the outer reaches of the Americas was transformed into a well-cultivated market garden capable of offering up astronomical riches to a small, powerful planter class.[16] By the mid-eighteenth

The engine at work. A detailed depiction of sugar production in the French West Indies in the seventeenth century, showing an evaporating furnace, grinding mill driven by oxen, dwellings for the slaves and a large plantation house. *Histoire générale des Antilles habités par les Françaist . . . enrichie de cartes et de figures* (Paris, 1667–71).

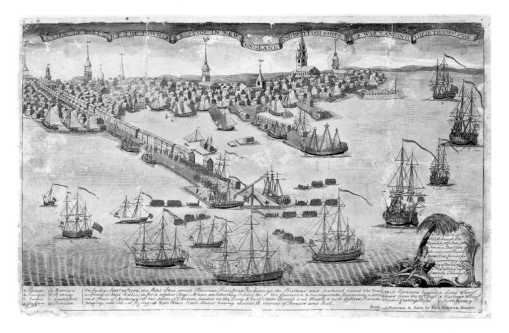

1. 'On Friday, September 30th, 1768, the ships of WAR, armed Schooners, Transports, etc. Came up the Harbour and Anchored round the TOWN.' Paul Revere's engraving of British troops landing at Long Wharf, Boston.

2. The execution of the innocents. Paul Revere's depiction of the 'Boston Massacre' of 1770, against a backdrop of the Old State House.

3. A view of Boston
Common in 1768, with
John Hancock's house
in the top right-hand
corner.

4. Samuel Adams
defending the Magna
Carta rights of Boston
against British tyranny, as
caught by John Singleton
Copley (1770).

5. An Empire of Goods. A British teapot (*c.* 1766–1770s), made in Derby, commemorating the repeal of the Stamp Act.

6. 'Boston Harbor a tea-pot this night!' An heroic depiction of the Boston Tea-Party, with the leaves falling into the waves and the rebels dressed as Mohawks, from the Reverend Mr Cooper's *History of North America* (1789).

7. 'This Little Spot of Ground ... has been as good as a Mine of Silver or Gold to the Crown of England.' The Nicholas Abbey plantation and sugar mills, the property of Sir John Gay Alleyne, Speaker of the House of Assembly (1767–97), were amongst the most productive in Barbados.

8. Barbados Governor Sir Thomas Robinson travels to St Michael's Church in this anonymous panorama of *c.* 1742. A busy Carlisle Bay is overlooked by the Charles and Willoughby forts, while the Bridgetown skyline shows the presence of Dutch gable roof tops.

9. Rachel Pringle –
slave; free-woman;
property owner;
associate of Prince
Henry – depicted
in her youth and
maturity by Thomas
Rowlandson (1796).

10. 'They will follow me wherever I go.' Leinster House, Dublin, print by Thomas Malton (1745).

11. Portico frieze of James Gandon's Custom House, Dublin, showing Hibernia and Britannia seated on a car of shell, Neptune driving away Famine and Despair, with a fleet approaching under full sail (1791).

12. The Corbally family in a Georgian interior in Dublin, 1770s, attributed to Strickland Lowry. Signs of prosperity abound: the fiddle-grate for coal-burning; Irish Chippendale chairs; patterned carpet; and costly wallpaper depicting classical architecture.

13. Henry Grattan (standing, on the right) addressing the Irish House of Commons, 1780, by Francis Wheatley.

14. Waves and clouds crashing around the whitewashed Dutch cityscape of Cape Town and the unmistakable rise of Table Mountain, painted by William Hodges (1772).

15. 'Considered as an entrepot between Europe and Asia, it has every advantage that can be wished.' East Indiamen off Cape Town, by Thomas Whitcombe (1820).

century there were some 4,000 resident landowners in Barbados, but the wealthiest planters had intermarried and consolidated their plantations – with just thirty estates accounting for almost 80 per cent of the island's 90,000 acres.[17] Generally, the lead planters controlled estates ranging between 200 acres and 1,000 acres: Henry Drax boasted 880 acres; Sir Peter Colleton 700 acres; the sugar baron John Pierce enjoyed the largest with some 1,000 acres under ownership. As they entered into their third generation, in the early eighteenth century the Barbadian plantocracy – the Alleynes, Cumberbatches, Freres, Osbornes, Beckles, Powells and Haynes – formed a solid socio-political elite: Anglican, loyalist and fabulously wealthy. They dominated the Barbadian Assembly, controlled the professions and endowed schools and churches across England, North America and the Caribbean.

As early as the 1650s, a land mass similar in size to the Isle of Wight was exporting some 8,000 tons of sugar a year to England, with a value of well over £3 million. The island was almost entirely given over to cane, with some 93 per cent of its total exports made up of sugar, rum and molasses. 'Sugar has contributed more to England's pleasure, glory, and grandeur than any other commodity we deal in or produce, wool not excepted,' was the judgement of merchant and imperial enthusiast Sir Dalby Thomas in the 1690s.[18] As a result, it was regarded as the richest spot in the New World, 'that fair jewell of your Majesty's Crown,' as Barbadian Governor Willoughby described it to King Charles II. Others called it the 'finest and worthiest island in the World' and 'the most flourishing colony the English have'.[19] John Oldmixon, in *The British Empire in America* (1708), was adamant that, 'When we examine the Riches that have been rais'd by the Produce of this little Spot of Ground, we shall find that it has been as good as a Mine of Silver or Gold to the Crown of England.'[20] The prospect of sharing in such riches might account for all the high-blown elegies offered up to Barbados. 'The whole is a sweet Spot of Earth, not a Span hardly uncultivated with Sugar-Canes; all sides bend with an easy Declivity to the Sea, and is ever green,' was what John Atkins, a surgeon in the Royal Navy, thought of it in 1735.[21] Catching sight of Barbados on a trip to Jamaica, the attorney and man of letters William Hickey thought:

this land presents to the eye one of the richest views that can be, one side being covered with the most luxuriant verdure, handsome buildings belonging to the planters, and windmills innumerable, the canes being ground by that machine. It did not appear to me that there was a single foot of uncultivated land upon the whole island. [22]

European society was drinking tea, coffee and chocolate in ever larger quantities during the 1700s and now adding sugar with even greater enthusiasm. As sugar made the transition from elite luxury to dietary staple, consumption in England rose from about 6lb per head in 1710 to over 23lb per head by the 1770s.[23] In the process, British culinary habits were transformed. 'Sugar achieved a revolution in eating habits,' according to the historian Matthew Parker.

> Along with coffee, tea, and cocoa, jams, processed foods, chocolate and confectionary were now being consumed in much greater quantities. Treacle was spread on bread and put on porridge. Breakfast became sweet, rather than savoury. Pudding, hitherto made of fish or light meat, now embarked on its unhealthy history as a separate sweet course . . . 'Sugar is so generally in use, by the assistance of tea,' read a 1774 report, 'that even the poor wretches living in almshouses will not be without it.'[24]

To satisfy this addiction, the British imported some 8,176 tons of sugar in 1663, almost 25,000 tons in 1710 and over 97,000 tons by 1775.

All of this demanded a massive West Indies workforce for the planting of cane, its cutting, crushing, boiling and barrelling. But Drax and his fellow planters were not offering to do it themselves. Instead, between 1662 and 1807, British ships carried around 3.25 million African slaves across the Atlantic to America and the Caribbean to work the land.[25] Around 40 per cent of these came from West Central Africa (Angola and the Congo); another 40 per cent from Benin and Biafra; some 15 per cent from the Gold Coast, Sierra Leone and Senegambia; and the remainder from other ports and slave forts in South-east Africa and Madagascar.[26] One such piece of human cargo was Olaudah Equiano, aka 'Gustavus Vassa, the African', whose account of his journey across the Atlantic 'middle passage' remains one of the most compelling testimonies to imperial barbarism.

The stench of the hold while we were on the coast was so intolerably loathsome, that it was dangerous to remain there for any time ... The closeness of the place, and the heat of the climate, added to the number in the ship, which was so crowded that each had scarcely room to turn himself, almost suffocated us ... This wretched situation was again aggravated by the galling of the chains, now become insupportable; and the filth of the necessary tubs, into which children often fell, and were almost suffocated. The shrieks of the women, and the groans of the dying, rendered the whole a scene of horror almost inconceivable ... One day, when we had a smooth sea, and moderate wind, two of my wearied countrymen, who were chained together, preferring death to such a life of misery, somehow made through the nettings, and jumped into the sea; immediately another quite dejected fellow, who, on account of his illness, was suffered to be out of irons, also followed their example.[27]

Unsurprisingly, mortality rates during the 'middle passage' stood at 9–18%.[28] Yet Britain was not the pioneer in this field – the Portuguese had been using African slaves, mainly shipped over from Congo and Angola, on their Brazilian plantations since the mid-1500s – but the British, French and Spanish industrialization of sugar production transformed the terms of trade. Indentured white servants, Carib Indians or the Irish prisoners of war who Cromwell exported to the West Indies in the 1650s just did not have the physical strength required for the work, heat and humidity of plantation life. The Irish labourers also had a history of rebellion, which put off the planters. As Vincent Harlow put it in his *History of Barbados* (1926): 'The planters discovered that labour of Negro slaves, accustomed as they were to intense heat and sudden cold, was more efficient ... consequently the British labourer ... gave place to the Negro. It was the triumph of geographical conditions.'[29]

For it was a hellish existence of often inhuman demands: the trench-digging, planting and slashing of the sugar cane under the broiling, semi-tropical sun in humid marshland; the transporting of huge cane bundles to the windmills for the crushing between the rollers; the refining in the boiler house amidst scalding heat (often at night to get through the harvest); then the barrelling and delivery.

'The Devil was in the Englishman,' was one slave saying, 'that he makes every thing work; he makes the Negro work, the Horse work, the Ass work, the Wood work, the Water work, and the Windework.' So, the business model worked much better with imported slaves, handled by the Crown-appointed slavers of the Royal African Company with its Caribbean headquarters in Bridgetown, and paid for with good credit lines from London and Amsterdam. In the mid-1640s, at the outset of sugar production in Barbados, the island housed a little more than 5,600 slaves. By 1680 that had become 38,000 and, with 1,300 arrivals a year, it reached 54,000 by 1700. For some, Bridgetown was a final destination, but for tens of thousands more African slaves it was a transit point for the wider West Indies, as the first port of call after the middle passage. Between 1708 and 1725 Bridgetown customs records reveal 321 ships anchoring in Carlisle Bay carrying 52,005 slaves. Equiano remembered landfall well.

> We came in sight of the island of Barbados, at which the whites on board gave a great shout, and made many signs of joy to us. We did not know what to think of this; but as the vessel drew nearer we plainly saw the harbour, and other ships of different kinds and sizes; and we soon anchored amongst them off Bridge Town. Many merchants and planters now came on board, though it was in the evening. They put us in separate parcels, and examined us attentively. They also made us jump, and pointed to land, signifying we were to go there.[30]

So began the Bridgetown slave auction:

> On a signal given, (as the beat of a drum), the buyers rush at once into the yard where the slaves are confined, and make choice of that parcel they like best. The noise and clamour with which this is attended, and the eagerness visible in the countenance of the buyers, serve not a little to increase the apprehension of the terrified Africans.[31]

John Oldmixon was present at one such sale. 'The Slaves are purchas'd by Lots, out of the Guinea Ships. They are all view'd stark naked, and the strongest and handsomest bear the best Prizes. They are allow'd to have two or three Wives, that they may encrease the Planter's Stock by Multiplication.'[32] The process naturally had its apologists. 'The sales, which formerly took place on board the ship, are now (most properly)

conducted on shore, and care is taken that no cruel separation of relations should take place,' was how one pro-slavery polemicist described
the auction. 'To behold a number of human beings, naked, captive,
exiled and exposed for sale, must, at first sight, affect the mind with
melancholy reflections; but the victims themselves seem to be hardly
conscious of their situation . . . In the market they display few indica-
tions of being deeply affected with their fate.'[33] Equiano recorded it
differently. 'In this manner, without scruple, are relations and friends
separated, most of them never to see each other again. I remember in
the vessel in which I was brought over, in the men's apartment, there
were several brothers, who, in the sale, were sold in different lots; and
it was very moving on this occasion to see and hear their cries at
parting.'[34]

The slaves, now the private property of their masters, were taken
from Bridgetown out to the sugar plantations. It was here, amid the
cane fields and boiling rooms, that the most appalling crimes and
torture were committed.

> There was no ingenuity that fear or a depraved imagination could
> devise which was not employed to break their [the slaves'] spirit and
> satisfy the lusts and resentment of their owners and guardians – irons
> on the hands and feet, blocks of wood that the slaves had to drag
> behind them wherever they went, the tin-plate mask designed to pre-
> vent the slaves eating the sugar-cane, the iron collar. Whipping was
> interrupted in order to pass a piece of hot wood on the buttocks of the
> victim; salt, pepper, citron, cinders, aloes, and hot ashes were poured on
> the bleeding wounds. Mutilations were common, limbs, ears, and
> sometimes the private parts, to deprive them of the pleasures which
> they could indulge in without expense. Their masters poured burning
> wax on their arms and hands and shoulders, emptied the boiling cane
> sugar over their heads, burned them alive, roasted them on slow fires,
> filled them with gunpowder and blew them up with a match.[35]

These were the plantation conditions in the French colony of
Saint-Domingue, as described by C. L. R. James in his classic history
of resistance *The Black Jacobins*. As abolitionist William Dickson's
harrowing accounts of slaves run through on spits and human mutila-
tions attested, the British were no better. On the plantations, the lash,

iron collar and straitjacket were regular remedies for poor behaviour. 'The English do not look after their slaves well,' noted Père Labat in Barbados.

> The overseers get every ounce of work out of them, beat them without mercy for the least fault, and appear to care far less for the life of a negro than for a horse . . . The clergymen do not instruct the slaves or baptize them, and the negroes are regarded more like the beasts to whom all license is permitted so long as they do their work properly.

If they ever tried to resist their enslavement, the planters' savagery knew no bounds. 'The slaves who are captured are sent to prison and condemned to be passed through a cane mill, or be burnt alive, or be put into iron cages that prevent any movement and in which they are hung up to branches of trees and left to die of hunger and despair.'[36]

And when the slaves were no longer fit enough to work the plantations, they were discarded like dogs. 'In Barbadoes, sir, I am sorry to say, there are some owners, who, when their slaves become incapable of labour, from age, ill usage, or disease, especially leprosy;

'Not a Span hardly uncultivated with Sugar-Canes'. Map from *A True and Exact History of the Island of Barbados*, by Richard Ligon (1657).

inhumanely expose them to every extreme of wretchedness, by turning them out to shift for themselves,' Dickson wrote. 'The poor creatures generally crawl to Bridge-town ... and they are often to be seen in the streets, in the very last stage of human misery, naked, famished, diseased and forlorn.'[37]

Such savagery kept up the need for imports. Records from one Barbadian plantation in the mid-eighteenth century show only one slave birth for every six slave deaths; and one birth a year for each hundred slaves.[38] Typically, the plantation owners had to replace their workforce at a rate of 2–5 per cent per annum to keep up with mortality levels. John Oldmixon explained this was because:

> The Negroes are generally false and treacherous ... They are apt to swell with a good Opinion of themselves, on the least occasion for it, to be very stubborn, are sullen and cruel, and their Masters are almost under a fatal Necessity to treat them inhumanely, or they would be ungovernable ... when we consider how lazy they are apt to be, and how careless, and that the Fortune of their Masters depends almost entirely on their Care and Labour, one can't blame the Overseers, for punishing the Idle and Remiss severely.[39]

Not least when such extraordinary wealth was at stake.

SO MANY PORTS, HARBOURS, CITTYES, HAVENS

Karl Marx called it 'primitive accumulation' – the initial influx of capital from the colonies which allowed the nations of Western Europe to kick-start the industrial revolution. 'The discovery of gold and silver in America, the extirpation, enslavement and entombment in mines of the aboriginal population, the beginning of the conquest and looting of the East Indies, the turning of Africa into a warren for the commercial hunting of black-skins, signalised the rosy dawn of the era of capitalist production,' as he put it in *Das Kapital*. And this accumulation of funds was essential for the development of industrial capitalism in the eighteenth century. 'The colonial system ripened, like a hot-house, trade and navigation,' he wrote. 'The colonies secured a market for the budding manufactures and, through the monopoly of the market, an increased accumulation. The treasures captured outside Europe by undisguised looting, enslavement, and murder, floated back to the mother country and were turned into capital.'[40] Daniel Defoe, with characteristic succinctness, spelt out the relationship:

> I must confess I do not know any thing in Trade that could befal us, *I mean that was ever probable to befal us*, that could be so great a Blow to Trade in general, as the Ruin of the *African* Trade in particular; and those who know how far our Plantation Trade is Blended and Interwoven with the Trade to *Africa*, and that they can no more be parted than the Child and the Nurse, need have no time spent to convince them of this; The Case is as plain as Cause and Consequence: Mark the Climax. *No African* Trade, *no* Negroes; *no* Negroes, *no* Sugars, Gingers, Indicos [indigo] etc.; *no* Sugars, etc. *no* Islands; *no* Islands, *no* Continent; *no* Continent, *no* trade.[41]

This was the interpretation which Eric Williams developed more fully in *Capitalism and Slavery* (1944), where he traced how profits from the slave trade 'fertilized the entire productive system' of Great Britain. The Welsh slate industry, Manchester textile production, Glaswegian, Bristol and Liverpool banking, ship-building and heavy engineering were all endowed by foreign funds drawn from the plantation system. 'It was the capital accumulation from the West Indies trade that financed James Watt and the steam engine,' writes Williams of the most celebrated of industrial innovations.[42] In 1741, the value of Barbadian exports alone to England (of which the vast majority was constituted by sugar) was £298,000. By 1763, the total value of Caribbean exports to England had risen to near £2 million. What was more, sugar had a multiplier effect, increasing domestic land values – as it was consumed with domestic fruits – and growing import duties on cocoa, tea and coffee.[43]

Since the publication of *Capitalism and Slavery*, many historians have sought to downplay such Marxist interpretations, suggesting that funds from the West Indies were falling by the late eighteenth century and that the industrial revolution was far more dependent upon new energy sources, systems of innovation, or nonconformist finance. Yet more recent scholarship has reasserted just how closely profits from advanced sugar production, as well as captive markets in the colonies, assisted the industrialization process. The slave trade provided important routes for British industry – notably textiles – to develop their competitive strengths in expanding markets. In 1772, 72 per cent of Yorkshire woollens and 90 per cent of broadcloth, and about 40 per cent of all English copper and brass was going abroad chiefly to Africa and the New World.[44] The Atlantic trade was the dynamo for British industrial development. Robin Blackburn has calculated that profits derived from the triangular trade could have furnished anything from 20.9 per cent to 55 per cent of Britain's gross fixed capital formation in 1770, crucially underpinning the prosperity of the UK economy as a whole and easing the financial or credit problems of technically advanced sectors in particular. It was not only investment in new technologies, but also the vital infrastructure of ports, new docks (most notably in London and Liverpool), canals, harbours and agricultural improvements which were made possible by the colonial tribute pouring in from the West Indies.[45]

As well as promoting industrial development, the Caribbean plantations funded the enforcement and expansion of Empire. It was a symbiotic process with increased revenue from the West Indies financing the Royal Navy's expeditions across the Atlantic and Pacific, which in turn secured further imperial possessions. During the rolling conflicts of the mid-eighteenth century, naval officers and colonial merchants worked closely together over victualling, enemy bounties and convoy security. The assistance even extended to the manning of empire, with West Indian merchant sailors being called upon in time of war. The planters' propagandist Bryan Edwards estimated that in 1787 the British West Indian trade employed 689 ships, totalling 148,176 tons and manned by nearly 14,000 seamen – all potential crewmen for the Royal Navy. When Captain Richard Wyvil, of the 79th Regiment of the British infantry, anchored in Carlisle Bay en route to Martinique, the harbour 'was so full of shipping [that] it was difficult to steer clear of them. Here lay the East Indiaman belonging to Admiral Sir Hugh Christian's fleet, with the troops still on board.'

Retaining control of the colonies and their merchant marine was an essential part of any European power's geo-political strategy. The wars of the eighteenth century saw extensive skirmishes between France, Britain, Holland and Spain centred on the West Indies, with the succeeding peace treaties of Utrecht (1713), Aix-la-Chapelle (1748) and Paris (1763) usually involving the return of whichever wealthy colony had been captured. 'Whenever the nations of Europe are engaged, from whatever cause, in war with each other, these unhappy countries are constantly made the theatre of its operations,' noted Bryan Edwards of the West Indies. 'Thither the combatants repair, as to the arena, to decide their differences.'[46] And such were the riches at stake that, at the Treaty of Paris for example, the French were willing to cede most of Canada in order to keep control of sugar-rich Guadeloupe and Martinique.

This military backdrop determined much of the physical infrastructure of Bridgetown – from parade grounds to barracks to hospitals and forts. In 1681 the commission granted to the governor of Barbados gave him the authority 'to erect, raise and build in the Island . . . so many fortes, platforms, castles, cittyes, burroughs, townes and fortifications' as he thought fit to defend the island. Time and again, in the ensuing century of global conflict, the vital guarantor of Barbadian autonomy was the defensive system around the coast of Bridgetown. 'The Wharfs and Keys are very neat and convenient; and the Forts to the Sea so strong, that there would be no taking it by Force, if they were as well mann'd and furnished with Ammunition as they ought to be,' was John Oldmixon's verdict in 1708.

> The first of these Forts Westward, is James Fort, near Stewart's Wharf. 'Tis mounted with 18 Guns . . . Next to this is Willoughby's Fort, built on a small Neck of Land, that runs out into the Sea. 'Tis mounted with 12 Guns . . . Above this Fort, and more within Land, the late Governor, Sir Bevill Granvill, began the Royal Cittadel . . . This will be the strongest in the whole Island, and stand the Country in above 30000 *l*. Sterling.[47]

These were the forts – the remnants of which now encircle the grassy, Garrison Savannah racecourse – which provided a protective cove for the Royal Navy, a home for the 2,700 troops stationed in Barbados and a base from which to launch invasions and counter-attacks into neighbouring Caribbean islands.

Bridgetown's Charles Fort and James Fort secured that same

'empire of goods' that connected the fortunes of Bridgetown and Boston with the colonial metropolis across the Atlantic. For the governor had also been authorized to 'order and appoint within our said Island ... respectively such and so many ports, harbours, cittyes, havens and other places for convenience and security of shipping and for the better loading and unloading of goods and merchandizes'.[48] If the rural sugar plantation was the *ingenio* of the colonial process, then Bridgetown provided the entrepôt – exporting the hinterland's sugar to Europe, and importing an ever-expanding range of British 'goods and merchandizes'.

It was in Bridgetown that the structures of an export economy were developed, where a market for British manufactured goods emerged – the townhouses of the plantation owners bedecking themselves in the same collection of Wedgwood ceramics, Chippendale furniture, linens and soft furnishings as were on display in Boston's Beacon Hill – and where idealized notions of English society were reflected back into urban life.[49] 'The great value of Barbados to Great Britain is best known from its vast consumption of British and Irish manufactures and commodities,' was the well-connected Bajan Henry Frere's judgement in the 1760s. 'The goods sent from Great Britain are chiefly woolen, linen, Manchester velvets, silk, iron, brass, copper, leather, laces for linen, hats, wigs, shoes, stockings, china, glass, earthen wares, pictures, clocks, watches, jewels, plate, gold and silver lace ...'[50] It was what one visitor called 'promoting Trade by a Magnificent way of living'.[51] Père Labat was certainly impressed by the levels of Caribbean consumption. 'The shops and stores are full of everything one could wish to buy, and their goods come from all parts of the world. There are a number of goldsmiths, jewellers, clockmakers and other artisans who drive a thriving trade and appear to be very comfortably off, and the largest business in "America" is carried on in this town.' For the plantocracy had no hesitation about showing off their wealth. 'One observes the wealth and good taste of the inhabitants in their furniture, which is very fine, and their silver, of which they have so large a quantity that were this island to be sacked the silver alone would be worth more than the value of several galleons.'[52]

So, alongside the forts, the domestic and commercial fabric of Bridgetown started to reflect these colonial economics. Although

British chroniclers were always keen to emphasize the fact that this was no Baroque city, laid out on a grid-pattern like the vainglorious French and Spanish colony ports, Bridgetown started to be widely admired for its elegance. 'The Bridge Town, or rather City, is certainly the finest and largest in all the Islands, if not in all the English Colonies abroad,' noted John Oldmixon in 1708. 'It contains 1200 Houses, built of Stone; the Windows glass'd, many of them sash'd; the Streets broad, the Houses high, and the Rents as dear in Cheapside, in the Bridge, as in Cheapside in London.'[53]

This was all the more surprising when one considers that the main focus of the sugar barons and slave traders was always the plantation house. One only has to visit St Nicholas Abbey in the north or Sunbury Plantation in the south to realize the time and energy which the planter class spent on exhibiting their prosperity in the drawing rooms, dining rooms and parlours of the great slave mansions. But what was so distinct about Barbados was that the plantocracy also had townhouses and took urban culture seriously. The diary of the prominent planter and member of St Michael's vestry, Francis Ford, reveals just such a high level of both urban attachment and English combination of country and city, *rus* and *urbe*. 'Early in the morning set out to Bridgetown,' he writes of 12 January 1790. 'Breakfasted with Beckles [town agent for Ford], attended the meeting of the Vestry . . . Saw Phillips about the sale of Codrington [estate], gave the paper to Beckles to prepare . . . Dined with the Vestry.' On 18 January, 'after breakfast went [to] Town, attended to Vestry, agreed to sign the sale for Codrington . . . returned home to dinner'. And on 27 January Ford only continued the pattern: 'Went to Bridgetown . . . took the Bay Rents [part of his responsibility as vestryman].' Numerous merchants, lawyers and professionals resided in Bridgetown to be close to the centre of judicial, military and political affairs, while the big planters retained a city residence. As the Royal Navy surgeon John Atkins described it, 'Bridgetown, the principal of the Island . . . is the Residence of the Governor, Factors, and Merchants, who transact their Business here and at their Plantations alternately.'[54] From a property list of 1706, for example, we know that Eliza Drax (of the Drax clan) kept a Bridgetown house, as did leading planters Richard Forstall, Samuel Hassall and John Blackman.

What is more, there emerged in the latter half of the eighteenth century a concerted attempt to beautify this civic environment. That Georgian vision of urban politeness – of neo-classical designs and uniform aesthetics – which was to refashion Bath, Newcastle and Edinburgh, also changed the face of Bridgetown, Barbados. Following a devastating fire in 1766, a series of ordinances were passed to promote the building of new homes in Bridgetown with 'uniformity and gracefulness'. Houses were not to be constructed higher than three storeys, with any parapet walls carried two and a half feet above the eaves. And when it came to materials, the building code included strict precautions against further infernos sweeping the city.

> The outside of all buildings within the limits of the said town, be henceforth made of brick or stone, or of bricks and stones together, except door-cases and window frames, which shall be made of any kind of wood and set four inches at least within the wall, and all buildings shall be covered with copper, slate, tile, sawed stone, or block-tin and not other materials.[55]

The townhouse style, meanwhile, was either Dutch-influenced with curvilinear gables, or a more classical Georgian aesthetic replete with tall windows, central entrances, minimal ornamentation and hip roofs with parapets (most of which would be blown apart in the hurricane of 1780).[56]

Alongside the Georgian townhouses, the commercial district of Bridgetown grew up around the Customs House on Cheapside. The same planters who took city residences, also owned storehouses for holding sugar between the harvest and its export. Cheapside, still lined today with three-storey, limestone warehouses built in the 1700s, was christened in a conscious declaration of Bridgetown's commercial dependence upon London. Alongside it, Cornhill and Broad Street provided a West Indian answer to the financial sector of the City of London. And the dependence of Barbados on the markets, financiers and politicians of London was made even plainer with the naming of Milk Street, London Street and Maiden Lane in honour of the capital; when textile imports from Manchester, slave ships out of Liverpool and other manufactured goods from industrial England started to arrive in Barbados, Bridgetown was swift to respond with the naming of Manchester, Liverpool and Lancaster Lanes. The biggest hardware warehouse in Bridgetown even adopted the title of Britain's metal-bashing metropolis: the 'Birmingham Warehouse'. The colonial fealty remained, even if it was becoming as much industrial as financial by the end of the 1700s.[57]

THE SPIRIT OF ENGLISHMEN
IN OUR HEARTS

Where did all this staggering sugar wealth end up? Barbados was by no means as bad as Jamaica and Antigua when it came to absentee landlords, but the profits from its plantations were always more likely to be found in Dorset, Surrey and Hampshire than in the parishes of St George, St Andrew and St Phillips. The history of the Lascelles family is telling. In the early 1700s, Henry Lascelles, son of a Conservative MP and part of a middling gentry family, left Yorkshire for Barbados to join his eldest brother George in the sugar-exporting and slave-importing business. Between 1713 and 1717, Henry Lascelles had shares in twenty-one slave ships, imported 1,101 Africans and used the profits to buy up plantations across the West Indies. He embedded himself further in the Barbados slavery business by marrying Mary Carter, the daughter of the leading Bridgetown slave-trader Edwin Carter. Together with his brothers Edward and George, Henry Lascelles established a London commission house, importing sugar from the West Indies, and also earning himself a lucrative income by landing the post of customs collector for Bridgetown in 1715 (a post he passed on to his brother Edward in 1734).

From 1738, Lascelles was an absentee owner of a plantation at Holetown. But he was far more notorious as the innovator of the so-called 'floating factory', which sought to apply the logistics of military planning to slave trafficking, with vessels stationed off the Guinea coast at Anomabu used as holding pens in place of incarcerating the slave cargo in troublesome African forts. It proved a highly profitable operation, with the Lascelles and their backers moving into the shipping of ivory and gold, as well as Africans. By 1787 the family held more than 27,000 acres in Barbados, Jamaica, Grenada and Tobago and sent their money back across the Atlantic, commissioning the gorgeous Harewood House, outside Harrogate in Yorkshire, as testimony to their commercial success (although its range of Chippendale furniture, Old Master paintings and Chinese wallpaper carefully hid the sources of the Lascelles' wealth).[58] However, Harewood was just one of a number of West Indian planter palaces springing up over the 1700s – there was Dodington Hall in Gloucester, where the Codrington family (who also endowed the Anglican seminary Codrington College in Barbados and the library of All Souls College at Oxford) sunk their riches; Charborough House in Dorset, where some of the Drax family funds went; their fictional correlative was Jane Austen's Mansfield Park, where the wealth of Sir Thomas Bertram seemed always shrouded in Antiguan, plantation mystery. So remarkable was this influx of Caribbean cash that the former prime minister Lord Shelburne exclaimed in 1778 that 'there were scarcely ten miles together throughout the country where the house and estate of a rich West Indian was not to be seen'.[59]

This 'mercantile-financial complex' also purchased the British establishment. It was not simply that the Lascelles and the Draxes from Barbados, or the Beckfords from Jamaica, the Martins from Antigua or the Stapletons from Nevis sat in the House of Commons; rather, the tentacles of plantation finance spread right through the British commercial, political and ecclesiastical classes. Following the death of Christopher Codrington, the Church of England – through its missionary arm, the Society for the Propagation of the Gospel in Foreign Parts – ran the 980-acre Codrington plantation in Barbados, helpfully branding its slaves on their chests with the word 'SOCIETY'. Junior princes of the royal family counted themselves staunch supporters of the slave-trading industry, with an equally large number of the British aristocracy heavily invested in its continued profitability. Industry, finance, faith and nobility were all bound into the West Indian trade.

Yet for all its political and economic intimacy with Britain, colonial Barbados was also involved in a different set of trade relationships that would – in the latter half of the eighteenth century – force the island to affirm its imperial identity. For the commercial traffic blocking up Carlisle Bay came as much from the ports of America's Thirteen

Colonies as it did from Bristol, London and Liverpool. Despite the failure of Henry Winthrop's tobacco crop, another of Governor Winthrop's sons, Samuel, decided in 1647 to leave godly Boston to start his own business shipping wine from Madeira to Barbados – before then settling there in 1648, 'where in all probability I can live better than in other places'. Austere as ever, Governor Winthrop simply noted of that year, 'it pleased the Lord to open us a trade with Barbados and other Islands in the West Indies'.[60] That trade accelerated in the ensuing decades. The public wharf in Bridgetown was renamed 'New England Row', which itself led on to 'New England Street', as more than 100 ships carrying timber, rice, fish and other provisions annually docked in Barbados from New England in the early 1700s. 'The commerce of the West India islands is a part of the American system of commerce,' wrote the Boston lawyer John Adams. 'They can neither do without us nor we without them. The Creator has placed us upon the globe in such a situation that we have occasion for each other.'[61] Indeed, the building of the sugar plantations was dependent upon the import of timber, shingles, horses and cattle – as well as fish, beef, pork and cereal products – from the American north, while Boston, New York and Charlestown spent their export profits on West Indian sugar and molasses. On 3 November 1785 seven ships arrived at Bridgetown, including a schooner from Philadelphia. Its cargo was typical of the time: 38 hogshead of corn, 27 kegs and 29 barrels of bread; 53 barrels and 4 hogshead of apples; 236 barrels of flour; 1 wheelbarrow; 55,000 shingles; 3,000 hoops; 6 kegs of sturgeon; 1 horse and 1,600 staves.[62] Similarly, the journey of the 40-ton barque *Palm Tree* provides an exemplary tale of commerce in the Georgian colonies. The ship set sail in October 1799 from Plymouth, England, taking the westerlies into the Channel, down the Portuguese coast to Madeira, then west along 13°N latitude, round the southern edge of Barbados and into Bridgetown some eight and a half weeks later. She exchanged her cargo of biscuit, cider and serges for rum, sugar and molasses, before sailing for ports in Virginia (taking a further five weeks). She then returned to England with tobacco, after a regular, nine-month, 16,000-kilometre circuit.[63]

Few embodied this trade between the British American colonies more obviously than Gedney Clarke Senior, who succeeded Edward

Lascelles as customs collector for Bridgetown and was, for some decades, one of the most successful transatlantic merchants, with interests covering South Carolina, Virginia, New England and Great Britain. His business life began in the late 1730s, exporting sugar and rum to Salem and bringing fish and whale oil back to Barbados. Clarke then developed a long-running business partnership with the Lascelles family, setting up a trading house in London specializing in sugar plantations, selling slaves and transporting military supplies, as well as investing in the coming Dutch colonies of Demerara and Essequibo in the West Indies. Operating out of Bridgetown, Clarke ran a highly successful trading corporation which took as much advantage of Britain's imperial-mercantilist trading system as possible.[64]

Gedney Clarke's close connections to the wealthy, landed Fairfax family of Virginia also meant that he was responsible for inviting a young Fairfax retainer and land surveyor, George Washington, to visit Barbados in 1751. Washington arrived with his half-brother Lawrence (who was hopeful that the blustery sea air might alleviate his tuberculosis) and spent a bucolic few months riding across the slave plantations, visiting the theatre, dining at the Anglophile Beefstake and Tripe clubs and generally taking in colonial society. He rented the house of Captain Crofton (at an exorbitant £15 per month 'exclusive of liquor and washing'), just south of Bridgetown – on the edge of the Garrison district – and took advantage of his host's military background to inspect the defences at James Fort and Charles Fort, guarding the entrance into Carlisle Bay. In the succeeding years, British soldiers would have a dual reason to curse Washington's time in Bridgetown: first, for his detailed knowledge of the principles of British defence fortifications; and, second, because he contracted smallpox during his stay, which ensured his later immunity against the disease, to which thousands of his fellow revolutionaries succumbed.

Even Washington's enjoyable time in Barbados, however, could not alter the fact that by the latter half of the eighteenth century the mutual interests of the West Indies and the Thirteen Colonies were starting to dissolve. When the much larger French colonies of Martinique and Saint-Domingue entered the sugar trade and were able to use their economies of scale to drive down production costs, the

Barbadian plantocracy found its American market drying up. By the 1730s, a gallon of molasses from Barbados could cost 10d but only 4d from Martinique – and the New England rum distillers wasted little time dropping British for French suppliers. The response of the Barbadian planters was not to cut costs or improve production, but to lobby the British parliament to impose a tax on foreign molasses. 'Molasses was an essential ingredient in American independence,' wrote John Adams looking back on the mercantilist Molasses Act (1733), which imposed an import duty of 6p per gallon on foreign molasses entering North America in order to protect the profits of the West Indian planters.[65] It was the first step along the path toward the the Stamp Act and taxation without representation – and Boston's merchants suspected the West Indian planters of egging on the British parliament. The next turn of the screw was the 1764 Sugar Act, which cut the duty on molasses but imposed a new tax on imported sugar and, in the opinion of many North American merchants, once more sacrificed the interests of the Thirteen Colonies 'to a few West-India planters'. Costs were being piled up in Massachusetts and Philadelphia to enrich the already prosperous Caribbean planters. When the Barbadian Assembly accepted the 1764 Stamp Act, out of 'a principle of loyalty to our King and country' it was clear that there was a gulf between Boston and Bridgetown as to the nature of the British Empire to which they wished to belong. 'Can no punishment be devised for Barbados and Port Royal in Jamaica, for their base desertion of the cause of liberty, their tame surrender of the rights of Britons, their mean, timid resignation to slavery?' asked John Adams. Barbados's exports were added to Boston's growing list of non-importation goods, and the island was denied 'the comfortable enjoyment of every delicious dainty from us . . . till they are brought to a state of despondency without anything but stinking fish and false doctrine'. The *Barbados Mercury* responded to Boston's insolence with a castigating assault on the 'set of men, who, under the specious name of asserters of their liberty, dare, contrary to all laws human and divine, break out into the most outrageous Acts of Rebellion against their Sovereign defender'.[66]

The tussle over molasses and money thus became a broader

divergence of views between the North American merchants and the West Indian planters. On the one hand, the ethos of self-government was just as proud in Bridgetown as in Boston. The Bridgetown Assembly – established in 1639 – was the third-oldest parliament in the British Empire after those of Virginia and Bermuda, and the island only agreed to its status as a Crown colony in the 1660s after King Charles II had promised to safeguard its autonomy. But whereas in the Thirteen Colonies a more obviously 'American' identity emerged out of the struggle against the Sugar Act, Stamp Act, and Townshend duties, the Barbadians responded to this Atlanticist crisis of imperial authority by embedding themselves even deeper in Britishness. 'British blood runs in our veins and the spirit of Englishmen in our hearts,' declared a local Bajan patriot.[67] And as the African slave population increased on the island, identification with white Europe was an important means of both retaining separation and cementing a sense of cultural superiority. 'It is to Great Britain alone that our West Indian planters consider themselves belonging,' in the words of Bryan Edwards. The inchoate British Empire of the mid-eighteenth century – that collection of plantations, cities, Crown colonies and trading companies – was a highly lucrative consortium for the planters of the Caribbean. With their finances and families divided between Britain and the West Indies, they had few doubts about standing by the colonial system.

In turn, London looked after the interests of its loyal, Anglican and well-connected plantocracy. If there was to be a struggle between the North American colonies and the West Indian interest, the Caribbeans were going to win every time – as the passage of the Molasses Act and the Sugar Act and the exclusion of plantation goods from the Townshend duties proved. As, indeed, did the miserably slow passage of William Wilberforce's Bill to abolish the slave trade, first raised in the House of Commons in 1789 and subject to relentless opposition by sugar- and slave-funded Members of Parliament. It also meant that when the Boston Tea-Party began the journey towards American independence, London proved more determined than ever to hold on to the West Indies. There could be no 'domino effect' in the Americas; the British Exchequer simply could not afford the loss of such a vital, colonial cash-cow.

THE GREAT CAPITAL

Yet by the time Washington was crossing the Potomac in December 1776 and the American Revolution was splintering the First British Empire, Barbados was in fact no longer proving quite such a lucrative possession for the Exchequer. It was still profitable, but more than a century of plantation farming and sugar cane monoculture had taken its toll on the island's soil. And it simply could not compete against the economies of scale offered either by the enormous French colonies of Saint-Domingue and Martinique, or by the prospering British islands of Jamaica and Antigua. Indeed, as early as the 1750s Jamaican sugar production was exceeding Barbados's output, while planters were having to expend ever more resources on labour, manuring and replanting in order to keep yields up. One solution was to refine further (or 'clay') the muscovado, providing the white sugar for the making of preserves which commanded a much higher price and smaller shipping costs. But it was only a stop-gap (as was a boom in prices following slave revolts in Saint-Domingue in 1794) in a trajectory of relative economic decline compared to other Caribbean colonies.

Falling yields from Barbados's plantations did little to detract from the importance of Bridgetown as a colonial city. By the 1740s, it could boast a population of some 10,600 inhabitants – the equal of Boston and New York in British colonial America. Equally attractive, for colonial society, was the much higher ratio of whites to blacks than in other West Indian colonies. In Jamaica it was one white to ten blacks and in Antigua as high as one to eighteen, but in Barbados only one to four.[68] This gave Bridgetown, the historic capital of the 'Mother-Colony' and 'very Mart of all other plantations in these parts', a powerful sense of racial and cultural security all amplified by that reassuring footprint of forts and garrisons overlooking Carlisle Bay. Within the city, a merchant class had developed, partly peopled by a growing Jewish community who were banned from owning slaves but able to make a good living in urban trading. With the development of a regional sugar and slave economy across the West Indies,

Bridgetown exploited its position as the easternmost island to become the Caribbean hub for market intelligence, military news, fashion, culture and influence.

For the medical doctor George Pinckard, sailing around the Caribbean in the 1810s, Barbados was 'the London of the West Indies – the great capital to which we anxiously look for events, and for news'.[69] The first destination of William Hickey's tour around the West Indies was Grenada, but, 'wishing to gain information', the captain naturally 'ran close in to Bridgetown, capital of Barbadoes, and there hove to. A boat, with only caffres in her, having fruit to sell, came off, and we purchased pines, oranges, plaintains, guavas, star apples, etc., all of which were highly acceptable.'[70] The Royal African Company instructed all its ships to dock first at Bridgetown to test the market for other islands. 'I have seen 300 sail of merchant ships, with their convoy, enter Carlisle Bay, in one fleet,' noted William Dickson in 1780, 'and have known large fleets of men of war, once as far as 32 ships of the line, besides frigates, at anchor, for a considerable time, in that harbour.'[71] In 1788 alone, over 350 ships left Bridgetown carrying nearly 38,000 tons of cargo. With its Cheapside warehouses, its merchant class and London connections, Bridgetown was easily the dominant trading and cultural centre of the British Empire in the West Indies.

And more than any of the other cities of the British West Indies – such as St John's, Antigua or Spanish Town, Jamaica – Bridgetown offered a way out of the tedium of plantation living. 'Being hot and moreover, not fit for Hunting or Hawking, the Planters and other Gentry here are obliged, for most part, to sedentary diversions at home: as cards, dice, tables, quoits, bowling, balls, and concerts,' was how one 1740s visitor described daily existence in the Barbados big house. Then, of course, there were the 'five or six Bottles of Madera wine, to their share, every Day, for which they find sweating the best Relief'.[72]

In Bridgetown, by contrast, there was culture and refinement: there were assembly rooms, racecourses, musical societies, dancing schools, bowling greens, coffee houses, taverns, inns, literary societies, Masonic lodges and a Society for the Encouragement of Arts, Manufacture and Commerce.[73] The *Barbados Mercury* was laden with adverts for events such as an 'Elegant Concert of Vocal and Instrumental Musick' (November 1784), or more excitingly, 'A Concert of Vocal and Instrumental Musick by the Gentlemen of the Musical Society. Proper MUSIC FOR DANCING after the Concert will be provided' (November 1787). And just as in pre-revolutionary Boston, so in Bridgetown the conspicuous display of consumer goods, the construction of Georgian mansions and the circulation of London novels and journals cemented an imperial, Atlantic identity. Above all, there was the theatre (much frequented by George Washington). While the Patagonian Theatre went highbrow with productions of Shakespeare's *Richard III*, the shows at the James Street theatre were a little more bawdy with titles such as *Beaux Stratagem* and *The Spouting Club, or Dick the Apprentice*. Indeed, the pages of the *Mercury* or the *Barbados Gazette* – founded in 1731 by Samuel Keimer (a former business associate of Benjamin Franklin) – were full of a vernacular, eighteenth-century humour straight from the pages of Grub Street. In between shipping announcements and 'Foreign Affairs' correspondence and minutes from the General Assembly, there were squibs from 'Celia Epigram' and a series of 'amusing' announcements: 'MISPLACED Three languishing glances, and as many *sighs*, which escaped from *Miss –*, and were directed to a gentleman in the grenadier company, who, it is shrewdly suspected, has a wife on the other side of the Atlantic'; 'LOST from the *bosom of Miss* – a very valuable *heart*, set around with *graces*, supposed to be dropt near a young *officer*, who it is hoped if he should have the luck to discover it, will make an honourable use of this accident'.[74]

We gain a rich sense of this urban, commercial society from the diaries of Eliza Fenwick, a flighty but well-connected young English actress, who arrived in 'Barbadoes' in 1811, to a welter of social invitations. 'After a short passage through purgatory, we arrived yesterday in Heaven,' she wrote back to her mother with a rather different version of the Atlantic 'middle passage'. 'This is indeed the Land of Promise, – I hope it is not too good to last.' Soon enough it was lunchtime.

> At 3 we sat down to a grand dinner: sucking-pig, fowls, soup, mutton, game, yams, plantain, sweet potatoes, sour cabbages, and a hundred

other nasty things . . . Afterwards they compelled me and Miss Simms to lie down. We slept till tea time, when Miss Lewellyn and her Negroes brought us tea, Coffee and cakes, made us take them in bed, and then rubbed our legs, which really were almost as big as our bodies. At 8 o clock we had Chocolate, and at 9 Supper. Miss L. gave us up her room and when we were in bed brought us up hot Madeira, bathed our feet with camphorated wine, and then all the ladies came and kissed us most affectionately.[75]

The ensuing weeks entailed only more lemonade, luncheons with the planters, piano duets and dinners with the Attorney General. It was such fun that she stayed for a decade, starred in many a Bridgetown production and even shipped over her mother.

Those 'Negroes' rubbing Eliza's legs highlight another unique aspect of Bridgetown life: a growing population of domestic servants, skilled slaves and freed coloureds who created a far more multicultural urban environment than the binary racism of the plantations. Between 1765 and 1818 the free coloured population of Barbados expanded from 500 to 3,000, almost all of them based in the capital. Their numbers shaped the relatively unusual topography of the city, as land shortages, high prices and the need for slaves and servants to live alongside their masters produced high levels of mixed-race living. Unlike other cities of the British Empire, there was no clearly segregated 'black town' or 'white town' (which would have had to include the Jewish residents and impoverished white labourers). Indeed, Bridgetown became notorious for the remarkable degree of social licence granted to the urban black community. 'The inhabitants of the towns may, in general, be said to be humane,' William Dickson noted carefully. 'Many of them, indeed, treat their domestics with a degree of indulgence, which in their present uncultivated state . . . they are in general but ill able to bear, and which they often abuse.' What Dickson regarded as unacceptable behaviour was most likely black urban culture – spread through kinship networks across different domestic settings – which found its voice during funerals, Saturday-night gatherings (unnerving white residents with drumming and dancing), storytelling and gaming. Just as concerning for many white residents was the economic challenge posed by this expanding, mixed-race community. As merchants, haberdashers, tavern- and innkeepers, tailors, jewellers and artisans, the skilled slaves and freed coloureds easily undercut the often unskilled, white working class. Dickson thought it was 'almost impossible for a poor free [i.e., white] man to find a market for his work, when it came into competition with the slaves of the rich'.[76] So time and again the planter-run Barbados House of Assembly had to resort to racial solidarity to pass laws limiting the competition that freed slaves could pose to white merchants. However, it could never eliminate this 'black' economy altogether – and Bridgetown received a powerful economic boost from the presence of such an aggressively entrepreneurial community.

One sector of the economy where the freed coloureds faced little competition was in the running of brothels. Across the colonial Caribbean, Bridgetown was also famous for a highly developed sex industry. This was partly the traditional product of a port servicing a large volume of sailors, but also because of the racial dynamics of the island – what the Barbadian historian Hilary Beckles calls 'the institutionalization of prostitution by the white elite'.[77] Within Bridgetown society, there were examples of more consensual intimacy, as revealed through the wills of various merchants seeking either to manumit a slave lover or provide for their joint offspring. The 1776 will of the merchant Richard Adamson, for instance, left his property to his mother, Jane Stoute, in trust for his slave mistress, Joan, and their seven children. The 1787 will of Charles Cross manumitted his three mulatto children, and made his 'negro woman' Nanny the property of their son George as a means of securing her freedom. In contrast to the brutalism of the plantation, the urban culture of Bridgetown appeared to offer some avenues for more loving relationships – albeit within a context of racial dominance.[78] For the most part, enslaved women would be coerced into relationships with plantation owners and powerful whites, who might then grant them their freedom. In turn, many of these free mulatto women branched out into running brothels. 'The hostess of the tavern is, usually, a black, or mulatto woman who has been the favoured enamorata of some *backra* [the negro term used for white] man, from whom she has obtained her freedom, and perhaps two or three slaves to assist her in carrying on the business of the house,' helpfully explained the army doctor George

Pinckard, following his visit in 1796. She then employs a series of young, good-looking assistants.

> One privilege, indeed, is allowed them, which, you will be shocked to know, is that of tenderly disposing of their persons. This offers the only hope they have of procuring a sum of money, wherewith to purchase their freedom: it is so common a resource among them, that neither shame nor disgrace attaches to it; but, on the contrary, she who is most sought, becomes an object of envy, and is proud of the distinction shown her.[79]

Bridgetown was populated by a series of internationally renowned brothel keepers, of whom by far the most celebrated was the lady known as Rachel Pringle. Today, a 1790s cartoon of her generous physique seated on a stool outside her tavern serves as a popular tourist print, highlighting her remarkable, transatlantic notoriety. Pringle's origins are shrouded in Bajan myth, but it is thought that Rachel was the daughter of an African slave woman and her master William Lauder, 'a Scotch schoolmaster'. Mr Lauder then sought to impose himself on young Rachel as well. 'Lauder's conduct to his offspring, is a damning proof how debasing to the human mind is the power given us over our fellow creatures by holding them in bondage!' was how a mid-Victorian pot-boiler described it. 'The ties of consanguinity were all merged in the authority of the master, and he saw but the slave in his own daughter! She ... awakened the libidinous desires of her disgraceful and sinful parent; who made many – but to her eternal honour be it spoken – unsuccessful attempts on her chastity.'[80] Thankfully, at this moment, the Royal Navy officer Thomas Pringle intervened to purchase her freedom and set her up in a house as his lover. But she soon tired of Thomas: she borrowed a child to fake a birth and so send Captain Pringle back to Britain. For by then she had found a new patron in the form of a Mr Polgreen – and Miss Rachel becomes Miss Rachel Pringle Polgreen. By the late 1780s she is listed in Bridgetown's tax records as having five properties, and by the 1790s as the owner of 'a large house, 2 side houses, 5 tenements in a yard, formerly Mary Ann Bellamy's and two houses'. This added up to a real estate fortune of over £1,300, combined with property (including slaves) at over £1,600.[81]

Her first 'tavern' or 'hotel' was in Canary Street, and it rapidly became the most sought-after brothel in Bridgetown – not least because of the patronage of one of Bridgetown's more surprising visitors, the priapic, red-haired Prince William Henry, the future King William IV. By the time he arrived in Bridgetown, the then Duke of Clarence was notorious as a drunken, bullying, coarse, self-regarding, lascivious letch. He was also a passionate pro-slavery advocate, using his maiden speech in the House of Lords – as 'an attentive observer of the state of the negroes' – to explain how well the slaves lived on the plantations, in their 'state of humble happiness'. Take away slavery, he argued, and the imperial edifice of navy, colonies and inward investment would crumble; he, naturally, neglected to explain how much he also enjoyed its freer, urban incarnations. Clarence repeatedly toured the West Indies in the 1780s as part of his duties in the Royal Navy as commander of the frigate *Pegasus* and, it seems, had a particular penchant for Rachel Polgreen. 'We perfectly recollect this immense mass of flesh (she was nearly as big as a sugar hogshead) walking with the Prince, actually leaning on the Royal Arm, and accompanied by other Naval officers, and a host of mulatto women, as His Royal Highness promenaded the crowded streets,' as *The Barbadian* magazine later recalled.[82] Indeed, the whole of Bridgetown gave itself over to festivities when the Prince sailed into Carlisle Bay. 'The short time which the prince remained in Barbados was the season of mirth and festivity,' as one history recalled. 'Besides the balls and entertainments given by Governor Parry in honour of his illustrious guest, his royal highness was sumptuously entertained by the legislature, at the public expense.'[83]

The problem came when he left. As the nineteenth-century collection of Barbadian tales *Creoleana* relates,

> His Royal Highness had dined with the mess of the 49th regiment, then on this station, and returning to the hotel in the evening, *more* than 'half seas o'er', accompanied by some of the choice *spirits* of the corps, he commenced a royal frolic by breaking the furniture, etc., and with the aid of his boon companions carried on the sport with such activity, that in a couple of hours every article was completely demolished – the very beds cut up, and their contents emptied into the street, and

the whole neighbourhood strewed with the feathers, representing a mimic snow storm! Crack went the pier glasses, pictures, chandeliers and lamps; smash went the decanters, goblets, wine glasses, porcelain and crockery, all, all went in the general havoc, while the sly and cunning Rachael sat quite passive in her great arm chair at the entrance door of the hotel. Servant after servant came running to announce to her the destruction that was going on, but the stoical hostess moved not! ... She would, as each fresh communication was made, reply with perfect nonchalance, 'Go, go long man, da' no King's son! If he no do wha' he please, who d'en can do'um? Let he lone! lay he muse he-self – da no King's son! Bless he heart! Da' no King's son' ... It was, however, now time for the Prince to return on board, and as he had literally (in nautical phrase) 'cleared the decks', he was 'taking his departure', when encountering Rachael still occupying the 'gang way', he bid her 'good night', and to crown his sport, upset her and chair together, leaving her unwieldy body sprawling in the street, to the ineffable amusement of the laughing crowd. Rachael showed no ire even at this – but calling out in her sweetest dulcet tones, 'Mas Prince! Mas Prince; you come ma-morning, to see wha' mischief you been do!' – and after a little floundering and much assistance, she was reseated.

But when she discovered the prince was to set sail for Saint Vincent the following evening, she took an inventory of all the damage the drunken royal had wreaked and duly presented him with a bill for a sizeable £700. 'Our most generous hearted Tar, with a magnanimity as conspicuous in him after he became sovereign, as at this juvenile and sailor-like period of his life, made no question of the correctness of the account, but sent her an order for the amount on Firebrace and Co., (merchants of the town,) which was duly paid.'[84] Rachel Pol-green used the funds to re-equip her hotel, which then recalled its distinguished visitor by renaming itself Bridgetown's 'Royal Naval Hotel'. Following Polgreen's death in 1791, the establishment was passed on to another free black woman, Nancy Clarke – who man-aged the establishment so successfully that by 1810 she had become, as an affidavit from the Lord Mayor of London decreed, 'Nancy Col-lins of the island of Barbados, free mulatto, now residing in Duke

Street, St James, in the Kingdom of Great Britain.' Charlotte Barrow was the last of the hotel's owners before it burned down in 1821.[85] With the inferno went an intriguing remnant of Barbadian history – on the one hand a familiar story of a plantation investor's exotic predilection for a mulatto lady; on the other, an account of bawdy, Bajan culture and a more complicated interracial relationship between a freed black woman and a prince of the realm which could only take place in Bridgetown.

Such tales – repeatedly recycled and embellished during the nineteenth century – connected the Barbadians with the metropole across the ocean. Prince William Henry was honoured with his own street in Bridgetown, as the public space of the port became increasingly codified around the imperial identifiers of Trafalgar Square, 'Wellington Stairs' and the Nelson monument. Of course, by that time Bridgetown's real contribution to the imperial story – sugar and slavery – had faded. Barbados's cane production had been overtaken by that of Jamaica, while William Wilberforce finally succeeded in abolishing the Atlantic slave trade in 1807. Indeed, many Barbadian planters even supported abolition as, by the beginning of the new century, they had barely enough work for their own slaves and didn't want further competition from other islands. The riches that had come from 'the civilized island' had done their work in Britain and abroad, providing capital for industrialization, funds for infrastructure and – via the merchant navy – much of the manpower for the Royal Navy. Bridgetown's finest exports had expanded the reach of Empire and helped to secure its economic foundations. And so, with its work done, Barbados remained for the Victorians, as it had been since 1625, 'little England' – a Caribbean paradise captured forever in aspic, with a society and economy pleasingly dependent upon the largesse of its colonial master.

The Cambridge academic Henry Nelson Coleridge recollected reaching Bridgetown in 1825:

> How a man's heart swells within him, when after sea and sky and sky and sea for nearly a month, he first sees the kindly land beckon to him over the salt waves! And that land tropical! Carlisle bay sleeping like an infant, and countenanced like the sky on a June morning, the

warrior pendants, the merchant signals, the graceful gleaming boats, the dark sailors, the circling town, the silver strand, and the long shrouding avenues of immortal palms greenly fringing the blue ocean! ... Barbados is the most ancient colony in the British empire. It has never changed hands, and been invaded once only by the forces of the Long Parliament.[86]

Here was an early taste of that imperial nostalgia which Barbados and Bridgetown would continue to elicit right up until the present day.

Early Bajan currency: the so-called 'Pineapple Penny' minted in England for commercial use in Barbados. The coin depicts, on the obverse, an African in profile wearing the royal diadem of the Prince of Wales with the motto 'I serve' inscribed beneath (1788).

3

Dublin

'One whole and integrated Empire'

'They will follow me wherever I go.' When the Earl of Kildare chose for the site of his townhouse a cheap, boggy plot of land on the south side of the River Liffey, polite society was appalled. Out at the rougher edges of Molesworth Fields, this was 'the lands of tib and tom', an almost rural outpost a long way from the theatres, drawing rooms and coffee-shops of fashionable north Dublin.

James and Emily Fitzgerald knew what they were doing. Delighted with the designs of Richard Cassels (or Castle) for their country seat of Carton House in Maynooth, County Kildare, they now set the German architect to work on Dublin's grandest private home. As the residence of Ireland's leading 'patriot' politician, a hugely wealthy landowner who always skilfully balanced the interests of Ireland and England with his own, Kildare House had to fulfil many expectations. Begun in 1745, its pedimented façade, ornamental railings and gilded interiors remain to this day a triumph of eighteenth-century English Palladian design – so much so that, across the Atlantic, the Irish architect James Hoban would later draw extensively on its styling for his own plans for George Washington's White House in the newly independent America.

In 1766 Kildare was elevated to the Dukedom of Leinster, and so Kildare House became Leinster House, an essential sight for anyone visiting Ireland's capital. 'Viewed the Duke of Leinster's house,' the agricultural economist and author Arthur Young reported in 1776, 'which is a very large stone edifice, the front simple but elegant, the pediment light. There are several good rooms, but a circumstance unrivalled is the court, which is spacious and magnificent. The opening behind the house is also beautiful.'[1] When the eponymous hero of *The History of Ned Evans* (1797) passed along Merrion Street, he too 'was infinitely struck with the grandeur of the Duke of Leinster's house. The beautiful opening at the back of that noble palace, and the elegant disposition of the ground, with the refreshing shrubs that surround it, charmed his fancy, and made him think it a dwelling fit for a sovereign.'[2]

This rural Elysium didn't last for long. As Kildare predicted, Dublin's smart set were quick to follow him across the Liffey, and the south side was soon being carved up for terraces, squares and five-storey townhouses. Today, Leinster House serves as the seat of Ireland's Houses of the Oireachtas or National Parliament and – despite all the dreadful emendations of state-bureaucratic interior design – in the two-storeyed great entrance hall, with its black and white squared floor, or the sweeping staircase or the grandiose Filippo Francini ceiling, you can still just capture a taste of that airy eighteenth-century Anglo-Irish world.

Leinster House is, however, more than just another aristocratic mansion converted to democratic use. Standing now between the National Library and the National Museums, just north of the business suites of St Stephen's Green and just west of the hotels and restaurants of Merrion Square, the house sits at the heart of what guidebooks like to call 'Georgian Dublin'. This is the Dublin of the twenty-first-century city-break: Trinity College, the National Gallery and the Shelbourne Hotel set in an affluent urban landscape of sash-windowed terraces, neo-classical elegance, 'colourful Georgian doors', high-end shopping and easily consumable culture. According to the 'Visit Dublin' website, an 'elegant Georgian metropolis with wide streets, gracious squares and great houses, neatly bordered by two canals . . . a city that will capture your heart'.[3] In short, an Irish capital focused on marketing the architecture and aesthetic of a colonial, Protestant past.

It was not always so. The preservationist impulse is a new phenomenon. In the aftermath of Ireland's independence in 1922 there was a concerted attempt to sweep away this Georgian history – the past of Leinster and Fitzwilliam, Rutland Square and St Stephen's Green. Eamon de Valera's interwar government thought the architecture

Dublin, *c.* 1800s

N

Dublin Bay

Royal Canal

Mountjoy Square

Rutland Square

North Great George's Street

Charlemont House ●

Hospital Rotunda ●

Sackville Street

Nelson Monument ●   **Custom House**

General Post Office ●

Carlisle Bridge

Wellington Monument

Essex Bridge   **Theatre Royal**   **Liffey Docks** ●

Four Courts   **Irish Houses of Parliament** ●

●   **Trinity College**

River Liffey   Parliament Street

Guinness Brewery ●   **Royal Exchange**   **Great Musick Hall**

Castle   Merrion Square

Leinster House   Merrion St.

Fitzwilliam Street

Fitzwilliam Street Lower

Grand Canal

¹/₂ mile

1 km

'un-national' and set out plans to demolish all of Merrion Square. In place of this imperial architecture, Dublin was to rise again as a peasant-Gaelic capital, shorn of the neo-classical detritus of the humiliating eighteenth century. In the early 1960s, one Irish government minister was positively gleeful about the swathe of demolition ripping through his city's terraces. 'I was glad to see them go,' he told a visitor, 'they stand for everything I hate.' Under the hand of usually Fianna Fáil politicians, Georgian Dublin was put to the wrecking ball, with the most egregious destruction being of sixteen Georgian terraced houses on Lower Fitzwilliam Street in 1963 to make way for the bland, modernist headquarters of the Electricity Supply Board. A decade later, as further developments were allowed to scythe through Kildare Place and Mountjoy Square, one nationalist letter writer to the *Irish Times* was wholly unapologetic about the elimination of this colonial legacy: 'Georgian buildings are an offence to all true-blue Irishmen, they are a hangover from a repressive past ... and they must go.'[4] In the doleful judgement of the leading historian of Georgian Dublin, Kevin Corrigan Kearns, 'Many Irishmen believe that the Georgian structures are English architectural types transplanted on Irish soil by the Anglo-Irish ... The call to erase the Georgian heritage from the Dublin cityscape has often been justified as an act of national purification on the premise that the architecture and structures are not Irish.'[5]

Instead, Dublin was to become a martyrs' memorial to those patriots who secured a pure, free Ireland liberated from the British Empire after a long and bloody struggle. This Dublin is the Dublin of the General Post Office, scene of the 1916 Easter Rising and the Proclamation of Independence, and the Jim Larkin Statue opposite it, commemorating the life of the great trade unionist and republican. This is the modern Dublin of the Famine Memorial, of the statue of Daniel O'Connell, which commands the O'Connell Bridge across the Liffey, of Croke Park (scene of a bloody and vengeful massacre by British special forces in 1920) and the Gardens of Remembrance.

Dedicated to the Irish patriot dead and opened in 1966 on the fiftieth anniversary of the Easter Rising, the Gardens of Remembrance also provided the most symbolic stop on the Dublin leg of Queen Elizabeth II's tour of Ireland in 2011 – the first state visit by a British monarch for over a century. 'The image of the Queen with her head bowed in the Gardens of Remembrance seemed to me a significant moment,' reflected the Irish author Colm Toibin. 'It suggested that now there is such ease and open harmony between our islands and our two governments, we can include without worry the Irish patriot dead.'[6] It was a sentiment which the Queen was subtly to endorse as she spoke at the Dublin Castle state dinner of the 'painful legacy' of a colonial rule that had not been 'entirely benign'. For Fintan O'Toole of the *Irish Times*, Elizabeth II's pitch-perfect progression around the one-time colonial capital suggested as much about Britain as Ireland:

> The familiar question that was posed was whether the Irish have got over their sometimes neurotic love-hate relationship with the Brits. But it was joined by a question that was completely unexpected: have the British got over their post-imperial delusions of grandeur? Or to put it another way, is Britain's self-image now sufficiently cleansed of the stains of empire that it can treat Ireland as an equal?[7]

All of which speaks to the deep, historic complexity of Britain's relationship with Ireland, a relationship that has shaped the streets and squares, the bridges and buildings of Dublin. For in what remains of eighteenth-century Dublin, one can begin to trace an important transition in the history of British colonialism, emerging from the failures of the so-called First Empire of the Thirteen Colonies and readying itself for a more expansionist Second Empire reaching eastward. The story of Dublin in the second half of the eighteenth century reflects the new global realities confronting London after defeat in America and escalating competition from France and Spain. In the face of such danger, there was a stark realization that the internal bonds of Empire had to be tightened: a secure perimeter around the island of Ireland was just as important as the promotion of Atlantic trade. In the aftermath of the American and French revolutions, the architects of the British Empire were forced to think much more intensively about the kind of Britishness their colonial project was premised on. It was a readjustment that would force Ireland to change from an uncomfortable colony into a component part of the British Isles – and one which had both to be defended against external invasion and fully integrated within the colonial economy. What was altogether more surprising about this shift was the extent to which so many of the most important elements within Ireland then became willing participants in the British Empire's global ambitions. How Ireland was transformed from a problem to a partner in imperialism can all be chronicled through the beautiful and ostentatious urban fabric of Georgian Dublin.

TOO GREAT TO BE UNCONNECTED

The complexity of Ireland's status in the British imperial imagination is partly the product of longevity. 'Ireland may be regarded as the earliest English colony,' noted Friedrich Engels in the 1850s, 'and one which, by reason of her proximity, is still governed in exactly the same old way; here one cannot fail to notice that the English citizen's so-called freedom is based on the oppression of the colonies.' Engels traced the 'English wars of conquest' back to the twelfth century, when Henry II gifted himself the 'Lordship of Ireland' and the Anglo-Normans picked up from where the Vikings had left off. 'Neither should it be forgotten, of course, that three hundred years of invasion and plunder by the Danes had already dragged the country considerably backwards.'[8]

But for the most part, Ireland as a colonial project only began to enter English and then, crucially, British consciousness in the sixteenth century. On the face of it, the island exercised a high degree of autonomy under colonial control. In 1541, Ireland was granted the formal status of a kingdom in her own right and, what is more, had a parliament of Commons and Lords whose history could be traced back to the Middle Ages. But from the 1590s, there were quickening calls for the destruction of the old Gaelic order and the colonization of Ireland under the plough of English settlers, whose task would be to establish a political and economic framework capable of civilizing the people and securing the Protestant faith. Royal policy and private enterprise came together as large allocations of farmland, beginning on the confiscated Munster estates of the rebellious Irish peer the Earl of Desmond, were handed out to English colonists for growing grain. Soon enough, some 12,000 English settlers were farming in the southern half of Ireland. Their numbers expanded exponentially in the early 1600s and then moved northward following the 1607 'flight of the earls' (which saw the leading Gaelic aristocracy flee to Europe in the hope of recapturing Ireland from the English with Spanish help) and the lucrative confiscation of estates across Ulster. King James I and VI parcelled these tracts out in smaller allotments in the hope of building up a more diverse and sustainable rural society. And just as James's kingship had personally combined the two crowns of England and Scotland, so the Ulster plantations offered an early example of lowland Scots and English settlers working together in an obviously 'British' colonial enterprise. By the 1630s Thomas Wentworth, the Earl of Strafford, could announce to James's son, Charles I, that the systematic settlement of English colonists was the best means for enriching the English government and for 'civilizing . . . this people, or securing this kingdom under the dominion of your imperial Crown'.* Prior to the outbreak of the English Civil War (or War of the Three Kingdoms) in 1641, some 100,000 people had migrated from England, Scotland and Wales *into* Ireland.[9] Remarkably, the liberating events of 1649 – the execution of a king; establishment of a republic – did little to alter official policy towards Ireland. Indeed, the Lord Protector, who came to political maturity amidst the 1641 Irish Rebellion and its lurid tales of Protestant settlers massacred by Irish Catholics, proved positively messianic about bringing the Pale to heel. 'We should see Oliver Cromwell's Irish policy as part of his general imperial policy,' explained his biographer Christopher Hill. 'The native Irish were treated much as the original settlers of New England

---

* Strafford's ingratiating use of the phrase 'your imperial Crown' needs some explanation. The Kings of England and then the United Kingdom did not generally title themselves 'Emperors' (until, that is, they became Emperors of India in the nineteenth century) but the Protestant Reformation of the mid-1530s and the creation of the Church of England had led England to declare itself autonomous, free from the jurisdiction of Rome. As the 1533 Act in Restraint of Appeals famously phrased it, 'this realm of England is an Empire governed by one Supreme Head and King having the dignity and royal estate of the imperial Crown of the same'. Phrases such as 'great Brittaines imperial crown' or 'the Empire of great Britaine' were common by the 1610s. Oliver Cromwell perhaps came closest to assuming the title 'Emperor' in the mid-1650s. See David Armitage, 'The Cromwellian Protectorate and the Language of Empire', *The Historical Journal*, 35 (1992).

treated the Indians.'[10] In 1649 the rebels of Drogheda and Wexford were put to the sword; the dispossessed were exiled to Barbados; and the practice of Catholicism was outlawed, with a few priestly lynchings to make the point. It was an early stage in the strategy of conquest and colonization.

In the aftermath of the 1690 Battle of the Boyne and the 1691 Battle of Aughrim – the conclusive clashes of the Glorious Revolution at which King William III consolidated his victory – there was further sequestration of indigenous lands. Protestant, colonial culture became far more assertive, with the 1720 Declaratory Act, which clarified the supremacy of the British parliament over Ireland. 'The ... Kingdom of Ireland hath been, is, and by Right ought to be subordinate unto and dependent upon the Imperial Crown of Great Britain, as being inseparably united and annexed thereunto.' All peoples of Ireland – both the conquered Irish Catholics and the British colonists – were declared subject to the 'full power and authority' of the Westminster parliament.[11] The 'Penal Acts' – a series of petty but savage measures primarily directed against Ireland's dominant Roman Catholic population – reaffirmed Ireland's subjugated status. In 1792, the Dublin-born politician and philosopher Edmund Burke, who would prove such a glittering critic of imperialism in the British Houses of Parliament, described the legislation 'as well fitted for the oppression, impoverishment, and degradation of a people, and the debasement in them of human nature itself, as ever proceeded from the perverted ingenuity of man'.[12]

And yet Ireland was neither an occupied territory nor a police state; it could not be viewed in the same light as Barbados, the Bahamas or the Thirteen Colonies. Its proximity to Great Britain and pre-history as a dependent kingdom stretching back to Henry II excluded such obvious imperial identification. 'By the late seventeenth century, Ireland resembled not so much a model colony, a *terra Florida* near home, drawn up in conformity with an official blueprint, but rather an unruly palimpsest, on which, though much rewritten and scored out, could be discerned in an untidy jumble: "kingdom", "colony", "dependency", and, faintly, "nation".' Ireland could not be set within the obvious 'imperial paradigm' of 'mother and child, metropolitan legislature and local Assembly, imperial core and colonial periphery'.[13] It was altogether more complicated – not least because of the Protestantism of the migrant communities from Scotland and England.

At the apex of that settler society stood the professional and landed elite of the so-called 'Protestant Ascendancy', a term coined in the 1790s to classify the ruling caste of Georgian Ireland. These were the descendants of the pioneer military and landowning classes of the Elizabethan plantations and comprised an entrenched clique oriented around the established, Anglican church and who effortlessly monopolized law, civil society and high politics. An official architecture and public ritual were designed to cement the colonial hegemony. Of the Ascendancy's centre of political power, the Irish Houses of Parliament, the Victorian historian W. E. H. Lecky wrote,

> The traces of recent civil war and the arrogance of a dominant minority were painfully apparent. The walls of the House of Lords were hung with tapestry representing the Siege of Derry and the Battle of the Boyne. A standing order of the House of Commons even excluded Catholics from the gallery. The anniversaries of the Battle of Aghrim, of the Battle of the Boyne, of the Gunpowder Plot, and, above all, of the discovery of the rebellion of 1641, were always celebrated.[14]

Roy Foster invites us to think of the Ascendancy as 'marginalized if not isolated' in the same manner as 'colonial Virginia, or even the Kenya highlands in the 1920s'.[15] But the Anglo-Irish Protestants themselves fiercely resented any attempt to put them alongside the rebellious colonists of Massachusetts or the Caribbean sugar barons. As 'English-born-in-Ireland', they wanted to be equal partners in Empire, not troublesome colonial cousins. Like their West Indian peers, they were militarily dependent upon the British state for protection against the indigenous (in this case, Catholic) majority but regularly felt aggrieved at their treatment by the mother country. As they expressed an ever greater emotional attachment to the island of Ireland, there was the lurking fear that Westminster, tiring of its obligations, might even one day sell them out. The emergent 'nationalism' of these Irish Protestants was 'a potent mixture of triumphalism, anxiety and wounded *amour-propre*' which constituted neither a plea for Irish secession nor a suspicion of Empire. It was, in fact, just a perfect recipe for misunderstanding, slights and religio-cultural confusion – neatly summed up in one 1780s diplomatic memo on the muddled status of Ireland within the British Empire: 'Ireland is too great to be unconnected with us and too near to be dependent on a foreign state and too little to be independent.'[16]

These tensions were magnified by the challenges confronting British imperialism in the later eighteenth century. As we saw in Boston, the extensive military expenditure necessitated by the Seven Years' War had required new sources of income to fund the burdens of Empire. The colonies needed to start paying their way, so it was no surprise that the 1760s presaged a new determination to exert parliamentary sovereignty over the various colonial assemblies which dotted the Atlantic seaboard in order to extract some financial recompense. In Ireland, under the viceroyalty of Field Marshal Lord Townshend (1767–72), this took the form of new systems of 'management' by the imperial administration to curtail the increasingly autonomous aspirations of the Protestant Ascendancy, reaffirm the powers of Westminster and deliver more secure sources of revenue for the British armed forces. A residential lord lieutenant or viceroy was appointed and the colony made much more responsible for bearing the fiscal cost of Britain's growing imperial commitments until, that is, a 'tea-party this night' in Boston starkly revealed the limits of London's centralizing strategy. In its wake, Britain's grand strategy for more direct imperial control came grinding to a halt. So after years of tight 'management', Ireland in the late 1770s and early 1780s enjoyed a period of relative autonomy and Ascendancy prowess.

The politician who led the charge for greater self-government was Henry Grattan – gifted rhetorician, Member of the Irish Parliament for Charlemont and coming man of the so-called 'Patriot' cause. Working closely with the middle-class militia of the Irish Volunteers (ostensibly formed to defend Ireland during the absence of British troops fighting in America, but soon a shadowy military force behind the Irish Patriot cause), Grattan successfully used the post-1776 hiatus to marshal a programme for repatriating powers from London to Dublin. His first line of attack was the economic restrictions which Irish industry suffered thanks to the old bugbear of the Navigation

Acts and the pejorative terms of trade Britain had demanded. While Ireland had enjoyed relatively favourable terms with Great Britain herself and enjoyed extensive imports of colonial goods, many of its industries were barred from exporting to the colonies except through British ports. In addition, the Irish wool, glass and beer industries were wholly excluded from competing with British exports. Grattan opened the 1779 Parliamentary session in Dublin demanding an end to these restrictive practices and the opening up of Irish ports 'for exportation of all its manufactures'. In London, the prime minister, Lord North, was struggling to contain the effects of the American Revolution and had no power to oppose such demands. The result was an end to trade restrictions and the opening-up of colonial markets for Irish goods 'upon equal conditions with Great Britain'.

All well and good, but not enough for Grattan. His next step was political. In January 1780, Grattan told the Dublin Guild of Merchants that it was his intention to 'strain every nerve to effectuate a modification of the Law of Poynings ... [and] to secure this country against the illegal claims of the British Parliament'. Dating back to the 1490s, Poynings' Law was just one part of the armoury of legislation – along with the Irish Mutiny Act and the Declaratory Act–designed to subjugate Ireland to Britain's imperial interests. By it, Irish Catholics were prohibited from holding all public office, intermarriage with Protestants, owning land or holding commissions in the British army or navy. Grattan wanted the laws repealed and new commitments made on the independence of the Irish judiciary and the passing of a Habeas Corpus Act. All of which, Grattan assured King George III, could be granted without any diminution of Ireland's place within the British imperial firmament. 'The Crown of Ireland,' he told the Irish parliament, was 'an Imperial Crown, inseparably annexed to the Crown of Great Britain, on which connection the interests and happiness of both nations essentially depend ... and ... the people of this kingdom have never expressed a desire to share the freedom of England without declaring a determination to share her fate likewise within the British nation.'[17] In London, Lord Rockingham had succeeded Lord North in 1782 but proved equally unable to contain the power of the Irish Patriot cause. Yorktown had fallen, America was lost, the Empire was in mortal danger, and no one wanted Ireland to go the same way. Grattan played his hand well and was granted almost all of his demands, the 'Constitution of 1782' giving Ireland an unprecedented degree of legislative independence while still under the banner of the British Crown. This was the high-point of Protestant or 'colonial' nationalism in Ireland. 'A new order of things is commencing,' noted Edmund Burke. 'The old link is snapped asunder. What Ireland will substitute in the place of it to keep us together, I know not.'[18]

The answer was a new cultural relationship between Ireland and Britain, much of which was manifested in the cityscape of Dublin. A new and different imperial identity was emerging within the Protestant Ascendancy: a sense of Irish nationhood which allowed for expressions of patriotism while still swearing fealty to the imperial British Crown. As ever, there were confusions and contradictions in this Anglo-Irish sensibility; it was also the product of a narrow urban elite. Nonetheless, the energy and ambition, the speed and purpose of the building works which raced along the River Liffey in the 1780s and '90s spoke to the renewed enthusiasm for a colonial relationship based upon greater equality and clear commercial advantage. 'You who were here so lately would scarcely know the city, so much is it improved, so rapidly is it continuing to improve,' was one Englishman's response to Dublin's rapid development in 1785. 'After the talk of the misery of the people in our Parliament, and in the Parliament here, I cannot but feel daily astonishment at the nobleness of the new buildings and the spacious improvements hourly making in the streets ... In a word, there never was so splendid a metropolis for so poor a country.'[19] The advantages of Empire were helping to fund the development of one of Britain's finest colonial cities.

DUBH LINN

Like so many cities of Empire, Georgian Dublin was layered upon previous colonial accretions. The Vikings began the development of modern Dublin in the ninth century. The dark bog waters provided the name 'black pool' – Dubh Linn in Irish, or Dyfflin in Norse – while the River Poddle gave a further boundary and natural clump of raised land that was a perfect setting for the construction of a castle. A bustling Viking fort and trading post emerged, with slaves and silver underpinning much of the commerce, all enriched by raiding parties cruising the Irish littoral. Under the Anglo-Normans in the twelfth century, the medieval city had the castle at its military and economic core. Always a successful commercial centre, Dublin retained its medieval fabric and relatively limited urban reach until the advent of the Tudor state in the sixteenth century and the beginnings of more extensive British intervention.

More important from an economic perspective was the arrival of French Huguenot artisans in the late seventeenth century and the transformation of the linen and woollen trade. The excellence of Irish wool and the cheapness of labour – combined with Huguenot artisan skill – nurtured a globally successful export trade. For all the restrictions of the Navigation Acts, managed trade with Britain's foreign colonies (with produce re-exported through British ports) and direct commerce with other foreign markets steadily lifted the Irish economy during the eighteenth century. From 1705, certain kinds of Irish linen were allowed to be directly shipped to the colonies, helping to take cloth exports up to 292,000 yards (267,000 metres) by 1768. But that was nothing compared to the agricultural economy. Barred by another series of protectionist measures from exporting cattle to England, Ireland started selling its beef around the world – with the American and Caribbean plantations being particularly strong markets for salted-beef products. Dublin took full advantage of its historic positions as a port and distribution centre. From the warehouses along the Liffey, dockers winched tons of linen as well as thousands of barrels of salted beef, butter, pork and cheese on to ships bound for those colonists in Bridgetown and Boston, Kingston and Philadelphia missing some of the old-country food. The Royal Navy proved to be among Ireland's best beef customer. Despite accounts of Irish agricultural poverty in the eighteenth century, there were also real-terms increases to butter prices, improvements in the dairy industry and quickening colonial demand. In the last three decades of the eighteenth century, Irish butter exports to Britain doubled, and those of pork increased eightfold. Other commodities for the colonial markets

included candles, fishing tackles, Kilkenny marble, soap, silk handker-
chiefs, ink and iron products.[20]

Alongside the booming docks, commerce and industry flourished in
the south-west of Dublin. Here were the breweries and the distilleries,
the soap manufactories and ceramicists, the silver-ware makers and
glass houses, the carrion houses and slaughterhouses. The work was
for the most part filthy, dangerous and exploitative; but it created an
increasingly vibrant urban economy. The prosperity was reflected in
the demography as Dublin's population climbed from some 100,000 in
the early 1700s to reach 180,000 by latter half of the century. Added
to this were the civic, professional and political advantages which the
city enjoyed as the site of Dublin Castle (the intermittent residency of
the lord lieutenant or viceroy, Britain's imperial administrator), the
national legislature, the seat of the judiciary, Trinity College, the
Church and the official bodies encircling them. 'The curse of absenteeism was little felt in Dublin,' noted Lecky, 'where the Parliament
secured the presence of most of the aristocracy and of much of the
talent of the country; and during the residence of the Viceroy the
influence of a Court, and the weekly balls in the winter time at the
Castle, contributed to the sparkling, showy character of Dublin society.'[21] All of which underwrote an expanding service and retail
economy and, with it, increasingly obvious signs of consumer affluence. Late eighteenth-century Dublin could boast some 25 coach
builders, over 30 gold and silversmiths, nearly 50 cabinet makers and
a rich choice of tea-houses and coffee-shops.[22]

This was the economic underpinning of the Protestant Ascendancy's manifestations of colonial confidence – a process of mutual
affirmation enacted through dinners, drinks parties, dances, races,
charitable events, gambling, eating, duelling and declarations of Protestant identity. 'Dublin, the second city in the British Empire, though
it yields in extent, yields not in architectural beauty to the metropolis
of England,' wrote one account of the capital at the end of the eighteenth century. 'Its progress was excessive – the locality of the
parliament – the residence of the nobility and commons – the magnificence of the viceregal court – the active hospitality of the people – and
the increasing commerce of the Port, all together gave a brilliant

prosperity to that splendid and luxurious capital.'[23] 'High living is too much the fashion here,' commented another. 'You are not invited to dinner to any private gentleman of £1,000 a year or less, that does not give you *seven* dishes at one course, and Burgundy and Champagne; and these dinners they give once or twice a week.'[24]

Certainly, there were some who expressed astonishment at Dublin's excesses in a country still mired in poverty. 'A city, which contains in miniature every thing to be met with in the great capital of the British empire, is an object of attraction, to the wealthy, the idle, and the dissipated,' thought the philanthropist Edward Wakefield.[25] High-minded critics like Wakefield were particularly perturbed by the coexistence in Dublin of conspicuous consumption with a growing proletariat. An American visitor, Edward Melville, was shocked by the 'half starved, half naked children [who] everywhere meet your eye!' It regrettably led him to conclude that 'a great deal of the pomp, splendour and high living, which struck me with such admiration and pleasure on my first arrival lays the foundation for a large share of the wretchedness every feeling heart must deplore'.[26] Mass rural immigration into the city, overcrowding and unemployment were producing some ugly social consequences. 'The vast inferiority of the lower ranks in Dublin, compared even with those of the country towns in England, is very striking,' remarked one chronicler. 'In a morning, before the higher classes are up, you would imagine that half the prisons in Europe had been opened, and their contents emptied into this place.'[27] On one of those early mornings, the Reverend James Whitelaw took a stroll through some of the ancient parts of Dublin. 'I have frequently surprised from ten to sixteen persons of all ages and sexes, in a room not fifteen feet square, stretched on a wad of filthy straw, swarming with vermin, and without any covering, save the wretched rags that constituted their wearing apparel.' And the sanitary conditions were even worse. 'Into the back yard of each house, frequently not ten feet deep, is flung from the windows of each apartment, the odour [sic] and other filth of its numerous inhabitants, from whence it is so seldom removed, that I have seen it nearly on a level with the windows of the first floor.' 'When I attempted, in the summer of 1796, to take the population of a ruinous house in Joseph's Lane, near Castle Market, I was interrupted in my progress by an inundation of putrid blood, alive with maggots, which had from an adjacent slaughter yard burst the door, and filled the hall to the depth of several inches.' Finally, in the garret, 'I found the entire family of a poor working shoemaker, seven in number, lying in a fever, without a human being to administer to their wants.'[28] The contrast of such poverty to the affluence of Merrion Square and Sackville Street, combined with a growing reputation for violence and robbery, led commentators time and again to compare Dublin to Naples – a city of swarthy, unstable Catholic extremes.

Arthur Young approached the city with greater emotional detachment. 'The town life at Dublin is formed on the model of that of London,' he explained. 'Every night in the winter there is a ball or a party, where the polite circle meet, not to enjoy but to sweat each other; a great crowd crammed into 20 feet square gives a zest to the agréments of small talk and whist.' Nevertheless, it made for 'a very good society in Dublin in a parliament winter; a great round of dinners, and parties, and balls and suppers every night in the week, some of which are very elegant'. When the young, romantic hero of *Ned Evans* enters the Dublin townhouse of the Anglo-Irish peer 'Lord Ravensdale' (a thinly disguised Duke of Leinster) he marvelled at the luxury. 'The room was 44 feet long, 34 feet wide, and 30 feet high:–it was hung with silk damask of an azure blue, chairs, sophas, and window curtains of the same . . . The ceiling and cornices were the finest stucco . . . from the centre hung a luster of cut glass, with branches for thirty-six candles.'[29] Among the most elegant of settings was that provided by Lord Charlemont's townhouse at the top of Rutland Square (now Parnell Square). Today it houses the admirable collection of the Dublin City Modern Art Gallery, and even in the late eighteenth century the rooms were already bristling with fine art:

> the apartments large, handsome, and well disposed, containing some good pictures, particularly one by Rembrandt . . . In the same room is a portrait of Caesar Borgia, by Titian. The library is a most elegant apartment of about 40 by 30 feet, and of such a height as to form a pleasing proportion; the light is well managed, coming in from the cove of the ceiling, and has an exceeding good effect; at one end is a pretty ante-room, with a fine copy of the Venus de Medicis.[30]

At the apex of high society was the viceroy's court and the colonial calendar set by Dublin Castle. In the 1770s, much of the crumbling, medieval castle was refitted to provide the right spaces for viceregal entertainment. 'The Court has nothing remarkable or splendid in it,' thought Young, 'but varies very much, according to the private fortunes or liberality of disposition in the Lord Lieutenant.' Charles Manners, fourth Duke of Rutland, was appointed in 1784 – on a salary of £20,000 p.a. – and certainly had the private fortune and disposition to support Dublin society, although he himself was not immediately enthusiastic about his posting. 'This city is in a great measure under the dominion and tyranny of the mob,' he wrote back concernedly to the prime minister, William Pitt the Younger, in 1785. 'Persons are daily marked out for the operation of tarring and feathering; the magistrates neglect their duty ... the state of Dublin calls loudly for an immediate and vigorous interposition of Government.'[31] This meant, in Rutland's case, excessive displays of Dublin hospitality and the introduction of all-night balls at Dublin Castle. 'The utmost magnificence signalled the entertainments of the viceregal court, and the duke and duchess were reckoned the handsomest couple in Ireland.' His dining-out was epic, his claret consumption unrivalled, and his ability to eat seven turkey eggs for breakfast might have assisted his untimely death from incurable liver disease in 1787.[32] The social baton was only intermittently taken up by his successors. In the early 1800s, one English visitor was impressed by the flummery attached to a visit by the viceroy, the Duke of Richmond, to Dublin's Theatre Royal. 'The cavalcade consisted of three carriages, with the servants in superb liveries, and the horses very richly decorated with ribbons, etc. Behind the first carriage were two footmen, the second three, and the last, in which were the Duke and Duchess, four, the same number as attend their Majesties upon similar occasions, in London.'[33]

Civil society prospered alongside the social whirl. 'Society was never anywhere, perhaps, more brilliant than in Dublin in the years which succeeded 1782,' wrote the historian J. A. Froude in the mid-nineteenth century. 'The great Peers and Commoners had cast in their lot with the national life. They had their castles in the country and their town houses in the Irish metropolis. Their lives had a public purpose. They were conscious of high responsibilities; and if they were not always wise, they had force and dignity of character.'[34] This civic sensibility made itself felt through organizations such as the Dublin Society, established in 1731 as a grouping of high-minded Ascendancy types committed to the 'improvement' of the city of Dublin and the development of a more sophisticated, metropolitan discourse. Georgian Dublin, during its 'winter season' of November to March, began to rival whatever Hanoverian London could offer. Clubland was well supplied by the Sackville, the Kildare and Daly's. The latest plays were quick to make their way on to the stage at the Theatre Royal, Smock Alley, Crow Street (said to be 'as ample and magnificent as Drury Lane') or Stretche's Theatre. The legendary eighteenth-century actor David Garrick played Hamlet in Dublin before taking it to London, whilst Thomas Sheridan performed a series of Shakespeare plays at Crow Street. A slightly more vernacular popular entertainment could be found at the Great Musick Hall in Fishamble Street or the Great Assembly Rooms in Brunswick Street. In the winter of 1764–5, for instance, there were thirteen grand balls advertised, thirteen assemblies, twenty-five concerts and one 'entertainment' sponsored by the lord lieutenant. Many of the concerts, balls and performances were put together for charitable causes, with the likes of the Duchess of Leinster and Lady Charlemont in charge of their promotion and patronage. Hospitals, baths and funds for the poor were the usual recipients of such social largesse.[35] Indeed, the most important musical event of eighteenth-century Dublin – the preview of Handel's *Messiah*, at the Fishamble Music Hall in 1742 – was a charitable performance in aid, at Handel's request, of Mercer's Hospital, the Charitable Infirmary and the Charitable Musical Society. The 700-strong crowd (with ladies asked to remove hoops from their skirts to allow for more audience members) which was lucky enough to hear the first expression of this defining contribution to Hanoverian culture raised £400 'for the relief of the Prisoners in several Gaols, and for the Support of Mercer's hospital in Stephen street, and of the charitable infirmary on the inn's quay'. And the city knew it had witnessed something special. 'On Tuesday last Mr Handel's Sacred Grand Oratorio, the MESSIAH, was performed at the New Musick-Hall in

Fishamble Street,' reported the *Dublin Journal*; 'the best Judges allowed it to be the most finished piece of Musick. Words are wanting to express the exquisite Delight it afforded to the admiring crouded Audience. The Sublime, the Grand, and the Tender, adapted to the most elevated, majestic and moving Words, conspired to transport and charm the ravished Heart and Ear.'[36]

An equally celebrated institution within Dublin civil society was Dr Bartholomew Mosse's Hospital Rotunda. 'They have devised in Dublin a rather singular form of entertainment, the proceeds of which are applied to the maintenance of a Maternity Hospital,' recorded the French cavalry officer Jacques Louis de Bougrenet on his travels through the city.

> It is called a Promenade, and the name made me wish to go and see one. The visitors walk in a circular hall called the Rotunda, and while there is somewhat more freedom than that which obtains at private entertainments, people only mix with, and speak to, members of their own circle. After a certain time a bell sounded, and the company hurried through a door just opened, and groups of friends settled round tea-tables.[37]

Seeking to raise funds for his Lying-in Hospital, the entrepreneurial Dr Mosse managed to establish the Pleasure Grounds ('a polite place of amusement') surrounding his maternity hospital – around Rutland Square, in the fashionable north of the city – as *the* place for conspicuous display by Dublin society. It was to be Dublin's answer to London's Vauxhall Gardens, where the smart set came to mingle and mutually admire. A series of balls, public subscriptions and levées managed to raise the funds Mosse needed to establish some decent maternity care within the city, along with one of Dublin's most recognizable medical institutions. Like Leinster before him (whose children he, in fact, helped to deliver), Mosse turned to the fashionable Richard Cassels to design the hospital, but it was Cassels' architectural successor John Ensor who in 1764 added the Rotunda as a space for further mingling, *conversazione* and fund-raising. 'Here they have an organ and orchestra for concerts, in the wet evenings of summer, and for balls in winter,' one visitor wrote admiringly in the 1770s. 'So that, upon the whole, this is the Vauxhall, Ranelagh, and Pantheon of Dublin.'[38]

NEVER SO SPLENDID A METROPOLIS

In contrast to both Bridgetown and Boston – whose urban plans had developed organically, even chaotically, as their colonial economies expanded – the architecture of Georgian Dublin was far more obviously shaped by a cohesive civic vision. As such, it exhibited markedly fewer spaces for meaningful interaction between different communities. There was little of that cross-cultural exchange evident in Bridgetown. Instead, in the second half of the eighteenth century, Dublin became a bullish colonial capital with a city centre controlled by the great Anglo-Irish aristocrats and their property development schemes. The Protestant Ascendancy followed the Duke of Leinster into the city from their vast, rural plantations and transformed the Anglo-Norman remnants of Dublin into a spectacular embodiment of their imperial identity.

Initially, these mid-eighteenth century developments were focused on the townhouses of Leinster House and Charlemont House, as well as the eponymous Powerscourt House on South William Street (designed by Richard Cassels for the third Viscount Powerscourt) and Tyrone House on Marlborough Street (for Marcus Beresford, Earl of Tyrone). The grandiose style and iconography of these houses represented a transfer of the system of Protestant landholding from the Irish countryside into the capital: this was plantation planning in an urban setting, displaying the same belief in asserting control and dominion through an architecture designed to defend the Ascendancy from the Catholic majority. It was what would mark Dublin out from both Edinburgh New Town (begun in the 1760s) and the building of Bath. Rather than submerging its streetscapes into classical uniformity, colonial Dublin prided itself on its brace of spectacular townhouses.

And it turned out that designs for rural Maynooth would work equally well in city-centre Mountjoy Square. The stately homes which dominated the Ascendancy's agricultural estates in plantation Ireland were assertions of cultural power over the indigenous peasantry, which drew upon Palladian designs stretching back to the Venetian Republic's colonialism in the sixteenth century.[39] This was the aesthetic which was now transplanted into Dublin as large private estates on the suburbanizing fringes, abutting the old city walls, were bought up by Anglo-Irish aristocrats as well as new-money merchants such as Luke Gardiner and Humphrey Jervis.

After the grand houses came the tree-lined squares and the high-windowed Georgian terraces which would come to symbolize the domestic architecture of Dublin. Here the comparisons with Edinburgh were more apparent as plots were leased to architects and developers, but styles and landscaping were tightly controlled with a series of clauses designed to secure a pleasing and profitable appearance. Leading up to Belvedere House (1786), for instance, was laid out North Great George's Street, which could still be described in the 1970s as 'the finest example ... of a complete Georgian avenue ... contain[ing] all the merits and traits of the period: iron snuffers, fine wrought iron work, fanlights, grilles, bell pulls and lanterns'. Around Mountjoy Square were erected the terraces of Fitzgibbon Street and Great Charles Street. Similarly, Fitzwilliam Street Lower, Merrion Street and Merrion Square (all named after the ancestral home – Merrion Castle – of the Viscounts Fitzwilliam) were developed in the 1790s with large mansions, four storeys over basement, and wide street frontages. In 1769 Mornington House, part of a set of terraces stretching along Merrion Street, would be the birthplace of one of the greatest warriors of the British Empire, Arthur Wellesley, the future Duke of Wellington, and provide the Dublin residence for the Mornington clan.

Those contracted to build such townhouses had to operate under highly exacting instructions. Mr Boylan, building on the west side of Fitzwilliam Street, was only to construct a 'good and substantial Dwelling House of the best Materials, well roofed and covered with Slates, [and] not less than three storeys and a half high above the cellars'.[40] Any deviation from these guidelines threatened to fall foul of the Wide Street Commissioners – Dublin's all-powerful enforcer of aesthetic rigour. The origins of this extraordinarily innovative planning committee can be traced to 1757 with the passing of an Act 'for making a wide and convenient Way, Street, or Passage, from Essex-bridge to the Castle of Dublin'. A consortium of MPs, aldermen, earls, viscounts, mayors and magistrates, christened 'the

Commissioners for Making Wide and Convenient Ways, Streets and Passages' (otherwise known as 'the Wide Street Commissioners'), was drawn together to oversee the implementation of the Act, and, over the ensuing decades, it was their tight grip over Dublin's urban plan which would furnish 'so splendid a metropolis for so poor a country'. The Act gave the Commissioners extensive powers over compulsory purchase (a jury having established the value of any property under seizure) and then the allocation of development rights to different contractors who had to build under a rigid series of stipulations.[41] Their philosophy was 'Order, Uniformity and Convenience', and their ambition was to unclog the arteries of the ancient Norman core: promote circulation, clear space for the erection of fine new buildings and create a cityscape more reflective of Dublin's place under the imperial Crown. Major axes, thoroughfares and *viae triumphales* were opened up linking the townhouses of the Protestant Ascendancy with the squares, terraces and civic monuments. The Commissioners' work entailed a comprehensive vision of the city as the stage-set for the display of colonial grandeur. As so often in the cities of the British Empire, improvement became the cloak for dominance.[42]

The rebuilding of Essex Bridge in the early 1750s was the initial spur to development. The architect George Semple drew upon the recently completed Westminster Bridge in London for inspiration, as well as 'the Methods which were at that Time in Agitation, for opening the Streets in London and Westminster'. However, the Pont Royal in Paris also 'led me to think of forming a Plan, to get a Street opened in a direct Line of 51 Feet broad from the Bridge to the Castle'.[43] Such a street, Parliament Street, linking Essex Bridge (now Grattan Bridge) to Dublin Castle, was opened in 1762. It was much more than a traffic-relief solution to the tight quayside of the Liffey; it was also a contribution to 'the adorning of those parts of the city' with a newly impressive approach to Dublin Castle from the river.[44] Buoyed with tax receipts from their municipal monopoly over coal sales, the Commissioners now pursued an assertive programme of beautification: Dame Street and Nassau Street were widened, Upper Merrion Street, Baggott Street and Westmoreland Street laid out. The Commissioners' greatest triumph, in conjunction with the wily property developer

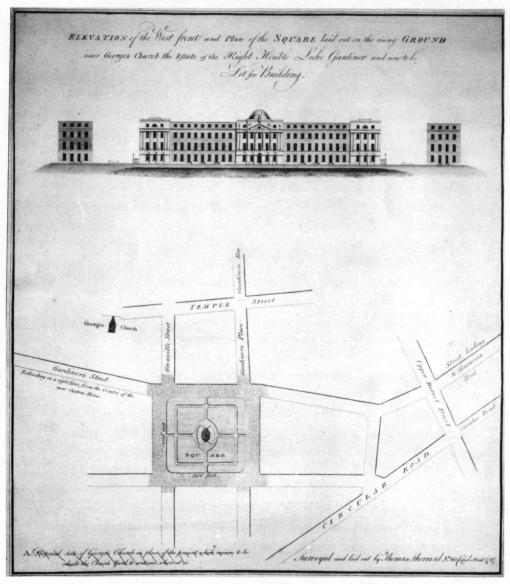

The work of the Wide Street Commission. Elevation of the west front and plan of Mountjoy Square laid out on the rising ground, near St George's Church (1787).

Luke Gardiner, was Sackville Street, stretching from the Rotunda
Hospital in the north across the newly built Carlisle Bridge and down
towards Trinity College. As today's O'Connell Street, the ambition of
the Wide Street Commissioners remains apparent – it is a resplendent,
commercial boulevard. 'By the end of the eighteenth century a person
wishing to travel from Dublin Castle to Rutland Square could proceed through an urban landscape that in scale and architectural
uniformity rivalled many a Continental city.'[45] Indeed, Dublin often
seemed to regard itself as a natural extension of continental Europe
with the Wide Street Commissioners involved in an urban project of
Enlightenment order, elegance and aesthetic harmony.

Visitors were certainly impressed by the transformation of the Irish
capital into a city of such metropolitan ambition. 'Few cities can boast
more extensive conveniences, more eminent beauties, than Dublin,'
wrote one architectural booster, 'in addition to its natural excellence,
its works of art rival, and in some instances excel, those appropriated
to the same purposes in any other country; it is still expanding, and as
it were, unfolding new lustre.'[46] Nathaniel Jefferys was particularly
taken with the unfolding urban vista. The new Dame Street, he
thought, was 'the greatest thoroughfare in Dublin for the carriages of
the nobility'.

> It is of a great width, and being filled with elegant shops of various
> descriptions, forms one of the most accustomed and amusing lounges
> in the city of Dublin; where, from the groups of elegant women con-
> tinually passing and repassing, and the numerous parties of military
> officers from the barracks, (foraging in fruit shops) it bears a strong
> resemblance to the London Bond-street.

Carlisle Bridge (O'Connell Bridge) was a further triumph – 'another
very elegant specimen of architectural taste, it consists of three arches,
and is ten feet wider than Westminster Bridge. It forms a very grand
communication between the north and south sides of the river, one
end of it leading through Westmoreland-street to College Green, and
the other opening immediately into Sackville-street.'[47] For others,
such obvious prosperity was all a little unreal. Dublin struck one English observer like being 'at table with a man who gives me Burgundy,
but whose attendant is a bailiff disguised in livery'.[48]

Yet it was not all just show: Georgian Dublin also witnessed the beginnings of a move from private ostentation to public spirit. The architecture of the city was extended beyond the great townhouses of the Ascendancy into buildings which celebrated a more civic sensibility. Central to this extension was the relationship between the architect James Gandon and John Beresford, chief commissioner of the Irish revenue and one of the most influential of the Wide Street Commissioners. Both men played vital roles in the migration of Dublin's development eastwards, and the visual elevation of the city with some of Europe's most striking Palladian works. There were, happily, some pre-existing artefacts to work with. Sir Edward Lovett Pearce's Irish Houses of Parliament (1729) on College Green was a monumental work of architecture designed to rival the Westminster parliament itself. 'No edifice that we recollect in the British metropolis can be compared for simple elegance with this,' wrote one visitor. 'It is perhaps in this respect the *chef d'oeuvre* of our imperial architecture.'[49] Its colonnade of Ionic columns, its three statues representing Hibernia, Fidelity and Commerce above the portico, and its array of Venetian windows spoke to a more extensive vision of Ireland's place in the imperial nexus than simple colony. In the 1780s, James Gandon was asked to add to the building's lustre with a new entrance for the House of Lords facing on to Westmoreland Street. Whilst the grubby MPs had to make do with an Ionic colonnade, the peers' portico enjoyed six fine Corinthian columns, above which sat three further statues signifying Wisdom, Justice and Liberty.*

Work on the Parliament House came after Gandon's success in designing his greatest commission, Dublin's new Custom House. But for the rattle of trains on the overhead bridge and the hum of traffic around Beresford Place, today the Custom House sits serenely on the banks of the Liffey near the remnants of the old docks. On the eastern edges of the city's commercial district, its location seems an obvious choice for ships accessing the Irish Sea. But at the time, John Beresford was involved in a bitter struggle to drag development downstream and away from the traditional legal and corporate centre around the old walled city. On marshy ground, a mile away from the original site

---

* Since 1803 the building has served as the Bank of Ireland, where appeals to Wisdom and Justice have not, in recent years, always been heeded.

on Essex Quay, the Custom House was to be another 'great and munificent improvement' which would add considerably to the 'ornament and convenience of the metropolis'. It took ten years to construct, with extensive engineering involved in the embedding of riverbank foundations, but was instantly heralded as a triumph of neo-classicism. 'The most sumptuous edifice of the kind in Europe,' exclaimed John James McGregor in his *New Picture of Dublin* (1821). 'It is finished in the Doric order, with an entablature, and bold projecting cornice. On the attic story, over the pillars of the portico, are statues of Neptune, Plenty, Industry and Mercury.' Crowning the dome was a 5-metre high statue of Hope, resting on her anchor.

Just as on Somerset House on London's Strand, riverine heads dotted the keystones above the doors and windows on the ground floor, here depicting the Liffey, the Foyle, the Boyne, the Shannon and other great waterways. The Custom House's most telling iconography, however, was a carving of the Arms of Ireland, a woman and a harp, being embraced by the Lion and the Unicorn of Great Britain. Figures representing Great Britain and Ireland 'are seated on a car of shell,' continued McGregor, 'Neptune, with his Trident, driving away Famine and Despair, while a fleet at a distance approaches in full sail.'[50] Should anyone remain in doubt about the message, the theme was the 'Union of Empire' representing 'the friendly union of Britannia and Hibernia, with good consequences relating to Ireland'.[51]

After the Custom House came the Four Courts, Gandon's second great civic building on the north bank of the Liffey, which allowed the Law Courts to leave their the cramped old conditions in Christ Church Cathedral. The domed roof of the Courts still provides one of Dublin's most instantly recognizable skylines. Its vaulted rotunda provides a perfect space under which clerks can gossip and lawyers confer with clients before disappearing into the court rooms, which siphon off the central hall. 'It is a truly magnificent pile of architecture,' thought Nathaniel Jefferys. 'The extent of its front toward the river is 433 feet, and from the uses to which it is applied, Englishmen naturally consider it as the Westminster Hall of Dublin.'[52] Edward Smyth, the sculptor of the Custom House, was let loose on the stonework and provided five powerful statues on the central block representing Wisdom, Justice, Moses, Mercy and Authority. The prospect of Dublin from Carlisle

Bridge, looking towards the Four Courts, now presented the pedestrian with 'such a cluster of architectural beauties grouped together, or scattered in every direction which he turns, as are not to be seen from any other spot in any other city . . . Strangers who visit Dublin are particularly struck with the beauty of this assemblage of objects.'[53]

These were the most celebrated buidlings, but across the city other parts of Georgian Dublin were being beautified and improved at a remarkable rate. There was the new King's Hospital in Blackhall Place; the Green Street Courthouse; the Guinness's Brewery; and the Royal Exchange, built in 1769–79 as part of the Wide Street Commissioners' plans for improvement around Essex Bridge. 'The inside of this edifice possesses beauties that cannot be clearly expressed by words,' noted one contemporary.

> The dome is spacious, lofty, and noble, and is supported by twelve Composite fluted columns, which, rising from the floor, form a circular walk in the centre of the ambulatory . . . Between two of the columns . . . on a white marble pedestal, is a statue in brass of his present

View of the Four Courts Looking Down the River Liffey, attributed to Henry Brocas Junior after Samuel Brocas (1818).

Majesty George III., in a Roman military habit, crowned with laurel, and holding a truncheon in his hand.[54]

Here was the King of Britain and of Ireland presiding as emperor, with Roman mien, over his emerging citadel. In April 1792 the Commissioners sent their surveyor Thomas Sherrard, 'to obtain Elevations of such range of Buildings or others in London as he may Judge will be of advantage towards furnishing design for the new Streets and places in this City'.[55] The Commissioners were always hungry for new maps of London or plans of prestigious schemes. And the flow of ideas and architects across the Irish Sea was extensive, with many of Dublin's leading designers gaining their groundings in Palladian rules from their time with London patrons. Indeed, the parallels between the capitals of King George's two kingdoms were made with gratifying frequency. John Gamble, an army surgeon from County Tyrone, expressing a common eighteenth-century refrain, was 'forcibly struck with the strong likeness [Dublin] bears to London, of which it is a beautiful copy – more beautiful, in truth, in miniature than the gigantic original'.[56]

Traditionally, this surge of development, the work of the Wide Street Commissioners and Dublin's broader sense of civic spirit in the 1780s and '90s have been interpreted as the product of the Grattan parliament and a renewed sense of *Irish* identity, the urban outflow of the cultural patriotism surrounding the 'Constitution of 1782', with its repeal of Poynings Law and cultural awakening of Irish nationalism. In fact, the Palladian designs, the iconography and the rhetoric show that Georgian Dublin was much more a robust expression of imperial affinity than Irish nationalism. From its colonial economy to its theatrical and literary culture to its civil society, Dublin was becoming more, not less, integrated with Britain during this period of so-called 'colonial nationalism' – and its cityscape said so. 'The initiative for public building came predominantly from the loyal "supporters of government" in Ireland,' explains the historian Murray Fraser, 'who aimed to maintain a social order and a colonial relationship they believed to be the best guarantee for Ireland's progress.'[57]

But Ireland, as we know, was always more than just a colony – 'rather an unruly palimpsest, on which, though much rewritten and scored out, could be discerned in an untidy jumble: "kingdom", "colony", "dependency", and, faintly, "nation"'. And in 1798 all those contradictions resurfaced with bloody force in the rebellion of the United Irishmen.

IRELAND OR EMPIRE?

Behind the colonial grandeur of Georgian Dublin, political tensions within the Irish state were intensifying. The 1790s were a tough economic decade, with debts running high and the public finances further undermined by the outbreak of war between Great Britain and revolutionary France in 1793. More worrying for the British Empire was the fact that republican France seemed to be garnering an increasing number of sympathizers within Ireland, who came together in the Society of the United Irishmen in 1791. In some ways, these constitutional activists were the ideological descendants of the Irish Volunteers and the 'patriot' cause, but their political demands were altogether more expansive. They urged the immediate and radical reform of parliament to include Catholic representation and a reconfigured relationship with Britain based on a reduced role for the Protestant Ascendancy. Much of their inspiration came from Thomas Paine, the early years of the French Revolution and a broader, Enlightenment belief in separating religion off from politics. Throughout the early 1790s Dublin booksellers stocked an extensive array of French revolutionary tracts and radical pamphlets. The United Irishmen's support was generally middle- rather than working-class (together with the odd aristocratic supporter, such as the Paine acolyte Lord Edward Fitzgerald of the Leinster clan), but also drew heavily upon a Presbyterian tradition of radical dissent. Nonetheless, at the core of the leaders' – Theobald Wolfe Tone and Thomas Russell – demands was a total commitment to reform of the anti-Catholic laws, which still discriminated against the indigenous Irish population, as part of a broader modernization programme for the Irish state based upon national determination. They wanted Ireland liberated from the imperial bonds. 'From my earliest youth I have regarded the connection between Ireland and Great Britain as the curse of the Irish nation, and felt convinced that, while it lasted, this country could never be free nor happy,' as Wolfe Tone later put it. 'In consequence, I determined to apply all the powers which my individual efforts could move, in order to separate the two countries.'

Unfortunately, space for progressive, liberal reform in 1790s Ireland was limited. First, the curse of sectarianism arose with the forming of Orange Order Lodges in the mid-1790s, 'to support the King and his heirs as long as he or they support the Protestant Ascendancy'. In response, networks of Catholic Defenders emerged to protect their communities from the early morning raids which the Protestant 'Peep o'Day Boys' liked to launch. In 1796, Ireland lurched into a rumbling rebellion as the United Irishmen (who were outlawed in 1794) sought an alliance with revolutionary France to oust the British; Catholic and Protestant militia terrified the countryside with sectarian assaults; and the threat of foreign invasion became a realistic prospect. In 1798 the United Irishmen pushed Leinster into open revolt, with County Kildare and County Wexford producing scenes of brutality not witnessed since the early 1640s. 'The 1798 rising was probably the most concentrated episode of violence in Irish history. Mass atrocities were perpetrated in circumstances of chaos and confusion, symbolized by the oddly assorted icons of the rosary and the "cap of liberty".'[58] By the end of the summer, the death toll stood at around 30,000 on both sides. Even the newly installed lord lieutenant, General Cornwallis, veteran of some of the bloodiest battles of the American War of Independence, was shocked to find a country 'streaming with blood'. He lamented how 'the only engines of government were the bayonet, the torch and the cat o' nine tails'. He marvelled at the 'bloodlust' of loyalist troops and the 'numberless murders which are hourly committed by our people without any process or examination whatever'. It only strengthened his deep, residual contempt for the colonial classes.[59]

Equally shocking was how close the French were to a well-armed invasion of Ireland and thence presumably across the Irish Sea into England. In 1795 the United Irish rebel Arthur O'Connor was in Paris, holding talks with the Revolutionary army about a French invasionary force. In 1796 a French expedition of 14,000 soldiers almost made a landing at Bantry Bay in west Cork, but the storm and fog prevented them from putting ashore; in August 1798 the French put ashore a small force of 1,000 soldiers at Kilcumin in County Mayo, of whom Cornwallis made short work; and, finally, in October 1798 a further landing was attempted off Lough Swilly in County London-derry. The sea battle was a triumph for the Royal Navy as seven of the ten French ships were captured, on board one of which was Wolfe Tone. In the end, no invasion could establish itself, but the repeated, dangerous assaults so close to the inner sanctum of Empire confirmed in the mind of the British prime minister, William Pitt, his own scheme for the future of Anglo-Irish relations.

'The idea of the present fermentation gradually bringing both parties to think of an Union with this country has long been in my mind,' Pitt had written as early as 1792 to the then lord lieutenant, the Earl of Westmorland. 'I hardly dare flatter myself with the hope of its taking place; but I believe it, though itself not easy to be accomplished, to be the only solution for other and greater difficulties.' The multiple invasions along the Irish coast at a time of seismic military crisis on the European continent cemented his belief in the need for a constitutional union between Ireland and Britain. On grounds of national security alone, the freedoms of 1782 and the autonomy of Grattan's parliament had to be superseded by direct control from Whitehall. Union with Ireland, Pitt explained to the House of Commons on 31 January 1799, 'would increase the general power of the Empire ... to a very great extent by a consolidation of the strength of the two kingdoms'.[60]

However, Union promised more than just protection against Irish rebellion and French invasion. There was the economic argument for the 'circulation of capital' and 'improved trade and commerce' between London and Dublin as a way of alleviating Ireland's deep-seated poverty. In return, Irish manpower and resources might be utilized more expansively through the Empire. And then there was the moral case for religious equity since, curiously enough, union with Protestant Britain offered the chance of solving the problem of Catholic emancipation in Ireland. By means of a single national parliament covering Great Britain and Ireland, the vast Irish Catholic vote – which so obviously threatened Protestant interests in a single Irish parliament – would be dissipated through a broader representative body. Catholics could vote and sit in an imperial parliament without becoming the majority. 'The admission of the Catholics to the ... suffrage could not then be dangerous,' explained Pitt. 'The Protestant interest – in point of power, property, and Church establishment – would be secure, because the decided majority of the supreme Legislature would necessarily be Protestant; and the great ground of argument on the part of the Catholics would be done away, as compared with the rest of the Empire, they would become a minority.'[61]

Such logical assurances about Ireland, Empire and the Catholic majority were not received well by the Protestant Ascendancy in Dublin. Henry Grattan certainly didn't like to hear what he called 'the novel and barbaric phraseology of empire'. But this was exactly what London had in mind: Ireland, like Scotland in 1707, was to move from kingdom-cum-colony to a true partner in Empire. 'By an incorporation of our legislature with that of Great Britain, it would not only consolidate the strength and glory of the empire, but it would change our internal and local government to a system of strength and calm security, instead of being a garrison in the island,' explained Pitt's ally in the Irish parliament, the acting chief secretary for Ireland, Viscount Castlereagh. He later added: 'it had been said that this measure would reduce Ireland to the state of a colony; was it by making her a part of the greatest and most powerful empire in the world? If I were called upon to describe a colony, I would describe it as something very like the present state of this country.'[62] Union, by contrast, offered an altogether more dignified future as a fellow beneficiary in the greatest Empire on earth. As the former Irish chief secretary Sylvester Douglas put it, 'Ireland, by an Union, no more becomes a *province* in any offensive sense of the word, than Great Britain: they both become provinces, or component parts of one whole and integrated Empire.'[63]

For all the lofty rhetoric of shared identities and imperial concerns, the means of achieving this Union were far from dignified. The turn of the century witnessed quite the grubbiest display of parliamentary graft since the 1707 Act of Union between England and Scotland, as Castlereagh showered peerages, pensions, dinners and gifts on to wavering Members of the Irish Parliament in order to force through the Union. An avalanche of money – estimated at some £32,336 in cash bribes alone – did the job as the completed Union Bill passed the Irish House of Commons on 7 June 1800 (though without the much promised clauses promising Catholic emancipation). Ireland's status as a separate kingdom or a separate colony – depending on your point of view – had come to an end. 'I see her in a swoon, but she is not dead,' was Grattan's melodramatic verdict on the passing of the Bill, 'though in her tomb she lies helpless and motionless, still there is on her lips a spirit of life, and on her cheek a glow of beauty.'[64]

Was Dublin now a fully fledged City of Empire, standing alongside her imperial partner, London? It turned out that she indeed now entered a swoon. All the energy of late eighteenth-century Dublin, fostered by the Protestant Ascendancy's sense of Irish pride and colonial affinity, faded away. 'Where are we now? – What are we about? – Where are we going?' asked *The Dublin Magazine* in the aftermath of Union.

> It might be answered – Not what we were twenty years ago. – We are an almost ruined people – we are doing worse than nothing ... At the time of the Union ... we then had a trade, flourishing in all its various directions ... Now, what with the removal of our parliament, the absence of our nobility and gentry, the inundation of British articles, and the strange contempt for our home-manufactures, numbers wander meal-less in our streets, [and] the fatigued eye of charity meets beggars in every direction.[65]

Prior to the Union, Dublin had been the regular residence of 271 peers and 300 Members of Parliament, as well as a powerful lord lieutenancy, and all the society and commerce that accompanied it. By 1821 there were only thirty-four peers, thirteen baronets and five Members of Parliament. Dublin felt their loss not so much on account of an absence of political leadership but because, as the army surgeon John Gamble put it, the 'three hundred Bacchanals, whose sun daily set in claret, spending six months every year with their wives and children in Dublin, must have been of infinite service; and their loss would for a time be severely felt'.[66] Visitors could not but comment on the straitened times facing the city. The travel writer James McGregor spoke of the 'depress[ed]' state of Dublin's 'Literature, Arts and Manufactures'.[67] The novel *Florence Macarthy*, published in 1818 by the Anglo-Irish writer Lady Morgan, described how:

The capital of Ireland, since the Union, has become a mere stage of passage to such of its great landholders as occasionally visit the kingdom for purposes of necessity. They consider this beautiful city only as a *pendant* to Holyhead; and take up their temporary lodging to await the caprice of wind and tide, in those mansions where a few years ago they spent a large part of their great revenues, drawn from their native soil.[68]

The fulcrum of power had crossed the Irish Sea: the capital's dynamism vanished, absenteeism returned and the big houses lost their patrons. 'Behold the reciprocity which Pitt has bequeathed to you by the union – to eat the crumbs which have fallen from the rich man's table,' thundered a Dublin pamphleteer in 1811.[69] Parliament House was offered up to the Bank of Ireland; the Royal Horticultural Society took over the Rotunda for annual exhibitions; Powerscourt House became the Stamp Office; Lord Castlereagh's house in Merrion Square was let to the Irish Canal Board; Lord Cloncurry sold Mornington House in 1801 for 30 per cent of what he had bought it for in 1791; and Leinster House itself – the epicentre of Georgian Dublin, the residence that had signified the city's renaissance – was sold to the Dublin Society, with a third of the price knocked off.

Similarly, the semi-autonomous, colonial culture of the Protestant Ascendancy was superseded by a more obviously aggrandizing, militaristic imperialism. On 8 November 1805 news of Vice Admiral Horatio Nelson's victory and death at the Battle of Trafalgar reached Dublin. The City Assembly swiftly met to prepare an address of congratulation to King George III, but also to call a public meeting to discuss rising popular demand for a monument honouring the 'immortal memory' of Nelson. On 15 February 1808, to mark the anniversary of Nelson's victory at the Cape St Vincent in 1797, the foundation stone of the 22-metre column (and 4-metre high statue) was laid amid huge, enthusiastic crowds.[70] 'The testimonials of national gratitude and admiration to the memory of this favourite naval hero are already numerous in the British dominions. That erected by public subscription in Dublin is perhaps the greatest of any of them,' noted one Dublin history of the city's newly carved Nelson's Pillar.[71] Built at a cost of £7,000 and officially opened in 1809, the Pillar joined the Wellington Monument, the new Viceregal Lodge in the Phoenix Park, improvements to the decaying Dublin Castle and, above all, the bombastic, magnificent General Post Office on Sackville Street as part of a new architecture of Empire celebrating the historic Union with Great Britain. The political and diplomatic clout of the capital might have disappeared, but the citizens of Dublin could now enjoy all the icons of British imperialism in their midst. The meaning of this architecture would not be lost on the Irish nationalist instigators of the 1916 Easter Rising, who used the GPO as the headquarters of their struggle against British rule, or the Irish Republican Army volunteers who partially destroyed Nelson Pillar in March 1966 as an unwanted residue of the colonial past.*

In the early 1800s, however, such anti-imperialism was a long way off. In fact, the talk was all of how the Irish would benefit from Empire. 'A man can not speak as a true Englishman, unless he speaks as a true Irishman; nor can he speak as a true Irishman, unless he speaks as a true Englishman,' Pitt the Younger waxed at the peak of his unionist enthusiasm.[72] After Union, 'the voice of Irishmen,' predicted Henry Dundas, the British war secretary, 'would be heard, not only in Europe but in Asia, Africa and America'.[73] And so it proved, with the Irish revealing themselves to be as enthusiastic proponents of Empire – as soldiers, traders, missionaries, sailors, civil servants, engineers and doctors – as the Scottish. What was more, Empire proved remarkably unsectarian: both Irish Catholics and Protestants benefited from the career opportunities it offered. Surreptitiously, the East India Company had long been recruiting Irish Catholics in the south and west of the island for military service, but now the pace of employment multiplied. By 1813 the Company had established recruiting offices in Dublin, Belfast, Enniskillen and Limerick, which went on to supply almost 50 per cent of the Bengal army's European recruits in the period 1815–50.[74] Meanwhile, among the industrious Irish middling sort there emerged a more global, British affiliation to compete

---

* The events of 1916 and 1966 were explicitly connected. At a meeting of the Dublin City Council on 7 December 1953, a letter was submitted from the Hon. Secretary, IRA Dublin Brigade, enclosing a copy of a resolution adopted by the Dublin Brigade Council calling for the removal of Nelson Pillar and the erection adjacent thereto of a memorial to the men of 1916. See Andrew O'Brien, 'The History of Nelson's Pillar', *Dublin Historical Record*, 60, 1 (2007).

with romantic notions of national identity – and Dublin, with its Nelson Pillar and Wellington Monument, only affirmed such imperial, rather than colonial, empathies. Here was 'the friendly union of Britannia and Hibernia, with good consequences relating to Ireland'. For a brief period, the Anglo-Irish imperial relationship was not perhaps quite as foreign and oppressive as Friedrich Engels and later Irish nationalists would descrie.

With Ireland secure and Dublin becalmed, a more obviously *British* Empire had emerged by the early nineteenth century, connecting the Celtic fringes of Great Britain under a unifying purpose. Resentment about England's historic dominance over Ireland and Scotland was subtly overcome by the collective opportunity of the imperial project. The divisions between Protestant and Catholic, patriot and Whig faded away in the face of employment and prosperity. Instead, there emerged a shared imperial identity built around monarchy, the Royal Navy, military bravura and a concerted attempt to confound the

Nelson's Column, illustration from G. N. Wright, *An Historical Guide to Ancient and Modern Dublin, Illustrated by Engravings after Drawings by George Petrie* (London, 1821).

common enemy of France. But after the attempted invasions of the 1790s, the focus of that struggle for colonial hegemony between Britain and France was shifting from the narrow passage of the English Channel to the warm waters of the Indian Ocean. Ten thousand kilometres south of Dublin another colonial city now stood ready to resist the French and help to secure for Britain the foundations of its resurgent empire.

4
Cape Town

*'The master link of connection between the
western and eastern world'*

Lady Anne's voyage was a long one. After passing Madeira and the
Canary Islands, and reaching the low latitudes of the Cape of Good
Hope, her ship, the *Guardian*, was blown into the ice-packs of the
southern Atlantic. Eventually, there came a change of wind and the
'joyful news' that land had been sighted. Alas, the sea mists and fogs
were still so thick as 'not to permit us to enjoy its appearance till we
were exactly placed in the Bay opposite to Cape Town . . . Then, as if
by one consent the Lion's Rump whisked off the vapours with its tail;
the Lion's Head untied, and dropped, the necklace of clouds which
surrounded its erect throat, and Table Mountain over which a white
damask table cloth had been spread half way down showed its broad
face and smiled.' As the *Guardian* glided into Table Bay in July 1797,
'guns from the garrison and from all the batteries, welcomed His Majesty's government'.[1] The Cape Colony had its first governor and its
capital, Cape Town, was about to embark on its 140-year history as a
British imperial city.

Anne Barnard's journey to the southernmost edge of British Empire
was not just a physical ordeal, but one equally laden with emotional
complexity. She was born Lady Anne Lindsay into Scotland's
eighteenth-century Enlightenment elite, the eldest daughter of James
Lindsay, 5th Earl of Balcarres. She was also a beauty and a wit. 'Her
face was pretty and replete with vivacity; her figure light and elegant;
her conversation lively; and, like the rest of the family, peculiarly
agreeable,' remembered a contemporary. She formed an early attachment to the ambitious Edinburgh advocate and eager political fixer

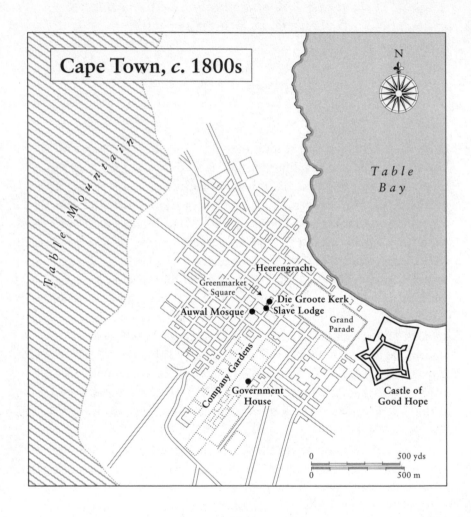

Cape Town, *c.* 1800s

N

Table Mountain

Table Bay

Heerengracht

Greenmarket Square

Die Groote Kerk

Auwal Mosque ● ● Slave Lodge

Grand Parade

Company Gardens

Government House ●

Castle of Good Hope

0   500 yds

0   500 m

Henry Dundas and, on moving to London (like so many smart Scots in the eighteenth century after the 1707 Act of Union), she worked tirelessly to promote Dundas as he sought to rise under the patronage of Pitt the Younger. Dundas proposed marriage – yet by then Lady Anne had fallen for another Georgian politician, William Windham. He might have been described as 'the first gentleman of his age', but Windham refused to commit to her (in Paris, during the height of the Robespierre Terror), so she returned to Dundas ready to serve as his wife. But he, by then, had married another.[2]

In 1793, at the age of forty-three, Lady Anne found herself betrothed to the unknown Andrew Barnard, an impoverished son of the Bishop of Limerick. Now all her formidable society skills were dedicated to the furtherance of his unpromising political career – and she demanded Dundas pay her back for her decades of devotion. 'You owe me some Happiness, – in Truth you do – pay me by making me the means of serving a man who has rebuilt in a considerable degree what tumbled to its foundations.' After much haranguing, Dundas, who had risen to home secretary and then secretary of state for war, gave in to her emotional pressure by granting Barnard a sinecure as colonial secretary to the Cape of Good Hope. In 1797, the ambitious diplomatic couple accompanied a new governor, Earl Macartney, to the new colony – Anne Barnard acting as de facto governor's wife in the absence of Lady Macartney – and carried a secret commission to report directly back to Dundas on the strategic value of the recently acquired South African outpost.[3]

For all the uniqueness of her mission, Lady Anne's first response to the natural beauty of Cape Town was intensely generic. Much more than Puritan Boston, fetid Bridgetown or familiar Dublin, the British fell in love with Cape Town from the outset.* A few years after Lady

---

* The acerbic Swedish doctor Andrew Sparrman had a simple explanation for such effusive praise. 'The Cape is usually mentioned in too high terms by sea-faring men; particularly by such as have been there only for a short time. The reason probably is, that people, who are weary of a long and tedious voyage of several months duration, are usually enchanted with the first spot of earth they set foot upon, of which they afterwards make their reports according to the impression it first made upon them. This is so much more likely to happen with respect to the Cape, as seafaring men are seldom used to stay there long enough to be weary of it.' See Andrew Sparrman, *A Voyage to the Cape of Good Hope* (Dublin, 1785), p. 7.

Anne's arrival, the naturalist William J. Burchell would be equally delighted to hear 'Land ahoy!' after four months at sea.

> At this pleasing intelligence we hastened up from the cabin, and although nothing could be seen but a small cloud, which seemed fixed on the horizon, and was at first not very easily to be distinguished, the captain, who was well acquainted with the singular appearance of the cloud which rests on the Table Mountain during a south-east gale, declared that the land which we had now before us was that of the Cape of Good Hope.[4]

And when the clouds dispersed, the stunning vista was revealed. Captain Robert Percival of His Majesty's Royal Irish Regiment was completely bewitched. 'Nothing can exceed the general effect of this scenery,' he wrote in 1804.

> After leaving Round-a-Bosch and proceeding two miles further, you find yourself on a line with the foot of Tiger or Devil Hill, which rises on your left hand; and on your right is the head of Table Bay, which with the town now opens to view. Here the stranger is greatly struck with the grand, beautiful, and variegated appearance of the prospect before him, and on each side of him.[5]

With its long pre-history of European colonization, stretching back through the Dutch in the seventeenth century to the Portuguese in the sixteenth century, Cape Town already had a cosmopolitan, European sensibility by the time the British took control in the 1790s. It was a place where they instantly felt comfortable. For all the strange, African 'Hottentot' peoples inhabiting the region, there would be no phobia of the 'Dark Continent' about the Cape Colony. Since the 1600s, Cape Town had grown as a staging post between the great oceans of east and west; it faced outwards to the lucrative trade winds of the world as 'a caravanserai on the periphery of the global spice trade'.[6] It was never much interested in its farmstead hinterland or the further African interior. 'Since the time of the Dutch, it has been suggested that if England were thus to cut off the Table Mountain with its adjacent land, England would have all of South Africa that it wants,' noted novelist Anthony Trollope in the 1870s, with uncomfortable precision.[7]

To modern critics of Cape Town, that same Eurocentricity remains all too redolent. In its politics (Democratic Alliance rather than African National Congress), its economic infrastructure of financial and legal services and its patterns of property ownership, the city's white European power-base seems to stand untouched by the advent of South African black majority rule. As in the apartheid years, Cape Town and its lush environs are still marketed to the world as a landscape of paddocks and cricket-pitches, rugby and wine-tasting, sun-downers and surfing, all set against the stunning natural beauty of Table Mountain, the Twelve Apostles and Camps Bay. 'There is nowhere like Cape Town,' as the Cape Town Tourism literature has it. 'Perched between the ocean and the mountain, with a national park at its heart, it's a place to renew and reconnect. Cape Town, the "Mother-City", is the oldest city in our country and has cultural heritage spanning more than 300 years.' For foreign visitors, when the 'real Africa' is encountered it is usually through a trip to the Robben Island museum for a glimpse of Nelson Mandela's cell, or a Cape Flats township tour ('experience a heartwarming tour of the Cape Black's townships ... and witness the reality of township folk').[8]

Understandably, this almost colonial branding of modern Cape Town has produced a political backlash. 'Black people feel this is the old South Africa,' in the words of Xola Skosana, a township pastor. 'If you come to Cape Town, you've come to the last post of the colonial history of this country. Both politically and economically, white people are in power.' South African president Jacob Zuma has described Cape Town as simply a 'racist' place, with an 'extremely apartheid attitude'. In part, such criticisms are the product of the city's refusal to bow to the ANC's political monopoly. Instead, it has stayed true to the metropolitan, melting-pot heritage of Cape Town, where black Africans have not formed a majority demographic for some 400 years. As a busy port city, Cape Town was from the 1600s a place of competing cultures and commerce, of multiple religions and ethnicities, of colonialism and anti-colonialism, and influenced as much by Malay, Indonesian and Dutch culture as by indigenous African.

Such cosmopolitanism, however, was of little concern to Europe's great powers at the end of the eighteenth century. In London, Paris and Amsterdam, the value of Cape Town lay purely and simply in its strategic significance. In the aftermath of American Independence and with growing interest in the potential riches from East India Company factories in Bengal, Britain's colonial interests shifted decisively from the Americas towards India. Cape Town proved to be the axis of the Empire's 'Swing to the East', a city which would be fought over and traded between multiple European empires – not for the riches of its African interior, but for its command of the open oceans. It was an Anglo-Dutch colonial city, the footprint of which has yet fully to recede, which signified the shift from the First British Empire of America to the Second British Empire of India. At the turn of the eighteenth and nineteenth centuries, its more explicit purpose was to secure India for the British and ensure the demise of French colonial competition.

KAAPSTAD

A 'Swing to the East' had certainly inspired the first European settlers of the Cape. Founded in 1602, the Verenigde Oostindische Compagnie (VOC) was the Dutch equivalent to England's East India Company, tasked with an equally aggressive approach to foreign markets. The Dutch States General granted it exclusive monopoly rights to engage in commerce with Asia, consolidating all of Holland's trade with the East Indies under it. In return, fleets of more than one hundred ships delivered staggering financial returns to the Company's six founding cities on the import of nutmeg, cloves and cinnamon, as well as Chinese porcelain, tea, coffee and cotton textiles. In many ways, the VOC enjoyed even greater licence than the East India Company, as it could make treaties, acquire land, build forts and generally provide the infrastructure of future colonization. Steadily, the spice islands of the East Indies – modern-day Indonesia – fell under Dutch control and Britain's East India Company was limited to the Indian subcontinent.[10]

But getting from Amsterdam to the Javanese capital of Batavia (now Jakarta), around the Cape of Good Hope, was never a smooth sail. The confluence of the warm Agulhas current of the Indian Ocean and the cold Benguela waters of the South Atlantic made for a treacherous passage. Rear Admiral Fitzroy, captain of Charles Darwin's ship the *Beagle*, describes the meteorological challenge well:

> Several causes combine to make the Cape of Good Hope a stormy promontory. High, steep, and salient, every wind must be more or less affected by it, as a mechanical obstacle, and by the relative temperatures surrounding, as well as immediately above, its ranges of mountainous land ... In the north are African deserts – towards the south, Antarctic ice, beyond a wide range of open sea, in which strong currents, like the Gulf Stream, run from thirty to eighty or more miles a day (off Cape Lagulhas). And this in that zone where incessant alternation occurs between the two greater air-currents: all which causes contribute to make that famous promontory truly 'El Cabo Tormentoso' or the 'Cape of Storms', as described by the early voyagers, and not in exaggerated terms.[11]

When the storms caught the ships, it was dangerous sailing indeed. 'Rapidly the swell increases, and like the water in a boiling cauldron, tosses the vessels to and fro, the brutal battering of the waves placing a heavy strain on the anchor ropes as they slacken and tighten suddenly with each wave,' was how one captain described a Cape north-wester. In the dangerous months of May to September, ship after ship could fall victim to the waves and the weather, even when anchored in Table Bay or False Bay. William Burchell spent days buffeted around the South Atlantic as his ship tried to drop anchor.

> The moment we had passed beyond the shelter of the Lion Mountain, a furious wind suddenly and unexpectedly assailed the vessel; pouring out of the clouds, as it seemed, its boisterous fury upon us ... The vessel was rapidly driving out to sea again: in the utmost hurry the sailors flew up the rigging, and took in all sail possible ... the fore top-sail being split, we were compelled to wear the ship, and retreat to the shelter of the Lion Mountain to bend another sail.[12]

It was the Portuguese mariner Bartolomeu Dias who first rounded the Cape in the 1480s and named it Cabo de Boa Esperanza, the Cape of Good Hope, since a successful passage opened up the route to

India. Another Portuguese explorer, António de Saldanha, is the first recorded European to set foot on the Cape, in 1503. In 1620 two British officers, Andrew Shillinge and Humphrey Fitzherbert, of East India Company fleets bound for Surat and Bantam, took 'quiet and peaceful possession' of Table Bay and 'of the whole continent near adjoining', in the name of 'the High and Mighty Prince James, by the Grace of God King of Great Britain'.[13] Their plans were to establish a plantation along the lines of Virginia, but the resources were never forthcoming. So in 1652 the Dutch agent Jan van Riebeeck took Table Bay as part of a deliberate move to exclude the English and, as the VOC bureaucrats put it, gain control of a refuelling station 'to provide that the passing and re-passing East India ships, to and from Batavia, respectively, may, without accident, touch at the said Cape or Bay, and also upon arriving there, may find the means of procuring herbs, flesh, water, and other needful refreshments, and by this means restore the health of their sick'.[14] Without such a stopping-off point at the Cape, the VOC would have been unable to operate on such a large scale. The sixty-odd Dutch ships that annually passed back and forth through the port during the eighteenth century deposited their sick and made some money by off-loading either European delicacies such as Dutch cheese and beer (on the outward-bound route) or spices and oriental artefacts (homeward-bound) in order to buy fresh meat, wine and vegetables. When the VOC rear admiral Johan Stavorinus, who was fastidious about the health of his sailors, passed through in 1774, he 'sent forty or fifty men on shore every day, in order, that by taking exercise among the hills, and by the effects of the land-air, the scorbutic tendency, which had already begun to manifest itself among them, might be combated'.[15]

'The Dutch never considered the Cape in a commercial view, but merely as a place of refreshment necessary for the carrying on their Commerce to India,' as one Royal Navy memo from the 1790s accurately put it. 'Considered as an entrepot between Europe and Asia, it has every advantage that can be wished, either in point of Situation, Climate, Soil, and Productions.'[16] So much so that other ships – British, French and American – started dropping in, all of whom were charged higher rates for their victuals by the VOC in order to subsidize the refuelling of Dutch East Indiamen.

One disadvantage of the incipient colony from the Dutch perspective was the attitude of the indigenous Khoekhoe (an ethnic grouping of the broader Khoe-San people, but usually described at the time as either 'Hottentots' or 'Bushmen'), who refused repeated attempts to corral them into labouring for the Europeans. For centuries, the Khoekhoe tribesmen had grazed sheep and then cattle around the lush pastures of the Cape in a nomadic, subsistence way of life. The Portuguese, in the 1480s, had bartered with yellow- and brown-skinned herders at Saldanha Bay, Table Bay and Mossel Bay and recorded their language as characterized by clicks. Moving with the seasons, they shepherded fat-tailed sheep and long-horned cattle in huge numbers, often with six head of cattle per person. The Khoekhoe drank the milk and skinned the carcasses, but fed themselves from hunting boar, fishing and collecting honey. To begin with, relations with the incoming Dutch were politely commercial, the VOC exchanging brass, iron and dress ornaments for beef and mutton. However, when the Dutch began to impinge on traditional grazing areas – by farming, initially, in the Rondebosch region – and claim novel rights of private ownership over common land, tensions escalated. By the 1670s, the Dutch settlers were using all the advantages of European technology to drive the Khoekhoe off their lands and, in a colonial experiment which would continue until the 1990s, deport the most troublesome suspects to Robben Island. Between 1662 and 1713, company records reveal that the VOC expropriated 14,636 cattle and 32,808 sheep, while Dutch colonists, spreading out as free burghers to farm wheat and tend vineyards on their own land (in contrast to the absentee landlord plantations of Barbados and Ulster), took the best pastures and expanded their control of territory up to 80 kilometres north and 65 kilometres east of Cape Town. Such systematic theft of livestock and land destroyed the Khoekhoe community: without large tracts of land, the Khoekhoe livestock economy faltered, the chieftain structure imploded, and the language faded. Then, in 1713, a homeward-bound Dutch ship docked and spread smallpox across the Cape colony, wiping out multiple indigenous tribes. The disease returned in 1735 and 1767, cutting the Khoekhoe population down from an estimated 200,000 in the mid-seventeenth century to approximately 20,000 by the opening of the nineteenth century.[17]

In the meantime, Dutch settlers got to work transforming the 'Cape Settlement' into Kaapstaad, or Cape Town. In its opening decades, the 'Brothel and Tavern of the Two Oceans' (as it was known) enjoyed a ragged reputation as little more than a stopping-off point for sailors, whalers and traders – with a service economy built around their various carnal needs. Unlike Boston or Bridgetown, Cape Town did not develop as an export dock for colonial produce. Instead, it was a refreshment stop with an urban economy of innkeepers and drink salesman, butchers and brewers, as well as masons, carpenters, smiths, wagonmakers, potters, shoemakers and tailors. The rich let out their houses to the officer class, and the less wealthy put up the sailors. Smuggling, private trading, prostitution and slaving kept the city afloat. 'Nothing can be more agreeable to the people of this place, than the arrival of an English ship,' commented a passing visitor in the 1760s, 'as it causes a circulation of money, and indeed it is chiefly by the English that most people in town are supported; not only by taking the captains, passengers, etc., to board at their houses, but by furnishing the ships with provisions.'[18]

The earthy realities of this port economy were masked by the city's stunning whitewashed fabric and natural magnificence. 'Nothing can be neater, or more pleasant, than the appearance which this town presents, spreading over the valley, from the sea-shore towards the mountains on each side,' thought Burchell.[19] 'The situation of Cape Town is singularly well chosen; and the Dutch certainly deserve great credit for the regularity and convenience with which it is laid out,' agreed Robert Percival of the Royal Irish.

> It is divided by five streets, running in a parallel direction from the shores or edge of the bay towards the Table Mountain, with five other streets, intersected by lanes at regular intervals, which cross the larger streets at right angles ... Most of the streets are wide, airy and spacious, planted with oak trees entwined in each other, which shade the houses and take off the great glare occasioned by the reflection of the sun from the white houses, and from the Table Mountain.[20]

Mrs Jemima Kindersley, in transit to Pondicherry in 1777, wrote how:

every one must be pleased with the town, which has all the regularity and neatness usual among the Dutch: the streets are all parallel to each other; and there is one large square with trees planted round, and a canal of water from springs running down: the houses are very good and have a neat appearance on the outside; which altogether make it a very pretty town and, some few circumstances excepted, equal in neatness to any of our sea-ports in England.[21]

A French author, Jacques Arago, was similarly effusive in his praise. 'From the brilliant whiteness of the houses of the Cape you would take it at a distance for the foundations of a city which is but just finished. The fronts of the houses, the windows, the steps, are all astonishingly clean. The streets are broad, as straight as a line, and in general bordered with trees which keep the apartments agreeably cool.'[22] The Dutch domestic architecture of flat roofs, bared joist ceilings, large windows and lofty rooms was widely admired, with the paved platform *stoep* (step) in front of each house a source of particular fascination – 'here the inhabitants frequently walk or sit, in the cool of the evening, and often at other times, to enjoy the air, or to converse with passing friends'.[23]

Others christened Cape Town 'Little Amsterdam' on account of its array of ditches, bridges, sluices and low-walled channels which diverted the mountain streams into watering the growing city. In succeeding decades, as the city's population expanded, these channels would become filled with filth and refuse, but in the late eighteenth century they still formed part of a broader cityscape dedicated to providing for the culinary passage of passing ships – since ninety days at sea on a diet of cheese, biscuits, salt meat and rum could be deadly for any crew's constitution. Johan Stavorinus liked to put three quarts of lemon-juice into his sailors' drinking water, and mix orange-peel into the rum rations. Previously, to keep the scorbutics at bay, the Dutch had planted fruit-trees and vegetables at regular inlets in Saint Helena and Mauritius. However, the miraculously fecund soil and sea air of Cape Town fertilized an exceptional array of fresh produce – oranges, lemons, grapes, melons, apples, pears, peaches, almonds, apricots, figs, walnuts, mulberries, quinces, chestnuts, bananas and guavas. And if it was too cold for mangoes and too warm for gooseberries, subtler gardeners could harvest strawberries, plums, raspberries and cherries to be sold to passing boats. For sailors, there was also the added attraction of the colony's celebrated 'pickled fish curry' prepared by Malay cooks. The moment Calcutta diarist William Hickey's ship, the *Sea-horse*, dropped anchor in False Bay en route to the Bay of Bengal in 1777, 'we instantly were regaled with the most delicious fruits'. The local 'Dutch Chief' also tried to sell them poultry, ham, tongues, sausages and, to the horror of the gluttonous Hickey, a truly execrable Constantia vintage – 'more like treacle and water than a rich and generous wine'.[24]

Wisely, the VOC prioritized the planting of market gardens, and the most impressive of these were the Company Gardens, fed by the waters of the Heerengracht (Gentlemen's Canal). Now a well-tended civic park dotted with First World War cannons and statues of Jan Smuts and Cecil Rhodes, it provides an elegant and shaded setting for the South African Parliament and National Gallery. In the 1700s, it was an altogether more industrious landscape. As well as an exhausting hike up Table Mountain ('we beheld beneath us both the Cape Town and that of False Bay, an immense tract of rich and fertile country, bounded by the ocean'), Hickey and his party 'walked in the Company's Gardens, which are well stored with curious plants, the choicest fruits and vegetables'.[25] Peter Kolben, a Prussian diplomat sent to investigate the Cape, thought the 40-acre Company Gardens simply 'the noblest and most beautiful Curiosities in all Afric. And I question whether there is a Garden in Europe, so rich and beautiful in its Productions as any one of 'em.' Not only did the Gardens provide the Cape with 'almost every Thing the Vegetable World produces by Way of Fruit and Flower', they were also gloriously free of artifice. 'The Gardens are not laid out and divided, perhaps, so curiously as are many in Europe ... Nature has Little or Nothing to set her off there besides her own Charmes and the Hand of the Gardener: And she is more charming than I have seen her in any other Part of the World.' Through the middle of the Gardens ran a public walkway overshadowed by oak trees 30 feet tall, while around the fruit trees were planted elm and myrtle to protect their delicate produce from the brutal south-east winds. Then there were the domestic gardens, encircling the whitewashed houses. ''Tis very delightful to visit 'em;

and they make a lovely Appearance in several Views of the Town. The Millions of Flowers in the Cape-Gardens replenish the Air with the most delicious Perfumes.'[26]

Close to where the Heerengracht would have once gushed into the sea still stands the most totemic edifice of the Dutch Cape: the Castle of Good Hope. 'The Castle is a large pentagonal fortress on the south-eastern or inland side of the town, close to the water's edge,' reported Burchell. 'It commands the jutty, or landing-place, and part of Table Bay, and completely controls the only road between the town and country.'[27] Built in the 1670s to replace van Riebeeck's initial mud, clay and timber fort, it was from the castle's stone bastions that the VOC imposed their will upon ocean and inland alike. Here was where the governor and his senior officials enacted the orders of the Council of Seventeen from Amsterdam and answered to the governor-general in Batavia. Today, on reclaimed land between the castle walls and the Atlantic shoreline, is the six-lane Strand freeway, the rail terminus, the central business district and then the Duncan Dock. But until the 1800s the spring tide used to come crashing in through the entrance gates. From the battlements and captain's tower (for a long time Cape Town's tallest building), the comings and goings of the Table Bay anchorage could be carefully scrutinized, with few ships escaping investigation by the Dutch authorities. Whilst the castle would be remodelled under British rule, its stonework still retains its VOC imprimatur. Above the main gates, the pediment bears the coat of arms of the United Netherlands, a clawed, crowned lion holding the seven arrows of unity in its paw. Carved on the architrave below are the arms of Van Hoorn, Delft, Amsterdam, Middelburg, Rotterdam and Enkhuizen – the six Dutch cities in which the United East India Company had chambers. The yellow brickwork, the VOC initials, the Dutch colonial styling, the sun dials, the shutters and statues of Neptune all give the castle an air of cloistered, colonial assertion even as twenty-first-century Cape Town's skyscrapers crowd over its courtyard. The courtyard itself is sliced in two by a 12-metre-high wall (with balcony for public pronouncements) which allowed for protection from attack from both Table Mountain to the north and the coast to the south.

The Dutch designed the castle, but they were not the ones who built

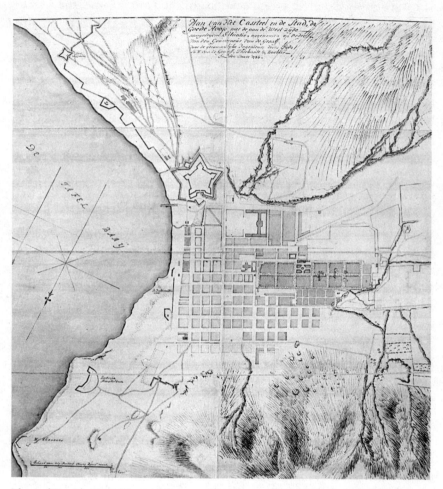

Plan of Dutch Cape Town. *Plan van Het Cassteel en de Stad, de Goede Hoop,* by Van de Graaff, Thiebault & Barbier (1786).

it. That task fell to the thousands of slaves sold into Cape Town. Wary of establishing a fully fledged colony rather than staging post, the VOC had refused van Riebeeck permission to enslave the local Khoe-khoe. So in 1658 he started importing slaves, and over the ensuing 150 years some 63,000 men, women and children entered the Cape Colony in bondage. Most came from the VOC's eastern empire, with Indonesia, Sri Lanka and Goa – as well as Madagascar, Zanzibar and Mozambique – providing the progenitors of the modern Cape coloureds and multicultural Cape Town. By the 1790s, compared to around 13,000 free burghers, there were already some 15,000 slaves (generally replenished through imports rather than births in the colony), and these were the men, women and children who built the infrastructure of the Cape economy. They laboured in the vineyards, the docks, the salt-works and the hospitals; they built canals, drains and public buildings; they worked as butchers, carpenters and barrel-makers. There was no plantation economy in the Cape, and so the diffusion of slaves through society was not concentrated on great estates but spread across different businesses and classes. In the 1750s, seven burghers had more than fifty slaves each, whilst it was common for a Dutch citizen of decent rank to keep ten to fifteen slaves (including women and children) to work as farm labourers and drivers, cooks and wetnurses. William Burchell reported that Malay slaves were the most prized possessions in Cape Town, the men working as carpenters, cabinet-makers, masons and tailors. Those from Mozambique and Madagascar were put to 'the most laborious' employments. In contrast to the Caribbean, manumission levels were very low, and the 'freed slave' community small, but the Cape did share with the West Indies a high degree of racial miscegenation, and it was quite common for a slave-owner to allow one of his female slaves to cohabit with a European as man and wife. None of this amused the VOC, which issued successive circulars deploring the fact that 'irresponsible people, both among the Company's servants in the garrison of this fortress, as also free settlers or inhabitants of this place', were living in open concubinage with coloured and slave women, siring illegitimate coloured children.[28] British commentators usually turned a blind eye to such practices and instead chose to criticize the practice of Cape slavery as another example of the slothful indulgence of the

Lady Anne Barnard, *View of The Gallows, Cape Town*, detail from a panorama of the distance is the building known as the Great Barracks. Lady Anne's panorama was

Cape Town. A slave in shackles repairs the castle walls while others rest in the sun. In
ntended as a gift for Governor Macartney (1797).

Dutch. 'There is, perhaps, no part of the world, out of Europe, where the introduction of slavery was less necessary than at the Cape of Good Hope,' thought John Barrow, private secretary to Earl Macartney. 'Nor would it ever have found its way into this angle of Africa, had the same spirit of Batavian industry, which raised a wealthy and populous republic out of the sea, impressed the minds of those who first formed the settlement.'[29]

If brutality on the scale of the West Indian plantations was a rarity in the Cape, the Dutch legal system nonetheless sanctioned an array of appallingly murderous and sadistic tortures – breaking on the wheel, boiling to death, burning alive, branding and whipping – to crush any dissenting slave spirit. The gallows and the rack formed an important part of Dutch public architecture (slaves who murdered their masters were sentenced to the most innovatively barbaric of deaths), whilst the conditions in which the VOC housed its chattels were equally inhuman. 'You have entered the oldest surviving slave building in South Africa,' explains the guide as you walk into the Slave Lodge in Adderley Street, at the bottom of the old Company Gardens. Now a fine museum dedicated to the history of slavery in South Africa, it was once the fetid home to some 1,200 slaves belonging to the VOC. 'The lodge for the government-slaves is a large, plain, oblong building, about eighty paces long, and twenty broad, with an area in the center,' as the American visitor Robert Semple described it. 'It stands between the church and the Company's garden, and has nothing in its structure worthy of notice.'[30] Indeed it didn't: originally, a single-storey rectangular structure of plastered brick, built around an open inner courtyard, much like a prison, its base conditions and overcrowded cells ensured a wretched mortality rate from smallpox, malnutrition and ill-treatment.

The church which Semple referred to, across Spin Street from the Lodge, is Die Groote Kerk. Home to the Calvinist Dutch Reformed congregation (which remained the Cape state church until 1780), the church has been described as the oldest place of Christian worship in southern Africa. It was rebuilt in the so-called 'Cape Gothic' style in the mid-nineteenth century on the foundations of an earlier edifice renowned for its Puritan simplicity. 'Nothing entertaining to the Eye is seen within the Church,' reported Peter Kolben. 'The Pulpit is plain wood, quite naked of Ornament. And the People sit on long Forms, planted in several Parallels, running this Way and that, before the Pulpit. But distinctions are observed in sitting nearer to or farther from the Pulpit, according to every one's Birth, Employment or Condition in Life.'[31] Christian worship was as important a part of Dutch Cape culture at the end of the eighteenth century as slave-trading and the city was noteworthy for its public displays of piety. 'The principal church near the grand parade, is a very handsome building,' reported Robert Percival. 'The church is well attended, and a great deal of solemnity and decorum observed in the worship.'[32] For those of a more ecumenical nature, the sumptuous Dutch Lutheran church – which was allowed to compete with Calvinists for souls from the 1780s – offered an alternative place of worship.

With its churches, whitewashed double-storey houses, canals, gardens, castle, hospital and barracks, the rough and ready 'Cape Settlement' had by the mid-1700s made the transition into the more civilized Kaapstad with a population and prosperity beginning to challenge the VOC's more developed East Asian ports. No building captures that sense of urban pride and cultural confidence more than the Old Town House on Greenmarket Square. Rising above the tourist tat for sale in the square's stalls, this resplendent display of whitewashed Cape Dutch architecture is a vainglorious celebration of 'European civilization' as it existed on the edge of the known world. Inside, the Dutch still-life watercolours, the dark mahogany furniture and the closed shutters transport you back to seventeenth-century Rotterdam or Amsterdam.

The Dutch had turned Cape Town into an eminently liveable, colonial backwater. Yet if it was recognized as a useful logistical asset, the Cape Colony rarely featured prominently in European colonial thinking in the eighteenth century. In the 1790s this low-key status was to be dramatically revised. And the man who proved so determined to transform the Cape from a second-tier refreshment station to axis of Empire was Lady Anne Barnard's mentor and husband manqué, Henry Dundas.

FEATHERS AND SWORDS

Today, Henry Dundas, first Viscount Melville, is a rather forgotten servant of Empire who rarely features in the higher imperial Pantheon of Clive, Pitt, Wellesley or Wolfe. Yet he was a pivotal architect of Britain's colonial strategy as it made the transition from the First Empire of the Americas to the Second Empire of India. Raised within the same Edinburgh circles as Lady Anne, he worked his way up Auld Reekie's political and legal ladder to become lord advocate, Scotland's chief officer of government. But he was determined to get to Westminster and, in 1774, Dundas was duly sent by the voters of Edinburgshire (Midlothian) to represent them in the House of Commons. Wisely, he allied himself early on to Pitt the Younger and assumed 'a powerful informal position as friend, advisor, and factotum' as Pitt plotted his way into Downing Street. Dundas did not entertain many high-minded notions about public service: he was happy to cut the deals, do the dirty work and give Pitt the glory. It was an approach to Westminster life which would generate plentiful evidence for his impeachment in 1806 on charges of siphoning off public funds. But that was all in the future: in the 1780s and '90s Dundas was beginning a brilliant government career which would culminate in his appointment as first lord of the Admiralty in 1804.

The American War of Independence had been the subject of Dundas's maiden speech in parliament in February 1775, and he had followed the consensus in supporting the Coercive Acts on Boston and urging the harshest possible reprisals against the rebels. The loss of America convinced him, however, of the pitfalls of any future involvement with territorial Empire. 'The peopling of colonies would, he believed, create demand for autonomy, then independence, with disruption or loss of British commerce.' The next phase of British imperialism, he argued, should be a trading rather than colonizing one, built on commercial outposts for the exploitation of resources.[33] It would be an Empire focused as much around the navy as the army and intimately connected with Britain's mercantile interests. 'We must be merchants while we are soldiers ... our trade depends upon a proper exertion of our maritime strength,' as one diplomatic memo put it, 'trade and maritime force depend on each other, and . . . the riches which are the true resources of this country depend on its commerce'.[34]

Yet Britain sought to erect this trade and maritime force in the face of a geo-political storm worthy of the Cape of Good Hope. The development of Boston on the back of an Atlantic war economy, the extraction of plantation riches from the Caribbean and the perennial fears of a foreign invasion of Ireland have all shown different aspects of the continuing battle for colonial supremacy in the eighteenth century between the British, French, Dutch and Spanish Empires. It was an epoch of 'total war', fought across oceans and continents at huge cost in treasure and men, to shape the pace of European imperialism. However, British victory in the Seven Years' War had transformed London's imperial strategy from a defensive control of existing plantations and settlements to a more aggrandizing posture focused on the taking and holding of locations in an effort to beat back the French. 'Great Britain can at no time propose to maintain an extensive and complicated war but by destroying the colonial resources of our enemies and adding proportionately to our own commercial resources, which are, and must be, the sole basis of our maritime strength,' as Dundas himself put it.[35] What was more, 'the primary object of our attention ought to be, by what means we can most effectually increase those resources on which depends our naval superiority'.[36]

Central to this strategy was indeed a hegemonic naval force – a military asset painfully lacking during the War of American Independence and regarded as increasingly essential in any future struggle against France. So, in the final decades of the eighteenth century, the might of the Royal Navy (and its place in British popular culture) expanded exponentially. During the Seven Years' War, there were on average 74,800 men serving in the navy, but by the early 1800s it had passed 120,000. From the Navy Board at London's Somerset House and from the dockyards of Deptford and Woolwich, and then Chatham and Plymouth, was hammered out an incredible escalation of naval capacity. 'The natural strength of the nation is its navy; the builders or first movers in our navy are the shipwrights . . . They set the great wheels of commerce and war in motion,' wrote the shipwright and Methodist pamphleteer William Shrubsole.[37] By 1805, the year of the Battle of Trafalgar, Britain could boast under the leadership of Pitt and Dundas over 120 ships of the line (massive warships, such as HMS *Victory*, able to take part in the line of battle with broadside attacks from cannon fire) and another 160 cruisers. The backbone of the Royal Navy was the 74-gunner, two-decked third rate warship, just one of which boasted more firepower than all Napoleon's artillery at the Battle of Austerlitz and helped to secure for Britain her command of the world's oceans. But an effective Royal Navy required more than just sail, timber and cannon: it needed victualling stations and refreshment stops to allow it to remain at sea and dominate the enemy. 'It is therefore as much the duty of those entrusted with the conduct of a British war to cut off the colonial resources of the enemy, as it would be that of the general of a great army to destroy or intercept the magazines of his opponent,' explained Dundas.[38] This meant the control of port cities such as Gibraltar (ceded to Britain from Spain by the 1713 Treaty of Utrecht), Bridgetown – and maybe even Cape Town.

Dundas's imperial scenario-planning was put to the test in 1793 when Britain went to war with a newly energized and revolutionary France. While France threatened Britain through attempted invasion of Ireland, the Royal Navy's response was swift: in 1793 Tobago, part of Saint-Domingue, Pondicherry and Miquelon were captured, while in Toulon the French Mediterranean fleet was seized without a shot being fired. In 1794 the West Indian islands of Martinique, Guadeloupe and St Lucia were taken, followed by the vital eastern territories of Ceylon and Malacca one year later. Over the next decade, the navy would press home its advantage by taking Dutch possessions in the East and West Indies, then Trinidad, the French colony at Madagascar and Minorca (an island endlessly traded between the great powers over the course of the eighteenth century). At home, the British public lapped up these stories of naval heroics. 'The extacy of joy displayed by the public on receiving the news of Lord Howe's glorious victory, proves how much more Britons are delighted by success at sea than on land,' exclaimed the London paper *St James's Chronicle* in the aftermath of the Battle of the Glorious First of June in 1794, when the British fleet bested the French in the mid-Atlantic. 'The sea is our protecting element, and as long as Britannia rules the waves nothing can hurt us. A victory at sea must ever give us more heart-felt pleasure than twenty victories on the Continent.'[39]

Early in the war against France, Dundas realized the strategic significance of Cape Town. Not lacking in ambition, France had declared war simultaneously on both Great Britain and the Dutch Republic. Any French conquest of the Netherlands, Dundas assumed, would also bring with it control of their colonial outposts. 'The preservation of the Cape of Good Hope is an object of so much importance, both to Holland and Great Britain, it is impossible for this Country to view with indifference any circumstance that can endanger the safety of that Settlement,' Dundas wrote to the foreign secretary, Lord Grenville, in April 1793. He wanted to know 'what is the Force now at the Cape, either Naval or Military, what is conceived to be sufficient for rendering the Possession of its perfectly secure ... and how far the Dutch are disposed to allow a Depot of British Troops to be placed at the Cape, either for its own Defence, or for acting offensively from it'.[40]

Other members of the British imperial establishment were equally concerned about a threat to the Cape of Good Hope. Sir Francis Baring, founder of Barings Bank and director of the East India Company, urged Dundas to launch an immediate assault before the French put a garrison down at Table Bay. Through a series of military alliances with Indian princes, the French were already putting Company interests in Bengal under pressure. If France gained control of the Cape, then British possessions in India – with all the wealth and power that came with them – could be lost. 'The importance of the Cape is in my opinion comprised under two heads – as a place of refreshment for our ships on their return from India ... Secondly, whoever is Master of the Cape will be able to protect, or annoy, our ships out and home, serving at the same time as an effectual check upon Mauritius etc.' When it came to mercantile competition, it was a zero-sum game: the French had to be kept out as much as the British let in. Military men were making the same point from the perspective of imperial security. As soon as the French invaded Holland in January 1795, Captain John Blankett of the Royal Navy wrote to Evan Nepean, under secretary of the War Department, with an urgent briefing on the likely loss of the Cape. 'Whatever tends to give to France the means of obtaining a footing in India is of consequence to us to prevent, it would be idle in me to say anything more to point out the consequence of the Cape than to say that what was a feather in the hands of Holland, will become a sword in the hands of France.'[41]

This was the nub of the matter. As British imperial concerns had started to turn, in the latter half of the eighteenth century, from the Atlantic to the Indian Ocean, so a secure route around the Cape of Good Hope had become ever more vital. 'It is our decided opinion . . . that whichever of these two great powers [Britain or France] shall possess the Cape, the same may govern India,' the East India Company had declared as early as 1781.[42] Captain Robert Percival was similarly convinced of the Cape's pivotal role in the imperial contest. 'For the purposes of defending our own foreign possessions, or keeping our enemies in check, no station can indeed be found comparable to the Cape of Good Hope,' he averred. 'Were the native princes of India to make such head against us, as that our army there required speedy reinforcements, we could from the Cape convey troops thither in less than half the time in which they could be sent from Europe.'[43] For Dundas, trade with India was the central pillar of his imperial plan and British control of the Cape – the 'Frontier fortress of India' – was a prerequisite for it. Cape Town could not be allowed to fall to France.

A PLACE WORTH RETAINING

The taking of the Cape by British troops was a rapid and bloodless affair. On 11 June 1795, Admiral Keith Elphinstone and Major-General James Craig sailed into False Bay with a force of 1,200 infantry and 200 artillery. The British usually liked to suggest some legalistic basis for their military adventures, and so Elphinstone and Craig carried with them the claims of Andrew Shillinge and Humphrey Fitzherbert to the Cape in the name of King James I in 1620. The Dutch, 'seeing the impossibility of defending Cape Town, and anxious to spare it from assault and plunder', swiftly surrendered. In turn, the British offered conciliatory terms with private property guarantees, no demands for reparations, and a commitment to uphold the local currency. This was, in their mind, a temporary occupation occasioned by the war with France, rather than the beginnings of British colonization.[44]

In addition to Cape Town, Elphinstone and Craig took possession (on behalf of His Britannic Majesty) of an extensive tract of Africa inhabited by some 20,000 Dutch-Afrikaans, over 25,000 slaves from East Africa and the East Indies, a collapsed Khoe-San population numbering around 15,000 and then, further east, a few thousand Bantu-speaking Africans.[45] Truth be told, the king's ministers had very little idea what to do with it all. Was the Cape to be held simply for the duration of the conflict with France, or should its obvious strategic benefits encourage Britain to develop the city and exploit the countryside? The agriculture and viticulture, the ship-building industry and East–West trading networks could all be usefully drawn into the service of the British Empire. Should Britain therefore start to populate its shores with industrious migrants, or continue to rely on the Dutch burghers and slave labour already in place? In 1797, in the face of continued French military threats, Dundas decided, for the time being at least, to hold on to the Cape. Lord Macartney was duly despatched to run the colony as military governor, with Andrew Barnard and Lady Anne in tow.

Macartney's first impressions were not sympathetic towards maintaining a long-term British presence. 'It does not indeed appear that this Colony is ever likely to become a source of very abundant revenue,' he reported back to Dundas in July 1797. 'Its chief importance to us arises from its geographical position, from its forming the master link of connection between the western and eastern world, from its being the great outwork of our Asiatic commerce and Indian Empire, and above all from the conviction that, if in the hands of a powerful enemy, it might enable him to shake to the foundation, perhaps overturn and destroy the whole fabric of our oriental opulence and dominion.' However, maintaining these strategic advantages would not come cheap. To defend the colony from French invasion and keep a grip on the Dutch, Cape Town would be transformed into a formidable arsenal – with '5 ships of the line, 2 of 50 guns, 7 frigates and 4 sloops or small vessels' as well as '4 battalions of infantry, 2 regiments of light dragoons and 2 companies of artillery'.[46]

As the year progressed, Macartney became ever less convinced of the capacity of the Cape Colony to sustain itself. The Dutch always ran the Cape at a large loss, and it seemed the Treasury was heading the same way. Macartney did, however, have a plan for the mainten-ance of British interests in the region. 'The more I consider the subject,' he explained in December 1797,

> the more I am confirmed in my opinion that the administration of this Colony, if retained at a Peace, should be committed to the charge of the East India Company. The possession of it ... whether in the hands of the Crown or the Company, must always be attended with a very great expence, and not a little embarrassment.

Unfortunately, the East India Company was just as adamant that it didn't want responsibility for the Cape. 'As a Colony it would be rather dangerous,' wriggled Sir Francis Baring, 'as there is too much encouragement for settlers and we have already too many drains upon our own population.'[47]

Some of Macartney's entourage were not nearly so unenthusiastic about British possession of the colony. Indeed, the wife of his colonial secretary was positively ebullient about her new life at the Castle of Good Hope. 'It is a palace, containing such a suite of apartments, as makes me fancy myself a princess when in it,' Lady Anne gleefully wrote,

> but not an Indian or Hottentot princess as I have fitted it all up in the style of a comfortable plain English house, Scotch carpets, English linen and rush bottom chairs with plenty of lolling sofas which I have had made by Regimental carpenters and stuffed by Regimental Taylors ... I shall not be stinted for room; as I have a Hall of sixty feet, a drawing room of forty, a dancing room of twenty, a tea room of thirty and three supper room.

As the Dutch moved out and the British moved in, Cape society became a little more frivolous, and the interior decoration a little more colourful. Under the professional stewardship of Lady Anne, the First Lady of the Cape, the castle's social diary rapidly filled up.

> In a week or two, I shall invite all who wish to be merry without cards, or dice, but who can talk or hop to half a dozen black fiddlers, to come

and see me on my public day which shall be once a fortnight, when the Dutch Ladys (all of whom love dancing or flirting still more) shall be kindly welcomed and the poor Ensigns and cornets shall have an opportunity of stretching their legs as well as the generals.[48]

Among those keenest to take up Lady Anne's invitation were the so-called 'Indians' or 'Hindoos' – the officers and administrators of the East India Company on their journey out east, or returning home to recover their health after years in the blistering Indian sun. For Cape Town's mild climate, refreshing south-east winds racing off Table Mountain (known as the 'Cape Doctor') and healthy diet were all greatly valued by sun-drenched soldiers and fever-ridden Company men. Rather than travelling all the way back to Britain for their leave, they took cottages in the suburbs – Kenilworth, Constantia, Plumstead or Wynberg – and came into Cape Town to complain about its lack of culture in contrast to the sophistication of Madras or Calcutta. But in Lady Anne the 'Indian men' clearly found a most worthwhile attraction, as she hosted enough guests for 'a Bengal levy every morning at breakfast'. At the centre of this circle was Lord Mornington, 'who seems anxious to gain all he can from them'.[49]

Richard Wellesley, Earl of Mornington, was the elder brother of Arthur Wellesley, future Duke of Wellington, and another favourite of Prime Minister Pitt. Born in 1760, he spent his childhood years living in the heart of Georgian Dublin in Mornington House, Merrion Street. After Eton and Oxford, where he developed a passion for the classics, he entered the House of Commons as MP for Windsor and then for the pocket borough of Old Sarum. Wellesley's growing interest in imperial politics saw him promoted to the Board of Control for India and then, to the surprise of many, appointed as governor-general of India aged only thirty-seven. Of smallish stature, at 1.7 metres, he had thick, dark hair, a high forehead, a straight Roman nose, large blue eyes and a powerful libido. The suspicious Andrew Barnard warned his wife of the 'inconsistencies' in Wellesley's character: 'he is clever but weak [and] proud . . . he will get through the task of what is entrusted to him to the satisfaction of his employers, but . . . in doing it he will get himself more looked up to than beloved'.[50]

In India, this ambitious imperialist would become known as 'the glorious little man', but in Cape Town en route to Calcutta he had more mundane issues to worry about. When he entered the Bengal breakfast one morning in November 1797 complaining of bed bugs at his own accommodation, Lady Anne took him up in an instant and moved him into the castle.

> Lord Mornington is lodged in one of our back parlours into which a little tent is put to hold the great Man and from which he has only to step out upon the bricks of our Balcony to enjoy the Cool air as it hangs over a basin full of pure water supplied by a fountain descending from the Table Mountain.

Soon enough, Mornington was also soaking up advice from the legion of India-men resting at the Cape. 'Every day produces something to entertain him, and he has a levee every morning of yellow Generals and Captains from India.' But the natural beauty of Cape Town was as equal an attraction, and Mornington liked little more than a hearty hike up Table Mountain with a furious south-easter at his back. On one such occasion the winds became too strong: '"So" said he "I laid me down with my face on the ground at the calm side of great Stone, took off my hat, tied my handkerchief round my head that it should not be blown off and while in that situation laughed most heartily at the idea of the "pomp and circumstance" in which the Governor General found himself.'[51]

During his sojourn Wellesley also had time to think more deeply about Cape Town's strategic value: its role in defending trade in the East Indies, securing territory in India and the profound threat posed by any enemy ownership. He too concluded it was a place worth retaining. In a letter to Dundas, he argued that 'as a military station I believe it to be one of the most advantageous which can be imagined to a power compelled to maintain a large European force in India'. Indeed, he doubted whether 'with the Cape in the hands of the enemy, it would be possible for you to maintain your Indian trade or empire, unless you could acquire some other settlement on the southern continent of Africa'. Characteristically, he also thought that the government of the Cape 'ought to be rendered subordinate to the governor-general, or lord lieutenant of India'.[52]

It was a view enthusiastically shared by Macartney's successor as governor of the Cape Colony. 'This country is improving fast,' wrote the former war secretary and old colonial hand Sir George Yonge when he took over from Macartney in 1799. In a series of memos sent back to Henry Dundas, Yonge urged Cape Town's retention on commercial as well as military grounds. 'Of the Importance of this Colony I need say nothing to you, but it grows in its every hour. It is and will become the Centre of Commerce with India, America, and Europe.' Indeed, 'there is not a Dominion of the Crown abroad that will be of the Value of this Colony to the Mother Country by the employment of its shipping and seamen, and by the Vent of its Manufactures . . . I know very well this has been represented as an useless Colony, and even a heavy Burthen, and a Place not worth retaining . . . the Assertion is false, and I assert that whoever has the Cape is Master of the Commerce of India.' Contrary to Macartney's plans, he urged Dundas not to push the colony off to the East India Company – 'which would be the most unwise, and I do not scruple to add, the most Dangerous Thing in the World. For the Example of American Independence teaches a Lesson on this Subject, which is against giving such great Means into the Hands of Distant Colonies to resist, or deny the Power or Rights of the Crown.'[53]

But London's imperial power-brokers were more inclined to Macartney's scepticism about the Cape's merits. Bonaparte's invasion of Egypt in 1798 led Admiralty strategists to put the claims of Malta above those of Cape Town, whilst some officers were so convinced of the Royal Navy's might to think the Cape 'a superfluous security'. What was more, the fall of Pitt's ministry in 1801 had led to the departure of Henry Dundas from government and, with him, the loss of the Cape's ablest defender. Lord Hobart, the new secretary for war and colonies, was markedly less enthusiastic. 'He could explicitly declare that he had scarcely ever met with one person who did not consider the Cape a burden rather than an advantage to this country . . . the expense of it had been enormous, its revenue did not pay its civil establishment, it was a peculiarly expensive station for ships.' Nelson himself was more damning. 'He had himself been there, and he considered it merely a tavern on the passage, which served to call at and thence often to delay the voyage. When the Dutch had it you could buy a cabbage there for twopence, but since it had been in our hands a shilling was obliged to be paid for a cabbage.'[54] (Sauerkraut was one of the more effective, if not popular, remedies for combating scurvy.)

General Sir David Baird leads the Highlanders into combat at the Battle of Blaauwberg. 1806, coloured aquatint by J. Clark and J. Hamble after William Marshall Craig,

So at the Treaty of Amiens in 1802, which produced a temporary truce between Britain and revolutionary France, the Cape Colony was handed back to Holland (then named the Batavian Republic). At the Castle of Good Hope, the commander of British forces, Lieutenant-General Francis Dundas (no relation), read out the terms of the Treaty. 'These are to signify to all the Inhabitants of this colony of every description and to all others who have taken the Oath of Allegiance to His Britannic Majesty, that from the day above mentioned they are absolved from the said Oath and return under the subjection of the Batavian Government.'

But within a year the Amiens peace was shredded, and in May 1803 Britain and France were back at war. Suddenly, the strategic significance of the Cape Colony was appreciated again and its abandonment keenly felt. In July 1805 there were growing reports of a French fleet ready to sweep into Table Bay. William Pitt, who had been in Downing Street when the French tried to invade Ireland in 1798, was now back in power and could not wait: fleets were despatched from Cork and Falmouth carrying 6,650 troops and ordered to rendezvous at Madeira, where Commodore Sir Home Popham took command. They sailed for another 120 days before anchoring in the roadstead off Robben Island. On 6 January 1806, after two days of pitching and tossing in Table Bay, General Sir David Baird led the Highlanders of the 71st, 72nd and 93rd Regiments ashore to recapture the colony. The second British invasion of the Cape was no repeat of 1795's parade, but involved a treacherous landing, with the

A view of the Cape of Good Hope. The Battle previous to the Surrender, 8 January published by Edward Orme (1806).

drowning of forty-one soldiers amid the crashing surf of Losperd's Bay, some 30 kilometres north of Cape Town. There was then an arduous trek, dragging cannons through the South African bush, before Dutch troops, under the command of Lieutenant-General J. W. Janssens, were confronted at the Battle of Blaauwberg. Over 500 casualties mounted up over the day, but in the end British military professionalism saw off the Dutch army of German mercenaries, Frenchmen, slaves and volunteer militia. Overnight, Baird pushed on towards Cape Town for a final confrontation with the Batavian forces. But Colonel Von Prophalow, commander of the Cape Town garrison, opted for surrender rather than slaughter and sent a white flag of truce out to the encircling British troops; the thick walls of the Castle of Good Hope managed to escape trial by cannonball.

On 11 January 1806, after new articles of Capitulation were signed at Papendorp, General Baird announced that, 'being in complete possession of the Town and principal Places, I am fully entitled to consider the whole of this Settlement as completely subject to His Majesty's Authority'. He was also adamant that any guerrilla resistance was futile. 'I wish lastly to point out to the whole Settlement the inevitable misery they must endure from a protracted state of warfare in the bosom of the Colony. Let them for a moment reflect on the uninterrupted state of prosperity they enjoyed a few years ago under the British Flag.'[55] The Union flag was fluttering again over Cape Castle – as it would do for the next 120 years.

ASSUMING A CHARACTER

Despite its obvious colonial affinities, the Cape turned out to be a surprisingly complex colony for the British to manage. 'As yet the people of the Cape are only about to assume a character,' thought Robert Semple. 'They are neither English, nor French, nor Dutch. Nor do they form an original class as Africans, but a singular mixture of all together, which has not as yet acquired a consistence, and is therefore almost impossible to be exactly represented.'[56] For all their shared northern European inheritance, the British found it difficult to make much headway with the Dutch and German settler communities who made up the Afrikaans-speaking population. Establishing terms of surrender and settlement was one thing, but reaching a shared social and cultural accommodation with the 'Cape Dutch' proved a more arduous task. Yes, they could be governed under the rule of law, and the Cape bureaucracy was able to make the initial transition to British administration without too many tantrums, but at heart the British did not take to the Dutch Afrikaners (a term, which gained usage from the early 1700s, to describe succeeding generations of Cape Dutch who started to speak the creole language of Afrikaans). 'Almost without exception ... you may observe the greatest coldness and indifference; and perfect apathy, mixed with a most inordinate share of pride, pervade all ranks of the Africanes,' was the view of the British author Richard Fisher. 'To Englishmen they appear an unsocial, inhospitable, and boorish race, and their actions entirely guided by mercenary and interested motives,' agreed Robert Percival. The narrow, money-grubbing commercialism of the Cape Dutch was a familiar complaint. 'Every man at the Cape is a merchant in some way or other; the whole study of the inhabitants being to make money, and they contrive to do so in numberless ways.' According to Robert Semple, 'Their ideas are almost entirely commercial; their general conversation is of buying and selling, and the best friends will sell to each other, and with a view of gain. No sooner are two or three met together, especially females, than the words dear, cheap, rix-dollars, so many schalins per ell, etc. are sure to strike the ear.'[57] As such, any display of religious piety was regarded as a sham. 'Their pretensions to religion are very slender; and, whatever little there is of it is principally among the female sex,' thought Fisher. Semple was even more damning. 'They go to church at the stated hours; they dress in black on sacramental days; they sing; they stand up and they sit down with the utmost propriety; but they do not seem to perceive the admirable adaptation of the precepts of Christianity to every situation of common life.'[58]

This was part of a broader critique of the vulgarity of the Afrikaners. Even the European Dutch were shocked at their uncouth laziness. 'The men, who are freemen of the town, are seldom seen abroad: they are generally at home, in an undress, and spend their time in smoking tobacco, and in loitering up and down the house,' complained Johan Stavorinus. 'After dinner, they take a nap, according to the Indian fashion [i.e., undressing fully], and in the evening they play a game at cards. They are not addicted to reading, and are, consequently, very ignorant.' Whilst the cities of the Dutch Republic – Amsterdam, Rotterdam and Delft – were renowned across the world for their culture and refinement, the Afrikaners were dismissed as boorish philistines. 'Few have any taste for reading, and none for the cultivation of the fine arts,' wrote John Barrow. 'They have no kind of public amusements except occasional balls ... Money-matters and merchandize engross the whole conversation.' Worst of all, they went to bed early. Whilst the British regarded colonial life as an ever-ready excuse for excessive drinking and late suppers, the Dutch conclaves of Cape Town would begin to echo to the sound of 'Welt e rusten' (May you rest well) from around 9 p.m. Perhaps what sent them to sleep so readily was the heavy cuisine. 'The manner of dressing and cooking [meat] is highly disgusting to an Englishman's palate, being so full of grease, so indifferently and dirtily dressed,' complained Percival. 'Though the meat may be good in itself, it is spoiled to us in the cooking, being soaked in stinking grease, or rank oily butter, or oil made from the fat of the sheep's tail.' Wellesley was forced to sit through many a dinner in his honour hosted by the Dutch community, with cow's heel, tripe, macaroni, boiled calf's head and finally, 'a Tureen of Bird's Nest Soup ... a mess of the most aromatic nastiness I ever tasted'.[59]

Leavening the boredom were the 'pretty, lively, and good-humoured' ladies of the Cape. John Barrow explained approvingly that the

'Dutch Frows' 'are generally of a small delicate form, below the middle size, of easy and unaffected manners, well dressed and fond of social intercourse'. Jemima Kindersley's description was a little double-edged. In contrast to the 'constitutional dullness' of the Dutch men, 'the women are more active: delicacy is not the characteristic of Dutch females, but they are decent, plump, healthy and cheerful'.[60]

But the Dutch residents – as well as the descendants of French Protestant Huguenot exiles and German and Danish merchants – were only one part of Cape Town's multicultural make-up. As we have seen, the European population of the Cape Colony was always outnumbered by both indigenous Africans and migrants from the East Indies. Then came the West African crewmen and Lascars (south Asian seamen) from the Royal Navy, a growing number of Irish and Scottish immigrants, as well as poorer British soldiers from the Highlands and northern England who ended up staying. All these helped to swell the city population to over 16,000 by the early 1800s. 'The town is composed of so many different nations,' the American missionary George Champion wrote in astonishment, 'Dutchmen, Englishmen, Germans, Scotch, Malays, Malagesh etc. and of so many different sects, Episcopalians, Dissenters, Wesleyans, Scotch, Dutch Reformed, Lutheran, Catholics, Unitarians, infidels, Mahometans, Pagans, that no general description will answer.'[61] British officials had no problem in embracing this cosmopolitan ethos. In contrast to the religious absolutism of the Victorian missionaries and governors of nineteenth-century Africa, the Georgian frame of mind was altogether more tolerant of both religious and racial diversity. And the skyline of Cape Town soon started to reflect the city's role as a place of interaction and exchange between the multiple elements of the British Empire.

Islam arrived in the Cape via the Indian Ocean slave routes, with Muslims among the thousands transplanted to the colony from the Dutch East Indies. Around one-third of slaves imported from Madagascar and East Africa were either practising Muslims or familiar with Islamic culture. What was more, many slaves converted to Islam at the Cape Colony, having quite understandably connected their own bondage with the Christian hypocrisy of their masters. 'Mahometanism is greatly on the increase in Cape-Town,' reported a worried John Campbell of the Missionary Society, called to South Africa to protect the souls of the British army in 1815. 'They have, I believe, five mosques, where they assemble for their worship. About twenty free Mahometans club together, and rent a large house, to which they invite poor ignorant slaves to gain them over to the party.' Not afraid to confront heterodoxy wherever it surfaced, Campbell ventured into a mosque. 'The place was small – the floor was covered with green baize, on which sat about a hundred men, chiefly slaves, Malays, and Madagascars. All of them wore clean white robes, made in the fashion of shirts, and white pantaloons, with white cotton cloths spread before them, on which they prostrated themselves.'[62] Campbell was right to highlight the strength of Islam. By the 1830s, there were 6,000 Muslims in Cape Town, served by a range of mosques, prayer rooms and madrasses. Campbell was probably unaware that the existence of the Cape Town mosques and the open practice of Islam were partly products of British rule. With no centre for assembly and with prayer forced to take place in the open, 'in the stone quarries at the head of the town, in 1797 Macartney had agreed to the establishment of a Muslim place of worship. This became the Auwal, South Africa's first official mosque. Its teachings were drawn from the Muslim Shafi'i tradition, reflecting the East Indies (or Indonesian) make-up of its worshippers, whilst its first imam was an influential Moluccan priest, the Dutch political prisoner and theologian imam Abdullah ibn Qadi Abd al-Salam. Indeed, Dutch attempts to silence political protest in Indonesia by exiling troublesome clerics to Cape Town was an important component in the growth of Islam in South Africa. Today, Friday prayers continue at the Auwal on Dorp Street in the beautiful, edgy, low-rise 'Cape Malay' Bo-Kaap district of Cape Town – the historic home of free blacks, coloureds and slaves in the city. The prayer site is now joined by a further ten mosques in the Bo-Kaap neighbourhood, whose minarets puncture the skyline at the foot of Table Mountain and provide a physical expression of the 'rainbow' diversity of Cape Town's heritage.

As well as a commitment to religious tolerance, the British were equally keen to disassociate themselves from the Dutch use of slavery. The gallows and the rack were publicly destroyed as the British announced an end to torture and a new policy of paternalistic 'benevolence' towards the indigenous and enslaved peoples. 'On hearing that the abolition of the rack and torture was likely to take place, he [the hangman] waited upon the chief magistrate to know whether it was the fashion among the English to break on the wheel. A few days later he was found hanging in his room,' according to John Barrow.[63] After centuries of slave-trading and murder, after the brutality of Bridgetown's Cage and the atrocities of the sugar plantations, a new conception of Britain as an 'Empire of Liberty', dedicated to the furtherance of human freedom, was just starting to dawn. In 1807 the British abolished the trade in slaves across its imperial possessions, and in the Cape Colony the administration was keen to publicize its emancipation credentials. In 1809 a 'Hottentot Code' was enacted in order to prevent Dutch landowners from enslaving what remained of the Khoekhoe people and to mitigate some of the abuses still meted out to them on the farmsteads.[64] The Slave Lodge was abolished and the building turned into the Cape's Supreme Court ('in the process, the Lodge was stripped of its slave history,' as the museum puts it). Then the Royal Navy raiding parties on 'illegal' slavers in the Indian and Atlantic Oceans began. 'A slave ship containing many slaves from Madagascar and Mozambique, was lately captured by one of our cruisers,' the missionary John Campbell recorded approvingly. 'The slaves were landed at Cape Town, and apprenticed to masters for 14 years, who are bound by agreement to treat them well, to teach them a trade, and to instruct them in reading and in the principles of the Christian religion.'[65] This 'apprenticeship system' – a mode of indentured labour – would continue even beyond the official abolition of slavery within the British Empire in 1834. In Cape Town the practice of enforced apprenticeships lasted until the late 1830s, but that did not stop the British presenting their rule in Cape Town as a beacon of civilization in contrast to that of the barbaric Dutch. At the beginning of British rule there genuinely was a conviction that this cosmopolitan port city would be governed on very different principles from those of their exploitative and abusive colonial predecessors.

For after the 1806 recapture of Cape Town it seemed certain that British rule would now extend into the future. The need to operate a safe commercial and military passage to India, to square off the French strategic threat, and to have a secure station for the Royal Navy (which moved from Table Bay to Simon's Bay in 1813) all necessitated a permanent presence at the Cape of Good Hope. As a result, the British colonial footprint began to spread across Cape Town. At its peak, in around 1810, the Cape garrison contained almost 6,500 soldiers, giving it a larger military capacity than either Gibraltar or Malta. In response, the cityscape of Cape Town, after over a decade of invasionary fear and to-and-fro warfare, was transformed into a mountainside of batteries, forts, towers, lighthouses, magazines and barracks – all set alongside the great castle itself. There was, for instance, the Chevone battery, which had, 'level with the sea, one great tier of guns, and farther back, but more elevated, another range, with a flanking redoubt at each end, to enfilade both edges of the shore. This battery is capable of greatly annoying ships standing into the bay, immediately on their rounding Green Point.' Five hundred metres along stood the Amsterdam battery, 'with a rampart round it, and bomb proof . . . It is capable of containing at least two hundred troops, in the ranges of barracks and store houses in the body of the work.'[66]

Along the coastline in Simon's Bay, the Royal Navy squadron consisted of some thirty to forty ships of the line alongside smaller cruisers and nearly 3,000 sailors housed in Simonstown (where the Royal Navy would remain until 1955). The symbolic significance of this naval base was richly apparent after 1815, when the defeated Napoleon Bonaparte was exiled to the island of St Helena until his death in 1821. With naval responsibilities stretching from Cape Verde around Agulhas to Mauritius, the provisioning of St Helena with Constantia wine, meats, fruits and other necessities fell to the sailors of Simonstown. The Royal Navy, which had kept Cape Town from becoming a sword in the hand of France, could enjoy its victory all the more now it was in charge of victualling its chief tormentor.

After the reinvasion of 1806, successive British administrators became more committed to the long-term prosperity of the Cape. British rule was no longer just a holding operation; it was a determination to develop southern Africa as a component part of the Empire. The debate of the 1790s between the East India Company grandees and Whitehall defence officials as to the viability of the Cape as an imperial possession was forgotten as the British government began to encourage trade in the colony's natural resources and use the port as a trading hub. Its perfect positioning as 'the master link of connection between the western and eastern world' meant the colony was well located for the East India Company flotillas sailing from Calcutta, Madras and Bombay back to Britain. Cape Town also developed a vibrant entrepôt trade in importing timber from Port Jackson, tobacco and cinnamon from Ceylon, Mauritian sugar, Réunion coffee and cloth from Madras. With the Cape now a component part of Empire, the colony's own wines, wheat and barley, its whale fisheries and merino wool were given easier access to UK markets, with often preferential tariffs. British merchant interest in Cape Town expanded markedly in the early 1800s, and it was not long before a Commercial Exchange, Cape of Good Hope Bank, joint-stock companies and insurance and legal services industry were springing up in the city.[67]

In one sense, this was Henry Dundas's vision of trade and territory, the Royal Navy and mercantilism, at work. Capture of the Cape Colony had given Britain control of the Indian Ocean and, in the process, helped to exclude the French from any sovereign threat to her Indian possessions. Yet, as the nineteenth century advanced, the British administration in the Cape did exactly what Dundas had warned against in 1775, by peopling the colony and establishing permanent settlements.

Symbolic of Cape Town's change in tone was the 1814 appointment of Lord Charles Somerset as the new governor. Born in 1767, the second of eight sons of Henry, Duke of Beaufort, Somerset was desperately proud of his Plantagenet bloodline stretching back to King Edward III; his youth at Badminton was spent riding to the Beaufort Hunt. In the early 1800s, he was a prominent member of the Prince Regent's louche circle in Brighton and London and was frankly horrified by the boondock philistinism he encountered on his arrival at the Cape. The locals were not too enamoured either. 'If England is determined to use us only as a depot for the dregs of her Aristocracy – if her surplus idlers are to be quartered upon us at this rate – we would ... advise our countrymen to avoid these shores,' was the response Somerset received from the radical journalist John Fairbairn in the pages of the *South African Commercial Advertiser*.[68]

From the outset, Somerset's ambition was to raise Cape Town to the kind of cultural sophistication evident in its sister imperial cities of Dublin and Bridgetown. He began with the 'dog-kennel', as he called it, of Government House, expanding it with new wings and a 23-metre ballroom decorated with blue and gold wallpaper in the Bourbon style, plaster mouldings on the ceiling, lead chandelier roses and cornices. At the summer residence of Newlands, he inserted two original French marble fireplaces. The modest burghers of Dutch, Calvinist Cape Town had never witnessed such splendour.

Most importantly of all for the future aesthetics of Cape Town, Somerset introduced the veranda into the new Government House. It marked the beginnings of an architectural transformation in the colony as Dutch domestic design started to make way for more flamboyant, Regency styles. Street lamps were attached to corner houses and ornamental ironwork, reminiscent of Merrion Square and St Stephen's Green, appeared on upper windows. Houses were now built with porticoes and light, latticed verandas with curving zinc roofs. Burchell's beloved *stoep* was abandoned for closed porches. Glass windows replaced shuttered windows, plastered ceilings infilled open beams, and thatched roofs were exchanged for tiles. There were now trellised balustrades and a new, naturalistic focus on garden design and the picturesque. Indeed, Lady Anne and Andrew Barnard themselves led the fashion by building 'The Vineyard', a simple cottage (sleeping ten) at the bottom of Table Mountain's eastern buttress, complete with rustic verandas and naturalistic charm.[69]

The interior life of Cape Town changed as houses became partitioned up into a series of social settings for the quickening round of visits: drawing rooms, dining rooms and the latest fashion of breakfast rooms. In place of the Spartan simplicity and cool emptiness of the Dutch homes, the British settlers now filled up their houses with chintz curtains, horsehair sofas, English carpets, marbled chimney pieces (following Somerset's lead), mahogany furniture, flounced dressing tables and Staffordshire ceramics. At Government House, 'instead of finding a dirty old house with a perpendicular staircase, up which Lord Macartney hopped, gout and all, like a parrot on its perch', as Lady Anne unkindly put it, there were now elegantly painted and wallpapered state rooms.[70]

Somerset's second significant innovation was in the sporting field, allocating a great deal of effort in building up the South African Turf

Club. William Burchell had once visited the Green Point racetrack to the west of Table Bay and rather enjoyed its ragged, multicultural point-to-point feel. 'Horsemen, without number, fly backwards and forwards to watch the fate of the day; and exhibit their prancing steeds of half Arab or English blood ... Nor is it less amusing to watch the motley group on foot: Malays and Negroes mingled with whites, all crowding and elbowing, eager to get a sight of the momentous contest.'[71] Somerset clearly felt there was not nearly enough 'English blood' in the Cape stables and he began importing thoroughbreds from Badminton.

His other import was foxhounds. British regimental officers had been hunting buck on the Cape Flats since the mid-1790s, but by the time Somerset turned up steenbuck were finished, and they usually had to make do with jackals. 'I have been three times a hunting and have had a very capital run each time,' he wrote to his brother in England after his arrival in 1814. 'They hunt Fox and two sorts of Deer, whichever they happen to find; the Duyker a large brown deer goes straight away and shows fine sport. The Jackhal is exactly our Fox except that he is larger and has rather a smaller Brush.' But while his horses were good enough for the chase, Somerset desperately needed a better class of dog. 'I should be very much oblig'd to you if you would save five couples of unenter'd draft hounds for me when your puppies come in next Christmas, and if you could also send me an old Dog Hound for a stallion Hound.'[72]

At work as well as in play, Somerset oversaw the steady Anglicization of Cape culture. In 1812, the Latin School in Cape Town was instructed by Government House 'to promote and establish the cultivation of the English language to the greatest extent among your pupils of the highest rank, as the foundation upon which they will in their future life best make their way'. Somerset took the policy further by replacing Dutch teachers 'by Englishmen of a superior class, as affording both the best means of making the English language more general in the Colony and improving the manners and morals of the people'. In official documentation, English took over from Dutch, and British jurisprudence subsumed Dutch law as the colony's legal system. In matters spiritual, Scottish Calvinist ministers started to assume the ministries at Dutch Reformed churches, and Anglican services became the norm. Increasingly frozen out of law, politics and business, Cape Town's original Dutch residents became progressively disillusioned and resentful of British rule – so much so that many allied themselves with the Boer farmers to join the Great Trek northward in the 1830s out of the Cape Colony and into the Transvaal.[73]

In addition to the English language, law, religion and domestic style, the Cape's civic infrastructure was also turning more obviously British with public libraries, museums, Royal Observatory and Mechanics' Institute all aping the mother country's civil society. Soon enough there were Union flags billowing in the Table Mountain breeze, amateur dramatic productions of *She Stoops to Conquer* playing at the African Theatre, the military band thumping out 'The British Grenadiers' from the castle parade ground, cricket games between 'Colonial Born' and 'Mother Country', a comforting Anglican spire at St George's Cathedral and whist at the Harmony Club. By the mid-nineteenth century the city and its suburbs had become, in the words of its foremost biographers, 'an identifiably British colonial city'.[74] 'The country, as far as Rondebosch, Wynberg, and Constantia, is really delightful, and more than any other part of the colony, resembles the rich, cultivated scenery of England,' happily concluded William Burchell.[75]

One of Cape Town's more popular new clubs was the Cape of Good Hope Association for Exploring Central Africa. Formed to finance a trip by the army doctor Andrew Smith into Natal, this committee of well-placed British settlers was perhaps the first sign of Cape Town's future function. For in the latter half of the nineteenth century, with the development of wheat fields and vineyard production, the discovery of diamonds in Kimberley and gold in Witwatersrand and the advent of the railways, the British Empire would become much more interested in what journalist John Fairbairn called the 'repelling genius' of the African interior. As it was, in the early 1800s, the importance of Cape Town still lay in its connections to the exterior world. Its vital position as the Gibraltar of the south, as the master connection between east and west, meant control of the Cape allowed sovereignty over India and, with it, the foundations of the Second Empire. Henceforth, no other European power would have the strength to match Britain as a global empire. The creation of naval supremacy, in which Cape Town played so significant a part, meant that the whole world was now Britain's market. In the words of *A Treatise on the Wealth, Power and Resources of the British Empire, In Every Quarter of the World, Including the East Indies* (1815), 'the magnitude and splendour of the resources which have been thus developed cannot fail to fill the mind of every British subject with exultation and gratitude to the Supreme Being for the numerous blessings conferred on this highly favoured nation'.[76]

No visitor to the Cape signified this role as the axis of east and west, the lynchpin of nineteenth-century imperialism, more than Richard Wellesley. From Cape Town, Wellesley continued his journey to what stood by the late eighteenth century as the richest and grandest metropolis in the British Empire. In May 1798, the new governor-general set sail for Calcutta.

5

Calcutta

'The City of Palaces'

Nothing could equal the magnificence of my approach to this town. For nearly three miles the river, which is as large as the Thames at London, is bordered by lovely well-built country houses with porticoes and colonnades. The town is a mass of superb palaces in the same style, with the finest fortress in the world – all this is, as in Rome, mixed up with miserable huts and gardens. The green of the lawns surpasses anything you can ever have seen – an extraordinary effect in so hot a country.[1]

It did not take long for the one-time classics scholar Richard Wellesley, as the incoming governor-general of India, to add his own Roman imprint to Calcutta. 'The state rooms were for the first time lighted up,' recalled the young Lord Valentia of the opening of Wellesley's Government House in 1803. 'At the upper end of the largest was placed a very rich Persian carpet, and in the centre of that, a musnud [throne cushion] of crimson and gold, formerly composing part of the ornament of Tipu Sultan's throne.' At about ten o'clock, Lord Wellesley, wearing the order of St Patrick, arrived from Fort William, 'attended by a large body of aide-de-camps, etc., and after receiving, in the northern verandah, the compliments of some of the native princes, and the vakeels [agents] of the others, took his seat. The dancing then commenced, and continued till supper'. After the 800 guests had dined in the marble hall, 'thence they were summoned about one o'clock to the different verandahs to see the fireworks and illuminations'.

Ceremony was integral to Wellesley's idea of Empire. Of course,

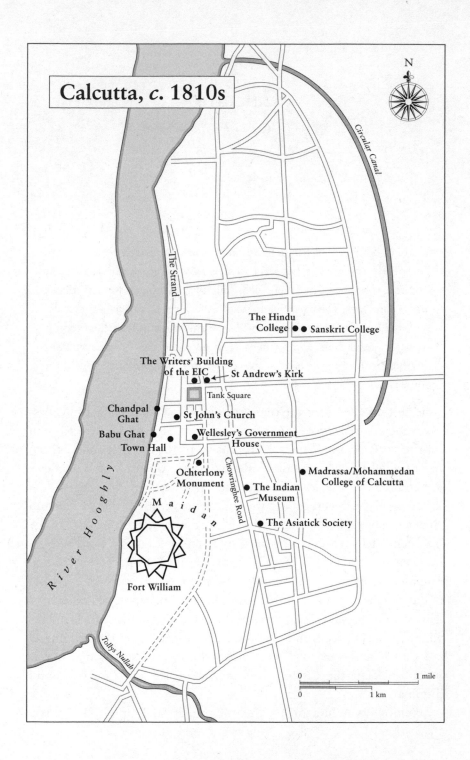

Calcutta, *c.* 1810s

N

Circular Canal

The Strand

The Hindu
College ●● Sanskrit College

The Writers' Building
of the EIC
● St Andrew's Kirk
☐ Tank Square

Chandpal
Ghat ● ● St John's Church

Babu Ghat ● ● Wellesley's Government
Town Hall House

Ochterlony
Monument

Madrassa/Mohammedan
College of Calcutta

● The Indian
Museum

Chowringhee Road

M a i d a n

● The Asiatick Society

River Hooghly

Fort William

Tolly's Nullah

0   1 mile
0   1 km

critics would grumble about the cost, admitted Valentia, 'but they ought to remember, that India is a country of splendour, of extravagance, and of outward appearance; that the Head of a mighty empire ought to conform himself to the prejudices of the country he rules over'. In short, Wellesley was determined for 'India to be ruled from a palace, not from a counting-house; with the ideas of a Prince, not with those of a retail dealer in muslin and indigo'.[2]

Such Augustan swagger was to define the ethos of Wellesley's Calcutta, a colonial citadel which cemented Britain's 'Swing to the East' and, with it, a much more stately and ambitious vision of Empire. The growth of Calcutta was both a symbol and signal of the expanding territorial might of the British Empire in India. And it was embodied in the neo-classical majesty of Wellesley's Government House and the rituals of oriental extravagance which enveloped it. This was a building designed to affirm an Empire of conquest as well as commerce, and as a conscious affront to the sprawling complex which stood opposite it – the Writers' Building of the East India Company. Looking like 'a shabby hospital, or poors-house', this elongated, Victorian Gothic edifice (built in the 1770s and renovated in the 1880s) originally contained 'apartments for the writers newly come from Britain'.[3] The writers were the teenage apprentices of the East India Company, shipped to Calcutta to run a counting-house Empire which Wellesley thought was corrupt, sordid and ignoble. These 'cheesemongers of Leadenhall Street' (the site of the Company's headquarters in London) 'are so vulgar, ignorant, rude, familiar and stupid', thought Wellesley, as to be 'disgusting and intolerable'.[4] Theirs was a cut-price approach to power, built on Bengal's muslin and silk trade, which could only reflect poorly on a Britain called forth to an altogether grander global purpose. That Atlantic empire of trade and commerce, slaves and sugar, even Henry Dundas's strategy of trading posts and naval forts had now to accede to Britain's grander Second Empire of sovereignty and dominion; the Writers' Building was going to make way for the primacy, across Dalhousie Square, of Government House.

Today, Government House is the Raj Bhavan, the governor's official residence, and the Writers' Building is base for the chief secretariat of West Bengal. Where once the pallid young men of the East India Company nursed their ledgers, shirt-sleeved functionaries now wander along the balconies, muttering on mobile phones. The building is, in the words of one architectural critic, 'a consummate manifestation of bureaucratic humanity'.[5] Above the balcony still stands the high Victorian statuary celebrating the achievements of 'Commerce' and 'Agriculture', while below West Bengal intellectual life flourishes amid the colonnades' bookstalls and newspaper vendors. But the incessant, noisy traffic they look out upon no longer crawls around Dalhousie Square (named after the former British governor-general), but Benoy-Badal-Dinesh Bagh – renamed in honour of three Indian nationalist martyrs who in 1930 shot dead Lieutenant-Colonel Norman Skinner Simpson, the inspector general of prisons, at the Writers' Building before fighting a pitched battle with the police along the corridors. In 2001, Calcutta completed its postcolonial renaming by rechristening the entire city with the more Bengali-sounding title of Kolkata.

Bengal's role within the story of Indian independence – providing the heartland of India's radical political tradition; forcing (as we shall see) the movement of the British capital to New Delhi in 1911; and fostering the most left-wing response to any vestige of colonial capitalism in its trenchant support for the Communist Party of India (Marxist) and Communist Party of India (Marxist-Leninist) – might naturally produce expectations of an unforgiving approach to its imperial past. And yet all around BBD Bagh, in the old Dihi Kalikata district, the imperial fabric is exceptionally well preserved. 'No longer is there an anxiety that we have to be anticolonial,' explains the municipal commissioner, Alapan Bandyopadhyay.[6] You certainly get a sense of that cultural confidence when stepping into the colonnaded portico of St Andrew's Kirk, a crisp Regency replica of London's St Martins-in-the-Fields, down the road from the Writers' Building and recently restored as a reminder of the Scottish contribution to the growth of early Calcutta. By contrast, the elegiac grandeur of nearby St John's Church is fiercely Anglican. Its steeple rises high above the skyline, its walls are littered with tablets to the fallen foot soldiers of the imperial mission – men like Michael Cheese Esq., 'Surgeon on the Honourable Company's Bengal Establishment, and Garrison Surgeon of Fort William. Dedicated by Public Contribution, In Token of the High Esteem of this Community for the Enlarged and Practical

Philanthropy of that Gentleman's Character'. The memorials continue in the church grounds, between the banana plants and corrugated iron railings, to the 'well-loved and respected' 'Begum' Frances Johnson (and her four marriages), Vice Admiral Charles Watson and 'Jobus Charnock' – Job Charnock, founder of modern Calcutta. Removed from Dalhousie Square in 1940, the Viceroy Lord Curzon's memorial to the Black Hole of Calcutta – 'To the Memory of 123 Persons, Who Perished in the Black Hole prison of Old Fort William, On the night of the 20th of June, 1756' – also lingers here as a reminder of one of the most elemental identifiers of Calcutta in the British colonial psyche and as justification for so much imperial assertiveness.[7]

Curzon's other great monument – the Victoria Memorial – retains its original position, resplendent on the southern edge of Kolkata's vast city park, the Maidan. Indeed, almost every element of central Kolkata retains its sweeping imperial sense of metropolitan enormity. Conceived in 1905 and completed in 1921, the memorial was to be the British Empire's answer to the Taj Mahal, using the same marble (from Makrana in Jodhpur) and combining grandiose, Edwardian Baroque architecture with Saracenic styling, 'a suggestion of orientalism in the arrangement of the domes and minor details'. Curzon wanted this sepulchral homage to the late queen empress to be 'a building stately, spacious, monumental and grand . . . where all classes will learn the lessons of history and see revived before their eyes the marvels of the past'.[8] Today, as a heritage site-cum-museum, it does just that. Of course, the collections have changed from the days of Curzon, when the monument's compact, little museum was replete with artefacts of colonial conquest; now, the installations tell the story of modern Bengal through its heritage of visual arts to a predominantly Indian audience of local sightseers. But in a corner of the Persian Room, the colonial past stands firm in the form of a very svelte statue of Wellesley – hand on hip; peerage robes, Caesar-cropped hair, angular nose, scroll in hand – looking every bit the imperial general. It was erected, the inscription reads, 'by the British inhabitants of Bengal in testimony of their high sense of the wisdom, energy, and rectitude of his administration'.

Such unexpected levels of preservation are partly the product of contemporary Kolkata's ex-urban growth. Even as the city revives its

Bengali heritage, the Bengali middle classes have been leaving the old municipal area.[9] The energy in this city is now on the boomburb rims – along the motorways, around the airport, hurtling into the countryside – as tower-blocks and commuter villages lure the professional and managerial classes away from the civic centre and into the eastern peripheries. Kolkata's traditional manufacturing economy of jute, engineering, steel and textiles has been superseded by a service economy of retail, hospitality and education suited to out-of-town business parks. And so the urban core of Kolkata is left to the past, with its crumbling warehouses, power outages, streets regularly flooded by rainstorms and political in-fighting between the Communist and Congress parties. This is a cityscape of walking tours through Rudyard's Kipling's Old Calcutta – 'the many-sided, the smoky, the magnificent', with its 'deep, full-throated boom of life and motion and humanity'.[10] It is, in the words of one *New York Times flâneur*, 'more a journey through the grimy layers of time. History is inscribed on every lane, like tattoos on an aging diva.'[11] And the *Chai* conversation is all of decline – how the one-time 'Second City of the British Empire' has, like Glasgow or Liverpool, been left behind as Mumbai, Bangalore and Delhi come to embody the materialist ambition of liberalized, 'BRIC' India: a nation whose accelerating growth rates, following the early 1990s deregulation, herald a very different 'Swing to the East'. It is a city out of joint with the times. 'India changed rapidly, often disturbingly, after 1991,' writes the novelist Amit Chaudhuri of his home city, 'Calcutta remained resistant to globalisation and the new world order, cultivating their irrelevance to itself, and its own to theirs.'[12]

In 2011, the Kolkata authorities had become so concerned by their relative decline that the new chief minister of West Bengal, Mamata Banerjee, decreed a £60 million development plan not just to match Mumbai or Chennai, but to turn the city 'into another London'.[13] Plans were announced for a Kolkata Eye, modelled on London's South Bank ferris wheel; the redevelopment of Alipore Zoo along the lines of London Zoo; and a redesign of Curzon Park as a Hooghly-side version of Hyde Park. In the face of declining business investment and urban irrelevance in the New India, a century of West Bengal anti-colonialism was done away with as Ms Banerjee looked, of all places, to the old imperial capital for inspiration and the past re-emerged replete with colonial irony. As Kipling himself had once written of Calcutta, 'Why, this is London! This is the docks. This is Imperial. This is worth coming across India to see!'[14]

THE PLASSEY REVOLUTION

'August 24. This day at Sankraal, I ordered Captain Brooke to come up with a vessel to Chuttanuty, where we arrived about noon, but found the place in a deplorable condition, nothing being left for our present accommodation, the rains falling day and night,' recorded Job Charnock, an agent in the East India Company, in his diary for 1690. 'In consideration that all the former buildings here are destroyed, it is resolved that such places be built as necessity requires and as cheap as possible ... these to be done with mud walls and thatched till we get ground whereon to build a factory.' So, at the tail end of the seventeenth century, the foundations of British Calcutta were laid among the Indian villages of Kolikata, Govindapore and Sutanuti –themselves surrounded by a series of smaller hamlets (*dihis*), formed of agricultural and fishing settlements, inhabited by weavers, potters, oil-pressers, as well as farmers and fishermen. This territorial toehold was the outcome of a disastrous military incursion by the Company into Bengal in 1686 to carve out a proper trading operation along the Hooghly River. In the event, British forces made little substantive progress against the Mughal emperor Aurangzeb. After three years of skirmishing – which 'only rendered our nation ridiculous', according to Charnock – they ended up with a small 'factory' and fort. Just as at Bridgetown, few were impressed with Charnock's original site. 'He could not have chosen a more unhealthful place in all the River,' commented Captain Alexander Hamilton. A nearby saltwater lake, subject to periodic droughts, meant that 'putrefaction affects the air with thick stinking vapours which the North-east winds bring with them to Fort William', so causing 'a yearly Mortality'.[15]

As with the Massachusetts Bay Company in Boston, the slave traders in Bridgetown, and the VOC in Cape Town, the original energy for Calcutta came from a semi-public corporation – in this case, the most powerful colonial agent of them all, the Honourable East India

Company, often known as 'John Company'. Established on New Year's Eve 1600 by Queen Elizabeth I as 'The Governor and Company of Merchants of London Trading to the East Indies', its remit was to bring back valuable commodities – pepper from Java, cloves from the Moluccas, tea from China – which should be 'bought, bartered, procured, exchanged, or otherwise obtained'. As part of its Royal Charter, the Company was also entrusted with a broader policy remit for the 'advancement of trade' for England (and eventually Great Britain) around the world. Accompanying the grant were a series of privileges, the most valuable of which was a monopoly over all commerce between England and the lands beyond the Cape of Good Hope.[16]

That meant India and, in particular, it meant Bengal. The quality of Bengal's cotton yarn and textiles – as well as its salt, opium, indigo and saltpetre – had been attracting European interest since the early 1500s. First the Portuguese and then the Dutch put down trading stations along the Hooghly River to warehouse and then export Bengal's material riches back to Europe. By the time the English established themselves, the Danes were at Serampore, the French at Chandernagore, and the Dutch at Chinsura. Taking ruthless advantage of the crumbling dominion of the Mughal Empire, the East India Company was quick to overtake its European competitors. In 1696, ramparts for Calcutta's first Fort William were constructed between the Hooghly on the west and Lal Dighi (a pool of fresh water) on the east, much of it where today's BBD Dagh roundabout now stands. It soon housed a trading hall, warehouses, the governor's residence, an armory, soldiers' barracks, and officers' lodgings for the East India Company. In 1698, Prince Azim-ush-shan, the Mughal emperor's viceroy for Bengal, Bihar and Orissa, was persuaded to grant the Company lordship or *zamindari* rights, including powers of tax collection, over the surrounding villages. 'The best money that ever was spent' was the judgement of Company directors in Leadenhall Street of the Bengal investment. By the early 1700s, some 90 per cent of East India Company cargoes were coming out of India: cotton textiles from Gujarat; pepper from Bombay; and silk and cotton cloth from Bengal. Just as sugar from Barbados changed the British diet, textile imports from Bengal transformed fashion and allowed for the mass consumption of cheap, lightweight fabrics. From the 1720s, assisted by the granting of further trading rights by the local governor (or *nawab*) of Bengal and working closely with local banking networks, shipments from Calcutta amounted to almost 50 per cent of Indian cargoes, with new wharfs (*ghats*) and factories established up and down the Hooghly to meet demand. By the mid-eighteenth century, the city of Calcutta building up around Lal Dighi could boast upwards of 100,000 people, making it larger than any British conurbation bar London.[17]

Soon enough, the East India Company started to break its contract with the Mughal princes. Contrary to agreement, agents started to dabble in duty-free private trade, while tax exemptions were sold to local merchants which deprived the *nawab* of his revenues. In 1756, the new, 21-year-old *nawab*, Siraj-ud-Daula – with assistance from the French – brought an end to the Company's illegal profiteering by storming Fort William and taking Calcutta. It was during the course of this assault that over 100 Company prisoners died, it was reported, of asphyxiation in the notorious 'black hole', a cell in the grounds of the fort. In turn, the 'Black Hole of Calcutta' became an indelible and useful tale of Indian barbarism and British stoicism – 'Many to the right and left sunk with the violent pressure, and were soon suffocated; for now a steam arose from the living and the dead, which affected us in all its circumstances, as if we were forcibly held with our heads over a bowl full of strong volatile spirit of hartshorn, until suffocated' – that would be recycled time and again to justify the extension of Empire across India.[18] The nature of the confinement and the numbers of casualties were nowhere near as dramatic as suggested. But all too real was the impact of Siraj-ud-Daula's capture of Calcutta: the East India Company share price collapsed, calico prices rose 50 per cent, and plans for a British counter-attack had to be rapidly drawn up.[19]

'We have always thought it strange,' the Victorian historian and Indian statesman Thomas Babington Macaulay would later muse in his celebrated 'Essay on Lord Clive':

> that while the history of the Spanish empire in America is familiarly known to all the nations of Europe, the great actions of our

countrymen in the East should, even among ourselves, excite little interest ... It might have been expected that every Englishman who takes any interest in any part of history would be curious to know how a handful of his countrymen, separated from their home by an immense ocean, subjugated, in the course of a few years, one of the greatest empires in the world. Yet, unless we greatly err, this subject is, to most readers, not only insipid but positively distasteful.

In Macaulay's judgement, this remarkable history of subjugation began with the retaking of Calcutta and Clive of India's victory at the 1757 Battle of Plassey.[20]

Robert Clive sprang from an unremarkable wing of the eighteenth-century Shropshire gentry and was sent off as a Company writer to Madras in 1742 to seek his fortune. Having been blooded in a series of battles against the French in the struggle for control of southern India, Clive advanced up the military wing of the Company. His martial capacities overshadowed his accountancy skills, but he was always very good at numbers when it came to his own enrichment. As victory followed victory, a relieved East India Company advanced the avaricious Clive suitably generous attestations of gratitude. So, together with Vice Admiral Watson, Clive was the obvious choice to lead the campaign against Siraj-ud-Daula. Calcutta was retaken in January 1757 and in June, at Plassey in Bengal, Clive's force of 3,000 troops (two-thirds of whom were Indian) routed the *nawab*'s army. Siraj-ud-Daula was deposed and then assassinated; in his place came the new *nawab*, Mir Jafar, installed as a client prince of the East India Company. In swift succession, French factories were eliminated, Clive garnered presents worth £234,000 alongside land revenue rights, and the Company extracted various compensation funds from the new *nawab*. 'This great revolution, so happily brought about, seems complete in every respect,' Clive breezily wrote back to the Company directors.[21]

In fact, it would take the deposition of a further succession of *nawabs* followed by the Battle of Buxar in 1764 against combined Mughal forces for the British to gain a total grip over Bengal. But it was worth the wait. The 1765 Treaty of Allahabad, signed by Clive and the Mughal emperor Shah Alam II, granted the Company the imperial post of *diwan*, or revenue collector, over the Mughal provinces of Bengal, Bihar and Orissa in return for military support and an annual tribute of 26 *lakhs* of rupees a year to the emperor (equivalent to £330,000). The settlement gave the British power to rule over some 20 million people in Bengal together with access to an annual revenue of around £2–3 million, which could be used to fund a 25,000-strong army and grow the Company's export business. This was Clive's so-called 'Plassey revolution', in which conquest, administration and trade were all now intimately connected: a series of military advances which vastly enriched the East India Company, expanded the reach of British influence up to the edges of Delhi and began the bleeding of Bengal. 'Enormous fortunes were thus rapidly accumulated at Calcutta, while thirty millions of human beings were reduced to the extremity of wretchedness,' wrote Macaulay of Clive's legacy. 'They had been accustomed to live under tyranny, but never tyranny like this. They found the little finger of the Company thicker than the loins of Surajah Dowlah.' Company rule, 'strong with all the strength of civilization', proved 'the most oppressive form of barbarian despotism'.[22]

The 'unrequited trade', as it was known, saw some 85 per cent of Bengal's external trade in the hands of the East India Company by the end of the eighteenth century, with funds leaving India for Britain at an annual rate of some £1.3 million. High levels of taxation, monopolistic trade practices, the squeezing of suppliers all served to beggar what had previously been one of the most prosperous and vibrant regions of India. The muslin weavers and silk winders felt the full force of Leadenhall economics as the open market for their goods was eliminated, prices slashed, and Company middle men enriched. According to the former Company official William Bolts's chronicle of British rule in Bengal, *Considerations on India Affairs* (1772), 'various and innumerable' were 'the methods of oppressing the poor weavers ... such as by fines, imprisonments, floggings, forcing bonds from them, etc. by which the number of weavers in the country has been greatly decreased. The natural consequences whereof have been, the scarcity, dearness and debasement of the manufactures, as well as a great diminution of the revenues.'[23]

And then the rains failed. Inadequate monsoons and the spectre of famine had long been a feature of Bengal life, to which the habitual response of Mughal rulers was to ease taxation and provide charitable relief. The approach of the East India Company was rather different: agents started to fuel price speculation by buying up rice grain and hoarding stock in Company warehouses. This was then not released to the starving Bengalis, but sold at inflated prices in Calcutta and Murshidabad. At the same time, Company agents hiked up land taxes. The inevitable result was a famine of grotesque proportions, needlessly exacerbated by the depravity of East India Company agents. 'We have another scene coming to light of a black dye indeed. The groans of India have mounted to heaven,' wrote the Whig politician Horace Walpole on 5 March 1772 in a letter to his friend, the British diplomat Sir Horace Mann. 'We have murdered, deposed, plundered, usurped – nay, what think you of the famine in Bengal, in which three millions perished, being caused by a monopoly of the provisions by the servants of the East India Company.'[24]

Just as bad, according to one Calcutta merchant, was the fact that these self-same Company servants who, 'after exhibiting such scenes of barbarity as can scarcely be paralleled in the history of any country, have returned to England loaded with wealth'.[25] With relatively low regular salaries, the writers enriched themselves through private practice. They piled on the perquisites by means of either 'country trade' – transporting goods in private British vessels westward to the Persian Gulf, or eastward to China and South-east Asia – or 'inland trade', which entailed taking loans from Indian merchants and using their positions of power within the Company to carry on their own commerce. In the event, huge fortunes were made. These were the wealthy, vulgar, louche 'nabobs' (most likely a play upon the Indian *nawab*) who had started to overtake West Indian planters in the stocks of public opinion. 'Arrived in England, the destroyers of the nobility and gentry of a whole kingdom will find the best company in this nation, at a board of elegance and hospitality,' thundered Edmund Burke during one his regular denunciations of the corruption, jobbery and immorality of Company rule in India. 'Here the manufacturer and the husbandman will bless the just and punctual hand, that in India has torn the cloth from the loom, or wrested the scanty portion of rice and salt from the peasants of Bengal.'[26] While an estimated 1.2 million Bengalis starved to death from famine (rather than Walpole's three million), the East India Company nabobs were swanning around Mayfair, buying up country seats and rotten boroughs, impregnating British society with their ill-gotten gains. As Britain's territorial and trading interests in India expanded, the notion of Empire was changing. What had once stood out as 'Protestant, commercial, maritime and free' – the Atlantic *imperium* of Boston and Bridgetown, of battling against the absolutism of Bourbon France, preserving Great Britain against foreign invasion and securing the passage of colonial traffic across the oceans – was now at risk of becoming visibly despotic, 'oriental' and corrupting. Empire as a bulwark of British liberty against the threat of continental tyranny was being undone by John Company's activities in the east.[27] 'The riches of Asia have been poured in upon us,' William Pitt the Elder warned, 'and have brought with them not only Asiatic luxury, but Asiatic principles of government.' And now the British were becoming just as bad as any grasping imperialists. 'Oh! my dear Sir, we have outdone the Spaniards in Peru!' exclaimed Walpole. 'They were at least butchers on a religious principle, however diabolical their zeal.' No one embodied this plague of foreign wealth and power more shamelessly than Lord Clive – the general whom Walpole thought 'seems to be Plutus, the daemon who does not give, but engrosses riches'.[28] Whilst the hero of Plassey always stood astonished at his own moderation, critics noted his fortune touching £400,000, his purchase of the Okehampton estate in Devon and the Claremont estate in Surrey (where he knocked down a Vanburgh-designed Palladian mansion for a new one by Capability Brown and Henry Holland) and his deployment of personal wealth in pursuit of parliamentary ambition with at least seven MPs on the payroll.

Yet Indian critics of British rule in Bengal had no need to look as far as Surrey or Devon to track the plunder of colonialism. The tribute of Empire stood there before them in the City of Palaces.[29]

LACE, SPANGLES AND FOIL

'Calcutta, you know is on the Hoogly, a branch of the Ganges, and as you enter Garden-reach which extends about nine miles below the town, the most interesting views that can possibly be imagined greet the eye.' If accounts of arriving at Cape Town evoked the journey in from the Atlantic and the dramatic lifting of the tablecloth, seeing Calcutta was an enchanted tale of steady revelation, travelling up river from the Bay of Bengal. 'The banks of the river are studded with elegant mansions ... These houses are surrounded by groves and lawns, which descend to the water's edge, and present a constant succession of whatever can delight the eye, or bespeak wealth and elegance in the owners.'[30] 'Imagine everything that is glorious in nature combined with everything that is beautiful in architecture and you can faintly picture to yourself what Calcutta is,' explained one junior writer. The scholar and tea magnate Thomas Twining, arriving in 1792, was equally rhapsodic at catching sight of the 'City of Palaces', 'with its lofty detached flat-roofed mansions and the masts of its innumerable shipping'. Maria Graham, the writer, illustrator and wife of a naval officer, stepped ashore in 1810. 'The river was covered with boats of every shape, villas adorned the banks, the scene became enchanting, all cultivated, all busy, and we felt that we were approaching a great capital,' she wrote in her *Journal of a Residence in India*. 'On landing I was struck with the general appearance of grandeur in all the buildings ... groups of columns, porticoes, domes, and fine gateways, interspersed with trees, and the broad river crowded with shipping, made the whole picture magnificent.'[31]

After the humiliation of Siraj-ud-Daula's capture of Fort William, the construction of a new stronghold after 1757 signalled the determination of the British to hold on to Calcutta. Positioned south of the city in the cleared village of Govindapore abutting the Hooghly, the new fort was a bricks-and-mortar testament to the Plassey settlement. With an irregular heptagon design of seven gates that conformed to the very latest in siege technology, able to mount 600 guns as well as accommodate 10,000 soldiers – and costing £2 million – it far outclassed the Castle of Good Hope. Its sophistication seemed to suggest that the fort was built as much as a bulwark against other predatory European powers as against domestic insurgents. 'No ship can pass up or down the Ganges without being exposed to the fire of this fort,' noted the Dutch admiral Johan Stavorinus when he sailed from the Cape to Calcutta in 1768–71. 'This nation [the British] have thus so firmly rooted themselves in Bengal, that, treachery excepted, they have little to fear from an European enemy, especially as they can entirely command the passage up and down the river.'[32] Around it stood a moat, then a wide expanse of scorched grassland, and finally cleared acres of jungle and marsh providing open sight lines and, in time, the landscape of the modern Maidan. Inside were the mansions of the British army top brass, the barracks for the soldiers and the Anglican St Peter's, often described as the finest garrison church in India.[33]

It was Fort William's size and modernity, the sense of permanence and power, which so impressed and assured European visitors. 'The new fort, an immense place, is on the river side about a mile below the town,' recorded Mrs Jemima Kindersley in 1768. 'If all the buildings which are intended within its walls are finished, it will be a town within itself; for besides houses for the engineers and other officers who reside at Calcutta, there are apartments for the company's writers, barracks for soldiers, magazines for stores etc.' Another Calcutta chronicler, Mrs Eliza Fay, was equally enthusiastic. 'Our Fort is ... so well kept and every thing in such excellent order, that it is quite a curiosity to see it – all the slopes, banks and ramparts, are covered with the richest verdure, which completes the enchantment of the scene.' For Maria Graham, after an evening spent bobbing aboard HMS *Fox* moored on the Hooghly banks, staring at the compound, 'nothing can be more beautiful than both the outside and inside of Fort-William'.[34] Today, the beauty of this military complex, headquarters of the Indian army's Eastern Command, is more difficult to grasp behind the fumes of the six-lane Khidirpur Road and the necessary security apparatus. But its self-separation from the city of Kolkata, its might and pugnacity remain eminently tangible.

With the new fort in place, British Calcutta grew rapidly. In the so-called 'White Town', around Lal Dighi or Tank Square, large merchant houses sprung up. 'The town of Calcutta is daily increasing in size, notwithstanding which, the English inhabitants multiply so fast that houses are extremely scarce,' noted Mrs Kindersley with pride. But construction often proved a clumsy affair as Calcutta was:

an awkward place ... and so irregular, that it looks as if all the houses had been thrown up in the air, and fallen down again by accident as they now stand: people keep constantly building; and every one who can procure a piece of ground to build a house upon, consults his own taste and convenience, without any regard to the beauty or regularity of the town.

Similarly, the attorney William Hickey commented on how during the 1770s the old Bengal style of mud houses was 'being replaced by well-constructed solid masonry' in the city-centre district around Chowringhee Road. Foreign visitors were even more amazed by the speed and style of Calcutta's growth. 'The city now contains around 5,000 two or three storey houses of stone or brick and stucco,' noted the Persian nobleman Abdul Lateef Shushtari in 1789. And the sanitation and refuse systems were just as impressive. 'Seven hundred pairs of oxen and carts are appointed by the Company to take rubbish daily from streets and markets out of the city and tip it into the river. All the pavements have drains to carry off the rain water to the river and are made of beaten brick so as to absorb water and prevent mud forming.'[35]

British residents would have been delighted by such commendations of modernity, for a fiercely Enlightenment notion of progress and improvement, crucial to European self-approbation, was evident in the development of Calcutta. Out of the dense jungle of Bengal and the thick swamps of the Hooghly there arose a glistening tribute to Western civilization protected by the might of Fort William. It was, as William Dalrymple puts it, 'as if Regency Bath had been relocated to the bay of Bengal'.[36] For Company denizens, neo-classical architecture was the order of the day, with white colonnaded verandas, arched porticoes, open terraces, Ionic and Doric columns all suggesting prosperity and permanence, the European ideal of civilization as transplanted to the subcontinent. In the words of Samita Gupta, British architecture 'reflected a classical vocabulary adapted to a tropical setting. Glistening white mansions, pedimented and porticoed set amidst the abundant greenery created exotic images which excited the admiration of visitors'.[37] Contemporaries were undoubtedly impressed. 'Gardens tastefully laid out and houses more resembling the palaces of Princes than the abodes of private gentlemen, certainly contribute to give the stranger a most favourable idea of the metropolis of the British Empire in the East,' purred one British surveyor of the city in 1809.[38] With a relatively small armed force, limited capital and a still jumpy East India Company all that supported British rule in India, the impression of invulnerability was expressed through the urban fabric. It could be seen most obviously in Calcutta's notoriously extravagant domestic architecture. 'Of European towns I am most reminded of Moscow,' thought the visiting Bishop Heber.* 'The size of the houses ... their Grecian architecture, their number of servants, the Eastern dresses and the hospitality of the place ... continually remind me of what I saw in a different climate.'[39] When Bengal's 'Prince of Merchants', the trader John Palmer, sought to consolidate his place within Calcutta society in the early 1800s he commissioned the master builder Richard Blechynden to demolish a large house on the shores of the Hooghly and reconstruct it on a more palatial footprint. He boasted to Blechynden that money was no object, as he had lavished over £2,000 on the compound alone. One of the most popular fictional accounts of eighteenth-century British India, *Hartly House, Calcutta: A Novel of the Days of Warren Hastings* (1789), described the travails of heroine Sophia Goldborne as she falls for a young Brahmin, tries to avoid being made a 'nabobess' and eventually fulfils expectations by becoming Mrs Doyly. She enters the eponymous Hartly House as a guest of Mr and Mrs Hartly, 'by means of a double flight of stone steps, at the top of which we found a spacious balcony called a veranda, covered in by Venetian blinds, and lighted up with wax candles'. Again and again, the anonymous author returns to the grandeur of this domestic palace – 'the roof whereof covers a most magnificent hall, or saloon, the whole length and breadth of

---

* The missionary Reginald Heber, Bishop of Calcutta (1823–26), was the author of that quintessentially colonial nineteenth-century hymn 'From Greenland's icy mountains' (1819):

> From Greenland's icy mountains,
> From India's coral strand,
> Where Afric's sunny fountains
> Roll down their golden sand,
> From many an ancient river,
> From many a palmy plain,
> They call us to deliver
> Their land from error's chain.

this central space ornamented at both fronts with balconies or verandas, that open by folding glass-doors of inconceivable grandeur'.[40]

These domestic palaces provided the stage set for the dissolute, Hogarthian life of Calcutta's ex-pat community. There were the young Griffins holed up in the Writers' Building hurling bread rolls at each other, downing bottles of 'lol shrob' (*lal sherab* – red wine) and belting out their favourite after-dinner ditty of 'A Lass and a Lakh a day', a pun on 'Alas and Alack-the-Day'. 'The costly champagne suppers of the Writers' Building were famous,' as one observer had it, 'and long did the old walls echo to the joyous songs and loud rehearsing tally-hoes.'[41] There were punch houses, horse-race days and repeat visits to the expanding array of brothels. There was a similar lowlife air to Calcutta high society. 'At the time I arrived in Bengal, everybody dressed splendidly, being covered with lace, spangles and foil,' William Hickey recalled in his memoirs of Calcutta in the 1780s. 'I, who always had a tendency to be a beau, gave into the fashion with much goodwill, no person appearing in richer suits of velvet and lace than myself. I kept a handsome phaeton and a beautiful pair of horses, and also had two noble Arabian saddle horses.' Hickey also had a strong constitution, vital for the endless array of socializing, dinner parties and conversations which took place in the new palatial, but domestic setting. 'It being the general custom of Bengal in those days to drink freely and to assemble in numerous parties at each other's houses, I, who had always been disposed to conviviality, soon rendered myself conspicuous, and by the splendour of my entertainments gained the reputation of being the best host in Calcutta.'[42] To his shame, however, Hickey disgraced himself at the consecration of St John's Church in 1787 by 'pouring down claret until eight in the morning' before rushing to the service with his drinking pals. 'It may easily be believed that in such a state we sadly exposed ourselves, drawing the eyes and attention of the congregation upon us as well as that of the clergyman, who took occasion to introduce into his sermon a severe philippic against inebriety.'[43] For the less exuberant, there were evening drives along the Course, a roadway which ran south from the Esplanade through the midst of the Maidan and east of Fort William; assembly balls; trips to the theatre; boating on the Hooghly – all promoted through the pages of John Hicky's *Bengal Gazette or the*

Calcutta General Advertiser, the essential source of society gossip in Calcutta.

At the centre of this socializing, there squatted the groaning English dinner table. 'We dine at two o'clock in the very heat of the day,' explained Eliza Fay. 'A soup, a roast fowl, curry and rice, a mutton pie, a fore quarter of lamb, a rice pudding, tarts, very good cheese, fresh churned butter, fine bread, excellent Madeira.' 'Dinner was served with a scrupulous exactness, the hour being four during the hot months, and three in the cooler,' reported William Hickey of hospitality at Government House.

> He [the governor-general] sat at the table for two hours, during which the bottles were in constant circulation. If any one of the company . . . inadvertently stopped their progress, or what was quite as serious an offence, passed them without putting in the corks, his lordship instantly attacked the defaulter . . . 'Pass the wine, Mr –', and in the latter, 'Fie, fie! Sir, how can you omit to put the cork into the bottle before you pass it?'[44]

With good reason, this meal was followed by a solid two-hour sleep, before the early evening social whirl kicked off again. 'Formal visits are paid in the evening; they are generally very short, as perhaps each lady has a dozen to make and a party waiting for her at home besides,' continued Mrs Fay. 'Gentlemen also call to offer their respects and if asked to put down their hat, it is considered as an invitation to supper. Many a hat have I seen vainly dangling in its owner's hand for half an hour, who at last has been compelled to withdraw without any one's offering to relieve him from the burthen.'[45]

ORIENTAL CALCUTTA

'I had often admired a lovely Hindustani girl who sometimes visited Carter at my house, who was very lively and clever. Upon Carter's leaving Bengal I invited her to become an inmate with me, which she consented to do, and from that time to the day of her death Jemdandee, which was her name, lived with me, respected and admired by all my friends by her extraordinary sprightliness and good humour.'[46] William Hickey's account of his relationship with the

Bengali woman Jemandee, after the death of his beloved wife Charlotte, points to a more cosmopolitan sensibility than his boorish
Englishness might suggest. Calcutta was, like Cape Town, an expressly
multicultural city. 'Chinese and Frenchmen, Persians and Germans,
Arabs and Spaniards, Armenians and Portuguese, Jews and Dutchmen, are seen mixing with the Hindoos and English, the original
inhabitants and the actual possessors of the country,' as Maria
Graham recounted it.[47] The Portuguese, of course, had come in the
1500s; the entrepreneurial Armenians arrived in the 1700s, setting
up import-export businesses in muslin, indigo and spices; a
Baghdadi-Jewish community developed soon after, with a similar
commercial bent, alongside Parsis from Surat, in western India. In
turn, these commercial enclaves competed with the Bengali trading
castes such as the Subarna Baniks, Kayasathas and the Brahmins –
among whom could be counted the celebrated Bengal dynasty of the
Tagores. The Chinese became involved in Calcutta's sugar mill industry from the 1780s, before branching out into cabinet-making,
ship-repair and shoe-making. And from the early 1800s, Calcutta's
Muslim community began to grow more obviously.[48] Even the European residency was not a uniform British bloc. According to a 'List of
Inhabitants Residing in Calcutta', drawn up in 1766 for Lord Clive,
only 129 out of 231 European men were English, Welsh or Scottish.
Twenty were Irish, another twenty from German states, and the rest
from Greece, France, Denmark and elsewhere. 'Inhabitants of every
clime might be seen in the streets, in their diversified and picturesque
costumes,' said one novel of early 1800s Calcutta, which reflected an
increasingly racialized language.

> Here a group of princely looking Persians, there a knot of majestic Turks,
> in flowing garments. Flat faced Chinese with their great straw hats like
> umbrellas, fans always in motion, and hair in a plait reaching to their
> heels ; broad featured Malays and Birmans . . . muscular robust Arabs,
> French, Dutch, Portuguese, Danes and Germans; native processions, and
> European carriages, palanquins and hackeries filled up the streets.[49]

This was the strange, foreign world which the young writers of the
East India Company – after an often gruelling five-month passage to
India – confronted in Calcutta. Many of them embraced the cultural

and sexual liberation it offered – dressing in Bengali attire, swapping 'roast fowl' and 'good cheese' for curries, fathering children and cohabiting with Indian women. 'It is a very general practice for Englishmen in India to entertain a *cara amica* of the Country,' decreed a popular 1805 guide for Company men. In the years 1780–85, one-third of wills filed in Calcutta included a bequest for Indian wives or companions or their natural children (sadly, Hickey's *bibi* Jemandee was to die giving birth to his son).[50] In the same period, over half of the children baptized in St John's Church were illegitimate. For while marriage was very rarely an option – less than 7 per cent of all European men were known to be married (to either European or Indian women) while serving in India – anywhere from 20 to 50 per cent were known to be involved in some sort of sexual liaison with a local woman. These relationships were rarely publicly acknowledged or legitimized and often resulted in a series of complicated legal cases for the East India Company.[51]

Such cross-cultural cohabitation had been sanctioned from the very top with the arrival of Warren Hastings as the first governor-general of India in 1773. He was born in 1732 to an established family of Worcestershire gentry, only to see his father abandon the family for Barbados, leaving the young Hastings to fend for himself as a junior East India Company official. Despatched to Bengal in 1750, his first period in Calcutta ended when the governor, Henry Vansittart, was recalled to Britain in 1765 after the Battle of Buxar, and the extension of territory which came with it, forced the Company to rethink its India strategy. But by then Hastings had been bewitched by the East. He drew up plans for a 'Professorship of the Persian Language' at Oxford and on his return to India in 1769 – first to Madras and then Calcutta – he sought to promote a new strategy of cultural engagement. If British influence was to be sustained in India, the writers needed to 'know' India: to be able to speak Urdu and Bengali, to immerse themselves in the literature and appreciate the history. So ancient and exotic a country as India had to be ruled according to its 'own' tradition and the governor-general lavishly subsidized those willing to study Indian languages and culture. Hastings himself collected Indian paintings, patronized Indian musicians, arranged for the Sanskrit scholar Charles Wilkins to translate the *Bhagavad Gita* into English for the first time and organized the publication of *A Grammar of the Bengali Language*.

Indeed, he all but inaugurated the printing industry in Calcutta, which would come to be such a hive of literary and journalistic culture. Hastings also served as patron of a newly established 'Society for enquiring into the History, Civil and Natural, the Antiquities, Arts, Sciences and Literature of Asia'. The Asiatick Society of Bengal, as it became known, was the prime vehicle for British officials to begin to understand Bengali arts and learning. 'Such studies,' Hastings hoped, 'independent of utility, will diffuse a generosity of sentiment . . . [the Indian classics] will survive when British dominion in India shall have long ceased to exist, and when the sources which it once yielded of wealth and power are lost to remembrance.'[52]

The driving force behind the Asiatick Society and embodiment of Calcutta's cosmopolitan ethos was the jurist, Sanskrit scholar and Enlightenment radical Sir William Jones. Appointed as a judge of 'his Majesty's supreme court of judicature at Fort William in Bengal' in 1783, Jones embraced the intellectual ambition of Hastings's Calcutta and immersed himself in the romance of Sanskrit literature. 'I am in love with the *Gopia*, charmed with *Chrishen*, an enthusiastic admirer of *Rām*,' while the warriors of the *Mahabaharat* 'appear greater in my eyes than Agamemnon, Ajax, and Achilles appeared, when I first read the Iliad'. He thought Sanskrit 'more perfect than the *Greek*, more copious than the *Latin*, and more exquisitely refined than either'. Jones's ideas for governing India were conservatively paternalist, but he stood in awe of the country's cultural and linguistic heritage. Month after month, he published papers for the Asiatick Society, setting out his translations, historical researches into Hinduism, and rediscoveries of Sanskrit texts. And while he failed in his attempts to secure entry to the Asiatick Society for Indian scholars, he did ensure their papers were published in the in-house journal *Asiatick Researches*, and he worked closely with Indian 'court-pundits' (assistants) to craft new legal manuals, on both *The Mohammedan Law of Inheritance* (1792) and the *Institutes of Hindu Law* (1794). 'Jones's close co-operation with Hindu pundits and Muslim maulavis provides a model of cultural contact between the European and Asiatic intelligentsia.'[53] Indeed, his activities exemplify the way in which the British authorities, rather than crushing Indian culture and learning, seemed keen to sustain and deepen it.

The unorthodox religious thinker Rammohun Roy (1772–1833) was another product of Bengal's thriving East–West exchange, living as a theist in Bengal and dying as a Unitarian in Bristol. His life as a scholar was funded by wisely managing his inheritance on the Calcutta money markets, securing returns from investments both in the East India Company and among private traders. In politics, he was a progressive actively opposed to the practice of suttee and he shared with Jones an interest in the linguistic history of Sanskrit and Bengali; but his real passion was for theological investigations into the roots of Hindu polytheism and Christianity. In pursuit of his conviction that 'the doctrines of the unity of God are real Hinduism', he established an Amitya Sabha ('friendly society') of like-minded free-thinkers. It was just one of a number of associations, or *sabha*, formed in early nineteenth-century Calcutta as part of the city's increasingly diverse civil society.[54] By far the most important was the Hindu College, forerunner of today's University of Calcutta, which was established in 1817 to introduce the Hindu elite to 'the literature and science of Europe' in a liberal manner and without any reference to Christianity. The curriculum comprised not only 'reading, writing, grammar and arithmetic' in both English and Bengali, but also 'instruction . . . in history, geography, chronology, astronomy, mathematics, chemistry and other sciences'.[55] Along with the Calcutta Book Society and the city's myriad newspapers – *Bengal Gazette*, *Calcutta Journal*, *Bengal Harkaru*, *India Gazette* – the College was another component of the city's confident intellectualism – 'a new social space for the activities of an urban public, mixed in its racial, religious, and caste composition'.[56]

These cosmopolitan sensibilities were reflected in the city's racial topography. Of course, there existed stark distinctions between the European 'White Town' around Tank Square in the southern half of the city and the indigenous 'Black Town' in the northern parts. 'The upper division to the north of Muchoa Bazar is, comparatively speaking, but thinly covered with habitations,' noted one British doctor. 'It is surprising how much of the condition of the native portion of the town has been neglected in this great city and its suburbs, in which are to be found all the faults of all the cities in India.'[57] The visiting Lord Valentia was altogether blunter about the state of Black Town. 'Its streets are narrow and dirty; the houses, of two stories, occasionally brick, but generally mud, and thatched, perfectly resembling the cabins of the poorest class in Ireland.'[58] However, between the extremities of north and south, black and white, there was a rewarding degree of racial intermingling. For all the Westerners' masonry walls and wrought-iron railings, the ethnic boundaries within Georgian Calcutta were remarkably fluid, and the self-declared White Town never carved out an exclusive, homogeneous space for European residents. What was more, both districts were also shaped by similar, internal differences of income and status: in the midst of the 'native' quarter there were large colonnaded mansions, rivalling Chowringhee's palaces, for the homes of such wealthy Indians as the Company agent and entrepreneur Dwarkanath Tagore and the merchant Maharajah Rajkissen.[59]

Mrs Kindersley would have liked a much more clearly demarcated Black Town – 'as in Madras' – for the servants to live in. Unfortunately, 'Calcutta is partly environed by their habitations, which makes the roads rather unpleasant . . . the smoke of the fires with which they dress their victuals, comes all out at the doors, and is perhaps more disagreeable to the passenger than to themselves.'[60] The trading, market and business bazaars which dotted Calcutta – most notably, the city central yarn and cloth market of Burrabazar – were places of informal ethnic and racial integration. The adventurous Maria Graham particularly enjoyed visiting the bazaars during the Kali Puja festival in late October. 'In all the bazaars, at every shop door, wooden figures and human heads, with the neck painted blood-colour, are suspended, referring, I imagine, to the human sacrifices formerly offered to this deity, who was, I believe, the tutelary goddess of Calcutta.'[61] In Leadenhall Street, such enthusiasm for the culture and civilization of Bengal only intensified suspicions towards the practices of its employees in Calcutta. There was a paranoia about local officials 'going native', adopting Asiatic habits and indulgences. Ironically enough, Warren Hastings's appointment as governor-general was an attempt to bring the East India Company to heel and prevent any spread of 'oriental corruption' within its lucrative Bengal operation.

For in the early 1770s the Company was facing growing financial and political pressure. As well as a failure to plan for the full costs of policing the new Company possessions in Bengal and the mismanagement of the Bengal famine, a minor military set-back in Madras in 1769 had punctured the equity bubble which had been inflating its stock over the previous decade. The shock sparked a set of painful readjustments in London's banks and merchant houses which, by the early 1770s, was sending over-leveraged financial institutions to the wall. 'There never was since the South Sea year [1720] so great a crush in stock matters,' wrote the financier Israel Barre.[62] The Company thought it could find a way out of falling revenue in Bengal by piling into the Chinese tea market – an equally disastrous venture that led to the dumping of excess supply in America and setting in train the events of the Boston Tea-Party (see p. 55 above). When that wheeze failed, the directors went cap in hand to His Majesty's Treasury to seek a £1.4 million bail out. Parliament was recalled as government ministers seized on this valuable opportunity to humble the over-mighty Company and its nabob allies by enacting the 1773 East India Regulating Act. The new legislation curtailed the Company's freedom to manage its own affairs in India, withdrew its privileges of commercial confidentiality, gave government ministers access to all correspondence and introduced the new post of governor-general of India based in Calcutta complete with powers over the other presidencies of Madras and Bombay. However, to prevent any whiff of 'Asiatic despotism' emerging from such an office, the governor-general was to be part of a five-person council of whom three members were nominated by parliament.

It was desperately unfortunate for Warren Hastings that among those first council appointees was the brilliantly destructive bureaucrat Sir Philip Francis, who made his primary purpose the forcing of the first governor-general from office. For much of the 1770s, Calcutta was engulfed in a dirty war of political attrition, as allegations of corruption, judicial murder, forced resignations, extra-marital affairs and dishonourable conduct – leading to a melodramatic, if non-fatal, duel between Hastings and Francis in 1780 – bedevilled the relationship between governor-general and council. This, in turn, spilled over into Westminster party politicking when Edmund Burke used these events to mount a broader condemnation of the plunder and corruption of the East India Company and led the charge for Hastings's impeachment on his return from India in 1785.

The trial lasted eight years and, at the end, Hastings was found not guilty.

In the interim, William Pitt the Younger set about trying to fix the remaining deficiencies of British governance in India. The outcome was the 1784 India Act, whose purpose, according to Pitt, was 'to give the crown the power of guiding the politics of India with as little means of corrupt influence as possible'. Against the spectre of 'Asiatic corruption' and nabob excess, the Act expanded parliamentary supervision over the Company, widely resented as an *imperium in imperio* of unaccountable wealth and power, and separated its civil service and military functions from its commercial operations, in the hope of ending the tension between the Company's roles as merchant and government in India. Lest anyone was in any doubt as to the future direction of British policy in Bengal, Pitt appointed as his new governor-general Charles, Earl Cornwallis – the bluff, colonial veteran of the American War of Independence (and future Viceroy of Ireland). Having endured the personal indignity of surrendering Yorktown to George Washington, Cornwallis brought to Bengal a joint appointment as commander-in-chief and governor-general with powers to override the council, and a bitter suspicion towards any settled colonial class which might grow to question British sovereignty (the same instinct he would show in dealing with the 1798 Irish Rebellion). None of this boded well for the cosmopolitan world of Warren Hastings's Calcutta.[63]

In fact, Cornwallis thought he had inherited 'a system of the dirtiest jobbery', and his mission was to bring to an end 'the good old principles of Leadenhall Street economy – small salaries and immense perquisites'. He set about raising salaries; banning Company writers from engaging in private trade on their own account; instituting a new system of law courts with 'European principles'; and reducing the role for Indians and mixed-race within the Bengal administration, to avoid any 'Asiatic contamination'. The political function of the East India Company was now separated off from the trading interests so that British civil servants in India – collecting taxes, adjudicating disputes and running the bureaucracy – would not be tainted by any commercial transactions. Most significant of all was Cornwallis's 'Permanent Settlement' of 1793, which aimed to end the cycle of crises wrought by the absence of a sustainable revenue base for the Company. The fault lay, it was decided, with the haphazard taxation and short-term leases of Bengali land tenure, which meant Indian farmers had no true financial incentive in cultivating their lands, leaving the Company with an unreliable income. There was, to British eyes, nothing more dangerous to good governance than insecure property ownership. So, the 'principle of property' had to be embedded in Bengali society, which would allow it to abandon its feudal, Mughal past and embrace the sound principles of Whig England: looking after the land and paying taxes. Working to a system drawn up by Sir Phillip Francis, Cornwallis's reforms ended the old arbitrary taxation of land and replaced it with a set revenue from Bengal at £3 million per annum, which, at the same time, allowed the creation of permanent private property rights for Indian landowners. This dramatically increased the value of Bengali land, with the aim of both spurring investment and securing stability at a time of renewed military danger from revolutionary France.[64] But it had an unexpected disadvantage: the effects of this transformation of land-ownership patterns sucked the mercantile energy out of Calcutta. Realizing that there were greater and more reliable riches to be made from being a *zamindar* (landlord) in country estates than being traders in Calcutta warehouses, the *banians* or agents of the eighteenth century became the rural *rentiers* of the nineteenth century and lost 'the instinct for business'.[65]

THE GLORIOUS LITTLE MAN

None of this bothered Cornwallis's fiercely aristocratic successor as governor-general, Richard Wellesley, who arrived in Calcutta from Cape Town in 1798 unconcerned about such technocratic reforms. His ambition was to craft an empire of military glory rather than commercial profits. In London, colonial officials had come to realize the limitations of the Cape Town model of light-touch mercantilism and patchwork naval bases; now, territorial Empire and the commercial and military power it brought were back in fashion. Securing India against competing European powers was a regrettable and expensive necessity for the maintenance of prosperity of the United Kingdom. The attempted invasion of Ireland in 1798 and the assault on British interests in the Caribbean had only underlined the global nature of the Anglo-French conflict. India had to be rid of French influence to create a bulwark against Napoleonic influence on the European continent – and Wellesley was the man to do it. His period of governor-generalship 'was to be the decisive phase in the establishment of British dominion over the Indian subcontinent and witnessed the beginnings of the projection of British military and maritime power into the Middle East and south-east Asia'.[66]

In the first instance, it was Tipu Sultan, the Muslim ruler of the southern Indian city of Mysore, whom Wellesley had in his sights. With a 'liberty tree' planted in his capital, Seringapatam, Wellesley regarded 'Citizen' Tipu – 'the tiger of Mysore' – as a tool of French interests whose ambitions constituted an unacceptable design on British rule in India. Within a year, the governor-general's aggressive militarism had provoked the sultan into war, and on 4 May 1799 British troops stormed Seringapatam, Tipu dying in battle. 'Seringapatam I shall retain in full sovereignty for the Company, as being a tower of strength, from which we may at any time shake Hindostan to its centre, if any combination should ever be formed against our interests,' Wellesley wrote back to Dundas in the afterglow of victory.[67] However, he did not assume this defensive stance for long, and internal conflicts between the major Maratha rulers – the governing princes of western and northern India – allowed him to pursue a strategy of divide, rule and conquer. In a succession of ruthless wars against the Marathas, conducted in part by Wellesley's younger brother Sir Arthur, the 'glorious little man' managed to stretch British power and influence into all corners of the Indian subcontinent. Victories at Assaye and Argaum, followed by General Lake's success at Laswari, laid the foundations of British paramountcy in India. The dark memory of defeat in the American War of Independence was shed once and for all as British forces took Delhi itself, ancient capital of the Mughal Empire, in 1803. With the taming of the Marathas, the last major rivals to British power and influence on the subcontinent were vanquished. Britain was now the Empire in India, and the governor-general a de facto emperor – all of which suited Wellesley rather well. In

Calcutta, victory over the Marathas would be commemorated with the Ochterlony Monument – a 49-metre fluted Doric column standing on a square Egyptian-style plinth and crowned with a Turkish cupola – dedicated to the heroism of Major-General Sir David Ochterlony in capturing and defending Delhi and providing one of the most recognizable icons in the city (now renamed Shaheed Minar in honour of the martyrs of the Indian independence movement).

It had been the disingenuous boast of Horace Walpole and others that, during the growth of the British Empire, 'a peaceable, quiet set of tradesfolks' had somehow become the 'heirs-apparent to the Romans'.[68] In the aftermath of the conquest of Mysore, such faux-diffidence would no longer do: the British presence in India was now there for all to see as a political as much as economic project. 'The Civil servants of the English East India Company ... can no longer be considered as the agents of a commercial concern,' Wellesley announced in 1800. 'They are, in fact, the ministers and officers of a powerful sovereign; they must now be viewed in that capacity, with reference, not to their nominal, but to their real occupations ... Their duties are those of statesmen in every other part of the world.' As such,

> their education should be founded in a general knowledge of those branches of literature and science which form the basis of the education of persons destined to similar occupation, in Europe. To this foundation should be added an intimate acquaintance with the history, languages, customs and manners of the people of India, with the Mahommedan and Hindoo codes of law and religion, and with the political and commercial interests and relations of Great Britain in Asia.[69]

Since the existing training for the John Company Griffins was so poor and parochial, Wellesley's plan 'for the improvement of the civil service at Bengal' involved the establishment of Fort William College as the training ground for a new cadre of officials destined to run an empire. In this 'Oxford of the East', writers would be instructed in 'the liberal policy which ought to actuate the government of a powerful empire' rather than 'the little spirit of a retail dealer'.[70] They would learn theology; Sanskrit, Arabic and the six major languages of their colonial subjects (Hindustani, Bengali, Telugu, Marathi, Tamil and

Kannada); Hindu, Islamic and English law; botany and chemistry; and the history and culture of India. Fort William College would 'cherish in the minds of the servants of the Company, a sense of moral duty, and teach those who fill important stations, that the great public duties which they are called upon to execute in India are not of a less sacred nature than the duties of similar situations in their own country'.[71] And Wellesley found 'the mischief [of "extravagance, profusion and excess"] to be so pressing' that he intended, 'without waiting for orders from home, to proceed to found such an institution at Calcutta'.[72]

The same certainty of purpose which Wellesley brought to the battlefield, he now applied to the establishment of the College of Fort William. The governor-general deliberately ignored the Writers' Building and opted for virgin land at Garden Reach, south of Fort William, to be drained and cleared for his new complex. The cosmopolitanism of Warren Hastings's and William Jones's Calcutta was revived as over a hundred original works in oriental languages were published by the college between 1801 and 1805. Among the first was *Rajabali* by Mrityunjay Vidyalankar, a chronicle of India in the Bengali language telling the history of 'the Rajas and Badshahs and Nawabs who have occupied the throne in Delhi and Bengal'. Young Company writers, expecting the dissolute nabob life of their predecessors, were now grilled in Persian, Arabic and 'Hindustani Languages' and inspired to interrogate the teachings of the Koran or ancient Sanskrit texts. They wrote essays with titles such as 'On the character and capacity of Asiaticks, and particularly of the natives of Hindoostan' and disputed in Persian on topics such as 'An Academical Institution in India, is advantageous to the Natives, and to the British Nation'. Wellesley himself, with orientalist flamboyance, took a personal interest in public examinations at the College. 'In a state chair covered with crimson velvet and richly gilt, with a group of aides-de-camp and secretaries standing behind him, sat the Governor-General,' was how one resident remembered his visit. 'Two servants with state punkahs of crimson silk were fanning him, and behind him again were several Native servants bearing silver staffs.' Protected by a bodyguard 'drawn up in full uniforms of scarlet with naked sabres', Wellesley sat alongside the professors, listening to the College disputants argue their case.[73] He was delighted with what he heard. 'The principles on which this Institution is founded, the spirit which it is designed to diffuse, and the purposes which it is calculated to accomplish, must enhance the importance of its success, in proportion to the exigencies of every public crisis, and to the progressive magnitude, power, and glory of the Empire.'[74]

Such extravagant, ornamental regard for the display and rituals of power was elemental to Wellesley's Empire. He believed in awing his Indian subjects with ceremony and, like Cornwallis, instilling some sense of civic discipline into Calcutta's dissolute ruling class. 'I am resolved to encounter the task of effecting a thorough reform in private manners,' Wellesley had written to the British foreign secretary, Lord Grenville, upon his arrival in 1798. 'The effect ... has been to compel me to entrench myself within forms and ceremonies, to introduce much state into the whole appearance of my establishments and household to expel all approaches to familiarity, and to exercise my authority with a degree of vigour and strictness nearly amounting to severity.'[75] The lax, dissolute Calcutta of William Hickey came under sustained assault from Wellesley's reformation of manners: extra-marital affairs, interracial liaisons, drinking and gambling and a critical, free press were all now subject to close supervision. In their place, the governor-general promoted a new code of colonial honour based upon the army, the Company and the Anglican church. Morality and pageantry, deference and duty were to provide the templates of colonial Calcutta, and they were all carefully codified in the design and iconography of his greatest architectural legacy to the city: Government House.

'Of all the public buildings of Calcutta, the government-house, built by Lord Wellesley, is the most remarkable,' eulogized Maria Graham.

> The lower story forms a rustic basement, with arcades to the building, which is Ionic ... The centre of the house is given up to two rooms, the finest I have seen. The lowest is paved with dark grey marble, and supported by Doric columns of chunam, which one would take for Parian marble. Above the hall is the ball-room, floored with dark polished wood, and supported by Ionic pillars of white chunam.

Then there was the throne room, in which sat, pride of place, Tipu Sultan's captured dais. Government House was, in the words of Jan Morris, 'the original great palace of British India'.[76]

Lieutenant Charles Wyatt of the Bengal Engineers was the architect of this pioneering display of neo-classical bombast in the capital of Bengal. He took for inspiration the work of his uncle, Samuel Wyatt, who collaborated with Robert Adam on Kedleston Hall in Derbyshire, the seat of Lord Scarsdale – the great-great-grandfather of the future Indian viceroy Lord Curzon (who would come to inhabit both buildings). It was a suitably authoritative and expensive prototype for the Augustan ambitions of the victor of Mysore. Just as the world was coming to appreciate Edward Gibbon's meditation on the collapse of Roman civilization in his *History of the Decline and Fall of the Roman Empire* (1772–89), on the banks of the Hooghly Richard Wellesley was confidently inaugurating a new era of imperial might. Calcutta's old Council House and 'sixteen other handsome private mansions' were ripped down for Wellesley's riposte to the counting-house ethos of the East India Company. The building was designed with four wings – in contrast to Kedleston's more modest two – a rounded and colonnaded south face with a large dome for a roof. An Ionic portico, complete with huge processional staircase, faced north towards the centre of Calcutta; looking south across the gardens, towards the Maidan, was a domed front, completed with a figure of Britannia. The high ceilings, wide passageways, Venetian blinds and windows with fretwork valances ensured the residency, in the words of Curzon, 'was admirably adapted to a climate where every breath of air from whatever quarter must be seized, and where a perpetual current relieves the petty aggravations of life'.[77]

Government House's comfort was always overshadowed by its pomp and circumstance: the arched and columniated gateways topped by sphinxes, lions and globes, all spoke to a conscious declaration of imperial power and success. It was the embodiment of Wellesley's serious, formal, Roman-style Empire, which he thought essential for the governance of India. Inside, protocol was everything. 'The Levees at the Government House will in general be holden in the centre room of the upper floor,' read an advertisement in the 1803 *Calcutta Gazette*, setting out the rigid social requirements of colonial hospitality.

'The general entrance into the Government House on all occasions is from the *northward*; but on Levee Days, Public Balls, and entertainments, the southern entrance will be open to the Chief Justice, Members of Council, Judges of the Supreme Court,' and so it went on.[78] Every visitor was unsurprisingly awed by Government House's neo-classical majesty. 'The length of the verandahs and the flights of stairs almost wore me out before we reached the principal reception room,' exclaimed one party-goer at a Government House ball. 'The *coup d'œil* of these rooms is indeed calculated to impress a young person with delight, particularly when filled by a brilliant assembly.'[79] The young Elizabeth, heroine of Anna Monkland's Calcutta novel *Life in India*, was certainly impressed on entering the ballroom – 'the roof supported by two rows of pillars running down each side, leaving within that beautifully chalked area for the dancers ... The quantity of red coats and jewels, to say nothing of ostrich plumes, adds much to the effect.' Indeed, Elizabeth perceptively concluded that, 'His Majesty on the throne of Britain is not a more sovereign prince than is the Governor-General of India.'[80]

But Wellesley nonetheless chafed at the restrictions on his power – particularly in governing his capital. 'Some doubts have arisen with regard to the legislative power of the Governor-General in council as applicable to the town of Calcutta,' he grumbled to Henry Dundas in 1799. The governor-general wanted a special Act of Parliament to allow total authority to reshape the city before it relapsed 'into its ancient state of filth, and unhealthiness' and become again 'fatal to European constitutions'. 'It is my intention immediately to proceed to improve the drains and roads, to widen the streets and avenues, to clear the jungles, and remove the [water] tanks, and other nuisances situated in the neighbourhood of the town.'[81] Unsurprisingly, he began with the environs of Government House, and plans for a trunk road linking his official residence to his country estate at Barrackpore, an exotic bungalow compound some 23 kilometres up the Hooghly River. This imperial boulevard never quite succeeded, but he had more success with laying out The Strand, a large, open avenue hugging the Maidan and then stretching along the banks of the Hooghly, which became a useful arterial road and an embankment for new warehouse developments. It was a perfect setting for the Ochterlony Monument, then the Victoria Memorial and the endless processions of imperial self-congratulation which cluttered up the Maidan.

Even the otherwise hostile William Hickey welcomed the new roads: 'A prodigious improvement it assuredly was, not only proving conducive to the health of the inhabitants in general, but likewise affording an agreeable morning or evening ride to those Europeans who were fond of exercise.'[82] Wellesley's upgrading of the city was taken over in 1803 by Calcutta's Town Improvement Committee, Bengal's answer to the Wide Street Commissioners of Dublin. The Committee embarked on a major programme of draining and cleaning; building new squares and opening up avenues; clearing the riverbank and constructing new ghats; setting building regulations and rules on public monuments. The domestic finery of the City of Palaces was gaining an improved urban infrastructure. 'The appearance and beauty of the town ... and every improvement which shall introduce a greater degree of order, symmetry, and magnificence in the streets ... will tend to ameliorate the climate and to promote and secure every object of a just and salutary system of Police,' explained the Committee.[83] City improvement would promote public health, which would foster civic pride and, with it, an instinctive sense of imperial virtue. But such a focus on magnificence, symmetry and public health did not extend to the 'Black Town' in the north of Calcutta. 'Whoever has visited the native portion of the town before sun-rise, with its narrow lanes, and "rankest compound of villainous smells that ever offended nostril", will require no argument in favour of widening the streets,' wrote a British doctor in 1837, noting the lack of attention the district received, 'so as to effect the two greatest improvements of all as respects the salubrity of a city, free exposure to the sun, to rarify and elevate the vapours, and to winds to dilute and dissipate them.'[84]

Nor did improvements to the 'White Town' come cheap. 'Marquis Wellesley was in no way sparing of the Company's cash,' recalled Hickey of the new roads, avenues and infrastructure. The price for the construction of Government House alone came in at some £168,000, while the costs of his ornate protocol and chivalry were also raising some hackles among 'the cheesemongers of Leadenhall Street' left to pick up the bill. The East India Company debt for the year

1805–6 reached a terrifying £28,523,804, two-thirds of which had been added during Wellesley's time in Bengal. From the Castle of Good Hope, his most devoted supporter, Lady Barnard, warned him that his enemies were circling:

> by the mouth of a certain party here you are positively recalled, as being too proud, too expensive and too successful ... in short your conquests have been too large – your reforms too large – your schemes too large – your house too large, and your pride and presumption on all you have done much too large and therefore it must be diminished.[85]

Leadenhall bureaucrats grumbled about his war-mongering, financial excesses, infringement of their trading monopolies and autocratic style. Wellesley had his own gripes. Chief among them was the humiliation of his 'potato peerage' – his elevation to the Irish peerage in 1799 under the title of Marquess Wellesley, following his victory over Tipu Sultan. He regarded the title as an unforgiveable humiliation since, at the very least, he deserved to be made a British baron. With his *amour propre* so grievously wounded, the arrogance of 'The Most Noble, the Governor General' now assumed self-destructive new heights.

Watching the approaching storm, wily Henry Dundas had sought to close off potential sources of tension between the Company and governor-general. He tried to steer Wellesley away from plans for Fort William College, with his 'considerable doubts about the suggestion'. Dundas thought the Company training in London perfectly adequate and doubted if 'any of the other accomplishments for Indian business are to be attained so well in any seminary of education'. Such reservations meant nothing to Wellesley – he was interested in imperial statecraft, not Indian business, and proceeded regardless. Dundas also warned Wellesley against over-expenditure and the growth of 'unwieldy and unmanageable' debt which might prevent Britain 'from the means of extricating our affairs when peace shall have returned'. Again and again, Dundas reminded Wellesley of the economic necessities underpinning the British presence in India. 'It is to the increased exports from India to Europe, that we are to attribute the increase of Indian prosperity, industry, population and revenue.'[86] But Wellesley had no thought of Britain extricating itself from India; he ran an Empire of timeless horizon, not a trading station.

Behind these tussles over costs and colleges was a more existential disagreement about the nature of Empire, between an East India Company which saw India as an economic venture necessarily accompanied by political consequences and Wellesley, who saw the British presence as fundamentally political with economic consequences.[87] Reviewing Wellesley's legacy in 'Notes on Some Viceroys and Governors General', Lord Curzon was ambivalent. 'One class of writers has seen in Wellesley the courageous and far-sighted architect of Empire, who carried out and expanded the great work of Warren Hastings and reared the central edifice, lofty and strong, of British dominion in the East. The opposite school regards him as the embodiment of vanity in high places ... The truth does not lie midway between these extremes. It is to be found in both of them.' Yet the city of Calcutta, Curzon thought, certainly benefited from Wellesley's reign. For, 'while Anglo-Indian society stood aghast at Wellesley's pretensions and was considerably awed by his magnificence, it regarded the presence and the patronage of the little autocrat as a compliment to itself, and saw a reflection of the nimbus which he habitually wore floating about its own head'.[88]

MAKING ANGLO-SAXONS
OF THE HINDOOS

The tripling of East India Company debt, the spiralling costs of the Maratha wars and accusations over 'illegal appointments' and 'evasion of the law' ensured Wellesley's recall in 1805. The Company Court of Directors had had enough of Wellesley's war-mongering and impossibly expensive territorial ambitions. He was succeeded as governor-general by Lord Cornwallis, who returned to Calcutta for a second tour of duty. 'Lord Wellesley, with his customary attention to parade and show, sent down all his carriages, servants, staff officers, and general establishment to receive his noble supercessor at the waterside,' Hickey recorded of the handover. But the austere Cornwallis ushered them all away and, with them, Wellesley's flamboyant ethos of Empire. 'Too civil, too civil by half. Too many people. I don't want them, don't want one of them, I have not yet lost the use of my legs.' And he walked the short journey to Government House – whose grandiosity he found equally ridiculous. 'It is as much too large as the other [Governor's house] was too small. I shall never be able to find my way about it without a guide, nor can I divest myself of the idea of being in a prison, for if I show my head outside a door, a fellow with a musket and fixed bayonet presents himself before me.'[89]

With the return of Cornwallis, the last embers of cosmopolitan Calcutta were snuffed out as a more assertive ideology of imperial righteousness took hold. In the few months before his death in October 1805, Cornwallis reasserted his strategy of racial hierarchy, anti-historicism and Utilitarian governance. High-level officials were now discouraged from keeping Indian companions, and lower-level soldiers and employees of the company were encouraged to turn to prostitutes to satisfy their impulses. Cornwallis also wanted a quick end to the 'unprofitable and ruinous' warfare against the Marathas. Any encouragement to Company officials to learn 'Hindustani languages' or 'know' Indian culture were quickly disavowed. Fort William College was a rapid casualty of this anti-orientalist agenda.

As in Cape Town, so now in Calcutta, there took place a sustained process of cultural Anglicization. The future of British India belonged to men like the East India Company deputy chairman Charles Grant, who regarded Wellesley's territorial project as 'the road to ruin' and sought to have the late governor-general – like Clive and Hastings before him – impeached for corruption. The East India Company College at Haileybury (founded in 1806), rather than Fort William College in Calcutta, was to be where the imperial ethos of the Victorian governing class would be laid. And in the quads of Hertfordshire, the young Company writers were taught the works of Adam Smith and Jeremy Bentham by the likes of Reverend Thomas Malthus. Free trade, transparent government, rational choice – these were to be the templates for governing the East. If students dared to know about Indian history and culture, it was most certainly not to the *Bhagavad Gita* they should turn; but rather James Mill's *History of British India*, whose author was a staunch defender of the Company with the critical advantage of never having actually been to India. 'We have to educate a people who cannot at present be educated by means of their mother tongue,' wrote Macaulay, who had joined the Supreme Council of India in 1834, in his influential 'Minutes on Education in India'. 'We must teach them some foreign language. The claims of our own language it is hardly necessary to recapitulate. It stands pre-eminent even among the languages of the West.'[90] The Minutes also crudely decreed that 'all the historical information which has been collected from all the books written in the Sanskrit language is less valuable than what may be found in the most paltry abridgments used at preparatory schools in England'. The public mind of India, which the British had found 'debased and contracted by the worst form of political and religious tyranny', had to be instructed in European knowledge and Enlightenment thinking. There was little of true value to be learned from Indian literature or civilization; this subject race had to be raised towards self-governance on a course of Western culture. And it would be a noble calling. As Macaulay told the House of Commons, 'To have found a great people sunk in the lowest depths of slavery and superstition, to have so ruled them as to have made them desirous and capable of all the privileges of citizens would indeed be a title to glory all our own.'[91] Macaulay's own work in Calcutta centred on crafting a new system of jurisprudence. In contrast to Sir William Jones, who worked with Indian assistants to reinterpret the Muslim and Hindu inheritance, Macaulay stuck to the Benthamite conviction that human nature was the same everywhere and would respond to the same mixture of pain and pleasure: what was wanted in India was clarity and uniformity, not tradition and custom.

Lord William Bentinck was the governor-general (1828–35) keenest to impose this Utilitarian, Anglicist orthodoxy on Bengal. Like Cornwallis, he abjured the flummery of Wellesley and, with it, any hint of orientalist sympathy. Bentinck dictated the sole use of English in legal and bureaucratic procedures, starved the Asiatick Society of funds and drove the Calcutta Madrasa and Sanskrit College almost towards extinction. The closed minds and cultural arrogance of the British Empire in India were beginning to crystallize, even in multicultural Calcutta. It was exactly what the 'orientalist' governor of Madras, Sir Thomas Munro, had feared might happen. 'The ruling vice of our Government is innovation,' he complained. In a letter to the former foreign secretary George Canning in 1821, he said: 'I fear some downright Englishman [at the India Board] ... will insist on making Anglo-Saxons of the Hindoos'. The truth was that 'the improvement of the character of a people, and the keeping them, at the same time, in the lowest state of dependence on foreign rulers to which they can be reduced by conquest, are matters quite incompatible with each other'.[92]

In Bengal, there was a more pressing fear that the best days of Calcutta were already behind it. The 1830 bankruptcy of John Palmer & Co. – the wealthiest and most reliable of Calcutta's agency houses, which had dominated the city's commercial life for forty years – on the back of a crisis in the indigo market, prompted financial contagion across all the major trading houses.[93] 'It ruined one half of the English society in Bengal and seriously injured the other half,' wrote Macaulay from Calcutta in 1836. 'A large proportion of the most important functionaries here are deeply in debt and, accordingly, the mode of living is now exceedingly quiet and modest. Those immense subscriptions, those public tables, those costly entertainments and equipages of which [Bishop] Heber and others who saw Calcutta a few years back, say so much, are never heard of.'[94] The fabled City of Palaces was starting on its long journey towards Rudyard Kipling's 'City of Dreadful Night', where 'death looked down'. From mid-century, the language of Calcutta shifted quite perceptibly: talk of the beauty, sophistication and majesty of the 'Second City of Empire' gave way to concerns about public health, dirt, disease and squalor. The amorphous stench of the city became a permanent source of British conversation. Kipling called it the Big Calcutta Stink, or B.C.S.

> There is only one. Benares is fouler in point of concentrated, pent-up muck, and there are local stenches in Peshawar which are stronger than the B.C.S.; but, for diffused, soul-sickening expansiveness, the reek of Calcutta beats both Benares and Peshawar. Bombay cloaks her stenches with a veneer of assafœtida and tobacco; Calcutta is above pretence. There is no tracing back the Calcutta plague to any one source. It is faint, it is sickly, and it is indescribable.[95]

The sense of decline was more than just environmental as the economic strength of Calcutta was challenged by other Indian cities more attuned to the industrial age. The illusion of permanence, of that imperial bravado which inspired a cityscape of neo-classical follies, was ebbing.[96]

What was certainly true was that the profits of the East India Company, whose agent Job Charnock had founded British Calcutta in 1690, had come to a precipitous end in Bengal and in 1833 its monopoly was finally annulled by the British government. Calcutta's hinterland had been stripped of its riches, and the British industrial revolution and rapid expansion of the Lancashire cotton industry undermined any profitable export industry from Bengal. India was now forced to import finished goods from Manchester, and the Company's income shrivelled. Abandoning its exhausted playground of Calcutta and hungry for new profits, British merchants now headed east out of the Bay of Bengal towards the Middle Kingdom of Qing China, to found the most potent city of free enterprise in the history of British imperialism.

6

Hong Kong

'A free port on British soil in China'

Holed up in the Portuguese trading enclave of Macao, the Scottish merchant James Matheson seemed to possess an uncanny ability to predict British policy in the East. 'Hong Kong is to be immediately occupied by our forces, and till Her Majesty's pleasure is known, will be garrisoned by about a thousand Europeans,' he wrote back to his business partner, William Jardine, in London. Thankfully, there would be no objection from the Royal Navy 'to our stowing opium there'.[1]

As Matheson predicted, on 26 January 1841 Her Majesty's ship *Sulphur* circumnavigated the island of Hong Kong and then landed at fifteen minutes past eight in the morning – 'and being the bona fide first possessors, her Majesty's health was drank with three cheers on Possession Mount'. The same day, the full British squadron arrived. 'The marines were landed, the union [flag] hoisted on our post, and formal possession taken of the island, by Commodore Sir J. G. Bremer, accompanied by other officers of the squadron, under a feu-de-joie from the marines, and a royal salute from the ships of war.'[2] Watching proceedings, bobbing in the choppy South China Sea, was Matheson himself. 'I witnessed the hoisting of the British flag at Hong Kong this 26th,' he reported back to Jardine.[3]

The British were not, in fact, the 'bona fide first possessors': an indigenous Chinese population existed on the island numbering up to 4,000 by the time the *Sulphur* dropped anchor. For centuries, they had been engaged in a subsistence economy of farming, fishing and stone-cutting in the shadow of the great trading hubs of Canton and Portuguese Macao across the Pearl River Delta. And so the arrival of Bremer's squadron in the stunning, rocky setting of Hong Kong, or

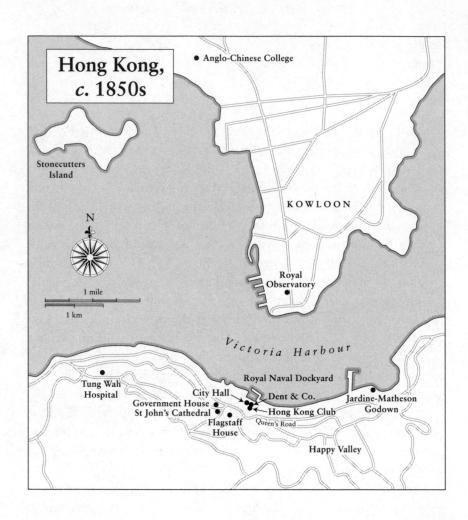

Hong Kong,
c. 1850s

Stonecutters
Island

N

1 mile

1 km

Anglo-Chinese College

KOWLOON

Royal
Observatory

Victoria Harbour

Royal Naval Dockyard

Tung Wah
Hospital

City Hall

Dent & Co.

Jardine-Matheson
Godown

Government House

St John's Cathedral

Hong Kong Club

Flagstaff
House

Queen's Road

Happy Valley

the 'Fragrant Harbour' as it was known in Cantonese, set in train the long, often discordant history of Sino-British involvement in building one of the most celebrated imperial cities in the world. It grew as a monument to an idea – free trade – as well as the less exalted colonial realities behind that nominally pacific ambition. In its port-and-peak natural beauty, its urban density and deep harbour, as well as its complex relationship with the mainland, Hong Kong would be a resplendent if uneasy monument to the global reach of the British Empire and to British imperialism at the height of its ideological self-confidence. Over the succeeding 150 years, this extraordinary city-state would also come subtly to reflect the shifting realities of world politics.

Today that means a declining West and a rising East – all readily traceable through the prism of Hong Kong's governance, from the contentious 1997 UK handover to the conclusive sealing of China's hegemony with the 2012 election of the pro-Beijing chief executive of Hong Kong, Leung Chun-ying. Yet, for all the centuries of geo-political struggle over this piece of East Asian real estate, there has remained one constant. As Hong Kong pro-democracy activist Emily Lau put it in 1997, 'Like many other governments, London's top priority is getting a slice of the huge China market. We have also not forgotten that trade was the reason why the colony of Hong Kong was founded in the nineteenth century.'[4] She was right. The British capture of Hong Kong symbolized a rejection of the East India Company, the mercantilism of Calcutta and the territorial vanity of the Marquis of Wellesley. Instead, the creation of a new city on a rocky outpost on the edges of the Pearl River would exemplify the energy of laissez-faire and the prowess of Britain's 'informal empire' of free trade. The history of Hong Kong reveals how the promotion of Britain's colonial interests worked hand in glove with a high-minded belief in the benefits of extending global commerce. Then, as now, whether it was aboard Her Majesty's ship *Sulphur* in 1841 or at the gathering of the Hong Kong association at the Mandarin Oriental in 2010, the port city would serve as an entry-point for British business into the vast riches of an untapped Chinese market – the only difference being that back then Hong Kong was 'ours', and now it is 'theirs'.

THE ACCURSED AND PROHIBITED
POISON

Looking round modern Victoria today it is curious to reflect that the men who founded the prosperity of this mundane granite citadel . . . first made their money by the sale of that most intangible of all commodities – illusion: for the opium trade, we may infer, provides the only example in mercantile history of massive and prosaic fortunes being made by selling the material for hallucination and artificially induced happiness.[5]

With typical insouciance, James Pope-Hennessy highlighted how the riches of harsh, rocky Hong Kong were erected on the whispery puffs of opium *and* that the Gospel of Free Trade had some truly fallen apostles. As Hong Kong vice consul Henry Sirr put it in the 1840s, opium was 'China's curse'.

By the sale of this pernicious drug Great Britain's sons gain gold; and earn opprobrium for dealing destruction around them, bringing into derision the name of a Christian country, by enabling the Chinese to violate the laws of their own nation, in obtaining the accursed and prohibited poison; the use of which entails destruction, mentally and bodily on its infatuated devotees.[6]

Some of the earliest accounts of the modern opium industry can be traced to the Dutch East Indies in the 1690s, when the VOC sold opium in Sumatra for an expanding drug market across the archipel-ago. It was, however, indigenous Chinese junk traders who were the first to bring opium on to the mainland and build up a demand for the drug in elite circles. This led in 1729 to an import ban into China by the Qing Empire except under licence for medical purposes.[7] To elim-inate any uncertainty, the smoking of opium was outlawed in 1796, and the importation block reasserted in 1800. None of these clear, legal prohibitions stopped the British East India Company from enter-ing the market. The Company had gained its first foothold in China in 1672, taking the place of the expelled Dutch VOC with a trading post in Taiwan. By the early 1700s it had built up a prosperous trading operation – working alongside the Hong merchants licensed to deal with foreign merchants – centred on its 'factory' at Canton. Indeed, the finances of Leadenhall Street were becoming increasingly oriented around the opium trade in the East Indies. Heavily dependent upon exporting tea from China into Europe, the Company discovered that the merchants of Shanghai had little interest in buying British produce in return. There were no reciprocal orders for Manchester cottons or Staffordshire pottery or Yorkshire woollens; the only currency the Chinese merchants, the Co-Hongs, were interested in was bullion – and the relentless drain of silver west to east was soon threatening to scupper the Company finances. It was among the poppy fields of Bengal that a solution was found to this fiscal crisis. 'Opium is the only ready money article sold in China,' as William Jardine succinctly put it.

From the early 1780s, Warren Hastings was already smuggling opium into China, and by the turn of the century it had become a core component of the East India Company's business. The opium was grown under Company monopoly in Bengal, sold at public auctions run by Company officials and branded with the Company's unique *chop* mark on each chest; its sales provided the Company with some 15 per cent of its tax revenue in India. Wary of provoking the Chinese authorities and risking any long-term damage to Sino-British trade, Leadenhall Street refused to allow Company ships directly to transport the cargo out of Calcutta. Instead, private merchants, known as 'country traders', were licensed to carry the chests laden with opium cakes into Canton, whereupon Chinese smugglers took the drug up country. With such extensive corporate resources behind it, the spread of opium into China 'crept in a most mysterious and fascinating manner into the homes of the rich and poor, and with its mystic fingers gripped the hearts of old and young', reported one shamed British missionary. 'Men became paralysed before this new force, and reason stood silent, and the highest ideals of human life slowly paled and vanished in the presence of this Indian mystery.'[8] However lamentable the effects, the profits were unanswerable. Chinese drug smugglers converted their cash payments into East India Company bills payable in London or Calcutta, and the flow of silver from west to east began to reverse its direction at a remarkable speed.

Leadenhall Street's balance of payments crisis faded thanks to another 'triangle trade' – this time an Asian nexus that saw the produce of Indian poppy fields arrive in City of London accounts via Canton agency houses.

With such massive profits on offer, the East India Company monopoly over trade with China was soon under pressure from aggressive pirate traders. British merchants started to seek out alternative sources of opium, and in princely Malwa, on the west coast of central India, they found a new fount of poppy production beyond the control of the British army or Company officials. From the 1810s Malwa opium started to enter the Chinese market, forcing the East India Company to slash the price of its own Bengal opium and leading to a surge of imports into Canton. From 5,000 chests in 1820, the East India

A busy drying room in the opium factory in Patna, India. The raw opium was formed into a ball about 1½ kilos in weight and wrapped in poppy petals to protect it from damage. The balls were then dried on shelves and boxed into chests each containing 25–40 balls before shipping to China and Europe. After W. S. Sherwill, lithograph (c. 1850).

Company was exporting over 19,000 chests by 1831. Leading the customs-busting operation was Jardine Matheson, which poured money into a new fleet of clipper ships to outmanoeuvre the competition (the *Red Rover* could race from the Hooghly to the Pearl River and back again in eighty-six days, with its company flag of a white diagonal cross on a blue field billowing through the South China Sea) as well as brigs and schooners to offload the drug along the China coast. Its efficient distribution infrastructure meant that by the late 1820s Jardine, Matheson & Co. was able to control up to a third of Canton opium deliveries. The firm was wholly unembarrassed about the basis of its prosperity: William Jardine thought the opium trade 'the safest and most gentlemanlike speculation I am aware of',[9] and James Matheson declared that 'During the twenty one years I have passed almost entirely in China, I can conscientiously declare that I have never seen a native in the least bestialized by opium smoking, like drunkards in Europe.' Jardine Matheson's only frustration was the unhelpful attitude of the Chinese authorities and, in the absence of a safe port in which to offload the cargo, the dangerous necessity for clippers to dock alongside floating warehouses. How much easier it would be if the British could get their hands on a nice, proper harbour – such as, for example, Hong Kong. Indeed, James Matheson's nephew, Alexander Matheson, came to think the island 'absolutely indispensable for the extension of British trade in China' and, in 1842, wanted it 'officially declared a British Colony with as little delay as possible'.[10]

But Hong Kong was never the ultimate objective; it was a way-station for the real prize of China. With a conviction that bordered on obsession, Europe was determined to 'open up' China to the wonders of modern, capital markets. 'The trade with China already is of equal if not greater importance than that with any other nation in the world, and, if judiciously fostered and encouraged, is capable of almost unlimited increase,' wrote the former East India Company merchant H. Hamilton Lindsay in an open letter to Viscount Palmerston in 1836.[11] British merchants and diplomats remained bewildered as to why the Qing Empire could possibly want to preclude itself from the wonders of Western civilization and commodity capitalism.

In fact, attempts to open China up to European imports had been going on since the ill-fated mission of the first British ambassador to China (and first ambassador to the Cape Colony), Lord George Macartney, in 1793–4. Despatched by Henry Dundas to seek some form of diplomatic representation at the Celestial Court in Peking and reveal to the Qing dynasty the virtues of the 'fair competition of the Market', the Macartney mission ended in one of the great fiascos of British diplomatic history as its leader was repeatedly humiliated and then expelled. 'Strange and costly objects do not interest me,' was the emperor's high-handed response to King George III. 'As your Ambassador can see for himself, we possess all things.' The lofty, Confucian ethos of the Qing court never had much admiration for the solid manufactures of Britain's industrial revolution. Yet the mission was not a total waste of time. From a military perspective, Lord Macartney realized that 'the empire of China is an old, crazy, first-rate Man of War . . . She may, perhaps, not sink outright; she may drift sometime as a wreck, and will then be dashed to pieces on the shores.'[12]

But to James Matheson's mind, it was positively wicked that the 'empire of China' could control such a 'vast portion of the most desirable parts of the earth' and not allow foreigners access to them. Instead, they selfishly wanted to 'monopolize all the advantages of their situation' and retain the domestic market for themselves.[13] It was all the more egregious since, according to the Manchester Chamber of Commerce and Manufacturers, 'no country presents to us the basis of a more legitimate and mutually advantageous trade than China'.[14] Its vast numbers and advanced urban centres but backward state of industrial production made the Middle Kingdom a tantalizing prospect for British manufacturers and merchants. What was more, it could be an important export market for India, the profits from which could then be spent on more imports from Manchester, Glasgow and Birmingham to Calcutta and Madras.

Legitimizing this commercial strategy for 'China Opened' was the Gospel of Free Trade – that self-righteous engine of nineteenth-century British imperialism. As the free-market ideas of Adam Smith and Utilitarian philosophy of Jeremy Bentham seeped through the British ruling class, the corrupt practices of the East India Company were condemned as an out-of-date, Hanoverian hangover. The Manchester

School of Political Economy, with its Trinity of competition, transparency and open markets – the aspiration of Jardine and Matheson – started to reframe colonial thinking. In 1823 the President of the Board of Trade, William Huskisson, introduced the Reciprocity of Duties Bill into parliament in an attempt to dismantle, as he put it, 'the bastions of our ancient colonial system': mercantilism gave way to open markets as Huskisson pursued a series of free-trade agreements with other trading nations, effectively ending the 200-year sway of the Navigation Acts. In 1833 the East India Company's monopoly was abolished by Act of Parliament, opening up the Empire to Adam Smith's invisible hand. In 1846 the Corn Laws would be repealed as a defining symbol of the abandonment of the protectionist past and the triumph of Manchester liberalism; in 1860, with the Cobden–Chevalier Treaty, even France and Britain would agree to a free-trade pact. 'The spirit which moved the British Parliament to wrench asunder the shackles in which British trade had been kept for two long centuries by the East India Company was the potent spirit of free trade,' explained the Hong Kong missionary Ernst Johann Eitel at the end of the nineteenth century, 'and in this general free trade movement we see above the dark horizon the first streak of light heralding the advent of the future free port of Hong Kong.'[15]

But before Hong Kong came Singapore – the first of those rays of light dispelling the mercantilist gloom from the British Empire. In 1819 the East India Company writer Stamford Raffles began negotiations with Sultan Hussein Shah to secure the island, which was located in a prime position on the trading route between India and China. Sat between the Malay peninsula and the Indonesian archipelago, Singapore was historically part of the Dutch sphere of influence. Raffles's achievement was to snatch it from under their nose in 1824, declare it a British possession and then institute a new model of colonialism predicated on the virtuous effects of free trade. 'It is the peculiar characteristic of Great Britain, that wherever her influence has been extended, it has carried civilization and improvement in its train,' he wrote in 1819. 'The acquisitions of Great Britain in the East have not been made in the spirit of conquest.'[16] Rather, in the spirit of raising the wealth of all nations, the Port of Singapore was declared 'a Free Port and the Trade thereof is open to Ships and Vessels of every Nation free of duty equally and alike to all'. The consequences were immediate as the traffic from China, Siam and Cochinchina – as well as German, Swiss, Dutch, Portuguese and British ships – began to pour into Singapore. In 1822, a total of 139 square-rigged vessels entered the port; by 1834, there were 517 ships carrying nearly 160,000 tons of cargo coming in.

Despite all the evidence of port tonnage and shared prosperity, there still remained certain civilizations unpersuaded of the merits of open markets. Nowhere was this obstinacy more apparent than in the major Chinese port of Canton, where foreign merchants were required to conduct all trade through a laborious cartel of Hong merchants. Added to this were the costs of compradors and linguists and then port charges and an ever-expanding array of other taxes the Canton governor wanted to add on. In 1827, James Matheson, who had ordered the works of Adam Smith and David Ricardo to be sent out to him in China, attempted to change the culture with a weekly paper, the *Canton Register*, in order to 'disseminate the principles of free trade'.[17] The paper even ran a £50 essay prize for any author able to illustrate 'the great principles of Political Economy, applicable to the errors and abuses which may exist in China'.

These were principles shared by the Scottish naval officer and veteran of the Battle of Trafalgar Lord Napier. Despatched to China as lord superintendent of trade in the aftermath of the abolition of the East India Company monopoly in 1833, he adopted an even more pugilistic approach than Matheson – confident that 'three or four frigates or brigs' and 'a few steady British troops' could settle things 'in a space of time inconceivably short'.[18] This would, he thought, speedily ensure British objectives of a resident embassy in Peking and open access to China's ports for London merchants. Despite clear instructions from Whitehall to 'observe all possible moderation' and 'conform to the law and usages of China' in pursuing the strategy, the old sea-dog sailed into Canton without approval, sent gunboats upriver to Whampoa, and paid absolutely no heed to Celestial protocol. This was to be free trade delivered from the barrel of a gun.*

---

* And it was all for a great cause. 'The war, when it comes, will not be for opium. It will be for a principle: for freedom – for the freedom of trade and for the freedom of the Chinese people' was how the sanctimonious Calcutta merchant Benjamin Burnham

In the event, Napier's ambitions were cut short when he contacted malarial fever and died at Macao in 1834. But he did not depart without planting in the mind of the Foreign Office a recommendation to occupy 'the island of Hong Kong, in the entrance of the Canton river, which is admirably adapted for every purpose'. As demands for the opening-up of China to Western commerce intensified and the profiteering of the opium merchants accelerated, the allure of the Fragrant Harbour grew stronger. 'If the lion's paw is to be put down on any part of the south side of China let it be Hong Kong,' wrote one correspondent in 1836 to James Matheson's *Canton Register*, 'let the lion declare it to be under his guarantee a free port, and in ten years it will be the most considerable mart east of the Cape!'[19]

GUNBOAT DIPLOMACY

'This little band of free traders, the Jardines, the Mathesons, the Dents, the Gibbs, the Turners, the Hollidays, the Braines, the Innes, unconsciously did for the future colony of Hong Kong what subsequently Cobden did for Manchester,' was how E. J. Eitel described the commercial transformation of the mid-nineteenth century. They 'prepared the public mind for future free trade in a free port on British soil in China'.[20]

Leading the pack were Messrs Jardine and Matheson, the outriders of British imperialism in the East. Born in Dumfriesshire in 1784 to a family of small farmholders, William Jardine was educated in medicine at the University of Edinburgh before securing a position with the East India Company as a surgeon's mate. He travelled back and forth to India and then China using his 'privilege tonnage' as a ship's surgeon for cargo space for private trade, mostly in cassia, cochineal and musk. His interest in commerce soon supplanted that in medicine, and in 1817 he resigned his commission with the East India

---

frames it in Amitav Ghosh's colonial-era novel *Sea of Poppies*. 'Free Trade is a right conferred on Man by God, and its principles apply as much to opium as to any other article of trade. More so perhaps, since in its absence many millions of natives would be denied the lasting advantage of British influence.' See Amitav Ghosh, *Sea of Poppies* (London, 2009), p. 120.

Company and became an independent country trader, working the Bombay to Canton route. And it was in Bombay in 1820 that he met a fellow Scot, James Matheson, then making his way in the export trade.

Twelve years younger than Jardine, Matheson was also a graduate of Edinburgh University and the East India Company. Various business ventures came and went until he based himself in Canton and Macau in the early 1820s and started earning proper money as an agent for merchants in Singapore and India. However, it was Jardine who transformed his prospects by bringing him into his trading company of Magniac & Co., which in 1834 was reconstituted as Jardine, Matheson & Co. Matheson was the more mercurial, entrepreneurial and intellectual of the two, but it was the brutish, Calvinist, austere Jardine who ground out the profits from their Canton factory at No. 4, The Creek. All time was God's time, and Jardine abhorred idleness; he kept only one chair in his office, on which he sat while visitors stood. Among the Chinese he was known as the 'Iron-Headed Rat', after an incident at Canton when he was struck on the head by a club and carried on as normal. Benjamin Disraeli, in his 1845 novel *Sybil*, offered a more acerbic pen-portrait after Jardine had returned from China and stood as Member of Parliament for Ashburton in Devon. 'A Scotchman, richer than Croesus, one McDruggy, fresh from Canton, with a million of opium in each pocket, denouncing corruption and bellowing free trade.'[21]

There was a third figure in the establishment of Jardine, Matheson & Co. – the Bombay-based Parsi merchant Jamsetjee Jejeebhoy. Born in 1783, Jejeebhoy worked his apprenticeship in his uncle's shop counting and selling empty bottles before joining the China trade as an accounts clerk for another Parsi merchant. On one journey in 1805, aboard the *Brunswick* (which would later be captured by French forces) he made friends with the ship's assistant surgeon, William Jardine, and was happy to enter into the opium business with him and Matheson. Jejeebhoy's supply routes out of Bombay and extensive trading contacts in Calcutta, Colombo, Singapore and Macao helped the two Scottish entrepreneurs build up the lucrative trade between Britain, India and China. They bought opium from Jejeebhoy or at auction in Calcutta, shipped it into Canton, sold it to the 'country

16. Fort William on the Hooghly River, here painted by Francis Swainer, gives visitors to Calcutta an immediate sense of the permanence and power of the British Empire in Bengal (1763).

17. Major-General Sir David Ochterlony, hero of the Maratha wars, smoking a hookah and embracing the Orientalist attractions of service in India (c. 1800).

18. 'It being the general custom of Bengal in those days to drink freely and to assemble in numerous parties at each other's houses.' William Hickey's Calcutta on display at a levée at Old Government House (1792).

19. The Glorious Little Man. Richard Wellesley, Governor General of India, by Thomas Lawrence (1813).

20. Kedleston in Calcutta: Wellesley's 'original great palace of British India', Government House (1848) painted by Charles d'Oyly.

21. 'The most gentlemanlike speculation I am aware of.' Opium Clipper *Waterwitch* in Calcutta (*c.* 1850).

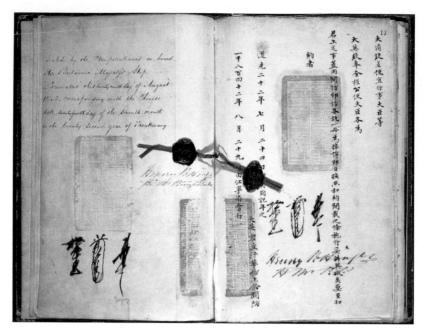

22. 'The imperial powers descended on China like a swarm of bees.' Treaty of Nanjing (1842).

23. East Point, Hong Kong, with the residence and godowns of Jardine, Matheson & Co (mid-nineteenth century).

24. The Fragrant Harbour becomes one of the busiest shipping stations in the world, as depicted in an 1860s watercolour by Marciano Baptista.

25. Queen's Road, Hong Kong, from the clock tower looking towards the east. Decorations for HRH the Duke of Edinburgh's visit can be seen on the buildings (1868).

26. Merchant prince, Parsi philanthropist and urban improver: Sir Jamsetjee Jejeebhoy and his Chinese servant, by George Chinnery (*c.* 1830s).

27. 'Bombay has long been the Liverpool of the East – she is now becoming the Manchester also.' Parsee cotton merchants of Bombay. Illustration from *The Countries of the World* by Robert Brown (London, 1876–92).

28. Engineer of Empire:
Sir Bartle Frere,
Governor of Bombay,
by Sir George Reid
(1881).

29. The Indo-Saracenic
Gormenghast of Bombay
Victoria Terminus
(*right*) – 'the truly central
building of the entire
British Empire' with the
Municipal Corporation
Building behind, as
photographed by Raja
Deendayal (*c.* 1893).

30. Ruskin's Venetian Gothic shapes the urban fabric of Victorian Bombay. Sir George Gilbert Scott's University Library, complete with Ca' d'Oro styling (1878).

31. Buried amidst the pineapples of Crawford Market, a gleefully ornamental water fountain designed by William Emerson and encased with decorative panels by Lockwood Kipling (1869).

traders' and then purchased Company bills, with the profits cashed back in London. The end of the East India Company monopoly in 1833 provided further opportunities for the firm in tea, silk, cotton, even insurance. But the opium trade remained at the core of their business, with chests of Malwa and Patna buying Jardine and Matheson country seats and securing the company its soubriquet, 'the Princely Hong'.

If Jardine and Matheson were admired in London as the buccaneering heroes of British free enterprise, the view from Peking was less adulatory. The criminality, drug addiction and sustained loss of silver bullion wrought by Jardine, Matheson & Co. were threatening to destabilize regional economies and undermine the finances of the Qing Empire. Despite repeated edicts outlawing the import of opium, British merchants had taken no notice. After debating the merits of legalizing the drug, Peking decided instead on a clampdown and appointed the experienced Qing official Lin Zexu as imperial commissioner in Canton with a licence to eradicate the problem. He first fired off a letter to Queen Victoria complaining of opium being planted 'from hill to hill' in British India, where 'its obnoxious odor ascends, irritating heaven and frightening the spirits'. He then announced that if 'the barbarian merchants of your country' wished to carry on doing business in China, they would be required 'to obey our statutes respectfully and to cut off permanently the source of opium'. Lin then rounded up the Chinese smugglers, confiscated 20,000 cases of British-owned opium and confined foreign merchants in their factories until all his requests were acceded to. This was just the kind of *casus belli* the China free-traders had been hoping for.[22]

In London, William Jardine raced round Whitehall to meet the foreign secretary, the roué Whig Lord Palmerston, to urge an overwhelming military and naval response to Lin Zexu's hostage-taking. 'My advice is to send a naval force to blockade the Chinese coast from the Tartar Wall [Great Wall] to Tienpack; the force to consist of two ships of the line, two frigates and two flat-bottomed steamers for river service with a sufficient number of transports to carry . . . six or seven thousand men.' The troops needed to head straight to Peking to demand an apology for the insult, 'payment for the opium given up, an equitable commercial treaty and liberty to trade with northern ports'.[23] In a further note to Palmerston, this plan of action became more succinct: 'You take my opium – I take your Islands in return – we are therefore Quits – and thenceforth if you please let us live in friendly Communion and good fellowship.'[24] Palmerston rarely needed much encouragement for a display of British imperial bravado, and the iron warship *Nemesis*, armed with rocket launchers and 32-pounder guns, soon left Portsmouth harbour for the Pearl River, and an expeditionary force set sail from India (carried, conveniently enough, by a Jardine Matheson clipper). With tensions rising, the British merchant community fled Canton for Macao and then the secure inlet of Hong Kong. As they departed, a Royal Navy force of sixteen men-of-war, four armed steamers and twenty-seven transport ships carrying 3,000 British troops arrived to avenge the Lin Zexu insult and prise open China once and for all.

As predicted, Macartney's 'old, crazy, first-rate Man of War' was dashed to pieces as British naval might smashed through the Qing defences. Sir Edward Belcher, now on the *Nemesis*, recorded the scene as the steam-powered battleship drew up close to the Chinese junks 'before opening fire' with 'several well-directed guns', throwing the Qing navy into confusion.

> The first rocket pitched into the magazine of the ship next to the admiral, and she blew up in great style . . . The boats then moved on, and set fire to the junks in the lower part of the river, but in ascending the main branch, those retreating under canvass kept up a very spirited fire on the chasing boats . . . The increase of force soon decided their fate; two ran on shore, and the remainder made their escape.[25]

Some of the naval encounters lasted barely an hour. The British battle-fleet cruised on to capture Amoy (Xiamen), Chushan, Chintu (Chengdu) and Ningpo (Ningbo). In the spring of 1842 Shanghai itself was taken; then the flotilla entered the lower Yangtze River with a view to storming Nanking (Nanjing) and cutting off supplies to Peking by controlling access to the Grand Canal.

An initial attempt at peace – the Chuan-pi Convention in January 1841 – drawn up by Chinese and British officials was dismissed by both Peking and London as a piece of diplomatic freelancing and an unacceptable, near-treacherous compromise. The British negotiator,

Captain Charles Elliot, had secured a $6 million indemnity, new terms of equality between British and Chinese merchants and a set of useful if unspecified rights over the island of Hong Kong – just enough to allow Sir J. G. Bremer and his troops to hoist the Union flag at Possession Mount. In London, however, Lord Palmerston was incandescent at the pusillanimity of it all. 'Throughout the whole course of your proceedings, you seemed to have considered that my instructions were waste paper,' he harangued Elliot. Nor was he very impressed with the prize of Hong Kong – 'a barren little island with hardly a house upon it'.[26] Queen Victoria was equally disappointed. 'All we wanted might have been got, if it had not been for the unaccountably strange conduct of Charles Elliot who completely disobeyed his instructions and *tried* to get the *lowest* terms he could,' she complained to her uncle, the King of the Belgians. There was one light-hearted consolation. 'Albert is so much amused at my having got the island of Hong Kong, and we think Victoria [her eldest daughter] ought to be called Princess of Hong Kong in addition to Princess Royal.'[27]

Another year of battering from the cannon of the *Nemesis* and the *Sulphur* resulted in the more acquisitive Treaty of Nanking of August 1842, negotiated by Elliot's successor, the experienced colonial governor Sir Henry Pottinger. Pottinger's task was an easier one than Elliot's. With Nanking on the precipice of destruction, the Qing diplomats were forced to sue for peace with a weakened hand: China agreed to pay an indemnity of 21 million silver dollars for the costs of war and the destroyed opium, transfer Hong Kong island and its harbour to British sovereignty 'in perpetuity', and to open up the five ports of Canton, Amoy, Foochow (Fuzhou), Ningpo and Shanghai to British traders and a British consulate. These 'Treaty Ports' and, in particular, Shanghai, became enormously significant to Sino-British trade from the mid-nineteenth century right through to the Second World War. With new rights of residence and business, the British merchants quickly exploited Shanghai's strategic location at the mouth of the Yangtze River and its much more developed commercial market. They ran the Chinese Maritime Customs, assumed political and military control of the urban core and turned Shanghai into, if not a colonial city, then certainly a colonial-concession city.[28]

Finally, it was hoped, China had been 'opened'. 'A war more unjust in its origin, a war more calculated in its progress to cover this country with permanent disgrace, I do not know, and I have not read of,' was William Gladstone's verdict on the Opium War and capture of Hong Kong. A child of Liverpool and the free-trading son of a corn merchant, he found it painful to see the Union flag, which had always been associated 'with the cause of justice, with opposition to oppression, with respect for national rights, with honourable commercial enterprize', now hoisted on the coast of China 'to protect an infamous contraband traffic'.[29]

Such righteous indignation was a minority view. Most commentators regarded the Opium War and the taking of Hong Kong as a golden opportunity to demonstrate the divine energy of free trade. In contrast to India, the British did not want a territorial empire in the Far East. 'I had no predilection in raising a colony at Hong Kong, or at any other place in China,' recalled Pottinger. Rather, he was convinced 'of the necessity and desirability of our possessing such a settlement as an emporium for our trade and a place from which Her Majesty's subjects in China may be alike protected and controlled'.[30] 'A secure and well regulated trade is all we desire,' cooed the new foreign secretary, Lord Aberdeen. Indeed the capture of Hong Kong was so high-minded a venture in free trade that Britain 'would seek no exclusive advantages, and demand nothing that we shall not willingly see enjoyed by the subjects of all other States'.[31]

In theory, the invisible hand of the free market would nurture a new era of Sino-British prosperity and peace, which would be willingly and selflessly shared out among other European and American merchants. In practice, the taking of Hong Kong was a textbook exercise in 'gunboat diplomacy', in which trading rights were acquired at the point of a warship's guns and British businesses were granted special dispensations through the imposition of unequal treaties on beaten powers. Palmerston, at least, was honest about his motives, when he thanked William Jardine, in a letter of April 1842, for the 'assistance and information' which he and other merchants provided 'to our affairs naval, military and diplomatic'. 'There is no doubt that this event, which will form an epoch in the progress of the civilization of the human races, must be attended with the most important advantages to the commercial interests of England.'[32] This was, in the formulation of historians John Gallagher and Ronald Robinson, the 'imperialism of free trade': the exertion of political, diplomatic and sometimes military influence to secure the kind of privileged free-trade regime which worked to the explicit advantage of the colonial powers.[33] Of course, British interests in Hong Kong were purely commercial – just so long as no one dared to question the political settlement underpinning them. In cruder terms, as Lord Aberdeen explained to the House of Lords, 'he did not wish to be understood to say, that at no time should any [free] port be without a British cruiser anchored there, but no port should be long without, and he trusted that each port would always have one, except when the exigencies of the naval service might require their temporary absence'.[34] The 'well-directed guns' of the *Sulphur* and the *Nemesis* became an essential adjunct to Adam Smith's *The Wealth of Nations*. The real winner, naturally, was British business. Within less than two years of the Treaty of Nanking, predicted the free-trade *Friend of China*, 'the Tartar of Central Asia will trim his beard with Sheffield scissors, and every spinster in Peking must have a Coventry ribbon'.[35]

To secure this kind of commercial access, however, the British merchants starting to operate out of Hong Kong wanted a commitment to retain the Fragrant Harbour and not return it in any future peace deal with the Chinese – which the Treaty of Nanking duly provided. Leading the pack was Jardine, Matheson & Co. 'Once thoroughly protected roads [anchorage] made and settlers encouraged it could hardly fail to become a considerable emporium,' James Matheson wrote to William Jardine. And so he was happy to sink the company's funds into new headquarters on the island's East Point. 'Our outlays in building an extensive godown [warehouse] etc. at HongKong will by and bye amount to perhaps 20,000 dollars – so that I am not disinterested in advocating its retention. Many prefer Cowloon Peninsula, but we ought to have both.'[36] By May 1842 Hong Kong was 'progressing with wonderful rapidity', agreed Alexander Matheson (who had assumed leadership of the firm from his uncle). 'Several large store godowns and dwelling houses are already finished, and many more in progress, and there is an immense Chinese Bazaar of brick houses exceeding in extent that of Macao; and with its fine anchorage, excellent roads [sheltered waters], and picturesque scenery, it has already thrown Macao into the shade.'[37] There was a growing conviction that Palmerston's 'barren little island' might just have something going for it. 'It struck me at that time, and circumstances have since borne me out, that we should never again relinquish this little spot,' wrote Captain Arthur Cunynghame in *An Aide-de-Camp's Recollections of Service in China* (1844). 'It seemed perfectly requisite for us to possess some portion of land, neighbouring the continent, where our own laws should be enforced, free from the chicanery and grasping insolence of the mandarins.' It would all help, he reflected, in compelling 'the Chinese authorities to respect the laws of civilized nations'.[38] By which, of course, he meant the laws of Britain.

GLEN AND GOLDTOWN

It was the very drama of the location – the rain and sun, the valleys and forests, the deep greens and shearing rocks – which so entranced the first European visitors. 'Both on the mainland and in the island itself, there are bold, rugged mountain outlines, often shrouded in a mist that reminds one of Scotland and Ireland; huge boulders of rock from which beautiful ferns of every variety grow in profusion,' wrote the British attaché at Peking, Lord Redesdale. The hills surrounding the bay offer a vista of 'a blue glen such as Sir Walter Scott might have described'.[39] The missionary and future Oxford Professor of Chinese, Reverend James Legge, would never forget the journey from Macao to Hong Kong and 'the sensations of delight with which . . . I contemplated the ranges of hills on the north and the south, embosoming, between them the tranquil waters of the bay. I seemed to feel that I had found at last the home for which I had left Scotland.'[40] It was Wong-nai-chong, or Happy Valley – where once 'there were to be seen only fields of rice and sweet potatoes' (and now is home to one of the most obviously urban racecourses in the world, with its floodlit track nestled in a modern valley of towering residential apartment blocks) – which seduced the incoming colonists.[41] Hong Kong vice consul Henry Sirr thought the valley's gushing streams made it 'the most picturesque portion of the Island', as the 'lover of nature' made his way up towards the peak, passing 'broken rocks relieved by stunted trees, clad in dark green, with occasionally a noble mangoe or lei-chee tree, the branches drooping under the weight of the delicious fruit' lining the route.[42] The travel writer Albert Smith, visiting in the 1850s, was equally delighted by 'the belts of mango and lychee trees' and the water cascading over the 'blocks of granite, with a charming Chamouni sound about it'.[43] It was a curious mix of the exotic and the familiar: a meteorology and geology like that of the Highlands or the Alps, but set above the South China Sea.

Along the foreshore, much of this sublime beauty would soon be obliterated by the speed of development. In Hong Kong's halcyon days at the start of the twentieth century, its Renaissance Revival cityscape of City Hall, Praya esplanade, Royal Square and Regatta Club would earn the colony the title of Pearl of the Orient. It was a sophisticated, elegant, if somewhat raffish destination on the rim of the exotic East. At the beginning, though, the colony had more the feel of midwest America in the midst of a gold rush. 'If you leave Hong Kong for a month, where you left a rock you find a drawing room in the height of Indian luxury – and a road where there was twenty feet of water,' reported Lieutenant Bernard Collinson of the Sappers in 1845, who also had the thankless task of producing Hong Kong's first map.[44] Queen's Road, originally a rough track straggling along the coastline, quickly emerged as the colony's main thoroughfare. 'Go where you would your ears were met with the clink of hammer and chisels, and your eyes were in danger of sparks of stone at every corner,' recalled the American traveller Osmond Tiffany. 'The buildings were run up and finished with magic ease; one day the cellar would be dug, and the next the roof was being finished.'[45] In between the construction sites were the tents and huts of the 55th Regiment, builders' yards, and then a Chinatown hinterland of squatters' huts, opium dens, temples, gambling-halls and duck-pens.[46] Out of the chaos came Hong Kong. 'Within one year from the completion of the first house, not only were regular streets and bazaars for the Chinese erected, but numerous large substantial warehouses were built, mostly of stone, some already finished, and others in progress.'[47]

Then as now, it was these commercial premises – the warehouses, banks, wharfs, jetties and factories – which provided the colony's defining architectural edifices. Pottinger's ambition to turn Hong Kong into 'a vast emporium of commerce and wealth' led him towards a policy of land auctions and peppercorn rents designed to attract the major East Asian merchants on to the island. It proved a remarkable success as the premises of Gibb, Livingston & Co. of Jamieson, How & Co., of Dent & Co., of the American firm Russell & Co. and of Lindsay & Co. overtook the waterfront. To store the huge quantities of stock – the woollens, silks, cottons, coal, earthenware, alcohol, timber, rice, nut oil, tea and opium – entering from Europe, India and China, merchant houses demanded extensive lots, and the 'Princely Hong' obviously required the largest. Just outside the centre, East Point might not have been the finest location on offer, but Jardine, Matheson & Co. managed to erect there a godown 'so extensive, as to form almost a town of themselves'.[48] Another witness thought the Jardine Matheson headquarters so grandiose that it resembled 'somewhat an independent though allied sovereignty of Hong Kong'.[49] These bastions of an informal empire were then joined by those more formal symbols of Empire such as the Royal Navy Dockyard, army barracks and hospital, government offices, St John's Cathedral and Flagstaff House, residence of the commander of British forces in Hong Kong – and all bearing witness, reflected Henry Sirr, 'to English perseverance, industry and energy'.[50]

In those pioneering days, not everyone shared Sirr's belief in the future of the Fragrant Harbour as a viable British colony. For all that broiling sun, sea mist and lashing rain fostered not a clean Highland air, but a deadly 'Hong Kong fever' which managed to wipe out scores of early colonists. Soldiers had the worst of it as poor housing, bad diet, exhaustion, venereal disease and drink took their toll. Smallpox, malaria and cholera did the rest. The mid-1840s saw a mortality rate approaching 20 per cent with 100 soldiers from the 55th Regiment dying between June and August 1843, and over 260 men, 4 women and 17 children from the 95th Regiment lost between 1847 and 1850; in the July and August of 1848 they were burying them at a rate of fifty a month.[51] 'The mortality was mainly owing to the want of accommodation for the multitudes who kept pressing into the new colony, and to the miasma set free from the ground which was everywhere being turned up,' thought James Legge. 'Then the drains were for the time all open, and an atmosphere of disease, which only the strongest constitutions and prudent living were able to resist, might be said to envelope the island day and night.'[52] Until the advent of a proper system of burial grounds (beginning around Happy Valley), effective sanitary reform and safe drinking water in the 1860s, the casualty rate was terrible, and few thought England had such human capital to spare. One Hong Kong resident concluded that the death rate meant 'the settlement on the Eastern coast of China must become a national burden, with no counterbalancing advantage'.[53] Even Victoria had heard tell of the island's insanitary mess. 'The Queen understands there is a notion of exchanging Hong Kong for a more healthy colony,' reads a January 1844 note to the foreign secretary. 'The Queen, taking a deep interest in all these matters, and feeling it her duty to do so, begs Lord Aberdeen to keep her always well informed of what is on the *tapis* in his Department.'[54]

Across Whitehall, there was growing scepticism about the wisdom of colonizing Hong Kong. As the five Treaty Ports on the Chinese coast opened up by the Treaty of Nanking allowed European merchants direct access to the mainland markets and took up most of the increased trade, and as the Qing authorities worked to block wealthy traders from moving to the island, the great Hongs started to take a hit on their investments. After a few years at his East Point godown, even Alexander Matheson no longer thought the colony 'absolutely indispensable for the extension of British trade in China'. Instead, he told a House of Commons Select Committee into 'The State of Our Commercial Relations with China' that if it were not for the amount of money sunk into real estate, most merchant houses would be looking to pull out of Victoria Harbour. 'From Hong Kong we cannot be said to have derived directly much commercial advantage, nor indeed does it seem to be likely, by its position, to become the seat of an extended commerce,' concluded the MPs in their July 1847 report.[55] Colonial Treasurer Robert Montgomery Martin was adamant about Hong Kong's death at birth. Following his brief and unhappy tenure in what some boosters had called 'the Carthage of the Eastern Hemisphere', he concluded in 1844 that 'there is scarcely a firm in the island but would, I understand, be glad to get back half the money they have expended in the Colony, and retire from the place'. Even after three years' residence, he still could not understand why the British Empire had sunk so much of the Nanking indemnity money into 'this wretched, barren, unhealthy, and useless rock, which the whole wealth, talent and energy of England would never render habitable, or creditable, as a colony, to the British name'. To talk of Hong Kong becoming a durable commercial emporium or emulating Raffles's achievements at Singapore was a delusion: 'There does not appear to be the slightest probability that, under any circumstances, Hong Kong will ever become a place of trade.'[56] Even the fervently free-trade *Economist* magazine was soon lamenting how the island was in danger of becoming, 'nothing now but a depot for a few opium smugglers, soldiers, officers, and men-of-war's men'.[57] This was certainly not the great citadel of laissez-faire economics they had hoped for.

THE GREAT BABYLON

Even if over-optimistic aspirations for Hong Kong as an eastern Carthage were not immediately realized, the colony did nonetheless grow as a busy trading hub. Initially this was down to foreign merchants involved in the China trade in opium, silk and tea, a growing ship-building and -refitting industry and financial and legal services in banking and insurance. Despite the naysayers, Hong Kong offered a secure, accessible and competitive staging post, tax-free and under British rule of law, on the India–China trade route. For all their shroud-waving and demands for government support, once Jardine, Matheson & Co. and Dent & Co. decided to station their headquarters on the island, its importance as a hub of Asian trade and finance expanded exponentially. Soon enough, French, Dutch, German, Parsi and Sephardic Jewish businesses (led by the entrepreneurial Sassoon family) were stationing themselves in the colony in a mutually reinforcing process of commercial growth. Together with Calcutta, Bombay and Canton, Hong Kong was where global trading information came to be exchanged, capital raised, prices fixed and international trading networks forged. For all Montgomery Martin's prophecies of collapse, commerce picked up as traders deposited their goods in 'insurable' godowns, waiting for the right moment to bring their wares to market. Between 1844 and 1861, the number of ship arrivals rose almost fivefold from 538 to 2,545, and total tonnage climbed almost sevenfold from 189,257 to 1,310,388 tons.[58] In 1847, for example, the chief countries from which they came were Great Britain, with 53 ships carrying 21,173 tons; India, with 114 ships, of 66,259 tons; Australia, with 33 ships, of 10,364 tons; and North America, with 16, of 8,175 tons.[59] The Fragrant Harbour became one of the busiest shipping stations in the world as Chinese ocean-going junks bobbed up against heavy Indian merchantmen, American whalers, tea clippers, gigs, paddle-steamers and gunboats. By the end of the nineteenth century, when over 11,000 ships entered and cleared every year, carrying over 13 million tons of cargo, Hong Kong would proudly claim the title of the Empire's third port after London and Liverpool.[60]

In the early years, it was above all else the opium business which kept Hong Kong going. 'The principal mercantile firms are engaged in the opium trade, who have removed hither from Macao as a safer position for an opium depot and which they frankly admit is the only trade Hong Kong will ever possess,' was Montgomery Martin's acid verdict in 1844.[61] He was wrong, but not yet. In the 1840s, the colony became known as 'the central warehouse' for 'British Indian produce' as it handled some 75 per cent of the entire Indian opium crop. 'Between 1845–9 some three-fourths of the opium crops were deposited in and reshipped from this harbour, which thus protected an immense amount of British property,' boasted one British diplomatic memo. In 1844, the second British governor of Hong Kong, Sir John Davis, thought that 'any scruples on our part' about Hong Kong becoming a transshipment centre for drug running were 'more than superfluous' given that the opium trade was 'now fairly established by general connivance along the whole coast of China'.[62] Opium dealing subsidized the rest of the expanding Hong Kong economy: Chinese traders came to the colony to trade in the drug; opium cakes became standard currency; and drug disputes dominated judicial proceedings. 'Then came on a troublesome case about selling a ball of opium,' recounted Albert Smith of a typical workload at the Magistrates Court. 'A swore that he ordered the ball of B, and paid for it, but that it was never sent home. B swore it was; and called C & D – his shopmen – to prove this. The books were also produced. B was a known respectable shopkeeper, so A was fined five dollars for telling lies and taking up the Queen's time.'[63] It was expected that Sino-British trade would move on from its dependence on opium into a broader commerce of goods and services between the kingdoms; in fact, the decision to continue drug trafficking, despite repeated demands by the Chinese authorities for the trade to end, dreadfully retarded any productive commercial relationship between Hong Kong and Peking.[64] Yet the British Empire had a characteristic answer to that problem: another bout of gunboat diplomacy.

For Karl Marx, the irony was delicious. It would be Sir John Bowring – 'the pet disciple of Jeremy Bentham', as Marx called him, 'the greatest-benefit-of-the-greatest-number man' and the leading member of the Peace Society – who would, as Hong Kong vice admiral, be the British official to instigate the Second Opium War. Bowring was indeed a true disciple of laissez-faire. Accredited with the early Victorian aphorism 'Jesus Christ is Free Trade and Free Trade is Jesus Christ', he passionately believed in the pacific, improving, enlightening virtues of commerce. Bentham had died in his arms; he was there at the founding of the Anti-Corn Law League in 1838; and he represented Bolton as a free-trade candidate in parliament for seven years. Few symbolized liberal commerce as Bowring did, and, as one of his earliest despatches revealed, he was an ardent advocate of the Hong Kong model of tax-free enterprise. 'Believing that the satisfactory development of our prosperity is mainly due to the emancipation of all shipping and trade from fiscal vexations and exactions, I trust no custom-house machinery will ever be introduced,' he intoned in language reminiscent of Huskisson's assaults on the Navigation Acts. 'Hong Kong presents another example of the elasticity and potency of unrestricted commerce which has more than counter-balanced the barrenness of the soil ... the disadvantages of its climate, and every impediment which would clog its progress.'[65]

Yet impediments still existed on the mainland. Despite the hopes invested by British merchants in the 1842 Treaty of Nanking, Qing officials still proved far too reluctant to open China up to trade. In Peking, the celestial emperor thought the Treaty had conceded too much, and his agents showed no inclination to honour its terms. As a result, the mid-1850s witnessed growing tension between British merchants and Chinese authorities over access to ports and trading rights. And when, in October 1856, Chinese soldiers boarded the *Arrow*, a British schooner registered in Hong Kong, roughed up the captain and pulled down the Union flag, it was Sir John Bowring of the multinational Peace Society who, in Karl Marx's description, 'preached red-hot shells' with a retributive bombardment of Canton.

The so-called Second Opium War (1856–60) saw an Anglo-French invasion of Canton, the occupation of Peking, the burning of the Summer Palace (preserved now as a crumbling monument to Western barbarism) and the flight of Chinese Emperor Xianfeng into exile. It was humiliation on a grand scale and, in London, the British press and parliament were full of chauvinistic self-congratulation. 'We hear nothing of the illicit opium trade, which yearly feeds the British treasury at the expense of human life and morality,' complained Karl Marx in his *New York Daily Tribune* column of the jingoism sweeping the capital. 'We hear nothing of the constant bribery of sub-officials ... We hear nothing of the bullying spirit ... or of the vice introduced by foreigners at the ports open to their trade.'[66] None of that mattered. Instead, the British pressed home their military advantage with the Treaty of Tientsin and then the Convention of Peking in 1860, which liberated ten more Chinese ports to foreign trade, allowed access to China's hinterland for British missionaries and merchants and by imposing a tariff on the importation of opium effectively normalized the trade. Crucial to the future sustainability of Hong Kong, the Convention also ceded to the British in perpetuity the southern part of the Kowloon peninsula and the Stonecutters Island, a small island to the west of Hong Kong. British territory in China increased to over ninety square kilometres, and another episode of gunboat diplomacy had paid off.

The religious imagery which enveloped the 'Gospel of Free Trade' and 'saving' of China was entirely purposeful. Across the British imperial landscape during the nineteenth century there was an increasing intimacy between commerce and Christianity, between the virtues of capitalism and the spread of Protestantism. The more cosmopolitan East India Company had always sought to keep the Church out of its colonial affairs, but as its monopoly ended and the evangelical movement gained greater sway in Westminster the spread of British civilization across the globe invited a more interventionist religious component. In southern Africa, the missionaries were said to come with 'the Bible in one hand and the gun in the other'; in South-east Asia, they arrived with a free-trade agreement and a cruiser at anchor. And just as British merchants went weak at the knees at the prospect of opening up the Chinese market to European trade, so Western missionaries delighted at the prospect of so many heathen, Chinese souls ripe for conversion. 'The high governor of all the nations has employed England to chastise and humble China,' proclaimed the American missionary Elijah C. Bridgeman. 'He may soon employ her to introduce the blessings of Christian civilization and free intercourse among her millions.'[67] 'Do we now wait for China? No! China waits for us!' responded the British missionary R. G. Milne. 'Providence, by commerce, has given us access to no fewer than five ports of that magnificent nation, and by conquest has facilitated our entrance among its inhabitants, as bearers of celestial light, as apostles of good tidings.'[68]

Of course, there was the bothersome business of illegal drug trafficking and war-mongering as the vehicle for divine opportunity. Some evangelicals did express concern at the method of entry into China (the leading evangelical Lord Shaftesbury condemned the First Opium War as 'one of the most lawless, unnecessary, and unfair struggles in the records of History'), but most missionaries were willing to overlook the chests of opium for the sake of advancing God's greater calling.[69] Hong Kong had been delivered into British hands for a purpose and, with the colony barely a few months old, the London Missionary Society, the American Episcopal Church and the Baptist Church sailed into Victoria Harbour. Special China Funds were raised in London to support a missionary programme of Christianization to be run out of Hong Kong. As with sales, so with souls: Hong Kong was the bridgehead into China. 'While contemplating this rapidly-formed colony ... and its probable influence on the future destinies of a race amounting to one-third of the estimated population of our planet, many novel considerations obtrude themselves on the mind of a British Christian,' mulled Reverend George Smith of the Church Missionary Society after his visit to Hong Kong in 1846.

Believing that his country has been honoured by God as the chosen instrument for diffusing the pure light of Protestant Christianity through the world, and that the permanency of her laws, institutions, and empire, is closely connected with the diffusion of evangelical truth, a British Missionary feels jealous for the faithfulness of his country to her high vocation, and 'rejoices with trembling' at the extension of her colonial empire.[70]

The most celebrated of the new missionaries was the Reverend James Legge of the London Missionary Society, who arrived on the island in 1843 and set up the Union Chapel as a starting point for conversion. 'I am very happy in my work. I opened a new chapel in the heart of the Chinese population in January which is attended in a very encouraging way. A-fat, the first Chinese Protestant convert, is labouring with me,' he wrote in February 1844. 'By and by, I hope to see a flourishing school and a Theological Seminary, with an Institute for native girls, all flourishing here. My hands will be full.'[71] An 'Anglo-Chinese College' (later, a theological college) did indeed spring up, as did the Morrison Education Society School and the Medical Missionary Hospital, all dedicated to the practical dissemination of the Gospel. They were followed by the high-Anglican edifice of St John's Cathedral, opened for divine service in March 1849. 'Ultimately, the island will become a hive,' predicted Legge, 'and I hope that many a Christian swarm will be thrown from it to settle on the adjoining continent.'[72]

In the event, Legge proved more of a scholar than charismatic missionary, and conversion in the colony was slow. Native Hong Kongers might have been amenable to education and healthcare provision from missionary societies, but the purer benefits of Protestantism were generally lost on them. Legge started to concentrate on translation work and theology, while missionary leaders openly questioned the resources allocated to Hong Kong when all of China remained unconverted. Yet the most formidable obstacle to building a Christian ministry was the unfortunate state of the Chinese population. 'While in the northern cities on the mainland of China daily intercourse may be held without restraint with the more respectable classes of native society,' continued Smith, 'at Hong Kong, on the other hand, missionaries may labour for years without being brought into personal communication with any Chinese, except such as are, generally speaking, of the lowest character, and unlikely to exert a moral influence on their fellow-country-men.' The Chinese population of the colony was made up, for the most part, of those 'of the lowest dregs' – coolies, stone-cutters, boatmen, junk crews, iron workers, handicraftsmen, pirates, brothel keepers, Triads and thieves. Very few of them provided receptive Christian material.[73]

Smith's characterization of the population was not unusual, and a hint of illegality suffused the entire island. Rubbing up against the incoming missionaries were the usual range of chancers attracted to a bustling, commercial melting pot on the contested edges of imperial authority. 'It was a seaport of the east, a garrison town, a smuggling centre, a haunt of pirates and racketeers, a drug market and among the most cosmopolitan of Her Majesty's possessions,' explains Jan Morris.[74] Those who were displaced by the Opium War made their way into the colony as well as a growing population of boatpeople drawn to the distribution and construction work on offer. It was a migrant, shifting, shady community whose loyalties were limited: few felt confident enough to predict the future control of Hong Kong, and public order, beyond the barracks, was difficult to maintain. 'In the early days there was next to no police guardianship; and the consequences were frequent disorders on the streets during the day, and many burglaries on a great scale at night,' recalled Legge.[75] Warehouses, public buildings (including Government House), shops, and domestic properties such as James Legge's were all broken into.

The rampant criminality only augmented the racism of the British colonial elite. From the very foundation of the colony, the abuse and occasional violence meted out towards indigenous and migrant Chinese by the Europeans was noticeable. 'The Europeans hate the Chinese, and the latter return the compliment with interest,' was Lord Redesdale's opinion.[76] In stark contrast to the early orientalists of Calcutta, there was little attempt on the part of imperial administrators in Hong Kong to read Chinese literature or understand Qing culture. 'At the present moment, the separation of the native population from the Europeans is nearly absolute,' noted Sir John Bowring in the 1850s.

'Social intercourse between the races is wholly unknown ... I do not believe there is a single merchant or tradesman in Hong Kong who speaks or understands the native dialect, who has seen a Chinaman at his table, or admitted him to the slightest confidential intimacy.'[77] The Reverend George Smith thought it worse than that. 'The Chinese are treated as a degraded race of people,' he noted. The British authorities responded to the volume of crime in May 1843 by prohibiting all Chinese boats from moving about the harbour after 9 p.m. and requiring all Chinese on shore to carry lanterns after dark and not be on the street after 10 p.m. These controls were escalated in 1844 with an ordinance to control the Chinese population through systematic registration and thereby block the influx of the 'scum' of the Chinese into the colony.[78] The result of this heavy-handed array of registrations and restrictions was the elimination of any hope of mutual trust in the colony. 'By these means, a race of people, the most alive to the influences of kind treatment, instead of being converted into friends of British connexion, become alienated, and return to their native soil with prejudices and heart-burnings increased to a ten-fold degree, to spread disaffection to Hong Kong, and hatred of the Western Barbarians.'[79]

At moments of heightened Sino-British tension, that prejudice and disaffection spilled over into communal acts of resistance and sometimes violence. When the 1844 registration requirements were announced, the Chinese community called a General Strike and forced the abolition of the scheme for all but the lowest classes. And then there were the poisonings. In July 1848 there was an attempted poisoning of twenty-five men of the Royal Artillery. But 'the diabolical attempt to poison a large number of the inhabitants of the Colony' came in the shadow of the *Arrow* incident and the run-up to the Second Opium War, when bread from the E-sing bakery was laced with arsenic. On 15 January 1857 James Legge was one of the 300 or so Europeans

> who partook of the poison. I did so twice; – early in the morning, and again at breakfast time; soon getting rid, however, of all the noxious matter through violent paroxysms of sickness. Never was such a day of excitement in the Colony; and had A-lum [the baker] been caught at

once, he would have been lynched beyond doubt; but he had gone off with all his family by the early steamer to Macao.[80]

Although a jury could come to no firm conclusion as to criminal intent behind the poisoning, in its aftermath, new controls were placed over the Chinese community, with more extensive registration schemes, licensing, corporal punishment, searches, deportations and curfews.

The bigotry was all the more self-defeating because, in the words of Governor Hercules Robinson in 1863, 'it is the Chinese who have made Hong Kong what it is and not its connection with the foreign trade'.*[81] It was Chinese labour, trade connections and entrepreneurialism which rescued Hong Kong's finances from their opium dependency and began to chart a more sustainable urban economy. The outbreak of the Taiping Rebellion across southern China in the early 1850s led a growing number of wealthy Cantonese families to make a base in the colony. Between 1853 and 1859, the Chinese population of Hong Kong rose from around 40,000 to around 85,000, and with them came new links to markets on the mainland, with lower overheads thanks to the absence of middlemen, as well as international networks. The growth of overseas Chinese communities in the American West (on the back of the California goldrush), South-east Asia and Australia in the latter half of the nineteenth century helped to turn Hong Kong into a transnational trading and labour hub. Attracted by the British system of private property rights, Chinese immigrants started sinking large funds into the Hong Kong economy, spurring a new wave of commercial development. Such was the growth of confidence that in 1864 the Hong Kong and Shanghai Bank was founded in the colony and, in 1872, Jardine, Matheson & Co. even felt sure enough of future profits to drop the opium trade. But it was Chinese industriousness which was the main source of the wealth creation, and the Chinese were the ones reaping the profits. In 1876 twelve of the twenty highest ratepayers were European firms; in

---

* A hundred years later Hong Kong's last governor, Chris Patten, put it in similar terms: 'A great Chinese city created by the fabulous energies of extraordinarily hard-working and audacious people' (*Financial Times*, 30 June 1997).

1881 only three European companies were among the top twenty. The rest were Chinese individuals or firms.

In the process, great fortunes were accumulated. The so-called *hanjian* or 'Chinese traitors', those smugglers, merchants and gang-masters who had thrown in their lot with the English early in the history of Hong Kong, did particularly well. The comprador Kwok-acheong was a pilot and then provisioner for the Royal Navy who later managed to gain a monopoly over cattle imports into the island and ended up with a personal fortune worth over half a million dollars. His business associate, Tam Achoy, followed the British fleet from the naval dockyard in Singapore to Hong Kong during the First Opium War. His fortune came from construction contracts, chartering emigration ships and then an extensive property portfolio along Victoria Harbour. There were numerous other Chinese 'hongs' grown rich from the cotton and silk trade, construction, real estate investment and the emigration business.[82]

Barred from the traditional avenues of social preferment and political power, Hong Kong's wealthy Chinese used philanthropy and voluntary association to develop an active civil society. These Chinese were not the passive victims of colonialism, but active partners in the development of the colony's social ecology. Charity on a grand scale was the vehicle of choice for ambitious Chinese former compradors, as they assumed the traditional civic function of public men in a commercial city. The creation of a District Watch Committee in 1866, followed by the Nam Pak Hong guild (a mutual assistance association 'to promote members' welfare and market prosperity'), the Tung Wah Hospital and the Po Leung Kuk (literally, 'protect virtue association', formed to stop kidnapping and prostitution) showed an increasingly self-confident mercantile Chinese elite in the second half of the nineteenth century. 'Since the founding of the Tung Wah Hospital, the members of its board of directors have begun to hold an annual gathering to celebrate the lunar new year,' reported Wang Tao, the Christian publisher and friend of James Legge. 'For the occasion they don all sorts of fine headgear and gowns, as if they were illustrious officials having an audience with the emperor! Sartorial splendour has supplanted the plainer styles of the past. At fashionable social gatherings, some spend tens of thousands of dollars on a single dinner.'[83]

For all the philanthropic venture and ostentatious display, the places on the Watch Committee, the Sanitary Board and the hospital, the real levers of power in Hong Kong – the Executive Council and Legislative Council (which supported the governor) – were closed to the Chinese. Demands for political representation were always resisted by both Crown authorities and the British business community. The Chinese could do the hard work, but the lion's paw remained on top. For E. J. Eitel it was the key to the colony's success: 'the rapid conversion of a barren rock into one of the wonders and commercial emporiums of the world has demonstrated what Chinese labour, industry and commerce can achieve under British rule'.[84] Despite the prosperity of many of the Chinese population, the colony's early racial absolutism also produced, as with so many of Britain's imperial cities, a chronically divided urban topography. 'In this island of contrasts none is greater than that between the European and Chinese quarters of the town,' thought Lord Redesdale. 'In the former the houses are large and well built of gray slate-coloured bricks and fine granite . . . In the latter, on the contrary, the houses are low and mean' and peopled 'by ugly old women and queer little yellow children'.[85] Despite the presence of an indigenous Hong Kong population, the British conviction of themselves as 'bona fide first possessors' spurred them to give an air of permanence to their Chinese colony. They would live and build in a British manner, cementing their ownership of the island through the design of its colonial institutions: the Gothic of St John's Cathedral (1849), recalling the Early English architecture of the thirteenth century; the neo-classical Government House (1855); the colonnades and cupolas of the Renaissance-styled City Hall (1869); the arches and verandas of the Royal Observatory Building (1883) – as well as all the vast godowns lining the harbour. This stood in sharp contrast to the supposed impermanence of the migrant Chinese population, housed in their shoddy shanty towns without classical or Gothic legitimacy. They were passing; the British were the possessors.

As in Calcutta and Bridgetown, separate living spurred racial consolidation as the British colonial elite hugged themselves together in a class hierarchy directly imitative of nineteenth-century England. Then as now, the pinnacle of domestic Hong Kong living was Victoria Peak, with its cool air, lush forest, stunning views and cloistered exclusivity. Today native Hong Kongers complain about the 'wall of money' coming over from China and buying up the best properties, but in colonial days it was China-free. In 1867 a summer lodge was erected for the British governor, and, during the second half of the nineteenth century, non-Europeans were progressively excluded from accessing the Peak. Finally, in 1904, after a deadly outbreak of bubonic plague on the island, they were banned from it altogether as Hong Kong consolidated its racial exclusivity and British expatriate life retreated to its rarefied air.

Even in the mixed areas of the island, there was not much mixing. For all the charity and philanthropy of the Chinese merchants, the British remained steadfast in their social segregation. Hong Kong's exclusive panoply of clubs, associations, sports, recreation, entertaining and civic functioning were the means by which the British maintained a colonial sense of purpose and, by excluding the Chinese, racial superiority. There was the Amateur Dramatics Club, the Victoria Club, the Peak Club, the Victoria Recreation Club and the Hong Kong Smoking Concert Club – all with complicated and fraught membership structures for upwardly mobile expats. Then there was the sporting life: the Victoria Regatta Club, the Hong Kong Boat Club, the Royal Hong Kong Yacht Club, the Hong Kong Rifle Association, the Hong Kong Athletics Club, the Hong Kong Cricket Club and, of course, the Hong Kong Jockey Club at Happy Valley (where the Jardines proved particularly successful trainers). However, since its foundation in 1846, the social summit of colony life was located at what was called, very simply, the Hong Kong Club. 'The Club will form a point of attraction which cannot fail to be most welcome,' declared its co-founder Donald Matheson. 'It will afford every variety of entertainment to give a stimulus to the enjoyment of literary and scientific society.'[86] Few would claim it has ever done that. Instead, with an aggressively discriminatory membership code – firmly excluding the island's petit-bourgeoisie, along with Indians, Chinese and women – it became the fulcrum of British colonial self-belief. To belong to the Hong Kong Club secured an elite status on the island and daily access to the governmental and business circle in charge of the colony's destiny. For all his wealth, and despite his place on the

Hong Kong Legislative Council, the Jewish trading dynast Frederick Sassoon never risked applying to join the club for fear of the dreaded black-ball. Today, the club still has an air of exclusivity, albeit now entirely corporate rather than racial. Rehoused in a rather drab, modernist three-storey block opposite the Legislative Council, the club comingles the super-rich of South-east Asia with some old China hands of pre-handover days. Humorous cartoons of various club chairmen playing rugby or drinking whisky, and the impressive fine-art collection of Landseer-lite depictions of Highland scenes, speak to a nostalgic colonial identity, but the club is clearly run with mainland China money. Hierarchy and prestige remain tangible, but the way in is now international finance.

In nineteenth-century Hong Kong, the club, the racing at Happy Valley and the cricket woe what made the climate, illnesses, absence of females and demands of work just about bearable. To Albert Smith, it was a life of relentless tedium and pettiness. 'The young men in the different large houses have a sad mind-mouldering time of it,' he thought. Tea-tasting demanded no great intellect, and so the colony's young clerks 'loaf about the balconies of the houses, or lie in long bamboo chairs, smoke a great deal, [and] play billiards at the Club, where the click of the ball never ceased from the earliest morning'.[87] Then there were the feuds, snubs and social climbing to contend with, the smallness of the island only adding to the pressure-cooker etiquette tussles. 'The little community, far from being a band of brothers, is split into numerous petty cliques or sets, the members of which never think of associating with those out of their own immediate circle,' wrote the clerk Alfred Weatherhead of mid-1850s Hong Kong.[88] This was the bitter-sweet nature of Hong Kong life: a place of remarkable beauty, global reach and offering the promise of great riches, but more often than not the setting for a claustrophobic, enervating colonial life. Rudyard Kipling thought it all too reminiscent of 'an India up-country station', where the inhabitants, surrounded by the open sea and high mountains, 'complain of being cooped in and shut up'. 'They have amateur theatricals and they quarrel and all the men and women take sides, and the station is cleaved asunder from the top to the bottom.'[89]

The warring merchants, officials, soldiers and spouses of the island

were all, however, united by the absolute conviction that the transformation of Hong Kong was the product of what Jules Verne called
'the colonizing genius of the English' allied with the elixir of free
trade. For Phileas Fogg, Verne's hero of *Around the World in Eighty
Days*, Hong Kong's 'docks, hospitals, wharves, Gothic cathedral, government house, macadamized streets' gave to the colony 'the appearance
of a town in Kent or Surrey, transferred by some strange magic to the
antipodes'. For British national identity in the Victorian era, increasingly configured around free trade and an imperial psyche deeply
antagonistic towards China, Hong Kong managed to assume a monumentality rarely reached by other possessions. Part of that was always
connected to the drama and emotion of the location – and, with it, the
legend of those pioneering, commercial adventurers, led by Jardine
and Matheson, crafting out a city-state from a barren rock in the face
of the mighty Middle Kingdom. To James Legge, looking back on
thirty years of Hong Kong missionary activity, such a transformation
could only signal a grander hand at work.

> When I contrast the single street, imperfectly lined with hastily raised
> houses, and a few sporadic buildings on the barren hill-side, with the
> city into which they have grown, with its praya, its imposing terraces,
> and many magnificent residences, I think one must travel far to find
> another spot where human energy and skill have triumphed to such an
> extent over difficulties of natural position.

He concluded his 1872 talk to the City Hall audience in Hong Kong
by imagining 'Britannia standing on the Peak, and looking down with
an emotion of pride on the great Babylon which her sons have built'.
Rudyard Kipling concurred. While he was always proud to see the
busy shipping lanes of Singapore, the poet of Empire wrote of swelling with patriotism 'as I watch the fleets of Hong-Kong from the
balcony of the Victoria Hotel'. 'No Englishman can land in Hong
Kong without feeling a thrill of pride for his nationality,' confirmed
Lord Curzon. 'Here is the furthermost link in that chain of fortresses
which from Spain to China girdles half the globe.'[90]

Any Englishman or -woman landing at Hong Kong now would be
hard-pressed to find much physical remnant of Britannia on her peak.
Of course, Wellington Street, Connaught Street, Stanley Street and

Queen's Road still exist. But with a brutal, rhythmic regularity, the old is ripped down for the new. In stark contrast to the imperial riches of Calcutta, Dublin or Cape Town, the British colonial footprint in Hong Kong is now limited to the tea museum at Flagstaff House (nestled in the midst of Hong Kong Park), the busy, whitewashed Gothic Revival St John's Cathedral, the Old Dairy Farm Building, Government House and the LEGCO Building on Statue Square (previously Royal Square), built in 1898 for the Supreme Court before becoming home to Hong Kong's Legislative Council.* The heart of activity of the island is in the Central skyscrapers, the Mid-Levels apartments and then in the haggling bustle of the Chinese markets heading west into Sheung Wan. The colonial sunsets of Somerset Maugham, veranda drinks and social *faux pas* on Victoria Peak are long gone.

What does remain is the mental architecture of Empire: the rule of law and private property rights; a free press, remnants of a parliamentary system and horse racing. Yet Hong Kong never achieved its defining purpose. For even after the addition of the New Territories in 1898 on a 99-year lease, the colony failed in its imperial mission to 'open up' China to the virtues of free trade. In fact, much of Hong Kong's prosperity in the twentieth century would be thanks to China 'closing down' to world trade under Communist rule – the advent of Maoism in 1949 and the imposition of US sanctions secured Hong Kong's position as a vital entrepôt for trading in the far East; the protection of private property and the rule of law made it a good place to do business; its free port and low taxes kept it globally competitive; and the pegging of its currency to the US dollar gave it sound money.

Another part of the success, however, was a planning policy predicated on the creative destructive power of capitalism. There has never been much room for architectural sentiment in Hong Kong, as progressive advances in engineering have made the capacity for urban densification and elevation ever easier. Today the modernist Jardine House, with its distinctive circular windows, is now overlooked by the glimmering skyscrapers of Standard Chartered Bank, Sir Norman Foster's Hong Kong Shanghai Banking Corporation Building

---

* From 2015, the building is set to revert to its original function as the Court of Final Appeal.

(complete with Scottish Saltire styling), International Finance Centre, Tower 2 and, most important of all, since 1990 the Bank of China Building.

What the skyscrapers conceal, however, is how since the 1840s Hong Kong's unabashed capitalism has also been the product of generous state support. Indeed, the landmass of modern Hong Kong is a creature of extensive government subsidy as the waterfront has receded in the face of sustained public reclamation projects taken deep into Victoria Harbour. In 1841, the sea lapped the shore at where Queen's Road stands – now a good half a kilometre from the Star Ferry Terminal over to Kowloon. In the most inhospitable of geological terrains, successive administrations have sought to provide, not least at Kowloon Docks, the perfect circumstances for commercial success. And this triumph of infrastructure is what is so striking about Hong Kong under Chinese rule: the super-efficient Chek Lap Kok Airport (now overlooked by the vast Tian Tan Buddha), the six-lane highways, and then the graceful suspension bridges linking Lantau Island and the New Territories, and then the smooth roadways into Hong Kong itself. In its statist efficiency, modern Hong Kong is a self-confident testament to capitalism with Chinese characteristics. For when China did finally open up to the merits of free markets in the early 1990s, it was time for Hong Kong to be handed back.

As just another global financial metropolis of the twenty-first century – alongside Doha, Singapore and Shanghai – Hong Kong's special purpose in the vanguard of free trade is no longer so obvious. Yet despite all its concrete and commuter villages, underpasses and train-tracks, global brand advertising and Americana shopping malls, the Pearl of the Orient's unique urban élan somehow still manages to impress. The lush greenery of Victoria Peak, the criss-crossing ferries between Hong Kong island and Kowloon, and then the silver canopy of skyscrapers combine to produce an unrivalled city sensation. It was just as beguiling a vision in 1997 as 1898 – and few British politicians wanted willingly to take leave of it.

But if British Hong Kong was born of the age of sail, by the latter half of the nineteenth century the steamer was taking over. A second industrial revolution of rail and steam was rolling across the Empire, and Curzon's chain of fortresses was coming to include the citadels of the manufacturer as well as the merchant. Jardine Matheson's ideology of free trade would remain, but the age of industry and mass production would change the function of imperial cities. And it would be William Jardine's business partner Jamsetjee Jejeebhoy, and his dirty, smoggy city of Bombay, which would come to take the colonial mantle from the Fragrant Harbour of Hong Kong.

7

Bombay

'City of the present and the future'

Struggling against the 'abominable filthiness' of Mango Senoy Street in the Fort district of Bombay, the deputy inspector general of hospitals was led by one enraged tenant to 'a range of latrines, where he indignantly showed to him what he and others were subjected by the landlord'. 'Both men and women, to avoid wading through the pool of ordure, had to use as stepping-stones some pieces of masonry that still projected a little above its surface,' reported the inspector, Andrew Leith. Alongside decomposing animal and vegetable refuse rotting in the streets, 'there is scarcely a part of the Fort or Native Town in which the ground along every dead wall is not wet or in pools from its being resorted to as an urinary'. Indeed, 'many instances occur where the walls of the adjoining houses are constantly wet with fœtid fluid which frequently affects the atmosphere of the rooms so as to render it impossible to keep food for one single night without its being tainted'.

Sewage was another problem for the city, as painstakingly recorded in the *Report on the Sanitary State and Sanitary Requirements of Bombay* (1852). 'The open drains, or rather uncovered receptacles of filth . . . do not deserve the name of drains: there is seldom any perceptible motion in the liquid contents of the majority of them.' One Bombay resident, the Parsi lawyer and politician Sir Dinshaw Wacha, well remembered how this refuse was dealt with. 'The black foul semi liquid stuff was first thrown out on both sides of a street or road in a heap and after a day or two carted away.' In the meantime, the 'decomposed gases emitted from the perforated covers saturated the atmosphere with foul exhalations'. It was all deeply unpleasant.

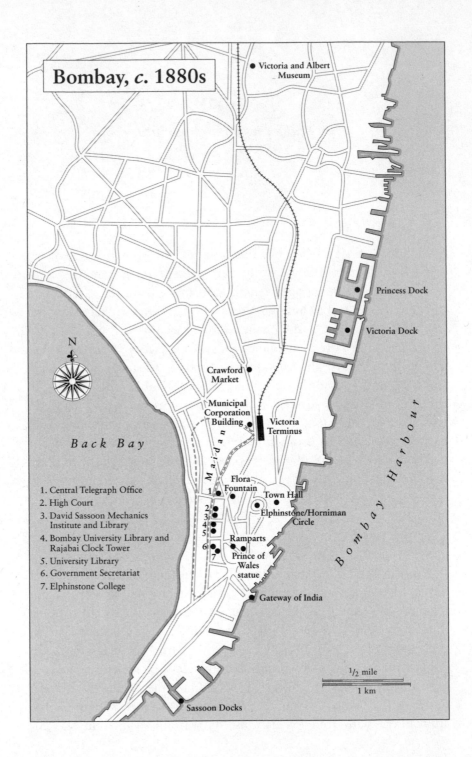

Bombay, *c.* 1880s

● Victoria and Albert
Museum

Princess Dock

Victoria Dock

N

Crawford ●
Market

Municipal
Corporation
Building

Victoria
Terminus

Back Bay

M a i d a n

Flora
Fountain

1. Central Telegraph Office
2. High Court
3. David Sassoon Mechanics
   Institute and Library
4. Bombay University Library and
   Rajabai Clock Tower
5. University Library
6. Government Secretariat
7. Elphinstone College

1

2
3
4
5

6
7

Town Hall

Elphinstone/Horniman
Circle

Ramparts

Prince of
Wales
statue

B o m b a y   H a r b o u r

● Gateway of India

¹/₂ mile

1 km

● Sassoon Docks

'Picture to yourself the life of a Hindu gentleman in the heart of the city,' pleaded one public official. 'Disturbed in the early morning, long before sunrise, by the sweepers at work, he gets up and goes to the verandah in front of his house to breathe the cool and refreshing air of the morning; but even that comfort – and how dear it is to all India! – is denied him, for he is driven from the verandah by the sweepers passing to and fro in front of his dwelling, and the horrid odours that taint the morning breeze.'

Then there were Bombay's public water tanks, which one sanitary reformer described as 'nothing more than huge cess-pools, in which persons and clothes, wash and are washed, in a water that is never changed'. Just as disconcerting was the dangerous proximity of sewers to drinking water – 'in some cases the distance between the privy and the well is as little as six or seven feet . . . there can be no doubt that into all these wells there is a large percolation of impure matter'. 'All was darkness in Bombay,' thought Sir Dinshaw of his native city in the 1850s, 'and one generation after another lived in a happy-go-lucky style oblivious of the heavy bill of annual mortality.' And it was quite a tab: cholera, smallpox, measles and a range of other diseases 'annually claimed a large holocaust' numbering in the tens of thousands. In 1865, over 65 per cent of the total mortality within the city of Bombay was attributed to 'fever'.[1]

'But by the side of this native town there is the modern European city, which in its regularity, magnificence, and beauty rivals any in the West,' countered James Furneaux, subeditor of *The Times of India*. If a visiting European tourist avoided the insanitary rookeries, he might not even think his steamship had landed him east of Suez. In fact, 'the stately pile of the Yacht Club, the imposing arcade of the Apollo Restaurant, and the electric lights around him, remind him of his own land'. This healthy, stately Bombay had for its motto 'Urbs Prima in Indis' and deserved it. 'By the largeness of its population, greatness of its extent, the excellence of its situation, the volume of its trade, the wealth of its inhabitants, by everything that contributes to material greatness, it stands out pre-eminently among all the cities of India, nay of the whole East.'[2] Far from the slums and open sewers, an array of grandiloquent, 'Bombay Gothic' edifices lined the city's Esplanade, lapped by the Arabian Sea, and highlighting the achievements of

Empire. Bombay's University Library and Convocation Hall, the High Court, the Government Secretariat and the Central Telegraph Office offered a well-crafted essay in colonial self-congratulation. 'The long and magnificent series of public buildings ... was one of the finest sights of its kind in the world,' thought the governor of Bombay in the 1870s, Sir Richard Temple. 'The buildings are in themselves grand, but other cities may have structures as grand, though probably separate. Bombay, however, has all her structures in one line of array, as if on parade before the spectator.'[3] It was always the case that a visiting Briton 'feels himself a greater man for his first sight of Bombay'.[4]

No building symbolized the meaning of the British Empire in the latter half of the nineteenth century more purposefully than Bombay's Victoria Terminus station. Officially opened in 1887 for the Golden Jubilee of Queen Victoria, Empress of India,* it served both as the lead terminal of the Great Indian Peninsula Railway and as an icon of colonial achievement. 'The Jewel of Bombay is the Victoria Railway Station,' thought the British writer G. W. Stevens, 'a vast domed mass of stone fretted with point and column and statuary and shrubbery, purple-belled creepers, scarlet-starred shrubs.'[5] From under its gaudy Indo-Saracenic domes – an overwhelming architectural mélange of London's Natural History Museum, Balmoral Castle and St Mark's, Venice – spread forth the infrastructure of British India, connecting this commercial metropolis with the lineaments of Empire round the world. Small wonder Jan Morris was moved to describe the station as 'the truly central building of the entire British Empire – the building which expresses most properly the meaning of the imperial climax'.[6]

It was equally understandable when British director Danny Boyle chose to make VT – by then renamed Chhatrapati Shivaji Terminus – the defining backdrop to his 2008 Bombay blockbuster *Slumdog Millionaire* (a cinematic adaptation of the novel *Q & A*, by Vikas Swarup). It was beneath the station's canopy of monkey-gargoyles, sculpted dripstones and corrugated iron-roofing, and among the overhead bridges, information boards and ticket offices, that the drama's final chase takes place. This was the film that acquainted mass

---

* The Conservative prime minister Benjamin Disraeli had flatteringly laid the title on her in 1876.

Western audiences with contemporary Mumbai: a rambling, quasi-Dickensian rendering (complete with the deliberate blinding of child beggars) of a slum megalopolis approaching 20 million inhabitants. In one sense, the screenplay was an easily consumable depiction of the 'familiar' India – of the Bandra, Dharavi and Annawadi slumdogs, of child poverty, immiseration and sanitary systems which would not have been unfamiliar to Andrew Leith in the 1860s. But this fable of doomed young lovers was also an introduction to the New India – of call centres, Bollywood, property development, fashion and multinational corporations. Mumbai was the obvious place to set it. For behind Sir Richard Temple's 'magnificent series of public buildings' that once dominated the Esplanade there now towers Bombay House, the global headquarters of India's industrial behemoth Tata Group, its satellite dishes and radio masts clashing with the Gothic of the University Library Clock Tower. Mumbai is now a commercial and cultural epicentre of twenty-first-century global capitalism; together with Shanghai, it serves as an urban shorthand for the assertive dynamism of the BRIC economies. When the 'Licence Raj' of postwar socialist development fell away in the early 1990s, Mumbai rose up as Asia's 'Maximum City' of wealth creation.[7] It was a city where the fabulously wealthy Ambani dynasty could build a twenty-seven-storey tower-block in the exclusive Malabar Hill as their own personal compound, while inequality and poverty still of Victorian levels flourished in coagulating 'Slumbai'. 'The inequalities that defined Bombay as a colonial port town have continued,' notes journalist Kalpana Sharma. 'Investment is always available to beautify the already well-endowed parts of the city. But there is no money to provide even basic services to the poorer areas.'[8]

Yet, for all these iniquities, there is little internal confusion about Mumbai's place in the world. In contrast to Calcutta, this 'City of Gold', as it became known in the nineteenth century, is relatively uninterested in its relationship with its British pre-history. It is the business of making money that drives Mumbai. The imperial past is demolished, the new rises up, hotels and skyscrapers, smart bridges and thrusting flyovers jostle for space as edifices of Old Bombay offer little in the way of nostalgia to Mumbai's youthful, globalized, middle class. The history which has re-emerged after the end of the Raj is the lost world of Shivaji, the seventeenth-century Maratha warrior who battled against the Mughal Empire and whom the Shiv Sena Hindu militant movement adopted as an all-purpose icon for Bombay's home state of Maharashtra in the mid-1990s. Statues, airports, roads and municipal offices all began to bear his name as part of a broader shedding of the English language and decolonization of public space. So, to the consternation of Urdu-speaking Muslims and middle-class protectors of the city's cosmopolitan spirit, in June 1995 Bombay became Mumbai – a 'proper' Indian city, with a name and an identity that honoured its cultural and linguistic heritage.[9] In turn, VT was swapped for CST, and the Victoria and Albert Museum became the Bhau Daji Lad Museum – in whose gardens were dumped the fallen heroes of Empire, angrily decapitated statues of Wellesley, Cornwallis and Sir Richard Temple among them. 'By Indianizing street and building names, by officially renaming Bombay Mumbai, the postcolonial present suggests control over the colonial past,' argues historian Gyan Prakash. 'It assumes that the colonial past can be bleached out of Mumbai's historical existence as a metropolis and neatly appropriated by the postcolonial era.'[10] For some, this aggressive anti-colonialism is self-defeating and only serves to undermine Mumbai's complex identity. 'By banishing the statues and symbols of the Raj to the Queen's gardens in Byculla, we have also turned our backs on the city's history which in turn formed its character,' says Pratapaditya Pal.[11]

The irony is that it was precisely this kind of confident, commercial and nostalgia-free ethos that was first adumbrated for the city by the rulers of British India themselves. In the 1890s, James Furneaux was already praising Bombay for the refreshing absence 'of historical associations clinging about it, as about many another Indian city ... it is essentially a modern city, a city of the present and the future, but not of the past'.[12] For Bombay's role was to display the technological and managerial capacity of British imperialism: unlike East India Company Calcutta or laissez-faire Hong Kong, Bombay would embody the Victorian spirit of Progress. Under beneficent colonial guidance, all the virtues of urban improvement – rail and trams, sewage and drinking water, municipal governance and higher education, industry and finance, architecture and planning – could be brought to the benighted East. And more so than with any previous imperial city, modern communications and the advancing science of urban planning meant that British debates about civic improvement informed the development of Bombay. The planning and civilization which had transformed the British cities of London, Birmingham and Glasgow were now to be unleashed on insanitary, ill-equipped India. Bombay would not represent British naval or military might, its mercantilist power or buccaneering free enterprise, but instead the Empire's awakening capacity for effective, technocratic governance. In Bombay the British Empire would build a monument to its own modernity.

TOWERING CHIMNEYS SOLEMN AND SOMBRE

Like Cape Town before it, the British Empire came to Bombay on the back of a competing imperial power – this time the Portuguese, who had started taking land from Gujarat Muslim chieftains in the early 1500s, steadily building up a small trading and fishing settlement on the islet they called *a ilha da boa vida*, or the island of good life. In stages, the name would change from the native Mumbai (after the local goddess Mumba) to Mumbaim, Mombaim, Boa Vida, Bombaim, Bom Bahia and thence Bombay. The islands' rulers gently prospered under Portuguese protection, and by the early 1600s both the British and Dutch East India Companies were eyeing the harbour with envy. Even amid the man-made docks and tugs of the Victorian age, the natural advantages of this Arabian Sea inlet were relentlessly praised. 'The soundings are of convenient depths, the holding ground good; and the strong ebb and flood tides . . . facilitate the entrance and exit of ships in all winds and all weathers,' thought the Calcutta-based writer James Silk Buckingham. 'No harbour in the world, perhaps, is better entitled than this to the original name given it by its first European possessors, the Portuguese, of "Bon Baia", or Good Bay, from whence the present name of Bombay is formed.'[13] These attractions would also be noted by the Bombay Marine (Indian navy), which controlled from here the Persian Gulf and so helped to maintain British influence over the growing number of East African colonies.

In the event, the British Crown beat off the Dutch when in 1661 Portugal gave the islands as a dowry for the marriage of Princess Catherine of Braganza to King Charles II. Seven years later, the colony was handed over to the East India Company with a mandate to grow it as a commercial centre. Under an active Company campaign to bring in migrant workers with the promise of religious liberty, Bombay soon attracted a multinational merchant community. The secure bastions and gates of Bombay Fort, built by the Company in the early 1700s, also proved an attractive draw for merchants, bankers and investors. Under the shadow of the fort's Apollo Gate, Church Gate and Bazaar Gate, a settlement of residential and commercial houses, shops, churches and temples grew up. A moat was added in 1743 and then an esplanade of wide, open land in the same manner as Calcutta's Maidan. The Parsi community from Surat were among the first to enter under the fort's ramparts in the latter half of the seventeenth century, to be joined later by Hindu and Jain merchants of the Bania caste, Brahmans from Salsette, Armenians and Jews (most notably, once again, the Sassoons). The traders initially settled in the Bazaar Gate area in the northern part of the fort. Outside the city walls were the Gujarati Muslim communities of Bohras and Khojas as well as merchants from as far afield as Afghanistan, Persia and Arabia. Abolition of the East India Company's monopoly over commerce in India in 1833 opened up further commercial opportunities, while Hong Kong's incessant demand for Malwa opium helped to endow the fortunes of such Parsi merchants as the Jardine and Matheson partner Sir Jamsetjee Jejeebhoy.[14]

It was the industrial revolution and then the political ramifications of the American Civil War that transformed Bombay's prospects. In Britain, the entrepreneur and inventor Richard Arkwright – who had pioneered cotton production at his Cromford mills along Derbyshire's Derwent Valley – was the first to use steam-power for the purposes of cotton-spinning in Manchester in the late 1780s. By 1830, there were more than 550 cotton mills in Lancashire with well over 100,000 workers. 'Hast thou heard, with sound ears,' asked the Victorian sage Thomas Carlyle, 'the awakening of a Manchester, on Monday morning, at half-past five by the clock; the rushing off of its thousand mills, like the boom of an Atlantic tide, ten-thousand times ten-thousand spools and spindles all set humming there, – it is perhaps, if thou knew it well, sublime as a Niagra, or more so.'[15]

Steam-power inaugurated a new urban era as iron and steel, glass and ceramics, woollen and worsted, silk, lace and above all cotton production transferred to cities. Beginning in the 1800s, hundreds of thousands of migrants flooded into Birmingham, Glasgow, Liverpool and London – bringing in their wake an industrial proletariat, collapsing life expectancy, sanitary horror and, for some, unprecedented prosperity.

As in Manchester in the 1780s, so in Bombay in the 1850s, the cotton industry sparked economic take-off. Luckily, the city was about to have a governor with a particular passion for weaving and spinning. 'Cotton has always been a special hobby of mine,' wrote Sir Bartle Frere in 1861 to a British business contact. 'The capacity of India to supply cotton is absolutely unlimited . . . if the demand for cotton continues, there can be no doubt we can supply you all you want.'[16] Traditionally, the cotton lords of Manchester had preferred the plants of the American South for their raw material, which was cheaper to import and generally of higher quality than the Indian. 'The supply in the English market from India is merely supplementary to that received from America, and the largest exports from India take place in those years in which there is a deficiency in the American crops,' noted a commercial report on western India for the Lancashire Chambers of Commerce in 1853.[17] In turn, the finished goods – made with either American or Indian cotton – were exported back to India, flooding the indigenous market with mass-produced mill-made cloth from the Lancashire factories. 'It was the British intruder who broke up the Indian hand-loom and destroyed the spinning wheel. England began with driving the Indian cottons from the European market; it then introduced twist into Hindostan, and in the end inundated the very mother country of cotton with cottons,' as Karl Marx put it. In 1824, Britain exported 1 million yards of cotton to India; by 1837 it was 64 million yards.[18]

Bartle Frere aimed to improve the supply of raw cotton, and its production, by appointing a cotton commissioner with a mandate to cut transport costs from the cotton fields to the docks and erect new mills in the northern Byculla quarter. 'I am convinced the growth of cotton factories in India is the very best thing which could happen for

Manchester,' he announced in 1862, with a frank expression of his priorities in India. It would improve the growing of raw cotton and act as a surplus source for Lancashire's trading houses.

> The first effect of an extension of mills in India will be an improvement in the quality of the cotton used for local purposes and by India manufacturers ... once improve the general quality of Indian cotton, so as to make it workable by such machinery, and you create a vast supply which is always in reserve for, and at the command of, the long purse of the English manufacturer.[19]

Yet it was events in America, rather than England, which were to spur the boom of the mills and blacken Bombay's skyline with smog. In April 1861, at the inception of the American Civil War, Northern Federal forces started to blockade the Southern Confederate cotton-exporting ports, ratcheting up the cost of freight and insurance and, above all, the price of cotton itself. Imports from the American South into Liverpool fell from 2.6 million bales in 1860 to fewer than 72,000 by 1862; in response, Surat cotton from India rose from 5 pence per lb to 24 pence per lb. Bombay seized the moment. 'The produce of all the great cotton-fields of India, Nagpur, Berar, Guzerat, the South Mahratta country, found its way to Bombay in order to be exported to England, with all possible despatch while the high prices ruled and the blockade of the South American ports lasted,' remembered Temple of the 1860s boom.[20] Cotton exports to Europe rose from 490,000 bales in 1859 to near 890,000 by 1865, the vast majority heading to Britain. Wisely, Bombay also started its own production lines. Parsi merchants, Jewish traders and Bhatia industrialists seized the opportunity by commissioning new steam-powered mills which employed tens of thousands of migrant labourers: in 1854 there was only the Bombay Spinning and Weaving Company mill at Tardeo in central Bombay; by the mid-1860s there were some 10 mills employing 7,000 workers; by the late 1870s near 30 mills employing over 13,000 hands; and by 1900 around 80 mills providing jobs for 73,000 workers (the industry having diversified, by then, into the China market for yarn). As early as July 1860 one Bombay newspaper could boast:

Capital was never more plentiful amongst us than at present, nor the spirit of enterprise more powerful. Money, to the amount of nearly a quarter of a million pounds sterling, has been invested during the last fortnight in the establishment of manufactories calculated to promote industry and assist in the development of the resources of the country. Bombay has long been the Liverpool of the East, and she is now become the Manchester also . . . In 1850 we question much if even the model of a cotton mill had found its way to Bombay: but now the tall chimneys of half-a-dozen factories tower solemn and sombre above the surrounding buildings.[21]

Underpinning the export surge was the development of rail infrastructure. Just as Newcastle, Glasgow and Birmingham had metamorphosed into industrial cities on the back of rail, so Bombay's exponential growth was made possible by steam transport. Its greatest promoter was Lord Dalhousie, governor-general of India (1848–56), who wrote in 1852 of rail's capacity to produce in India 'some similar progress in social improvement that has marked the introduction of improved communications in various Kingdoms of the Western World'. Education would spread, the caste system would crumble amid the enforced intimacy of third-class carriages, and new lines would ensure 'the prevention of local famine and the uniform dispersion of food'.[22] The first 34 kilometres of railway in India were laid by the Great Indian Peninsula Railway in 1853 between Bombay and Thana, but the real ambition was always to link up the Deccan plateau of west-central India with Bombay port. This involved boring through the Western Ghat mountain range to the east of Bombay and so providing James J. Berkley, chief resident engineer of the GIPR, with a perfect opportunity to show India the might of British engineering. 'The passage of the Ghauts has always been a costly and serious obstruction to the trade of India,' he explained in a paper to the Bombay Mechanics Institution in 1850. But with some 30,000 men working on his celebrated Bhore Ghaut Incline (with its terrifying mountaintop reversing station), Berkley judged that 'it has always appeared to me to be impossible that the liberality and devices of English enterprise could so fail in their operation upon the industrial classes of India, as not to procure an ample supply of labour for the completion of undertakings materially affecting the prosperity of commerce, the public revenue, and the convenience of the people'.[23] English technological efficacy combined with a vast resource of Indian labour would build the railways. The young Dinshaw Wacha attended Berkley's talk. 'It was a thrilling narrative of what the great railway engineer had accomplished in the way of tunnelling the two Ghats and the innumerable difficulties he had to surmount,' he recalled. 'Those tunnels are a permanent monument of his engineering skill and ingenuity.'[24] They also accelerated the movement of industry into Bombay and boosted exports by connecting hinterland to port. At the same time, the Bombay, Baroda and Central India Railway was surging northwards to link the cotton fields of Gujarat with the mills of Bombay – one of Bartle Frere's essential requirements to boost competitiveness. In 1862 there were only 917 kilometres of rail open for traffic within the Bombay region; by 1867 it had reached 1,865. But more infrastructure was needed.

'At present your railways are like the *Great Eastern*, with nothing but canoes and catamarans to load and unload her,' complained Frere to the Indian Supreme Council at Calcutta, referring to Isambard Kingdom Brunel's epic ship. 'We are doing well in this Presidency as regards traffic on all open lines, but I see everywhere that it can be increased, perhaps doubled, by a good network of roads affording the necessary complement to the great carrying engine already provided.'[25] The Council obliged, and in the wake of the railway main lines came deeper docks, more roads, better bridges, a growing suburban network and, above all, an extensive programme of land reclamation. During the second half of the nineteenth century, in a quintessentially Victorian display of urban engineering, Bombay's natural archipelago of seven islands was bolted together (like Boston) into the single littoral recognizable today. Bombay became a city of iron and steel, earning its identity as one of the great railway cities of the world – still obvious today in the daily mass commute of some 6 million Mumbaikers in and out of the city.

Together with the cotton came new communities migrating into Bombay – from Gujarat and the Deccan – along the railway routes. Having stood at some half a million residents in the mid-1840s, by 1872 Bombay's population had reached more than 644,000 (overtaking that of Calcutta) and climbed to 773,196 by the census of 1881. Of that cohort, 50 per cent had come from Bombay's hinterland and spoke Mararthi as their native tongue (itself subject to some thirty or forty regional dialects), 28 per cent spoke Gujarati, 12 per cent Urdu, and just 1 per cent used English. Only 28 per cent of the city's dwellers had been born in Bombay. This overwhelming multiculturalism – the religions, languages, ethnicities and dress – was an abiding feature of commentary on nineteenth-century Bombay. Already in the 1820s, Mrs Anne Elwood, visiting her brother-in-law, the governor Mountstuart Elphinstone, thought the street scenes reminiscent of the last days of the Florence Carnival. Yet, 'even in a fancy ball in London, or during the Carnival in Italy, where every one strives to be in a particular and original costume, it would be impossible to meet with a greater variety than ... what may be seen every day in the Island of Bombay'. 'On all sides, jostling and passing each other, are seen – Persian dyers; Bannian shop-keepers; Chinese with long tails; Arab horse dealers; Abyssinian youths ... Armenian priests, with flowing robes and beards; Jews in long tunics and mantles,' reported Viscountess Falkland in her *Chow-Chow: Being Selections from a Journal Kept in India, Egypt and Syria* (1857). G. W. Stevens commented on how 'every race has its own costume; so that the streets of Bombay are a tulip-garden of vermilion turbans and crimson, orange and flame colour, of men in blue and brown and emerald waistcoats, women in cherry-coloured satin-drawers ... of blazing purple or green that shines like a grass-hopper'. G. W. Forrest, author of *Cities of India* (1903), described Bombay as simply 'a world of wonder'. 'Here all races have met: Persians in huge shaggy hats, and British sailors in white; the strong, lithe, coal-black Afreedee seaman, tall martial Rajpoots, peaceful Parsees in cherry-coloured silk trousers, Chinamen with the traditional pigtail, swaggering Mussulmans in turbans of green, sleek Marwarees with high-fitting parti-coloured turbans of red and yellow.'[26]

Such high levels of migration and ethnic diversity made for a much more complicated colonial geography than the traditional European 'White Town' *versus* Indian 'Dark Town'. Of course, a racial divide overlaid the city, and West remained distinct from East. 'Cross but one street and you are plunged in the native town,' explained G. W. Stevens. 'In your nostrils is the smell of the East, dear and never to be forgotten; rapturously you snuff that blending of incense and spices and garlic, and sugar and goats and dung.'[27] A visiting Scottish missionary, Norman Macleod, recorded the inequalities in less romantic terms. 'As to the native town, no Irish village of the worst kind has a look of greater poverty, confusion and utter discomfort,' he wrote in *Peeps at the Far East: A Familiar Account of a Visit to India* (1871). 'The low huts covered with palm leaves – the open drains – the naked children, with their naked fathers and miserable-looking mothers ... present a most remarkable contrast to the wealth and luxury of the neighbouring city.'[28]

But in Bombay, wealth as well as race played its part in the social topography as a prosperous elite clustered along the south and west side of the city while the poor were shunted together amid ill-planned and insanitary alleys north of the fort. Industrialization – the arrival of tens of thousands to work in the docks, the mills and the railways – intensified the demarcations with workers huddled in overcrowded tenement *chawls* around their factories on the north of the island, while the middle classes sought refuge up-wind. In 1881, the British-dominated section of the South Fort had a density of 27 persons per acre; in the Indian-occupied North Fort there were 258 per acre and outside the city walls it could reach 700 per acre.[29] At the height of mill production, Girangaon – 'the village of the mills' – stretched over 1,000 acres across the centre of Bombay. Along the eastern foreshore, in Dongri and Majid Bunder, the dockworkers stayed in *kholis* consisting of a single room or two. Within these slums, elements of a multicultural proletariat could also be found as poor Europeans were housed cheek by jowl with poor Indians. An 1863 'Report on European Pauperism' commented how 'European operatives on the railway are more constantly and closely connected with the natives than any other class of Europeans, and for this reason their moral condition has an important national significance which cannot be safely over-looked.'[30] Indeed, European vagrancy after 1857–8 became a growing concern as ever greater numbers of labourers arrived to take up construction and manual work. At the other extreme, Bombay's wealthy merchant princes could just as easily be found living within European neighbourhoods. Yet, in Bombay, it was congestion that

shaped the fabric of the city more than cosmopolitanism. Sir Bartle
Frere was determined to liberate the fetid urban core.

FRERE TOWN

Standing above a crown of yucca plants in the gardens of London's
Victoria Embankment is a brass statue of Sir Bartle; with his back to
Whitehall's great offices of state, he looks thoughtfully out towards
the River Thames. It is a perfect site for this engineer of Empire:
beneath his feet flow some of the 134 kilometres of sewer mains
installed by Sir Joseph Bazalgette as well as the tube trains of London
Underground's District Line. Indeed, the Victoria Embankment as a
whole stands as a concrete testament to the mid-Victorian determination to use all their advances in engineering, technology and planning
to tame Britain's filthy, insanitary cities. This was not simply a
phenomenon of London. In Paris in the 1850s Georges-Eugène Haussmann, *préfet* of the Seine *département*, began to cut great boulevards
through the *arrondissements* of medieval Paris to create a capital fit
for Emperor Napoleon III. 'Second Empire' Paris, with its grandeur,
apartment blocks, train termini, parks and cafés, was the epitome of
modernity – 'the capital of the nineteenth century'. In Vienna, the
thirteenth-century walls of the city were demolished to make way for
Emperor Franz Joseph I's Ringstrasse, along which were built museums, university departments, government ministries and other
embodiments of state power. This was the European vision of improvement and progress which Bartle Frere was ready to transfer to India.

Born in 1815 to an East Anglian family with a lineage of parliamentary and diplomatic service, Frere was trained up for the East
India Company at Haileybury before beginning his Company career
as a writer in Bombay in 1834. His apprenticeship took him across
the Bombay Presidency (the administrative region for the British
Empire in the west of India) and then Karachi and Calcutta. At each
posting, Frere showed a passion for public works – water supplies
and education in the Maratha state of Satara; irrigation and harbour
works in Karachi; and railways everywhere. When he returned to

Bombay in 1862 as governor, Sir Bartle and Lady Frere journeyed by the first train to cross India from the Indian Ocean to the Arabian Sea. It was a suitable preamble to his plans for the city.

With a booming population and accelerating economy, Bombay Fort's gates and bastions, ramparts and moat were anachronistic obstacles to economic progress. It was a seventeenth-century relic of when the East India Company ruled Bombay as a garrison town, and not a credible urban setting for the industrial age of railway, steamboats and telegrams. 'The maintenance of the Fort of Bombay,' wrote the *Times* correspondent as early as 1841, 'is not only useless, but has become a downright and most serious nuisance to the inhabitants at large. It is the source of a ridiculous waste of money to Government itself.'[31] Bombay resident James Gray criticized the government residence within the fort as 'much more like a prison than a vice-regal abode'.[32] Others thought the entire fort 'cramped in space, badly situated and imperfectly ventilated . . . erected at a time when civilization was but little advanced in the settlements of the East India Company'.[33] There had been previous attempts to open up the fort, notably in 1787, when a Special Committee (along the lines of Dublin's Wide Street Commissioners) urged the widening of principal streets in the town, but planning reform was made more urgent by the 1857 Indian Mutiny, or First War of Indian Independence, and its aftermath. The rebellion was a seismic assault on British power in India. It began with a revolt of sepoy soldiers in the Bengal army (angry over mistreatment and threats to their military privileges) before cascading into a much broader civil uprising and culminating in an assault on Delhi to restore Mughal power across India. Fed on lurid tales of massacres at Kanpur and the defiling of English women by rapacious Moors (Indians), the British army steadily and bloodily restored colonial rule. In Bombay, investment in technology and urban planning was accelerated as part of this reassertion of imperial hegemony. This signalled the transition of the city from a Western defence fort into a presidency capital of India – in the words of Sharada Dwivedi and Rahul Mehrotra, 'the metamorphosis of Bombay from a trading centre into a multifunctional industrial port-town'. And, in the aftermath of the Mutiny, there was now the money to reshape the city, since over

£80 million had poured into Bombay during the five-year export boom brought about by the American Civil War.[34]

In January 1863 the three great gates of the fort's ramparts – Apollo, Church and Bazaar – were levelled, then the water tanks sealed, the encircling swamps drained and further consolidation between the Bombay islands approved. The Ramparts Removal Committee succeeded in widening roads, erecting bridges, building houses and joining the fort area to the city. In London, the 1860s were known as the 'time to pull down', as the Underground, the Embankment and new boulevards and railway lines honeycombed the capital; in Bombay, these were known as the 'years of improvement', as Frere's embrace of modernity displayed a similar absence of nostalgia. Yet the resulting urban plan was not without elegance. On top of the spot where Church Gate had stood, Flora Fountain was erected as a conscious act of beautification for the new Bombay. Designed by R. Norman Shaw and sculpted in fine Portland stone, the Roman goddess Flora stands above some bullish-looking carp, from whose mouths jets of water shoot out into the open clams below. The statue could have been removed from the Boboli Gardens or a Roman mansion, but today resides in the midst of Mumbai as a glistening, whitewashed traffic island, opposite the modernist martyrs' memorial of Hutatma Chowk. Due east from Flora's Fountain, in front of the city's neo-classical town hall, erected in the 1830s as both a symbol of the British Empire's Roman aspirations and as a meeting-place for the Royal Asiatic Society, Frere then laid out Elphinstone Circle, an urban park in the heart of the old fort, in honour of his predecessor. The circular garden's lawn and Banyan trees are themselves encircled by a terrace of uniform, classical buildings, with an ornamental arcade beneath them that would not have looked out of place in Regency Brighton. This was to be Frere's commercial district, built on the back of the cotton boom, and its first tenant was the Bank of Bombay. Today, Horniman Circle (as it was later renamed in honour of Benjamin Horniman, pro-independence editor of the *Bombay Chronicle*) retains that self-same corporate sensibility: beneath the Circle's sand-blasted stonework, dotted with neo-classical keystone heads, a Hermès flagship store and other global boutiques now occupy the arcade.

Frere would have approved, because his Bombay was a business city. 'It has never in past times been the proud capital of a mighty empire like Delhi; it has not even been the seat of a wealthy provincial kingdom like Ahmeddabad or Bijapur. It has never been the centre of a great historical religion likes Benares,' explained James Furneaux.[35] As a result, Bombay contained, in the words of an 1880s pamphlet, 'no elaborate antique structures, no features of ancient greatness, which people run to see with heightened curiosity . . . There is no "Taj Mahal" of spotless marble masonry and unblemished purity.'[36] Instead, this was a workaday city, 'with an air of businesslike activity pervading every street'.[37] Visitors to Manchester at the height of its industrial might in the 1830s always marvelled at the unnatural speed of the people and the crush of the streets: Alexis de Tocqueville described how 'crowds are ever hurrying this way and that . . . their footsteps are brisk, their looks preoccupied and their appearance sombre and harsh'.[38] So commentators on Victorian Bombay complained of 'the rush of agents and merchants immersed in large-scale financial speculation; the more or less rushed pace of official and private employees going to work, checking their watches; every person concentrating hard on his work and walking fast and straight without looking around'. In one Maratha account of this increasingly foreign-feeling city, money-making had subsumed the entire urban ethos. 'In Bombay, even soil has a price,' noted the *Mumbaicha Vrittanta* (1889). 'It is not possible to spend even a single day in this city without money. Everything has to be bought.'[39] The sensitive Sir Dinshaw Wacha lamented the ignoring of antique structures or features of ancient greatness, deeply regretting how 'Bombay has been intensely shopkeeping, and that is the reason why the temples, the mosques and other places of worship inspire neither reverence nor awe, let alone beauty and joy'.[40]

Frere's ambition was to intensify the shopkeeping. 'When the Bombay walls fell, great was the fall thereof . . . Bombay now threw out her arms like a giant refreshed in a new atmosphere and Samson-like burst away the bonds of a hundred years,' was how one resident remembered the impact of Frere's assault on the fort.[41] Just as Haussmann had opened up medieval Paris to allow for the free circulation of capital, goods and services (as well as soldiers) across the city, so

Frere Town's easy access betwixt the docks, the mills, the banks and the trading floors would ensure the future prosperity of Bombay. As such, it makes sense to think of Sir Bartle Frere less as a Baron Haussmann and more of a Joseph Chamberlain. As mayor of Birmingham, Chamberlain cut Hill Street and New Street through the cramped quarters of the inner-city St Mary's ward, lined the new Corporation Street with offices and shops and beautified the urban core complete with Council House and Victoria Square as symbols of civic pride. What is more, he ensured that the council retained the freehold and operated an aggressive leasing strategy in order to retain any surplus for the ratepayers. Chamberlain's genius was to combine profit with civic dignity; to use commercial acumen for the glory of the conurbation. 'Birmingham is above all else a business city, run by business men on business principles,' as an American magazine admiringly put it in 1890. Frere might have hoped for similar approbation as he auctioned off land-sites made available by the fort demolition process to private developers and diverted the funds back into urban renewal projects. It was a virtuous circle which redeveloped the fort quarter (whose seventeenth-century origins are now totally obliterated) and helped Bombay's economy scale dangerously inflated heights.

'How many alive still remember those silver times?' asked Arthur Crawford, the former municipal commissioner, of booming 1860s Bombay,

> ... when there was a new bank or new 'Financial' almost every day – when it was a common thing, in strolling from your office to the dear old Indian Navy Club, to stop a moment in the seething Share Market and ask your broker, 'Well, Mr B. or Bomanji! What's doing?' before then going for tiffin and ordering a pint of champagne – no one ever drank anything but champagne in those days.[42]

With tens of millions of pounds flooding into Bombay from Lancashire's cotton orders (which, despite the city's expanding domestic production, still constituted a sizeable part of the urban economy), all sorts of investment schemes miraculously appeared to soak up the surplus capital. 'Financial associations formed for various purposes sprung up like mushrooms; companies expanded with an inflation as that of bubbles; projects blossomed only to decay,' recalled Sir

Richard Temple. By January 1865 the 'City of Gold' could boast 31 banks, 16 financial associations, 8 land companies, 16 cotton press companies, 10 shipping companies, 20 insurance companies and 62 joint stock companies, most of them the product of the previous five years. The land companies, or *khados*, offered by far the most inflated business enterprises with their dock construction projects and reclamation projects. The Back Bay, Mody Bay, Apollo Bay and Mazagon reclamation companies collectively accounted for 94.5 per cent of the 206 million rupees of paid-up capital for companies registered in 1863–5.[43] 'Not only were baseless schemes put forth,' continued Sir Richard, 'but also schemes, which originally had a sound foundation were pushed forward so imprudently that they ended in becoming unsound and involving in loss or ruin those who were concerned in them.'[44]

No matter. While the Bombay bubble kept floating upwards, vast riches were accumulated by the city's merchant princes, headed by the 'Supreme Pontiff of Speculation' Premchund Roychund. This Hindu merchant's early fortune had been made by his speed to market with privileged information on cotton pricing. Before British ships lowered anchor, Roychund's network of sailors and dockers managed to ascertain for him the London and Liverpool prices and he then speculated accordingly on the Bombay exchange. 'His bark rode on the crest of the wave, and he was the acknowledged leader among the knot of speculators from whom many financial associations had their origin,' in Temple's judgement.[45] Roychund nursed his fortune carefully enough to become a major shareholder in the Bank of Bombay as well as a leading public dignitary. But while the modest Roychund was personally frugal with his wealth, other profiteers took to the lush, breezy heights of Malabar Hill, then as now Bombay's most exclusive suburb, for a display of conspicuous consumption. 'The immense bungalows of the rich merchants and the high government officials are ranged, with their gardens and terraces, along the side of the hill,' was how the French writer Louis Rousselet described the plutocratic neighbourhood, revealing again Bombay's racial intermingling. 'Some of the houses display a richness and sumptuousness truly Asiatic. Columns support the verandahs and porticoes, and large flights of steps, bordered by China vases, lead to terraces on which are collected works of art both of Europe and Asia.'[46] 'Rich foliage plants in profusion adorn the entrances, where well-attired servants, assuming a conscious air of importance, stand about in readiness to obey orders,' said another account of the Malabar lifestyle. 'Carriages well appointed with liveried servants drive up in a style that accords with the air of luxury and ease apparent everywhere.'[47]

But then, half a world away, General Robert E. Lee surrendered the Army of Northern Virginia to General Ulysses S. Grant at Appomattox on 9 April 1865. The American Civil War had been lost by the South, and it was only a matter of time before the Northern blockade would be lifted and cotton shipments resume to Lancashire. 'The price of Bombay cotton fell fast, property in produce estimated at many millions sterling declined in a few weeks to less than half the value.' Banks crashed, financial associations folded, pyramid investment schemes collapsed, and the merchants of Malabar Hill went into liquidation. The bubble had burst, and the cotton mania was over. Some 40 per cent of Bank of Bombay debts had to be written off, and Premchund Roychund was among the most high-profile casualties. 'Never had I witnessed in any place a ruin so widely distributed, nor such distress following so quickly on the heels of such prosperity,' said Temple.[48]

HANDMAIDENS OF CIVILIZATION

The crash cascaded through all elements of 'society', and those already on the bottom rung of Bombay life had an even harder time to deal with than the fallen merchant princes. Conditions in the northern half of the city, around the mills and tenements, in the alleys and lanes, were existentially miserable both before and after 1865. An essential precondition of improving them was official acknowledgement of the reasons behind such Dickensian squalor. 'The present sanitary movement in England is even there of very recent origin,' wrote Henry Conybeare, architect, engineer and superintendent of Bombay repairs, in 1852, 'and the great importance of the subject had been as yet scarcely recognized in India.' Unlike in Britain, where a library of sanitary reports, parliamentary investigations and official publications from the registrar general to local medical officers of health had been exposing the wretched state of industrial cities since the 1820s, there was a crippling absence of comparable information about Victorian Bombay. What was more, public opinion still seemed to care far more about law enforcement than public health. 'In fact, the general impression seems to be, that a defective police is a greater municipal evil than a defective sanitary condition.' It was a ridiculous position, thought Conybeare, 'for the only object of a police is the protection of life and property; and . . . what is this to the thousands of lives which it can be proved annually lost in Bombay "for want of the most evident sanitary precautions"'. Indeed, the superintendent of repairs was willing to estimate that 'a very large proportion, probably nearly one-half of the deaths, from 12,000 to 16,000 in number, that annually occur in this island, are preventable'.[49] This was the conclusion which eventually secured the establishment of a proper ethnographic census for the city, a Sanitary Commission, a Public Health Commission, a Commission on the Drainage and Water Supply of Bombay and a concerted programme of municipal improvement to sanitary infrastructure. It was almost a textbook replica of the process of sanitary improvement which had been adopted in British cities.

In the process, many lives would be saved and harm prevented to those living under British rule. Yet this public health programme also entailed strong components of colonial ambition: the cleaning and draining of Bombay would provide a glistening testimonial to the technological capacity of the British Empire. The debate which had earlier engulfed Macaulay's Calcutta – between those who believed in ruling in the slipstream of the culture and traditions of India and those who thought it wholly lost to superstition and so deserving of Western enlightenment – had been conclusively won by the Westernizers. Haileybury's finest were now in charge of British policy in the East and the European virtues of evangelical Protestantism and Utilitarian governance were the lodestars of post-1850s imperial rule. Any vestiges of 'oriental despotism', with its heathen practices and caste discrimination, were to be dismantled.[50] Embodying the new imperial ethos was the lieutenant-governor of Bengal and then governor of Bombay, Sir Richard Temple. He had passed out top of his class at Haileybury and, in the 1870s, unleashed all he had learned at the school of Malthus upon the starving Deccan of the Bombay Presidency. For if British policy was about saving lives in the city, when it came to managing the famines of rural India (whose victims soon started to flood the streets of Bombay) Temple emphasized the subordination of everything 'to the financial consideration of disbursing the smallest sum of money consistent with the preservation of human life'. Under pressure from the Indian viceroy and governor-general Lord Lytton* to minimize any expenditure on famine in the Bombay Presidency, Temple defended the free market, blocked government intervention and put starving Indians to work on physically demanding public works projects. Infamously, his rigid Utilitarianism allocated the famished Indian peasantry a 'Temple wage' of one pound of rice per diem – significantly fewer calories than would later be provided to inmates of the Buchenwald concentration camp in Nazi Germany. As with the Bengal famines, grain was stockpiled in the cities, and between 1876 and 1878 some 1.2 million Indians in the Bombay province died of starvation. Rather than preventing famine, the new network of railways expedited the hoarding of rice in urban distribution centres and rural desolation. It is small wonder that Sir Richard Temple has been described by one modern historian as 'the personification of free market economics as a mask for colonial genocide'.[51]

But in the city a different type of efficiency was also in evidence. Here Utilitarian reform offered a test case not of inhumanity and penny-pinching, but of the superiority of British civilization – and into Bombay came a cadre of imperial administrators determined to show just how beneficent colonialism could be. Their vehicle was not the Royal Navy or British army, the Mission or Exchange, but the Department of Public Works, the Board of Conservancy and the Sanitary Commission; their philosophy was not about the divinity of free trade or an Empire of liberty, but the pragmatic capacity of the British Empire to improve urban conditions. Despite the administrators' best attempts, their rational utility could never fully obliterate the

---

* The title 'viceroy and governor-general' was another innovation following the Indian Mutiny, signalling the expanded role of the governor-general now that the British government had assumed the functions of the East India Company. The viceroy was the sovereign's representative in India.

cosmopolitan complexities of Bombay's ethnic and caste make-up. Yet their science of government certainly transformed the urban landscape.

Not least because they were determined to replicate tried and tested strategies which had worked at home, where sweetness and light had been brought to the 'dark continents' of inner-city London and Birmingham beginning in the 1830s. In Bombay, British colonial officials committed themselves to following the methods by which the likes of Victorian sanitary pioneers such as Edwin Chadwick and John Simon had investigated the industrial city; they mistakenly accepted the same flawed science of 'miasma' to explain the spread of fever (the 'noxious matters', 'poisonous gases' and 'accumulated filth' which they assumed were killers); and they aped their British predecessors in lambasting the unclean, immoral and feckless habits of the poor as mutually reinforcing components of urban pollution. Henry Conybeare thought that 'municipal improvements can only provide the means of cleanliness to those who are willing to avail themselves of them' and that many of the inhabitants of Bombay were sadly lost to filth.[52] 'At home and abroad, rulers and reformers identified the same practical problems, the unhygienic habits of the working class or native city dweller, and the same abstract predicament, the moral degeneration of townspeople living among "filth", and applied the same environmental solutions,' suggests historian John Broich. 'In both places, British authorities saw reconfiguring the environment as a powerful tool for reforming society ... Bombay and Manchester were "colonized" in the same way.'[53]

Among the most dedicated advocates of this purifying imperialism was none other than the Lady of the Lamp, Florence Nightingale herself. Just as with James Mill, Karl Marx and an array of Victorian pundits on British policy in the subcontinent, Nightingale never travelled to India, though to her credit she did want to. 'While others try to run away from India, I would desire more than anything else which I do desire ... to go to India,' she wrote to a friend. 'I have studied the country so much, I seem to know so well what to do there, it appears to me as if I would be going home, not going to a strange country. But alas for me, it is quite impossible.'[54] So, she sent missives from afar, drawing on her experience of the ill-effects of poor sanitation and lax public health in the Crimean War. This background in nursing reform made her an obvious candidate for membership of the Royal Commission on the Sanitary State of the Army of India (1859–63). Beginning with the question of army barracks and military hospitals, she then went on to write a series of tracts demanding extensive sanitary reform within British India – including *How People May Live and Not Die in India* (1863); *Suggestions in Regard to Sanitary Work for Improving Indian Stations* (1864); and, co-authored with Sir Bartle Frere, *Report on Measures Adopted for Sanitary Improvements in India 1868–69* (1869). Nightingale's success in public policy had always partly been a question of nobbling the right kind of people, and she was soon in close correspondence with Indian viceroys, Presidency governors and fellow reformers like Andrew Leith and Sir Bartle. She also had direct contact with Indian activist organizations such as Poona Sarvajanik Sabha of the Bombay Presidency Association and would, in time, come to support the ambitions of the Indian National Congress, especially its female pioneers.

Nightingale was shocked by the Empire's lethargy in transferring the technological advancements it had made in British cities to India. 'At home there have been great improvements everywhere in agriculture and in town drainage, and in providing plentiful and pure water supplies,' she complained. 'There is nothing of the kind in India. There is no drainage either in town or country.' Contrary to popular opinion about the climate, deficient drainage and overcrowding, she believed 'there is not a shadow of proof that India was created to be the grave of the British race'. The place simply needed a decent sanitary infrastructure: hygiene was the 'handmaiden of civilization'. And if Britain was to have any ethical claim to Empire it had to 'bring the appliances of a higher civilization to the natives of India'. 'In holding India, we must be able to show the moral right of our tenure,' and that meant practical improvement. 'There is not a town which does not want – water supply; drainage; paving; cleansing. Healthy plans for arranging and constructing buildings.'[55] Whenever the reforming impetus looked like faltering, her compelling persona was quick to urge it on. 'We *have* made an impression on the sanitary state of that vast country,' she declared in 1874, 'but "impression" so far as this: only to show us the immense work that remains to be done; the immense success that *can* attend it.' She had a particular hope for the Bombay Presidency: 'Bombay, hitherto the pioneer; Bombay the active, not to say restless, the energetic Bombay. Bombay has for years done everything to drain itself, except doing it ... it has had enough surveys, plans, reports, paper and print ... The only thing it has *not* done is *to do it*.'[56]

Nightingale's criticisms caught the colonial mood, as the British Empire sought to prove itself by building up a healthy, stately Bombay. The sustainable growth of British industrial cities in the nineteenth century had been heavily dependent upon access to a clean water supply. In Bombay this was doubly needed: first on public health grounds and, secondly, because demand for water was increasing so rapidly from both domestic and industrial users that it was now having to be transported into the city by boat and rail. As a result, the periodic droughts which hit the Presidency saw the city's water supplies run dry with worrying frequency. By early June of the arduous summer of 1854 only thirty-seven of Bombay's 136 public wells and monsoon tanks had any water in them. As Nightingale suggested, the solution was to follow the British model of urban improvement, so the city's chief engineer, Henry Conybeare, was despatched to tour the great municipal water projects of Liverpool, Bristol and Glasgow. He returned with his own plan for a Maharashtra Lake Katrine: like Glasgow, Bombay would be watered by a reservoir to the north through pipes flowing down to the city. What was more, in another precursor of Joseph Chamberlain-style 'gas and water socialism', the reservoir and transport costs would be borne by a general water rate. The Vihar water project (named after the Vihar valley in Salsette, 23 kilometres north of the fort) was the first municipal water project in India, begun in 1856 and completed in 1860. Despite numerous problems involving the transfer of Scottish Highland technology to west India – bursting pipes under the saline soil, lake algae formed by tropical sun – by the end of the decade, some 7,500 houses were connected to the Vihar pipes, reaching about 220,000 people. In the following decade water from the Tasso River was diverted into the Vihar Lake, and proper reservoirs were built first at Malabar Hill and then at Bhandarwada. The handmaiden of civilization was at work: Bombay now had the water it needed to grow.[57]

With clean water coming in, there was an equally urgent demand to have human waste going out. The piles of excrement lining the streets, which Sir Dinshaw had complained of, were both an obvious public health risk and a source of civic embarrassment. 'Of the many evils that the inspection of Bombay has disclosed that which is most prominent and at the same time most open to immediate remedy is filthiness,' Andrew Leith stressed in 1864. 'The maintenance of thorough cleanliness cannot be looked for without a general and efficient house drainage.'[58] His *Report on the Sanitary State of the Island of Bombay* recommended the execution of a new drainage scheme, but also urged a series of intermediate measures – a larger number of filth-carts, a Building Act requiring the construction of proper privies, deodorizing drains and sewers with carbolic acid, widening streets to improve ventilation. In Britain, the problem of night-soil had been solved with a massive expansion of sewerage systems. As Henry Conybeare noted as early as 1852, London with a population of some 1.8 million had more than 1,100 kilometres of sewers, while Bombay with a population approaching half a million had less than 23 kilometres (most notably, the notorious Main Town Drain or 'monster nuisance of Bombay' down to Love Grove). Liverpool – with a population of some 370,000 – had built 27 kilometres in a year. Instead, Bombay's excrement was carted off from the gullies between houses to beaches or dumped at sea – a practice which accelerating land reclamation projects and rising mortality levels made increasingly untenable. So the Victorians began in Bombay what they had done to their own cities some twenty years previously: building pumping stations and outfall posts and a sewerage system of drainage pipes which has lasted, like those in British cities constructed at the same time, to this day. When combined with Leith's other improvements and the new Vehar Lake water supply, the effects on life expectancy were marked. 'Bombay has had a lower death-rate on the last two years than London – the healthiest city in Europe,' Nightingale gushed to Sir Bartle in 1869. 'This is entirely your doing.' Indeed, 'if we do not take care Bombay will outstrip us in the sanitary race. People will be ordered for the benefit of their health to Bombay or to Calcutta, which is already healthier than Liverpool or Manchester.'[59]

Not all were so effusive. Leading members of Bombay's Indian merchant class were uncomfortable with the financing of the city's sanitary improvements. 'The project of bringing water from Vihar does not find favour with the community in general,' Sir Jamsetjee Jejeebhoy informed the governor in 1854.

> Many persons ... do not think that it should rest with any Engineer or Architect, however high his repute or abilities, to have the devising and execution of the plans, an almost unlimited power of expending the public money ... without any control whatever on the part of those who have to pay for the works.[60]

In Britain, numerous ratepayer associations had been formed in the 1830s to oppose the cost of capital improvements to their city's infrastructure. Local elections were won and lost on the cost of reservoirs, drainage schemes and water supplies. 'The tyranny of the petty tradesman is a serious evil in municipal life,' as George Bernard Shaw later put it. 'The small shopkeeper does not understand finance, nor banking, nor insurance, nor sanitary science.'[61] In Bombay there developed an equally well-organized resistance to the administration's grand public health schemes, when many believed a more localized, organic series of changes would suffice. Inevitably, in British India, the issue of cost was also overlaid with that of imperial inequality, for behind much of the British Empire's sanitary strategy was a determination to improve the health of its own military personnel in barracks and the living conditions of the governing class. Rate-paying, indigenous Indians were forced to fund major capital projects which more often than not benefited the colonial class and its contractors in charge of the piping, masonry and machinery shipped in from Leeds and Glasgow. It was Bombay's European quarters which received the Vihar water and could afford to pay the rates, whilst the Native Town residents had their public wells closed and endured only a highly irregular supply from Vihar. Within Victorian Bombay, water and waste policy were not value-neutral tools of improvement; in fact, they subtly codified the inherent stratifications of urban colonialism. A small appendix to the 1869 *Report of the Commission on the Drainage and Water Supply of Bombay* deftly captures the frustrations of Bombay's resident Indians. After complaining about leaking pipes, poor pressure rates which didn't even push the water supply up to the second floor and the need for Parsi families to have a good 14 gallons per head per day, Mr Cursetjee Framjee made a more general point. 'The natives look to the great wastage of Vihar water in watering our streets,' he told the commission; 'as only royal streets are watered, the poor envy the least drop of water wasted for the convenience of the rich. They would wish rather that water found its way in their mouths.'[62]

The object of Framjee's ire was the municipal authority as, once again, the British experience of managing industrial cities at home shaped the development of urban plans for India. Following the 1832 Great Reform Act, the 1835 Municipal Corporations Act had inaugurated the modern era of local government, when the medieval system of guild corporations which had historically ruled Britain's towns and cities started to be replaced by democratically elected municipal authorities. By the mid-nineteenth century, Britain's leading conurbations had accumulated a series of tax-raising and expenditure powers which allowed them not only to civilize their cities with sanitary improvements, but to beautify them with town halls and parks and enlighten them with libraries and art galleries. Bombay's 1865 Municipal Act aimed for something similar, but with much more power vested in the single person of the municipal commissioner, who was appointed by the government for three years with extensive powers over the governance of the city. Supporting the commissioner was a controller of municipal accounts, a health officer (a statutory requirement in Britain since 1848) and an executive engineer, who combined to deliver exactly the kind of improvements urged by Andrew Leith's 1864 *Report on the Sanitary State of the Island of Bombay.**

Bombay's first commissioner was thirty-year-old Arthur Travers Crawford (chronicler of the booming Bombay of the early 1860s), who set to work with gusto: polluting industries were outlawed, burial grounds were cleared, refuse collection upgraded, slaughter-houses relocated, cholera-swamps drained, and old bazaars pulled down and the new Crawford Market erected – from whose stalls could be

---

* In its corporate, technocratic structure, the office of the commissioner is probably best compared with London's Metropolitan Board of Works, which was allowed unfettered authority in the aftermath of the 1858 'Great Stink' (when the Thames nearly stopped flowing outside the Houses of Parliament due to the amount of human waste clogging it up) and placed in total charge of improvements to the capital in order to by-pass the ancient nexus of warring parishes and councils.

purchased, in the 1880s, 'oranges from Nagpore, apples from America, grapes from Cabul, dates from the Persian Gulf'.[63] 'A vigorous administration, comprising a Health Department, is doing much good,' noted the Sanitary Commission of 1865. 'Drainage works are begun and increase to the water supply is contemplated; gas is used in lighting the streets.'[64] The *Bombay Builder* concurred, suggesting in 1867 that 'more has been done for the advancement of important works during the present than during any previous administration'.[65] Indeed, Crawford's zeal in office brought to mind Joseph Chamberlain's great claim for his time in Birmingham: 'The Town will be parked, paved, assized, marketed, Gas-and-Watered and *improved* – all as the result of three years' active work.'[66]

However, the Haussmannesque arrogance of Crawford's reign proved too much for many Bombay residents: the paving, draining, street-widening and improving were carried out at a speed which showed little sensitivity to the city's complicated caste and ethnic politics. As with the Vihar water project, there were allegations of favouring improvements to the European quarter at the expense of the rest of the city as well as a careless approach to costs in a post-crash era when the city could ill-afford unnecessary expenditure. Many wealthier residents were also uncomfortable with Crawford's detailed property survey and ensuing demand for retrospective taxes. Just as London's Metropolitan Board of Works would finally be replaced by the democratically elected London County Council in 1888, so Commissioner Crawford was removed, and in 1872 the Bombay Municipal Act established a Municipal Corporation, half of whose sixty-four members were to be elected by ratepayers. It was on the Corporation that the future British Member of Parliament for Central Finsbury, Naoroji Dadabhai, garnered his taste for politics. A brilliant Bombay polymath – combining roles as a cotton trader with a professorship in mathematics and natural philosophy at Elphinstone College – Dadabhai progressed from the Corporation to the Bombay legislative council, thence to the Indian National Congress, before fighting seats in the British General Elections of 1886 and 1892. Spectacularly disproving the future Liberal prime minister Lord Rosebery's prediction that the people of London would never elect a 'black man', Dadabhai became an active figure in British radical circles and a conspicuous embodiment of Bombay's colonial, cosmopolitan ethos.

In London, the County Council sought to transform the British capital into a city worthy of its imperial calling by laying out the sweeping boulevards of Holborn Kingsway and the Aldwych, as well as expanding Trafalgar Square. In Bombay, the Corporation was the instrument for an equivalent programme of modernization and extolling of Empire: the transformation of the 'Queen of Isles' into a colonial city, 'her population expanded to an extent, unparalleled in past eras; and those great works of public convenience and adornment, which fitted her to take high rank among the most beautiful possessions of a world-wide empire, were by the exertions and genius of her leading men brought to completion'.[67] In a 'business city' such as Bombay, the Corporation was just the vehicle to exploit the age of steam and progress, technology and improvement, the Suez Canal and the quickening use of telegram from the 1860s. Under its aegis would come all the other evidence of civilization – the train stations and the docks, the post offices and courts, the gas and sewerage, the land reclamation and tram tracks – working steadily to reveal the worthy, pragmatic benefits of Empire. And its architecture would say so. In contrast to the fine, classical delicacy of the old town hall, the bombastic Municipal Corporation Building erected in 1884 was a red-blooded statement of the place of Bombay within the British Empire and the function of local government. With a 72-metre tower fronting this riot of Bombay Gothic styling (or 'free treatment of early Gothic with an Oriental feeling', as the architect put it), the building was a championing of municipal modernity. Its hydraulic lifts, fire-proofing and electricity were a testament to the improving spirit of the times and corporate purpose of Bombay. Unsurprisingly, the designs drew heavily upon Joseph Chamberlain's Venetian-inspired Council House in Birmingham and had emblazoned upon them an equally adamant belief in the virtues of municipal action: on the front façade hovered an enormous winged figure representing *Urbs Prima in Indis* – the First City of India.

MERCHANT PRINCES: ICONS OF PROGRESS

'Though many distinguished Britons played a great part in the making of Bombay ... the city is essentially the handiwork of the Indian communities also,' Sir Lovat Fraser, editor of the *Times of India*, generously conceded. 'Hindus and Mussulmans and Parsees and Jews, have in equal measure spent themselves and their wealth in the advancement and embellishment of the Gate of India. To their enterprise and generosity, not less than to the prescient control of capable Englishmen, we owe the magnificent capital of Western India as it exists today.'[68]

Despite the Empire's obvious gifts to Bombay, the British were always more willing to concede that indigenous residents might have played a greater role in its development than they had in the case of Calcutta. Coming from Bengal, the Bombay governor Mountstuart Elphinstone was immediately impressed with the greater 'zeal and liberality' he saw on display in 'the construction of roads and public buildings'. Indeed, from the early 1850s, commentators keen to debate the reasons as to why Bombay was rising and Calcutta was falling focused on the differing approaches of their native elite. While the Calcutta merchant classes, it was said, tended to retreat to country estates to live as landed *rentiers*, the Parsis and Muslim Gujaratis of Bombay had little opportunity for rural investment and no other home than the city. 'Bombay's affairs were taken over by a band of dedicated industrialists, businessmen and entrepreneurs who were large in vision, big in money and unsparing of effort,' as the Calcutta historian Asok Mitra puts it. 'Bombay was their passion, their destiny and apart from straining all their surplus energy for the good and prosperity of the city, they gave away their own money in trusts and charities to make Bombay strong, cultured, beautiful.'[69]

The very same ethos which inspired Victorian merchant princes to endow the art galleries, museums, schools, universities, medical colleges and parks of urban Britain was at play in Bombay – but on an even grander scale. 'There are many valuable charitable institutions in Bombay, all of which are liberally supported by the rich Natives, as well as by the English,' wrote James Gray in his 1852 *Life in Bombay*. 'Amongst these is one especially worthy of notice, the Jamsetjee Jejeebhoy Hospital, built and endowed at the joint expense of the munificent Parsee Knight, and the East India Company.'[70] After Jejeebhoy had made his money shipping opium with Jardine, Matheson & Co., before then branching into cotton, banking and shipping, he poured the profits back into the civic fabric of Bombay – endowing a further obstetric hospital, school of industry and school of art. (It was to the last of these that the sculptor John Lockwood Kipling would come from Stoke-on-Trent to teach. His son Rudyard was born in a bungalow on the art school grounds.) What was so remarkable about Bombay was that the liberal Jejeebhoy was just one philanthropist of many.

David Sassoon was born in Baghdad in 1792 to a Sephardic family of financiers and religious scholars. He arrived in Bombay in 1832, fleeing persecution of the Jews, and soon set up a small counting house, then a carpet warehouse, before providing finance to other industrialists and emerging as one of the city's leading commodity traders. The Sassoon portfolio ranged wide as he bought up companies, turned around commercial failures and invested in new enterprises to take advantage of Bombay's transit point between the markets of Europe and China. 'Silver and gold, silks, gums and spices, opium and cotton, wool and wheat – whatever moves over sea or land feels the hand or bears the mark of Sassoon & Co.,' was how one contemporary explained the breadth of his business.[71] His eldest son, Abdullah (later Sir Albert), grew the family firm – branching into cotton-weaving and then building the vast Sassoon Docks in 1875 – and continued the philanthropic ethos. The Sassoons endowed synagogues, schools, boys' reformatories, hospitals, convalescent homes and, perhaps most famously, the David Sassoon Mechanics Institute and Library, which stands to this day, in all its Venetian Gothic finery, on Mahatma Gandhi Road in the 'Kala Ghoda' district. The origins of the library go back to 1847, when a group of young mechanics and foremen of the Royal Mint and Government Dockyard decided to establish a museum and library of mechanical models and architectural designs. Sassoon then funded its development as a sanctuary of learning and improvement for Bombay's industrious

'Kala Ghoda'. Albert Sassoon presents Bombay with Statue of the Prince of Wales (1879), with the Mechanics Institute and Library in the background.

classes (which the cloistered calm of its reading rooms still admirably sustains); he was rewarded for his patronage with a fine marble statue in the entrance hall. Opposite the library there also used to stand the 13-foot, bronze statue of the Prince of Wales (the future King Edward VII) on his 'black horse' donated by Sir Albert Sassoon to the city in commemoration of the Prince's visit in 1875. In 1965, the 'Kala Ghoda' (as it was known) was removed to the graveyard of Empire in the Byculla Gardens – to be replaced, in a superb display of Mumbai's unrepentant modernism, by a carpark.

Besting even Jejeebhoy and Sassoon was the Hindu banker Prem-chund Roychund. 'During his prosperity he strove to make the best use of his money, and gave several of the noblest benefactions for the service of education and of charity that have ever been given by a Native of India,' thought Sir Richard Temple.[72] The University Library and Rajabai Clock Tower, which was named after his mother and whose bells used to peel out of a Sunday 'God Save the Queen!', instilling the merits of both patriotism and punctuality, stands testimony to Roychund's extensive urban philanthropy, which continued even after his losses in the cotton crash of '65. There were other equally generous donors: businessman Gokuldas Tejpal funded a hospital; Mulji Jetha built the largest textile market in the city, still carrying his name; Mangaldas Nathubhai encouraged education by establishing scholarships; and the 'Peabody of the East', Sir Cowasji Jehangir Readymoney, used his trading fortune, built up from working first as a lowly godown keeper, to give Bombay a convocation hall, an ophthalmic hospital, an art gallery and forty water fountains.[73]

One of Mumbai's most telling testimonies to this civic culture of philanthropy is the Bhau Daji Lad Museum, in the northern Byculla district. In the aftermath of the 1851 Great Exhibition of the Works of Industry of All Nations in London's Hyde Park – when the diffuse riches of Empire had been brought together for the admiration of the British people under Joseph Paxton's 'Crystal Palace' – the governor of Bombay, Lord Elphinstone, appointed a committee to establish a 'Museum of Economic Products' that would similarly showcase 'the raw products of Western India and the methods of converting them into manufactured articles and to gather together a collection of natural history specimens'. And just as South Kensington was to establish a Museum of Science and Art, soon known as the Victoria and Albert Museum, so Bombay would have its own museum to prove its contribution to the age of Progress and Improvement. What was more, a Bombay museum would offer the city's merchant princes an opportunity to demonstrate their loyalty to the Crown in the aftermath of the 1857 Mutiny. In the words of businessman Sir Jagannath Shankarseth, president of the Museum Committee, the new institution would be a tribute 'worthy of the august and good sovereign who wielded the scepter of the mightiest and most beneficent empire the globe has ever bowed beneath'. So Shankarseth joined together with the merchants Mangaldas Nathubhai, Rustomjee Jejeebhoy and David Sassoon – as well as Sir George Birdwood of the Grant Medical College, Dr George Buist of the *Bombay Times* and physician and surgeon Dr Bhau Daji Lad and others – to build a Victoria and Albert Museum at the Botanical Gardens. The foundation stone was laid by Sir Bartle Frere in 1862, with a clear injunction that he did not want a 'mere collection of rarities and curiosities', but an improving display of Indian and Eastern economic products to promote manufacturing, engineering and craft. The displays would be housed in a resplendent Palladian building, more Calcutta than Bombay, with plinths, friezes and Corinthian columns full of neo-classical bravura about the purpose of Empire. Inside, however, stone gave way to iron as the pillars and railings of the upper balcony spoke to the museum's consciously urban, mid-Victorian sensibility. In many ways, the BDL is a generic site of the British Empire – with its statue of Prince Albert (donated by David Sassoon, complete with Hebrew inscription), its busts of Victoria, its display cabinets of brassware and copper, ceramics and silverware, it clearly has the same instincts behind it as the Manchester Royal Institution or the Melbourne Royal Exhibition Building. After a brilliant restoration project in 2007, its gaudy, overflowing and inchoate style manages to capture the spirit of 1860s Bombay and its essential conviction in the power of technology, progress and wealth creation.[74]

The V&A and the Municipal Buildings would not be Bombay's only monuments to modernity. Across the city, the ideology of the later nineteenth-century British Empire was coming to be revealed through an architecture unrivalled for its heterogeneity.* Fronted by an esplanade of resplendent colonial edifices, Bombay stood ready to take from Calcutta the title of 'City of Palaces'. 'Her public buildings are remarkably handsome and imposing, beautifying her broad streets and adorning her common resorts,' thought Sir Richard Temple. 'Few cities in the world can show a finer series of structures.'[75] This was not, however, the initial sentiment. 'When the English nation suddenly found itself the possessor of a great empire and of its great works of architecture, architecture in England was at such a low ebb that we could not realise what was essential to the progress of art in India,' reflected Sir Bartle Frere in 1870. 'Our ancestors in consequence left no good architecture behind them in India.'[76] What Frere had in mind was the unsympathetic neo-classicism of Wellesley's Calcutta, as well as Bombay's Regency town hall (described by the *Bombay Builder* in the 1860s as 'a decayed old beau of the last century, whose wig sits awry and whose false teeth are falling out').[77]

For there had erupted in India, some two decades after England, a colonial version of the 'Battle of the Styles', which pitted the supporters of classicist and Italianate design against the Gothicists. In Britain, such battles had usually centred around the construction of provincial town halls in cities such as Manchester, Northampton and Liverpool, as well as major national buildings including the India Office and the Grand Midland Hotel at St Pancras Station. In Bombay, the debate had begun in the late 1840s with the construction of the Afghan Memorial Church of St John the Evangelist at Colaba in the south of the city. Dedicated to the British victims of the First Anglo-Afghan War (1839–42), it was designed by the ubiquitous Henry Conybeare, working from outline proposals by George Gilbert Scott, its

---

* Not all of it to critical approval. By the interwar years, Bombay's architecture was regularly attacked for its garish miscegenation. The critic and traveller Robert Byron called Bombay an 'architectural Sodom', arguing that 'the nineteenth century devised nothing lower than the municipal buildings of British India. Their ugliness is positively daemonic. The traveller feels that the English have set the mark of the beast on a land full of artistry and good example.' Aldous Huxley concurred, thinking Bombay was 'one of the most appalling cities of either hemisphere. It had the misfortune to develop during what was, perhaps, the darkest period of all architectural history.' See Philip Davies, *Splendours of the Raj* (London, 1985).

'Early English' styling beginning the move away from classicism towards more Gothic fashioning. In Britain, the nuances of the Gothic Revival were highly complex terrain – with the precise details of Early English, domestic, thirteenth-century French and later Venetian Gothic all aggressively contested by architects and commentators alike. The chief protagonist in these architectural struggles was often the *Ecclesiologist*, the journal of the Camden Society dedicated to reviving 'the principles which guided medieval builders' and always keen to excommunicate transgressors. In 1846 the journal decreed two colonial styles for India: 'Hyperborean' for the north of the country, based on the native, vernacular style; and 'Speluncular' for the south, involving heavy planes and a lot of polychrome masonry. The latter pointed to the Venetian Gothic styling of pointed arches and sculptural ornament, of coloured stonework and free design which John Ruskin would popularize so successfully in *The Stones of Venice*; more importantly for Bombay, it was the favoured architectural idiom of Sir Bartle Frere. So, when the rampart walls came down, the domes, turrets and towers of 'Bombay Gothic' rose in their place.[78]

The contribution of Indian merchant princes to this aesthetic is particularly interesting. For all Bombay's later role in the development of Indian national consciousness – as the foundation city of the Indian National Congress and starting point for Gandhi's 1942 'Quit India' campaign – in matters of art and design the Parsi elite appeared more than happy to allow European idioms (such as the classical temple housing the Victoria and Albert Museum) to dominate their cityscape. There existed a form of deep cultural hesitation to beautifying the city in indigenous styles. Only Sir Jamsetjee Jejeebhoy's School of Art seemed interested in preserving and developing traditional Indian pottery, carving and architecture. And through the teachings of Lockwood Kipling and others at the school, there began to emerge that fusion of English Gothic and so-called Indo-Saracenic designs which would come to reshape the face of Bombay and change British architecture in India for good.

Across the road from the School of Art, heading north towards the Muslim district lining Mohammed Ali Road, stands a glorious product of this cultural fusion. Commissioner Crawford's Market (since renamed Mahatma Phule Market), built to eradicate the unhygienic bazaars but now something of a public health challenge itself, is a gaudy mix of Flemish-Moorish, even Norman, styling. Its three large gateways, whose arches are distinctly coloured with bright red stone from Bassein, are interlaid with sculpted marble panels in bas-relief celebrating commerce and industry, and all overseen by a 39-metre-high clocktower. The market is now disfigured with a corrugated iron roof, collapsing guttering and fume-blackened sculpture, but among the pineapple, onion and lime sellers in the interior, it manages to hold on to its greatest secret. There, between sleeping vendors and water-melons, is a gleefully ornamental water fountain designed by William Emerson and then encased with decorative panels by Lockwood Kipling. These playful, naturalistic designs – mixing gargoyles, god-desses (now with red *bindi* marks), monkeys and alligators – might have come straight from the pages of Ruskin's 'The Nature of Gothic'. It symbolizes the evolution of the Gothic Revival away from church design and its transformation of the secular architecture of Bombay.

Bombay Gothic grew to maturity along the Esplanade. Sir George Gilbert Scott's University Library and Rajabai Clock Tower, which now overlooks the cricket games and tea-tents along the Oval Mai-dan but once stood at the sea's edge, is a more free-flowing account of Gothic Revivalism. Loosely modelled on the tower of Big Ben, Scott's design deployed the coloration of the local Porebunder stone with a thirteenth-century French Romanesque styling. Twenty-four statues representing the castes of western India are combined with busts of Shakespeare and Homer. 'They are the mild Hindu; the shrewd Kutchi; the traditionally fierce Rajput . . . a praying Parsee . . . a sleek, high-caste Brahman', as one contemporary British guide described the Rajabai Clock Tower.[79] Next to the university is the Government Sec-retariat Building, designed in more orthodox Venetian Gothic style by Colonel Henry St Clair of the Royal Engineers and completed in 1874. The front elevation is a textbook translation of the Doge's Pal-ace, but again the use of local stone gives this otherwise drab design an unexpected colour and lift. Completing the Maidan's array of departmental buildings is the High Court, which deployed all the might of Gothic design to elevate the majesty of British justice. A ser-ies of subversive interior sculptures – a fox wearing lawyers' bands; a monkey with an eye-patch holding a scale – attempt to puncture the pomposity, but ultimately can do little to leaven the turrets, towers and black stone of officialdom. This was exactly the 'fine series of structures' colonial mandarins like Sir Richard Temple so admired.[80]

The Victoria Terminus itself, bespeaking 'the incomparable power and beauty of steam, and the unaccountable blessings of empire too', stood as flamboyant testimony not to the bureaucracy of East India Company clerks, but to the technological power of the Empire and its relentless modernity in the British imagination.[81] Lodged between the Sassoon Docks and the business district, connecting the Municipal Buildings to the General Post Office, the station stood at the fulcrum of East and West, truly the central building of the British Empire; the transit point from Suez to the world through the axis of British India. Born a stone's throw from the VT site, no wonder Rudyard Kipling called Bombay,

> Mother of cities to me,
> For I was born in her gate,
> Between the palms and the sea,
> Where the world-end steamers wait.

It would be his own father's students, the alumni of the JJ School of Art, who would embed that Bombay ethic so dramatically in the VT fabric.

The station's lead architect was F. W. Stevens, who was brought up amid the uniformity of Bath but nurtured his eclectic style at the Victoria and Albert in South Kensington, and was assisted by Sitaram Khanderao Vaidya as assistant engineer and M. M. Janardhan as supervisor. Appointed in 1877, Stevens's first act was a ten-month study trip of European termini as he worked out how to combine the Gothic Revival with emergent Indo-Saracenic designs. The result was costly, but a stunning triumph. 'The style of architecture is Italian Medieval Gothic, and the detail of the whole scheme is most elaborate,' as James Furneaux of the *Times of India* described the terminus soon after its opening.

> The hall is as large as that so familiar at Euston but infinitely grander. Within its four walls there is a wealth of columns of choice Italian marble, and polished Indian blue stone; elaborate stone archways covered

with carved foliage and grotesque heads of men and animals; a groined roof rich in blue and gold decorations, a tessellated floor, a dado of art tiles; stained glass windows, galleries of highly ornamented iron work; long counters made of differently coloured woods, exquisitely carved and polished and fitted with brass work and brass railings of artistic designs.[82]

What this description doesn't bring out is the joyful chaos: the riot of pediments, sculpture, tympanums and ironworks – mongooses, monkeys and peacocks alongside busts of Sir Bartle Frere and railway worthies. Just as on Dublin's Custom House the Arms of Ireland are embraced by the Lion and the Unicorn of Great Britain, the VT west front displays its imperial purpose though a sculpture of a lion and tiger couchant, representing England and India. There were so many other startling feats to the station: the marble columns, the cantilevered staircase, the stained-glass windows, the courtyards, verandas, the sheer enormity of a 100-metre-high and 366-metre-long train shed – and, above all, the high dome of dovetailed ribs, built without centring, Bombay's answer to Brunelleschi's Florence Cathedral. Just as with London's Euston Arch, or St Pancras Station, the designers of Victoria Terminus sought to encase one of the great engines of modernity – the steam train – in an architecture reminiscent of the classical or medieval past. But in Bombay, 'a city of the present and the future, but not of the past', the symbolism was contemporaneous and unrepentant in its embrace of modernity. On each of the main gables were placed sculptures representing Engineering, Commerce and Agriculture. On top of the central dome of the tallest tower in western India was a statue of Progress herself, carrying aloft a flaming torch and a winged wheel at her side.

The goddess of Progress stood as the crowning monument to the colonial system in Bombay. Forged into a single metropolis from seven islands, this wealthy, well-run, well-connected metropolis was a symbol of the industry and improvement which came with British rule. The very same municipal, sanitary and civic progress that had transformed the domestic cities of Manchester, London, and Birmingham could now be seen abroad on the island of good life. In Victorian Bombay, Empire had a modernity and practical application which allowed its administrators to convince themselves they had the best interests of the colonized at heart. Many of the institutions which the British and Parsi elite established in Bombay – secular spaces such as such as libraries, colleges, art galleries, parks, railway carriages and hospitals – did indeed have the effect of modernizing Indian society by confronting caste and religious identities and, in the process, updating the city's historic, cosmopolitan sensibility.

For all the multiculturalism of Bombay, Empire in India still remained a question of ruler and ruled, European and Indian. It would take the transformation of a former convict settlement, on the final stop of Kipling's world-end steamers, to develop an idea of Empire owing as much to Commonwealth as colonialism.

8

Melbourne

'The very counterpart of England'

British civilization reached Australia on 26 January 1788, when Captain Arthur Phillip and his cargo of convicts first anchored in what became Sydney harbour. Yet, 100 years on, it was the city of Melbourne, not Sydney, that was chosen to commemorate the anniversary. The 1888 Melbourne Centennial International Exhibition opened with a 7,000-strong procession of firemen, trade unionists, friendly society members, even druids marching behind a living Britannia, complete with her trident. Following her were the six governors of Britain's Australian colonies (New South Wales, Queensland, South Australia, Tasmania, Victoria and Western Australia) riding in open carriage up to the festooned arches of the Royal Exhibition Building. Spread out before them, beneath the building's vast dome, were 33 acres of display space bursting with global and colonial ephemera – a giant bust of Captain Cook; dioramas of Botany Bay; marble statues of Queen Victoria and the late Prince Albert; Irish linen; wire mattresses; a model Westminster parliament; and then a range of 'wine and beer tasting outlets'. There were orchestras and hydraulic lifts, electric lighting and banners decorated with improving words of Victorian wisdom: 'Experience is by Industry Achieved'; 'The Wheels of Progress do not Stop'. To launch the formal proceedings, the city choir sang a centennial cantata, penned by a local Melbourne minister:

> Where the warrigal whimpered and bayed,
> Where the feet of the dark hunter strayed,
> See the wealth of the world is arrayed.
> Where the spotted snake crawled by the stream,
> See the spires of a great city gleam.[1]

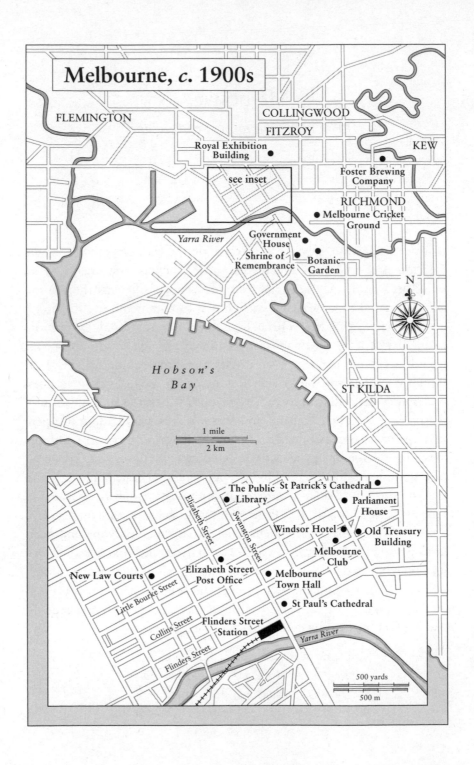

Melbourne, *c.* 1900s

FLEMINGTON

COLLINGWOOD

FITZROY

KEW

Royal Exhibition
Building

Foster Brewing
Company

see inset

RICHMOND

Melbourne Cricket
Ground

Yarra River

Government
House

Shrine of
Remembrance

Botanic
Garden

N

*Hobson's
Bay*

ST KILDA

1 mile

2 km

The Public
Library

St Patrick's Cathedral

Parliament
House

Elizabeth Street

Swanston Street

Windsor Hotel

Old Treasury
Building

Melbourne
Club

New Law Courts

Elizabeth Street
Post Office

Melbourne
Town Hall

Little Bourke Street

St Paul's Cathedral

Collins Street

Flinders Street
Station

Yarra River

Flinders Street

500 yards

500 m

In its avenues and halls, its hundreds and thousands of square feet of products and artefacts, the International Exhibition revealed what colonial Australia – and more particularly Victoria – thought it stood for. Like pre-revolutionary Boston, Victoria styled itself a prosperous partner in an updated 'Empire of goods' that successfully connected Britain's disparate possessions together under the banner of material improvement. Indeed, it seemed only natural that 'Marvellous Melbourne' – with its department stores, suburban mansions and glitzy hotels – rather than lumbering, slothful Sydney (with its unfortunate penal past) should be the locus of the centenary celebrations.

Yet the International Exhibition was also keen to explain how the bonds of colonial fraternity went beyond mere commercial advantage. Australia had also bound herself to a deeper sense of shared, imperial identity: Victoria, and its capital Melbourne, conceived of themselves as part of a Greater Britain, whose blood loyalties flowed out from the British Isles all the way to the Bass Strait. The International Exhibition identified a notion of Empire very different to the kind of autocratic governance the British state had pursued in Africa or the caste politics it had deployed in India. It was premised, first of all, on a decision to treat the indigenous inhabitants of Australia – the Aborigines – as beyond redemption. Imperial commentators and administrators in Britain and Australia regarded the Aboriginal tribes as lost to civilization and, as such, they were widely excluded from elite debate as to how to govern the colonies. 'The Aboriginal Australian blacks . . . were so extraordinarily backward a race as to make it difficult to help them to hold their own,' explained Charles Dilke, a British Member of Parliament, in the 1860s. 'They were rapidly dying out, and it is hard to see any other fate could be expected for them.' In the chilling words of Anthony Trollope, 'it was their [the Aborigines'] fate to be abolished'.[2] So late nineteenth-century Australia saw no attempts by Haileybury cadres to Westernize the backward mores of the populace or refashion their habits. Instead, as in 1760s Boston, debate focused on the relationship between the British settler class and the mother country. And that came down to the 'crimson thread of kinship', in the words of the colonial secretary, Joseph Chamberlain, that connected Australia to Great Britain. In the urban centres of the 'white colonies' – South Africa, Canada and New Zealand as much as Australia – a conception of Empire emerged as a partnership between an Anglo-Saxon tribe separated by oceans but connected by race. It was to this belief in a shared purpose, of struggle and responsibility, in which all 'European' parts of the Empire were engaged, that the imperial city of Melbourne bore witness.

But pass through Melbourne's Carlton Gardens today, from the beautifully restored Royal Exhibition Building (where generations of Melbourne students have sat their school exams) round the corner to the ultra-modern, glass and steel Melbourne Museum and that colonial history is shed like the skin of the cantata's spotted snake. The antagonism of the new museum's angular architecture towards the Renaissance aesthetic of the Royal Exhibition Building is reaffirmed by the curatorial hostility. The museum's main 'Story of Melbourne' gallery is a postmodern exercise in historical amnesia, as meandering displays of Ned Kelly and Phar Lap (the legendary Melbourne Cup racehorse) undermine any chronological understanding or insight into the city's imperial history.

The same is true elsewhere. Metropolitan, Pacific-rim, China-focused, itchingly republican Melbourne has no need or desire to dwell upon its colonial past. The remnants of imperial rule – martial statues, the King George V memorial in the Kings Domain parkland, road names and busts – are neither revered nor removed. There are no Mumbai-style decapitations of Wellesley or Cornwallis here, no dumping of old monuments in the distant corner of a park. Of course, there are fierce debates between conservationist groups and property developers over the colonial fabric, with Melbourne Heritage Action bravely resisting the destruction of some fine Victorian buildings in the downtown Hoddle Grid district. Yet these preservation battles are played out on purely architectural grounds just as in San Francisco or Glasgow, with none of the post-imperial angst of Dublin, Calcutta or Hong Kong. For the official ideology of modern Melbourne is consciously multicultural. Mundanely self-branded as 'one of the world's most liveable cities', its official literature foregrounds not the British past but the postwar story of Chinese, Greek, Italian and Vietnamese migration. The only element of imperial history with which the city is concerned is the unresolved legacy of internal colonization and

Aboriginal genocide.* 'The City of Melbourne respectfully acknowl-
edges that it is located on the traditional land of the Kulin Nation', as
the official website of the urban authority guiltily admits. 'This special
place is now known by its European name of Melbourne.'[3]

But despite this prioritization of other pasts, the Empire heritage is
nonetheless remarkably well preserved in modern-day Melbourne.
The city's colonial-era fabric remains among the world's finest, rivalled
only by that of Glasgow or Liverpool. On swaggering Collins Street
and Swanston Street, beneath the Gothic spires of St Paul's and St Patrick's, in the alcoves of Melbourne Town Hall, the vestibule of the
Melbourne Club and the tea room of the Windsor Hotel, the city's
unique mix of imperial bombast and gold-digger vulgarity is still
tangible beneath the New Australia modernity. Melbourne came to
maturity as the greatest urban embodiment of a mid-Victorian belief
in imperial solidarity, Anglo-Saxon brotherhood and civic pride. Like
Bombay, it prided itself on being a city of modernity and progress. But
in Australia, the British Empire aspired to be an exercise in communal
endeavour rather than an assertion of colonial superiority.

AUSTRALIA FELIX

It was on 20 June 1837 that Her Majesty commenced that long and
eventful reign which makes so wonderful an era in the history of human
kind. The first land sale of Melbourne had taken place twenty days before,
and we may well suppose that it was just about the time when the girl
Queen was roused from her slumbers at break of day to be informed of
her uncle's death that the pioneers of Melbourne, having bought their
allotments, began to lay the foundations of those permanent buildings
which constituted the real beginnings of what is now so handsome a city.[4]

---

* The indigenous population of Australia declined from approximately 750,000 in
1788 to 31,000 in 1911 (*The Encyclopaedia of Aboriginal Australia*, Volume 2 (Canberra, 1994)). In 2011, the Australia Bureau of Statistics listed the Aboriginal and
Torres Strait Islander population as 548,370.

In fact, the foundations of Melbourne – contrary to this 1888 centenary account – had been laid during the reign of King George III in the early 1800s. Some fifteen years after Captain Phillip's landing in Botany Bay in 1788, British ships were dropping anchor around the southern Australian coast in the protected harbour of Port Phillip Bay. Lieutenant John Murray, aboard the *Lady Nelson*, observed in January 1802 an 'apparently fine harbour of large extent'; Captain Matthew Flinders of HMS *Investigator* found the land around Port Phillip had 'a pleasing, and in many places a fertile appearance'; only Captain David Collins, of HMS *Calcutta*, was less enamoured. After landing a party of marines, free settlers and convicts in 1803, the absence of fresh water forced him to abandon the site for Van Diemen's Land (Tasmania) across the Bass Strait. It would be another thirty years before British settlers, led by the bushranger John Batman, sought to reacquire the site – principally through a series of treaties, purchases and then forcible acquisitions from the indigenous Aboriginal people. In September 1836, in response to the quickening commercial interest in the Port Phillip Bay area, the Crown authorities issued an official settlement order, sparking a frenzied land grab. As the colony of Victoria would not be legally established until 1851, overseeing the initial auction was the governor-general of New South Wales, Sir Richard Bourke, and his assistant surveyor-general, Robert Hoddle, whose grid-iron development plan for the city further augmented the plot values. With sweeping colonial bravado, he laid out forty-eight rectangular blocks, with three main east–west streets, each some 99 feet across, four 'little' east–west streets and then the main north–south avenues. Hoddle purchased a couple of lots for himself, and in time did very nicely from them. When it came to the name for this emergent conurbation, Bourke wisely alighted upon the new sovereign's first prime minister and avuncular favourite – William Lamb, Viscount Melbourne.[5]

The new city expanded furiously, putting on some 10,000 residents by 1840 and reaching 126,000 by 1861. It was an extraordinary boom, yet in tune with the peculiarly urban nature of the British Empire in Australia. Towards the end of the nineteenth century, the American sociologist A. F. Weber commented on the uniqueness of British colonialism in Australia: how 'the most remarkable concentration, or rather centralization, of population occurs in that newest product of civilization, Australia, where nearly one-third of the entire population is settled in and about capital cities'. Other countries contained a larger proportion of urban population, 'but in none of them is it so massed in a few centres'.[6] As with America, there was initial resistance towards populating the rural interior and, instead, there took place an intensive clustering of populations along the coastal cities. Nowhere more so than in Melbourne, which housed two-fifths of the residents of Victoria and, in the words of one British guidebook, 'has somehow amassed a population out of all proportion to the numbers of people settled in the rest of the colony'.[7] 'The metropolis of Victoria is inordinately overgrown,' agreed the Victoria MP William Shiels. 'I forget who it was that compared London to a wen on the face of England; but what would he [William Cobbett] have said to a metropolis of a new and still undeveloped country, which has gathered to itself more than one-third of the total population of the community?'[8]

Balancing such fears of demographic sinks and urban sprawl was admiration for Melbourne's ambition. Travelling for the first time to Australia and New Zealand in 1871 to visit his younger son Frederic, who was working on a sheep farm in New South Wales (and would become the inspiration for his 1874 novel *Harry Heathcote of Gangoil: A Tale of Australian Bush Life*), Anthony Trollope thought Melbourne 'the undoubted capital not only of Victoria, but of all Australia'.[9] The travel writer Isabella Bird described Melbourne as 'the great capital of Australia Felix, the child of gold and wool', shimmering betwixt the blue waters of Port Phillip Bay and the green woods lining the River Yarra.[10] Clara Aspinall, author of *Three Years in Melbourne*, was impressed by the transformation of the bay from the land of the whimpering warrigal (or dingo) and straying dark hunter into such a civilized city. 'I did not expect to find myself in such a handsome city,' she wrote, 'the streets wider than those of any provincial town I had ever seen in England.' She was most shocked by the prosperity of the retail boulevard Collins Street – 'lined on each side with handsome shops, banks, and private houses, three or four storeys high worthy of the neighbourhood of Hyde Park. Melbourne in reality is quite a different place to the Melbourne I imagined'.[11]

'When looked into, all this success means gold,' was the brutal conclusion reached by travelling British MP Charles Dilke. 'There is industry, there is energy, there is talent, there is generosity and public spirit, but they are the abilities and virtues that gold will bring, in bringing a rush from all the world of dashing fellows in the prime of life.'[12] Just as cotton transformed the prospects of Bombay, so the gold fields of Mount Alexander and Ballarat poured a molten prosperity on to Melbourne. On 9 July 1851, a public meeting subscribed a 200 guineas reward for the first 'strike' within 200 miles (320 kilometres) of the city. Over the next decade, the Australian colonies would extract some 25 million ounces of gold, amounting to 40 per cent of the world's output and accounting for two-thirds of the value of Victoria's total exports; between 1851 and 1861, Victoria produced 88 per cent of Australia's gold. Yet the first impact of the gold-strike was rapid depopulation. 'The whole city is "gold mad",' reported the *Melbourne Morning Herald*. 'Richmond [suburb] is a deserted village, so far as the lords of creation are concerned, only one grey-headed old gentleman of some 70 summers being left'. 'Within the last three weeks the towns of Melbourne and Geelong and their large suburbs have been in appearance nearly emptied of their male inhabitants,' complained Charles La Trobe, the first lieutenant-governor of Victoria, in October 1851, in a letter to the colonial secretary, Lord Grey. 'Not only have the idlers thrown up their employment and run off to the workings, but responsible tradesmen, farmers, clerks and not a few of the superior classes have followed. Cottages are deserted, houses to let, business is at a standstill, and even schools are closed.'[13]

It did not take long for the population tide to turn, and soon enough Melbourne was wrestling with an influx of gold-diggers, prospectors, prostitutes, merchants and lawyers. A pioneer colonial community became a gold-mine metropolis and, almost overnight, a city with 'American' levels of entrepreneurial bravado. Stock exchanges, banks, building societies, investment companies, brokers' offices and mercantile houses sprang up across the city centre. 'As we cross Elizabeth-street and think of the muddy gully of fifty years ago, the eye is lost in amazement at the magnificent vista of warehouse, bank and public building that stretches on either hand,' wrote a contemporary, in language reminiscent of the early days of Hong Kong. 'Standing at the corner it is possible to count some twenty banks, most of them housed in buildings on which no money has been spared.'[14] In contrast to 'staid and steady' Sydney, there were now 'the bustling, gold-digging, go-ahead Victorians'. 'Were I ever to return to Australia, I should pitch my tent in Melbourne,' wrote the British author and journalist Frank Fowler in 1859. 'The lively, business-like character of the place and people pleases me . . . At any hour of the day, thousands of persons may be scurrying along the leading thoroughfares, with true Cheapside bustle and eagerness.'[15] Like Bombay, Melbourne was a place of business. 'Is there a company to be got up to stock the wilds of Western Australia, or to form a railway on the land grant system in Queensland, to introduce the electric light, or to spread education amongst the black fellows, the promoters either belong to Melbourne or go there for their capital,' wrote the Anglo-Australian journalist Richard Twopeny. 'There is a bustle and life about Melbourne which you altogether miss in Sydney. The Melbourne man is always on the look-out for business, the Sydney man waits for business to come to him.'[16]

Yet Australia Felix was a child of wool as well as gold, and for all the Ballarat mining boom total gold exports to Britain were still less than one-third of those of the Australian wool trade. With easy capital from the London clearing houses behind them, smart Victoria middle-men bought up vast tracts of cheap Australian land and exported the produce (on ships like the *Cutty Sark*) to London and Liverpool. In the 1880s, the development of refrigerated shipping meant that butter and meat from the dairy market could be added to the cargo. The colonial economy worked well for Australia, with a lucrative export industry and high levels of domestic investment on the back of lax credit. Between 1860 and 1890, the Australian colonies were the principal imperial borrowers of funds from the City of London, rising from £400,000 in 1873 to £10.8 million in 1879 to £51.4 million in 1883–6. By 1890 the Australasian colonies had accumulated greater debts per head than anywhere else in the world.[17] 'Mountains of sugar from the Mauritius, tea from China, and of everything else that man can want, from every part of the world, are reared, pile upon pile, in and about Flinders Street,' marvelled Edwin Carton Booth. 'Farther north, so as to be equally convenient for the railway station and the wharf, larger and more imposing-looking buildings still, have been erected for the special purpose of storing wool, sent down from the up-country stations, and awaiting its shipment to England.'[18] For Froude, the trade and energy of Melbourne's Williamstown port instantly recalled the great imperial docks of Merseyside. 'Huge steamers – five, six, or seven thousand tons – from all parts of the world . . . Steam launches, steam ferry-boats, tugs, coasting steamers were flying to and fro, leaving behind them, alas! black volumes of smoke, through which the city loomed as large as Liverpool.'[19]

ANOTHER ENGLAND

It was a source of great angst amongst the proponents of the British Empire that the affinities between Melbourne and Merseyside were not sufficiently appreciated back in the mother country. 'There is something very characteristic in the indifference which we show towards this mighty phenomenon of the diffusion of our race and the expansion of our state,' wrote the historian J. R. Seeley in 1883. 'We seem, as it were, to have conquered and peopled half the world in a fit of absence of mind . . . thus, if we are asked what the English population is, it does not occur to us to reckon-in the population of Canada and Australia.'[20] Seeley's *Expansion of England* was the most influential text in a growing body of literature in the late nineteenth century urging the British public and their political leaders to embrace colonies like Australia and reimagine their approach to Empire.

It was an imperial ideology that had its own roots in the mid-Victorian upsurge of interest in Britain's Saxon past. 'A Saxon race, protected by an insular position, has stamped its diligent and methodic character on the century,' explained the mystical Sidonia in Benjamin Disraeli's novel *Tancred, or The New Crusade* (1847). 'And when a superior race, with a superior idea to Work and Order, advances, its state will be progressive, and we shall perhaps follow the example of the desolate countries. All is race; there is no other truth.' In a similar collection of works, historians such as Sharon Turner, William Stubbs and Henry Hallam successfully popularized this highly racial understanding of

British identity in which the main constituents of English blood, character and language could be traced back, through the Norman Conquest, to the early Anglo-Saxons. 'The chief element of our nation is Germanic, and we have good cause to be proud of our ancestry,' became the established view, as expressed by Sir Edward Creasy, Professor of History at the University of London in the 1850s and '60s. 'Freedom has been its hereditary characteristic from the earliest times at which we can trace the existence of the German race.'[21] Seeley's contribution, together with the likes of polemicist-historians J. R. Green and J. A. Froude and politician Sir Charles Dilke, was to broaden out that sense of a unique, Anglo-Saxon inheritance from England on to the shores of the 'English-speaking, white-inhabited, and self-governed lands' of the Empire.[22]

So, rather than grumbling about the financial burden of the colonies, Seeley urged his readers to regard these distant lands as fondly as they would the counties of Kent or Cornwall. 'When we have accustomed ourselves to contemplate the whole Empire together and call it all England, we shall see that here too is a United States. Here too is a great homogeneous people, one in blood, language, religion and laws, but dispersed over a boundless space.'[23] Such a fraternal approach would prevent exactly the kind of misunderstandings between mother country and colonies which had led to the Boston Tea-Party: Seeley was adamant that the precedent of division set by the American Revolution was far from inevitable. Yet it was also true that, if the Empire was to survive, then London would need to deploy a different method of governing. 'The English race do not like to be parts of an empire,' explained J. A. Froude, with unconscious hypocrisy. What the English-speaking peoples of the Dominion of Canada (brought together in 1867 with the union of Canada, Nova Scotia and New Brunswick), Australia and other white settler states wanted was a more egalitarian form of Commonwealth, 'held together by common blood, common interest, and a common pride in the great position which unity can secure'. To prove his point, Froude embarked on a round-the-world trip to speak to this settler diaspora. 'Amidst the uncertainties which are gathering round us at home,' he reported back optimistically, 'it is something to have seen with our own eyes that there are other Englands besides the old one, where the race is thriving with all its ancient characteristics.'[24]

It was a beguiling philosophy of racial destiny, colonial conquest and Saxon freedom – an 'empire of liberty' – which rapidly made its way from the pages of history books into politicians' speeches. 'I believe in this race, the greatest governing race the world has ever seen,' exclaimed the Colonial Secretary Joseph Chamberlain, 'in this Anglo-Saxon race, so proud, so tenacious, self-confident and determined, this race which neither climate nor change can degenerate, which will infallibly be the predominant force of future history and universal civilization.'[25] For all the innate superiorities of the Anglo-Saxon peoples, however, global hegemony was by no means assured. Indeed, the colonial secretary was increasingly exercised at the strategic threat posed to the Empire by the military and demographic rise of Russia, Germany and the United States. Chamberlain's solution was for Great Britain to take advantage, economically and politically, of the expanse of its empire. The later nineteenth century had witnessed a surge of colonial aggrandizement, the so-called 'Scramble for Africa'. The diamond and railway magnate Cecil Rhodes set the tone in southern Africa by declaring, in his 1877 'Confession of Faith', that it was Britain's duty 'to seize every opportunity of acquiring more territory' because 'we are the finest race in the world and . . . the more of the world we inhabit, the better it is for the human race'. From the 'Cape to Cairo' was Rhodes's mantra as the British Empire finally expanded out of the Cape Colony into 'Rhodesia', Sudan, Egypt and Kenya, as well as Uganda, Nigeria and Ghana. In addition to this, east of Suez, the colonial partition of South-east Asia brought Burma, Malaya and Borneo into London's portfolio. And just as important was the development of already existing colonial interiors. The railway revolution begun in Bombay also now opened up mineral riches and prime agricultural land in tropical Africa, in Canada and in Australia. During the last quarter of the nineteenth century, the British Empire grew by over 4 million square kilometres and added an extra 57 million subjects.

Such expansion offered the prospect of exciting new consumer markets for British manufacturers. 'In the multiplying numbers of our own fellow-citizens animated by a common spirit, we should have purchasers for our goods from whom we should fear no rivalry,' as Froude put it.[26] In the first instance, that meant copying the example of the United States by erecting import duties and introducing tariff reform among the British colonies. 'Sugar has gone; silk has gone; iron is threatened; wool is threatened; cotton will go! How long are you going to stand it?' Chamberlain demanded. 'Let us claim some protection like every other civilized nation.'[27] The former Birmingham screw manufacturer endorsed the stance taken by the liberal polemicist J. A. Hobson: that the economics of the late nineteenth-century British Empire was enriching the finance houses of the City of London – the Rothschilds, the Barings and the Coutts – but beggaring British industry and so, in the long run, undermining national competitiveness. The country that had fired up the industrial revolution was now sliding towards what the Russian revolutionary leader V. I. Lenin would later call 'the "rentier" state, the usurer state, in which the bourgeoisie to an ever-increasing degree lives on the proceeds of capital exports and by "clipping coupons"'.[28] Between 1870 and 1914, the accumulated total of British assets abroad grew from c. £700 million to almost £4 billion, returning an income of roughly £300 million per annum – which was then re-exported and put to work on high-yielding infrastructure projects abroad. London had become, as Chamberlain put it, 'the clearing house of the world', which yielded high returns by shovelling cheap money into the colonies while starving manufacturing at home of investment. While the gentleman capitalists of the south of England might have been doing well, northern industrialists and Midlands farmers were struggling under the impact of an increasingly liberalized global market. In 1854 manufactured imports into Great Britain from other competing economies were equivalent to just 10 per cent of the UK's manufactured exports; by 1913, that figure had topped one-third. And the growth of imports was so rapid that, between 1870 and 1913, *net* manufactured exports (exports minus imports) grew at only 0.4 per cent per annum. In 1902 net exports of manufactures fell to their lowest point at less than £20 million, and Britain, once the Workshop of the World, endured the ignominy of a trade deficit to foreign countries on the most highly finished goods.[29]

In Chamberlain's analysis, all of this proved that the school of free trade and minimal government (the ideology that had built Manchester and Hong Kong) was redundant in an age of competing imperial powers. In its place, as the city's former mayor, he posited 'the Birmingham school' of state intervention, both to strengthen the Empire and to improve the welfare of the British people. In policy terms, that meant an imperial free-trade area to coalesce the economic interests of the colonies and prove the Empire's worth to the industrial conurbations of Britain. Chamberlain's ambition was for a colonial *Zollverein*, a customs union, with 'a treaty of preference and reciprocity' with Britain's global possessions, which would allow the mother country to take advantage of their expanding populations whilst also protecting indigenous industry against unwelcome Russian, American and German competition. Chamberlain thought it could be 'the strongest bond of union between the British race throughout the world'.[30]

The political accompaniment to tariff reform would be imperial federation, with a single shared parliament and executive ruling over the White Dominions or 'British nations'. 'England may prove able to do what the United States does so easily,' thought Seeley, 'that is, hold together in a federal union countries very remote from each other. In that case England will take rank with Russia and the United States in the first rank of state.' For it was essential to remember that 'Greater Britain is not a mere empire . . . Its union is of the more vital kind. It is united by blood and religion.'[31] The challenge was to use the communications revolutions of the steamship and telegram to craft a transnational system of governance which combined colonial diversity with more centralized governance. It was a problem Joseph Chamberlain had begun to wrestle with after a trip to Canada in the late 1880s – the 'working out', as he phrased it, 'of the great problem of federal government'. Terrified at the prospect of Canada and America joining together in a customs union, Chamberlain used a speech in Toronto in 1887 to champion 'the greatness and importance of the distinction reserved for the Anglo-Saxon race, that proud, persistent, self-asserting and resolute stock which no change of climate or condition can alter, and which is infallibly bound to be the predominant force in the future history and civilization of the world'. His ultimate ambition was to federate 'all these great independencies of the British Empire into one supreme and Imperial Parliament, so that they should all be units of one body, that one should feel what the others feel, that all should be equally responsible, that all should have a share in the welfare . . . of every part'.[32]

Australia was among the greatest of those independencies. 'Nestling down in the most southerly and most pleasant corner of the great Australasian island-continent, there lies a land in many respects the very counterpart of England,' wrote the author of *Another England: Life, Living, Homes and Homemakers in Victoria* (1869).*

> The habits of life, the tone of thought, many of the experiences, and all the affections of its sparse population are essentially English . . . The laws under which these far-off Britons live, the customs they observe, the houses they build, the towns they inhabit, the institutions they support, and the industries they pursue, all possess a strong family likeness to the same things at home.[33]

'How the Australians do like to copy Old England!' continued Charles Rooking Carter, 'a colonist of twenty years standing' in his colonial elegy *Victoria, The British 'El Dorado'; or, Melbourne in 1869*.

> There is no place like it, they say; they are proud of it – of having sprung from it; and this sentiment is almost as strongly cherished by the new generation, who have never set foot on the ancestral soil, as it is by native-born Britons . . . Does Great Britain take note of and value this loyalty? If on no other account but for the sake of her own greatness, let us hope that she does.[34]

But as Seeley and others had feared, too little was made of this sentiment; the federal bonds between Australia and England were being allowed to atrophy. The premier of Victoria in the 1880s, Robert Service, had 'hoped to see England grow more conscious of the value of the colonies to her, and the colonies of the consequence attaching to them as members of a great empire,' noted J. A. Froude. 'They

---

* The literature of the late nineteenth century on 'Greater Britain' and the 'Expansion of England' used English and British fairly interchangeably. If there was a difference, there was a sense of *English* cultural sensibilities and habits, while *British* identity emphasized a harder-edged, geo-political reality – neither of which precluded the other.

resented – knowing that they were as English as ourselves – being treated by English ministers as if they were strangers accidentally connected with us, as if blood and natural affection were to go for nothing.'[35]

MARVELLOUS MELBOURNE

In few cities was this affection for England, and the aspiration to be part of a Greater Britain, more apparent than in Melbourne. In 1878, some 3,000 Melbournians had turned up at the Town Hall to a rally in support of Disraeli's pro-Turkish policy against Russia in the so-called 'Eastern Question'. 'These meetings will convince the Earl of Beaconsfield and his colleagues of the strength of the imperial sentiment, even in the most distant portions of the Empire,' the *Melbourne Argus* loyally reported, 'and will help, we hope, to invigorate the feeling in England in favour of a closer union between all its members, and of the transformation of Great into Greater Britain.'[36] Similarly, Queen Victoria's Golden Jubilee of 1887 'was celebrated in Melbourne with an enthusiasm that was not excelled in any part of the Empire,' wrote the Melbourne banker and man of letters Henry Gyles Turner.[37]

Accompanying the public culture of imperialism was an urban fabric highly conscious of its imperial affinities. 'Melbourne spreads around over an immense area of ground,' wrote Mark Twain, touring Australia on a lucrative speaking tour, in the aftermath of the mid-century improvements. 'It is a stately city architecturally as well as in magnitude. It has an elaborate system of cable-car service; it has museums, and colleges, and schools, and public gardens, and electricity, and gas, and libraries, and theatres, and mining centres and wool centres and centres of the arts and sciences . . . In a word, it is equipped with everything that goes to make the modern great city.'[38]

The sense of colonial prowess was captured first in the Old Treasury Building (now City Museum) at the top of Collins Street, constructed in the late 1850s to guard the gold coming in from the Victoria mines. Today, its underground vaults house a social history of the gold rush, but in the mid-nineteenth century their secure enormity symbolized the city's prosperity. The building's youthful architect, John James Clerk of the Public Works Department, instinctively knew that the style which would best capture that sense of mercantile, civic enrichment was Italianate. Like an Antipodean Strozzi Palace, the colonnaded arcade, loggia and elaborately detailed pediments of the Old Treasury Building hinted at the kind of commercial city-state which newly minted Melbourne might like to aspire to. Its natural accompaniment was the Melbourne Club, down the hill at 36 Collins Street. With its elevated stucco front and vast windows, this exclusive private members' club (still very much gentlemen only) could have been lifted straight from St James's in London. The 'massive simplicity of its freestone walls' suggested 'a plain, unvarnished potency of some sort'. And when complemented with its full-liveried servants, racquet-court, library, and 'very fair table', it was the toast of every traveller's sojourn and a symbol of Melbourne's growth from grubby gold-town to civilized metropolis. 'The luxury within, the dinners of a dozen courses, the iced champagne, and the evanescent bewitchments of French cookery' were all a sharp rejoinder, one commentator thought, to the 'slab huts, the damper, the fat mutton, and the milkless tea to which these same portly gentlemen did honour, with good open-air appetites' some forty years previously.[39]

'With regard to their public institutions, the colonists are like children with a new toy,' Richard Twopeny unkindly observed, 'delighted with it themselves, and not contented until everybody they meet has declared it to be delightful.'[40] So each visiting dignitary had to take in the Public Library ('a noble building of Corinthian architecture', housing some 63,000 volumes); the New Law Courts (all 130 rooms, with a 42-metre-high dome modelled on Dublin's Four Courts); and the classical-cum-Second Empire architecture of the Elizabeth Street Post Office. Added to which were the other civic hallmarks of a Victorian city – Athenaeums, Mutual Improvement Societies, Mechanics' Institutes, Trades Hall Literary Institutes. Then there was the stately, neo-classical Parliament House ('the grandest in the Empire outside Westminster', in imitation of Cuthbert Brodrick's Leeds Town Hall) and the Town Hall itself, with its Birmingham-style clock-tower campanile and Second Empire mix of Italianate and Gothic styles.[41] (Today, the Town Hall's gas lamps and civic emblems, its masonry and roll call of former mayors instantly evoke the municipal pride of the 1860s, but with no proper use for the building beyond occasional concerts it has the sad feel of a fading regional theatre: a modern-day Nellie Melba would not debut here.) Close by, the Gothic Revival – or 'Gothic transitional' (part Early English, part Decorated) – reaches an apogee in the three spires of William Butterfield's St Paul's Cathedral, one of the Empire's finest contributions to Decorated Gothic, whose polychrome stonework, naturalistic masonry and Tasmanian black-wood provide a soaring testament to the architectural capacity of colonial Anglicanism. Outside its walls the rush-hour chaos and dingy grime of Flinders Street station fills the Melbourne streets, but inside the cathedral visitors and worshippers are immediately transported back to the age of Pugin and Ruskin, the Oxford Movement and the Gothic Revival. Without ever visiting Australia, Butterfield picked the stones from examples sent back to England, and the poly-chrome interior is rightly regarded as the Victorian architect's final masterpiece.

St Paul's Gothic spires offer a distinct contrast to the institution of which Melbournians were themselves most proud – the Royal Ex-hibition Building. Commissioned for the 1880–81 International Exhibition,* the architect Joseph Reed plundered a medley of Euro-pean styles – from the German *Rundbogenstil* (a round-arched mode drawing upon the Romanesque and Lombardic) to Norman but-tresses to ornamental Italianate. But what really mattered was the massive central dome beneath which an exhibition space could be shifted about depending upon the event. This double-shelled dome, the largest in the southern hemisphere and higher than London's St Paul's, was a symbol of Melbourne's ballooning ambitions, while the accompanying Tuscan palazzo designs sat well with the aesthetic of the nearby Treasury Building.[42] 'Altogether the public buildings of Melbourne do the greatest credit to the public spirit of the colonists and the thoroughness of their belief in the future of their country,' concluded Twopeny. 'There is certainly no city in England which can boast of nearly as many fine buildings, or as large ones, proportion-ately to its size, as Melbourne.'[43]

* See below, pp. 337–8.

It even had its own Boboli Gardens. 'It is of vital importance to the health of the inhabitants that there should be parks,' thought Melbourne Town Council. 'Experience in the mother country proves that where such public places of resort are in the vicinity of large towns, the effect produced on the minds of all classes is of the most gratifying character.'[44] In 1833, the Parliamentary Select Committee on Public Walks had urged Britain's industrializing cities to open up their tight, urban terraces and narrow, unhealthy courts to public parks. The first fruits of reform came with John Claudius Loudon's Derby Arboretum in 1840, and in the ensuing decades Manchester, Liverpool, London and Birmingham would gain free, open, public spaces as a means for the rational improvement of the working masses and a touch of inner-city aestheticism. In Melbourne, they were even more ambitious and in 1846 opened a Botanic Garden on the south side of the Yarra River, 'affording free instruction to the labourer and mechanic, as well as to the clerk and showman'.[45]

The Gardens' success was down to a planting system which subtly appeased the bifurcated identities of the Victorian colonists: fine, old English elms, oaks, planes and poplars along with an array of indigenous Tasmanian blue gums, hoop pine and Moreton Bay figs. To complete this Anglo-Australian scheme was a Firewheel Tree – native to the Australian rainforests – as planted by His Royal Highness the Prince of Wales (the future King Edward VIII) in 1920. 'The heaps of rustling leaves, as they chase each other on the gravelled walks, give an English air to the scene,' wrote one nineteenth-century visitor, 'which is, however, soon dispelled by the sight of a well clad gum tree, the feathery plumes of the tall pampas grass, the graceful fronds of the tree fern.'[46] Accompanying the naturalistic landscaping, there was a highly technical programme of plant breeding, herbarium and seed banking run by the overbearing director, Dr Ferdinand von Mueller. Today the Gardens are a well-used public park and high-end corporate venue, but in the 1870s there was a great deal of grumbling that Baron von Mueller had allowed his passion for botanical science to get in the way of providing a suitable pleasure ground for picnicking families. Too many conifers; not enough planting beds – 'more in the nature of a scientific herbary than a recreation ground and botanic garden combined'.[47] The conservative-minded Anthony Trollope thought the gardens spacious but not charming, 'and the lessons which they teach are out of the reach of ninety-nine in every hundred. The baron has sacrificed beauty to science, and the charm of flowers to the production of scarce shrubs.'[48] By contrast, Clara Aspinall thought the Botanic Gardens 'excessively pretty'.

> The grounds are undulating, and green with British vegetation, and command a view of Hobson's Bay and the town in the distance. The first time I saw them, on an exquisite March day, it did not require a very powerful stretch of the imagination to try and realise the idea that it was Mount Edgecumbe Park in which I was standing, and that I was overlooking the Bay and town of Plymouth.[49]

And playing the role of Mount Edgcumbe House – the stately home in the midst of Mount Edgcumbe Park in south-east Cornwall – was Government House, the official home of the Governor of Victoria complete with an explicit imitation, in fine white stucco, of Queen Victoria's Osborne House. After its construction in 1876, the residence provided another sense of English affiliation, reminding each visitor of Her Britannic Majesty's ultimate sovereignty.

The 1880s marked the defining years of what the London journalist George Augustus Sala christened 'Marvellous Melbourne' – a decade of rapid population growth (from 281,000 in 1880 to 500,000 by 1890), soaring land prices, housing bubbles, railway boondoggles, new coal and copper prospectuses, and cheap money raised on the London markets. 'The winter season of that year [1887] was made memorable to the rising generation by brilliant illuminations and imposing pageants; official and social entertainments crowded upon one another ... everybody believed in 1887 that he was making money, and on the high road to affluence,' remembered Henry Gyles Turner.[50]

As with Bombay, the boom would soon turn to bust, and the over-stretched Melbourne economy crashed spectacularly in the late 1880s – but it was one swell party while it lasted, as carriages bowled along Collins Street and Melbourne's theatres, concert halls, dinners, dances and *conversazione* bloomed. 'Melbourne is one of the gayest places in the world,' gushed Clara Aspinall, 'and the ladies and gentlemen (those in the gay circles) are the most indefatigable, and I believe the most accomplished, dancers in the world.' There were luncheons at Picnic Point in Brighton; archery parties at Government House; balls for the Royal Navy officers lately arrived into port. Richard Twopeny concurred: 'If you are a man of leisure you will find more "society" in Melbourne, more balls and parties, a larger measure of intellectual life' than in drab Sydney. In short, 'the people dress better, talk better, think better, are better'. Charles Rooking Carter concurred:

> I have seen the 'Row', in Hyde Park, and Regent Street in London; the Champs Elysées in Paris; the great square of St Mark's, Venice; the Corso and the Pincian at Rome; and the Toledo at Naples; and in the matter of dress, I would undertake to match the ladies of Melbourne against the fashionable dames who frequent the promenades in question: in short, they dress in the extreme of fashion.

And what was so comforting for any new arrival in town was, like Hong Kong before it, how familiar the social scene felt. 'Party followed party, and it was English life all over again: nothing strange, nothing exotic, nothing new or original, save perhaps in greater animation of spirits,' wrote a relieved Froude. 'All was the same – dress, manners, talk, appearance.' John Freeman, the Melbourne chronicler of high and low life, agreed: 'The social habits of the Melbourne people are British in every sense. We are fond of dinners, parties, balls, picnics and social gatherings of all kinds.'[51]

Only one visiting party seemed to find Melbourne society unsuited to their tastes. On a tour of municipal systems around the world, the austere Fabian couple Sidney and Beatrice Webb progressed through Victoria in the late 1890s. There they found the upper chamber of the Legislative Council 'the most reactionary in the British Empire' and the state legislators, 'a mean undignified set of little property owners, with illiterate speech and ugly manners'; they were horrified to discover Labour Party politicians 'playing billiards and smoking, evidently finding life extremely agreeable under the Capitalist system'. Astonishingly, given their disagreeableness, the two municipal socialists were then invited to a series of Melbourne dinner parties held in their honour. 'The houses and entertainments have been of the same type, costly and pretentious, wines and expensive food being lavishly supplied,' the ingrates grumbled. And while the Webbs did agree with Richard Twopeny that Melbourne men were a cut above their Sydney counterparts, 'the women, alas! are equally intolerable, untrained minds, over-dressed bodies, and lacking in the charm of physical vigour or grace of manner'. Perhaps because he was from a less puritanical wing of the socialist movement, the Marxist radical Henry Hyndman disagreed with the Webbs. He thought he had 'never lived in any city where the people at large, as well as the educated class, took so keen an interest in all the activities of human life, as in Melbourne . . . Art, the drama, music, literature, journalism, wit, oratory, all found ready appreciation. The life and vivacity of the place were astonishing.'[52]

The summit of Victoria society was then as now the Melbourne Cup. Just as in Bridgetown, Bombay, Hong Kong and Cape Town, 'wherever a community of the Anglo-Saxon race pitch their tents, one of the first things they think of is a race-course'.[53] Come November, Melbourne turned into the 'Mecca of Australia', according to Mark Twain, as every man and woman who could afford the expense 'begin to swarm in by ships and rail, and they swarm thicker and thicker day after day until all the vehicles of transportation are taxed to their uttermost . . . and all hotels and lodgings are bulging outwards'. On race day, Guy Fawkes Day (that most British of national fête days), the Flemington Course was a resplendent sight.

> And so the grand stands make a brilliant and wonderful spectacle, a delirium of colour, a vision of beauty. The champagne flows, everybody is vivacious, excited, happy, everybody bets, and gloves and fortunes change hands right along all the time . . . and when each day is done, the people dance all night so as to be fresh for the race in the morning.[54]

Even the unappreciative Sidney and Beatrice Webb appeared to enjoy their day at the races. After spending a little time on the 'Flat' – alongside 'thousands of working men' – they quickly made their way up to the Hill, 'ending up in the Governor's Box in which were gathered all the Governors and Governesses of Australia'. Quite the thing.[55]

IN SUBURBIA

For all the urban energy of the Hoddle Grid and the champagne lunches in the Flemington boxes, the essence of Melbourne was to be discovered a few kilometres away in the villas and mansions of its fast-expanding suburbs. 'A walk down Collins Street or Flinders Lane would astonish some of the City Crœsuses,' explained Richard Twopeny.

> But if a visitor really wishes to form an idea of the wealth concentrated in Melbourne, he cannot do better than spend a week walking round the suburbs, and noting the thousands of large roomy houses and well-kept gardens which betoken incomes of over two thousand a year, and the tens of thousands of villas whose occupants must be spending from a thousand to fifteen hundred a year.[56]

Whilst Cape Town would only later develop its exclusive suburbs of Constantia and Plumstead, Melbourne sprawled outwards from its inception, combining a central core with a growing constellation of suburban villages stretching along the shore line. In this, Melbourne very accurately reflected the shifting topography of British cities during the latter half of the nineteenth century. 'The greatest advance of the decade is shown,' reported the journalist Sidney Low in 1890,

> not in the cities themselves, but in the ring of suburbs which spread into the country around them ... The centre of population is shifting from the heart to the limbs. The life-blood is pouring into the long arms of bricks and mortar and cheap stucco that are feeling their way out to the Surrey moors, and the Essex flats, and the Hertfordshire copses.[57]

The roots of Britain's suburban efflorescence were variously cultural, economic and technological. Its origins could be traced back to the Protestant evangelical revival of the late eighteenth century, with its emphasis upon the virtue of domesticity, the homely sphere of the wife and the sanctity of the hearth. In its aftermath, there emerged a growing emphasis upon the sinfulness of the city in contrast to the capacity of a separate, suburban lifestyle to nurture a godly family. This thinking would blossom, during the mid-nineteenth century, into

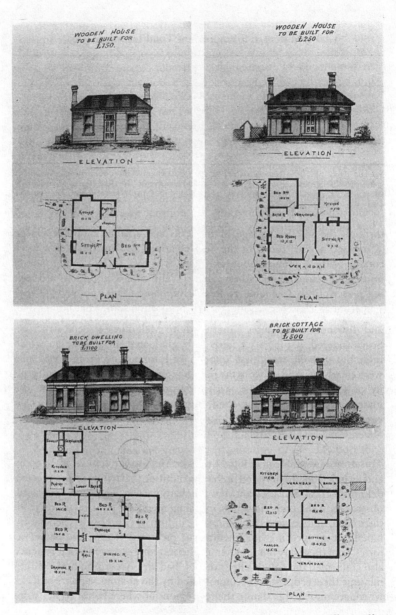

Melbourne suburban house plans, from Sands & McDougall, *Melbourne Directory* (1885). Top left: 'Wooden house to be built for £150' (1 bed); top right 'Wooden house £250' (2 beds, bathroom and veranda); bottom left: 'Brick Dwelling £1100' (4 beds and servants' quarters); bottom right: 'Brick Cottage £500' (2 beds)'.

that remarkably sentimental cult of the Home. 'The great store that the English still set by owning their home is part of this powerful sense of the individual personality,' wrote the London-based Prussian diplomat Herman Muthesius in 1904. 'The Englishman sees the whole of life embodied in his house. Here, in the heart of his family, self-sufficient and feeling no great urge for sociability, pursuing his own interests in virtual isolation, he finds his happiness and his real spiritual comfort.'[58] 'Home, Sweet Home' became the motto for millions of middle-class suburbans as, *The Times* reported, 'the habit of living at a distance from the scene of work [has] spread from the merchant and the clerk to the artisan'.[59]

The suburban ethic was transported wholesale to the Australian colonies. Indeed, 'Home, Sweet Home' was taken as the anthem of the Victoria stand at the 1880 International Exhibition, as low-density Melbourne championed the virtues of *rus in urbe* living. As in the mother country suburbs, the same faux rural name-plates were hammered on to houses, the intense focus on domestic improvement and gardening, passionate concern for family life and clearly demarcated gender divides. 'Nearly everybody who can lives in the suburbs,' explained Twopeny. 'It is strange that the Australian townsman should have so thoroughly inherited the English love of living as far as possible away from the scene of his business and work during the day.'[60] And as in Britain, the clerks and professionals were connected between the downtown and the shoreline by a highly effective transport system. Just as the Metropolitan Railway Company and the Great Eastern Railway (under pressure from the 1883 Cheap Trains Act, which necessitated the provision of workmen's fares) opened up London's suburbs to working-class commuters, so from the early 1880s the Melbourne Tramway and Omnibus Company started to connect Melbourne's outer edges to the urban core. By 1891 Melbourne's 76 kilometres of double-track line was the world's biggest and most efficient integrated cable system, carrying nearly fifty million passengers a year, with trams passing in some places once every four to five minutes, into the leafy suburban enclaves.[61] This was in addition to the railway lines which had opened up, in the 1850s, from Flinders Street and then Spencer Street stations, to take the wealthier Melbournians out to their beach-side retreats. 'A quarter of an hour will bring you ten miles to Brighton, and twelve minutes will take you to St Kilda, the most fashionable watering-place,' boasted Twopeny. 'Within ten minutes by rail are the inland suburbs, Toorak, South Yarra and Kew, all three very fashionable.'[62] And on the back of the tram and train networks came further housing developments and land speculation, sending the boundaries of the metropolis way beyond Port Phillip Bay.

Yet it would be a mistake to regard the Melbourne suburbs as dormitory commuter-villes. What Sidney and Beatrice Webb dismissed as a 'muddled and unsystematic organisation', with its '23 local authorities, called 8 cities, 7 towns, 2 boroughs, and 6 shires', was, in fact, the basis for a remarkable degree of suburban pride.[63] Just as the outer London boroughs of the later nineteenth century bedecked themselves in town halls, parks, museums, fire stations, libraries and swimming baths as monuments to their civic worth, so Melbourne's confederation of suburbs cemented their identities through public institutions and municipal monuments. 'Though the suburbs of Melbourne are in fact parts of the town,' commented Anthony Trollope, 'they seem to have built on separate plans, and each to have had a ceremonial act of founding or settlement on its own part, – being in this respect unlike suburbs, which are usually excrescences upon a town, arising as haphazard as houses are wanted.'[64]

Part of the attractiveness of the Melbourne suburbs was to be found in their contrasting characteristics. So the inner suburban, working-class district of Collingwood (the most heavily populated neighbourhood, christened in honour of Admiral Lord Collingwood, who commanded the British fleet at the Battle of Trafalgar) had little of the café Boho-chic its fast-gentrifying streets have today. Instead, it was described as 'radical and riotous': 'The shops and public-houses have a mildewy look about them. In class and character they are something between those of Whitechapel and the Edgware Road, joined to an evident tendency to run to a state of seediness.' Nearby Fitzroy, by contrast, was 'conservative and quiet'. Edwin Carton Booth thought there was 'a good deal of the solemn respectability of a small cathedral town about Fitzroy'. Richmond was even smarter. 'The shops and shop-keepers have a comfortable and contented look, and in many respects Richmond on the Yarra-Yarra has a strong family likeness to Richmond on the Thames.' Surmounting them all was St Kilda, Melbourne's answer to Bombay's Malabar Hill. 'Its residents are among the most wealthy and best known of the merchants and professional men of the metropolis', who were drawn to the glorious local beaches, 'exceeding in beauty and extent the beaches of Ramsgate, Margate, Brighton and Eastbourne, all put together'.[65]

The suburbs' autonomy was underscored by the individuality of the domestic architecture. The feverish creativity of nineteenth-century British design was brought to bear on the mansions, semis and villas of suburban Melbourne – Scots Baronial, Venetian Gothic, Indo-Saracenic, Moorish, Spanish and, most favoured of all, Italian Renaissance in rendered stucco. In *Great Expectations*, Charles Dickens had enjoyed taking a humorous swipe at the expense of the lower middle-class, suburban affectation for over-decorating homes. Deep in the south London suburb of Wandsworth, the solicitor's clerk Wemmick boasted a tiny little terraced house, which was then festooned with Gothic windows and a flagstaff. 'The bridge was a plank,

A suburban palace: Enderby, South Yarra, residence of William J. Mountain Esq. in south Melbourne (1888).

and it crossed a chasm about four feet wide and two deep. But it was very pleasant to see the pride with which he hoisted it up and made it fast; smiling as he did so, with a relish and not merely mechanically.' So too in Melbourne, homes became castles – with titles such as Kew, Windsor, Balmoral and Buckingham – as the suburban classes expressed themselves and their colonial identity through a proliferation of towers, verandas, balconies, summer houses and conservatories . Even the smaller cottages of Richmond, Carlton and Fitzroy bedecked themselves in cast-iron tracery and stucco decorations. And, whichever suburb you headed into, there was a tangible urge to be as English as possible. When J. A. Froude drove round the Melbourne environs, 'among endless suburban residences, like ours at Wimbledon', he could not but comment on their desire 'to surround themselves with graceful objects, and especially with the familiar features of their old home – oaks, maples, elms, firs, planes and apple-trees'. Another visitor, Henry Cornish, thought the 'snug villas and cosy retreats' of suburban Melbourne 'remind you strongly of Clapham'. Clara Aspinall was more inspired and suggested that sunset on a summer's day at St Kilda could, with a little imagination, remind one 'of the East and West Cliffs of Brighton, in Sussex'.[66]

Alongside the allure of a seaside Sussex town, the escalating sanitary crisis affecting the inner city was also propelling residents into the suburbs. For 'Marvellous Melbourne' had also gained the soubriquet 'Smellbourne' as a result of both its antiquated sewerage system and the untreated filth emanating from the bay's slaughterhouses, brass foundries, timber yards, boot factories and brick plants. Melbourne's plentiful human waste poured into the Yarra, where it mixed with 'large quantities of bloodstained fluid from the city abattoirs' and 'the contents of intestines from gut factories' to turn a fast-flowing river into something 'now little better than the main sewer of a large city'.[67] As the otherwise laudatory Charles Rooking Carter put it, 'here before the eyes of the public, a foul-looking and still more foul-smelling fluid runs its daily and appointed course – a filthy compound of liquids discharged from factories, dyehouses, workshops and private dwellings – emitting vapours which are anything but "odorous" – especially in hot weather'.[68] With the wind in the wrong direction the stench could sometimes waft all the way to the leafy enclaves of Malvern, South Yarra and Kew. 'I was staying at one time in a handsome house where the atmosphere of the sitting-rooms was, at certain times, and more especially in wet weather, so obnoxious, that we could not remain in them, feeling that we were inhaling poison,' exclaimed Clara Aspinall.[69]

Those left behind in the inner-city districts, or proximate suburbs of Collingwood and Flemington, faced housing conditions just as unpleasant as the insanitary stench. 'I know from experience something of the chronic domestic dirt which prevails amongst the lower classes in the manufacturing towns of England,' wrote the British doctor J. E. Neild, 'but nothing that I have ever witnessed in the West Riding of Yorkshire and in South Lancashire, equalled in repulsiveness what I have found in Melbourne.' Of particular horror was the cottage death-bed of a local bootmaker. 'The utter filth of this place was beyond description ... It was literally not fit for a pig to live in, and the body of the man who had for some time lived in it was a great deal dirtier than that of many pigs.'[70] As Henry Mayhew and Charles Dickens had explored the underworld of London's Seven Dials and Jacob's Island, so Melbourne's growing army of social scientists and journalists started slumming it along Little Bourke Street to expose the hidden terrain of colonial Victoria.[71] Suckled by the miasma of Melbourne's polluted lanes and sewers, brought up in criminal habits, crowded together with no conception of family bonds, this urban residuum constituted an embarrassing and dangerous threat to the city's reputation. 'On the breaking out of the first French Revolution, fifty thousand human beings came forth from the various holes and corners of Paris,' wrote the hack John Freeman, in Lights and Shadows of Melbourne Life (1888). 'We, too, have a dangerous class in our midst lurking in holes and corners away from public gaze, where they mature undisturbed their plans against society.' Their abodes were the little streets running off the great boulevards, where they coagulated in 'tumble-down wooden shanties ... dirty, alive with vermin, close and foetid, with the sharp pungent odour of decaying wood ever appealing to your nostrils'.[72] The young men inhabiting these slums were the dreaded 'larrikin', or 'colonial rough' – Melbourne's answer to the 'hoodlum' of San Francisco or Artful Dodger of Dickens's London. 'The "larrikin" is an embryo ruffian, a boy in years, but a man in vices,' explained Isabella Bird. 'He gambles, cheats, drinks, chews, smokes, sets outhouses on fire, rifles drunken citizens' pockets, insults respectable women.'[73] In another diagnosis, 'he is generally a weedy youth, undersized and slight, but like all Australians, who are cast in a lanky not thickset mould, he is wiry and active. He has a repulsive face, low forehead, small eyes, a colourless skin, and irregular discoloured teeth.'[74] They came out at night and, like 'pariah dogs', hunted in a pack. They were the scrawny, flashy, cowardly ne'er-do-wells who haunted the Hoddle Grid and drove decent families into the suburbs.

Rubbing up alongside the 'larrikins' of Little Bourke Street were the equally indigent Chinese, who had migrated to Victoria in their thousands in the 1850s to work the gold-mines and then drifted back to Melbourne when the rush receded. To the urban chroniclers of Outcast Melbourne, they formed another component of an inner-city eugenic sink. 'The smell of roast pork comes from several Chinese eating-houses. Here is a Chinese drug store with mysterious preparations on all sides; dried lizards and shrivelled up snakes,' recalled John Sutherland of his journey along Little Bourke Street. 'But the Chinese in Melbourne are mostly of the poorer sort. They spend the day in hawking through the suburbs, and they crowd into these narrow lanes after dark to gamble and smoke opium.' Charles Rooking Carter thought that the 'flat and tawny visages, peculiar dress and manners' of the city's Chinese denizens 'form one of the singular sights of Melbourne'.[75]

Even the suburbs had their divides. As we have seen, the inner-suburban neighbourhoods of Collingwood and Richmond, South Melbourne and North Melbourne, endured their share of pollution and poor housing. And whilst there was no Dark Town versus White Town apartheid in colonial Melbourne, there was certainly a yawning distance between the upper reaches of Kew and the tight terraces of Flemington. For the most part, aside from the growing Chinese quarter, the urban separation was based on class and money, not race and religion. The key dividing line was the Yarra River – almost a *cordon sanitaire*, as one historian puts it, between working-class and middle-class Melbourne.[76] North of the Yarra, the neighbourhoods were low-income with high-density developments and heavy levels of industrial smog. South of the Yarra and then east-ward along the coastline, the houses became villas, the air fresher and the vistas more beguiling. The omnibus system and train network, combined with boosterish municipal councils and speculative private developers, augmented the separateness of these wealthy suburbs from the urban problems of downtown Melbourne. And when Mel-bournians thought about their cultural identity, it was this suburban, domestic civilization – as much as the fine public institutions and bustling dockyards of metropolitan Melbourne – that they celebrated. 'The mansions in the fashionable suburbs are only less gratifying evi-dences of the prosperity of the people than the thousands of pleasant cottages which one sees on every road within a few miles of the city,' declared Victoria's official prospectus at the 1886 Colonial and Indian Exhibition in London.[77] 'People even of moderate means live in the country air and have gardens and pleasant houses,' agreed Trollope. 'On two sides, south and east, Melbourne is surrounded for miles by villa residences.'[78] What they had so successfully nurtured at Port Phillip Bay was a distinctive urban form, a middle-class conurbation based upon social mobility and an almost Garden City-like combin-ation of country and city.

This was why the authorities so abhorred the curse of 'larrikinism' and the spectre of a British-style urban residuum of which it reminded them. As a result, they were always keen to maintain that the worst of Little Bourke Street had nothing on the rookeries and tenements of Berlin, Marseilles or London. 'Nowhere is there any sign of poverty or anything at all resembling Stepney [East London] or the lower parts of an European city,' Richard Twopeny stated firmly.[79] Indeed, it became an increasingly popular trope to compare the expensive, cramped, unhealthy lives of British residents with the clean living of Victoria. The 1892 novel *Uncle Piper of Piper's Hill* chronicled the journey of the grand but impoverished Cavendish family from nervous, class-ridden London to Marvellous Melbourne and their realization of an alternative colonial future. After travelling the length of mighty Collins Street, they head south-east to the home of their generous uncle Piper in the suburbs of South Yarra: 'the carriage turned suddenly off the main road through two wide-open gates of wrought iron, and rolled swiftly and smoothly up a broad and perfectly-kept avenue. To the right lay a lawn as soft as velvet pile, dotted with flower-beds.' And then there was the house. 'At the foot of the flight of steps leading up to the verandah, upon which the great entrance-door seemed to open by magic as the carriage approached, stood two mighty marble vases, whence trailers of the scarlet passion flower, now little but a mass of light-green foliage, threw out long tendrils that twined themselves around the balustrade.' Such wealth and space were in stark contrast to the pollution, overcrowding and genteel poverty of life in the mother country. 'To the Cavendish family it seemed large enough as they approached to have held a whole row of London terrace-houses of the cramped kind to which they had been accustomed.'[80]

There was an intense pride in the suburbs of colonial Melbourne and the domestic, familial culture they secured. In contrast to Britain, there was very little of that snobbery and venom towards suburban living: no angst at the extending tentacles of the city; no fear of sprawl or lower-middle-class vulgarity. This was the liberal author Charles Masterman on London's swelling tide of suburban commuters: 'A turbid river of humanity, pent up by the narrow bridge, is pouring into London; aged men in beards and bowlers shambling hastily forward; work girls, mechanics, active boys, neat little clerks in neat little hats shining out conspicuous in the rushing stream ... The abyss is disgorging its denizens for the labour of the day.'[81] In Melbourne, by contrast, such suburban industriousness was a testament to the settler spirit, the natural beauty and the egalitarian, affordable living offered by the White Dominions. Towards the end of John Sutherland's account of *Victoria and Its Metropolis – Past and Present* (1888), he uses the scene of Flinders Street train station at rush hour to paint a very different picture of a virtuous, bourgeois, suburban civilization steadily taking shape before his eyes.

> For the great crowds that descend Elizabeth Street are people who have finished their day's labour, and the mind follows them to many a suburban home, the cheery meal, the expectant children, the social evening; and exults at the wide ocean of happiness that underlies the turmoil of human lives. And the scene is picturesque. The tram-cars lit with fairy-gliding lights of many colours; the clock tower with its shining

face; the wreathing smoke beyond, and the lines of tapering masts against the feeble glow of the western sky, all contribute to the striking effect of a most characteristically metropolitan prospect.[82]

PLAY UP AND PLAY THE GAME

In the steady application of the Flinders Street commuters were the germs of a startling, new notion: that the racial strength of the Empire was now more likely to be found in far distant colonies than in Great Britain itself. There was a growing concern that living conditions in Britain's polluted cities were undermining the nation's inner Saxon fortitude, while at the same time the Kiwis, the Aussies, the Canadians and the Cape dwellers were only growing in stature. 'A race of men sound in soul and limb can be bred and reared only in the exercise of plough and spade, in the free air and sunshine, with country enjoyments and amusements, never amidst foul drains and smoke blacks and the eternal clank of machinery,' mulled J. A. Froude in 1887. Thankfully, in its fit of absence of mind the British Empire had prepared precisely for this eugenic crisis by extending England across the world.

> English enterprise had occupied the fairest spots upon the globe where there was still soil and sunshine boundless and life-giving; where the race might for ages renew its mighty youth, bring forth as many millions as it would, and would still have means to breed and rear them strong as the best which she had produced in her early prime.

It was Froude's mentor, Thomas Carlyle, who was most explicit in recounting the coming purpose of Britain's possessions. 'According to him England's business, if she understood it, was to gather her colonies close to her, and spread her people where they could breathe again, and send the stream of life back into her loaded veins.'[83] If the Empire was to survive, the decaying Anglo-Saxon population of Old England needed a racial transfusion from the vigorous, sun-drenched young men and women of the White Dominions. After travelling through Australia and New Zealand (as well as the Cape Colony),

Trollope was convinced 'that the born colonist is superior to the emi-grant colonist ... the emigrant is superior to his weaker brother whom he leaves behind him. The best of our workmen go from us, and produce a race superior to us.' These second- and third-generation settlers, born under the Southern Cross, were the 'coming men' of the imperial project. And this was obviously the case in Melbourne. Froude regarded 'the principal men in Melbourne' as of 'exceptional quality', since their weaker brethren had been lost to the gold mines of Ballarat. Those who survived the digging and sifting, Froude sug-gested in a chilling display of social Darwinism, were a 'picked class, the seeming fittest, who had the greatest force, the greatest keenness, the greatest perseverance'.[84] The consequence of this breeding-out of the weaker human bloodlines could be seen in the startling vitality of the coming colonial generation. As the visitor passes through Melbourne's broad streets, wrote John Freeman, 'he will notice the well-to-do look of the people he meets; he will admire the grace and demeanour of the women, and the manly, independent bearing of the men'.[85] Melbourne's sea-air suburbia was producing a colonial master race in whose hands the future of the Empire could safely be placed. 'I would say to any young man whose courage is high and whose intelligence is not below par, that he should not be satisfied to remain at home; but should come out to Melbourne,' proposed Trollope, 'and try to win a higher lot and better fortune than the old country can afford to give him.'[86] In barely 100 years, a settler bay on the south-west edge of Australia, peopled by convicts, sailors and gold-diggers, had been identified as the imperial gene-pool of the future.

From an Australian perspective, it was not so clear-cut. By the 1880s, a tapered, dual identity as both Australians and Brits had begun to develop across Victoria. In most instances, this could safely be packaged under the banner of 'Britannic Nationalism', a shared racial and ethnic sensibility united through the global purpose of Greater British imperialism to spread civilization, trade and Chris-tianity around the globe. In Adelaide, Sydney and Melbourne, Australian urban society was able to offer the institutions and public spaces for the working out of this identity. And among the most popu-lar forms of urban culture was the cascade of jubilee, centennial and then international exhibitions which in their artefacts, iconography and ritual provided opportunities for exploring the ambiguous colonial status of Melbourne's subjects. In the shadow of a huge rhombic dodecahedron, representing 50 million ounces of gold valued at some £200 million, the opening cantata for the 1880–81 Melbourne International Exhibition summed up the sense of a shifting but shared cultural inheritance:

> And that true spirit of the British race
> Which makes the wilderness a dwelling place,
> And wrestles the desert into fruitful soil;
> Swift on the track of the bold pioneer
> Science and learning and the arts appear.

The themes of this 1880–81 exhibition outlined both a narrative of Australian progress in agriculture and industry – with displays from milliners, furniture makers, state forests, railways and Collingwood's celebrated Foster Brewing Company – and a reminder of the elemental ties which connected Victoria both to the mother country and to her fellow colonies around the world. Browsing the British pottery, the Indian silverware and the Irish linen, taking pride in their own displays of gold and wool, the Turner watercolours and the historical dioramas helped to nurture within Melbourne residents an imperial sensibility, allowing them to feel right at the centre of a virtuous, modern, wealth-creating Empire. This vernacular and highly popular exhibition format could also present all of Joseph Chamberlain's complex ambitions for an imperial federation and a trading *Zollverein* in the guise of an enjoyable, family day out attracting millions of visitors. 'God bless them both, old England and the new ... / Each helping each other, each to the other true ...' as the official ode of the 1887 Adelaide jubilee exhibition put it.[87]

Yet even the success of Melbourne's exhibitions paled when compared to the most popular passion of the 'Queen-City of the South'. 'Among many other essentially British attributes which the Victorian transplanted with himself to this adopted country, love of sport has taken the deepest root,' explained 'Tom Brown', sports commentator for the *Australasian* newspaper. 'Racing, rowing, cricketing all flourish here even to a greater extent, in proportion to our population, than they do in the old country.'[88] In Melbourne, the one sport to rival the horse-racing Cup was the British Empire's great gift to the world, cricket. It had been played in Australia since the 1810s, but public enthusiasm surged mid-century. In 1869, the Bishop of Melbourne even revoked the ban on diocesan clergy playing the game. 'The mania for bats and balls in the broiling sun during the last summer exceeded all rational excitements,' declared the usually anodyne *Australian Facts and Prospects*. 'The very walls of Melbourne became infected and threatening. Whichever way you turned a cricket ball met your eyes.'[89] It remains the case today: Melbourne is a sports-mad city with the entirety of its downtown handed over to whichever cricket, soccer, Australian rules football or rugby league match is in progress. Then as now the centre of this commotion was the vast Melbourne Cricket Ground, relocated in the 1850s to the east of the city next to Richmond, with a 213-metre grandstand able to accommodate some 6,000 spectators. In the 1870s it was reconfigured (as it would be again for the 1950s Olympic Games and then the 2006 Commonwealth Games) with swivel seating to enable fans to watch cricket in summer and football on Richmond Park during the winter season.

It was here that the All England Eleven – the first international cricket team to tour Australia – played their inaugural match in 1861, having been carried into Melbourne from Sandridge dock in a coach drawn by eight grey horses. Their trip was funded by Spiers and Pond, operators of a well-known restaurant in Melbourne, who booked the bowlers and batsmen only after Charles Dickens turned down the offer of a twelve-month reading tour. It was a smart second choice as 40,000 Melbournians came to welcome the tourists to the MCG and, in the words of *Bell's Life* magazine, to demonstrate that 'the race which inhabits Australia is essentially English in all its feelings and amusements; and that in changing our sky we have not lost our old love for the manly sports of the mother country'.[90] The series was such a triumph that another tour followed in 1863, before the legendary W. G. Grace himself arrived in 1873–4 – for the not inconsiderable fee of £1,500 (plus extras). It was worth every penny. 'As a judge of a run and for speed between the wickets he is unequalled in the world,' the *Australasian* gushed. 'The ease and power with which the leviathan played the bowling, the shooters, and bumpers, met equally coolly, not hitting the ball over the moon, but making runs simply and rapidly without apparent effort . . . all this was as near perfection as it is possible to be.'[91] What could match this? Only the triumphant return to Melbourne of the Australian cricketers who beat the English at Lord's during the celebrated 1882 tour, after which the *Sporting Times* announced that English cricket had died and 'the body will be cremated and the ashes taken to Australia'. The victors were greeted on arrival by a torchlight procession of 700 firemen, marching bands from the Victorian Navy and a procession numbering tens of thousands striding into the MCG to the tune of 'See the Conquering Hero Come' under the din of fireworks and cheering crowds.

For cricket fans and colonists alike, the 'Ashes' victory over the English on English soil was a pivotal moment. For 'test' cricket between England and Australia had become exactly that – a test of the virility and manhood of the colonies in combat with the mother country. In the 1990s, the British Conservative politician Norman Tebbit would seek to gauge the level of 'Britishness' amongst UK immigrant populations with his 'cricket test': when the West Indies or Pakistan teams were playing a cricket series against England, if second-generation Caribbean British or Pakistani British citizens of immigrant descent did not support England against the teams of their parents' birth nation then they had failed to integrate properly. Cricket was, for Tebbit, a useful arbiter of the health of immigrant patriotism and the level of multiculturalism the UK had reached. In 1880s Melbourne, cricket worked the other way by helping to undermine any unitary sense of Britishness. In fact, it was a very powerful means of generating a more cohesive national Australian identity and shedding that unclear affiliation of being southern hemisphere Englishmen split between six different colonies. The *Australasian* magazine was quick to remark on how different the cricket tours of the 1870s felt to those of the early 1860s, when 'the national or Imperial sentiment was dominant in men's minds, and the local or colonial sentiment was comparatively weak. But during the last decade all this has obviously undergone a striking change. The Imperial feeling has not been weakened, we would fain believe but there has grown by the side of it a healthy and vigorous Australian feeling.'[92] And this was only added to by the growing number of native-born Australians, descended from the

Celtic fringes of Great Britain, within the Melbourne crowds. By the 1860s, just over 30 per cent of the city population had been born in England, with Irish descent accounting for 16 per cent, Scots 11 per cent, and a further 9 per cent from outside the British Empire. Increasingly, the watching crowd was divided into two camps: 'the Englishmen, particularly those from the cricketing counties, were eager for the success of their champions, [but] the Irish, the Scotch and the Australians were burning for their adopted country'.[93] Of the latter, Tebbit would have approved.

These increasingly frequent cricketing duels allowed Australian commentators to dwell further upon the healthy, virile nature of their sporting young men; how the bowlers and batsmen of Victoria and New South Wales could match, in bone and muscle, run for run, the sportsmen of Surrey or Yorkshire. The Victorian Eleven's crushing victory over James Lillywhite's tourists (who grumbled about beer rather than champagne being served at the pre-match lunches) at the MCG in 1877 was a moment for the Sydney *Daily News* to reflect: 'For all that the sceptre has passed away so to speak, the flag is struck. It may console them to note that the English race is not degenerating, and that in the distant land and on turf where lately the blackfellow hurled his boomerang, a generation has arisen which can play the best bowlers of the time.'[94] Indeed, just as Trollope and Froude could point to a new imperial energy coming from the White Dominion stock, so England and Australia's shifting fortunes on the cricket pitch sanctioned a deeper reflection on the changing power dynamic between metropole and colony. Cricket allowed all those slights and snobberies with which the British Establishment had dismissed the colonies – 'being treated by English ministers as if they were strangers accidentally connected with us, as if blood and natural affection were to go for nothing', as the Victoria premier Robert Service had put it – to be bowled back down the wicket at them with the power of a yorker. The test series was a way of both defining a sense of Australian nationhood *and* cementing that Commonwealth of colonial equals which Froude and Chamberlain so desired. There was also a little Oedipal fun to be had. 'The passion for cricket burns like a flame in the Australian blood,' explained a leading Australian journal, 'and in the case of an All England Eleven, the passion is intensified by an unfilial yearning on the part of young Australia to triumphantly thrash the mother country.'[95]

A STERNER TEST

Across the Empire, cricket was regarded as the supreme test of character. It was, stated one Australian newspaper, 'A well known fact . . . that one of the most powerful influences . . . in moulding the character of the . . . spirited English boy into that of the steady, fearless, hearty Englishman – able to command and willing to obey – is the emulation, the discipline and the enthusiasm of the cricket field.' In the later nineteenth century, this language of 'manfulness' and sporting endeavour segued into a more obviously martial rhetoric. It was the sport which turned 'the boys of Eton, Rugby and of Harrow into the men of Alma, Inkerman and of Balaklava' – and the manful, sporting ethos was now working its magic in the colonies.[96] After Australia's victory in the Ashes tour, the *Australasian* noted that 'Mr Murdoch and his merry men would acquit themselves as gallantly upon the battle-field as they have upon the cricket-ground, and so would every true Australian.'[97] To the beat of an ever louder drum, the ties of Commonwealth and imperial federation were assuming a military air, with a looming sense of the need to defend the colonies against unspecified, looming threats. The newly established Empire Day of 1905 celebrated the military heroism of Nelson and Wolfe, and commemorated the sacrifice of General Gordon, while the sporting-cum-martial valour of Henry Newbolt's 1892 poem 'Vitaï Lampada' was echoing across the colonies:

> There's a breathless hush in the Close to-night –
> Ten to make and the match to win –
> A bumping pitch and a blinding light,
> An hour to play and the last man in.
> And it's not for the sake of a ribboned coat,
> Or the selfish hope of a season's fame,
> But his captain's hand on his shoulder smote
> 'Play up! play up! and play the game!'

The sand of the desert is sodden red, –
Red with the wreck of a square that broke; –
The Gatling's jammed and the Colonel dead,
And the regiment blind with dust and smoke.
The river of death has brimmed his banks,
And England's far, and Honour a name,
But the voice of a schoolboy rallies the ranks:
'Play up! play up! and play the game!'

In turn, a generation of Australian children were taught the jingo-istic words of the Australian politician Kenneth Mackay's poem 'The Song That Men Should Sing' (1899):

So our lads must learn there's a sterner task
Than playing a well-pitched ball;
That the land we love may some day ask
For a team when the trumpets call.

A team that is ready to take the field
To bowling with balls of lead,
In a test match grim, where if one appealed,
The umpire might answer 'dead'.[98]

The 'crimson thread of kinship' would soon demand a blood sacrifice – and all those long innings at the Melbourne Cricket Ground crease provided the perfect schooling. 'They acknowledge a duty to the mother country as they understand it,' J. A. Froude confidently predicted. 'It used to be pretended that if England fell into a war which might threaten the Colonial port towns, they would decline to share its burdens or its dangers. This will never be. The Colonies will not desert us in time of trial.'[99] Indeed, fighting in defence of the mother country was a means of proving, at one and the same time, colonial fealty and an independent sense of nationhood. 'Boys have a habit of developing into men,' John Freeman wrote of the Melbourne corps, 'and, by-and-by, these youngsters will be a body of well-trained soldiers, on whom we may rely in the hour of need.'[100] A martial spirit, an imperial ideology premised on spreading civilization and the progress of humanity and an urge to prove a nation's manhood on the field of battle – these were the sentiments which would be drawn upon to such deadly effect when the hour of need did arrive in 1914.

The First World War came as little surprise to Lenin. For him, it was an 'imperial war' and the natural by-product of the cartel capitalism of the preceding twenty years – 'Monopolies, oligarchy, the striving for domination and not for freedom, the exploitation of an increasing number of small or weak nations by a handful of the richest or most powerful nations'.[101] The struggle for global markets between the competing European powers inevitably led to conflict between them and their dependencies. And having benefited so richly from the cheap capital of finance imperialism, the white settler colonies were now willing to play their part in shoring it up. India was the largest single colonial contributor to the British war effort in 1914, but Canada, Australia, New Zealand and South Africa, with populations some twenty times smaller, collectively matched the Raj's manpower. Such sacrifice for the imperial cause would entail a staggering loss of life.

The Australian Imperial Force alone mobilized some 330,000 soldiers, 13 per cent of the white male population. Melbourne was not slow in contributing its share. When war broke out, the city was soon awash in a tide of jingoism, patriotism and colonial ardour. 'My fellow Britishers,' was how the Premier of Victoria began a call-up meeting at Melbourne Town Hall. If the Germans had expected Australia to use the war as a convenient point of separation from the mother country, commented a popular history of the period, they might have 'as truthfully prophesied that Yorkshire would declare its independence or that Manchester would become a republic'.[102] Instead, the healthy, athletic, virile young men of the Melbourne suburbs signed up for the infantry units of the AIF's 6th Battalion – and, within a year, found themselves on the blood-soaked sands of Anzac Cove and evacuating Gallipoli. Over 60,000 Australian lives would be bowled out on the cricket ground of the 'Great War'. But 'its men had proved themselves worthy of the highest traditions of the British race', according to the Melbourne *Age*.[103]

Today, at the other end of central Melbourne, south of the Yarra, stands the natural counterpoint to the Royal Exhibition Building. If the REB was a 'Marvellous Melbourne' monument to the prosperity and purpose of Empire – the material goods, Saxon kinship and civilizing mission – the city's Shrine of Remembrance is an austere reminder that Greater Britain could yield another kind of dividend. Completed in 1934 and set amid the statues and memorials of the Kings Domain parkland, this monument to the fallen of the First World War (and succeeding conflicts) is a bizarre architectural conflation of Greek and Egyptian designs. In the inner sanctuary of the shrine is the Stone of Remembrance, which is aligned with an aperture in the roof that allows a ray of sunshine to shine a light upon the inscriptions at 11 a.m. on 11 November every Remembrance Day. The accompanying inscription is clear about the cause of the losses *and* about the imperial pride which the city of Melbourne took in that supreme sacrifice:

THIS MONUMENT WAS ERECTED BY A GRATEFUL PEOPLE TO THE HONOURED MEMORY OF THE MEN AND WOMEN WHO SERVED THE EMPIRE IN THE GREAT WAR OF 1914–1918.

9

New Delhi

'The Rome of Hindustan'

'The Rome of Hindustan lies on a scorched and windswept plain, historied with tumbledown memorials of the Mohammedan conquerors. Across this plain glitters now an English Delhi, a vision of domes and towers, pink and cream against the morning blue and new green trees below.' Even the great travel writer Robert Byron thought words could barely do justice to this virgin city: the monumentality of New Delhi had to be seen to be believed – 'dome, tower, dome, tower, dome, red, pink, cream, and white, washed gold and flashing in the morning sun. The traveller loses a breath, and with it his apprehensions and preconceptions. Here is something not merely worthy, but whose like has never been.'[1]

The new city's inauguration, which began with a thirty-one-gun salute booming out from the gardens of the Viceroy's House, appropriately reflected its imperial grandeur. 'The cold weather sunlight shone down on a brilliant spectacle staged between the north and south blocks of the twin Secretariats,' reported *The Times* of 11 February 1931. 'The guards of honour mounted by the 2nd Battalion, The York and Lancaster Regiment on the one hand and the 1st Royal Battalion, The 9th Jat Regiment on the other, took up position. There were marching and counter-marching by the band of The Royal Fusiliers from Agra.'[2] Then there were investitures at the Durbar Hall, banquets at the Viceroy's House, fly-bys from the RAF 'after the manner of the Hendon display', a 'Hog Hunters Ball' at the Imperial Delhi Gymkhana Club, polo tournaments, garden parties, as well as a People's Fête on the sand banks between the Red Fort and the River Jumna – telling the story, in case anyone missed the point, of imperial

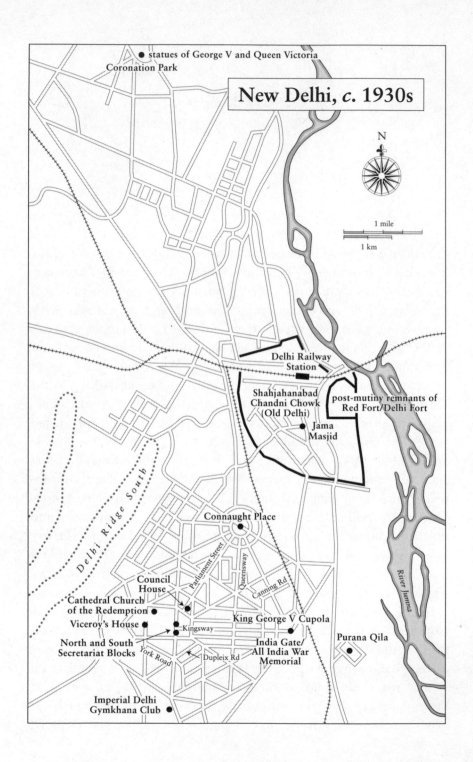

statues of George V and Queen Victoria
Coronation Park

New Delhi, *c.* 1930s

N

1 mile

1 km

Delhi Railway Station

Shahjahanabad Chandni Chowk (Old Delhi)

post-mutiny remnants of Red Fort/Delhi Fort

Jama Masjid

Delhi Ridge South

Connaught Place

Parliament Street

Queensway

Canning Rd

Council House

Cathedral Church of the Redemption

Viceroy's House

Kingsway

King George V Cupola

North and South Secretariat Blocks

York Road

Dupleix Rd

India Gate/ All India War Memorial

Purana Qila

River Jumna

Imperial Delhi Gymkhana Club

rule through military drill and martial music. The festivities came to a climax on 15 February with the consecration of New Delhi's Cathedral Church of the Redemption, as the Bishop of Lahore led the congregation in the hymn 'City of God': 'Let us build the city of God / May our tears be turned into dancing / For the Lord our light and our love has turned the night into day.'

But even with such festivities, *The Times* was forced to admit 'it would be idle to pretend that the ceremony had any popular support'. All the approaches to the capital were 'plastered with armed police' and 'attendance was confined entirely to those admitted by official invitation'.[3] 'So New Delhi is inaugurated in an atmosphere of political uncertainty rather than of political confidence,' thought the *Yorkshire Post*. 'There are in India those who see in it a memorial, indeed, to British enterprise and orderly development, but also a sepulchre of British influence and authority in India. It appears to them the tombstone of the British Raj.'[4]

The real engine of history was elsewhere. Two days after the cathedral's consecration, with the marquees slowly being dismantled, Mahatma Gandhi entered Delhi from Allahabad, in a third-class train compartment. 'Huddled in a blanket, Mr Gandhi ... drove up the stately avenues, which only last week were coloured with all the pageantry of the inauguration of Imperial Delhi.' At 2.30 p.m., he ascended the steps of the Viceroy's House to be greeted by Lord Irwin – 'and it was not until nearly four hours later that he drove away again'. This time there was no doubting the level of popular support. A crowd of 80,000 – 'a blaze of colour, as hundreds had discarded the white *khaddar* (home-spun) for the many-coloured garments worn at the traditional celebration of the Eid festival' – surged into the Queen's Gardens to hear the apostle of independence ready the Indian people for further sacrifice on the road to freedom.[5]

In London, there was no such enthusiasm for Gandhi's arrival into New Delhi. From an imperial city designed to show the permanence of British rule, its architecture dripping in the invincibility of mission, it seemed government officials were preparing to surrender the Jewel in the Crown. Having at vast expense restored Delhi as the capital of India, the British now looked ready to quit. At a gathering of the West Essex Conservative Association in February 1931, Winston Churchill could do little to repress his repugnance at both the weakness of Viceroy Irwin (his future bête noire, the pro-appeasement Earl of Halifax) and the impudence of Gandhi:

> It is alarming and also nauseating to see Mr Gandhi, a seditious Middle Temple lawyer, now posing as a fakir of a type well known in the East, striding half-naked up the steps of the Viceregal palace, while he is still organising and conducting a campaign of civil disobedience, to parlay on equal terms with the representative of the King-Emperor.[6]

Churchill knew that the loss of India meant the end of Empire. When the French prime minister, Georges Clemenceau, walked the New Delhi construction site in 1920, he had thought the same. 'This will be the finest ruin of them all,' he gleefully remarked.

Except, of course, it isn't. After Indian independence in 1947, the architecture and edifices designed by Edwin Lutyens and Herbert Baker were seamlessly adopted by the liberated Indian nation.* The Viceroy's House became the Rashtrapati Bhavan, the president's official residence; the Council House became the Parliament House, with its lower Lok Sabha and upper Rajya Sabha; the Kingsway became the Rajpath; and Connaught Place would, in theory at least, turn into Rajiv Chowk. The statues of King George V and Queen Victoria were removed, and the road names of York and Canning were changed, but at the midnight hour New Delhi's bureaucratic fabric continued as a place of power – just with a different set of rulers. Today the generals, ministers, planners and plutocrats of the confident, prosperous New India speed along Akbar Road into government departments or head down Lodi Road to berate international development agencies. New Delhi's clean, wide boulevards, five-star hotels, high-security apparatus, lush planting and cordoned-off villas provide an air of exclusivity

---

* It is interesting to contrast Jawaharlal Nehru's inheritance of New Delhi with his comments on Punjab's new capital city of Chandigarh. 'I am very happy that the people of Punjab did not make the mistake of putting some old city as their new capital. It would have been a great mistake and foolishness. It is not merely a question of buildings. If you had chosen an old city as the capital, Punjab would have become a mentally stagnant, backward state. It may have made some progress, with great effort, but it could not have taken a grand step forward.' See Pavan K. Varma, *Becoming Indian* (New Delhi, 2010), p. 115.

and authority for the governing classes which sits well with the advancing geopolitical ambitions of modern India. As such, New Delhi can feel all too reminiscent of old Empire. In the judgement of two contemporary Indian commentators,

> Today, Lutyens's Delhi houses the seat of government segregated from the chaos and vitality of this country. It has its own municipality, has been designated a 'VIP' zone, and remains insulated from the truth and idea of India. The retreating colonial power handed the baton to free India's ruling class that continues to live in quarantine, in a free-from-squalor, unreal disconnected compound 'city'.[7]

For the Delhi-based British writer Sam Miller, the Lutyens Bungalow Zone, where the political elite reside in exclusive, low-rent accommodation, 'is one of the most tangible vestiges of a dying British Empire in India, a place which was deliberately designed to exclude the ruled'.[8]

This contemporary hostility towards the elitism of New Delhi might go some way to explain the remarkable absence of celebration on the centenary of its foundation in 2011. '"Official" India, which otherwise loves to organise tacky commemorations by producing unappealing postage stamps, gave this event a wide birth,' commented journalist Swapan Dasgupta. Historian Malvika Singh similarly noted the commemorative vacuum. 'Any other nation would have had the prime minister marking the occasion by addressing the people in a live broadcast,' she wrote in the *Telegraph*. Instead, 'the Centre' thought the anniversary had no need 'to be commemorated or celebrated because those who rule us see it as a colonial legacy'. For Singh, this smacked of 'a deep-seated insecurity, a disease that has overwhelmed an "immature" leadership that does not have the emotional or the intellectual wherewithal to embrace 200 or more years of the nation's history, its more recent past, and, like it or not, the legacy of India'.[9] Dasgupta agreed that this refusal to engage with the imperial past meant 'India had yet to develop the necessary self-confidence to view history as history'.[10]

Such political trepidation was just the most recent manifestation of a deep-seated ambivalence about the meaning and purpose of New Delhi that has long been a part of the city's history. Often regarded as the pinnacle of imperial self-confidence, the foundation of the capital of British India was wrought with ambiguity about the nature of Empire from the start.

NINEVEH AND TYRE

The spectre of decline consumed the late Victorian imagination. Naturally, they turned for guidance on the topic to the sublime prose of Edward Gibbon's *History of the Decline and Fall of the Roman Empire* (1776–89). 'The decline of Rome was the natural and inevitable effect of immoderate greatness,' Gibbon told them. 'Prosperity ripened the principle of decay; the causes of destruction multiplied with the extent of conquest; and as soon as time or accident had removed the artificial supports, the stupendous fabric yielded to the pressure of its own weight.'[11] As a twenty-year-old cavalry subaltern stationed in Bangalore in 1895, the young Winston Churchill spent his leisure hours digesting these lessons of the imperial past: 'All through the long glistening middle hours of the Indian day, from when we quitted stables till the evening shadows proclaimed the hour of Polo, I devoured Gibbon. I rode triumphantly through it from end to end and enjoyed it all.'[12] On his return to England in 1897, the year of Queen Victoria's Diamond Jubilee, he discovered he was not alone in his enthusiasm for Gibbon's enlightened scepticism. 'There were not wanting those who said that in this Jubilee year our Empire had reached the height of its glory and power, and that now we should begin to decline, as Babylon, Carthage and Rome had declined.'[13] One of those siren voices was none other than the child of Bombay, Rudyard Kipling, whose Jubilee ode 'Recessional' gave voice to the looming end of Empire:

> Far-called, our navies melt away;
> On dune and headland sinks the fire:
> Lo, all our pomp of yesterday
> Is one with Nineveh and Tyre!
> Judge of the Nations, spare us yet,
> Lest we forget – lest we forget!

Paradoxically such fears escalated during the greatest assertion of British power since the eighteenth century: between 1860 and 1909, the territorial extent of the British Empire grew from 24.6 million square kilometres to 32.9 million, putting some 444 million people under some form of British rule. For Joseph Chamberlain and his Imperial Federation ideologues, an expanding Empire and a Greater Britain posed a public policy problem of economic tariffs and systems of international governance. To disciples of Gibbon, however, such enormous expansion hastened a more existential crisis. 'The power of Imperial Rome was broken in conquering the world; it dwindled away, century after century,' the Anglo-Australian politician Robert Lowe warned the House of Commons in 1878.[14] It was overstretch which had undermined the Roman Empire, and now Britain was repeating the mistake.[15] The signal moment for such fears was the calamity of the Second Boer War (1899–1902), when the Dutch exiles of the Cape Colony (whom we last saw starting out upon the Great Trek in the 1830s) sought to resist the conversion of the Transvaal and Orange Free State – with their untapped gold-mines – into British colonies. For three years, the Boers' sharp-shooting and guerrilla tactics managed to outfox the might of the British army. In the 'Black Week' in December 1899, nearly 3,000 British troops were killed, wounded or captured at the Battles of Stormberg, Magersfontein and Colenso. 'The condition of South Africa today is the most bitter commentary on our supposed imperial strength,' declared Lord Milner, high commissioner for South Africa. 'Here is a single Colony, not by any means one of the largest in the Empire, in which a bare majority of disaffected people is able to disorganise our whole South African policy ... and threaten the foundations of the Empire itself.'[16]

In Britain, the military and imperial weaknesses exposed by the Boer War produced a paroxysm of soul-searching. The rot was located in the 'heart of Empire' itself – the big cities of Britain which had succumbed to indolence, luxury, homosexuality and racial degeneration. They were responsible for pretty much every ill which it was hoped the clean-living suburbs of Melbourne and the pure-bred colonial race of the White Dominions would cure. The social reformer Lord Brabazon thought that if a gentleman took a walk through the streets of London, 'Should he be of average height, he will find himself a head taller than those around him; he will see on all sides pale faces, stunted figures, debilitated forms, narrow chests, and all the outward signs of a low vital power.' He feared that 'large numbers of the inhabitants of our cities are physically unfitted, though in the prime of life, to defend the country in time of war'. And when the call up came for the Boer War, tens of thousands of recruits were indeed turned down for military service, leading to the establishment of an Interdepartmental Committee on Physical Deterioration in 1904. 'With a perpetual lowering of the vitality of the Imperial Race in the great cities of the kingdom,' warned the lead critic of urban England Charles Masterman, 'no amount of hectic, feverish activity on the confines of the Empire will be able to arrest the inevitable decline.'[17]

When these fears were combined with the rise of American and German military power, the moral costs of colonialism exposed by the use of concentration camps during the Boer War and the fiscal damage produced by an economy over-dependent upon imperial finance, the longevity of the British Empire looked precarious. So much so that in 1905 a young Tory pamphleteer, Elliott Mills, penned *The Decline and Fall of the British Empire* – a spoof work of futuristic history, published in 'Tokio, 2005' and appointed for use in the 'National Schools of Japan', which recounted the loss of British India to Russia, the South African colonies to Germany and all of Australia to Japan. Its thesis was clear: 'Had the English people, at the opening of the Twentieth Century, turned to Gibbon's *Decline and Fall of the Roman Empire*, they might have found in it a not inaccurate description of themselves. This they failed to do, and we know the results.'[18] Clearly, such doubts had to be dispelled. 'Do not believe these croakers,' countered Churchill, 'but give the lie to their dismal croaking by showing by your actions that the vigour and vitality of our race is unimpaired and that our determination is to uphold the Empire ... and carry out our mission of bearing peace, civilisation and good government to the uttermost ends of the earth.'[19] India – 'the most truly bright and precious jewel in the crown of the King' – was the obvious place to begin.

DURBAR IMPERIALISM

'The day on which the Durbar was held was a perfect winter's day with a bright sun, blue sky and cool breeze,' proudly remembered the Indian viceroy, Lord Hardinge, of his 1911 Delhi durbar for King George V and Queen Mary. 'The spectacle was really as magnificent as it was possible to imagine.'[20] Beginning in the spring, some 20,000 Indians had been at work transforming the barren fields around Delhi Ridge – where the British had made their last stand during the 1857 Indian Mutiny – into Coronation Park, a neverland of royal-imperial pomp and circumstance. Today the park has returned to scrubland, encircled by a roaring ring-road, bland commercial developments and exposed drains. Some vestiges of colonial pre-history are kept on life-support (as in Mumbai's Byculla Gardens) in a gated pen of deposed imperial statues, peopled by the likes of Viceroy Irwin and even King George himself, having been removed from the Rajpath. It would take a heroic leap of imagination now to conceive of this grubby wasteland, consumed by the urgent urbanism of the New India, as playing host to the British Empire's most spectacular display of faux-regal chivalry.

> The Royal pavilion rose from a broad base in three tiers, ascended by broad stairways, to a central structure supported by four slender columns and surmounted by a huge gilt bulbous dome. This dome rose out of a kind of balustrade of gilt fretted work with four small domes at the four corners, beneath which extended a kind of gilt verandah, and beyond this a canopy of crimson velvet with a broad straight fringe of crimson and gold.

Here the Imperial Thrones, 'resplendent in crimson and gold', sat 20 feet above the ground, awaiting Their Imperial Highnesses.

> Both were arrayed in Royal attire; the King in the raiment of white satin which he wore at the Coronation in Westminster Abbey ... The Queen was dressed in white embroidered with gold, with a robe of purple, a circlet of emeralds and diamonds on her head, and the Orders of the Garter and of the Crown of India.

A salute of 101 guns at midday was the signal for 100,000 spectators to stand and cheer the arrival of the royal couple's open landau, escorted by the 10th Hussars, V Battery of Horse Artillery and the Eighteenth Indian Lancers – 'all this long parti-coloured procession, winding its devious way half seen above the immovable forest of turbans, helmets, bayonets and lance-pennons, presented a spectacle of amazing majesty and grandeur'. Arriving at a royal canopy beyond the central pavilion, the new king-emperor gave a short speech – 'To all present, feudatories and subjects, I tender my loving greetings' – and then the serious business of paying homage started. The viceroy genuflected first, 'bowing low thrice as he approached the throne, and finally kneeling to kiss His Majesty's hand, a distinction confined to him alone. To Lord Hardinge succeeded the members of his Executive Council; and then followed the Ruling Chiefs of Hyderabad, Baroda, Mysore, Kashmir, Rajputana, Central India, Baluchistan, Sikkim and Bhutan.' When the kow-towing of the Indian princes had finally subsided, the king and queen walked to the main pavilion, and then came the drum and trumpets summoning the herald. 'Through the gap in the vast Mound rode the tall soldierly Delhi Herald, General Peyton, in a tabard bearing the Royal Standard front and back, together with the Assistant-Herald, Malik Umar Hayat Khan, a Punjab magnate of martial bearing.' After reading out the king-emperor's proclamation, the chief herald doffed his helmet, called for three cheers for the king and queen and brought the official ceremony to an end. After Their Royal Highnesses had exited the pavilion, 'the people rushed down . . . and prostrating themselves, pressed their foreheads against the marble steps. Soon, as the crush became too great, they were fain to touch the pavilion with their hands and press their fingers to their foreheads, content with this, so only they could pay homage to the one supreme ruler of all India.'[21]

Luckily, *The Times* was on hand to decipher the meaning of this gaudy, medieval ritual – acted out amid the modern age of steamships, telephones, global capital flows and immunization. 'The ceremony at its culminating point exactly typified the Oriental conception of the ultimate repositories of Imperial power,' the newspaper explained. 'The Monarchs sat alone, remote but beneficent, raised far above the multitude, but visible to all, clad in rich vestments, flanked by radiant emblems of authority, guarded by a glittering array of troops, the cynosure of the proudest Princes of India.' It reassured its British readership: 'The Durbar has been far more than a mere success. It has been a triumphant vindication of the wise prescience which conceived and planned it.'[22]

In fact, it represented the culmination of an imperial strategy which had been pursued since the catastrophe of the 1857 Mutiny. The longer-term response of the British government to rebuilding imperial authority in India, after they had exiled the Mughal emperor and putative Mutiny ringleader Bahadur Shah II (Zafar), was not simply to disband the East India Company and transfer authority to the Crown, with a secretary of state for India in the Cabinet and a viceroy on the ground. It was also to reimagine the very nature of that authority. The Utilitarianism of Thomas Malthus's Haileybury, of Lord Macaulay and William Bentinck would no longer do; nor would the bureaucratic municipalism of Bartle Frere in Bombay. Instead, the ambition was to reach back to the kind of imperial grandeur which Richard Wellesley – for whom India should 'be ruled from a palace, not from a counting-house' – had first attempted in 1800s Calcutta and so manipulate Indian hierarchies of caste and princeship into the service of the British Empire. Rather than battling against the grain of Indian society, attempting to Westernize the colony with the high-flown theorems of Bentham and Mill ('making Anglo-Saxons of the Hindoos', as Sir Thomas Munro put it), the idea now was to marshal the native princes of India into governing under the imprimatur of the British Empire. Benjamin Disraeli's Royal Titles Act of 1876 signalled the new approach in anointing Queen Victoria as empress of India. 'This audacious appropriation consolidated and completed the British-Indian hierarchy,' as historian David Cannadine puts it, 'as the queen herself replaced the defunct Mughal emperor at the summit of the social order: she was now an eastern potentate as well as a western sovereign.'[23]

Only such a strategy of 'Ornamentalism', as Cannadine has coined it, can explain the appointment of the poet, novelist, socialite and diplomat-dilettante Edward Bulwer-Lytton as viceroy of India in 1876. His remit was to deploy all of his Romantic, imaginative flair in making flesh this new imperial philosophy. With his gifted feel for melodrama, Lord Lytton chose as his vehicle one of the most ancient rituals of the Mughal empire – the durbar display of princely fealty. The first great durbar took place in Delhi on 1 January 1877 to celebrate the proclamation of Victoria as queen-empress, with over 400 Indian princes paying homage to Lytton as the Crown's representative (even as hundreds of thousands of other Indians died of famine in Madras and the viceroy instructed Sir Richard Temple not to alleviate the starving of Bombay). In the capital of what was once the Mughal Empire, it was a visual affirmation of the new imperial settlement: a symbolic display of choreographed power to show the British Crown working in alliance with a subordinate hierarchy of indigenous princes, ruling India as if by consent.

When his time came, the maniacally competitive Lord Curzon would seek to outdo Lord Lytton's 1877 pageant. Appointed viceroy in 1899 in Government House, the Calcutta residence which Lord Wellesley had modelled on Curzon's ancestral seat of Kedleston Hall, George Nathaniel Curzon was passionate about the archaeology and ancient history of India.[24] He passed an Ancient Monuments Bill, oversaw repairs to artefacts across India and was closely involved in the restoration of the Taj Mahal at Agra. The notion of a durbar was instinctively compelling to a viceroy who saw the British Empire as the natural successor to his beloved, vanished Mughal dynasties. It too had a quasi-divine calling. He told his officials:

> To remember that the Almighty has placed your hand on the greatest of his ploughs . . . to drive the blade a little forward in your time, and to feel that somewhere among these millions you have left a little justice or happiness or prosperity, a sense of manliness or moral dignity, a spring of patriotism, a dawn of intellectual enlightenment, or a stirring of duty, where it did not exist before.[25]

Curzon was adamant that India was the lynchpin of British imperial hegemony around the world – as had been demonstrated when the British expeditionary force sailed from India to capture Hong Kong in 1842.

> If you want to save your Colony of Natal from being over-run by a formidable enemy, you ask India for help, and she gives it; if you want to rescue the white men's legations from massacre at Peking, and the need is urgent, you request the Government of India to despatch an expedition . . . It is with Indian coolie labour that you exploit the

plantations equally of Demerara and Natal; with Indian trained officers that you irrigate and dam the Nile; with Indian forest officers that you tap the resources of Central Africa and Siam.[26]

As long as Britain ruled India, it remained the greatest empire in the world: 'if we lose it, we shall drop straight away to a third-rate power'. Like Churchill, he refused to believe the dismal croakings. 'Let no man admit the craven fear that those who have won India cannot hold it,' Curzon insisted in 1904. 'This is not my forecast of the future. To me the message is carved in granite, it is hewn out of the rock of doom – that our work is righteous and that it shall endure.'[27] In Calcutta, his response to the spectre of decline was the marble grandeur of the Victoria Memorial; in Delhi, it was the durbar of January 1903 to celebrate the accession of King Edward VII to the throne. Curzon's durbar, in the self-same Coronation Park, was even bigger, grander and more expensive than that of 1877 – affirming to Indian princes and Westminster politicians alike both the unquestioning commitment of British rule in India and the naturalness of their Empire as heirs to the Mughal tradition.

Curzon's other attempt to sustain British hegemony in India, the partition of Bengal, was noticeably less successful. The Bengal province, which also included Assam, Bihar and Orissa and a combined population of 80 million Indians, was too large to govern effectively, and partition had been debated for decades. The viceroy's solution was to split it into a new, Muslim-dominated province of East Bengal and Assam and, in the west, a combination of Bengal, Bihar and Orissa with a non-Bengali majority population. Yet the politics of partition were just as urgent as the administrative demands, since the vocal nationalism of the Indian National Congress in Calcutta had started to unnerve Government House. 'Bengal united is a power; Bengal divided will pull in different ways,' noted Curzon's home secretary. 'One of our main objects is to split up and thereby weaken a solid body of opponents to our rule.'[28] But rather than undermining nationalism, splitting Bengal unleashed years of struggle against British rule. Furious at the prospect of partition, the Swadeshi or home-industry movement was born as Bengalis, in an echo of their colonial forebears in 1760s Boston, started to boycott British-made goods, before moving on to demonstrations and civil disobedience. The British reacted with a twentieth-century version of the Coercive Acts (which had sought to eliminate civil disobedience in Boston after the Tea-Party),* complete with arbitrary arrests and detention, all of which served only to heighten Bengali anger and to leave Calcutta increasingly exposed as the capital of British India.

With Canada, the Commonwealth of Australia, New Zealand, Newfoundland and the Union of South Africa all enjoying the much greater political autonomy which came with 'Dominion' status within the British Empire, there were growing calls in the 1900s for India to enjoy similar rights to self-government and equality to the United Kingdom. Part of the official British response to such pressure was to accelerate political reforms to deepen Indian participation in the institutions of government. In 1909 John Morley, the secretary of state for India, worked with Lord Minto, Curzon's successor as viceroy, to pass the Indian Councils Act allowing for non-official Indian majorities in the provincial legislatures. It was a conscious attempt to divide the Indian population and conciliate the urban intelligentsia, but it stopped well short of full representative government. What was more, there was no question of the Indian Civil Service – the day-to-day rulers of the Raj – being opened up to suitably qualified Indians. The Indian had a long way to go, British officialdom concluded, before the responsibility of sovereignty could be handed down. In the meantime, there would be further attempts to introduce limited forms of self-government, as part of a route towards Dominion status – all of which would continue to be managed for the foreseeable future under the righteous banner of Empire.

The king-emperor himself suggested a different response to the rise of Indian nationalism. 'Ever since I visited India five years ago [as Prince of Wales] I have been impressed by the great advantage which would result from a visit by the sovereign to that great Empire,' King George V wrote to Lord Morley in 1910. 'I am convinced that if it were possible for me, accompanied by the Queen, to . . . hold a Coronation Durbar at Delhi, where should meet all the Princes, officials and vast numbers of the People, the greatest benefits would accrue to

* See above, p. 62.

the Country at large.' To allay the revolutionary impulse in India, the answer was less democracy and more pageantry. What was more, the king had a clever idea to mark the first visit of a ruling British sovereign to India and becalm the partition fury. 'Why not make the two Bengals into a Presidency like Bombay and Madras? This would flatter the Bengalis very much, allay discontent and stop sedition, and would be well worth the extra cost to the country. Think it over!'[29] When a clever mandarin, Sir John Jenkins, suggested that the king's scheme could be combined with the removal of the capital from Calcutta – which allowed the reunification of Bengal to be presented as part of a strategic plan, rather than a hurried surrender to nationalist agitation – the unexpected finale of the 1911 durbar was assured. 'The trumpeters sounded another fanfare, and then to the general surprise, for the official programme gave no hint of such a thing, His Majesty rose, holding a paper in his hand. With clear voice and just emphasis he announced that the capital of India would be transferred from Calcutta to Delhi.' This declaration of a New Delhi flew, we are told, from the centre of Coronation Park, 'to both flanks with a buzz as of passing bees'.[30]

THE EMPRESS OF CITIES

King George V also decreed that the future capital of British India would be an entirely new city to be set against the historic backdrop of Old Delhi. 'It is my desire that the planning and designing of the public buildings to be erected will be considered with the greatest deliberation and care, so that the new creation may be in every way worthy of this ancient and beautiful city.'[31] But why Delhi? Why, at a cost of some £4 million, move the capital of British India from the City of Palaces to start all over again on a site notorious for its searing heat, terrible sanitation and malarial air? There were, in the first place, the obvious security advantages for decamping from an increasingly dangerous Bengal. Then there was Delhi's strategic location, close to the North-West Frontier, from which the British were increasingly determined the Russians had to be kept away. Additionally, it stood equidistant between the great ports of Karachi, Bombay and Calcutta; it was close to

Simla, the summer capital of the Raj, which would reduce the cost of the annual transhumance; and it was well served – for both provisions and military power – by six major railway lines. But far more alluring than all of that, there was the meaning of Delhi.[32]

If Bombay was a city of the future, Delhi was about the past – in particular, the imperial past. 'Delhi is the Empress of Indian cities,' wrote G. W. Forrest, ex-director of records for the government of India, in 1903.

> She has often been sacked and left naked and desolate. But she could not be despoiled of the incomparable situation which marks her for the metropolis of a great Empire . . . Scattered over this wild stretch of land are surviving ruins, remnants of mighty edifices, tombs of warriors and saints, which convey a more impressive sense of magnificence than Imperial Rome. They are memorials not of a single city but of supplanted nations.[33]

Unlike the other Garden City capitals of the British Empire – most notably Australia's Canberra and South Africa's Pretoria – Delhi was the very opposite of a *tabula rasa*. Indeed, her lineage as the ancient city of Indraprastha stretched back millennia to the age of the Pandavas, as chronicled in the Sanskrit epic *Mahabharata* and as testified by the still-standing Purana Qila fort. Even more powerfully, Delhi had ruled India as the centre first of Hindustan and then the Mughal Empire right up until 1857. Shahjahanabad, the walled city now known as Old Delhi, was built by the fifth Mughal emperor, Shah Jahan, and opened as his capital in 1648 – this was the glisteningly seductive, imperial cityscape of the Red Fort, the Jama Masjid mosque and Humayun's Tomb.* As King George put it to the Delhi Municipal Council in December 1911, 'The traditions of your City invest it with a peculiar charm. The relics of the dynasties of by-gone ages that meet the eye on every side, the splendid palaces and temples which have resisted the destroying hand of time, all these witness to a great and illustrious past.'[34]

In short, Delhi had a magnetic effect for empires; it was 'still a name to conjure with', thought Lord Hardinge. So, 'to the Mahomedans it

---

* In fact, Shahjahanabad was regarded as the seventh city of Delhi. The others, beginning in the tenth century, were Quila Rai Pithora, Mehrauli, Siri, Tughlakabad, Firozabad and Shergarh. New Delhi was promoted by the British as Delhi's eighth and final city.

would be a source of unbounded gratification to see the ancient capital of the Mughals restored to its proud position as the seat of the Empire', he explained in a memo to the secretary of state for India. 'The change would strike the imagination of the people of India as nothing else could, would send a wave of enthusiasm throughout the country and would be accepted by all as an assertion of an unfaltering determination to maintain British rule in India.' Secretary of State Lord Crewe concurred. He thought that the ancient walls of Delhi had a tradition comparable 'with that of Rome itself' and that the Indian mind, so addled by legend and myth, would read the transfer of power to Delhi as a 'promise [of] the permanence of British sovereign rule over the length and breadth of the country. Historical reasons will thus prove to be political reasons of deep importance and of real value in favour of the proposed change'.[35]

Delhi was also a place of more recent history: it was at Delhi Ridge in 1857 that the Mutiny was reversed and the Empire in India saved. The siege of Delhi was, in William Dalrymple's phrase, the Raj's Stalingrad, with the seat of the Mughal emperor serving as both the principal centre of the uprising and then the setting for some of the worst excesses of British military vengeance in the aftermath of victory.[36] Old Delhi was sacked and looted, whilst the exquisite Mughal architecture of the Red Fort was flattened to make way for a line of barracks (which still mar the courtyards and gardens some 150 years later). This was a city which witnessed one of the most dramatic and ugly reassertions of Empire within British India, the triumphalism of which was only augmented by the durbar pageants of 1877, 1903 and 1911. The psychology was obvious: the British ruled as the natural inheritors of the Mughal tradition, by might in 1857 and by right in 1911.

Within the imperial establishment, there was only one discordant voice. Of course, Lord Curzon was angry with the reversal of his policy of dividing Bengal and greatly resented the flight from Calcutta:

> I have a very warm feeling for Calcutta myself. It has always seemed to me to be a worthy capital and expression of British rule in India. It is English built, English commerce has made it the second city in the Empire . . . and from the offices of the Government in Calcutta English statesmen, administrators, and generals have built up to its present commanding height the fabric of British rule in India.

Yet as the viceroy who had urged the righteousness of Empire be carved in granite, one might have thought that he would have supported the grandeur of a new city erected on one of India's ancient capitals. Not a bit of it. He interpreted the lessons of history differently. 'I do not deny the glamour of the name of Delhi or the stories that cling about its dead and forgotten cities,' he warily informed the House of Lords. 'But if we want to draw happy omens for the future the less we say about the history of Delhi the better. Of course, there were capitals there before it, but all have perished, one after another.' Curzon thought the city's 'mass of deserted ruins and graves' was a fateful testimony to 'the mutability of human greatness'.[37]

Though Delhi's history was a powerful imperial aphrodisiac, the designers of *New* Delhi were not interested in updating the past. 'We are building a new city,' explained the *British Architect* journal.

A great imperial city from whence to hold and secure the roots of Empire. We are not going to trifle with the old Delhi of the Chandni Chowk and its jewellers, the weird, wonderfully streeted maze of crenellated caravanserai and picturesque squalor, dominated by piled fort and dull-red *musjeed* . . . We are Britons, the tombs and temples of alien faiths, though of unspeakable charm and lofty, dreamful beauty, do not concern us as builders.[38]

Instead, the vision was to build an entirely new city, which implicitly aligned itself with Delhi's imperial Mughal heritage but also constituted a modern, Western, civilized contrast to the decay and disarray of Shahjahanabad. As such, it marked the final fulfilment of a system of city planning in India which had developed since 1857. As we have seen in Calcutta and Bombay, there had long existed civic divisions between the White Towns and Black Towns, between the European and indigenous Indian quarters. But in the aftermath of the Mutiny, when, as Rudyard Kipling had urged in 'Beyond the Pale', one must let 'the White go to the White and the Black to the Black', the spatial apartheid of the colonial city became all the more obvious. Whether it was dressed up under sanitary legislation or security, an ideology of distance produced urban plans predicated upon Military Cantonment, 'Civil Lines' (where the European civilians lived) and bungalow compounds. The Europeans retreated from the native city

32. 'The heaps of rustling leaves, as they chase each other on the gravelled walks, give an English air to the scene.' Melbourne viewed from the Botanic Garden, by Henry Gritten (1867).

33. 'And that true spirit of the British race / Which makes the wilderness a dwelling place.' Cantata from the 1880–81 Melbourne International Exhibition.

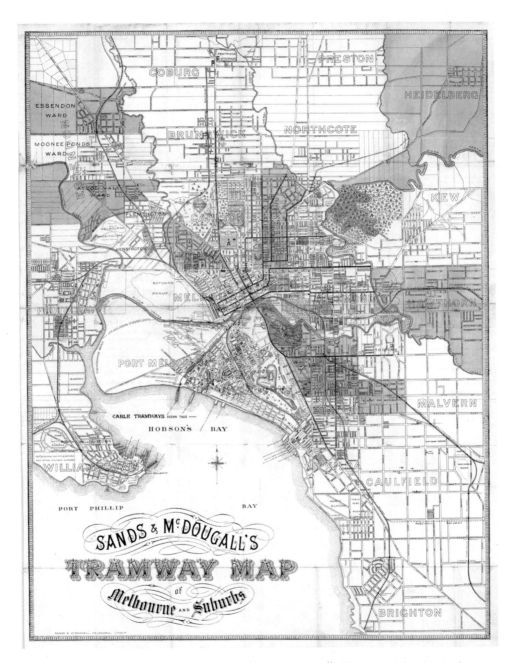

34. Melbourne's suburban civilization. Sands & McDougalls Tramway Map (1880s).

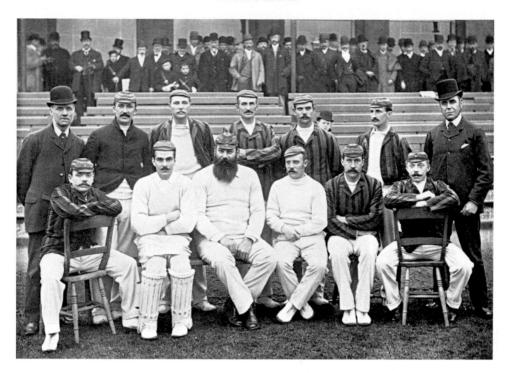

35. W. G. Grace and other members of the England national cricket team take advantage of Australia's 'old love for the manly sports of the mother country' with a 29-match tour (1891–2).

36. The 'crimson thread of kinship' demands the ultimate sacrifice. The Australian Imperial Force parading through Collins Street, Melbourne, before departing for the battlefields of the First World War (1915).

37. Osman Ali Khan, the
Nizam of Hyderabad,
pays homage to
King-Emperor George V
and Queen Mary
at the Delhi Durbar
(1911).

38. The Versailles of British
India. An aerial view looking
East, showing Kingsway
(the Rajpath) with Viceroy
House and Gardens (1947).

39. 'It must not be Indian, nor English, nor Roman, but it must be Imperial.' View of the east end of Herbert Baker's North Block, Secretariat Building, with Council House in background (1931).

40. A seditious Middle-Temple lawyer and Rear-Admiral Lord Mountbatten of Burma take tea at the Viceroy's House on the eve of Indian Independence (1947).

41. 'Today, all seas lead to Liverpool.' Merseyside's Atlantic traffic as charted in
a Dominion Line poster (1899).

42. View outside the Chinese shops in Pitt Street, Liverpool, from H. Scheffauer's article, 'The Chinese in England: A Growing National Problem', in the *London Magazine*, June 1911.

43. 'Abundant signs of illimitable expansiveness and invincible virility.' Liverpool caught at the peak of its powers in a panorama by Walter Richards (1907).

44. Everything going wrong: rioting on the streets of Toxteth, 6 July 1981.

45. Gateway of Empire. The prospective Liverpool Waters as imagined by the Peel Group, with the original Three Graces in the foreground.

to spacious, green and well-guarded stations as racial segregation dictated the living patterns of ruler and ruled. The cosmopolitanism of Bombay was abandoned for the ritual and hierarchy of the later Raj. In Lucknow and Allahabad, a form of 'death-dealing Haussmannising' (as the town planner Patrick Geddes called it) was enacted as the old cities were demolished, boulevards cut through the native quarters, military cantonments erected in the urban core, and the British officials bunkered down behind the Civil Lines. In post-Mutiny Delhi, the same logic had been at work. Great swathes of the city were cleared, with mosques, shrines, Mughal palaces and 80 per cent of the Red Fort demolished – the remnants were transformed into 'Delhi Fort', a massive military cantonment in the midst of the old city. With Delhi now little more than a military camp, the Europeans headed north-west to the growing suburbs of Civil Station beyond the city walls. The destruction of Old Delhi and the white flight were a useful reminder that behind all of the British Empire's Ornamentalist social hierarchy, of princes and pageants chained together in a multiracial caste system, there sat the urban reality of racial supremacy.[39]

If New Delhi was indeed to be a distinct development separate from Old Delhi, the question was where to put it. A committee of experts, peopled by British architects and engineers and chaired by Captain Swinton of the London County Council, was given the task of finding the spot. Coronation Park, to the north of Delhi, was rejected on health and drainage grounds; construction among the European community within the Civil Lines was deemed too disruptive; and appropriating the Sabzi Mandi district would upset the industrialists. Instead, the committee mounted their elephants and headed south of Shahjahanabad to find a suitable location amid fauna of all description: 'buck of all sorts, baboons, monkeys, jackals, hare, porcupine, water snakes, great fish, great tortoise which eat babies, snake, bats, flying fox, vultures, weird birds and many lovely ones', as one member put it.[40] Near the village of Malcha, the committee thought it had found the perfect spot. But Viceroy Hardinge was not convinced. 'The moment I saw the selected site I realized its objections. It would be hot; it had no views; and it had no room for expansion ... I told the assembled staff that I would rather not build a new capital at all than build it on that site.' So Hardinge commandeered a horse and 'galloped over the plain to a hill [Raisina] some distance away. From the top of the hill there was a magnificent view embracing old Delhi and all the principal monuments situated outside the town, with the River Jumma [sic] winding its way like a silver streak in the foreground at a little distance. I said at once ... "This is the site for Government House." '41 Forcibly relocating the 300 Indian families of Raisina and Malcha was also a lot easier than rehousing the officer class of the Civil Lines.

Just as crucial as finding the site was the appointment of an architect. From Dublin to Melbourne, the British Empire had asserted its colonial vision through the civic fabric of its cities: this was the canvas upon which the ideology of Empire could be painted. In architectural styling, city planning and urban iconography the shifting meanings of the imperial project were explored. Both the virgin soil of New Delhi and its development amid such fraught introspection about the nature of Empire placed the significance of the city's design on an altogether higher plane. 'We are endeavouring to place before the peoples of India our distinctive British ideals, and to adapt to their use the principles of government on which British power has thriven,' suggested *The Times*. 'The new capital has been decreed to carry on and consolidate those aims, and it should bear the impress of them in stones.'42 Lord Stamfordham, private secretary to King George V, thought it a golden opportunity to show the Indians, amid their ancient imperial capital, 'the power of Western science, art and civilization'. But again and again, it was the memory of an earlier empire – in the legends and history of which they had been immersed since their earliest days at public school and then university – which seemed to haunt the British imperial mind. 'It is not a cantonment we have to lay out at Delhi,' argued the India Office's Sir George Birdwood, 'but an Imperial City – the symbol of the British Raj in India – and it must like Rome be built for eternity.'43

Luckily, New Delhi's lead architect was a man brimming with colonial self-confidence. Sir Edwin Landseer Lutyens was born in London in 1869 and learned his craft at the National Art Training School in South Kensington before taking articles in the practice of Ernest George and Peto. But his real inspiration was drawn from the Arts and Crafts style of Richard Norman Shaw and Philip Webb. In the

1890s, he joined forces with the *grande dame* of British landscape gardening, Gertrude Jekyll, to design a series of Surrey and Home Counties houses which made his name as a domestic architect in the English vernacular tradition. His reputation was further enhanced by his work on Henrietta Barnett's model village of Hampstead Garden Suburb – which stood in relation to Hampstead village as New Delhi would to Old Delhi. Lutyens's contribution, most notably his churches and the Central Square, fitted well with the low-density, tree-lined retreat laid out by Raymond Unwin as part of a conscious rejection of the filthy, stinking, overcrowded rookeries of London. In 1912 Lutyens was asked to join the expert committee on finding the New Delhi site, and in January 1913 he was appointed architect. It had not harmed his chances of preferment that his wife was Lady Emily Bulwer-Lytton, daughter of the late viceroy.[44]

Lutyens saw his purpose as nothing less than rescuing architecture in India – first of all from the Indians. 'Personally, I do not believe there is any real Indian architecture or any great tradition,' he wrote to Lady Emily during his initial tour of India in 1912. 'They are just spurts by various mushroom dynasties with as much intellect in them as any other *art nouveau.*' The Mughal court in Delhi was 'all tommy rot'. And as for the Hindu tradition, 'Hindon't I say. It is not architecture – the best just clever children, though I own to some of their detail being beautiful.'[45] Secondly, it had to be rescued from the British. Because just as bad were those Bombay Gothic or Indo-Saracenic monstrosities, designed by Scott and Stevens, which had sprung up during the second half of the nineteenth century. For Lutyens and his followers, the Victoria Terminus was not the central building of the British Empire but a grotesque 'half-caste' of architectural forms. 'I do want old England to stand up and plant her great traditions and good taste where she goes and not pander to sentiment and all this silly Moghul-Hindu stuff.'[46] Despite his occasional reactionary outbursts ('India – like Africa – makes one very Tory and pre-Tory Feudal!'), it would be a mistake to regard Lutyens as a chauvinist.[47] Rather, he was an aesthete with an absolute conviction that the architectural principles of classicism should just as well be applied to the plains of Delhi as the estates of Surrey.

To temper Lutyens's absolutism, Lord Hardinge appointed Herbert

Baker to design the city's Secretariat buildings. Baker was the most dependable of British imperial architects, schooled for the task by Cecil Rhodes himself. Baker's initial commission for the Cape prime minister was his official residence, Groote Schuur, after which Rhodes packed him off on a study tour of Europe with a remit to introduce the classical tradition into imperial African architecture. Classical design, Rhodes thought, could give visible expression to imperialism and draw men into its purpose. The fruits of Baker's indoctrination can still be seen, at the base of Table Mountain's Devil Peak, in the Rhodes Memorial, modelled as an open Doric colonnade in the form of a Greek Temple. After Cape Town, Baker moved to Pretoria and, with the patronage of Jan Smuts, was awarded the design for the Union Buildings of the now self-governing Union of South Africa. This time, the Athenian Acropolis served as inspiration for a vast government edifice which, with its columned loggias and self-aggrandizing blocks with twin towers (symbolizing the 'two races of South Africa' – British and Dutch), was an obvious precursor to his New Delhi designs.

Baker, much more than Lutyens, was personally committed to the civilizing mission of the British Empire and instantly realized the

'In spite of our long friendship, there might be troubles ahead.' Sir Herbert Baker and Sir Edwin Lutyens on an elephant (1913).

magnitude of New Delhi. 'It is a question of Imperial as well as of artistic importance,' he wrote to *The Times* in October 1912, in something of a job application, 'as an event in the history of architecture it may be perhaps compared to the building of Constantinople.'[48] Since the purpose of architecture was to express the ideals of Empire, the question of style was a relatively simple one. 'It must not be Indian, nor English, nor Roman, but it must be Imperial. In 2000 years there must be an Imperial Lutyens tradition in Indian architecture, as there now clings a memory of Alexander.'[49] The defining attribute of British imperial rule, thought Baker, was the imposition of 'order, progress and freedom within the law', which then allowed the flourishing of each national civilization 'on the lines of their own tradition and sentiment'.[50] The British imperial genius was its ability to coalesce the chaos of castes, races and religions under the beneficent suzerainty of the Crown. What the design of New Delhi had to do was capture that 'spirit of British sovereignty' in 'stone and bronze'. 'The new capital must be the sculptural monument of the good government and unity which India, for the first time in its history, has enjoyed under British rule. British rule in India is not a mere veneer of government and culture. It is a blend of the best elements of East and West.'[51] On a personal level, as an old friend of Lutyens's, Baker was delighted with the chance to collaborate with him on the capital. Yet mindful of his friend's 'wilful masterfulness', he also 'foresaw that, in spite of our long friendship, there might be troubles ahead when we came to collaborate in the sensitive realms of art'.[52]

If the relationship between Lutyens and Baker did not provide enough potential for creative conflict, there were also the views of Lord Hardinge himself to take into account. To Lutyens's aestheticism and Baker's imperialism, the viceroy pushed for some form of Indo-Saracenic design as a mark of respect to Indian sensibilities. In the light of the partition violence and the conciliatory Morley-Minto reforms of 1909, Hardinge didn't want New Delhi to appear too triumphalist. Its architecture had to make some allowance to indigenous culture as part of a Curzon-like ambition to present British rule in India as an organic outcome of the nation's history. To that end, Hardinge appointed Sir Swinton Jacob, the leading Indianist architect, whose Albert Hall Museum in Jaipur was a classic of

Indo-Saracenic design, as a planning consultant. All of this interference and politicking drove Lutyens to distraction: 'The Viceroy changes his mind every time I see him,' he fumed to Lady Emily. 'I am afraid he will make work very difficult ... all he will think about [is] what the place will look like in three years time. Three hundred is what I think of ... This is the building of an imperial city!'[53]

DOME, TOWER, DOME, TOWER, DOME

Out of this cauldron of political and architectural ambition, a scheme for New Delhi emerged. 'Delhi is to be an Imperial capital and is to absorb the traditions of all the ancient capitals,' concluded the *Final Report of the Delhi Town Planning Committee* (1913). 'It is to be the seat of the Government of India. It has to convey the idea of a peaceful domination and dignified rule over the traditions and life of India by the British Raj.'[54] In planning terms, Lutyens achieved this through a remarkable combination of both hexagonal road patterns, linking governmental, commercial and leisure activities with the residential areas, and grand boulevards. The most impressive was Kingsway (now Rajpath), which connected the Viceroy's House, through the middle of the North and South Block Secretariats, down to the All India War Memorial (now India Gate), with the King George V cupola behind it. The Queensway (Janpath) intersected it at right angles to provide a direct route to the shopping hub of Connaught Place from the bungalow compounds of York Road (Motilal Nehru Marg). In this respect, New Delhi was the culmination of all the Wide Street Commissions since Dublin in the 1760s – here were boulevards of stupendous width, complete with the kind of vistas and dramatic sweeps every colonial administrator longed for. The avenues heightened the sense of New Delhi's modernity and rationality ('the power of Western science, art and civilization,' in Lord Stamfordham's words), by accentuating the contrast with Old Delhi. In streetscape and axial intersections, the ability of Empire to impose order on chaos was reaffirmed. Not only were the roads straight and broad, with their symmetry and size affirming the legitimacy of Britain's imperial claim, but their horizons ended with the crumbling monuments and lost glories of Shahjahanabad. The line of Parliament Street (Sansad Marg) concluded at the Jama Masjid mosque; the central vista of Kingsway would have reached the ancient fort of Purana Qila if it had proceeded as initially planned. Under the historic shadow of the empress of cities, the contrast of old and new was all the sharper.[55]

Embedded within the New Delhi scheme were all sorts of town planning philosophies accumulated over previous centuries. Most obviously, there was the inspiration of Pierre Charles L'Enfant's design for Washington, DC, with its diagonal roads bifurcated by north–south and east–west streets, as well as the grand avenues of the National Mall and Pennsylvania Avenue, connecting Congress to the White House. There was the more contemporaneous City Beautiful or Beaux Arts influence, which would come to remodel the south side of Chicago in the interwar years along similarly monumental lines to New Delhi, with landmarks, vistas and broad, tree-lined avenues. This was certainly the inspiration for those other notable imperial cities erected at the same time – Canberra in Australia and Pretoria in South Africa – but there the dull governmentality and architectural self-importance managed to suffocate any of the more inventive elements of the Beaux Arts school. By contrast, New Delhi succeeded by drawing on Lutyens's other roots in the Garden City tradition. Even on the scale of this imperial city, Lutyens's designs managed to add some of the playfulness and intimacy, the characterfulness and humanity, which Henrietta Barnett had demanded in Hampstead Garden Suburb. And then, of course, there was the extraordinary greenery which still envelops New Delhi in a cool canopy: to counter the furnace-like urbanity of Old Delhi, Lutyens planted 10,000 trees (laburnum, gulmohar, jacaranda and Asok), over 100 kilometres of hedges and bushes of bougainvillea and well-tended plant beds to ease the heat island and provide a very English, *rus in urbe* naturalism of which Gertrude Jekyll would surely have approved. This was the striking originality of New Delhi – a compelling combination of Garden City and Beaux Arts, domestic architecture and urban monumentalism in the most difficult of settings.[56]

Yet New Delhi's real success lay not in the plan, but in the buildings that populated it. The transcendent genius of the city's architecture is

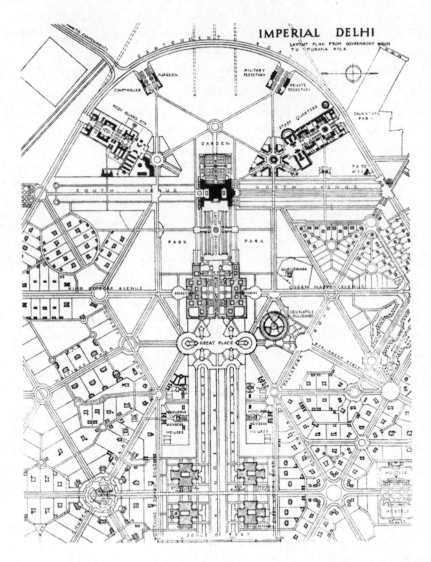

Edwin Lutyens, 'Imperial Delhi: Layout Plan from Government House to Purana Qila' (detail).

found in Lutyens's decision to meet Hardinge on his own terms, offering a new interpretation of the classical tradition upon Indian soil. 'Like all humanists, Sir Edwin Lutyens had drunk of the European past, and he now drank of the Indian,' as Robert Byron put it. 'In so doing, he has accomplished a fusion between East and West ... he has made of them a unity, and invested it with a double magnificence.'[57] Or, as Lutyens himself phrased it:

> East and West can and do meet, with mutual respect and affection ... There are two ways of building in India, one to parade your building in fancy dress ... or to build as an Englishman dressed for the climate, conscious only that your tailor is of Agra or Benares, and not of Savile Row or Petticoat Lane.[58]

Lutyens retained his horror for gauche Indo-Saracenic designs and never accepted that early Hindu architecture could be aped, but his initial condescension faded as he came to realize the impossibility of building in India without drawing upon indigenous designs and motifs. He also started to appreciate the particular demands which the climate placed upon the urban architecture – the need for shade, ventilation, flowing water and use of certain materials. As Byron describes it, 'while holding fast to the first principles of humanist architecture, line, proportion, and mass, he discovered, from the Mogul builders, how those principles might be adapted to a land whose natural conditions necessitate their modification'.[59]

So, into Lutyens's designs crept the red sandstone of Fatehpur Sikri and the cream stone of Agra, the overhanging cornice to block the sun and monsoon rains (*chujja*); the Rajasthani latticed marble window which admitted air but not sunshine (*jali*); and the miniature roof pavilion (*chattri*). The playful Mughal, Hindu and Buddhist traditions of Indian design – as well as a characterful oriental iconography of lions, snakes, elephants, crescents and lotus-blossoms – can be seen in the defining edifices of Lutyens's Delhi: the bungalows, princely palaces, the All India War Memorial, the King George V pedestal and, designed by Baker, the Council House. Today, the Council House is Parliament House – a mix of the Roman and the Mughal, with Coliseum-like corridors that encircle the two Legislative Assemblies (decorated with ornate curved *jalis* along the veranda walls) and provide a perfect setting for gossiping, plotting parliamentarians. There are memories of Britain in the green carpet of the Lok Sabha, akin to that in the House of Commons, and the more lordly red of the Rajya Sabha. Look carefully and you can find copies of the Westminster procedural bible, *Erskine May*, on the clerks' table and 'Fried Fish (with chips)' for lunch in the canteen.

Yet even the Council House pales in comparison with Lutyens's masterpiece, the Viceroy's House. Robert Byron could hardly contain his admiration – 'so arresting, so unprecedented, so uninviting of comparison with known architecture'. What he particularly admired was its instant monumentality – 'it seems not to have been built, but to have been poured compact from a mould, impermeable to age, destined to stand for ever, to watch the rise of an eighth Delhi and a hundredth Delhi'.[60] Lutyens and his extensive team of predominantly Sikh engineers and builders worked on the house for seventeen years (finally handing it over in 1929), and it represented the pinnacle of both his domestic and imperial architectural career. Perhaps it is the sheer scale, the still thunderous enormity of the building, which remains so startling to the eye. Larger than the Palace of Versailles, the façade runs 192 metres, while the residence contained 340 rooms including the circular, neo-classical temple of the Durbar Hall and a state dining room some 30 metres long. Pamela Mountbatten, daughter of the last viceroy, was terrified by the immensity of the house and thought the place made 'no sense whatever but just consists of vast corridors leading nowhere'.[61] However, Lutyens never allowed its enormity to undermine precision, as he applied all the refined luxury of the Palladian country house tradition to the furniture, panelling, woodwork and upholstery. He thought about the people who would live here and put particular effort into the nursery and drawing rooms, hoping to offer a familiar Home Counties aesthetic amidst the alien Delhi heat. The viceroy's vast gardens – some 360 metres by 180 metres – were a further testament to the double magnificence of East and West, combining the Mughal tradition of cascading water-channels, fountains and pools with Gertrude Jekyll's broad-brushed Surrey planting. Lutyens was proud of the fact that the Viceroy's House and garden was most definitely 'a gentleman's house', but also profoundly original 'in that it is built in India, for India, Indian'.[62]

He instinctively understood, however, that this building was more than some expansive domestic commission. Perched on the top of Raisina Hill, complete with bells hewn from stone so they would never be able to ring the death-knell of Empire, it was also meant to stand as the *ne plus ultra* of British colonial certainty. It was a calling Lutyens sought to signify in the vast dome which crowned the Viceroy's House, combining the Roman Pantheon with the Mughal and Buddhist traditions, and unequivocally demonstrating British technical achievement. 'The dome stood at the heart of the Indian Empire as a palpable reminder of British sovereignty,' in the words of historian Robert Grant Irving.[63] The Viceroy's House now surely took the place of Bombay's VT as the central building of the British Empire.

In front of it were Sir Herbert Baker's two Secretariat buildings, North and South Block, home to that 'kingdom of magistrates', the highest echelons of the Indian Civil Service. The gradient at which the blocks straddled Raisina Hill was the subject of a furious spat with Lutyens since the route's dramatic steepness obscured the view of the Viceroy's House from the Kingsway. Lutyens complained to Lady Emily that he had met his 'Bakerloo' – 'he [Baker] has designed his levels so that you will never see Government House at all (!) from the Great Place. You will see [only] the top of the dome! He is so obstinate and quotes the Acropolis at Athens, which is in no way parallel.'[64] In style, however, the Secretariat was a perfect complement, representing Baker's finest attempt at an imperial architecture blending the best elements of East and West. The open veranda, the *chujja* and *jalis*, the water gardens, were all corralled under an architecture of beautiful symmetry and classical precision, giving the Secretariat something of the cloistered calm of an Oxbridge college combined with the Mughal styling of the Taj Mahal. Here were housed the Indian government's departments of state; here was where the White Man's Burden was shouldered. 'Liberty does not descend to a people. A people must raise themselves to liberty. It is a blessing that must be earned before it can be enjoyed,' read an accompanying placard. To emphasize the point, four Dominion Columns representing Australia, New Zealand, South Africa and Canada were erected between the North and South Block, to indicate the long road which India would have to travel before it was granted full self-government. This was a landscape of imperial theatre – a place of processions, pageants and self-regard. When the historian and wartime intelligence operative Hugh Trevor-Roper visited in 1944, he was overcome with the imperial ambition of New Delhi. 'A fantastic growth, it seemed to me . . . a style without ancestry, without posterity, an architectural sport; and I compared it, according to my varying mood, now with the Pyramids of Egypt, now with the great statues of Easter Island, now with the megaliths of Avebury or Stonehenge.' In the end, Trevor-Roper tellingly reached for his copy of *The Decline and Fall of the Roman Empire* to understand the achievement. 'All the same, as my eye sought to comprehend that great pink and white symmetry of palaces and pagodas, fountains and obelisks, ornamental ponds and regal statues, I couldn't help thinking of those Roman magnificos of whom Gibbon wrote, who "were not afraid to show that they had the spirit to conceive, and the wealth to execute, the most grandiose designs".'[65]

For Sir Herbert Baker, New Delhi signalled the end point of the Indian capital's epic history: that long past of Indraprastha and Shahjahanabad, of risen and fallen empires captured in a cityscape of tombs and mosques, all culminated with the construction of British Delhi. Delhi, a city of the past, had met its destiny. Part of the reason he was so adamant about the gradient of Raisina Hill was because of his vision of future British imperialists stepping out on to the veranda of the Secretariat and lifting up their hearts 'over the far ruinous sites of the historic cities of the Hindu and Mahommedan dynasties to the new Capital beneath them that unites for the first time through the centuries all races and religions of India'.[66]

MODERN MUGHALS

What was it to live amid all this monumentalism? We catch a glimpse from the diary of twenty-something Viola Bayley, married to a Delhi police superintendent in the dying days of the Raj. In the winter of 1936, the Bayleys attended a ceremonial ball to welcome the new viceroy, Lord Linlithgow, to his capital. 'For sheer pageantry, it could hardly have been equalled,' Bayley recalled.

The dinner was held in an immense shamiana, a marquee of the most magnificent order, in the gardens of Viceroy's House. I suppose we must have sat down several hundred strong with almost as many khitmagars in red and gold standing behind our chairs ... Jewels flashed in every direction, from diadems in turbans, from ear-rings and necklaces. The difficulty was not to stare too hard. It was the most fantastic and Arabian-night-like scene that one could have witnessed.[67]

The paradox of New Delhi was that, as Viola Bayley depicted it and Robert Byron described it, the city was 'a slap in the face of the modern, average man', but it was also an intensely modernist project. The most up-to-date theorems of town planning, transport management, landscape architecture and City Beautiful styling were transplanted on to one of the most ancient sites of India. 'It all runs according to plan with great vistas and arches, parks and roundabouts and looks lovely at night with some of the buildings lit up,' thought Pamela Mountbatten. The contrast with 'colourful, crowded, smelly' Old Delhi was all the starker.[68] New Delhi was a place of cars, shopping, telephone lines and technology. This was where the modern Empire was to be ruled from with all the appendages of an industrial, Western state on display. It was as true for retail as administrative life, with Connaught Place 'Army and Navy' style shops specifically designed for a shut-off ICS cadre shuttled about in chauffeured cars, in contrast to the fluid bazaars and street life of Old Delhi. To accentuate that contrast – between colonial modernity and indigenous, oriental decay – the city of Old Delhi was progressively starved of investment. As energy and water, manpower and resources were poured into the blossoming Garden City, Shahjahanabad was left to crumble. Old Delhi's population density multiplied, death rates climbed, infant mortality accelerated, and infrastructure frayed. The legendary Delhi of Mughal beauty and sophistication – a city renowned across civilizations for its architecture, poetry, visual arts and literature – was now identified with filth, backwardness and superstition. The British project of urban colonialism, of developing an imperial hegemony through the assertion of cultural and geographical modernity, was advancing with apparently unstoppable success.[69]

Yet it was precisely that reviled civilization, the ethos of sixteenth-century Shahjahanabad and the durbar pageants of the Mughal Court (Viola Bayley's 'Arabian Nights' excess), which dictated official life in New Delhi. In its hierarchy, ritual, vanity and snobbery all the caricatures of oriental luxury were resuscitated under the British viceroy. There were no democratic or social advances to match the modernity of the motor car and telephone. Instead, New Delhi was a stage-set for a perpetual social durbar, amid the most up-to-date building styles and interior decor. Highly stratified principles of order and deference, as refracted through the occupational, social and racial criteria of New Delhi's official class, were reflected in the allocation of housing.

A Versailles-like system of social decorum was set out by the Warrant of Precedence, which listed the 175 colonial roles in descending order of social significance, beginning with the viceroy and ending up with the assistant chief controller of stores and superintendent of central jails. With *ancien régime* precision, each individual's status within the New Delhi hierarchy was classified and their housing allocated accordingly. What is now known as the Lutyens Bungalow Zone was carved up between the officials and soldiers, the clerks and elites of the British Empire as colonial couples went to war over compound acreage, servants' quarters and proximity to power. A Member of Council could expect to receive a decent 6-acre site, in contrast to Members of the Legislature, who were merely democratically elected representatives, and who had to make do with bungalows on a quarter acre. A clear pattern of social and racial segregation, of a caste hierarchy topped by European superiority, was laced through the New Delhi grid with the British elite huddled close to the Secretariat around York Place, Hastings Road, King George's Avenue and Dupleix Road and the Indian clerks and peons were despatched to the urban edges. Only the richest and grandest of Indian princes, notably the Nizam of Hyderabad, were able to break the racial barrier and embed themselves within the inner circle. Lutyens himself designed Hyderabad House with a restrained display of East-West humanism, and other, competing maharajas sought to insert themselves into the colonial geography. For the vast majority of Indians, however, New Delhi was testament to the Empire's racial apartheid, cocooning an elite ruling class in as gilded a setting as any ancient, Mughal court.[70]

'How often, while at Delhi, I thought of [Marcel] Proust and wished that he might have known the place and its inhabitants,' wrote Aldous Huxley after a brief stop-off in New Delhi in 1926. 'For the imperial city is no less rich in social comedy than Paris; its soul is as fertile in snobberies, dissimulations, prejudices, hatred, envies.'[71] The stage set for such snobberies and envies was the legion of clubs and societies which the British, with their innate genius for sport and drinking, populated the new capital (as they had in Hong Kong). There was the Gymkhana Club and the Chelmsford, the Delhi Hunt and the Annual Flower Show, the Imperial Horse Show and the Annual All-India Polo Tournament, the cricket club and golf club – as well as the clubs for high-ranking Indians such as the New Delhi Club, the Municipal Club and the Chartered Bank Club. The institutions codified the rigid, structured, stifling patterns of the Raj. 'Life was very formal,' remembered Viola Bayley.

> Winifred and I would be driven out to the shops or to pay calls in the morning, for which, even if only a shopping expedition, one wore hat and gloves . . . After tea, unless one had been taken to watch polo, there was possibly a stroll round the race-course that lay beyond the garden or a visit to the club library.[72]

The formality of it all appalled Huxley. 'From the Viceroy to the young clerk, who, at home, consumes high tea at sunset, every Englishman in India solemnly "dresses". It is as though the integrity of the British Empire depended in some directly magical way upon the donning of black jackets and hard-boiled shirts.'[73] Accompanying the uniform came the same obsession about hierarchy and protocol which had dictated housing allocations: the Warrant of Precedence dictated not just the bungalows, but which couples were invited to what parties and who sat where. Women, 'unless by virtue of holding an appointment themselves they are entitled to a higher position in the table,' were always allotted a place in the seating plan entirely dependent upon their husband's Warrant status. And, more often than not, the dinner-parties and cocktail sets were made up of the same tight circle of civil servants, officers and diplomats. Pamela Mountbatten found it all a dreadful bore – the city had no atmosphere; the people were desperately artificial. 'I went to the most extraordinary cocktail party given by Lady Tymms full of horrifying specimens and swarms of the huntin', shootin', and fishin' type who bombarded me with indignant demands as to why I hadn't been out with the hounds every morning since my arrival,' she wrote, four months before her father handed it all over to Nehru.[74]

Others enjoyed the last days of the Raj with more abandon. 'The atmosphere was too giddy,' recalled Iris Portal, daughter of the Indian Civil Service mandarin Sir Montagu Butler and future historian of India. 'It was all riding, picnics, dancing, dashing young men, and beautiful polo players.' Among these was her husband, the British army officer Gervas Portal.[75] 'During the so-called cold-weather season in Delhi, life is just one whirl of gaiety,' explained a visitor in 1933. 'Horse Show week is particularly marvellous. Balls, picnics, and parties; visitors come from miles around . . . Indian princes bringing magnificent jewels leave their native states to add splendour to Delhi.'[76] Huxley was bowled over by the sheer extravagance of the princes. 'The hotels pullulated with despots and their viziers. At the Viceroy's evening parties the diamonds were so large that they looked like stage gems; it was impossible to believe that the pearls in the million-pound necklaces were the genuine excrement of oysters. How hugely Proust would have enjoyed the Maharajas!'[77]

As Huxley intimated, the pinnacle of New Delhi society could only be glimpsed at the Durbar Hall and in the State Dining Room of Lutyens's Viceroy's House. But there, protocol was everything, from the wearing of sixteen-button, white kid-gloves to the act of homage to the king's representative. 'Dinner at Viceroy's House was a rather awe-inspiring affair, particularly the custom of dropping a full curtsey to the Viceroy as the ladies left the dining-room,' Viola Bayley recalled. 'Even less exalted dinners were very formal, great care being given to precedence.'[78] This Mughal Palace of British India could draw on a staff of 6,000 servants and an entertainment budget unrivalled across the Empire. The future King Edward VIII once remarked that he had never known what authentic regal pomp really meant until he stayed at the Viceroy's House. India was finally being ruled from a palace and not a counting house. And as at Louis XVI's Versailles Palace, the obsession with precedent and formality provided a cover for the creeping sclerosis.[79]

THE FALL OF ROME

From its inception, New Delhi was overshadowed by the Recessional gloom of Indian independence. On his first state entry into the city as viceroy, Lord Hardinge had had a taste of the struggle to come. After arriving at Delhi railway station on 23 December 1912, Hardinge and his wife progressed on a caparisoned elephant towards the ancient Mughal seat of power, the Red Fort. When the procession arrived at the Punjab National Bank along the old Delhi thoroughfare of Chandni Chowk – that foreign Indian cityscape of 'crenellated caravanserai and picturesque squalor', as the *British Architect* journal put it – a needle bomb was thrown into the viceroy's carriage (or *howdah*), killing his support staff and ripping an eight-inch gash in Hardinge's back and neck. A Bengali terrorist group with close connection to the anti-colonialist movement was blamed for the bomb plot. At the foundation moment of the greatest city of Empire, the endgame of Empire had begun.

Over the next thirty years demands for independence became more insistent and more sophisticated. Congress-led campaigns of civil disobedience – ranging from boycotts to shutdowns to tax protests – were countered by the British with violence (as at the Amritsar Massacre of 1919), the jailing of Gandhi and Nehru and emergency laws. On the other hand, a series of reforms, beginning with provincial self-government, were also passed to enable India to pursue a pathway towards Dominion status. But the advent of the Second World War accelerated the timetable. Congress reacted with fury when the British viceroy peremptorily announced India's entry into the war and initiated the 'Quit India' campaign in August 1942. Before the year was out, some 60,000 Indians had been jailed, 600 flogged and 900 reported killed.

Oblivious to it all, New Delhi's riding, dancing, cocktail-mixing durbar grandeur lasted until the final moments of the Raj and the birth of an independent India. Indeed, in Britain's final viceroy, Rear Admiral Lord Mountbatten of Burma, the pageantry and vanity of imperial Delhi produced its most consummate figurehead. Very much a product of the Lytton-Curzon school of colonial showmanship,

Mountbatten was determined to prove that the British could pass on a colony with dignity and élan. Before his flight into Delhi in March 1947, 'he was chiefly concerned with what he should wear on arrival,' according to his confidant Woodrow Wyatt.

> 'They're all a bit left wing, aren't they? Hadn't I better land in ordinary day clothes?' He was delighted when I said, 'No, you are the last Viceroy. You are royal. You must wear your grandest uniform and all your decorations and be met in full panoply and with all the works. Otherwise they will feel slighted.' And that is what he did, to everyone's pleasure.[80]

Not least his own. 'What a ceremony!' he said of his investiture as viceroy.

> Everyone who mattered was there. All the Princes. All the leaders. All the diplomats. I put on everything. My white full dress uniform. Orders, decorations, medals, the whole lot ... Obviously I wore the Garter. Then I wore the Star of India ... I wore the Star of the Indian Empire and then I wore the Royal Victorian Order and that made the four; that's all you're allowed to wear.[81]

Mountbatten was a clarifying embodiment of New Delhi's alien ethos and a desperate anachronism. The midnight hour presaged the triumph of the middle class of Calcutta and Bombay, not the colonial aristocracy of the Secretariat; it was a victory for the intelligentsia of the Indian National Congress and the urban radical activists, rather than the Ornamental *noblesse oblige* of Viceroy's House. Indeed, independence was an epic denial of the lofty condescension of New Delhi – of liberty being generously granted to the people of India by their colonial masters, rather than being taken by Indians as right through struggle.

The fall of New Delhi also signalled something more profound for the future of the British Empire. Lutyens's stone bells were now tolling as the straitened finances of a postwar economy and the growing ambitions of the American and Soviet empires ushered in the beginning of the end of the British imperial project. Winston Churchill's long-feared decline and fall of the British Empire – in which he had always regarded the loss of India as instrumental – had come to pass. By 1947 the Rome of Hindustan was awash in the blood of

India–Pakistan partition, as communal tensions spilled over into attacks on Delhi's Muslim neighbourhoods and the imperial elite danced out their final days.

Friday, 15 August 1947 was Independence Day in Pamela Mountbatten's diary – when India was made free, Daddy an earl and Mummy a countess.

> Mummy wore a long gold lamé dress and a little wreath of gold leaves on her head. With the golden thrones and golden carpets and the red velvet canopies over the thrones spot-lit it was very sumptuous. The trumpeters in scarlet and gold had heralded a splendid entrance. At the end of the ceremony the great bronze doors were thrown open and 'God Save the King' was followed by the new Indian national anthem, 'Jana Gana Mana' . . . Then Mummy and Daddy, escorted by the Bodyguard, drove in the state carriage down to the Constituent Assembly. I was already sitting with the staff but when the carriage arrived the Council House was entirely surrounded by a quarter of a million frenzied people chanting 'Jai Hind'.[82]

Rome had fallen, and another Delhi consumed by this graveyard of dynasties. Among the millions of Indians caught up in the excitement of the city's transition to independence was G. D. Khosla, a judge in the High Court of Lahore. 'In a few moments I would be a free citizen of India,' he wrote of the celebrated midnight session, as Nehru addressed the nation from inside Baker's Parliament House. 'Everyone in the hall would be free. Everyone outside and beyond the hall would be free . . . I had a sudden impulse to stand up and shout: *Civis Indicus sum*.'[83]

Another new Delhi, another new Rome, had been born.

10

Liverpool

The Janus Face of Empire

On 22 April 1981 the end of the British Empire hit home. After 112 years of business, the sugar giant Tate & Lyle closed the doors on its Liverpool refinery with the loss of 1,600 jobs. Whereas once the Merseyside warehouses had been piled high with the harvests of Caribbean plantations, the docks now stood idle. With sugar cane from the Commonwealth unable to compete with subsidized sugar beet from the Continent, Tate & Lyle chairman Lord Jellicoe described the Love Lane refinery as 'a victim' of UK membership of the European Economic Community. The terms of Britain's trade with the world were changing, and the port of Liverpool was stranded on the wrong side of history. Only the day before the refinery closure, the Liverpool Steamship Owners' Association had announced a further haemorrhaging of business. Foreign and coastwise cargo into the Mersey docks had slumped by 19 per cent over the year; the port had lost 957 berthings during the previous two years; and the container trade was withering. 'And now came the news that Tates was to be shut,' as the sugar company's historian describes it. 'Tates, the house-hold name, probably the one plant in Liverpool that everybody knew about. Tates with its long tradition of family service and its unique place in the minds of Liverpudlians. That this was to go was unbeliev-able, this was the ultimate blow.'[1]

The social effects of the port of Liverpool's slow-motion collapse were apparent across Merseyside: falling population levels; spiralling unemployment; declining business confidence; and rising child poverty. All of this was exacerbated by the economic recession of the early 1980s and heavy cuts to local government spending. In Liverpool, over 80,000 unemployed were chasing just over 1,000 vacancies. So when in July 1981 the disaffected, jobless and frequently brutalized inner-city youth of the 'Liverpool 8' district took to the streets, few were surprised. In that long summer of riots – sparked by unemployment, thuggish policing and what a later inquiry would call a culture of 'institutional racism' in the police towards Britain's black and minority ethnic urban populations – which spread from Brixton in London to Moss Side in Manchester to Handsworth in Birmingham, the events in 'Liverpool 8' (or Toxteth) were among the most despairing. Over four days and nights of rioting, while seventy properties went up in smoke, cars were torched, 460 policemen injured and hundreds arrested, CS gas was used for the first time on the British mainland. 'Outside, the entire skyline is an angry crimson,' was how one local resident described the night of 3 July 1981.

> Dense banks of black smoke hang threateningly above the rooftops. The silhouette of Tiber Street School, five hundred yards away, is framed by huge tongues of green and lilac flame, licking skyward. Over by the Anglican Cathedral is a colossal blaze, the like of which we've never seen in our lives . . . the view is like a Hieronymous Bosch painting of Hell.[2]

Liverpool, the Queen City of the Mersey, whose warehouses had supplied the industrial revolution and whose St George's Hall stood as the defining symbol of Victorian civic pride, the city that had commanded global trade since the 1700s and had boasted more millionaires than anywhere in the UK outside London, was ablaze. Merseyside's proud history as the 'Gateway of Empire' was going up like the city's torched Rialto Ballroom.

'Alone, every night, when the meetings were over and the pressure was off, I would stand with a glass of wine, looking out at the magnificent view over the river and ask myself what had gone wrong for this great English city.' Michael Heseltine was the government minister who relocated himself from London to Liverpool, in the aftermath of the Toxteth riots, to try to rebuild the shattered city.

> The Mersey, its lifeblood, flowed as majestically as ever down from the hills. Its monumental Georgian and Victorian buildings, created with

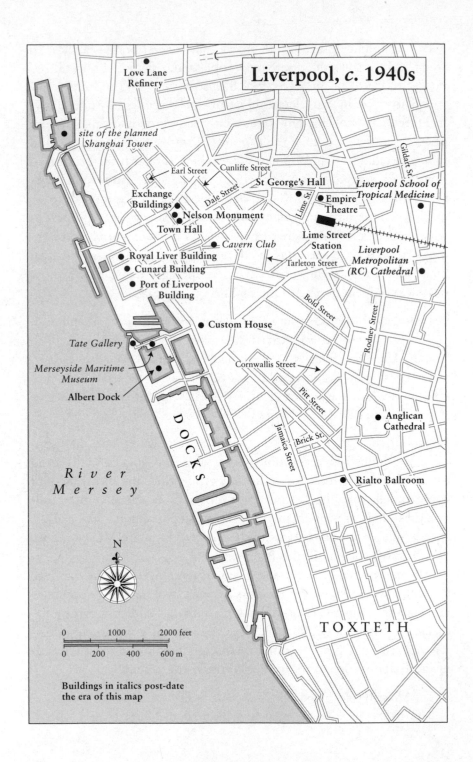

Liverpool, *c.* 1940s

Love Lane Refinery

site of the planned Shanghai Tower

Earl Street
Cunliffe Street
Exchange Buildings
Dale Street
Nelson Monument
Town Hall
St George's Hall
Lime St.
Empire Theatre
Liverpool School of Tropical Medicine
Gildart St.

Cavern Club
Royal Liver Building
Cunard Building
Port of Liverpool Building

Lime Street Station
Tarleton Street
Liverpool Metropolitan (RC) Cathedral

Custom House

Bold Street

Rodney Street

Tate Gallery

Merseyside Maritime Museum
Albert Dock

Cornwallis Street

Pitt Street

Jamaica Street
Brick St.

Anglican Cathedral

D O C K S

River Mersey

Rialto Ballroom

N

TOXTETH

0   1000   2000 feet
0   200   400   600 m

Buildings in italics post-date the era of this map

such pride and at such cost by the city fathers of a century and more earlier, still dominated the skyline. The Liver Building itself, the epicentre of a trading system that had reached out to the four corners of the earth, stood defiant and from my perspective very alone. The port had serviced an empire and sourced a world trade.

But since then, thought Heseltine, 'in truth, everything had gone wrong'.[3]

Here was the Janus face of Empire. Since Liverpool's merchants had first set out across the Atlantic for Boston and Bridgetown, or south to the Coast of Guinea, sailing between the West African slave forts, Britain had been enriched by Empire. What Karl Marx called the 'primitive accumulation' of colonialism had ensured the prosperity of the UK's great port cities – Glasgow, London, Bristol and Liverpool. But Indian independence signalled the start of a terrible turn in fortunes for these imperial cities of the British metropole. Autonomy for New Delhi meant the economic underpinning of their imperial wealth was ripped away and, in the aftermath of the end of Empire, their urban civilization came crashing down. Colonial liberation abroad produced postcolonial cities at home: metropolises crippled by both a vanishing economic rationale and the loss of any coherent sense of their place in the world. Overseas, in the 1980s, Britain camouflaged decline by running its most assertive foreign policy for decades. With the support (sometimes passive, sometimes active) of the American Empire, it would recapture the Falkland Islands in 1982, square up against the Soviet Union and support any number of military sorties in the Middle East. This was Britain 'punching above its weight', sustaining its semi-imperial role on the world stage with its fiercely guarded permanent seat on the United Nations Security Council, long after the Empire itself had gone. In the cities of northern England and Scotland, the reality of decline was harder to disguise. Here, at home, the end of Empire spelt deindustrialization, depopulation and unrest. What had once made Liverpool now unmade her: as the riches of Empire receded, urban bravura gave way to urban ruin.

THE BRICKS OF LIVERPOOL

Even today, after Second World War bombing raids, 1970s brutalism and relentless regeneration schemes, the origins of Liverpool's imperial economy can still be read in the city's fabric. Begin with the Town Hall, as the most obvious architectural remnant of how the city once sought to define itself. Long since overshadowed by the mighty St George's Hall, this neo-classical gem was erected at the heart of the city's commercial district, on the busy junction of High Street and Dale Street, in the 1750s. Jealous of Bristol's fine Exchange, Liverpool's civic elite poached its architect, John Wood, for a replica commission on the Mersey with the instruction to lavish extra attention on the wealth and trade that had made its commission possible. So, on the high reliefs between the square Corinthian piers, and above the teeming merchant streets, were carved a series of exotic stone panels revelling in Liverpool's proud history of human trafficking and colonial trade. 'Busts of Blackamoors and Elephants with the Teeth of the Latter, with such like emblematical Figures, representing the African Trade and Commerce,' as one admiring contemporary put it in the 1780s.[4]

The West African business, slavery, sugar and all the byways of colonial commerce were drilled through the stones of Liverpool. Jamaica Street and Rodney Street (named after Admiral Lord Rodney, who defeated the French at St Lucia in 1782) spoke to the city's Caribbean connections. Liverpool's gratitude to the Royal Navy for keeping the trade routes open was further acknowledged in 1813 with a public subscription for a Nelson Monument. Placed between the Exchange and the Town Hall, this macabre bronze composition of flags, cannon, captives and a skeletal figure of Death (so much more melodramatic than Bridgetown's statue of Nelson) remains one of Merseyside's most familiar monuments. Close by, the nautical theme continues with the slave-trading dynasties of Earle, Tarleton, Cunliffe, Gildart and Bold giving their names to some of the city's finest boulevards – the latter described in the 1820s as an 'imperial trading street . . . and such shops! Paramount, princely, nay imperial in their way. Here taste, elegance and display are in their element.'[5] From the dock warehouses to the family banks, from Pier Head to Rope Walk, the iconography and architecture of Liverpool were a physical reminder of the city's origins in an eighteenth-century imperial economy. The same power of commerce and slavery as had spurred the growth of Boston and Bridgetown had built cities on the eastern edges of the Atlantic too. Or as the Reverend William Bagshaw Stevens put it more explicitly in 1797, 'throughout this large-built Town every Brick is cemented to its fellow Brick by the blood and sweat of Negroes'.[6]

It was in the second half of the seventeenth century that Liverpool started to challenge nearby Chester as the leading port of north-west England. The size of its harbour on the Mersey, compared to Chester's on the Dee, made it more convenient for ocean-going vessels to manoeuvre, and its ready access to the clothmaking districts of south Lancashire offered an excellent export base for markets in Spain and the Mediterranean. Its traders then started to experiment first with salt exports and Irish commerce, before following Glasgow into the tobacco and sugar businesses. During the 1660s, some 320 years before Tate & Lyle's closure of Love Lane, Liverpool's refining of West Indian cane began in the vicinity of Dale Street. The displacement of London shipping during the plague and fire years of the Restoration only helped Merseyside expand its Atlantic networks. Customs revenue and shipping tonnage both accelerated steadily over the course of the eighteenth century, providing a far-sighted Liverpool Corporation with the funds to invest in the world's first commercial enclosed wet dock, then ape Dublin in widening and improving its streets. Indeed, Liverpool proved far more effective than the myriad of competing London dock companies in investing in its infrastructure and providing cheaper port facilities. The population grew from 5,715 in 1700 to some 78,000 by 1801.[7] Yet behind all this prosperity was the lynchpin of Liverpool's Georgian economy – the 'blood and sweat' of those Africans whose visages peered out from the high reliefs of the Town Hall.

'The West Indian sugar trade brought wealth to many, and in connection therewith the African slave trade grew to enormous proportions,' admitted an early twentieth-century history of Merseyside. 'It cannot be denied that Liverpool took a prominent part in this trade, and that many of the leading Liverpool families of the eighteenth century rose to wealth and distinction through the traffic.' But, the author averred, 'it is to be remembered that public opinion in those days, at home and abroad, held very different views on the slavery question from those held today'.[8] He was right in both respects. The 1750 African Trade Act undermined the monopoly of the London-based Royal African Company, whose Caribbean headquarters had been based in Bridgetown, and opened up the trafficking market to new entrants. Bristol, Whitehaven, Glasgow and above all Liverpool seized the opportunity, Merseyside overtaking its competitors to become Britain's leading slave port between 1750 and 1770. Over the course of the eighteenth century, some 5,000 slaving ships set sail from Liverpool, constituting around 50 per cent of slave-trading voyages. They journeyed south to the African coast, then across the Atlantic to the Caribbean, before completing the triangle trade and returning home to the Mersey laden with cane, molasses, cotton and foodstuffs. Alongside cotton, coal, sugar, tobacco and salt, slavers could account for up to a seventh of the tonnage clearing Liverpool's docks in the second half of the eighteenth century, the profits then cascading through the city's shipyards, shopkeepers, bankers, linen merchants and property speculators.[9] Indeed, large parts of Britain's Midlands and north-west economy would benefit from Liverpool's bloody enterprise, from the chain-makers of Dudley to the gun merchants of Birmingham and the cotton lords of Manchester, Burnley and Blackburn.

In 1807, after years of effort by William Wilberforce, supported by the highly principled but electorally doomed Liverpool MP William Roscoe, the trade in slaves was abolished across the British Empire. Merseyside was furious, but by then its economy had successfully diversified into servicing the surrounding centres of industrial production, which had been joined to the national and international markets by the expanding canal network. As the Liverpool Daily Post would later put it, 'Liverpool was called into being . . . as a junction for the landing, embarkation and storage of vast wealth exchanged between the North and Midlands of England and the overseas world.'[10] The Mersey docks brought in the raw materials from West Africa, the West Indies and North America (timber, sugar, grain), and then shipped out finished wares (Birmingham's metal goods, Staffordshire ceramics, Sheffield steel) to the world. With its hinterland of industrial Lancashire and Cheshire, served by an expanding array of turnpikes and canals, Liverpool was the port of choice for the Workshop of the World. And above all, it was the cotton industry that secured Liverpool's exponential growth. By the 1860s, the docks were handling some 2.6 million bales of cotton sailed in from the American South to feed the 2,000 mills which clacked and shuttled across Lancashire. The tonnage of shipping using Liverpool doubled between 1815 and 1830, and doubled again by 1845. As in Bombay, the advent of the railway in the 1840s only accelerated the port's entrepôt role, while the construction of Clarence Dock in 1830 had provided dedicated steamship facilities with substantial cargo holds, creating new commercial opportunities for ships to service distant Chinese, Indian and South American markets. 'The commerce of Liverpool extends to every port of importance in every quarter of the globe,' local journalist Thomas Baines could announce in 1852. 'In this respect it far surpasses the commerce of any city of which we have a record from past times, such as Tyre, Venice, Genoa, Amsterdam, or Antwerp, and fully equals, if it does not surpass, that of London and New York.'[11]

The commercial heart of Liverpool lay in the hundreds of acres of quayside that lined the sides of the Mersey. 'For seven miles and a quarter, on the Lancashire side of the river alone, the monumental granite, quarried from the [Mersey] Board's own quarries in Scotland, fronts the river in a vast sea wall as solid and enduring as the Pyramids, the most stupendous work of its kind that the will and power of man have ever created,' wrote the Liverpool historian Ramsay Muir in the early 1900s.[12] 'In olden times it used to be said that "all roads lead to Rome". Today all seas lead to Liverpool,' chimed the Liverpool historian W. T. Pike. 'There is no part of the globe, however remote, whose natives may not be met on the Liverpool landing stage, and there is no territory so distant whose products do not pass from time to time through the docks and warehouses of Liverpool.'[13] Across the Mersey, at the Birkenhead Iron Works, the boilermaker William Laird and his son John were building the iron ships to carry the wares to and from Liverpool. In 1903, Laird Brothers Ltd merged with the Sheffield steel firm of Charles Cammell and Co. to create the ship-building behemoth Cammell Laird. Between 1829 and 1947, over 1,100 vessels of all kinds were built and launched from their Birkenhead dockyards into the Mersey.

In Liverpool, each dock had its job: the Old Dock (opened in 1715) for the West India and Africa trade; the Salthouse Dock (1740s) for the corn and timber business; St George's Dock (1771) as an alternative for the Caribbean merchants; King's Dock (1788) for American and Baltic concerns; Queen's Dock (1799) for the Greenland fishery. The flotilla of vessels lining the quayside, the army of dockers loading and unloading made for a remarkable scene. 'All kinds of hardware, railway supplies, iron in all shapes, of all kinds and sizes, sheet, wire, bar, spring etc.; bales, boxes, casks, wines, spirits, ales, for India, Madagascar, Asia, Persia, the Continent and America,' marvelled a visiting New Yorker. 'Thousands of men are here measuring packages, invoicing goods, shipping merchandise; the tramp of horses, songs of stevedores, and shouts of sailors make a very Babel of industry.'[14] Then came Canada Dock, Princes Dock, Clarence Dock, Stanley Dock and – fully revitalized today – the elegant Albert Dock of 1847, designed by the great dock engineer Jesse Hartley. 'For sheer punch there is little in the early commercial architecture of Europe to emulate it,' was Pevsner's judgement on the sublime utility of Albert Dock. Its confident mix of austere classicism and brick functionalism – a product of Liverpool's commercial self-image, confident enough of its urban civilization to echo the architecture of ancient Greek city-states, combined with practical demands for fire-proof warehousing – underscored the city's transition to a mercantile-industrial metropolis.[15]

The busy dockscape also pointed to another part of Liverpool's make-up. 'Unlike the dwellers in most English towns, all of us in Liverpool are, to a great extent, citizens of the world,' explained the *Liverpool Critic* of 1877, 'for everything around us tells us of far-off countries and foreign ways, and in our midst are constantly natives of so many distant lands that we insensibly imbibe and learn to practice peculiarities not British.'[16] Ramsay Muir spoke of Liverpool's 'amazingly polyglot and cosmopolitan population' as the product of its port economy. 'The Liverpool citizen, therefore, from youth upwards, is familiar with the shipping of the world,' concurred the chairman of the Liverpool Chamber of Commerce. The daily sight of cotton bales from America, wool from New Zealand, canned meats from Argentina and raw sugar from the West Indies 'develops that cosmopolitan atmosphere and interest which distinguishes the Liverpool citizen from the inhabitants of other commercial towns'.[17] In contrast to the introverted textile communities of Oldham or Bradford, Liverpool was a world city, the 'New York of Europe', whose wharfs and piers were a melting-pot of peoples, products and cultures.

The initial ingredients for multicultural Liverpool came from across the UK itself. 'She is the meeting place of the Four Kingdoms,' boasted Ramsay Muir, 'with more Welsh citizens than any Welsh town but Cardiff, more Irish citizens than any Irish town but Dublin and Belfast, more Scottish citizens than any but some three or four of the great towns of Scotland.'[18] By far the largest foreign contingent in the city was poor Irish migrants. Poverty and immiseration caused by successive years of potato blight had been exacerbated by reactionary land policies to produce the Great Famine of 1845–52. As the death toll escalated, those who could emigrate caught the so-called 'coffin ships' for New York, Glasgow and Liverpool – entering through the gates of Clarence Dock for a scarcely less destitute life in the cellars and workhouses of Everton and Vauxhall. Such was the mid-Victorian influx that, by 1851, over 22 per cent of Liverpool residents (some 83,000) were Irish-born, leading some to describe the city as the capital of Ireland in England, 'a piece cut off from the old sod itself'. By the early years of the twentieth century, the number of Liverpool Irish and Catholics, regarded as synonymous terms at the time, was calculated at up to 200,000: roughly one-third of the population.[19] Accompanying the Irish immigrants was a relatively substantial African and West Indian community, drawn initially from freed black slaves (often the mixed-race sons and daughters of Caribbean plantation owners) and discharged, loyalist soldiers from the American War of Independence, whose numbers were then augmented by the typical port population of sailors, chefs, stewards and dockers. This was the means of entry for the Liberian Kru migrants, but also the Chinese community centred around Cornwallis Street and Lascars from the Indian subcontinent. 'Most of my early life was spent on Brick Street, a street of abominably overcrowded shacks,' remembered Liverpool resident Pat O'Mara, on growing up near Queen's Dock. 'Negroes,

Chinese, Mulattoes, Filipinos, almost every nationality under the sun, most of them with white wives and large half-caste families, were our neighbours, each laying claim to a certain street.'[20]

Such exceptional multiculturalism meant that, as early as the 1830s, Liverpool could begin to exchange its blood-soaked slave trading reputation for a more benign 'world city' image. 'In Liverpool indeed the Negro steps with a prouder pace, and lifts his head like a man; for here, no such exaggerated feeling exists in respect to him, as in America,' remarked young Wellingborough Redburn, the semi-autobiographical hero of Herman Melville's novel *Redburn* (1849). 'Three or four times, I encountered our black steward, dressed very handsomely, and walking arm in arm with a good-looking English woman. In New York, such a couple would have been mobbed in three minutes; and the steward would have been lucky to escape with his whole limbs.' As a result, 'the black cooks and stewards of American ships are very much attached to the place and like to make voyages to it'.[21] None of this multicultural balm prevented Liverpool from supporting the slave-owning South, whose cotton bales were such an important source of revenue, against the Yankees in the American Civil War of the 1860s. The Confederates poured resources, spies and propaganda into Merseyside, while Laird Brothers built the cruise ship CSS *Alabama*, deployed to break the blockade of Southern ports. 'We are southern almost to a man,' was the succinct verdict of one Liverpudlian merchant.[22]

Finally, there were the Liverpool immigrants who just got off at the wrong stop – the thousands of migrants from central Europe and Russia who thought they had reached New York, but instead found themselves in Merseyside. Some 12 million passengers passed through Liverpool between 1825 and 1913 and quite a few of them literally missed the departing boat, adding their own ethnic contribution to this powerfully diasporic city.

Victorian Liverpool was thus a cosmopolitan commercial emporium; a peaceful, free-trading gateway, building 'innumerable ties of friendship and interest, amongst nations formerly hostile and rival'; a second Tyre, Venice or Athens. It was 'beside the docks, that the citizen of Liverpool can best feel the opulent romance of his city, and the miracle of transformation which has been wrought since the not distant days when, where the docks now stand, the untainted tides of the Mersey raced past a cluster of mud hovels amid fields and untilled pastures'.[23] Yet beyond the docks there were ever grander urban testaments to the fruits of free trade, cultural exchange and commerce. In front of the Old Dock, a colossal, neo-classical Custom House rose up, paid for with the tributes of trade (sadly bombed beyond repair during the Second World War and demolished). And then, in 1854, Harvey Lonsdale Elmes's St George's Hall, the pinnacle of Liverpool's Classical Revival, was opened, a vast civic temple whose Minton tile-decorated interior sought to recreate the Roman Baths of Caracalla. Saved from demolition in the 1960s, its enormous, brooding, classical triumphalism catches your breath even today as you step out of Liverpool Lime Street Station into the blustery Scouse air. It was, rightly, hailed at the time as 'a design at the head of our public buildings, and worthy to take rank with those of the purest age of Grecian art'.[24] Even better, it was untainted by the crimes of the past. 'There is no drawback to damp the ardour of enthusiastic admiration: these stones, at least, are not cemented with the blood of negroes; these ornaments and decorations are not insulting trophies to grinding oppression,' glowed an 1855 guide to Liverpool. 'The fountain of wealth expended in erecting this pile was unpolluted; it is a temple erected to the genius of Commerce – bartering fairly, justly, freely.'[25] And yet in the hall's encircling friezes could still be seen a depiction of 'Commerce and the Arts Bearing Tribute to Britannia', at the centre of which appeared a kneeling African slave. Old habits evidently died hard.

QUEEN OF THE MERSEY

By the early 1900s, however, the call of Empire had crowded out free and just commerce. In the succeeding half-century, Liverpool's urban identity perceptibly shifted from the global to the colonial, as she draped herself ever more fulsomely within the folds of a popular imperialism and its economic advantages. Increasingly, official Liverpool imagined herself less as a free-trading city of commerce and more as the premier ocean port of the British Empire. All the tributes of Britain's formal as well as informal empire (those 'spheres of influence' which stretched into markets in Argentina, Brazil, China and parts of Africa) came pouring into the Mersey's wharfs and docks, with manufactured goods produced from the factories and mills of northern England then shipped out again. Unsurprisingly, Joseph Chamberlain's vision of imperial federation was a popular cause in the council chambers and club rooms of Liverpool. The advent of steam in the 1830s, the opening of the Suez Canal in 1869 and the beginning of liner traffic across the Atlantic only extended the city's reach. The Cunard Company started a weekly service to New York and fortnightly to Boston in the 1860s, and the White Star Line's third-class compartments became the major exporter of hundreds of thousands of European emigrants to America. Steaming off in the other direction were the three great transporters of the Ocean Steam Ship Company, *Agamemnon, Ajax* and *Achilles* (christened in honour of Homer, the supreme author of global odysseys), each capable of carrying 3,000 tons. This trio were the core of the great Liverpool shipping tycoon Alfred Holt's Blue Funnel Line, whose imperial routes dominated the import of China tea, Malay tin and Australian wool. 'We considered Bombay and Calcutta, but finally settled on China mainly because tea was a very nice thing to carry,' as Holt disarmingly put it.[26] His ships returned to dock with hundreds of Chinese seafarers, who helped to add to Pitt Street and Cornwallis Street's emergent 'China Town'.* Buoyed by a healthy balance sheet, Holt's group purchased wharfage facilities in Hong Kong and office complexes in Singapore, before entering the growing West African market by buying up the Elder Dempster shipping line, whose steamers returned from Zambia, Liberia, Guyana and the Cameroons laden with mahogany, coffee, rubber, palm oil and ginger – all to be unloaded in the Toxteth dock.[27]

It was no accident that one of the largest shareholders in the Ocean Steam Ship Company was another Liverpudlian, Lord Leverhulme, whose soap and cosmetics business, Lever Brothers, was heavily dependent upon West African palm oil extracted from the British

---

* A plaque on the wall of the nearby Nook pub (now boarded up) on Nelson Street declares itself, 'the centre of the oldest Chinatown in Europe and this pub, The Nook, became the Chinese "local" in 1940'.

protectorate of Nigeria (as well as King Leopold's Belgian Congo). The lines of Vim household cleaner, of Lux and Pears soap, pouring out of the factories of Lever's 'Port Sunlight' model village bound Liverpool and the Wirral peninsula ever closer to the rhythms of colonial trade. The *Red Book of West Africa* was Liverpool's in-house directory of those many merchants running operations in and out of the four British colonies of Nigeria, Gold Coast, Sierra Leone and the Gambia, and by the early 1900s the African Section of the Liverpool Chamber of Commerce was one of the city's most powerful lobby groups. Soap production was just one of a number of new businesses growing up around the Liverpool import trade: close by there were cigarette makers rolling tobacco leaf imported from South Africa; mills grinding Canadian grain and Indian rice; and sugar refineries, like Tate & Lyle, refining West Indian cane for the biscuit business.[28] A successful industrial eco-system flourished around the dockyards, turning raw materials from the Empire into manufactured goods.

But Liverpool was ultimately a place of exchange and evaluation, rather than a manufacturing economy. In the 1870s, a visiting clergyman paid a call on the Liverpool Exchange and watched in awe:

> a crowd of merchants and brokers swarming and humming like a hive of bees on the floor of the vast area below. All around the enormous hall were desks or screens or easels or huge slates covered with the latest telegrams, notices of London stock and share lists, cargoes, freights, sales, outward and homeward bound ships, times of sailing, state of wind and weather, barometer readings.[29]

W. T. Pike similarly thought the Exchange 'a wonderful scene of business activity' with its 'vast transactions by metal merchants and wool brokers, leather brokers, and representatives of every branch of home and foreign trade'.[30] This was the Liverpool of underwriting, exchanges, insurance and banking; a financial centre of ship-owners, traders, commodity-brokers, insurers, processors and bankers that could give the City of London a run for her money. Tom Best, a docker working for the Lancashire Cotton Corporation, recalled:

> a Jewish guy in Liverpool, he used to trade in futures, in cotton that hadn't even grown then. He made a million in a day, and lost a million

in a day. You bought bales at a certain price [before the cotton was grown] and if the crop was good, you were quids in, and if the crop was bad, well, you took a chance.

If the cotton bales were damaged, 'An insurance claim would be made. Insurance was another big business in Liverpool. Everything was insured.'[31] At the social apex of this shipping and insurance economy were the super-wealthy Rathbones and Roscoes, the shipping magnate Booths and Holts, who combined to ensure Liverpool easily outclassed Birmingham, Manchester, Glasgow or Leeds in its making of millionaires. The forces of imperial finance capital which so enriched Melbourne were equally evident in endowing the shipping and banking dynasties of Liverpool.

So, the port of Liverpool entered the twentieth century full of vigour, replete with the trade of an empire whose boundaries were stretching ever further across Africa and South-east Asia. On Merseyside, there were precious few fears of Gibbonian decline and fall. 'At the end of her seventh century as a chartered borough, Liverpool finds herself amongst the three or fourth greatest ports of the world,' as one history put it in 1907. 'She conducts one-third of the export trade, and one-fourth of the import trade, of the United Kingdom. She owns one-third of the total shipping of the kingdom, and one-seventh of the total registered shipping of the world.'[32] Contrary to the warnings of Chamberlain and Churchill, there was no evidence 'of either degeneracy or stagnation to be seen here. There are, on the contrary, abundant signs of illimitable expansiveness and invincible virility, not alone in trade and profit making, but in learning, culture, and all the arts of human progress and civilization,' wrote Pike.[33] The socialist writer and activist George Garrett, growing up by the Salthouse Dock in the early 1900s, remembered the trade and prosperity. 'Everywhere, ships; more steam than sail, charging the air with smoke and noise. Coal barges, trawlers, small coasters, ocean liners and cargo boats. Tramps of all nationalities, represented by the flags that flew at every stern, but all outnumbered by the Red Ensign, which fluttering from most of the flagstaffs, indicated Britain's far-flung trade.'[34]

For local journalist Michael O'Mahoney Liverpool was nothing less than a 'threshold to the ends of earth' and the confidence was there for all to see in the skyscrapers now going up along Liverpool's Pier Head. On the site of the 1770s George Dock were erected 'Three Graces', the iconic emblems of twentieth-century Liverpool and the city's answer to the fifth-century Athenian beauties of Aglaia, Euphrosyne and Thalia. First came the domed, Baroque, almost Saracenic headquarters of the Mersey Docks and Harbour Board (1903–7); then the towering Royal Liver Building (1908–11), built for the Royal Liver Assurance group and crowned by a statue of two liver birds, the cormorant-like symbol of Liverpool's connection with the sea, with seaweed in beak; and, to complete the trio, the stone, palazzo-style Cunard Building (1914). Today, the Three Graces stand horribly mutilated by a growing array of ugly additions to this once majestic waterfront, but in their day they symbolized the global ambition of this home-grown colonial city. Pevsner had it right: 'They represent the great Edwardian Imperial optimism and might indeed stand at Durban or Hong Kong, just as naturally as at Liverpool.'[35]

Alongside the architecture, the working and the middle classes of Liverpool embraced a public culture of imperial optimism. True, there were strands of radical anti-colonialism in support of the Fenian movement in Ireland and the Pan-African Congress, but majority opinion was more inclined to celebrate the relief of Mafeking than sympathize with liberation struggles. 'The city became increasingly identified with imperial and international affairs,' wrote W. T. Pike. The veterans returning from colonial conflicts in the Crimea, the Indian Mutiny and the Boer War paraded through the streets. 'Livingstone, H. M. Stanley, and other peaceful explorers and pioneers of civilization in savage lands, were entertained and cheered in their undertakings by the cordial sympathy of Liverpool citizens.'[36] There were West India Associations and East India Associations, there was the Royal Empire Society Liverpool and the Orange Order Lodges (with their unshakeable support for British rule in Ireland). There was the Empire Theatre and the world-famous Liverpool School of Tropical Medicine to assist those seafarers and salesmen who picked up something nasty in Niger. Meanwhile, the civic calendar became dominated by a multiplying array of colonial-themed events, exhibitions and festivals. In 1886 Liverpool hosted the International Exhibition of Navigation, Travelling, Commerce and Manufacture, opened by Queen Victoria herself, complete with an Indian village, dwarf elephants, dancing girls and commemorations of heroic British conquests. The first Colonial Products Exhibition also came to Liverpool in 1903 to celebrate the Empire as the 'wonder, admiration and envy of the whole civilised world'. The slightly less successful Liverpool Exhibition of 1913 gave rise to Orange Order demonstrations against Irish Home Rule. There were pageants based on the 1877 Delhi durbar and Trafalgar Day (21 October) parades around the Nelson Monument.[37]

The high point of this urban-imperial culture was the annual celebration of Empire Day on 24 May. Inaugurated in Canada in the late 1880s as Victoria Day and celebrated widely across the White Dominions, it made its way to Britain in 1904, where, in the north of England, it was often elided with the Whitsun festivities. Promoted relentlessly by the Earl of Meath, a Conservative peer and ardent imperialist in both England and Ireland, it was a day of loyal, royal demonstrations to give thanks for the blessings of an overseas empire and the racial superiority of the British, and to indoctrinate the next generation in its values of duty and sacrifice. 'In the forenoon the head teachers addressed the children upon the true significance of patriotism and Imperialism,' reported the *Liverpool Daily Post* of the wartime festivities of May 1915. 'The scholars rendered patriotic songs and the National Anthem of the Allies, and saluted the Union Jack.' At the Arnot Street Council School in Walton, its 2,500 pupils paraded through the playground before listening to an address by Archdeacon Spooner on 'the extent of the British Empire, its purpose, and the personal responsibility of each unit, whether man, woman, or child', for its future. At the Lister Drive Council School, 400 children processed around the main hall carrying a flag, before then forming 'tableaux representative of the Allies and our Colonial kith and kin'.[38] The sons of Melbourne, dying for the Empire in the eastern Mediterranean, were at least being thought about in the schools of Liverpool and Birkenhead.

As seen in Chapter 8, the First World War only served to strengthen the ties of Empire. The contribution of troops from all corners of the Empire was taken as evidence of the unshakeable bond of colonial kith and kin, while the additions of Egypt, Transjordan,

Iraq, Palestine and other African territories to Britain's dominion at the Versailles peace talks expanded the Empire to its geographical peak. After 1918, the British Empire covered a quarter of the world's territory and incorporated nearly a quarter of the world's population: here, at last, was the Empire of the never-setting sun. And, at home, the official forces of colonial propaganda, led by the Empire Marketing Board and the Imperial Economic Committee, escalated their promotion of the merits of Empire to the British people. There were Empire exhibitions at Glasgow and Wembley; booklets, pamphlets and postcards extolling the merits of colonialism; documentary films on the Empire's achievements abroad; imperial-themed posters for the London Underground; and lecture tours organized through networks of Rotary Clubs and Women's Institutes. For all the fears of decline and fall, and the superseding of Anglo-Saxon civilization, popular imperialism proved a powerful current in British interwar culture. From the popularity of Elgar's compositions and A. C. Benson's lyrics ('Wider still and wider shall thy bounds be set; / God, who made thee mighty, make thee mightier yet') to the poetry of Rudyard Kipling; from the heroism of T. E. Lawrence to the adventures of John Buchan; from stamps to imperial recipe books, the virtues of Empire were the product of artistic celebration, commercial endorsements and relentless official propaganda.[39]

Liverpool was immersed in this culture of colonialism – not least because the economics of Empire continued to prove highly lucrative for the city, with business actually accelerating in the interwar years. In the 1930s imperial trade topped 50 per cent of Liverpool's total, overtaking commerce with the United States and Latin America. As the Empire prospered, so did Liverpool. And as if any further proof were needed of Liverpool as an imperial city, there stepped forth, fresh from his exploits in New Delhi, the great architect of Empire, Sir Edwin Landseer Lutyens himself.

'I went to Liverpool and arrived just before lunch,' Lutyens recalled of his interview with Richard Downey, the Roman Catholic archbishop of Liverpool. 'I was shown into a large dull-gloomed room, and waited, feeling nervous and rather shy, till in came His Grace – a red biretta on his head and a voluminous sash round his ample waist ... His pectoral Cross swung towards me, and the first words he said were, "Will you have a cocktail?" [40] And with that, Lutyens was commissioned to build 'a cathedral in our time'. Twice as large as St Paul's in London and with a dome wider than that of St Peter's in Rome, Liverpool's Roman Catholic cathedral would be Merseyside's answer to New Delhi's Viceroy's House. But even more complicated: all the layered geometry of Lutyens's War Memorial Arch in New Delhi and his Thiepval memorial to the missing of the Somme were to be brought together in a space of cumulative, brilliant mathematical sophistication. The architectural historian Sir John Summerson thought the cathedral plans 'an architectural creation of the highest order, perhaps the latest and supreme attempt to embrace Rome, Byzantium, the Romanesque and the Renaissance in one triumphal and triumphant synthesis'. [41] There were apses, and chapels, and narthexes, and a 155-metre dome, and a transept with double aisles, and pretty much anything else Lutyens could gut from St Paul's and St Peter's and then mould into one. It was set to be a monument of mixed imperial meaning: an obvious affirmation of the might and power of Liverpool, Gateway of Empire, but also a tribute to those hundreds of thousands of Irish migrants who brought their faith and made their lives there. Unfortunately, it was never built: the foundation stones were laid on Whit Monday 1933, and work on the crypt and foundations continued until 1941, at which point wartime exigencies took over. Lutyens himself died in 1944, surrounded, it is said, by his drawings of Liverpool Cathedral. In 1953 the scheme was cancelled, and whilst the city's Anglican Cathedral, designed by Sir Giles Gilbert Scott, would come to rise above the skyline, Roman Catholic Liverpool was eventually given a cathedral of ungainly modernist design in the shape of an upturned funnel by Sir Frederick Gibberd, unkindly derided by Scouse wags as 'Paddy's Wigwam'.

If the construction of Lutyens's Viceroy's House was a monument to British imperial hubris in India, the failure to build Lutyens's cathedral in Britain was just as ominous a sign for the future of Liverpool. For after the initial post-First World War boom on the back of growing imperial markets, by the mid-1930s the first whispers of decline swirled through the quays and docks of Merseyside. Liverpool oversaw some 31 per cent of all UK trade in the years prior to the First World War. By 1938, this had dropped to 20.8 per cent, whilst

London (on the back of a rapidly growing, light-industrial economy in the south-east) had rocketed to 38.1 per cent.[42] The declining competitiveness of the traditional exports of northern England was beginning to affect shipping through the Mersey docks, while competition between the London docks, which had spare capacity, meant the capital's handling costs undercut Liverpool. The adamantine place of Liverpool in the British import trade was beginning to look more fragile.

In 1907, the municipal historian and Liverpool patriot Ramsay Muir had mulled on the future prospects of his beloved city. 'Will travellers come to Liverpool in the spirit in which we may go to Carthage, to view the inexpressive relics of a people that pursued gain with remorseless energy, and then were blotted out?' he asked. 'Or will they come in the spirit in which we still visit Athens or Florence, to see the real city, a city whose very atmosphere enriched the lives of all its citizens, a city which, for that reason, the world can never allow itself to forget?' The playwright and essayist J. B. Priestley had an answer. Visiting Liverpool on his *English Journey* of 1934, he found a city with neither the romance of Carthage nor the prosperous energy of Athens or Florence. 'The centre is imposing, dignified and darkish, like a city in a rather gloomy Victorian novel,' he wrote. It was a city for whom Empire now seemed more of a burden than a lifeforce. 'Here, emphatically, was the English seaport second only to London. The very weight of the stone emphasised that fact . . . We arrived at the edge of the Mersey, and below us was a long mud-bank . . . I have rarely seen anything more spectral and melancholy.' For all the antics of the Empire Marketing Board, Priestley regarded the glories of Empire, like Nineveh and Tyre, belonging to history. 'Here, a hundred years ago, the comfortable Liverpool merchants lived, going in and out of these charming doorways and beneath these fine old fanlights, thinking about their cargoes of cotton and tobacco from New Orleans and of rum and sugar from Jamaica . . . Liverpool must have been a town worth loitering in then.' But like the White Star Line's most infamous vessel of all, RMS *Titanic*, the city seemed oblivious to its imminent peril. The cinemas, theatres, dance halls, grill-rooms, boxing matches and cocktail bars were all in full swing, blissfully ignoring the approaching catastrophe. 'The Adelphi Hotel had dressed for the evening, was playing waltzes, and for the time being did not care a fig about the lost Atlantic traffic.'[43]

DECLINE AND FALL

The Second World War was the iceberg on which Liverpool, like the rest of the British Empire, would founder. The war's economic and strategic effects would scythe through the imperial cities of Britain – though not immediately. In the long run, the outcome of the fight against Hitler was the systematic dismemberment of the British Empire, under American pressure and domestic financial duress. But in the midst of battle, the Allied effort was celebrated in part as another glorious display of imperial cooperation. For all the iconography of May 1940, our finest hour and Britain standing alone against the forces of continental Fascism, the war also revealed the continuing, global potency of 'Britannic Nationalism'. All those Empire Days paid off as another generation of Australian, West Indian, Canadian, South African, New Zealand and Indian servicemen and -women laid down their lives in the service of the mother country. In his Christmas Day broadcast of 1941, King George VI spoke of 'one great family . . . the family of the British Commonwealth and Empire'.[44]

In Liverpool, the aftermath of war proved the benefits of Commonwealth and Empire to the city's economy. Demand which had been suppressed, but had not disappeared, during wartime burst on to the global economy in the late 1940s and '50s, and the docks boomed again. The intangible whiff of decline which Priestley had picked up in 1934 could now be downgraded to a minor, interwar hiccup in Liverpool's story of ever-ascending progress. Once more, ships lined the Mersey, the warehouses were bursting, and the quaysides bustling. New markets in Latin and South America offered growing opportunities for the port, as did the emerging cargo trade with independent Pakistan, India and even Egypt. The traditional trade connections to West Africa managed the transition out of Empire, with cocoa, nuts, palm oil and fruit carried into Liverpool on the newly established Black Star Line. The shipping trade was certainly helped by the British government's determination to ensure that those countries within the

Sterling Area – including Australia, New Zealand and South Africa – had their dollar spending capped and prioritized the purchase of sterling goods.* As a result, colonial and postcolonial trade flourished as Britain used what remained of the overseas empire to refloat its war-shattered economy. In July 1965 the Mersey Docks and Harbour Board announced that the previous financial year had witnessed a record 28.5 million tons of cargo pass through Liverpool. On the back of the boom, the city diversified into light manufacturing, with industrial estates at Speke, inward investment by Kodak and expanding car production lines for Ford, Leyland and Standard Triumph.[45] Low unemployment, high wages and a baby-boom saw the city foster a world-famous popular culture in its theatres, comedians, footballers, designers and musicians. By the early 1960s, the 'Mersey sound' or 'Merseybeat' boasted an estimated 400 groups, all trying to make a name for themselves on the stage of the Cavern and Iron Door clubs. And here was an irony of history: the British city that had done more than any other to undermine African culture by ferrying millions of slaves across the Atlantic now had its own culture transformed on the back of a transplanted African-American musical tradition. The R&B and Blues revolution of black America, of Ray Charles and Chuck Berry, made its way back across the sea lanes, carried by the 'Cunard Yanks' working the Liverpool–New York line, to inspire the songs of Gerry and the Pacemakers, the Remo Four and, of course, the Beatles. Even then, Liverpool remained a city of the Atlantic and the Empire, with its music inspired by slave descendants and its Swinging Sixties prosperity sitting on the infrastructure of the old colonial system.

Even with the advent of Indian and then Burmese independence in 1948, there was still little sense in swinging Liverpool that the end of Empire was imminent. British politicians might subtly have dropped the talk of colonies for the more consensual-sounding Commonwealth (now transformed from its pre-war identity as a White Dominion club into a more multiracial entity), but there remained

---

* The Sterling Area was a collection of mostly colonies and dominions of the British Empire (after 1949, the Commonwealth) which were heavily dependent upon the British market, did most of their trade in sterling, fixed their own currencies in relation to the pound and held some or all of their reserves in sterling.

a strong political conviction of the moral virtue and strategic necessity of Empire. Indeed, a renewed commitment to the bonds of Empire could be seen in the 1948 British Nationality Act, which gave all citizens of the Empire the right to live and work in the United Kingdom. In the eyes of the mother country all subjects of the Crown were equal – and soon enough the SS *Empire Windrush*, en route from Australia to England, dropped anchor at Kingston, Jamaica to pick up its 493 Caribbean passengers destined to dock at Tilbury in Essex in June 1948 (the dockyard from which Queen Elizabeth I had rallied her troops on the eve of the Spanish Armada in 1588). The *Empire Windrush*'s transatlantic voyage was followed later that year by the docking of SS *Orbita* with its 108 Caribbean migrants and SS *Reina del Pacifico* with its thirty-nine Jamaicans in Liverpool herself.

During the 1950s, in the wake of India and Burma, numerous other colonies would gain independence. Ghana and Nigeria, Jamaica, Trinidad and Barbados would, in the colonial mind-set of the day, be guided by British colonial officials towards autonomy, with ensuing membership of the Commonwealth the mark of their maturity. Even in the act of granting independence, Britain still regarded itself as a colonial power. The fiasco of the 1956 Suez Invasion of Egypt might reveal the dependency of the British military on US approval, and Prime Minister Harold Macmillan might tell the South African parliament in 1960 of the 'wind of change' blowing through the Continent, yet Britain remained convinced that some kind of colonial world-system, run through Whitehall, remained a viable possibility. There was a great deal of talk of 'managed withdrawals' and maintaining 'British connections' with former colonies under the tutelage of Westminster-style parliaments, the rule of law, embedded intelligence services and helpful trade contacts.

But the allure of liberty was altogether too powerful. Between 1945 and 1965 the number of people living under British colonial rule shrank from 700 million to 5 million, and the pace of decolonization accelerated with every passing year. With twenty-six countries gaining their independence from the British, an entire empire melted away within a generation. It was no wonder that mandarins in the Colonial Office, which once held sway over palm and pine across the globe, now fretted that their great department of state was being reduced to a ministry of 'rocks and islands', with little more than Gibraltar, Diego Garcia and the Falkland Islands to its name.[46]

The reality was that a decreasingly competitive British economy could no longer fund the military and organizational overheads of Empire. Britain's national debt levels and declining overseas income – in the face of Japanese, American and revived German competition – steadily crippled its economic capacity to act as a great power. As the pound sterling declined in value, its attractiveness as a reserve currency for Commonwealth countries similarly ebbed. Freer trade, the reduction in exchange controls and the increased attractiveness of the dollar all served to undermine the importance of the sterling area and, with it, some of the last advantages of Empire. Between 1950 and 1970, Britain's share of world exports dropped from 25 per cent to 8 per cent, and the amount of world trade denominated in sterling fell from 50 per cent to more like 20 per cent. For all the martial rhetoric, military adventurism and talk of colonial leadership, Britain no longer had the financial muscle to sustain its imperial ambition. What was more, the nature of global trade was changing: in place of the old model of shipping in raw materials to Liverpool and Glasgow, and turning out finished goods from Manchester and Clydeside, Britain's 'never had it so good' homeowners started to import consumer durables from America and Japan. After the initial postwar trade surge, the connection to smaller, less competitive and poorer Commonwealth markets began to crumble. Trade liberalization and the reviving markets of Western Europe came at the expense of traditional commercial ties to Britain's colonies.[47]

When the Empire did finally and conclusively capitulate, the consequences for a colonial city like Liverpool were catastrophic. The move away from a British economy based around raw material extraction on the edges of Empire and manufacturing production at the core – with the import-export business that all entailed – signalled a killer-blow to the shipping, storage, insurance, finance and trading activities of Merseyside. The port of Liverpool had been made by Empire, and as decolonization gathered pace, it was apparent it would be unmade by the end of Empire, just as rapidly and messily as those final years of imperial retreat. The bloody chaos of Kenya, Cyprus and Rhodesia found a domestic echo in the political and economic destruction of Liverpool.

The foreign consulates in Liverpool started to close, and less and less cargo found its way through the docks as colonial markets stagnated and the European Economic Community became a more lucrative trading bloc. As a result, Britain's port economy shifted south and east: between 1966 and 1985 Liverpool's share of all ship arrivals in the UK was halved, while Dover's increased by four and a half times. In the late 1960s Liverpool was still handling some 23 per cent of Britain's manufacturing exports, but a decade later this had fallen to under 10 per cent. Accompanying the changing trade patterns was the move from cargo liners to container ships, which had no need of the wharfs, quays and narrow docks of Liverpool. Instead, the containerization revolution of the 1960s concentrated larger vessels into fewer ports, with Felixstowe and Harwich gaining hold of the European cargoes coming in from Hamburg and Rotterdam. Liverpool responded with the development of its Seaforth docks in 1971, but it could do little to stem the haemorrhaging of trade. In 1985 Felixstowe berthed 496 container vessels of 20,000+ tons, Southampton managed 272, London 156, while Liverpool could only entice 76.[48] Containerization also meant much reduced local employment as cranes and terminals took the place of stevedores and dockers. By 1980 the number of dockworkers had fallen from its 1920 high of around 20,000 to little more than 4,000 (out of a total of over 600,000 jobs in the Merseyside area).[49] If that wasn't damaging enough, the growth of transatlantic air travel and the accompanying decline of the deep-sea passenger liners meant fewer city-centre hotels, waterfront business and ship repairs. For the port of Liverpool and its granite quaysides once as mighty as the Pyramids, decolonization and technological innovation combined to produce a perfect storm of economic immiseration.[50]

To which could then be added the effects of deindustrialization. The postwar expansion into light industry and car production had focused heavily on attracting foreign direct investment by the likes of Ford and Kodak, which meant that when the business cycle sagged strategic decisions about future capacity were rarely taken with the interests of Liverpool in mind. Too often, Merseyside resembled a branch-plant economy, and multinational corporations increasingly saw the merits of shifting production into cheap-labour, non-unionized developing nations and out of the old industrial centres. Absentee employers had little compulsion in closing plants and rationalizing production: between 1966 and 1977 nearly 350 factories in Liverpool closed, causing 40,000 job losses and a collapse in employment in the city by one-third.[51] In the words of Liverpool historian Stuart Wilks-Heeg, 'There can be no more dramatic a case of a city that had been a key driver of globalisation subsequently becoming one of its most significant victims.'[52]

Accompanying the flight of both trade and industry was the abdication of Liverpool's civic elites. The historian A. J. P. Taylor had once described his anguish at the decline of industrial Manchester and the postwar gentrification of its urban patriciate. 'The merchant princes have departed,' he mournfully noted in the 1950s. 'They are playing at country life in Cheshire or trying to forget Manchester in Bournemouth or Torquay. There are no more dinner-parties, no more bustle of social occasions.'[53] So too with Liverpool, as a series of amalgamations, take-overs and consolidations concentrated finance, management and legal services in London and threatened to turn Liverpool itself into a distant branch office. In 1969 Barclays Bank bought out the Bank of Liverpool and Martins Ltd, and the only major British bank with a head office outside London was gone. The great Merseyside businesses which had been built up around the shipping industry – its insurance, mergers and acquisitions, stock exchange – similarly sailed south. With the flight of white-collar work and the decline of regional financial systems, much of the upper-middle-class leadership evaporated. 'In Toxteth, the boarded-up properties, the empty, derelict, rubbish-strewn sites and the pervading street-corner atmosphere of hopelessness were proof of the long-term decline of the wider city,' concluded Michael Heseltine. 'The middle and professional classes, who had once inhabited this part of Liverpool, had long moved out to a more salubrious suburbia.'[54] Liverpool's tight civic circle of the exchange and the bank, town hall and chapel, lodge and liberal club was swapped for villas in the Wirral and the metropolitan power centres of Westminster and the City. As governor-generals lowered the Union flag across the capitals of the decolonizing British Empire, Merseyside's great commercial dynasties decamped from Liverpool.

Equally in danger was the city's proud heritage of multicultural equanimity. In truth, it had been under pressure since the early 1900s, when Liverpool's more assertive imperial identity started to crowd out the mid-nineteenth-century cosmopolitanism. Fears of mass Jewish migration, the rhetoric of the 1905 Aliens Act (restricting immigrants from outside the Empire), concerns about drugs and prostitution in Chinatown and dockside brawling by 'coloured seamen' tempered all that self-congratulation about Liverpool men being 'citizens of the world'. Instead, the *Liverpool Courier* ran prurient, fear-mongering features about Lascars and negroes 'Where East meets West', around St James's Place. 'You glimpse black figures beneath the gas lamps, and somehow you think of pimps, and bullies, and women, and birds of ill-omen generally, as now and again you notice a certain watchful callousness that seems to hint of nefarious trades and drunkenness in dark rooms.'[55] The expansiveness of Liverpool's horizon as a fulcrum of global trade and culture, the 'New York of Europe', was progressively challenged by a fear of migrants, ethnicity and miscegenation.

For all the lofty rhetoric of equal imperial citizenship behind the 1948 British Nationality Act, the Gateway of Empire now seemed to resent human remnants of Empire arriving on its shores. Notions of 'Britannic Nationalism' and the imperial family didn't extend to the hundreds of demobilized black British soldiers milling around Merseyside in the aftermath of the First World War. Having fought for the mother country during the war, they were then stranded in Liverpool with some waiting for the Colonial Office to repatriate them and others deciding to stay. In the summer of 1919, postwar unemployment, poverty and scarce resources in the city saw racial tension tip over into violence with an 'anti-black reign of terror' gripping dockside Liverpool on the nights of 9 and 10 June. Black seamen and sailors barricaded themselves into the Ethiopian Hall in the face of 5,000-strong white mobs chasing, beating, stabbing and even drowning any African they cornered – such as twenty-four-year-old Charles Wootton. D. T. Aleifasakure Toummanah, secretary of the Ethiopian

Hall, couched his demands for protection and support in the traditional language of colonial righteousness. 'Some of us have been wounded, and lost limbs and eyes fighting for the Empire of which we have the honour to belong . . . We ask for British justice, to be treated as true and loyal sons of Great Britain.'[56] Unfortunately, the officers in charge of administering that justice had a rather different perspective. 'The negroes would not have been touched but for their relations with white women. This has caused the entire trouble,' was the police response.[57] As a result, fifteen 'coloured men' found themselves at Liverpool Assizes in November 1919 on charges of 'riotous assembly and assault'.[58]

History repeated itself in 1948, when postwar demobilization of colonial soldiers led to more racial tension and rioting in Liverpool. Hostels for black seamen were attacked, Indian restaurants smashed up, and more random violence was inflicted on Africans and West Indians. Once again, the forces of law and order proved much keener on arresting black men than on protecting them from attack. Indeed, allegations of police brutality and racism towards Liverpool's black residents would be a long-running sore in the city, resurfacing with deadly anger in the Toxteth riots of 1981. By then, the cosmopolitanism of Liverpool was seen as much as a problem as a virtue, and a disaffected, alienated and unemployed black youth blamed for much of the disturbances. It was the second-generation offspring of Empire who were now blamed for bringing the Second City of Empire to its knees.

A TALE OF TWO TATES

By the time Liverpool 8 was alight and the Rialto Ballroom in flames, the decaying, declining Merseyside had become a postcolonial city. The *coup de grâce* had been delivered in 1968 when the Labour Party prime minister Harold Wilson announced the withdrawal of Britain's military commitments east of Suez. The winding-down of British bases in Singapore, Aden, Bahrain and Borneo signalled a final, clinical abandonment of Britain's Empire ambitions. Famously, the postwar American secretary of state Dean Acheson once remarked that Britain had lost an empire but was yet to find a role on the world stage. Three years after Wilson's announcement, in 1971, the Conservative prime minister Edward Heath sought to resolve any lingering confusions about the UK's post-imperial identity when he secured terms for Britain's entry into the European Economic Community. The Commonwealth and the old colonial order, it was announced, could no longer offer Britain 'comparable opportunities to membership of the European Community'. It was an unsentimental but acute reflection of commercial reality: in 1948 Britain sent 17.9 per cent of its visible exports to what would become EEC trading partners; by 1983 the EEC accounted for 43.4 per cent. Meanwhile, exports to the White Dominions and former colonies had declined from around 25 per cent of visible exports to more like 6 per cent over the same period. It was unavoidably apparent that the European Community was to fill the hole left by the dismemberment of Empire. None of this was good news for Liverpool.[59]

In 1747 the German scientist Andreas Sigismund Marggraf had discovered that sucrose could be isolated from beetroot, and a new crop entered into European agricultural production: sugar beet. The British blockade of France during the Napoleonic Wars, cutting off traditional supplies of sugar cane from her West Indian colonies, forced a much wider planting of the crop and, over the next 200 years, it became a staple part of northern European farming, until by the latter half of the twentieth century it was a cheaper alternative to African and Caribbean cane. Only Britain, led by Tate & Lyle, kept up decent trade connections with their former colonial cane exporters. Joining the European Economic Community on 1 January 1973 changed all that. In an instant, the big refineries switched from sugar cane to sugar beet: British farmers started to grow it, continental producers flooded the market with it, and European quotas ensured a steady supply. Though quietly investing in beet sugar processing plants in France, the colonially minded Tate & Lyle loudly bemoaned the impact of 'unfair' competition from Common Market sugar producers. By the late 1970s, the move to sugar beet was hammering the company's finances as it confronted falling profits, overcapacity and, in Liverpool, an increasingly uncompetitive refinery that cost £1.8 million a year to run. A child of Empire not Europe, facing westward not southerly, the beleaguered Love Lane sugar plant was a reluctant symbol of the desperate economic challenge Liverpool now faced.[60]

Its closure in 1981 marked the beginning of one of the bleakest decades in Liverpool's long history. During the riots, spiralling unemployment, strikes and urban flight that followed, Liverpool's population crashed from over 840,000 in the 1930s to some 500,000 in the early 1980s (settling, in 2011, at a figure of 466,400). 'They should build a fence around [Liverpool] and charge admission,' sighed the *Daily Mirror*. 'For sadly, it has become a "showcase" of everything that has gone wrong in Britain's major cities.'[61] Amid the economic meltdown, political extremism flourished. Liverpool had a long history of radical, progressive politics stretching back to the Independent Labour Party of the 1890s, the 1926 General Strike and continuing struggles over organized labour on the docks. But the city's dependence upon casual labour meant that a powerful, moderate trade union movement had never fully developed in the city (in contrast to, say, Manchester) and left the local Labour Party vulnerable to exploitation by Trotskyists. Under the banner of 'Militant Tendency', a powerful clique led by the charismatic Derek Hatton managed to gain control of the city council and systematically scare off any prospective investment, wreck the municipal finances and destroy the city's reputation. In Westminster, Cabinet ministers thought Liverpool almost beyond redemption. Worried about the heavy public cost of refloating the city, the chancellor of the exchequer, Sir Geoffrey Howe, urged instead a policy of strategic withdrawal. 'It would be regrettable if some of the brighter ideas for renewing economic activity were to be sown only on relatively stony ground on the banks of the Mersey,' he explained in a secret memorandum to Prime Minister Margaret Thatcher. 'I cannot help feeling that the option of managed decline is one which we should not forget altogether. We must not expend all our limited resources in trying to make water flow uphill.'[62]

Even worse than the government's policy of 'managed decline' was the way in which terrible events such as the 1989 Hillsborough disaster – when ninety-six football fans were crushed to death because of serious overcrowding at a match between Liverpool and Nottingham Forest at the Hillsborough Stadium in Sheffield – were turned against

Merseyside, as another example of the 'self-pity city', a lost civilization of welfare-dependent Scousers who refused to take responsibility for their lives. In the words of the *Spectator* magazine, it was part and parcel of the 'mawkish sentimentality', 'vicarious victimhood' and 'flawed psychological state' the entire city suffered from.[63] 'At the lowest point of its decline in the early 1990s, Liverpool descended into mass redundancy, failed strikes, depopulation, the anarchy of gang, gun and drug culture, the bottom of the league tables in all the indices of poverty and social exclusion,' recalled the Liverpool novelist Linda Grant. But what was worse was the 'venomous derision' for Liverpudlians, 'a form of racism' which condemned them all as 'thieves and scallies, rob-dogs and whiners'. 'You felt as if the rest of the country wanted Liverpool drowned just off the coast of Ireland with all its whingeing population. Liverpool was Britain's Detroit, a city that had died through its own irrelevance to the modern economy.'[64]

Eventually, assistance arrived – from the most unlikely of sources. The European Community might have pushed Liverpool to the brink of irrelevance, but now its Structural Funds Programme was set to return a pride and belief in the shattered city through a welcome wave of investment. Bullied by the European Commissioner for Regional Policy and ex-Glasgow MP Bruce Millan, the bureaucrats of Brussels, whose Common Agricultural Policy and Single Market had gutted the Liverpool economy, now poured tens of millions of pounds back into Merseyside. In 1993, the shocking state of Liverpool's post-industrial, post-imperial decline secured the city a much coveted Objective One status, triggering a cascade of Euro-cash for infrastructure, training and regeneration. The waterfront was beautified; the Rope Walks rebuilt; new galleries, museums and offices opened. In Jesse Hartley's Albert Dock, where sugar cane from the Caribbean had once sailed in, been warehoused and then transferred to the refineries, an altogether different branch of Tate now opened. In the mid-1980s the Tate Gallery (itself the product of sugar philanthropy) had decided to establish a regional outpost and, in the aftermath of the Toxteth riots, committed itself to Liverpool with a refitted site in the Albert Dock. In the north-west corner of Hartley's masterpiece, architects James Stirling and then Michael Wilford carved out a light, spacious, simple gallery for modern art that proved vital in anchoring the city's incremental, dockside regeneration. Soon, cafés, smart shops and TV studios lined the neo-classical arcades, and the Merseyside Maritime Museum became the most visible remaining link to the city's old shipping economy. The city which had once been the site of Tate's Love Lane refinery, now played host to Tate Liverpool, a media rather than manufacturing hub, underpinned by European rather than imperial riches.

Merseyside's assumption of its Continental identity was completed in 2008, when the city won the title of European 'Capital of Culture'. Its successful bid was built around the slogan 'The World in One City', a very conscious throw-back to the global, cosmopolitan Liverpool of the mid-nineteenth century. It was convincing enough to induce the Duke of Westminster, one of Britain's richest landowners, to sink £920 million into the Liverpool One shopping precinct close by the old docks. This was Liverpool as the Bilbao of northern England, with a regeneration strategy built around retail, the creative arts and an inclusive, trans-European identity. Suppressing a colonial past which had ended only a few decades previously, this increasingly prosperous, rebranded and better-governed Liverpool had no desire to point to its heritage as Queen of the Mersey, the Gateway of Empire. The memories of that recent past, which had taken the city to such heights of wealth and then plunged her into such despair, were too raw.

And yet, and yet, is there something in the spirit of Liverpool, with that taste of sea and sail in the air, the skeleton of docks and quays, the Liver Building and Nelson Monument, which still draws the city back to Empire? For all the European Union's Objective One generosity, Liverpool remains a port city, an outward-looking city, ineluctably attracted back to the rhythms of trade and power that encircle great empires. And in the twenty-first century, power has shifted from the Atlantic to the Pacific, from West to East. So, it is no surprise that Liverpool, more than any other British city, has decided its future fortunes lie with the largesse of a rising China.

This study of imperial cities began in the Mandarin Oriental Hotel, with British tai-pans of the Hong Kong Association paying court to the Chinese ambassador. The luncheon was a potent acknowledge-ment that Hong Kong – which for centuries had symbolized the aggressive, acquisitive, lucrative colonialism of the British abroad – had now itself become a symbol of Beijing's geo-political dominance. The handover was a passing of the baton from one power to another, readily traceable through the governance and culture of the 'Pearl of the Orient'. Now we have reached the end of the British Empire, this history ends in the city of Liverpool with the same forces at work. Just as those shifting ideologies and financial interests driving British colo-nialism had reshaped the civic fabric, economies, material culture and infrastructure of Bridgetown, Calcutta and Cape Town, so the con-cerns of China and India are reshaping our own cities.

For, as European funds decline, Liverpool's civic leaders have con-cluded that regeneration lies with the renminbi: the city has 'twinned' with Shanghai (whose celebrated pedestrian promontory, the Bund, was inspired by elements of the Liverpool waterfront), despatched Everton Football Club on a series of 'soft-power' friendlies, spruced up its own 'Chinatown', and opened the Liverpool Vision investment fund to lever-in Chinese resources. In a calculated display of 'win-win' harmony-building, the new Liverpool Museum has a special Liver-pool/Shanghai Exhibition, sponsored by Barclays Wealth, exploring the historic trading connection between Merseyside and 'The Paris of the Orient'.

Driving this Sino-Scouse collaboration is the Peel Group, which is hoping to revive the region's entrepôt economy with its £10 billion Liverpool Waters and Wirral Waters redevelopment scheme. This property fund-cum-investment vehicle is aiming at nothing less than rebuilding Liverpool as the Gateway of Empire with a £300 million port enlargement, centred on a deepwater quay on the Mersey to accommodate larger container ships (some coming from an expanded Panama Canal) and relieve docking congestion in the south-east. The 'Liverpool 2' terminal extension, set to open in 2015 with a 854-metre-long quay, will double the port's capacity and mean that container ships no longer have to pass through a series of restrictive locks.

But it is now a different empire that the Port of Liverpool is ser-vicing. In a total reversal of Lancashire and Liverpool's old export economy, the plan is for Chinese imports to be sailed down the Mersey and then transported along the Manchester Ship Canal straight into the north-west of England. This is Britain and Europe 'opened up'. Whereas once the produce of Chester, Manchester, Blackburn and Stoke-on-Trent would have flowed out of the Mersey to the free ports of Shanghai, Ningpo and Canton, now the consumer durables of Shenzhen, Tianjin and Guangzhou are heading into Britain through the Liverpool littoral. Their plastic and electronic wares will be unloaded at the 'trading outpost' of the £175 million Peel International Trade Centre, a vast warehousing and wholesaling facility. This modern-day godown – essentially a version of Jardine and Matheson's dockside developments of 1840s Hong Kong – is a 232,000-square-metre centre providing self-contained units for over 1,000 companies, drawn mainly from China and India, to sell, exhibit and distribute goods to European wholesale buyers. The International Trade Centre is set to complement the 'multimodal freight terminal' of Port Salford (with its 153,000 square metres of warehousing) and the suitably titled 'East Float' development at Wirral Waters. Behind Peel's development plans is a powerful set of Chinese investors. Heading the consortium is the Sam Wa Group, 'a global minerals importer and exporter based in Hong Kong and Jiangsu'. The Sam Wa Group's wealth is rooted in a series of exotic interests – jewellery exports to Jordan, manganese and copper mining in the Philippines, the American Banking Centre in Guangzhou (old Canton) – reminiscent of Joseph Conrad-style trading companies. And, as with many of the best colonial concerns, few in Liverpool seem interested in questioning the origins of these investment funds.[65]

Most startling of all within the Peel Group master scheme is its proposal to transform the UNESCO-listed Liverpool waterfront. Right next to the Three Graces, elegantly and elegiacally set back from the Mersey's edge, is planned a sixty-storey Shanghai Tower, which will entirely dwarf the Royal Liver Building. With it will come a 'Shanghai-style' high-rise waterfront – the Bund returning to reshape the cityscape which first inspired it – as well as 9,000 flats, office blocks, hotels, shops and restaurants. Not everyone along the Mersey is enamoured of the scheme. Faced with the transformation of its peninsula by Peel Holdings, in 2010 the Wirral Society of local conservationists condemned those 'who are dead set on restructuring the riverside entrance into the port of Liverpool in the style of Sydney, New York or Shanghai'. In the diffident language of a regional conservation group, they suggested, 'it is very feasible that many Wirralians will not like the idea of being Shanghai'd'. By contrast, in terms immediately reminiscent of those civic leaders in Dublin and Mumbai keen to expunge the remnants of a colonial history and embrace the globalized future, the leader of Liverpool City Council defended the Peel Group plan. 'We do not live in the past. We are not a museum.' Progress and growth mean facing up to often uncomfortable imperial realities.[66]

The people of the Wirral might well not want to be Shanghai'd. But, as Joseph Conrad first warned, Empire 'is not a pretty thing when you look into it too much'. After centuries of exporting our power abroad, Britain is now on the receiving end of Empire. American money is retreating and, in its place, influence and investment from China, India, South America and the Gulf States is flooding in. These sovereign wealth funds, well-oiled dynasties and state-backed banks are buying out businesses and funding infrastructure; taking over football clubs and endowing art galleries; reshaping neighbourhoods and concentrating wealth. A new imperial landscape is emerging. As in the British Empire before it, this history is being revealed through the streets and squares, sewers and monuments, architecture and corporations of our own freshly colonized cities.

Bibliography

Primary sources in chapters 1–10 are listed before secondary works.

GENERAL

British Parliamentary Papers.
The Economist.
Financial Times.
Liverpool Daily Post.
Louis, W. R. (ed.), *Oxford History of the British Empire*, 5 vols. (Oxford, 1998–9).
Marx, K. and Engels, F., *Collected Works* (New York, 1976–2004).
Oxford Dictionary of National Biography (Oxford, 2004–).
The Times.

INTRODUCTION

Beverley, E. L., 'Colonial Urbanism and South Asian Cities', *Social History*, 36, 4 (2011).
Blair, T., *A Journey* (London, 2010).
Campbell, A., *Diaries*, vol. 2: *Power and the People 1997–1999* (London, 2011).
Canny, N. (ed.), *The Oxford History of the British Empire*, vol. 1: *The Origins of Empire* (Oxford, 1998).
Chatterjee, P., *The Black Hole of Empire* (Princeton, 2012).
Conrad, J., *Heart of Darkness* (London, 1975).
Cunningham, P. (ed.), *The Letters of Horace Walpole, Earl of Oxford* (London, 1858).

Darwin, J., *Unfinished Empire: The Global Expansion of Britain* (London, 2012).

Davis, M., *Planet of Slums* (London, 2006).

Dirks, Nicholas B., *The Scandal of Empire: India and the Creation of Imperial Britain* (London, 2006).

Engelhart, K., 'Rule Britannia: Empire on Trial', *World Policy Journal*, 29, 4 (2012–13).

Ferguson, N., *Empire: How Britain Made the Modern World* (London, 2003).

Gott, R., *Britain's Empire: Resistance, Repression and Revolt* (London, 2011).

Harvey, D., 'The Right to the City', *New Left Review*, 53 (2008).

Kwarteng, K., *Ghosts of Empire: Britain's Legacies in the Modern World* (London, 2011).

Morris, J. and Winchester, S., *Stones of Empire* (Oxford, 2005).

Patten, C., *East and West: China, Power and the Future of Asia* (London, 1998).

Paxman, J., *Empire: What Ruling the World Did to the British* (London, 2011).

Porter, A. (ed.), *The Oxford History of the British Empire*, vol. 3: *The Nineteenth Century* (Oxford, 1999).

Ross, R. and Telkamp, G. J. (eds.), *Colonial Cities* (Leiden, 1985).

Said, E., *Culture and Imperialism* (London, 1994).

Sassen, S., *The Global City* (Princeton, 1991).

Seeley, J. R., *The Expansion of England* (London, 1895).

Urban World: Mapping the Economic Power of Cities, McKinsey Global Institute Report, March 2011.

CHAPTER 1: BOSTON

Burnaby, Rev. A., *Travels through the Middle Settlements in North-America. In the Years 1759 and 1760* (London, 1775).

Butterfield, L. H. (ed.), *The Adams Papers: Diary and Autobiography of John Adams* (Cambridge, Mass., 1961).

Cobbett, W., *Parliamentary History of England* (London, 1806–20).

Dunn, R., Savage, J. and Yeandle, L. (eds.), *The Journal of John Winthrop* (Cambridge, Mass., 1996).

Dunton, J., *John Dunton's Letters from New England* (Boston, 1867).

Ferguson, C., *A Letter Address'd to Every Honest Man in Britain* (London, 1738).

Franklin, B., *The Autobiography of Benjamin Franklin* (1793) (Philadelphia, 2005).

Franklin, B., *The Works of Benjamin Franklin* (Boston, 1837).

Jameson, J. F. (ed.), *Johnson's Wonder-Working Providence of Sion's Saviour in New England* (1654) (New York, 1910).

Labaree, L. W. (ed.), *The Papers of Benjamin Franklin* (New Haven, 2006).

Mather, Rev. C., *Magnalia Christi Americana; Or, The Ecclesiastical History of New England* (London, 1702).

Morton, N., *New England's Memorial* (Boston, 1772).

Nathaniel, B., *A Topographical and Historical Description of Boston* (Boston, 1871).

Neal, D., *History of New England* (London, 1720).

Papers of John Adams, Massachusetts Historical Society, 1977.

Pownall, T., *Administration of the Colonies* (London, 1764).

Shurtleff, N. B., *A Topographical and Historical Description of Boston* (Boston, 1871).

Strype, J., *Annals of the Reformation and Establishment of Religion and Various Other Occurrences in the Church of England*, vol. 2 (London, 1725).

Van Doren, M. (ed.), *Samuel Sewall Diary* (New York, 1963).

Winship, G. (ed.), *Boston in 1682 and 1699: A Trip to New England by Edward Ward and A Letter from New England by J. W.* (Providence, 1905).

Winsor, J. (ed.), *The Memorial History of Boston* (Boston, 1882).

Winthrop, J., *The Journal of John Winthrop, 1630–1649* (Cambridge, 1996).

Winthrop, J., *A Model of Christian Charity* (1630).

Winthrop, J., *Reasons for the Plantation in New England* (c. 1628).

Winthrop, R. (ed.), *Correspondence of Hartlib, Haak, Oldenburg and Others of the Royal Society with Governor Winthrop of Connecticut, 1661–1672* (Boston, 1878).

Wood, W., 'New England's Prospect', in Alexander Young (ed.), *Chronicles of the First Planters of the Colony of Massachusetts Bay* (Boston, 1846).

Young, A. (ed.), *Chronicles of the First Planters of the Colony of Massachusetts Bay* (Boston, 1846).

Alexander, J. K., *Samuel Adams: America's Revolutionary Politician* (Oxford, 2002).

Armitage, D., *Greater Britain, 1516–1776: Essays in Atlantic History* (Aldershot, 2004).

Armitage, D., *The Ideological Origins of the British Empire* (Cambridge, 2000).

Armitage, D. and Braddick, M. J. (eds.), *The British Atlantic World* (Basingstoke, 2002).

Bailyn, B., *The Ideological Origins of the American Revolution* (Cambridge, Mass., 1992).

Bailyn, B., '1776: A Year of Challenge – a World Transformed', *Journal of Law and Economics*, 19 (1976).

Bailyn, B. and Denault, P. L. (eds.), *Soundings in Atlantic History* (Cambridge, Mass., 2009).

Baltzell, E. D., *Puritan Boston and Quaker Philadelphia* (London, 1979).

Baxter, W. T., *The House of Hancock* (Cambridge, Mass., 1945).

Beach, S., *Samuel Adams: The Fateful Years* (Cornwallis, 1965).

Breen, T. H., '"Baubles of Britain": The American and Consumer Revolutions of the Eighteenth Century', *Past and Present*, 119 (1988).

Breen, T. H., 'An Empire of Goods: The Anglicization of Colonial America', *Journal of British Studies*, 25, 4 (1986).

Bremer, F. J., *John Winthrop* (Oxford, 2003).

Bridenbaugh, C., *Cities in Revolt: Urban Life in America, 1743–1776* (Oxford, 1955).

Bridenbaugh, C., *Cities in the Wilderness* (Oxford, 1970).

Bushman, R. L., *King and People in Provincial Massachusetts* (Chapel Hill, 1992).

Carp, B. L., *Defiance of the Patriots: The Boston Tea Party and the Making of America* (London, 2010).

Carp, B. L., *Rebels Rising: Cities and the American Revolution* (Oxford, 2007).

Deetz, J., *In Small Things Forgotten: The Archaeology of Early American Life* (New York, 1977).

DeJohn Anderson, V., 'New England in the Seventeenth Century', in Nicholas Canny (ed.), *The Oxford History of the British Empire*, vol. 1: *The Origins of Empire* (Oxford, 1998).

Gaustad, E., *Benjamin Franklin* (Oxford, 2006).

Gould, E. H., 'Revolution and Counter-Revolution', in D. Armitage and M. J. Braddick (eds.), *The British Atlantic World* (Hampshire, 2002).

Greene, J. P., *Pursuits of Happiness: The Social Development of Early Modern British Colonies and the Formation of American Culture* (Chapel Hill, 1988).

Hutson, J. H., *John Adams and the Diplomacy of the American Revolution* (Lexington, 1980).

Kay, J. H., *Lost Boston* (Boston, 1980).

McConville, B., *The King's Three Faces: The Rise and Fall of Royal America, 1688–1776* (Chapel Hill, 2006).

McCusker, J. J. and Menard, R. R., *The Economy of British America* (Chapel Hill, 1985).

MacInnes, A. I. and Williamson, A. H. (eds.), *Shaping the Stuart World* (Leiden, 2006).

Magra, C. P., *The Fisherman's Cause: Atlantic Commerce and Maritime Dimensions of the American Revolution* (Cambridge, 2009).

Marshall, P. J. (ed.), *The Oxford History of the British Empire*, vol. 2: *The Eighteenth- Century* (Oxford, 1998).

Miller, P., *Defining the Common Good: Empire, Religion and Philosophy in Eighteenth-Century Britain* (Cambridge, 2004).

Morgan, E., *The Puritan Dilemma: The Story of John Winthrop* (Boston, 1958).

Morison, S. E., *The Founding of Harvard College* (Cambridge, Mass., 1995).

Nash, G. B., *The Urban Crucible: The Northern Seaports and the Origins of the American Revolution* (Cambridge, Mass., 1986).

Parker, M., *The Sugar Barons: Family, Corruption, Empire and War* (London, 2011).

Reps, J. W., *The Making of Urban America* (New Jersey, 1965).

Rowe, A. (ed.), *Letters and Diary of John Rowe* (New York, 1969).

Rutman, D., *Winthrop's Boston: Portrait of a Puritan Town* (Chapel Hill, 1965).

Simms, B., *Three Victories and a Defeat* (London, 2007).

Stanwood, O., *The Empire Reformed: English America in the Age of the Glorious Revolution* (Philadelphia, 2011).

Stark, J. H., *The Loyalists of Massachusetts* (Boston, 1910).

Steele, I. K., *The English Atlantic 1675–1740: An Exploration of Communication and Community* (Oxford, 1995).

Thompson, E. P., 'The Moral Economy of the English Crowd in the Eighteenth Century', in E. P. Thompson, *Customs in Common* (London, 1993).

Tourtellot, A. B., *Benjamin Franklin: The Shaping of Genius* (New York, 1977).

Unger, H. G., *John Hancock* (New York, 2000).

Vaughan, A. T. (ed.), *The Puritan Tradition in America* (Hanover, NH, 1997).

Wright, E., *Benjamin Franklin: His Life as He Wrote It* (Cambridge, Mass., 1990).

CHAPTER 2: BRIDGETOWN

Anon., *News from Barbadoes* (London, 1676).

Atkins, J., *A Voyage to Guinea, Brazil and the West Indies* (1735) (London, 1970).

Bowen, E., *A Complete System of Geography* (London, 1747).

Coleridge, H. N., *Six Months in the West Indies in 1825*, 4th edition (London, 1841).

Dickson, W., *Letters on Slavery* (London, 1789).

Dickson, W., *Mitigation of Slavery* (1814) (Westport, 1970).

Eaden, J. (ed.), *The Memoirs of Père Labat* (1693–1705) (London, 1931).

Edwards, B., *The History Civil and Commerical, of the British West Indies* (London, 1819).

Edwards, B., *The History Civil and Commercial, of the British Colonies in the West Indies* (London, 1798).

Entick, J., *The Present State of the British Empire* (London, 1774).

Equiano, O., *The Interesting Narrative and Other Writings* (London, 1794).

Frere, H., *A Short History of Barbados* (London, 1768).

Froude, J. A., *The English in the West Indies* (London, 1888).

The Life and Works of John Adams (Boston, 1853).

Ligon, R., *A True and Exact History of the Island of Barbados* (London, 1673).

Madden, R. A., *A Twelvemonth's Residence in the West Indies* (London, 1835).

Oldmixon, J., *The British Empire in America* (London, 1708).

Orderson, J. W., *Creoleana: or, Social and Domestic Scenes and Incidents in Barbados in Days of Yore* (London, 1842).

Pinckard, G., *Notes on the West Indies*, 2nd edn (London, 1816).

Poyer, J., *The History of Barbados* (London, 1808).

Quennell, P. (ed.), *Memoirs of William Hickey* (London, 1960).

Smith, A., *An Enquiry into the Nature and Causes of the Wealth of Nations* (1776) (Harmondsworth, 1986).

Wedd, A. F. (ed.), *The Fate of the Fenwicks: Letters [Mainly Written by E. Fenwick] to Mary Hays (1798–1828)* (London, 1927).

The Winthrop Papers, vol. 1: *1498–1628* (Boston, 1925).

Alleyne, W., *Historic Bridgetown* (Bridgetown, 1978).

Armitage, D. and Braddick, M. J. (eds.), *The British Atlantic World* (Basingstoke, 2002).

Beckles, H. M., *A History of Barbados* (Cambridge, 1990).

Blackburn, R., *The Making of New World Slavery* (London, 1997).

Bowden, M. J., 'Three Centuries of Bridgetown: An Historical Geography', *Journal of the Barbados Museum and Historical Society*, 49 (2003).

Canny, N. and Pagden, A. (eds.), *Colonial Identity in the Atlantic World* (Princeton, 1987).

Connell, N., 'Prince William Henry's Visits to Barbados in 1786 and 1789', *Journal of the Barbados Museum and Historical Society*, 25, 4 (1958).

Devine, T. W., *To the Ends of the Earth: Scotland's Global Diaspora, 1750–2010* (London, 2011).

Drayton, R., 'The Collaboration of Labour: Slaves, Empires and Globalizations in the Atlantic World, *c.* 1600–1850', in A. G. Hopkins (ed.), *Globalization in World History* (London, 2002).

Duffy, M., *Soldiers, Sugar, and Seapower* (Oxford, 1987).

Earle, P., *The World of Defoe* (London, 1976).

Fraser, H., 'Historic Bridgetown – Development and Architecture', in W. Marshall and P. Welch (eds.), *Beyond the Bridge* (Cave Hill, 2005).

Greene, J. P., 'Changing Identity in the British Caribbean: Barbados as a Case Study', in Nicholas Canny and Anthony Pagden (eds.), *Colonial Identity in the Atlantic World* (Princeton, 1987).

Greene, J. P. (ed.), *Exclusionary Empire: English Liberty Overseas 1600–1900* (Cambridge, 2010).

Greene, J. P., 'Liberty and Slavery', in J. P. Greene (ed.), *Exclusionary Empire: English Liberty Overseas 1600–1900* (Cambridge, 2010).

Harlow, V. T., *A History of Barbados* (Oxford, 1926).

Hopkins, A. G. (ed.), *Globalization in World History* (London, 2002).

James, C. L. R., *The Black Jacobins* (London, 2001).

Marshall, P. J. (ed.), *The Oxford History of the British Empire*, vol. 2: *The Eighteenth Century* (Oxford, 1998).

Marshall, W. and Welch, P. (eds.), *Beyond the Bridge* (Cave Hill, 2005).

Marx, K., *Capital* (London, 1990).

O'Shaughnessy, A. J., *An Empire Divided: The American Revolution and the British Caribbean* (Philadelphia, 2000).

Parker, M., *The Sugar Barons: Family, Corruption, Empire and War* (London, 2011).

Potter, R. (ed.), *Urbanization, Planning and Development in the Caribbean* (London, 1989).

Potter, R. B. and Wilson, M., 'Barbados', in R. B. Potter (ed.), *Urbanization, Planning and Development in the Caribbean* (London, 1989).

Sheridan, R. B., 'Caribbean Plantation Society, 1689–1748', in P. J. Marshall (ed.), *The Oxford History of the British Empire*, vol. 2: *The Eighteenth Century* (Oxford, 1998).

Sheridan, R., *Sugar and Slavery* (London, 1974).

Smith, S. D., 'Gedney Clarke of Salem and Barbados: Transatlantic Super-Merchant', *The New England Quarterly*, 76, 4 (December 2003).

Smith, S. D., *Slavery, Family and Gentry Capitalism in the British Atlantic: The World of the Lascelles, 1648–1834* (Cambridge, 2006).

Solow, B. L. and Engerman, S. L. (eds.), *British Capitalism and Caribbean Slavery* (Cambridge, 1987).

Steele, I. K., *The English Atlantic 1675–1740: An Exploration of Communication and Community* (Oxford, 1986).

Walvin, J., *Atlas of Slavery* (Edinburgh, 2006).

Watson, K., *The Civilised Island, Barbados: A Social History, 1750–1816* (Bridgetown, 1979).

Welch, P., *Slave Society in the City: Bridgetown, Barbados, 1680–1834* (Oxford, 2003).

Williams, E., *Capitalism and Slavery* (Chapel Hill, 1944).

CHAPTER 3: DUBLIN

Anon., *The History of Ned Evans* (London, 1797).

Barnes, G., *A Statistical Account of Ireland Formed on Historical Facts* (London, 1811).

Barrington, J., *Historic Memoirs of Ireland* (London, 1835).

Campbell, T., *A Philosophical Survey of the South of Ireland* (London, 1777).

Carr, J., *The Stranger in Ireland; or, a Tour in the Southern and Western Parts of That Country in the Year 1805* (London, 1806).

Cooke, E., *Pro and Con: Being an Impartial Abstract of the Principal Publications on the Subject of Legislative Union* (Dublin, 1800).

Copeland, T. et al. (eds.), *The Correspondence of Edmund Burke* (Cambridge, 1958–70).

Cromwell, T., *Excursions Through Ireland* (London, 1820).

De Latocnaye, *A Frenchman's Walk through Ireland* (1798) (Cambridge, 1984).

Gamble, J., *Sketches of History, Politics and Manners in Dublin and the North of Ireland in 1810* (London, 1826).

Gilbert, J. T., *A History of the City of Dublin* (Dublin, 1859).

Jefferys, N., *An Englishman's Descriptive Account of Dublin* (London, 1810).

Lecky, W. E. H., *Ireland in the Eighteenth Century* (1892) (London, 1913).

McGregor, J. J., *New Picture of Dublin* (Dublin, 1821).

Malton, J., *A Picturesque and Descriptive View of the City of Dublin* (1799) (Dublin, 1980).

Melville, E., *Sketches of Society in France and Ireland in the years 1805–6–7 by a Citizen of the United States* (Dublin, 1811).

Owenson, S., *Florence Macarthy* (1818) (New York, 1979).

Parliamentary History, 34 (London, 1815).

Pool, R. and Cash, J., *Views of the Most Remarkable Public Buildings, Monuments & Other Edifices in the City of Dublin* (Dublin, 1780).

Speech of the Rt. Hon. William Pitt in the British House of Commons on Thursday 31 January 1799 (London, 1799).

Stanlis, P. J. (ed.), *Edmund Burke: Selected Writings and Speeches* (New Brunswick, 2009).

Two Views of British India: The Private Correspondence of Mr Dundas and Lord Wellesley, 1798–1801, ed. Edward Ingram (Bath, 1970).

Wakefield, E., *An Account of Ireland Statistical and Political* (London, 1812).

Warburton, J., Whitelaw, J. and Walsh, R. (eds.), *History of the City of Dublin from the Earliest Accounts to the Present Time* (London, 1818).

Young, A., *A Tour in Ireland* (Cambridge, 1983).

Ardill, J. R., *The Closing of the Irish Parliament* (Dublin, 1907).

Bartlett, T., 'Ireland, Empire, and Union, 1690–1801', in Kevin Kenny (ed.), *Ireland and the British Empire* (Oxford, 2004), pp. 60–71.

Bartlett, T., '"This Famous island set in a Virginian Sea": Ireland in the British Empire, 1690–1801', in P. J. Marshall (ed.), *The Oxford History of the British Empire*, vol. 2: *The Eighteenth Century* (Oxford, 2001), pp. 253–75.

Bew, J., *Castlereagh* (London, 2011).

Bew, P., *Ireland: The Politics of Enmity 1789–2006* (Oxford, 2007).

Boyd, G. A., *Dublin 1745–1922: Hospitals, Spectacle and Vice* (Dublin, 2006).

Brady, J. and Simms, A. (eds.), *Dublin through Space and Time* (Dublin, 2001).

Brown, M., Geoghegan, P. M. and Kelly, J. (eds.), *The Irish Act of Union 1800* (Dublin, 2003).

Burns, K., 'The History of 29 FitzWilliam Street', *Dublin Historical Record*, 57, 1 (2004).

Butel, P. and Cullen, L. M. (eds.), *Cities and Merchants: French and Irish Perspectives on Urban Development, 1500–1900* (Dublin, 1986).

Clark, P. and Gillespie, R., *Two Capitals: London and Dublin, 1500–1800* (Oxford, 2001).

Clarke, H., *Dublin* (London, 1976).

Connolly, S. J. (ed.), *Kingdoms United? Great Britain and Ireland since 1500* (Dublin, 1999).

Craig, M., *Dublin, 1660–1860: A Social and Architectural History* (Dublin, 1969).

Crosbie, B., *Irish Imperial Networks: Migration, Social Communication and Exchange in Nineteenth-Century India* (Cambridge, 2012).

Darwin, J., *Unfinished Empire: The Global Expansion of Britain* (London, 2012).

Dickson, D. (ed.), *The Gorgeous Mask: Dublin, 1700–1850* (Dublin, 1987).

Foster, R. F., *Modern Ireland 1600–1972* (London, 1988).

Fraser, M., 'Public Building and Colonial Policy in Dublin, 1760–1800', *Architectural History*, 28 (1985).

Hague, W., *William Pitt the Younger* (London, 2004).

Hill, C., *God's Englishman: Oliver Cromwell and the English Revolution* (London, 2000).

James, F. G., 'Irish Colonial Trade in the Eighteenth Century', *The William and Mary Quarterly*, 3rd Series, 20, 4 (1963).

Kearns, K. C., *Georgian Dublin: Ireland's Imperilled Architectural Heritage* (London, 1983).

Kearns, K. C., 'Preservation and Transformation of Georgian Dublin', *Geographical Review*, 72, 3 (1982).

Kelly, J., 'The Origins of the Act of Union: An Examination of Unionist Opinion in Britain and Ireland, 1650–1800', *Irish Historical Studies*, 25 (1986–7).

Kenny, K. (ed.), *Ireland and the British Empire* (Oxford, 2004).

Keogh, D. and Whelan, K. (eds.), *Acts of Union* (Dublin, 2001).

Kincaid, A., *Postcolonial Dublin* (Minneapolis, 2006).

Livesey, J., *Civil Society and Empire* (London, 2009).

Luckett, R., *Handel's Messiah: A Celebration* (London, 1992).

Lynch, P., 'A Dublin Street: North Great George's Street', *Dublin Historical Record*, 31, 1 (1977).

McCullough, N., *Dublin: An Urban History* (Dublin, 1989).

McCullough, N., *A Vision of the City: Dublin and the Wide Street Commissioners* (Dublin, 1991).

McDowell, R. B., *Ireland in the Age of Imperialism and Revolution* (London, 1991).

McParland, E., 'Strategy in the Planning of Dublin, 1750–1800', in P. Butel and L. M. Cullen (eds.), *Cities and Merchants: French and Irish Perspectives on Urban Development, 1500–1900* (Dublin, 1986).

McParland, E., 'The Wide Streets Commissioners', *Quarterly Bulletin of the Irish Georgian Society*, 15, 1 (1972).

Marx, K. and Engels, F., *Collected Works*, vols. 40 and 43 (New York, 1983).

Maxwell, C., *Dublin under the Georges* (London, 1956).

Maxwell, C., *The Stranger in Ireland* (London, 1954).

Mooney, T. and White, F., 'The Gentry's Winter Season', in David Dickson (ed.), *The Gorgeous Mask: Dublin, 1700–1850* (Dublin, 1987).

Nash, R. C., 'Irish Atlantic Trade in the Seventeenth and Eighteenth Centuries', *The William and Mary Quarterly*, 3rd Series, 42, 3 (1985).

O'Brien, A., 'The History of Nelson's Pillar', *Dublin Historical Record*, 60, 1 (2007).

O'Brien, G., '"What can possess you to go to Ireland?": Visitors' Perceptions of Dublin, 1800–30', in G. O'Brien and F. O'Kane (eds.), *Georgian Dublin* (Dublin, 2008), p. 23.

O'Brien, G. and O'Kane, F. (eds.), *Georgian Dublin* (Dublin, 2008).

Ohlmeyer, J. H., '"Civilizinge of those Rude Partes": Colonization within Britain and Ireland, 1580s–1640s', in Nicholas Canney (ed.), *The Oxford History of the British Empire*, vol. 1: *The Origins of Empire* (Oxford, 1998).

Sheridan, E., 'Designing the Capital City: Dublin, 1660–1810', in Joseph Brady and Anngret Simms (eds.), *Dublin through Space and Time* (Dublin, 2001).

Sheridan-Quantz, E., 'The Multi-Centred Metropolis: The Social Topography of Eighteenth-Century Dublin', in Peter Clark and Raymond Gillespie (eds.), *Two Capitals: London and Dublin, 1500–1840* (Oxford, 2001).

Somerville-Large, P., *Dublin: The First Thousand Years* (London, 1988).

CHAPTER 4: CAPE TOWN

Barrow, J., *An Account of Travels into the Interior of South Africa* (London, 1801).

Burchell, W. J., *Travels in the Interior of Southern Africa* (London, 1822).

Campbell, J., *Travels in South Africa, Undertaken at the Request of the Missionary Society* (London, 1815).

Champion, G., *The Journal of an American Missionary* (Cape Town, 1968).

Colquhoun, P., *A Treatise on the Wealth, Power and Resources of the British Empire, in Every Quarter of the World, Including the East Indies* (London, 1815).

Fisher, R. B., *The Importance of the Cape of Good Hope, as a Colony to Great Britain, Independently of the Advantages It Possesses as a Military and Naval Station, and the Key to Our Territorial Possessions in India* (London, 1816).

Fitzroy, R., *The Weather Book: A Manual of Practical Meteorology* (London, 1863).

Ingram, E. (ed.), *Two Views of British India: The Private Correspondence of Mr Dundas and Lord Wellesley* (Bath, 1970).

Kindersley, J., *Letters from the Island of Teneriffe, Brazil, the Cape of Good Hope, and the East Indies* (London, 1777).

Kolben, P., *The Present State of the Cape of Good Hope* (London, 1731).

Lewin Robinson, A. M. (ed.), *The Cape Journals of Lady Anne Barnard, 1797–1798* (Cape Town, 1994).

Lewin Robinson, A. M. (ed.), *The Letters of Lady Anne Barnard to Henry Dundas from the Cape and Elsewhere, 1793–1803* (Cape Town, 1973).

Parliamentary Register, vol. 14 (London, 1801).

Percival, R., *An Account of the Cape of Good Hope* (London, 1804).

Quennell, P. (ed.), *The Memoirs of William Hickey* (London, 1960).

Semple, R., *Walks and Sketches at the Cape of Good Hope* (London, 1805).

Shrubsole, W., *Plea in Favour of the Shipwrights Belonging to the Royal Dock Yards* (Rochester, 1770).

Sparrman, A., *A Voyage to the Cape of Good Hope* (Dublin, 1785).

Stavorinus, J., *Voyages to the East Indies* (London, 1798).

Theal, G. M. (ed.), *Records of the Cape Colony* (London, 1897–1905).

Trollope, A., *South Africa* (London, 1878).

Bayly, C. A. *Imperial Meridian: The British Empire and the World, 1780–1830* (London, 1989).

Bickford-Smith, V., 'Creating a City of the Tourist Imagination', *Urban Studies*, 46, 9 (2009).

Boxer, C. R., *The Dutch Seaborne Empire* (London, 1977).

Bradlow, F., *Early Cape Muslims* (Cape Town, 1978).

The Buildings of Central Cape Town, vol. 1: *Formative Influences and Classification* (Cape Town, 1978).

Burman, J., *The Bay of Storms* (Cape Town, 1976).

Darwin, J., *Unfinished Empire: The Global Expansion of Britain* (London, 2012).

Duffy, M., 'World-Wide War and British Expansion, 1793–1815', in P. J. Marshall (ed.), *The Oxford History of the British Empire*, vol. 2: *The Eighteenth Century* (Oxford, 1998).

Hamilton, C., Mbenga, B. K. and Ross, R. (eds.), *The Cambridge History of South Africa*, vol. 1 (Cambridge, 2010).

Irwin, D. A., 'Mercantilism and Strategic Trade Policy: The Anglo-Dutch Rivalry for the East India Trade', *Journal of Political Economy*, 99, 6 (1991).

Jasanoff, M., *Edge of Empire* (London, 2006).

Kennedy, P. M., *The Rise and Fall of British Naval Mastery* (London, 1976).

Knight, R., *Britain Against Napoleon* (London, 2013).

Malherbe, V., 'Christian-Muslim Marriage and Cohabitation: An Aspect of Identity and Family Formation in Nineteenth-Century Cape Town', *Journal of Imperial and Commonwealth History*, 36, 1 (2008).

Marshall, P. J., 'Britain and the World in the Eighteenth Century, I: Reshaping the Empire', *Transactions of the RHS*, 6th Series, 8, 10 (1998).

Marshall, P. J. (ed.), *The Oxford History of the British Empire*, vol. 2: *The Eighteenth Century* (Oxford, 1998).

Millar, A. K., *Plantagenet in Africa: Lord Charles Somerset* (Cape Town, 1965).

Pama, C., *Bowler's Cape Town* (Cape Town, 1977).

Pama, C., *Regency Cape Town* (Cape Town, 2008).

Porter, A. (ed.), *The Oxford History of the British Empire*, vol. 3: *The Nineteenth Century* (Oxford, 1999).

Rodger, N. A. M., *The Command of the Ocean* (London, 2004).

Ross, R. and Telkamp, G. (eds.), *Colonial Cities: Essays on Urbanism in a Colonial Context* (Dordrecht, 1985).

Saunder, C. and Smith, I. R., 'Southern Africa, 1795–1910', in A. Porter (ed.), *The Oxford History of the British Empire*, vol. 3: *The Nineteenth Century* (Oxford, 1999).

Seemann, U. A., *Fortification of the Cape Peninsula* (Cape Town, 1997).

Thompson, L., *A History of South Africa* (London, 1990).

Turner, L. C. F., 'The Cape of Good Hope and Anglo-French Conflict, 1797–1806', *Historical Studies, Australia and New Zealand*, 9, 36 (1961).

Viney, G. and Brooke Simons, P., *The Cape of Good Hope* (Houghton, 1994).

Willis, S., *In the Hour of Victory* (London, 2013).

Wilson, M., 'The Hunters and the Herders', in Monica Wilson and Leonard Thompson (eds.), *A History of South Africa to 1870* (London, 1982).

Wilson, M. and Thompson, L. (eds.), *A History of South Africa to 1870* (London, 1982).

Worden, N. (ed.), *Cape Town: Between East and West* (Auckland Park, 2012).

Worden, N., van Heyningen, E. and Bickford-Smith, V., *Cape Town: The Making of a City* (Claremont, 1998).

CHAPTER 5: CALCUTTA

Anon., *Hartly House, Calcutta: A Novel of the Days of Warren Hastings* (1789)(London, 1989).

Bolts, W., *Considerations on India Affairs* (London, 1772).

Cunningham, P. (ed.), *The Letters of Horace Walpole, Earl of Oxford* (London, 1858).

Curzon, Lord, *British Government in India* (London, 1925).

Dowie, J. (ed.), *Macaulay's Essay on Clive* (1840) (London, 1900).

Essays by Students of the College of Fort William in Bengal (Calcutta, 1820).

Fay, E., *Original Letters from India* (Calcutta, 1817).

Fenton, E., *The Journal of Mrs Fenton. A Narrative of Her Life in India, the Isle of France, and Tasmania During the Years 1826–30* (London, 1901).

Gleig, G. R., *The Life of Major-General Sir Thomas Munro* (London, 1830).

Graham, M., *Journal of a Residence in India* (Edinburgh, 1813).

Hudson, R. (ed.), *William Hickey: Memoirs of a Georgian Rake* (London, 1995).

Ingram, E. (ed.), *Two Views of British India: The Private Correspondence of Mr Dundas and Lord Wellesley* (Bath, 1970).

Kindersley, J., *Letters from the Island of Teneriffe, Brazil, the Cape of Good Hope, and the East Indies* (London, 1777).

Kipling, R., *The City of Dreadful Night and Other Places* (Allahabad, 1891).

Lewin Robinson, A. M. (ed.), *The Letters of Lady Anne Barnard to Henry Dundas from the Cape and Elsewhere, 1793–1803* (Cape Town, 1973).

Martin, J. R., *Notes on the Medical Topography of Calcutta* (Calcutta, 1837).

Martin, M. (ed.), *The Despatches, Minutes and Correspondence of the Marquess Wellesley K. G., During His Administration in India* (London, 1836).

Monkland, A. C ., *Life in India: Or, The English at Calcutta* (London, 1828).

Owen, S. J. (ed.), *A Selection from the Despatches, Treaties, and Other Papers of the Marquess Wellesley, K.G. during His Government of India* (Oxford, 1877).

Pearce, R. (ed.), *Memoirs and Correspondence of the Most Noble Richard, Marquess Wellesley, K.G.* (London, 1861).

Quennell, P. (ed.), *Memoirs of William Hickey* (London, 1960).

Seton-Karr, W. S. (ed.), *Selections from Calcutta Gazettes* (London, 1864–9).

Shushtari, S., *Kitab Tuhfat al-'Alam* (Bombay, 1847).

Stavorinus, J., *Voyages to the East Indies* (London, 1798).

Trevelyan, G. O., *Life and Letters of Lord Macaulay* (London, 1881).

Valentia, George, Viscount, *Voyages and Travels to India* (London, 1809).

Woodrow, H., *Macaulay's Minutes on Education in India, Written in the Years 1835, 1836, and 1837* (Calcutta, 1862).

Bach, B. P., *Calcutta's Edifice: The Buildings of a Great City* (New Delhi, 2006).

Banerjea, D., *European Calcutta* (New Delhi, 2005).

Butler, I., *The Eldest Brother: The Marquess of Wellesley, the Duke of Wellington's Eldest Brother* (London, 1973).

Chatterjee, P., 'Are Indian Cities Becoming Bourgeois At Last?' in P. Chatterjee, *The Politics of the Governed* (New York, 2004).

Chatterjee, P., *The Black Hole of Empire* (Princeton, 2012).

Chatterjee, P., *Empire and Nation* (New York, 2010).

Chatterjee, P., *The Politics of the Governed* (New York, 2004).

Chattopadhyay, S., 'Blurring Boundaries: The Limits of "White Town" in Colonial Calcutta', *Journal of the Society of Architectural Historians*, 59, 2 (2000).

Chattopadhyay, S., *Representing Calcutta: Modernity, Nationalism, and the Colonial Uncanny* (London, 2005).

Chaudhuri, K. N., *The English East India Company* (London, 1965).

Chaudhuri, S. (ed.), *Calcutta: The Living City* (Oxford, 1990).

Dalrymple, W., *White Mughals* (London, 2004).

Dirks, N. B., *The Scandal of Empire* (London, 2006).

Ghosh, D., *Sex and the Family in Colonial India* (Cambridge, 2006).

Ghosh, D. and Kennedy, D. (eds.), *Decentring Empire: Britain, India and the Transcolonial World* (New Delhi, 2006).

Guha, R., *A Rule of Property for Bengal* (New Delhi, 1981).

Gupta, P. D., *Ten Walks in Calcutta* (Kolkata, 2008).

Gupta, S., 'Theory and Practice of Town Planning in Calcutta, 1817–1912', *Indian Economic and Social History Review*, 30, 1 (1993).

Hawes, C. J., *Poor Relations: The Making of a Eurasian Community in British India, 1773–1833* (London, 1996).

Kincaid, D., *British Social Life in India, 1608–1937* (London, 1938).

Kling, B. B., *Partner in Empire: Dwarkanath Tagore and the Age of Enterprise in Eastern India* (Calcutta, 1981).

Kopf, D., *British Orientalism and the Bengal Renaissance: The Dynamics of Indian Modernization, 1773–1835* (Berkeley, 1969).

Losty, J. P., *Calcutta: City of Palaces* (London, 1990).

Marshall, P. J. (ed.), *The British Discovery of Hinduism* (Cambridge, 1970).

Marshall, P. J., 'The British in Asia, 1700–1765', in P. J. Marshall (ed.), *The Oxford History of the British Empire*, vol. 2: *The Eighteenth Century* (Oxford, 1998).

Marshall, P. J., *The Making and Unmaking of Empires: Britain, India and America* (Oxford, 2005).

Marshall, P. J. (ed.), *The Oxford History of the British Empire*, vol. 2: *The Eighteenth Century* (Oxford, 1998).

Marshall, P. J., 'The White Town of Calcutta under the Rule of the East India Company', *Indo-British Review*, 21 (1996).

Moon, P., *The British Conquest and Dominion of India* (London, 1989).

Moorhouse, G., *Calcutta* (London, 1998).

Morris, J. and Winchester, S., *Stones of Empire* (Oxford, 2005).

Mukherjee, S. N., *Calcutta: Essays in Urban History* (Calcutta, 1993).

Raj, K., 'Colonial Encounters and the Forging of New Knowledge and National Identities: Great Britain and India, 1760–1850', *Osiris*, 2nd Series, 15 (2000).

Raj, K., *Relocating Modern Science: Circulation and the Construction of Knowledge in South Asia, 1650–1900* (Basingstoke, 2007).

Robins, N., *The Corporation that Changed the World* (London, 2006).

Severn, J., *Architects of Empire: The Duke of Wellington and His Brothers* (Norman, 2007).

Sinha, P., 'Calcutta and the Currents of History, 1690–1912', in Sukanta Chaudhuri (ed.), *Calcutta: The Living City* (Oxford, 1990).

Sreemani, S., *Anatomy of a Colonial Town: Calcutta, 1756–1794* (Calcutta, 1994).

Stokes, E., *The English Utilitarians and India* (Oxford, 1963).

Teltscher, K., *India Inscribed: European and British Writings on India, 1600–1800* (New Delhi, 1995).

Travers, R., *Ideology and Empire in Eighteenth-Century India* (Cambridge, 2007).

Webster, A., *The Richest East India Merchant: The Life and Business of John Palmer of Calcutta* (Leicester, 2007).

CHAPTER 6: HONG KONG

Belcher, E., *Narrative of a Voyage Round the World, Performed in Her Majesty's Ship Sulphur, during the Years 1836–1842* (London, 1843).

Bingham, J. E., *Narrative of the Expedition to China, from the Commencement of the War to Its Termination in 1842* (London, 1853).

Cunynghame, A., *An Aide-de-Camp's Recollections of Service in China* (London, 1844).

Disraeli, B., *Sybil, or, The Two Nations* (1845) (London, 1980).

Eitel, E. J., *Europe in China* (1895) (Oxford, 1983).

Endacott, G. B. (ed.), *An Eastern Entrepôt* (London, 1964).

Hall, W. H. and Bernard, W. D., *Narrative of the Voyages and Services of the Nemesis* (London, 1845).

Hamilton Lindsay, H., *Letter to the Right Honourable Viscount Palmerston on British Relations with China* (London, 1836).

Hodder, E. (ed.), *The Life and Work of the Seventh Earl of Shaftesbury, K.G.* (London, 1886).

Kipling, R., *From Sea to Sea: Letters of Travel* (London, 1888).

Legge, H. E., *James Legge: Missionary and Scholar* (London, 1905).

Legge, Rev. J., 'The Colony of Hong Kong' (1872), *Journal of the Royal Asiatic Society Hong Kong Branch*, 11 (1971).

Le Pichon, A. (ed), *China Trade and Empire: Jardine, Matheson & Co. and the Origins of British Rule in Hong Kong 1827–1843* (Oxford, 2006).

The Letters of Queen Victoria: A Selection from Her Majesty's Correspondence between the Years 1837 and 1861, vol. 1: *1837–1843* (London, 1907), vol. 2: *1844–1861* (London 1908).

Macgowan, J., *How England Saved China* (London, 1913).

Matheson, J., *The Present Position and Prospects of the British Trade with China* (London, 1836).

Milne, R. G., *Sinim: A Plea for China. A Discourse Delivered in Providence Chapel, Whitehaven* (London, 1843).

Minute by Sir T. S. Raffles on the Establishment of a Malay College at Singapore, 1819, British Library D742/38, Microfilm No. NAB 083.

Nicolson, H., *Curzon* (London, 1934).

Redesdale, Lord, *The Attaché at Peking* (London, 1900).

Report from the Select Committee on Commercial Relations with China (London, 1847).

Sirr, H. C., *China and the Chinese: Their Religion, Character, Customs and Manufactures* (London, 1849).

Smith, A., *To China and Back* (1859) (Hong Kong, 1974).

Smith, G., *A Narrative of an Exploratory Visit to each of the Consular Cities of China and to the Islands of Hong Kong and Chusan* (London, 1847).

Tao, W., 'My Sojourn in Hong Kong', translated by Yang Qinghua, in *Renditions*, Special Issue, 29–30 (1988).

Tiffany, O., *The Canton Chinese: or, The American's Sojourn in the Celestial Empire* (Boston, 1849).

Verne, J., *Around the World in Eighty Days* (1873) (London, 2012).

Wood, W. M., *Fankwei: or, The San Jacinto in the Seas of India, China and Japan* (New York, 1859).

Bickers, R., *The Scramble for China* (London, 2011).

Bickers, R., 'Shanghailanders: The Formation and Identity of the British Settler Community in Shanghai 1843–1937', *Past and Present*, 159 (1998).

Blake, R., *Jardine Matheson: Traders of the Far East* (London, 1999).

Brook, T. and Wakabayashi, B. T. (eds.), *Opium Regimes: China, Britain and Japan* (London, 2000).

Carroll, J. M., *A Concise History of Hong Kong* (Plymouth, 2007).

Carroll, J. M., *Edge of Empire: Chinese Elites and British Colonials in Hong Kong* (London, 2005).

Chan, M. K. (ed.), *Precarious Balance: Hong Kong between China & Britain, 1842–1992* (New York, 1994).

Crisswell, C., *The Taipans: Hong Kong's Merchant Princes* (Oxford, 1981).

Endacott, G. B., *A History of Hong Kong* (London, 1958).

Faure, D. (ed.), *Society: A Documentary History of Hong Kong* (Hong Kong, 1997).

Gallagher, J. and Robinson, R., 'The Imperialism of Free Trade', *The Economic History Review*, 6, 1 (1953).

Ghosh, A., *Sea of Poppies* (London, 2009).

Greenberg, M., *British Trade and the Opening of China 1800–1842* (Cambridge, 1951).

Holtrop, P. N. and McLeod, H. (eds.), *Missions and Missionaries* (Woodbridge, 2000).

Home, R. K., 'Colonial Town Planning in Malaysia, Singapore and Hong Kong', *Planning History*, 11 (1989).

Hsü, I., *The Rise of Modern China* (Oxford, 2000).

Kong, W. M., *James Legge: A Pioneer at Crossroads of East and West* (Hong Kong, 1996).

Kwan, C. W., *The Making of Hong Kong Society* (Oxford, 1991).

Liu, L. H., *The Clash of Empires: The Invention of China in Modern World Making* (Cambridge, Mass., 2009).

Lowe, K., 'The Beliefs, Aspirations and Methods of the First Missionaries in British Hong Kong, 1841–5', in Pieter N. Holtrop and Hugh McLeod (eds.), *Missions and Missionaries* (Woodbridge, 2000).

Meyer, D. R., *Hong Kong as a Global Metropolis* (Cambridge, 2000).

Morris, J., *Building Hong Kong* (Hong Kong, 1995).

Morris, J., *Hong Kong: Epilogue to an Empire* (London, 1997).

Mote, F. W., *Imperial China 900–1800* (Cambridge, Mass., 2003).

Munn, C. M., *Anglo-China: Chinese People and British Rule in Hong Kong 1841–1880* (Richmond, 2001).

Munn, C. M., 'The Hong Kong Opium Revenue, 1845–1885', in T. Brook and B. T. Wakabayashi (eds.), *Opium Regimes: China, Britain and Japan* (London, 2000).

Pope-Hennessy, J., *Half-Crown Colony* (London, 1969).

Sayer, G. R., *Hong Kong: Birth, Adolescence, and Coming of Age* (London, 1937).

Smith, C., *A Sense of History: Studies in the Social and Urban History of Hong Kong* (Hong Kong, 1995).

Stanley, B., *The Bible and the Flag* (Leicester, 1990).

Steeds, D. and Nish, I. H., *China, Japan and Nineteenth-Century Britain* (Dublin, 1977).

Trocki, C. A., 'Drugs, Taxes and Chinese Capitalism in Southeast Asia', in Timothy Brook and Bon Tadashi Wakabayashi (eds.), *Opium Regimes: China, Britain and Japan* (London, 2000).

Tsai, J.-F., *Hong Kong in Chinese History* (New York, 1993).

Welsh, F., *A History of Hong Kong* (Plymouth, 2007).

White, B.-S. (ed.), *Hong Kong: Somewhere between Heaven and Earth* (Oxford, 1996).

Wong, J. Y., *Deadly Dream: Opium, Imperialism and the 'Arrow' War in China* (Cambridge, 1998).

CHAPTER 7: BOMBAY

Anon., *Bombay and Its Ducks of 1882 by One of the Latter* (Bombay, 1882).

Berkley, J. J., *Paper on the Thul Ghaut Railway Incline* (Bombay, 1850).

Buckingham, S., 'Autobiography', in R. P. Karkaria (ed.), *The Charm of Bombay* (Bombay, 1915).

Carlyle, T., 'Chartism', in *Selected Writings* (Harmondsworth, 1986).

Carpenter, M., *Six Months in India* (London, 1868).

Conybeare, H., *Report on the Sanitary State and Requirements of Bombay, Selections from the Records of the Bombay Government*, New Series, vol. 11 (Bombay, 1855).

Conybeare, H., *Report on the Sanitary State and Sanitary Requirements of Bombay* (Bombay, 1852).

De Tocqueville, A., *Journeys to England and Ireland* (1835) (London, 1958).

Edwardes, S. M., *The Rise of Bombay: A Retrospect* (Bombay, 1902).

Elwood, A. K., *Narrative of a Journey Overland from England . . . to India* (London, 1830).

Falkland, Viscountess, *Chow-Chow: Being Selections from a Journal Kept in India, Egypt and Syria* (London, 1857).

Forrest, G. W., *Cities of India* (London, 1903).

Furneaux, J. H., *Glimpses of India* (Bombay, 1895).

Gray, J., *Life in Bombay and the Neighbouring Out-Stations* (London, 1852).

Kabraji, K. N., *Fifty Years Ago: Reminiscences of Mid 19th Century Bombay* (Bombay, 1901).

Karkaria, R. P. (ed.), *The Charm of Bombay* (Bombay, 1915).

Ledbetter, J. (ed.), *Dispatches for the New York Tribune: Selected Journalism of Karl Marx* (London, 2007).

Leith, A., *Report on the Sanitary State of the Island of Bombay* (Bombay, 1864).

Mackay, A., *Western India: Reports Addressed to the Chambers of Commerce of Manchester, Liverpool, Blackburn, and Glasgow* (London, 1853).

Macleod, N., *Peeps at the Far East: A Familiar Account of a Visit to India* (London, 1871).

Macpherson, W. J., 'Investment in Indian Railways, 1845–75', *The Economic History Review*, 8, 2 (1955), p. 177.

Martineau, J., *The Life and Correspondence of Sir Bartle Frere* (London, 1895).

Marx, K., 'The British Rule in India' (1853), in James Ledbetter (ed.), *Dispatches for the New York Tribune: Selected Journalism of Karl Marx* (London, 2007).

Nightingale, F., *How People May Live and Not Die in India* (London, 1863).

Nightingale, F., *Life or Death in India* (London, 1874).

Report of the Commission on the Drainage and Water Supply of Bombay (Bombay, 1869).

Report of the Sanitary Commission for Bombay, 1865 (Byculla, 1866).

Rousselet, L., *India and Its Native Provinces: Travels in Central India and in the Presidencies of Bombay and Bengal* (London, 1875).

Shaw, G. B., *The Common Sense of Municipal Trading* (London, 1904).

Stevens, G. W., 'All India in Miniature', in R. P. Karkaria (ed.), *The Charm of Bombay* (Bombay, 1915).

Temple, Sir R., *A Bird's Eye View of Picturesque India* (London, 1898).

Temple, Sir R., *Men and Events of My Time in India* (London, 1882).

Vallée, G. (ed.), *Florence Nightingale on Health in India* (Waterloo, 2006).

Wacha, D., *Shells from the Sands of Bombay – Being My Recollections and Reminiscences, 1860–1875* (Bombay, 1920).

Broich, J., 'Engineering the Empire: British Water Supply Systems and Colonial Societies, 1850–1900', *Journal of British Studies*, 47 (2007).

Chandavarkar, R., *History, Culture and the Indian City* (Cambridge, 2009).

Chopra, P., *A Joint Enterprise: Indian Elites and the Making of British Bombay* (Minneapolis, 2011).

Davies, P., *Splendours of the Raj: British Architecture in India, 1660 to 1947* (London, 1985).

Davis, M., *Late Victorian Holocausts* (London, 2001).

Dossal, M., 'The "Hall of Wonder" within the "Garden of Delight"', in P. Rohatgi, P. Godrej and R. Mehrotra (eds.), *Bombay to Mumbai* (Mumbai, 1997).

Dossal, M., *Imperial Designs and Indian Realities* (Bombay, 1991).

Dossal, M., *Mumbai: Theatre of Conflict, City of Hope* (Oxford, 2010).

Drèze, J. and Sen, A., *An Uncertain Glory: India and its Contradictions* (London, 2013).

Dwivedi, S. and Mehrotra, R., *Bombay: The Cities Within* (Bombay, 1995).

Dwivedi, S. and Mehrotra, R., *Fort Walks* (Mumbai, 2003).

Ganachari, A., '"White Man's Embarrassment": European Vagrancy in 19th Century Bombay', *Economic and Political Weekly*, 37, 25 (2002).

Hansen, T. B., *Wages of Violence: Naming and Identity in Postcolonial Bombay* (Princeton, 2001).

Judd, D., *Radical Joe: A Life of Joseph Chamberlain* (Cardiff, 1993).

Kosambi, M., 'British Bombay and Marathi Mumbai: Some Nineteenth-Century Perceptions', in S. Patel and A. Thorner (eds.), *Bombay: Mosaic of Modern Culture* (Bombay, 1995).

London, C. W., *Bombay Gothic* (Mumbai, 2002).

Mazumdar, R., 'Spectacle and Death in the City of Bombay Cinema', in G. Prakash and K. M. Kruse (eds.), *The Spaces of the Modern City* (Princeton, 2008).

Mehta, S., *Maximum City: Bombay Lost and Found* (London, 2004).

Misra, M., *Business, Race and Politics in British India* (1999).

Mitra, A., *Calcutta's Indian City* (Calcutta, 1963).

Morris, J. and Winchester, S., *Stones of Empire* (Oxford, 2005).

Pal, P., 'Introduction', in P. Rohatgi, P. Godrej and R. Mehrotra (eds.), *Bombay to Mumbai* (Mumbai, 1997).

Patel, S. and Thorner, A. (eds.), *Bombay: Mosaic of Modern Culture* (Bombay, 1995).

Porter, A. (ed.), *The Oxford History of the British Empire*, vol. 3: *The Nineteenth Century* (Oxford, 1999).

Prakash, G., *Mumbai Fables* (New Delhi, 2011).

Prakash, G. and Kruse, K. M. (eds.), *The Spaces of the Modern City* (Princeton, 2008).

Ramanna, M., 'Florence Nightingale and Bombay Presidency', *Social Scientist*, 30, 9–10 (2002).

Ramanna, M., *Western Medicine and Public Health in Colonial Bombay* (London, 2002).

Ranade, R., *Sir Bartle Frere and His Times: A Study of His Bombay Years* (New Delhi, 1990).

Rohatgi, P., Godrej, P. and Mehrotra, R. (eds.), *Bombay to Mumbai* (Mumbai, 1997).

Sharma, K., *Rediscovering Dharavi* (Delhi, 2000).

Tindall, G. E., *City of Gold: The Biography of Bombay* (London, 1982).

Vallée, G. (ed.), *Florence Nightingale on Health in India* (Waterloo, 2006).

Washbrook, D. A., 'India, 1818–1860: The Two Faces of Colonialism', in A. Porter (ed.), *The Oxford History of the British Empire*, vol. 3: *The Nineteenth Century* (Oxford, 1999).

Zaheer, B., *The Science of Empire* (1996).

CHAPTER 8: MELBOURNE

Aspinall, C., *Three Years in Melbourne* (London, 1862).

Austin, A. G. (ed.), *The Webbs' Australian Diary* (1898) (Bath, 1965).

Booth, C., *Another England* (1869).

Boyd, C. W. (ed.), *Mr Chamberlain's Speeches* (London, 1914).

Carter, C. R., *Victoria, The British 'El Dorado'; or, Melbourne in 1869* (London, 1870).

Carton Booth, E., *Another England: Life, Living, Homes and Homemakers in Victoria* (London, 1869).

Cornish, H., *Under the Southern Cross* (Madras, 1880).

Creasy, E. S., *The Rise and Progress of the English Constitution* (London, 1858).

Dilke, C. W., *Greater Britain: A Record of Travel in English Speaking Countries During 1866 and 1867* (London, 1869).

Dilke, C. W., *Problems of Greater Britain* (London, 1890).

Fowler, F., *Southern Lights and Shadows: Being Brief Notes of Three Years' Experience of Social, Literary and Political Life in Australia* (London, 1859).

Freeman, J., *Light and Shadows of Melbourne Life* (London, 1888).

Froude, J. A., *Oceana, or England and Her Colonies* (Leipzig, 1887).

Grant, J. and Serle, G., *The Melbourne Scene* (Melbourne, 1957).

Hoffenberg, P. H., *An Empire on Display* (London, 2001).

Hyndman, H. M., *Record of an Adventurous Life* (London, 1911).

Illustrated Handbook of Victoria, Australia, Colonial and Indian Exhibition, London (1886) (Melbourne, 1886).

Lenin, V. I., 'Imperialism', in *Selected Works* (New York, 1976), vol. 1.

Low, S., 'The Rise of the Suburbs', *Contemporary Review*, 60 (1891).

Martin, A. P., *Australia and the Empire* (Edinburgh, 1889).

Masterman, C. F. G., *From the Abyss; of Its Inhabitants by One of Them* (London, 1902).

Muthesius, H., *The English House* (London, 2007).

The New Australian School Series Fourth Reader (Sydney, 1899).

Otter, R. H., *Winters Abroad: Places Visited by the Author on Account of his Health* (London, 1882).

Pollard, N. W., *Homes in Victoria* (Melbourne, 1861).

Seeley, J. R., *The Expansion of England* (London, 1895).

Sutherland, J., *Victoria and Its Metropolis – Past and Present* (Melbourne, 1888).

'Tasma', *Uncle Piper of Piper's Hill* (London, 1892).

Trollope, A., *Australia and New Zealand* (London, 1873).

Turner, H. G., *A History of the Colony of Victoria* (London, 1904).

Twain, M., *More Tramps Abroad* (London, 1897).

Twopeny, R. E. N., *Town Life in Australia* (London, 1883).

Weber, A. F., *The Growth of Cities in the Nineteenth Century: A Study in Statistics* (1899) (Ithaca, 1967).

Bell, D., *The Idea of Greater Britain* (Oxford, 2007).

Bird, I., 'Australia Felix: Impressions of Victoria', in J. Johnson and M. Anderson (eds.), *Australia Imagined* (Crawley, 2005).

Bolton, G., 'Money: Trade, Investment and Economic Nationalism', in Deryck M. Schreuder and Stuart Ward (eds.), *Australia's Empire* (Oxford, 2008).

Cain, P. J. and Hopkins, A. G., *British Imperialism: Innovation and Expansion 1688–1914* (Harlow, 1993).

Cannon, M., *Life in the Cities* (South Yarra, 1983).

Carter, P., *The Road to Botany Bay* (London, 1987).

Damousi, J., 'War and Commemoration: "The Responsibility of Empire"', in D. M. Schreuder, and S. Ward (eds.), *Australia's Empire* (Oxford, 2008).

Darian-Smith, K. (ed.), *Seize the Day* (Monash, 2010).

Davison, D., Dunstan, D. and McConville, C. (eds.), *The Outcasts of Melbourne* (Sydney, 1985).

Davison, G., *The Rise and Fall of Marvellous Melbourne* (Melbourne, 1979).

Dunstan, D. (ed.), *Victorian Icon* (Victoria, 1996).

Dunstan, K., *The Paddock That Grew: The Story of the Melbourne Cricket Club* (London, 1962).

Encyclopaedia of Aboriginal Australia (Canberra, 1994).

Frost, W., 'Heritage, Nationalism, Identity: The 1861–62 England Cricket Tour of Australia', *The International Journal of the History of Sport*, 19, 4 (2002).

Garvin, J. L., *Life of Joseph Chamberlain* (London, 1933–5).

Johnson, J. and Anderson, M. (eds.), *Australia Imagined* (Crawley, 2005).

Judd, D., *Radical Joe: A Life of Joseph Chamberlain* (Cardiff, 1993).

McCarty, J. W. and Schedvin, C. B. (eds.), *Australian Capital Cities* (Sydney, 1978).

Mandle, W. F., 'Cricket and Australian Nationalism in the Nineteenth Century', *Journal of the Royal Australian Historical Society*, 59, 4 (1973).

Mandle, W. F., 'Games People Played: Cricket and Football in England and Victoria in the Late Nineteenth Century', *Historical Studies*, 15, 60 (1973).

Pescott, R. T. W., *The Royal Botanic Gardens Melbourne* (Melbourne, 1982).

Schreuder, D. M. and Ward, S. (eds.), *Australia's Empire* (Oxford, 2008).

Turner, I., 'The Growth of Melbourne', in J. W. McCarty and C. B. Schedvin (eds.), *Australian Capital Cities* (Sydney, 1978).

White, R., *Inventing Australia: Images and Identity, 1688–1980* (Sydney, 1981).

Whitehead, G., *Civilising the City* (Melbourne, 1997).

Willingham, A., 'A Permanent and Extensive Exhibition Building', in David Dunstan (ed.), *Victorian Icon* (Victoria, 1996).

Wilson, G. and Sands, P., *Building a City: 100 Years of Melbourne Architecture* (Melbourne, 1981).

Wright, R., *The Bureaucrats' Domain: Space and the Public Interest in Victoria 1836–84* (Melbourne, 1989).

CHAPTER 9: NEW DELHI

Baker, H., *Architecture and Personalities* (London, 1944).

Bayley, V., *One Woman's Raj*, Viola Bayley Papers Collection, Centre for South Asian Studies, University of Cambridge, 1976.

Brabazon, Lord, *Social Arrows* (London, 1886).

Byron, R., 'New Delhi', *The Architecture Review*, 69 (1931).

Byron, R., 'New Delhi', *Country Life*, 6 June 1931.

Churchill, R. S., *Churchill* (London 1967).

Churchill, W., *My Early Life* (London, 1943).

Corfield, W., 'New Delhi', *The British Architect*, October 1912.

Curzon, Lord, *Lord Curzon's Farewell to India: Being Speeches Delivered as Viceroy and Governor of India during Sept.–Nov. 1905* (Bombay, 1907).

Curzon, Lord, *Speeches on India* (London, 1904).

Davenport-Hinds, R. (ed.), *Hugh Trevor-Roper: The Wartime Journals* (London, 2012).

Final Report of the Delhi Town Planning Committee on the Town Planning of the New Imperial Capital (London, 1913).

Forrest, G. W., *Cities of India* (London, 1903).

Fortescue, J. W., *Narrative of the Visit to India of Their Majesties King George V and Queen Mary: And of the Coronation Durbar held at Delhi* (London, 1912).

Gibbon, E., *The History of the Decline and Fall of the Roman Empire* (1776–89) (London, 1837).

Greenwall, H. J., *Storm over India* (London, 1933).

Hardinge of Penshurst, Lord, *My Indian Years, 1910–1916* (London, 1948).

His Majesty King George's Speeches in India (Madras, 1912).

Huxley, A., *Jesting Pilate: The Diary of a Journey* (1986) (London, 1985).

Masterman, C. F. G. (ed.), *Heart of the Empire* (London, 1901).

Mills, E., *The Decline and Fall of the British Empire* (London, 1905).

Percy, C. and Ridley, J. (eds.), *The Letters of Edwin Lutyens to His Wife Lady Emily* (London, 1985).

Raleigh, T. (ed.), *Lord Curzon in India* (London, 1906).

Rhodes James, R. (ed.), *Winston S. Churchill: His Complete Speeches, 1897–1963* (London, 1974).

AlSayyad, N. (ed.), *Forms of Dominance: On the Architecture and Urbanism of the Colonial Enterprise* (Aldershot, 1992).

Baker, H., *Architecture and Personalities* (London, 1944).

Cannadine, D., *Ornamentalism: How the British Saw Their Empire* (London, 2002).

Collins, L. and Lapierre, D., *Mountbatten and the Partition of India* (Michigan, 1982).

Dalrymple, W., *The Last Mughal: The Fall of Delhi 1857* (London, 2009).

Gilmour, D., *Curzon: Imperial Statesman* (London, 2006).

Green, E. H. H., 'The Political Economy of Empire, 1880–1914', in A. Porter (ed.), *The Oxford History of the British Empire*, vol. 3: *The Nineteenth Century* (Oxford, 1999).

Home, R., *Of Planting and Planning* (London, 1997).

Hopkins, A. and Stamp, G. (eds.), *Lutyens Abroad: The Work of Sir Edwin Lutyens Outside the British Isles* (London, 2002).

Hussey, C., *The Life of Sir Edwin Lutyens* (London, 1953).

Irving, R. G., 'Bombay and Imperial Delhi: Cities as Symbols', in A. Hopkins and G. Stamp (eds.), *Lutyens Abroad: The Work of Sir Edwin Lutyens Outside the British Isles* (London, 2002).

Irving, R. G., *Indian Summer: Lutyens, Baker and Imperial Delhi* (London, 1981).

Jyoti, H., 'City as Durbar: Theatre and Power in Imperial Delhi', in Nezar Al-Sayyad (ed.), *Forms of Dominance: On the Architecture and Urbanism of the Colonial Enterprise* (Aldershot, 1992).

Kennedy, P., *The Rise and Fall of Great Powers* (London, 1988).

King, A. D., *Colonial Urban Development* (London, 1976).

Lahiri, N., *Delhi's Capital Century (1911–2011): Understanding the Transformation of the City* (Yale, 2011).

McKitterick, R. and Quinault, R. (eds.), *Edward Gibbon and Empire* (Cambridge, 2002).

Metcalf, T., 'Architecture and the Representation of Empire: India, 1860–1910', *Representations*, 6 (1984).

Metcalf, T., *Forging the Raj: Essays on British India in the Heyday of the Raj* (New Delhi, 2005).

Metcalf, T., *Ideologies of the Raj* (Cambridge, 1998).

Miller, S., *Delhi: Adventures in a Megacity* (London, 2009).

Moore, R. J., 'Imperial India, 1858–1914', in A. Porter (ed.), *The Oxford History of the British Empire*, vol. 3: *The Nineteenth Century* (Oxford, 1999).

Mountbatten, P., *India Remembered* (London, 2007).

Porter, A. (ed.), *The Oxford History of the British Empire*, vol. 3: *The Nineteenth Century* (Oxford, 1999).

Pothen, N., *Glittering Decades: New Delhi in Love and War* (New Delhi, 2012).

Quinault, R., 'Winston Churchill and Gibbon', in R. McKitterick and R. Quinault (eds.), *Edward Gibbon and Empire* (Cambridge, 2002).

Singh, M. and Mukherjee, R., *New Delhi: Making of a Capital* (New Delhi, 2009).

Volwahsen, Andreas, *Imperial Delhi: The British Capital of the Indian Empire* (Munich, 2003).

Wolpert, S. A., *Shameful Flight: The Last Years of the British Empire in India* (Oxford, 2006).

CHAPTER 10: LIVERPOOL

Baines, T., *History of the Commerce and Town of Liverpool* (Liverpool, 1852).

Gawthrop, H., *Fraser's Guide to Liverpool* (Liverpool, 1855).

Heseltine, M., *Life in the Jungle: My Autobiography* (London, 2003).

Holt, A. (ed.), *Merseyside* (Liverpool, 1923).

Jones, C. W., *Pioneer Shipowners* (London, 1938).

Melville, H., *Redburn: His First Voyage* (1849) (New York, 1983).

Muir, R., *A History of Liverpool* (Liverpool, 1907).

Percy, C. and Ridley, J. (eds.), *The Letters of Edwin Lutyens to His Wife Lady Emily* (London, 1985).

Picton, J. A., *Memorials of Liverpool, Historical and Topographical* (London, 1873).

Pike, W. T. (ed.), *Liverpool and Birkenhead in the Twentieth Century* (Brighton, 1911).

Priestley, J. B., *English Journey* (Leipzig, 1935).

Belchem, J., *Irish, Catholic and Scouse* (Liverpool, 2007).

Belchem, J. (ed.), *Liverpool 800* (Liverpool, 2006).

Brendon, P., *The Decline and Fall of the British Empire* (London, 2007).

Chandler, G., *Liverpool Shipping: A Short History* (Liverpool, 1960).

Clark, P. (ed.), *The Cambridge Urban History of Britain*, vol. 2 (Cambridge, 2000).

Clarke, P., *The Last Thousand Days of the British Empire* (London, 2007).

Cornelius, J., *Liverpool 8* (London, 1982).

Couch, C., *City of Change and Challenge: Urban Planning and Regeneration in Liverpool* (Liverpool, 2003).

Darwin, J., *Unfinished Empire: The Global Expansion of Britain* (London, 2012).

Dudgeon, J. P., *Our Liverpool* (London, 2010).

ExUrbe, 'Peel and the Liverpool City Region: Predatory Capitalism or Providential Corporatism?', March 2013. www.exurbe.org.uk.

Foreman, A., *A World on Fire* (London, 2011).

Fryer, P., *Staying Power: The History of Black People in Britain* (London, 1984).

Haggerty, S., Webster, A. and White, N. J. (eds.), *The Empire in One City?* (Manchester, 2008).

Hyde, F., *Liverpool and the Mersey: An Economic History of a Port* (Newton Abbot, 1971).

Kumar, K., 'Empire, Nation, and National Identities', in Andrew Thompson (ed.), *Britain's Experience of Empire in the Twentieth Century* (Oxford, 2012).

Lane, T., *Liverpool: Gateway of Empire* (London, 1987).

Lewis, B., *'So Clean': Lord Leverhulme, Soap and Civilisation* (Manchester, 2008).

Mahler, V., 'Britain, the European Community, and the Developing Commonwealth: Dependence, Interdependence, and the Political Economy of Sugar', *International Organization*, 35, 3 (1981).

May, R. and Cohen, R., 'The Interaction between Race and Colonialism: A Case Study of the Liverpool Race Riots of 1919', *Race and Class*, 16, 2 (1974).

Munck, R. (ed.), *Reinventing the City? Liverpool in Comparative Perspective* (Liverpool, 2002).

Sacks, D. H. and Lynch, M., 'Ports 1540–1700', in P. Clark (ed.), *The Cambridge Urban History of Britain*, vol. 2 (Cambridge, 2000).

Sharples, J., *Liverpool*, Pevsner Architectural Guides (London, 2004).

Steele, M., 'Transmitting Ideas of Empire: Representations and Celebrations in Liverpool, 1886–1953', in S. Haggerty, A. Webster and N. J. White (eds.), *The Empire in One City?* (Manchester, 2008).

Summerson, J., *The Unromantic Castle and Other Essays* (London, 1990).

Taylor, A. J. P., 'Manchester', *Encounter*, 8, 3 (1957).

Thompson, A. (ed.), *Britain's Experience of Empire in the Twentieth Century* (Oxford, 2012).

Tomlinson, J., 'The Empire/Commonwealth in British Economic Thinking and Policy', in A. Thompson (ed.), *Britain's Experience of Empire in the Twentieth Century* (Oxford, 2012).

Watson, J. A., *The End of a Liverpool Landmark: The Last Years of Love Lane Refinery* (London, 1985).

White, N. J., 'Liverpool Shipping and the End of Empire: The Ocean Group in East and Southeast Asia, 1945–1973', in S. Haggerty, A. Webster and N. J. White (eds.), *The Empire in One City?* (Manchester, 2008).

Wilks-Heeg, S., 'From World City to Pariah City? Liverpool and the Global Economy, 1850–2000', in R. Munck (ed.), *Reinventing the City? Liverpool in Comparative Perspective* (Liverpool, 2002).

Notes

INTRODUCTION

1. Chris Patten, *East and West* (London, 1998), pp. 84, 85.
2. *The Economist*, 28 June 1997.
3. *Daily Mail*, 25 June 1997.
4. *New Statesman*, 11 July 1997.
5. *Independent*, 1 July 1997.
6. Tony Blair, *A Journey* (London, 2010), p. 126.
7. Quoted in *Daily Mail*, 23 February 2006.
8. For the most popular recent works, see: Richard Gott, *Britain's Empire* (London, 2011); Kwasi Kwarteng, *Ghosts of Empire* (London, 2011); Jeremy Paxman, *Empire* (London, 2011); John Darwin, *Unfinished Empire* (London, 2012); as well as the multiple publications emerging from the Oxford History of the British Empire series. For an insightful commentary on this cultural moment, see Pankaj Mishra, 'Guilt and Glory', *Financial Times*, 22–3 October 2011.
9. Niall Ferguson, *Empire: How Britain Made the Modern World* (London, 2003), pp. xxi, 358.
10. Gott (2011), pp. 1–8.
11. See Katie Engelhart, 'Rule Britannia: Empire on Trial', *World Policy Journal*, 29, 4 (2012–13).
12. *Hansard* (Commons), 6 June 2013, c. 1692.
13. *Guardian*, 18 January 2003.
14. Jan Morris and Simon Winchester, *Stones of Empire* (Oxford, 2005), p. 196.
15. Darwin (2012), p. 11. See also, Andrew Porter, 'Introduction', *The Oxford History of the British Empire*, vol. 3: *The Nineteenth Century* (Oxford, 1999). Nicholas B. Dirks is withering about such 'nuance': 'a post-imperial sigh of relief has been almost audible in some recent

445

writing, in which the historical stance of objectivity is said to be possible now that historians no longer need to take sides ... It is one thing to argue that the experience and ideological presuppositions of the colonizers are deserving of historical attention ... It is altogether different to assert that because there were perceived "affinities", say, between metropolitan and colonial elites, the fundamental notions of empire were not driven by racial and cultural prejudice.' See Dirks, *The Scandal of Empire* (London, 2006), pp. 27, 332–3.

16. Peter Cunningham (ed.), *The Letters of Horace Walpole, Earl of Oxford* (London, 1858), vol. 3, p. 496; J. R. Seeley, *The Expansion of England* (London, 1895), p. 10; Kwarteng (2011), p. 3.

17. Joseph Conrad, *Heart of Darkness* (London, 1975), p. 14.

18. Partha Chatterjee, *The Black Hole of Empire* (Princeton, 2012), p. xii.

19. Nicholas Canny, 'The Origins of Empire: An Introduction', in Nicholas Canny (ed.), *The Oxford History of the British Empire*, vol. 1: *The Origins of Empire* (Oxford, 1998), p. 10.

20. See Robert Ross and Gerald J. Telkamp (eds.), *Colonial Cities* (Leiden, 1985).

21. See Anthony D. King, 'Colonial Cities: Global Pivots of Change', in ibid.

22. *Urban World: Mapping the Economic Power of Cities*, McKinsey Global Institute Report, March 2011.

23. Saskia Sassen, *The Global City* (Princeton, 1991), pp. 3–4.

24. *The Sunday Times*, 31 January 2010.

25. Mike Davis, *Planet of Slums* (London, 2006), p. 96. See also Eric Lewis Beverley, 'Colonial Urbanism and South Asian Cities', *Social History*, 36, 4 (2011).

26. Edward Said, *Culture and Imperialism* (London, 1994), p. 15.

27. Dirks (2006), p. 330.

CHAPTER 1: BOSTON

1. The above account is based on Benjamin L. Carp, *Defiance of the Patriots: The Boston Tea Party and the Making of America* (London, 2010), pp. 117–40.

2. John Strype, *Annals of the Reformation and Establishment of Religion and Various Other Occurrences in the Church of England*, vol. 2 (London, 1725), p. 595, quoted in Francis J. Bremer, *John Winthrop* (Oxford, 2003), p. 181; see also Bremer's entry on Winthrop in *Oxford Dictionary of National Biography* (Oxford, 2004).

3. John Winthrop, *Reasons for the Plantation in New England* (c. 1628), quoted in Alden T. Vaughan (ed.), *The Puritan Tradition in America* (Hanover, N. H., 1997), p. 26.

4. Nathaniel B. Shurtleff, *A Topographical and Historical Description of Boston* (Boston, 1871), p. 16.

5. John Winthrop, *A Model of Christian Charity* (1630), p. 1, quoted in Bremer (2003), p. 179.

6. Nathaniel Morton, *New England's Memorial* (Boston, 1772), p. 91, quoted in Shurtleff (1871), p. 28.

7. See Darrett B. Rutman, *Winthrop's Boston* (Chapel Hill, 1975).

8. William Wood, 'New England's Prospect', in Alexander Young (ed.), *Chronicles of the First Planters of the Colony of Massachusetts Bay* (Boston, 1846), pp. 397, 398–9; quoted in Shurtleff (1871), pp. 40, 41.

9. John Winthrop to Henry Oldenburg, 12 November 1668, in Robert Winthrop (ed.), *Correspondence of Hartlib, Haak, Oldenburg and Others of the Royal Society with Governor Winthrop of Connecticut, 1661–1672* (Boston, 1878), pp. 34–5.

10. See Virginia DeJohn Anderson, 'New England in the Seventeenth Century', in Nicholas Canny (ed.), *The Oxford History of the British Empire*, vol. 1: *The Origins of Empire* (Oxford, 1998).

11. Vaughan (1997), p. 29.

12. John Winthrop, *The Journal of John Winthrop 1649* (1996), pp. 280–81.

13. Mark van Doren (ed.), *Samuel Sewall Diary* (New York, 1963), p. 29.

14. Samuel Eliot Morison, *The Founding of Harvard College* (Cambridge, Mass., 1995).

15. J. Franklin Jameson (ed.), *Johnson's Wonder-Working Providence of Sion's Saviour in New England* (1654) (New York, 1910), p. 71.

16. Winthrop (1996), p. 72.

17. Justin Winsor, *The Memorial History of Boston* (Boston, 1882), vol. 1, p. 496.

18. George Winship (ed.), *Boston in 1682 and 1699: A Trip to New England by Edward Ward and A Letter from New England by J. W.* (Providence, 1905), p. 43, quoted in Shurtleff (1871), p. 56.

19. Winthrop (1996), p. 432.

20. See Owen Stanwood, *The Empire Reformed: English America in the Age of the Glorious Revolution* (Philadelphia, 2011), p. 96.

21. Van Doren (1963), p. 21.

22. Ibid.

23. B. Franklin, *The Autobiography of Benjamin Franklin* (1793) (Philadelphia, 2005), p. 10.

24. Winsor (1882), vol. 1, p. 483.
25. Quoted in Rutman (1975), p. 272.
26. Christopher P. Magra, *The Fisherman's Cause: Atlantic Commerce and Maritime Dimensions of the American Revolution* (Cambridge, 2009), p. 79.
27. Shurtleff (1871), p. 50.
28. James H. Stark, *The Loyalists of Massachusetts* (Boston, 1910), p. 298.
29. See Gary B. Nash, *The Urban Crucible: The Northern Seaports and the Origins of the American Revolution* (Cambridge, Mass., 1986).
30. Winsor (1882), vol. 1, p. 499.
31. John Dunton, *John Dunton's Letters from New England* (Boston, 1867), p. 67.
32. Rev. Cotton Mather, *Magnalia Christi Americana; or, The Ecclesiastical History of New England* (London, 1702), p. 31.
33. L. H. Butterfield (ed.), *The Adams Papers: Diary and Autobiography of John Adams* (Cambridge, Mass., 1961), vol. 1, p. 81.
34. Daniel Neal, *History of New England* (London, 1720), p. 225.
35. Dunton (1867), pp. 68–9.
36. Neal (1720), p. 225.
37. Dunton (1867), pp. 78, 79, 80, 88.
38. See Benjamin L. Carp, *Rebels Rising: Cities and the American Revolution* (Oxford, 2007); Carl Bridenbaugh, *Cities in the Wilderness* (Oxford, 1970).
39. Neal (1720), p. 228.
40. See 'The British Conception of Empire in the Eighteenth Century', in David Armitage, *Greater Britain, 1516–1776: Essays in Atlantic History* (Aldershot, 2004); David Armitage, *The Ideological Origins of the British Empire* (Cambridge, 2000); John J. McCusker and Russell R. Menard, *The Economy of British America* (Chapel Hill, 1985).
41. T. H. Breen, '"Baubles of Britain": The American and Consumer Revolutions of the Eighteenth Century', *Past and Present*, 119 (1988), p. 86.
42. C. Ferguson, *A Letter Address'd to Every Honest Man in Britain* (London, 1738), p. 17.
43. Located online in Adams Papers of the US National Archives: http://founders.archives.gov/documents/Adams/01-04-02-0001-0035.
44. John Adams, 'Essay No. III – On Private Revenge', *Boston Gazette*, 5 September 1763.
45. Brendan Simms, *Three Victories and a Defeat* (London, 2007), pp. 426, 393.

46. Harlow Giles Unger, *John Hancock* (New York, 2000), p. 52.
47. Esmond Wright, *Benjamin Franklin: His Life as He Wrote It* (Cambridge, Mass., 1990), p. 155.
48. See Unger (2000).
49. See W. T. Baxter, *The House of Hancock* (Cambridge, Mass., 1945).
50. Butterfield (1961), vol. 1, p. 294.
52. Bernard Bailyn, '1776: A Year of Challenge – a World Transformed', *Journal of Law and Economics*, 19 (1976), p. 447.
53. Leonard W. Labaree (ed.), *The Papers of Benjamin Franklin* (New Haven, 2006), vol. 4, p. 229.
54. Franklin (2005), p. 11.
55. Carp (2010), p. 56. See also, pp. 49–57.
56. Information provided by Dr Gaye Blake-Roberts, director of the Wedgwood Museum, Barlaston, Stoke-on-Trent.
57. Shurtleff (1871), pp. 64, 88.
58. James Deetz, *In Small Things Forgotten: The Archaeology of Early American Life* (New York, 1977), p. 38. See also, T. H. Breen, 'An Empire of Goods: The Anglicization of Colonial America, 1690–1776', *Journal of British Studies*, 25, 4 (1986).
59. Brendan McConville, *The King's Three Faces* (Chapel Hill, 2006), p. 7.
60. See Richard L. Bushman, *King and People in Provincial Massachusetts* (Chapel Hill, 1992).
61. Quoted in McConville (2006), p. 260.
62. Anne Rowe (ed.), *Letters and Diary of John Rowe* (New York, 1969), p. 117.
63. Ibid., p. 68.
64. Ibid., p. 114.
65. Rev. Andrew Burnaby, *Travels through the Middle Settlements in North-America. In the Years 1759 and 1760* (London, 1775), p. 142. See also Holtz Kay, *Lost Boston* (1980).
66. Shurtleff (1871), p. 69.
67. Thomas Pownall, *Administration of the Colonies* (London, 1764), p. 9, quoted in Peter Miller, *Defining the Common Good: Empire, Religion and Philosophy in Eighteenth-Century Britain* (Cambridge, 2004), p. 211.
68. See P. J. Marshall, 'Introduction', *The Oxford History of the British Empire*, vol. 2: *The Eighteenth Century* (Oxford, 1998).
69. *The Works of Benjamin Franklin* (Boston, 1837), vol. 4, p. 89, quoted in Simms (2007), p. 539.

70. See Eliga H. Gould, 'Revolution and Counter-Revolution', in David Armitage and Michael J. Braddick (eds.), *The British Atlantic World* (Basingstoke, 2002).

71. Quoted in Matthew Parker, *The Sugar Barons: Family, Corruption, Empire and War* (London, 2011), p. 322.

72. Rowe (1969), p. 89.

73. See E. P. Thompson, 'The Moral Economy of the English Crowd in the Eighteenth Century', in E. P. Thompson, *Customs in Common* (London, 1993).

74. Butterfield (1961), vol. 2, p. 74.

75. John K. Alexander, *Samuel Adams: America's Revolutionary Politician* (Oxford, 2002), p. 20; see also Stewart Beach, *Samuel Adams: The Fateful Years* (Cornwallis, 1965).

76. Rowe (1969), p. 95.

77. Butterfield (1961), vol. 1, p. 316.

78. Carp (2010), p. 55.

79. Unger (2000), p. 133.

80. Breen (1988), p. 92.

81. Carp (2010), pp. 67–9.

82. Quoted in Carp (2007), p. 23.

83. Rowe (1969), p. 198.

84. Butterfield (1961), vol. 3, pp. 291–2.

85. Rowe (1969), p. 199.

86. Carp (2010), p. 21.

87. Papers of John Adams (Massachusetts Historical Society, 1977), p. 147.

88. Rowe (1969), p. 254.

89. Butterfield (1961), vol. 2, p. 86.

90. Ibid., p. 86.

91. Rowe (1969), p. 291.

92. Carp (2010), p. 191.

93. William Cobbett, *Parliamentary History of England* (London, 1806–20), vol. 18, cols. 798–9.

CHAPTER 2: BRIDGETOWN

1. William Dickson, *Letters on Slavery* (London, 1789), pp. 29–30.

2. See Pedro Welch, *Slave Society in the City: Bridgetown, Barbados, 1680–1834* (Oxford, 2003), pp. 164–5.

3. Adam Smith, *An Enquiry into the Nature and Causes of the Wealth of Nations* (1776) (Harmondsworth, 1986), p. 489.

4. H. Frere, *A Short History of Barbados* (London, 1768), pp. 115–16.
5. A. J. O'Shaughnessy, *An Empire Divided: The American Revolution and the British Caribbean* (Philadelphia, 2000), p. 3.
6. Richard Sheridan, *Sugar and Slavery* (London, 1974), p. 124.
7. J. A. Froude, *The English in the West Indies* (London, 1888), p. 38.
8. Quoted in Welch (2003), p. 54.
9. Quoted in Robert B. Potter and Mark Wilson, 'Barbados', in Robert B. Potter (ed.), *Urbanization, Planning and Development in the Caribbean* (London, 1989), p. 123.
10. *The Winthrop Papers*, vol. 1: *1498–1628* (Boston, 1925), pp. 356–7.
11. Hilary M. Beckles, *A History of Barbados* (Cambridge, 1990), pp. 6–13.
12. John Oldmixon, *The British Empire in America* (London, 1708), pp. 78–9.
13. Richard Ligon, *A True and Exact History of the Island of Barbados* (London, 1673), p. 25.
14. John Eaden (ed.), *The Memoirs of Père Labat (1693–1705)* (London, 1931), p. 120.
15. Ligon (1673), p. 85.
16. See Jack P. Greene, 'Changing Identity in the British Caribbean: Barbados as a Case Study', in Nicholas Canny and Anthony Pagden (eds.), *Colonial Identity in the Atlantic World* (Princeton, 1987).
17. Beckles (1990), p. 27.
18. Quoted in Richard Drayton, 'The Collaboration of Labour: Slaves, Empires and Globalizations in the Atlantic World, *c.* 1600–1850', in A. G. Hopkins (ed.), *Globalization in World History* (London, 2002).
19. Anon., *News from Barbadoes* (London, 1676), p. 26.
20. Oldmixon (1708), p. 162.
21. John Atkins, *A Voyage to Guinea, Brazil and the West Indies (1735)* (London, 1970) p. 206.
22. Peter Quennell (ed.), *Memoirs of William Hickey* (London, 1960), p. 190.
23. See Robin Blackburn, *The Making of New World Slavery* (London, 1997).
24. Matthew Parker, *The Sugar Barons: Family, Corruption, Empire and War* (London, 2011), p. 296.
25. James Walvin, *Atlas of Slavery* (Edinburgh, 2006).
26. See Blackburn (1997).
27. Olaudah Equiano, *The Interesting Narrative and Other Writings* (London, 1794), p. 51.
28. See Blackburn (1997).
29. V. T. Harlow, *A History of Barbados* (Oxford, 1926), pp. 292–3.
30. Equiano (1794), p. 54.
31. Ibid., p. 56.

32. Oldmixon (1708), p. 117.
33. Bryan Edwards, *The History Civil and Commercial, of the British Colonies in the West Indies* (London, 1798) pp. 186, 187.
34. Equiano (1794), p. 57.
35. C. L. R. James, *The Black Jacobins* (London, 2001), p. 10.
36. Eaden (1931), p. 126.
37. Dickson (1789), p. 34.
38. See Blackburn (1997).
39. Oldmixon (1708), pp. 118–19.
40. Karl Marx, *Capital* (London, 1990), pp. 915, 918.
41. Daniel Defoe, *Review*, 44, 10 January 1713, p. 89, quoted in Peter Earle *The World of Defoe* (London, 1976), p. 130.
42. Eric Williams, *Capitalism and Slavery* (Chapel Hill, 1944), p. 102.
43. See Welch (2003), p. 57; Richard B. Sheridan, 'Caribbean Plantation Society, 1689–1748', in P. J. Marshall (ed.), *The Oxford History of the British Empire*, vol. 2: *The Eighteenth Century* (Oxford, 1998).
44. Drayton (2002).
45. See Blackburn (1997). For new thinking on the impact of slave financing on Scotland's textile industry, see T. W. Devine, *To the Ends of the Earth: Scotland's Global Diaspora, 1750–2010* (London, 2011).
46. Bryan Edwards, *The History, Civil and Commercial, of the British West Indies* (London, 1819), vol. 3, p. 433.
47. Oldmixon (1708), pp. 79–80.
48. Welch (2003), p. 35.
49. See Welch (2003).
50. Frere (1768), p. 112.
51. Atkins (1970), p. 206.
52. Eaden (1931), p. 121.
53. Oldmixon (1708), p. 79.
54. Atkins (1970), p. 206.
55. Welch (2003), p. 45.
56. See Henry Fraser, 'Historic Bridgetown – Development and Architecture', in Woodville Marshall and Pedro Welch (eds.), *Beyond the Bridge* (Cave Hill, 2005).
57. See Martyn J. Bowden, 'The Three Centuries of Bridgetown: An Historical Geography', *Journal of the Barbados Museum and Historical Society* (2003), 49, 1–138.
58. See S. D. Smith, *Slavery, Family and Gentry Capitalism in the British Atlantic* (Cambridge, 2006).
59. Quoted in O'Shaughnessy (2000), p. 11.

60. Parker (2011), pp. 17, 37.

61. *The Life and Works of John Adams* (Boston, 1853), vol. 8, p. 74, quoted in Karl Watson, *The Civilised Island, Barbados: A Social History, 1750–1816* (Bridgetown, 1979), p. 14.

62. Welch (2003), p. 59.

63. See Ian K. Steele, 'Introduction', *The English Atlantic 1675–1740: An Exploration of Communication and Community* (Oxford, 1986).

64. See Smith (2006); S. D. Smith, 'Gedney Clarke of Salem and Barbados: Transatlantic Super-Merchant', *The New England Quarterly*, 76, 4 (December 2003).

65. Parker (2011), pp. 241, 320.

66. O'Shaughnessy (2000), pp. 66, 98–9.

67. Quoted in Jack P. Greene, 'Liberty and Slavery', in Jack P. Greene (ed.), *Exclusionary Empire: English Liberty Overseas 1600–1900* (Cambridge, 2010), p. 61.

68. See Parker (2011).

69. George Pinckard, *Notes on the West Indies* (London, 1816), vol. 1, p. 346.

70. Quennell (1960), p. 190.

71. William Dickson, *Mitigation of Slavery* (1814) (Westport, 1970), p. 374.

72. E. Bowen, *A Complete System of Geography* (London, 1747), vol. 2, p. 752.

73. See Watson (1979).

74. *Barbados Mercury*, 27 October 1781.

75. A. F. Wedd (ed.), *The Fate of the Fenwicks: Letters [Mainly Written by E. Fenwick] to Mary Hays (1798–1828)* Anon. (London, 1927), pp. 62–3.

76. Dickson (1789), pp. 38–9, 26.

77. See Beckles (1990).

78. Welch (2003), pp. 151–7.

79. Pinckard (1816), vol. 1, pp. 115, 116.

80. J. W. Orderson, *Creolena: or, Social and Domestic Scenes and Incidents in Barbados in Days of Yore* (London, 1842), pp. 95–6.

81. Welch (2003), p. 172.

82. *The Barbadian*, 21 May 1842, quoted in Neville Connell, 'Prince William Henry's Visits to Barbados in 1786 and 1789', *Journal of the Barbados Museum and Historical Society*, 25, 4 (1958), pp. 157–64.

83. John Poyer, *The History of Barbados* (London, 1808), p. 576.

84. Orderson (1842), pp. 99–101, 102.

85. See Welch (2003), p. 172; W. Alleyne, *Historic Bridgetown* (Bridgetown, 1978).

86. Henry Nelson Coleridge, *Six Months in the West Indies in 1825*, 4th edition (London, 1841), pp. 37–8.

CHAPTER 3: DUBLIN

1. Arthur Young, *A Tour in Ireland* (Cambridge, 1983), p. 4.
2. Anon., *The History of Ned Evans* (London, 1797), vol. 2, p. 38.
3. http://www.visitdublin.com/downloads/georgianguide.pdf (accessed 19 December 2011).
4. Quoted in Kevin Corrigan Kearns, *Georgian Dublin* (London, 1983), p. 70.
5. Kevin Corrigan Kearns, 'Preservation and Transformation of Georgian Dublin', *Geographical Review*, 72, 3 (1982), pp. 273–4.
6. *Guardian*, 21 May 2011.
7. *Observer*, 22 May 2011.
8. Karl Marx and Friedrich Engels, *Collected Works* (New York, 1983), vol. 40, p. 49; vol. 43, p. 409.
9. See Jane H. Ohlmeyer, '"Civilizinge of those Rude Partes": Colonization within Britain and Ireland, 1580s–1640s', in Nicholas Canney (ed.), *The Oxford History of the British Empire*, vol. 1: *The Origins of Empire* (Oxford, 1998).
10. Christopher Hill, *God's Englishman: Oliver Cromwell and the English Revolution* (London, 2000), p. 146.
11. John Darwin, *Unfinished Empire: The Global Expansion of Britain* (London, 2012), p. 76.
12. Peter J. Stanlis (ed.), *Edmund Burke: Selected Writings and Speeches* (New Brunswick, 2009), p. 319.
13. Thomas Bartlett, 'Ireland, Empire, and Union, 1690–1801', in Kevin Kenny (ed.), *Ireland and the British Empire* (Oxford, 2004), pp. 60–71.
14. W. E. H. Lecky, *Ireland in the Eighteenth Century* (1892) (London, 1913), vol. 1, pp. 321–2.
15. See R. F. Foster, *Modern Ireland* (London, 1988), p. 170.
16. Thomas Bartlett, '"This Famous island set in a Virginian sea": Ireland in the British Empire, 1690–1801', in P. J. Marshall (ed.), *The Oxford History of the British Empire*, vol. 2: *The Eighteenth Century* (Oxford, 2001), p. 253.
17. 'Henry Grattan', *Oxford Dictionary of National Biography* (Oxford, 2010).
18. Burke to the Duke of Portland, 25 May 1782, in T. Copeland et al. (eds.), *The Correspondence of Edmund Burke* (Cambridge, 1958–70), vol. 4, p. 455, quoted in Bartlett (2004), p. 78.
19. Quoted in Constantia Maxwell, *Dublin under the Georges* (London, 1956), p. 89.

20. Foster (1988), p. 201. See also, Francis G. James, 'Irish Colonial Trade in the Eighteenth Century', *The William and Mary Quarterly*, 3rd Series, 20, 4(1963); R. C. Nash, 'Irish Atlantic Trade in the Seventeenth and Eighteenth Centuries', *The William and Mary Quarterly*, 3rd Series, 42, 3(1985).

21. Lecky (1913), vol. 1, p. 325.

22. See Kieran Burns, 'The History of 29 FitzWilliam Street', *Dublin Historical Record*, 57, 1 (2004).

23. Sir Jonah Barrington, *Historic Memoirs of Ireland* (London, 1835), vol. 1, p. 7.

24. Quoted in Maxwell (1956), p. 102.

25. Edward Wakefield, *An Account of Ireland Statistical and Political* (London, 1812), vol. 2, p. 783.

26. Edward Melville, *Sketches of Society in France and Ireland in the years 1805–6–7 by a Citizen of the United States* (Dublin, 1811), vol. 1, pp. 111–12.

27. T. Campbell, *A Philosophical Survey of the South of Ireland* (London, 1777), p. 29.

28. Quoted in Wakefield (1812), vol. 2, pp. 789–90.

29. Anon. (1797), p. 46.

30. Young (1983), pp. 4, 5, 203.

31. Quoted in William Hague, *William Pitt the Younger* (London, 2004), p. 186.

32. 'Charles Manners, Fourth Duke of Rutland', *Oxford Dictionary of National Biography* (Oxford, 2010).

33. Nathaniel Jefferys, *An Englishman's Descriptive Account of Dublin* (London, 1810), p. 57.

34. John Roche Ardill, *The Closing of the Irish Parliament* (Dublin, 1907), p. 140.

35. See Tighearnan Mooney and Fiona White, 'The Gentry's Winter Season', in David Dickson (ed.), *The Gorgeous Mask: Dublin, 1700–1850* (Dublin, 1987).

36. Richard Luckett, *Handel's Messiah: A Celebration* (London, 1992), p. 125.

37. De Latocnaye, *A Frenchman's Walk through Ireland* (1798) (Cambridge, 1984), p. 24.

38. Campbell (1777), p. 26.

39. See Gary A. Boyd, *Dublin 1745–1922: Hospitals, Spectacle and Vice* (Dublin, 2006).

40. Paula Lynch, 'A Dublin Street: North Great George's Street', *Dublin Historical Record*, 31, 1 (1977), p. 14; Kieran Burns, 'The History of 29 FitzWilliam Street', *Dublin Historical Record*, 57, 1 (2004).

41. See Edward McParland, 'The Wide Street Commissioners', *Quarterly Bulletin of the Irish Georgian Society*, 15, 1 (1972).

42. See Andrew Kincaid, *Postcolonial Dublin* (Minneapolis, 2006).

43. Edward McParland, 'Strategy in the Planning of Dublin, 1750–1800', in P. Butel and L. M. Cullen (eds.), *Cities and Merchants: French and Irish Perspectives on Urban Development, 1500–1900* (Dublin, 1986).

44. See Edel Sheridan-Quantz, 'The Multi-Centred Metropolis: The Social Topography of Eighteenth-Century Dublin', in Peter Clark and Raymond Gillespie (eds.), *Two Capitals: London and Dublin, 1500–1840* (Oxford, 2001).

45. See Edel Sheridan, 'Designing the Capital City: Dublin, 1660–1810', in Joseph Brady and Anngret Simms (eds.), *Dublin through Space and Time* (Dublin, 2001).

46. James Malton, *A Picturesque and Descriptive View of the City of Dublin* (1799) (Dublin, 1980), p. ii.

47. Jefferys (1810), pp. 55, 85.

48. Quoted in Foster (1988), p. 186.

49. Thomas Cromwell, *Excursions Through Ireland* (London, 1820), p. 71.

50. John James McGregor, *New Picture of Dublin* (Dublin, 1821), pp. 75–6.

51. See Murray Fraser, 'Public Building and Colonial Policy in Dublin, 1760–1800', *Architectural History*, 28 (1985), p. 111.

52. Jefferys (1810), p. 82.

53. J. Warburton, J. Whitelaw and K. Walsh, *History of the City of Dublin from the Earliest Accounts to the Present Time*, 2 vols. (London, 1818), vol. 2, p. 1081, quoted in Sheridan-Quantz (2001), p. 286.

54. Quoted in J. T. Gilbert, *A History of the City of Dublin* (Dublin, 1859), vol. 2, pp. 57, 58.

55. See Fraser (1985), p. 115.

56. John Gamble, *Sketches of History, Politics and Manners in Dublin and the North of Ireland in 1810* (London, 1826), p. 22.

57. Fraser (1985), p. 117.

58. Foster (1988), p. 280.

59. John Bew, *Castlereagh* (London, 2011), pp. 119–20.

60. *Speech of the Rt. Hon. William Pitt in the British House of Commons on Thursday 31 January 1799* (London, 1799), p. 43.

61. Quoted in Hague (2004), p. 435.
62. Quoted in Bew (2011), pp. 132, 150.
63. Edward Cooke, *Pro and Con: Being an Impartial Abstract of the Principal Publications on the Subject of Legislative Union* (Dublin, 1800), p. 6, quoted in Bartlett (2004), p. 88.
64. Quoted in Bew (2011), p. 156.
65. *The Dublin Magazine*, 1 (1812–13), p. 392.
66. Gamble (1826), p. 64.
67. McGregor (1821), p. viii.
68. Sydney Owenson (Lady Morgan), *Florence Macarthy* (1818) (New York, 1979), vol. 1, p. 54.
69. George Barnes, *A Statistical Account of Ireland Formed on Historical Facts* (London, 1811), p. 16.
70. Andrew O'Brien, 'The History of Nelson's Pillar', *Dublin Historical Record*, 60, 1 (2007).
71. Warburton, Whitelaw and Walsh (1818), vol. 2, p. 1100.
72. *The Speech of the Rt. Hon. William Pitt in the British House of Commons on Thursday, 31 January 1799* (Dublin, 1799), p. 127, quoted in Paul Bew, *Ireland: The Politics of Enmity 1789–2006* (Oxford, 2007), p. 54.
73. *Parliamentary History*, 34 (London, 1815), p. 351.
74. See Barry Crosbie, *Irish Imperial Networks: Migration, Social Communication and Exchange in Nineteenth-Century India* (Cambridge, 2012), p. 85.

CHAPTER 4: CAPE TOWN

1. Lady Anne Barnard to Henry Dundas (Viscount Melville), 10 July 1797, in A. M. Lewin Robinson (ed.), *The Letters of Lady Anne Barnard to Henry Dundas from the Cape and Elsewhere, 1793–1803* (Cape Town, 1973), p. 37.
2. Roger Knight, *Britain Against Napoleon* (London, 2013), p. 72.
3. See 'Lady Anne Barnard [née Lindsay]', *Oxford Dictionary of National Biography* (Oxford, 2004).
4. William J. Burchell, *Travels in the Interior of Southern Africa* (London, 1822), vol. 1, p. 1.
5. Captain Robert Percival, *An Account of the Cape of Good Hope* (London, 1804), p. 103.
6. The phrase belongs to historian Richard Elphick. See Leonard Thompson, *A History of South Africa* (London, 1990), p. 39.

7. Anthony Trollope, *South Africa* (London, 1878), p. 81.

8. See Vivian Bickford-Smith, 'Creating a City of the Tourist Imagination', *Urban Studies*, 46, 9 (2009).

9. Quoted in the *Observer*, 9 October 2011.

10. See Douglas A. Irwin, 'Mercantilism as Strategic Trade Policy: The Anglo-Dutch Rivalry for the East India Trade', *Journal of Political Economy*, 99, 6 (1991), p. 1300.

11. Rear Admiral Fitzroy, *The Weather Book: A Manual of Practical Meteorology* (London, 1863), pp. 143–4.

12. Burchell (1822), p. 4.

13. See Nigel Worden, Elizabeth van Heyningen and Vivian Bickford-Smith, *Cape Town: The Making of a City* (Claremont, 1998), p. 12.

14. Carolyn Hamilton, Bernard K. Mbenga and Robert Ross (eds.), *The Cambridge History of South Africa*, vol. 1 (Cambridge, 2010), p. 174. See also Nigel Worden (ed.), *Cape Town: Between East and West* (Auckland Park, 2012).

15. John Stavorinus, *Voyages to the East Indies* (London, 1798), vol. 2, p. 55.

16. George McCall Theal (ed.), *Records of the Cape Colony* (London, 1897–1905), vol. 1 (1897), p. 23.

17. See Monica Wilson, 'The Hunters and the Herders', in Monica Wilson and Leonard Thompson (eds.), *A History of South Africa to 1870* (London, 1982); Thompson (1990).

18. Jemima Kindersley, *Letters from the Island of Teneriffe, Brazil, the Cape of Good Hope, and the East Indies* (London, 1777), letter dated February 1765 from Cape Town, quoted in C. R. Boxer, *The Dutch Seaborne Empire* (London, 1977), p. 245.

19. Burchell (1822), p. 70.

20. Percival (1804), p. 108.

21. Kindersley (1777), p. 53.

22. Anthony K. Millar, *Plantagenet in South Africa: Lord Charles Somerset* (Cape Town, 1965), p. 61.

23. Burchell (1822), p. 71.

24. Peter Quennell (ed.), *The Memoirs of William Hickey* (London, 1960), p. 224.

25. Ibid., p. 225.

26. Peter Kolben, *The Present State of the Cape of Good Hope* (London, 1731), vol. 1, pp. 351–2.

27. Burchell (1822), p. 73.

28. Boxer (1977), p. 263.

29. John Barrow, *An Account of Travels into the Interior of South Africa* (London, 1801), pp. 45–6.

30. Robert Semple, *Walks and Sketches at the Cape of Good Hope* (London, 1805), p. 18.

31. Kolben (1731), vol. 1, p. 350.

32. Percival (1804), p. 273.

33. See 'Dundas, Henry, First Viscount Melville', *Oxford Dictionary of National Biography* (Oxford, 2004).

34. Lord Holderness, secretary of state, dispatch to Mitchell, 1757, quoted in Paul M. Kennedy, *The Rise and Fall of British Naval Mastery* (London, 1976), p. 106.

35. *Two Views of British India: The Private Correspondence of Mr Dundas and Lord Wellesley, 1798–1801*, ed. Edward Ingram (Bath, 1970), p. 206, quoted in Michael Duffy, 'World-Wide War and British Expansion, 1793–1815', in P. J. Marshall (ed.), *The Oxford History of the British Empire*, vol. 2: *The Eighteenth Century* (Oxford, 1998), p. 191.

36. Quoted in Kennedy (1976), p. 129.

37. W. Shrubsole, *Plea in Favour of the Shipwrights Belonging to the Royal Dock Yards* (Rochester, 1770).

38. *Parliamentary Register*, vol. 14 (London, 1801), 25 March 1801, p. 577.

39. Quoted in Sam Willis, *In the Hour of Victory* (London, 2013), p. 21.

40. Theal (1897–1905), vol. 1, p. 10.

41. Ibid., vol. 1, pp. 17, 22, 26.

42. Quoted in L. C. F. Turner, 'The Cape of Good Hope and the Anglo-French Conflict, 1797–1806', *Historical Studies, Australia and New Zealand* 9, 36 (1961), p. 368.

43. Percival (1804), p. 335.

44. See Worden et al. (1998).

45. See Christopher Saunder and Iain R. Smith, 'Southern Africa, 1795–1910', in Andrew Porter (ed.), *The Oxford History of the British Empire*, vol. 3: *The Nineteenth Century* (Oxford, 1999).

46. Theal (1897–1905), vol. 2 (1898), pp. 114.

47. Ibid., vol. 2, p. 214; vol. 1, p. 17.

48. Lewin Robinson (1973), p. 43.

49. Ibid., p. 101.

50. A. M. Lewin Robinson (ed.), *The Cape Journals of Lady Anne Barnard, 1797–1798* (Cape Town, 1994), pp. 260, 265.

51. Ibid., pp. 260, 265.

52. Edward Ingram (ed.), *Two Views of British India: The Private Correspondence of Mr Dundas and Lord Wellesley* (Bath, 1970), pp. 41–2, 305.

53. Ibid., pp. 30, 94, 97.

54. Turner (1961), pp. 371–2.

55. Theal (1897–1905), vol. 5 (1899), pp. 267–8.

56. Semple (1805), p. 26.

57. Richard Barnard Fisher, *The Importance of the Cape of Good Hope, as a Colony to Great Britain, Independently of the Advantages It Possesses as a Military and Naval Station, and the Key to Our Territorial Possessions in India* (London, 1816), p. 26; Percival (1804), pp. 252, 256; Semple (1805), p. 33.

58. Fisher (1816), p. 27; Semple (1805), p. 32.

59. Stavorinus (1798), vol. 1, p. 565; Barrow (1801), p. 48; Percival (1804), p. 261; Lewin Robinson (1994), p. 266.

60. Barrow (1801), pp. 49, 50; Kindersley (1777), p. 64.

61. George Champion, *The Journal of an American Missionary* (Cape Town, 1968), p. 28, quoted in Vertrees Malherbe, 'Christian-Muslim Marriage and Cohabitation: An Aspect of Identity and Family Formation in Nineteenth-Century Cape Town', *Journal of Imperial and Commonwealth History*, 36, 1 (2008), p. 6.

62. John Campbell, *Travels in South Africa, Undertaken at the Request of the Missionary Society* (London, 1815), pp. 7, 495.

63. Barrow (1801), p. 44.

64. See Chris A. Bayly, *Imperial Meridian: The British Empire and the World, 1780–1830* (London, 1989).

65. Campbell (1815), p. 8.

66. Percival (1804), p. 105.

67. See Worden et al. (1998).

68. *South African Commercial Advertiser*, 17 May 1826.

69. See Graham Viney and Phillida Brooke Simons, *The Cape of Good Hope* (Houghton, 1994).

70. Worden et al. (1998), p. 117.

71. Burchell (1822), p. 28.

72. Millar (1965), p. 64.

73. C. Pama, *Regency Cape Town* (Cape Town, 2008), p. 79.

74. See Worden et al. (1998); Viney and Simons (1994).

75. Burchell (1822), p. 74.

76. Patrick Colquhoun, *A Treatise on the Wealth, Power and Resources of the British Empire, in Every Quarter of the World, Including the East Indies* (London, 1815), p. 88; see alse John Darwin, *Unfinished Empire: The Global Expansion of Britain* (London, 2012).

CHAPTER 5: CALCUTTA

1. Quoted in Iris Butler, *The Eldest Brother: The Marquess of Wellesley, the Duke of Wellington's Eldest Brother* (London, 1973), p. 134.
2. George, Viscount Valentia, *Voyages and Travels to India* (London, 1809), vol. 1, pp. 61–2, 235–6.
3. Maria Graham, *Journal of a Residence in India* (Edinburgh, 1813), p. 138.
4. Quoted in Sir Penderel Moon, *The British Conquest and Dominion of India* (London, 1989), p. 312.
5. Brian Paul Bach, *Calcutta's Edifice: The Buildings of a Great City* (New Delhi, 2006), p. 189.
6. *New York Times*, 29 April 2009.
7. On the cultural significance of the Black Hole and the manipulation of its memory, see Partha Chatterjee, *The Black Hole of Empire* (Princeton, 2012).
8. Jan Morris and Simon Winchester, *Stones of Empire* (Oxford, 2005), pp. 116–17.
9. Partha Chatterjee, 'Are Indian Cities Becoming Bourgeois At Last?', in *The Politics of the Governed* (New York, 2004).
10. Rudyard Kipling, *The City of Dreadful Night and Other Places* (Allahabad, 1891), p. 1.
11. Somini Sengupta, 'A Walk in Calcutta', *New York Times*, 29 April 2009.
12. *Guardian*, 2 February 2013.
13. *Financial Times*, 10 June 2011.
14. Kipling (1891), p. 2.
15. Geoffrey Moorhouse, *Calcutta* (London, 1998), pp. 31–2.
16. See Nick Robins, *The Corporation That Changed the World* (London, 2006), pp. 8, 27–8, 43.
17. See P. J. Marshall, 'The British in Asia, 1700–1765', in P. J. Marshall (ed.), *The Oxford History of the British Empire*, vol. 2: *The Eighteenth Century* (Oxford, 1998).
18. John Horwell, *A Genuine Narrative of the Deplorable Death of the English Gentlemen, and Others, Who were Suffocated in the Black-Hole in Fort William, in the Kingdom of Bengal; in the Night Succeeding the 20th Day of June, 1756*, quoted in Chatterjee (2012), p. 23.
19. Robins (2006), pp. 68–9.
20. John Dowie (ed.), *Macaulay's Essay on Clive* (1840) (London, 1900), pp. 1–2.
21. See H. V. Bowen, 'Robert Clive', *Oxford Dictionary of National Biography* (Oxford, 2008).

22. Dowie (1900), pp. 74–5.
23. William Bolts, *Considerations on India Affairs* (London, 1772), p. 74.
24. Horace Walpole's *Correspondence*, vol. 23, p. 387: http://images.library. yale.edu/hwcorrespondence.
25. Bolts (1772), p. v.
26. Edmund Burke, 'Speech on Mr Fox's East India Bill', 1 December 1783.
27. See Robert Travers, *Ideology and Empire in Eighteenth-Century India* (Cambridge, 2007).
28. Walpole, *Correspondence*, vol. 23, pp. 381, 387: http://images.library. yale.edu/hwcorrespondence.
29. See Pradip Sinha, 'Calcutta and the Currents of History, 1690–1912', in Sukanta Chaudhuri (ed.), *Calcutta: The Living City* (Oxford, 1990).
30. Eliza Fay, *Original Letters from India* (Calcutta, 1817), p. 238.
31. Quoted in Denis Kincaid, *British Social Life in India, 1608–1937* (London, 1938), p. 22; quoted in J. P. Losty, *Calcutta: City of Palaces* (London, 1990), p. 45; Graham (1813), pp. 132–3.
32. John Stavorinus, *Voyages to the East Indies* (London, 1798), vol. 1, pp. 497–8.
33. See Losty (1990); Dhrubajyoti Banerjea, *European Calcutta* (New Delhi, 2005).
34. Jemima Kindersley, *Letters from the Island of Teneriffe, Brazil, the Cape of Good Hope, and the East Indies* (London, 1777), pp. 277–8; Fay (1817), p. 240; Graham (1813), p. 153.
35. Kindersley (1777), pp. 278, 274; Peter Quennell (ed.), *Memoirs of William Hickey* (London, 1960), p. 237; S. Shushtari, *Kitab Tuhfat al-'Alam* (Bombay, 1847), p. 427, quoted in William Dalrymple, *White Mughals* (London, 2004), p. 408.
36. See Dalrymple (2004).
37. Samita Gupta, 'Theory and Practice of Town Planning in Calcutta, 1817–1912: An Appraisal', *Indian Economic and Social History Review*, 30, 1 (1993), p. 34. See also Swati Chattopadhyay, *Representing Calcutta: Modernity, Nationalism, and the Colonial Uncanny* (London, 2005).
38. G. G. Nichols, 'Field Book, Survey of a Part of Calcutta' (1809), MS Collection in the National Library of India, Calcutta, quoted in S. N. Mukherjee, *Calcutta: Essays in Urban History* (Calcutta, 1993), p. 59.
39. Quoted in Moorhouse (1998), p. 75.
40. Anon., *Hartly House, Calcutta: A Novel of the Days of Warren Hastings* (London, 1989), pp. 13, 18.
41. Quoted in Dalrymple (2004), p. 411.
42. Quennell (1960), pp. 240, 248.

43. Losty (1990), p. 56.
44. Roger Hudson (ed.), *William Hickey: Memoirs of a Georgian Rake* (London, 1995), pp. 386–7.
45. Fay (1817), pp. 255, 271.
46. Hudson (1995), p. 388.
47. Graham (1813), p. 139.
48. See Prosenjit Das Gupta, *Ten Walks in Calcutta* (Kolkata, 2008), pp. 8–10.
49. Anne Catherine Monkland, *Life in India: or, The English at Calcutta* (London, 1828), vol. 1, pp. 192–3.
50. C. J. Hawes, *Poor Relations: The Making of a Eurasian Community in British India, 1773–1833* (London, 1996), pp. 3–4.
51. See Durba Ghosh, *Sex and the Family in Colonial India* (Cambridge, 2006).
52. P. J. Marshall (ed.), *The British Discovery of Hinduism* (Cambridge, 1970), p. 189. See also P. J. Marshall, 'Warren Hastings', *Oxford Dictionary of National Biography* (Oxford, 2004).
53. See Michael J. Franklin, 'Sir William Jones', *Oxford Dictionary of National Biography* (Oxford, 2004).
54. See Dermot Killingley, 'Rammohun Roy', *Oxford Dictionary of National Biography* (Oxford, 2004).
55. See Kapil Raj, *Relocating Modern Science: Circulation and the Construction of Knowledge in South Asia, 1650–1900* (Basingstoke, 2007).
56. Chatterjee (2012), p. 129.
57. J. R. Martin, *Notes on the Medical Topography of Calcutta* (Calcutta, 1837), p. 19.
58. Valentia (1809), vol. 1, p. 237.
59. See Swati Chattopadhyay, 'Blurring Boundaries: The Limits of "White Town" in Colonial Calcutta', *Journal of the Society of Architectural Historians*, 59, 2 (2000).
60. Kindersley (1777), p. 277.
61. Graham (1813), p. 134.
62. Quoted in Robins (2006), p. 89.
63. See C. A. Bayly and Katherine Prior, 'Charles Cornwallis', *Oxford Dictionary of National Biography* (Oxford, 2004).
64. See Ranajit Guha, *A Rule of Property for Bengal* (New Delhi, 1981).
65. See Blair B. Kling, *Partner in Empire: Dwarkanath Tagore and the Age of Enterprise in Eastern India* (Calcutta, 1981).
66. See C. A. Bayly, 'Richard Wellesley', *Oxford Dictionary of National Biography* (Oxford, 2004).

67. *The Despatches, Minutes and Correspondence of the Marquess Wellesley K.G., During His Administration in India*, ed. Montgomery Martin (London, 1836), vol. 2, pp. 38–9, quoted in John Severn, *Architects of Empire: The Duke of Wellington and His Brothers* (Norman, 2007), p. 103.

68. Peter Cunningham (ed.), *The Letters of Horace Walpole, Earl of Oxford* (London, 1858), vol. 3, p. 496.

69. Sidney J. Owen (ed.), *A Selection from the Despatches, Treaties, and Other Papers of the Marquess Wellesley, K.G. during His Government of India* (Oxford, 1877), p. 722.

70. Valentia (1809), vol. 1, p. 251.

71. Owen (1877), p. 687.

72. Edward Ingram (ed.), *Two Views of British India: The Private Correspondence of Mr Dundas and Lord Wellesley* (Bath, 1970), p. 201. See also, Kapil Raj, 'Colonial Encounters and the Forging of New Knowledge and National Identities: Great Britain and India, 1760–1850', *Osiris*, 2nd Series, 15 (2000), p. 125.

73. 'Sketches of India', *Calcutta Journal*, New Series, 1 (3 January 1822), p. 26, quoted in David Kopf, *British Orientalism and the Bengal Renaissance: The Dynamics of Indian Modernization, 1773–1835* (Berkeley, 1969), p. 63.

74. *Essays by Students of the College of Fort William in Bengal* (Calcutta, 1820), vol. 2, p. xii.

75. Mornington to Grenville, 18 November 1798, Dropmore Papers, British Library, 4:382–4, quoted in Severn (2007), p. 90.

76. Morris and Winchester (2005), p. 67.

77. Lord Curzon, *British Government in India* (London, 1925), vol. 1, p. 41.

78. W. S. Seton-Karr (ed.), *Selections from Calcutta Gazettes* (London, 1864–9), vol. 3, 24 March 1803.

79. E. Fenton, *The Journal of Mrs Fenton. A Narrative of Her Life in India, the Isle of France, and Tasmania During the Years 1826–30* (London, 1901), p. 249.

80. Monkland (1828), vol. 1, pp. 198, 200.

81. Ingram (1970), pp. 145, 240.

82. Quoted in Losty (1990), p. 71.

83. Quoted in Chattopadhyay (2005), p. 87.

84. Martin (1837), p. 23.

85. A. M. Lewin Robinson (ed.), *The Letters of Lady Anne Barnard to Henry Dundas from the Cape and Elsewhere, 1793–1803* (Cape Town, 1973), p. 274.

86. Ingram (1970), p. 287; Owen (1877), p. 697.

87. Severn (2007).

88. Curzon (1925), vol. 2, pp. 173–4.

89. Hudson (1995), p. 405.

90. H. Woodrow, *Macaulay's Minutes on Education in India, Written in the Years 1835, 1836, and 1837* (Calcutta, 1862), 2 February 1835.

91. Macaulay in *Hansard* (Commons), 10 July 1833, vol. 19, cc. 585–6, quoted in E. Stokes, *The English Utilitarians and India* (Oxford, 1963), p. 45.

92. G. R. Gleig, *The Life of Major-General Sir Thomas Munro* (London, 1830), vol. 2, pp. 57, 58; vol. 3, p. 381.

93. See Anthony Webster, *The Richest East India Merchant: The Life and Business of John Palmer of Calcutta* (Leicester, 2007).

94. George Otto Trevelyan, *Life and Letters of Lord Macaulay* (London, 1881), p. 308.

95. Kipling (1891), p. 1.

96. See Mukherjee (1993).

CHAPTER 6: HONG KONG

1. Letter from James Matheson to William Jardine, 22 January 1841, Jardine and Matheson Archive, Cambridge University: C5–6, pp. 51–2, quoted in Alain Le Pichon (ed.), *China Trade and Empire: Jardine, Matheson & Co. and the Origins of British Rule in Hong Kong 1827–1843* (Oxford, 2006), pp. 464–5.

2. Sir Edward Belcher, *Narrative of a Voyage Round the World, Performed in Her Majesty's Ship Sulphur, During the Years 1836–1842* (London, 1843), vol. 2, pp. 147–8.

3. James Matheson to William Jardine, 30 January 1841, Jardine and Matheson Archive, Cambridge University: C5–6, pp. 64–5, quoted in Le Pichon (2006), p. 468.

4. *Independent*, 5 July 1997.

5. James Pope-Hennessy, *Half-Crown Colony* (London, 1969), p. 34.

6. Henry Charles Sirr, *China and the Chinese: Their Religion, Character, Customs and Manufactures* (London, 1849), p. 2.

7. See Carl A. Trocki, 'Drugs, Taxes and Chinese Capitalism in Southeast Asia', in Timothy Brook and Bon Tadashi Wakabayashi (eds.), *Opium Regimes: China, Britain and Japan* (London, 2000).

8. John Macgowan, *How England Saved China* (London, 1913), pp. 304–5.

9. 'William Jardine', *Oxford Dictionary of National Biography* (Oxford, 2004).

10. Jardine and Matheson Archive, Cambridge University: B2/12/21, 24 September 1839; C6/2, 25 May 1842, quoted in Chan Wai Kwan, *The Making of Hong Society* (Oxford, 1991), pp. 24, 23.

11. H. Hamilton Lindsay, *Letter to the Right Honourable Viscount Palmerston on British Relations with China* (London, 1836), p. 19.

12. F. W. Mote, *Imperial China 900–1800* (Cambridge, Mass., 2003), p. 913.

13. James Matheson, *The Present Position and Prospects of the British Trade with China* (London, 1836), p. 1.

14. Ibid., p. 122.

15. E. J. Eitel, *Europe in China* (1895) (Oxford, 1983), p. 25.

16. *Minute by Sir T. S. Raffles on the Establishment of a Malay College at Singapore, 1819*, British Library, D742/38, Microfilm No. NAB 083.

17. Eitel (1983), p. 25.

18. See Robert Bickers, *The Scramble for China* (London, 2011), pp. 37–40.

19. Quoted in Kwan (1991), p. 21.

20. Eitel (1983), p. 23.

21. See Le Pichon (2006); 'William Jardine', *Oxford Dictionary of National Biography* (Oxford, 2004); 'James Matheson', *Oxford Dictionary of National Biography* (Oxford, 2004); Benjamin Disraeli, *Sybil, or, The Two Nations* (1845) (London, 1980), p. 74.

22. Lydia He Liu, *The Clash of Empires: The Invention of China in Modern World Making* (Cambridge, Mass., 2009), p. 237.

23. Robert Blake, *Jardine Matheson: Traders of the Far East* (London, 1999), p. 93.

24. 'William Jardine', *Oxford Dictionary of National Biography* (Oxford, 2004).

25. Belcher (1843), vol. 2, p. 143.

26. Immanuel Hsü, *The Rise of Modern China* (Oxford, 2000), pp. 187–8.

27. Queen Victoria's letter to the King of the Belgians, 13 April 1841, *The Letters of Queen Victoria: A Selection from Her Majesty's Correspondence between the Years 1837 and 1861*, vol. 1: *1837–1843* (London, 1907), quoted in Barbara-Sue White (ed.), *Hong Kong: Somewhere between Heaven and Earth* (Oxford, 1996), p. 26.

28. See Robert Bickers, 'Shanghailanders: The Formation and Identity of the British Settler Community in Shanghai 1843–1937', *Past and Present*, 159 (1998).

29. *Hansard* (Commons), 8 April 1840, vol. 53, cc. 749–837.

30. Quoted in Le Pichon (2006), p. 51.

31. *Hansard* (Lords), 6 February 1844, vol. 72, cc. 263–8.

32. Michael Greenberg, *British Trade and the Opening of China 1800–1842* (Cambridge, 1951), p. 215.

33. See John Gallagher and Ronald Robinson, 'The Imperialism of Free Trade', *The Economic History Review*, 6, 1 (1953).

34. *Hansard* (Lords), 6 February 1844, vol. 72, cc. 263–8.

35. *Friend of China*, 6 April 1843, p. 15, quoted in C. M. Munn, *Anglo-China: Chinese People and British Rule in Hong Kong 1841–1880* (Richmond, 2001), p. 28.

36. Letter from James Matheson to William Jardine, 23 August 1841, Jardine and Matheson Archive, Cambridge University: C5–7, pp. 121–5, quoted in Le Pichon (2006), p. 497.

37. Kwan (1991), p. 24.

38. Arthur Cunynghame, *An Aide-de-Camp's Recollections of Service in China* (London, 1844), vol. 1, pp. 83–4.

39. Lord Redesdale, *The Attaché at Peking* (London, 1900), p. 14, quoted in White (1996), p. 67.

40. Rev. James Legge, 'The Colony of Hong Kong' (1872), *Journal of the Royal Asiatic Society Hong Kong Branch*, 11 (1971), p. 172.

41. Ibid., p. 175.

42. Sirr (1849), pp. 4–5.

43. Albert Smith, *To China and Back* (1859) (Hong Kong, 1974), p. 39.

44. Letter dated 26 January 1845, Letters of Lieutenant Collinson (Collinson MSS) in Hong Kong Public Records Office, quoted in Frank Welsh, *A History of Hong Kong* (Plymouth, 2007), p. 168.

45. Osmond Tiffany, *The Canton Chinese: or, The American's Sojourn in the Celestial Empire* (Boston, 1849), pp. 259–60, quoted in White (1996), p. 40.

46. See Jan Morris, *Hong Kong: Epilogue to an Empire* (London, 1997).

47. W. H. Hall and W. D. Bernard, *Narrative of the Voyages and Services of the Nemesis* (London, 1845), p. 254.

48. Ibid., p. 256.

49. W. M. Wood, *Fankwei: or, The San Jacinto in the Seas of India, China and Japan* (New York, 1859), p. 267, quoted in Bickers (2011), p. 91.

50. Sirr (1849), p. 3.

51. Munn (2001).

52. Legge (1971), p. 176.

53. Sirr (1849), p. 38.

54. *The Letters of Queen Victoria*, vol. 2: *1855–1861* (London, 1908), p. 4, quoted in Geoffrey Robley Sayer, *Hong Kong: Birth, Adolescence, and Coming of Age* (London, 1937), p. 138.

55. *Report from the Select Committee on Commercial Relations with China* (London, 1847), p. viii.

56. Robert Montgomery Martin, 'Report on Hong Kong', 24 July 1844, National Archives, London, CO/129/18, quoted in G. B. Endacott (ed.), *An Eastern Entrepôt* (London, 1964), pp. 99, 102.

57. *The Economist*, August 1846.

58. David R. Meyer, *Hong Kong as a Global Metropolis* (Cambridge, 2000).

59. G. B. Endacott, *A History of Hong Kong* (London, 1958).

60. Morris (1997).

61. Quoted in Endacott (1964), p. 98.

62. Ibid., pp. 81–2.

63. Smith (1974), p. 28.

64. See Christopher M. Munn, 'The Hong Kong Opium Revenue, 1845–1885', in Brook and Wakabayashi (2000).

65. Quoted in Eitel (1983), p. 571.

66. *New York Daily Tribune*, 16 March 1857, 10 April 1857.

67. *The Chinese Repository*, 11 (1842), p. 628, quoted in Wong Man Kong, *James Legge: A Pioneer at Crossroads of East and West* (Hong Kong, 1996), p. 35.

68. R. G. Milne, *Sinim: A Plea for China. A Discourse Delivered in Providence Chapel, Whitehaven* (London, 1843), p. 3, quoted in Kong (1996), p. 38.

69. E. Hodder (ed.), *The Life and Work of the Seventh Earl of Shaftesbury, K.G.* (London, 1886), vol. 1, p. 440, quoted in Brian Stanley, *The Bible and the Flag* (Leicester, 1990), p. 106.

70. Reverend George Smith, *A Narrative of an Exploratory Visit to each of the Consular Cities of China and to the Islands of Hong Kong and Chusan* (London, 1847), p. 446.

71. Letter from Hong Kong, 25 February 1844, quoted in Helen Edith Legge, *James Legge: Missionary and Scholar* (London, 1905), p. 49.

72. Quoted in Kate Lowe, 'The Beliefs, Aspirations and Methods of the First Missionaries in British Hong Kong, 1841–5', in Pieter N. Holtrop and Hugh McLeod (eds.), *Missions and Missionaries* (Woodbridge, 2000), p. 106.

73. Smith (1847), p. 448.

74. Morris (1997).

75. Legge (1971), p. 177.

76. Redesdale (1900), p. 5, quoted in White (1996), p. 65.

77. Bowring to Lytton, 18 September 1858, CO 129/69, 247–8, National Archives (London), quoted in Munn (2001), p. 1.

78. See Jung-Fang Tsai, *Hong Kong in Chinese History* (New York, 1993).
79. Smith (1847), p. 447.
80. Legge (1971), p. 185.
81. John M. Carroll, *Edge of Empire: Chinese Elites and British Colonials in Hong Kong* (London, 2005), p. 53.
82. Kwan (1991).
83. Wang Tao, 'My Sojourn in Hong Kong', translated by Yang Qinghua, in *Renditions*, Special Issue, 29–30 (1988), p. 39, quoted in White (1996), p. 64.
84. Eitel (1983), p. v.
85. Quoted in White (1996), p. 65.
86. Quoted in Kwan (1991), p. 36.
87. Smith (1974), p. 33.
88. Kwan (1991), p. 44.
89. Rudyard Kipling, *From Sea to Sea: Letters of Travel* (London, 1888), pp. 289–90.
90. Jules Verne, *Around the World in Eighty Days* (1873) (London, 2012), p. 87; Legge (1971), p. 175; Kipling (1888), p. 249; Harold Nicolson, *Curzon* (London, 1934), p. 13.

CHAPTER 7: BOMBAY

1. *Report of the Commission on the Drainage and Water Supply of Bombay* (Bombay, 1869), p. vi; Henry Conybeare, *Report on the Sanitary State and Sanitary Requirements of Bombay* (Bombay, 1852), p. 17; Andrew Leith, *Report on the Sanitary State of the Island of Bombay* (Bombay, 1864), pp. 12, 15; Sir Dinshaw Wacha, *Shells from the Sands of Bombay – Being My Recollections and Reminiscences, 1860–1875* (Bombay, 1920), pp. 467, 478; Gillian E. Tindall, *City of Gold: The Biography of Bombay* (London, 1982), p. 201; Mridula Ramanna, *Western Medicine and Public Health in Colonial Bombay* (London, 2002).
2. J. H. Furneaux, *Glimpses of India* (Bombay, 1895), pp. 200, 196.
3. Sir Richard Temple, *A Bird's Eye View of Picturesque India* (London, 1898), p. 20, quoted in Sujata Patel and Alice Thorner (eds.), *Bombay: Mosaic of Modern Culture* (Bombay, 1995), p. 168.
4. G. W. Stevens, 'All India in Miniature', in R. P. Karkaria (ed.), *The Charm of Bombay* (Bombay, 1915), p. 81.
5. Ibid.
6. Jan Morris and Simon Winchester, *Stones of Empire* (Oxford, 2005), p. 133.

7. Suketu Mehta, *Maximum City: Bombay Lost and Found* (London, 2004).

8. Kalpana Sharma, *Rediscovering Dharavi* (Delhi, 2000), p. 8. See also Ranjani Mazumdar, 'Spectacle and Death in the City of Bombay Cinema', in Gyan Prakash and Kevin M. Kruse (eds.), *The Spaces of the Modern City* (Princeton, 2008); and Jean Drèze and Amartya Sen, *An Uncertain Glory: India and its Contradictions* (London, 2013).

9. See Thomas Blom Hansen, *Wages of Violence: Naming and Identity in Postcolonial Bombay* (Princeton 2001).

10. Gyan Prakash, *Mumbai Fables* (New Delhi, 2011), p. 29.

11. Pratapaditya Pal, 'Introduction', in Pauline Rohatgi, Pheroza Godrej and Rahul Mehrotra (eds.), *Bombay to Mumbai* (Mumbai, 1997).

12. Furneaux (1895), p. 196.

13. Silk Buckingham, 'Autobiography', in Karkaria (1915), p. 64.

14. See Sharada Dwivedi and Rahul Mehrotra, *Bombay: The Cities Within* (Bombay, 1995).

15. Thomas Carlyle, 'Chartism', in *Selected Writings* (Harmondsworth, 1986), p. 211.

16. John Martineau, *The Life and Correspondence of Sir Bartle Frere* (London, 1895), p. 399.

17. Alexander Mackay, *Western India: Reports Addressed to the Chambers of Commerce of Manchester, Liverpool, Blackburn, and Glasgow* (London, 1853), p. 5.

18. Karl Marx, 'The British Rule in India' (1853), in James Ledbetter (ed.), *Dispatches for the New York Tribune: Selected Journalism of Karl Marx* (London, 2007), pp. 215–16.

19. Martineau (1895), vol. 1, p. 399.

20. Sir Richard Temple, *Men and Events of My Time in India* (London, 1882), p. 268.

21. S. M. Edwardes, *The Rise of Bombay: A Retrospect* (Bombay, 1902), p. 265. See also Prakash (2011); Rekha Ranade, *Sir Bartle Frere and His Times: A Study of His Bombay Years* (New Delhi, 1990).

22. W. J. Macpherson, 'Investment in Indian Railways, 1845–75', *The Economic History Review*, 8, 2 (1955), p. 177.

23. James J. Berkley, *Paper on the Thul Ghaut Railway Incline* (Bombay, 1850), p. 6.

24. Wacha (1920), p. 165.

25. Martineau (1895), vol. 1, p. 402.

26. Mrs Anne Elwood, *Narrative of a Journey Overland from England ... to India* (London, 1830), vol. 1, p. 378; Viscountess Falkland,

Chow-Chow: Being Selections from a Journal Kept in India, Egypt and Syria (London, 1857), vol. 1, p. 8; Stevens (1915), p. 83; G. W. Forrest, *Cities of India* (London, 1903), pp. 33–4.

27. Stevens (1915), p. 82.

28. Norman Macleod, *Peeps at the Far East: A Familiar Account of a Visit to India* (London, 1871), p. 26.

29. See Meera Kosambi, 'British Bombay and Marathi Mumbai: Some Nineteenth-Century Perceptions', in Patel and Thorner (1995).

30. 'Report on European Pauperism', December 1863, p. 19 (Maharashtra State Archives Judicial Department/1867/vol. 13/140), quoted in Avarind Ganachari, '"White Man's Embarrassment": European Vagrancy in 19th Century Bombay', *Economic and Political Weekly*, 37, 25 (2002), p. 2477.

31. Edwardes (1902), p. 265.

32. James Gray, *Life in Bombay and the Neighbouring Out-Stations* (London, 1852), p. 239.

33. Edwardes (1902), p. 283.

34. Dwivedi and Mehrotra (1995).

35. Furneaux (1895), p. 196.

36. Anon, *Bombay and Its Ducks of 1882 by One of the Latter* (Bombay, 1882), p. 7.

37. Mary Carpenter, *Six Months in India* (London, 1868), vol. 2, p. 1.

38. Alexis de Tocqueville, *Journeys to England and Ireland* (1835) (London, 1958), p. 108.

39. Quoted in Kosambi (1995), pp. 19, 22.

40. Wacha (1920), p. 319.

41. Quoted in Dwivedi and Mehrotra (1995), p. 86.

42. Quoted in Tindall (1982), p. 223.

43. Mariam Dossal, *Mumbai: Theatre of Conflict, City of Hope* (Oxford, 2010).

44. Temple (1882), pp. 269–70.

45. Ibid., p. 259.

46. L. Rousselet, *India and Its Native Provinces: Travels in Central India and in the Presidencies of Bombay and Bengal* (London, 1875), p. 14, quoted in Dwivedi and Mehrotra (1995), p. 76.

47. *Bombay and Its Ducks of 1882* (1882), pp. 64–5.

48. Temple (1882), p. 273.

49. Conybeare (1852), pp. 2, 21, 39.

50. See D. A. Washbrook, 'India, 1818–1860: The Two Faces of Colonialism', in Andrew Porter (ed.), *The Oxford History of the British Empire*, vol. 3: *The Nineteenth Century* (Oxford, 1999).

51. Mike Davis, *Late Victorian Holocausts* (London, 2001), pp. 37, 39.

52. H. Conybeare, *Report on the Sanitary State and Requirements of Bombay, Selections from the Records of the Bombay Government*, New Series, vol. 11 (Bombay, 1855), Appendix H, 'A Comparison between Different Methods of Conveyancing and Ultimately Disposing of Night Soil', p. 28, quoted in Rajnarayan Chandavarkar, *History, Culture and the Indian City* (Cambridge, 2009), p. 48.

53. John Broich, 'Engineering the Empire: British Water Supply Systems and Colonial Societies, 1850–1900', in *Journal of British Studies*, 47 (2007), p. 365.

54. Letter from Florence Nightingale to James Pattison Walker, 3 January 1865, Florence Nightingale Museum, London, quoted in Gérard Vallée (ed.), *Florence Nightingale on Health in India* (Waterloo, 2006), pp. 8–9. See also, Mridula Ramanna, 'Florence Nightingale and Bombay Presidency', *Social Scientist*, 30, 9–10 (2002), pp. 31–46.

55. Florence Nightingale, *How People May Live and Not Die in India* (London, 1863), pp. 6, 7, 8.

56. Florence Nightingale, *Life or Death in India* (London, 1874), pp. 3, 16.

57. See Mariam Dossal, *Imperial Designs and Imperial Realities* (Bombay, 1991).

58. Leith (1864), p. 36.

59. Martineau (1895), vol. 1, pp. 463, 464.

60. Jamsetjee Jejeebhoy to Lord Elphinstone, 26 October 1854, India Office Records MSS Eur F87/163, British Library, 5, 8, 10, quoted in Broich (2007), p. 361.

61. G. B. Shaw, *The Common Sense of Municipal Trading* (London, 1904), pp. 110–11.

62. *Report of the Commission on the Drainage and Water Supply of Bombay* (1869), p. 71.

63. *Bombay and Its Ducks of 1882* (1882), p. 5.

64. *Report of the Sanitary Commission for Bombay, 1865* (Byculla, 1866), p. 10.

65. Edwardes (1902), p. 284.

66. Joseph Chamberlain to Jesse Collings, 26 April 1875, Chamberlain Papers (University of Birmingham), quoted in Denis Judd, *Radical Joe: A Life of Joseph Chamberlain* (Cardiff, 1993), p. 67.

67. Edwardes (1902), p. 261.

68. Quoted in Dwivedi and Mehrotra (1995), p. 147.

69. Asok Mitra, *Calcutta's Indian City* (Calcutta, 1963), pp. 39–40.

70. Gray (1852), p. 248.

71. Quoted in Tindall (1982), p. 212.

72. Temple (1882), p. 259.

73. See Dwivedi and Mehrotra (1995).

74. See Mariam Dossal, 'The "Hall of Wonder" within the "Garden of Delight"', in Rohatgi, Godrej and Mehrotra (1997).

75. *Bombay and Its Ducks of 1882* (1882), p. 5; Temple (1882), p. 277.

76. *The Building* News, 18 (1870), quoted in Christopher W. London, *Bombay Gothic* (Mumbai, 2002), Appendix.

77. Quoted in Tindall (1982), p. 236.

78. See Philip Davies, *Splendours of the Raj: British Architecture in India, 1660 to 1947* (London, 1985).

79. Preeti Chopra, *A Joint Enterprise: Indian Elites and the Making of British Bombay* (Minneapolis, 2011), p. 69.

80. See Sharada Dwivedi and Rahul Mehrotra, *Fort Walks* (Mumbai, 2003).

81. Morris and Winchester (2005), p. 133.

82. Furneaux (1895), p. 203.

CHAPTER 8: MELBOURNE

1. See David Dunstan (ed.), *Victorian Icon* (Victoria, 1996); Kate Darian-Smith (ed.), *Seize the Day* (Monash, 2010).

2. Charles W. Dilke, *Problems of Greater Britain* (London, 1890), p. 214; Anthony Trollope, *Australia and New Zealand* (London, 1873), vol. 1, p. 75.

3. www.melbourne.vic.gov.au.

4. John Sutherland, *Victoria and Its Metropolis – Past and Present* (Melbourne, 1888), p. 490.

5. See Ian Turner, 'The Growth of Melbourne', in J. W. McCarty and C. B. Schedvin (eds.), *Australian Capital Cities* (Sydney, 1978).

6. A. F. Weber, *The Growth of Cities in the Nineteenth Century: A Study in Statistics* (1899) (Ithaca, 1967), p. 138.

7. Henry Cornish, *Under the Southern Cross* (Madras, 1880), p. 94.

8. Mr Shiels, MLA, *Victoria Parliamentary Papers*, vol. 58 (1888), p. 1318, quoted in McCarty and Schedvin (1978), p. 69.

9. Trollope (1873), vol. 1, p. 383.

10. Isabella Bird, 'Australia Felix: Impressions of Victoria', in Judith Johnson and Monica Anderson (eds.), *Australia Imagined* (Crawley, 2005), p. 62.

11. Clara Aspinall, *Three Years in Melbourne* (London, 1862), p. 7.
12. Charles W. Dilke, *Greater Britain: A Record of Travel in English Speaking Countries During 1866 and 1867* (London, 1869), vol. 2, p. 22.
13. *British Parliamentary Papers*, vol. 34 (1852), p. 1508.
14. Sutherland (1888), p. 545.
15. Frank Fowler, *Southern Lights and Shadows: Being Brief Notes of Three Years' Experience of Social, Literary and Political Life in Australia* (London, 1859), p. 16.
16. R. E. N. Twopeny, *Town Life in Australia* (London, 1883), pp. 2–3.
17. Geoffrey Bolton, 'Money: Trade, Investment and Economic Nationalism', in Deryck M. Schreuder and Stuart Ward (eds.), *Australia's Empire* (Oxford, 2008).
18. Edwin Carton Booth, *Another England: Life, Living, Homes and Homemakers in Victoria* (London, 1869), p. 269.
19. J. A. Froude, *Oceana, or England and Her Colonies* (Leipzig, 1887), p. 89.
20. J. R. Seeley, *The Expansion of England* (London, 1895), p. 10.
21. E. S. Creasy, *The Rise and Progress of the English Constitution* (London, 1858), p. 16.
22. Dilke (1869), vol. 2, p. 149.
23. Seeley (1895), p. 184.
24. Froude (1887), pp. 20–21, 25.
25. J. L. Garvin, *Life of Joseph Chamberlain* (London, 1933–5), vol. 2, p. 27.
26. Froude (1887), p. 25.
27. Denis Judd, *Radical Joe: A Life of Joseph Chamberlain* (Cardiff, 1993), p. 252.
28. V. I. Lenin, 'Imperialism', in *Selected Works* (New York, 1976), vol. 1, p. 260.
29. P. J. Cain and A. G. Hopkins, *British Imperialism: Innovation and Expansion 1688–1914* (Harlow, 1993), pp. 173–4, 166–7.
30. See Duncan Bell, *The Idea of Greater Britain* (Oxford, 2007), p. 58.
31. Seeley (1895), pp. 18–19, 60.
32. Charles W. Boyd (ed.), *Mr Chamberlain's Speeches* (London, 1914), vol. 1, p. 279.
33. Carton Booth (1869), p. 1.
34. Charles Rooking Carter, *Victoria, The British 'El Dorado'; or, Melbourne in 1869* (London, 1870), p. 67.
35. Froude (1887), p. 99.
36. A. Patchett Martin, *Australia and the Empire* (Edinburgh, 1889), p. 74.

37. H. G. Turner, *A History of the Colony of Victoria* (London, 1904), vol. 2, p. 262.

38. Mark Twain, *More Tramps Abroad* (London, 1897), pp. 102, 103.

39. Sutherland (1888), p. 543.

40. Twopeny (1883), p. 5.

41. N. W. Pollard, *Homes in Victoria* (Melbourne, 1861), p. 25; Granville Wilson and Peter Sands, *Building a City: 100 Years of Melbourne Architecture* (Melbourne, 1981).

42. See Allan Willingham, 'A Permanent and Extensive Exhibition Building', in Dunstan (1996).

43. Twopeny (1883), p. 11.

44. R. Wright, *The Bureaucrats' Domain: Space and the Public Interest in Victoria 1836–84* (Melbourne, 1989), p. 34.

45. *Illustrated Handbook of Victoria, Australia,* Colonial and Indian Exhibition, London (1886) (Melbourne, 1886).

46. Georgina Whitehead, *Civilising the City* (Melbourne, 1997), p. 84. See also R. T. W. Pescott, *The Royal Botanic Gardens Melbourne* (Melbourne, 1982).

47. James Grant and Geoffrey Serle, *The Melbourne Scene* (Melbourne, 1957), p. 149.

48. Trollope (1873), vol. 1, p. 393.

49. Aspinall (1862), p. 89.

50. Turner (1904), vol 2, p. 262.

51. Aspinall (1862), p. 36; Twopeny (1883), p. 3; Carter (1870), pp. 61–2; Froude (1887), p. 98; John Freeman, *Light and Shadows of Melbourne Life* (London, 1888), p. 10.

52. A. G. Austin (ed.), *The Webbs' Australian Diary* (1898) (Bath, 1965), pp. 66, 69, 71 H. M. Hyndman, *Record of an Adventurous Life* (London, 1911), p. 100.

53. Freeman (1888), p. 54.

54. Twain (1897), p. 103.

55. Austin (1965), p. 89.

56. Twopeny (1883), p. 16.

57. Sidney Low, 'The Rise of the Suburbs', *Contemporary Review*, 60 (1891), p. 550.

58. Hermann Muthesius, *The English House* (London, 2007), vol. 1, p. 2.

59. *The Times,* 25 June 1904.

60. Twopeny (1883), p. 17.

61. See Michael Cannon, *Life in the Cities* (South Yarra, 1983).

62. Twopeny (1883), p. 16.

63. Austin (1965), p. 76.
64. Trollope (1873), vol. 1, p. 389.
65. Carton Booth (1869), pp. 277–8, 279, 280, 284.
66. Froude (1887), p. 103; Cornish (1880), p. 91; Aspinall (1862), p. 17.
67. Cornish (1880), p. 140.
68. Carter (1870), pp. 24–5.
69. Aspinall (1862), p. 14.
70. Cannon (1983), p. 266.
71. See D. Davison, D. Dunstan and C. McConville (eds.), *The Outcasts of Melbourne* (Sydney, 1985).
72. Freeman (1888), pp. 14–15.
73. Johnson and Anderson (2005), pp. 171–2.
74. E. Kinglake, *The Australian at Home*, quoted in James Grant and Geoffrey Serle, *The Melbourne Scene* (Melbourne, 1957), p. 155.
75. Sutherland (1888), p. 557; Carter (1870), p. 55.
76. See Graeme Davison, *The Rise and Fall of Marvellous Melbourne* (Melbourne, 1979).
77. *Illustrated Handbook of Victoria, Australia* (1886).
78. Trollope (1873), vol. 1, p. 396.
79. Twopeny (1883), pp. 4–5.
80. 'Tasma', *Uncle Piper of Piper's Hill* (London, 1892), p. 144.
81. Charles F. G. Masterman, *From the Abyss; of Its Inhabitants by One of Them* (London, 1902), p. 5.
82. Sutherland (1888), p. 547.
83. Froude (1887), pp. 18, 19, 140.
84. Ibid., p. 143.
85. Freeman (1888), p. vii.
86. Trollope (1873), vol. 1, p. 401.
87. See Darian-Smith (2010); Peter H. Hoffenberg, *An Empire on Display* (London, 2001).
88. *Australasian*, 3 January, 1873, quoted in W. F. Mandle, 'Cricket and Australian Nationalism in the Nineteenth Century', *Journal of the Royal Australian Historical Society*, 59, 4 (1973), p. 232.
89. Grant and Serle (1957), p. 111.
90. *Bell's Life*, 28 December 1861, quoted in W. Frost, 'Heritage, Nationalism, Identity: The 1861–62 England Cricket Tour of Australia', *The International Journal of the History of Sport*, 19, 4 (2002), p. 59.
91. Keith Dunstan, *The Paddock That Grew: The Story of the Melbourne Cricket Club* (London, 1962), p. 38.

92. Mandle (1973), p. 232.
93. Frost (2002), p. 64.
94. Dunstan (1962), p. 48.
95. Mandle (1973), p. 242.
96. Frost (2002), pp. 59, 60.
97. W. F. Mandle, 'Games People Played; Cricket and Football in England and Victoria in the Late Nineteenth Century', *Historical Studies*, 15, 60 (1973), p. 527.
98. The poem in *The New Australian School Series Fourth Reader* (Sydney, 1899). See Richard White, *Inventing Australia: Images and Identity, 1688–1980* (Sydney, 1981), p. 81.
99. Froude (1887), p. 145.
100. Freeman (1888), p. 6.
101. Lenin (1976), vol. 1, p. 260.
102. Schreuder and Ward (2008).
103. Joy Damousi, 'War and Commemoration: "The Responsibility of Empire"', in Schreuder and Ward (eds), *Australia's Empire* (2008).

CHAPTER 9: NEW DELHI

1. Robert Byron, 'New Delhi', *Country Life*, 6 June 1931; Byron, 'New Delhi', *The Architecture Review*, 69 (1931), p. 2.
2. *The Times*, 11 February 1931.
3. Ibid.
4. *Yorkshire Post*, 11 February 1931.
5. *The Times*, 18 February 1931, 21 February 1931.
6. Robert Rhodes James (ed.), *Winston S. Churchill: His Complete Speeches, 1897–1963* (London, 1974), vol. 5, p. 4985.
7. Malvika Singh and Rudrangshu Mukherjee, *New Delhi: Making of a Capital* (New Delhi, 2009), p. 73.
8. Sam Miller, *Delhi: Adventures in a Megacity* (London, 2009), p. 74.
9. *Telegraph* (India), 18 November 2011, 13 December 2011.
10. *Sunday Times of India*, 18 December 2011.
11. Edward Gibbon, *The History of the Decline and Fall of the Roman Empire* (1776–89) (London, 1837), p. 611.
12. Winston Churchill, *My Early Life* (London, 1943), p. 125.
13. R. S. Churchill, *Churchill* (London, 1967), vol. 1, Companion, part 2, p. 774: W. S. Churchill to the Bath Habitation of the Primrose League, 26 July 1897, quoted in Roland Quinault, 'Winston Churchill and

Gibbon', in R. McKitterick and R. Quinault (eds.), *Edward Gibbon and Empire* (Cambridge, 2002), p. 320.

14. *Hansard* (Commons), 1 August 1878, vol. 242, c. 886.

15. For the history of imperial overstretch see the classic work by Paul Kennedy, *The Rise and Fall of Great Powers* (London, 1988).

16. Milner to C. Dawkins, 4 January 1902, Milner Papers, Bodleian Library, Oxford, MSS Eng. Hist. C. 68, ff. 4–6, quoted in E. H. H. Green, 'The Political Economy of Empire, 1880–1914', in A. Porter (ed.), *The Oxford History of the British Empire*, vol. 3: *The Nineteenth Century* (Oxford, 1999), p. 361.

17. Lord Brabazon, *Social Arrows* (London, 1886), pp. 13–14; C. F. G. Masterman (ed.), *Heart of the Empire* (London, 1901), p. 25.

18. Elliott Mills, *The Decline and Fall of the British Empire* (London, 1905), p. 7.

19. Churchill (1967), vol. 1, Companion, part 2, p. 749.

20. Lord Hardinge of Penshurst, *My Indian Years, 1910–1916* (London, 1948), p. 50.

21. John William Fortescue, *Narrative of the Visit to India of Their Majesties King George V and Queen Mary: And of the Coronation Durbar held at Delhi* (London, 1912), pp. 143–65.

22. *The Times*, 13 December 1911.

23. David Cannadine, *Ornamentalism: How the British Saw their Empire* (London, 2002), p. 46.

24. See David Gilmour, *Curzon: Imperial Statesman* (London, 2006).

25. Lord Curzon, *Lord Curzon's Farewell to India: Being Speeches Delivered as Viceroy and Governor of India during Sept.–Nov. 1905* (Bombay, 1907), p. 13, quoted in Thomas Metcalf, *Ideologies of the Raj* (Cambridge, 1998), p. 168.

26. Speech, 20 July 1904, in T. Raleigh (ed.), *Lord Curzon in India* (London, 1906), p. 35, quoted in Robin J. Moore, 'Imperial India, 1858–1914', in A. Porter (ed.), *The Oxford History of the British Empire*, vol. 3: *The Nineteenth Century* (1999), p. 443.

27. Lord Curzon, *Speeches on India* (London, 1904), p. 21, quoted in Metcalf (1998), p. 169.

28. Quoted in Singh and Mukherjee (2009), p. 18.

29. Quoted in Andreas Volwahsen, *Imperial Delhi: The British Capital of the Indian Empire* (Munich, 2003), p. 11.

30. Fortescue (1912), p. 164.

31. *His Majesty King George's Speeches in India* (Madras, 1912), p. 129.

32. See Robert Grant Irving, *Indian Summer: Lutyens, Baker and Imperial Delhi* (London, 1981).

33. G. W. Forrest, *Cities of India* (London, 1903), p. 133.

34. *King George's Speeches* (1912), p. 126.

35. *The Times*, 13 December 1911.

36. William Dalrymple, *The Last Mughal: The Fall of Delhi 1857* (London, 2009).

37. *Hansard* (Lords), 21 February 1912, vol. 11, c. 158.

38. Wilmot Corfield, 'New Delhi', *The British Architect*, 18 October 1912.

39. See Metcalf (1998); Anthony D. King, *Colonial Urban Development* (London, 1976); Robert Home, *Of Planting and Planning* (London, 1997).

40. Quoted in Singh and Mukherjee (2009), p. 12.

41. Hardinge (1948), p. 72.

42. *The Times*, 3 October 1912.

43. See Irving (1981).

44. See 'Sir Edwin Landseer Lutyens', *Oxford Dictionary of National Biography* (Oxford, 2004).

45. Clayre Percy and Jane Ridley (eds.), *The Letters of Edwin Lutyens to His Wife Lady Emily* (London, 1985), 4 June 1912, 16 September 1912.

46. Quoted in Thomas Metcalf, 'Architecture and the Representation of Empire: India, 1860–1910', *Representations*, 6 (1984), p. 61.

47. Percy and Ridley (1985), 14 April 1912.

48. *The Times*, 3 October 1912.

49. Quoted in Christopher Hussey, *The Life of Sir Edwin Lutyens* (London, 1953), p. 247.

50. See Robert Grant Irving, 'Bombay and Imperial Delhi: Cities as Symbols', in Andrew Hopkins and Gavin Stamp (eds.), *Lutyens Abroad: The Work of Sir Edwin Lutyens Outside the British Isles* (London, 2002).

51. *The Times*, 3 October 1912.

52. Herbert Baker, *Architecture and Personalities* (London, 1944), p. 64. See also, 'Sir Herbert Baker', *Oxford Dictionary of National Biography* (Oxford, 2004); Thomas Metcalf, *Forging the Raj* (New Delhi, 2005).

53. Percy and Ridley (1985), 7 January 1913.

54. *Final Report of the Delhi Town Planning Committee on the Town Planning of the New Imperial Capital* (London, 1913).

55. See Nayanjot Lahiri, *Delhi's Capital Century (1911–2011): Understanding the Transformation of the City* (Yale, 2011).

56. See Irving (1981).

57. Byron, 'New Delhi', *Architecture Review* (1931), p. 30.

58. See 'Sir Edwin Landseer Lutyens', *Oxford Dictionary of National Biography* (Oxford, 2004).

59. Byron, 'New Delhi', *Country Life*, 6 June 1931.

60. Byron, 'New Delhi', *Architecture Review* (1931), p. 6.

61. Pamela Mountbatten, *India Remembered* (London, 2007), p. 51.

62. Quoted in Singh and Mukherjee (2009), p. 68.

63. Irving (2002).

64. Quoted in Singh and Mukherjee (2009), p. 66.

65. Richard Davenport-Hines (ed.), *Hugh Trevor-Roper: The Wartime Journals* (London, 2012), p. 198.

66. Baker (1944), p. 69.

67. Viola Bayley, *One Woman's Raj* (Viola Bayley Papers Collection, Centre for South Asian Studies, University of Cambridge, 1976), pp. 25–6.

68. Mountbatten (2007), p. 62.

69. See Hosagrahar Jyoti, 'City as Durbar: Theatre and Power in Imperial Delhi', in Nezar AlSayyad (ed.), *Forms of Dominance: On the Architecture and Urbanism of the Colonial Enterprise* (Aldershot, 1992).

70. See King (1976).

71. Aldous Huxley, *Jesting Pilate: The Diary of a Journey* (1926) (London, 1985), pp. 103–4.

72. Bayley (1976), p. 3.

73. Huxley (1985), p. 107.

74. Mountbatten (2007), p. 78.

75. Quoted in Nayantara Pothen, *Glittering Decades: New Delhi in Love and War* (New Delhi, 2012), p. 47.

76. H. J. Greenwall, *Storm over India* (London, 1933), p. 161.

77. Huxley (1985), p. 106.

78. Bayley (1976), p. 29.

79. See Cannadine (2002).

80. Quoted in Stanley A. Wolpert, *Shameful Flight: The Last Years of the British Empire in India* (Oxford, 2006), pp. 130–31.

81. L. Collins and D. Lapierre, *Mountbatten and the Partition of India* (Michigan, 1982), vol. 1, p. 24.

82. Mountbatten (2007), p. 143.

83. Pothen (2012), pp. 135–6.

CHAPTER 10: LIVERPOOL

1. J. A. Watson, *The End of a Liverpool Landmark: The Last Years of Love Lane Refinery* (London, 1985), p. 51. See also *Liverpool Daily Post*, 23 January 1981, 21 April 1981.
2. John Cornelius, *Liverpool 8* (London, 1982), pp. 119–21.
3. Michael Heseltine, *Life in the Jungle: My Autobiography* (London, 2003), p. 217.
4. John Prestwich, 1780s, quoted in Joseph Sharples, *Liverpool*, Pevsner Architectural Guides (London, 2004), p. 43.
5. *The Liverpool Repository of Literature, Philosophy and Commerce* (1826), quoted in ibid., p. 192.
6. Ibid., p. 10.
7. See David Harris Sacks and Michael Lynch, 'Ports 1540–1700', in Peter Clark (ed.), *The Cambridge Urban History of Britain*, vol. 2 (Cambridge, 2000).
8. W. T. Pike (ed.), *Liverpool and Birkenhead in the Twentieth Century* (Brighton, 1911), p. 23.
9. See John Belchem (ed.), *Liverpool 800* (Liverpool, 2006).
10. Quoted in Tony Lane, *Liverpool: Gateway of Empire* (London, 1987), p. 26.
11. Thomas Baines, *History of the Commerce and Town of Liverpool* (Liverpool, 1852), p. 840.
12. Ramsay Muir, *A History of Liverpool* (Liverpool, 1907), p. 300.
13. Pike (1911), p. 13.
14. Lane (1987), p. 26.
15. Sharples (2004), p. 103.
16. Belchem (2006), p. 319.
17. Alfred Holt (ed.), *Merseyside* (Liverpool, 1923), pp. 179–80.
18. Muir (1907), p. 2.
19. See John Belchem, *Irish, Catholic and Scouse* (Liverpool, 2007).
20. Quoted in J. P. Dudgeon, *Our Liverpool* (London, 2010), p. 70.
21. Herman Melville, *Redburn: His First Voyage* (1849) (New York, 1983), p. 222.
22. Amanda Foreman, *A World on Fire* (London, 2011), p. 272.
23. Muir (1907), p. 302.
24. J. A. Picton, *Memorials of Liverpool, Historical and Topographical* (London, 1873), p. 567.
25. Hugh Gawthrop, *Fraser's Guide to Liverpool* (Liverpool, 1855), p. 188.
26. C. W. Jones, *Pioneer Shipowners* (London, 1938), p. 118.

27. See Nicholas J. White, 'Liverpool Shipping and the End of Empire: The Ocean Group in East and Southeast Asia, 1945–1973', in S. Haggerty, A. Webster and N. J. White (eds.), *The Empire in One City?* (Manchester, 2008).

28. See Lane (1987), p. 117; Brian Lewis, *'So Clean': Lord Leverhulme, Soap and Civilisation* (Manchester, 2008).

29. Lane (1987), p. 25.

30. Pike (1911), p. 59.

31. Dudgeon (2010), pp. 96–7.

32. Muir (1907), p. 298.

33. Pike (1911), p. 69.

34. Dudgeon (2010), p. 72.

35. Sharples (2004), p. 67.

36. Pike (1911), p. 32.

37. See Murray Steele, 'Transmitting Ideas of Empire: Representations and Celebrations in Liverpool, 1886–1953', in Haggerty, Webster and White (2008).

38. *Liverpool Daily Post and Mercury*, 22 May 1915.

39. See Krishan Kumar, 'Empire, Nation, and National Identities', in Andrew Thompson (ed.), *Britain's Experience of Empire in the Twentieth Century* (Oxford, 2012).

40. Clayre Percy and Jane Ridley (eds.), *The Letters of Edwin Lutyens to His Wife Lady Emily* (London, 1985), p. 395.

41. John Summerson, *The Unromantic Castle and Other Essays* (London, 1990), p. 256.

42. Francis Hyde, *Liverpool and the Mersey: An Economic History of a Port* (Newton Abbot, 1971).

43. J. B. Priestley, *English Journey* (Leipzig, 1935), pp. 242, 244, 247, 252, 257.

44. Kumar (2012).

45. Belchem (2006); see also John Darwin, *Unfinished Empire* (London, 2012); George Chandler, *Liverpool Shipping: A Short History* (Liverpool, 1960).

46. Piers Brendon, *The Decline and Fall of the British Empire* (London, 2007); see also, Peter Clarke, *The Last Thousand Days of the British Empire* (London, 2007).

47. See Jim Tomlinson, 'The Empire/Commonwealth in British Economic Thinking and Policy', in Thompson (ed.), *Britain's Experience of Empire* (2012).

48. Lane (1987).

49. Chris Couch, *City of Change and Challenge: Urban Planning and Regeneration in Liverpool* (Liverpool, 2003).

50. Belchem (2006).

51. Ibid.

52. Stuart Wilks-Heeg, 'From World City to Pariah City? Liverpool and the Global Economy, 1850–2000', in Ronaldo Munck (ed.), *Reinventing the City? Liverpool in Comparative Perspective* (Liverpool, 2002).

53. A. J. P. Taylor, 'Manchester', *Encounter*, 8, 3 (1957).

54. Heseltine (2003), p. 218.

55. Quoted in Peter Fryer, *Staying Power: The History of Black People in Britain* (London, 1984), p. 302. See also Roy May and Robin Cohen, 'The Interaction between Race and Colonialism: A Case Study of the Liverpool Race Riots of 1919', *Race and Class*, 16, 2 (1974).

56. Belchem (2006), p. 377.

57. Fryer (1984), p. 302.

58. *Liverpool Daily Post and Mercury*, 8 November 1919.

59. Wilks-Heeg (2002).

60. Watson (1985); see also Vincent Mahler, 'Britain, the European Community, and the Developing Commonwealth: Dependence, Interdependence, and the Political Economy of Sugar', *International Organization* 35, 3 (1981).

61. *Daily Mirror*, 11 October 1982.

62. BBC News Website, 30 December 2011.

63. *Spectator*, 16 October 2004.

64. *Guardian*, 5 June 2003.

65. The exception being the ExUrbe think-tank. See, 'Peel and the Liverpool City Region: Predatory Capitalism or Providential Corporatism?', March 2013, www.exurbe.org.uk. See also *Financial Times*, 29 November 2013, which noted that the chairman of Sam Wa Resources Holding, Stella Shiu, had other business partners who included 'an Iranian pomegranate juice exporter and an investment adviser in New Jersey who recently settled US Securities and Exchange Commission allegations of fraud and violation of securities regulation'.

66. 'Liverpool Reaches for the Sky to Thrive', *Financial Times* 12 March 2012; see also *Financial Times*, 13 November 2012; *The Economist*, 3 September 2012.

Index

Page references in *italic* indicate illustrations and maps.

About the Author

TRISTRAM HUNT is the author of *Marx's General: The Revolutionary Life of Friedrich Engels* and *Building Jerusalem: The Rise and Fall of the Victorian City*. One of Britain's leading young historians, he writes regularly for *The Guardian*, *The Observer*, and *The Times*, and has broadcast numerous series for the BBC. A lecturer in history at the University of London, Hunt represents Stoke-on-Trent in the British Parliament, where he serves as the education spokesman for the Labour Party.